POWER AND RESPONSIBILITY

The Life and Times of
THEODORE ROOSEVELT

POWER AND RESPONSIBILITY

THE LIFE AND TIMES

OF *Theodore Roosevelt*

By William Henry Harbaugh

FARRAR, STRAUS AND CUDAHY • NEW YORK

The author gratefully acknowledges permission to quote brief extracts
from the following books: Howard K. Beale, *Theodore Roosevelt and the
Rise of America to World Power,* The Johns Hopkins Press; Elting E.
Morison, *Turmoil and Tradition: A Study of the Life and Times of
Henry L. Stimson,* Houghton Mifflin Company; Elting E. Morison and
John M. Blum (editors), *The Letters of Theodore Roosevelt,* copyright
1951, 1952, 1954 by the Harvard University Press; George E. Mowry,
The Era of Theodore Roosevelt, Harper & Brothers; George E. Mowry,
Theodore Roosevelt and the Progressive Movement, The University of
Wisconsin Press; Theodore Roosevelt, African Game Trails (Vol. IV of
the National Edition of *The Works of Theodore Roosevelt*), and Theodore
Roosevelt, *An Autobiography* (Vol. XX of the National Edition), Charles
Scribner's Sons. Further acknowledgment will be found in the Preface of
this book (page v) and in the Notes (page 523).

PREFACE

This biography is written for the general reader—for the man or woman with a broad interest in American history, and for the college student. I have based it partly on original sources, partly on memoirs and other works by Theodore Roosevelt's contemporaries, and partly on the collection of Roosevelt's letters and the numerous scholarly reappraisals of his turbulent career published in the last fifteen years. Throughout, I have tried to keep Roosevelt in the context of his times while yet exercising the historian's heavy and sobering responsibility of judging his subject's deeds in the perspective of time.

Inevitably, I am heavily obligated—to my friend and former professor, Arthur S. Link of Princeton, on whose urging I decided to undertake the project; to Elting E. Morison of M.I.T. for his thoughtful appraisal of the entire manuscript; to Hermann Hagedorn, director emeritus of the Theodore Roosevelt Association, for the generous gift of his time and for his many provocative and informative suggestions; to Alfred Young of Patterson State College for his numerous perceptive criticisms of the whole; and to Richard Lowitt of Connecticut College for Women, who was a source of intellectual sustenance throughout, criticizing, encouraging, and sharing always his own vast knowledge of the period.

I am also grateful to numerous other friends, colleagues, or graduate students for reading particular chapters or discussing special topics with me. Among them are Louis L. Gerson, Peter Schroeder, John Thorkelson, and Sam Witryol of the University of Connecticut; Norman Enhorning and Ronald Grele, formerly of that institution; Ernest Cawcroft of Jamestown, New York; Alexander M. Bickel and Ward S. Bowman, Jr. of the Yale Law School; Thomas N.

Bonner of the University of Omaha; John Wells Davidson and David W. Hirst of The Papers of Woodrow Wilson; and Captain David Horner of the United States Military Academy.

Edmund A. Moore, my former chairman at the University of Connecticut, and Harrison W. Carter, dean of the college of arts and sciences, gave me the understanding without which books can hardly be written under the new dispensation of overcrowded classes and increased teaching schedules. Calvin Woodard read the galleys and caught a number of errors of fact and interpretation. Frances Stearns met my typing deadlines with skill and equanimity.

I am also indebted to Robert H. Haynes, curator of the Theodore Roosevelt Collection at Harvard University; to Leslie C. Stratton, formerly director of the Theodore Roosevelt Association, and to Helen MacLachlan, the Association's curator; to Roberta Smith, reference librarian at the University of Connecticut; and to the staff of the Manuscript Division of the Library of Congress.

I should like further to record my warm pleasure in the stimulating cooperation of John Farrar, friend, editor, and publisher, and of John Peck, associate editor of Farrar, Straus and Cudahy.

Finally, I am indebted to my wife, Wayne Talbot Harbaugh, for more than the usual reasons. She not only compiled the index, she made clear, logical, and penetrating criticisms of many parts of the manuscript. In a different way I am also grateful for the diversions afforded by the invasions of my study by Lyn, who has grown to learn that daddy was not really writing a story about her teddy bear; by her friend Clemency, who was always a little skeptical; and more recently by Billy, to whom teddy bear and Teddy Roosevelt are just now becoming synonymous.

Out of personal affection, and in appreciation of his long and fruitful service to the scholarship and memory of a great and controversial man, I dedicate this book to Hermann Hagedorn.

CONTENTS

PART V: THE HIGH TIDE OF PROGRESSIVISM

PART VI: ONE LAST GREAT CAUSE

PART I

THE MAKING OF A MAN

CHAPTER 1

THE FIRST BATTLE

> When I went into politics at this time I was not conscious of going in with the set purpose to benefit other people, but of getting for myself a privilege to which I was entitled in common with other people.
>
> —Theodore Roosevelt, *An Autobiography*

An air of anticipation fell over the gilded Chamber of the State House in Albany, New York, early in the afternoon of April 5, 1882, as Theodore Roosevelt, a twenty-three-year-old freshman assemblyman from New York City's twenty-first district, started to speak.

Roosevelt was already a young man apart. He stood only five feet eight inches high and weighed perhaps 140 pounds; but his head was so large and distinctive that it made his muscular shoulders appear slight. It rested on a bull-like neck and was crowned by a shock of wavy blond hair parted a bit off center. Beneath a moderately low brow, blue-gray eyes squinted behind thick pince-nez, and a full blond mustache set off a squaring face framed by extraordinarily small ears knit close to the head. Roosevelt wore his finely tailored clothes with a flair that belied their conservative cut, and his manner was at once appealingly callow and offensively self-assured. Though he pronounced his A's with a broad accent and his R's with a soft roll, there was a kind of suppressed vehemence about his speech even in conversation, and when excited his voice would shift involuntarily from a resonant tenor to a shrill falsetto.

"What on earth will New York send next?" an upstate newspaperman had reflected on meeting him at the start of the legislative session.

"We almost shouted with laughter to think that the most veritable representative of the New York dude had come to the Chamber," one of his friends recalled long afterward.

Roosevelt's remarks that April afternoon were exceptional, even for him. In words so bold that the press described them as "almost startling," he demanded that the Assembly investigate reports that T. R. Westbrook, a Republican-appointed justice of the State Supreme Court, had colluded with Jay Gould, Russell Sage, and Cyrus Field in a "stock-jobbing" deal for control of the Manhattan Elevated Railway. The professionals were shocked. Neither the G.O.P. regulars nor the Tammany Democrats wished to cross the notorious Gould or to impugn state officials who owed their positions to behind-the-scenes arrangements by the leaders of both parties; they designed to ignore the matter. But Roosevelt, who had obtained an unpublished letter in which Westbrook promised Gould that he would "go to the very verge of judicial discretion" to advance the financier's interests, insisted on pressing for an investigation.

The youthful crusader was peremptorily crushed both then and on the following day, April 6. Roosevelt's charges had so aroused civic leaders, however, that when the Assembly reconvened after the Easter holidays, the Republican leader, Thomas Alvord, and John Kelly, his Tammany counterpart, temporarily lost control of their forces. In spite of Alvord's sarcastic assertion that the only people upholding the attack on Westbrook were the "unnaturalized Englishmen who edited the *New York Times*" and the publisher of the New York *Herald* who "desired merely to get a strike at John Kelly," Roosevelt's resolution for an inquiry was approved on April 12 by 104 to 6.

The victory proved short-lived, the Judiciary Committee exonerating Westbrook late in May over the young New Yorker's outraged protest. "To you, members of the Legislature of the greatest Commonwealth in this great Federal Union," Roosevelt grandiloquently declared following his rebuff, "I say you cannot by your votes clear the Judge. He stands condemned by his own acts in the eyes of all honest people. All you can do is shame yourselves and give him a brief extension of his dishonored career. You cannot cleanse the leper. Beware lest you taint yourself with his leprosy."

The Westbrook affair was a political landmark for Theodore Roosevelt. For the first time he had tasted popular favor, and for the first time he had emerged as the leader of a faction. Although his brashness had incited resentment, especially among the regulars, his courage and persistence had also won begrudged respect. From then until he came out for James G. Blaine in the presidential campaign of 1884 his reputation as a reformer with the temerity to act on his principles burgeoned; and from then until 1884 his influence on independent-minded men inside and outside the legislature heightened. "I think he grew faster than anybody I ever knew," Isaac Hunt, a taciturn farmer-lawyer-assemblyman from Jefferson County later mused. "He increased in stature, in strength, mentally all the time. . . . I thought I knew more than he did, but before we got through he grew right away from me."

Superficially, the way had been easy for this scion of the old New York aristocracy. Born into an established family of comfortable means, Theodore had enjoyed numerous advantages—a warm and wholesome family circle, tutors, vacations in the country and travel abroad, a gentleman's education at Harvard, and a modest inheritance on reaching age. Had his background been different, in fact, had he not been known as an educated, high-minded gentleman of independent income, he would not even have been nominated for the legislature in the autumn of 1881.

Yet the difference between outward appearances and inner strivings is often great. The courageous, fearless man whom the world eventually came to know—the crusader against crime and corruption, the heroic soldier, the assailant of big business, the creator of a national political party—was not always the man that Roosevelt himself knew, or had known. His vaunted self-confidence was genuine; but it seems to have been more the product of experience and achievement than of inherent security. Roosevelt's is the story of a man driven: of a man whose strength derived from the conquest of fear, not from the lack of it; of a man compelled again and again to prove himself and possessed, happily, of the moral and physical stamina to do so.

Theodore had been asthmatic from birth, rarely a day or a night passing during which the baby, the boy, or the adolescent did not in some degree suffer. One of his earliest recollections, he later said, was of his father "walking up and down the room with me in his arms at night." Relief was temporary when it came. Summers in the Hudson River country or the New Jersey highlands failed to induce a cure; nor did a tour of Europe help. "I was very sick last night and Mama was so kind telling me storys (*sic*) and rubbing me with her delicate fingers," Theodore wrote from abroad when he was eleven years old. "I am here in Richfield now," he reported the following year. "Of course I came here because I was sick." By then, however, the tide had begun to turn. Told by his father that he would have to build himself by his own efforts, the twelve-year-old youngster had thrown back his head, flashed his already prominent teeth, and asserted: "I'll make my body."

That fall Theodore began daily workouts in a gymnasium and on apparatus installed on the back porch of his house; and whether because of these exertions or natural causes, he improved so markedly by the following summer that asthma or other sickness never thereafter seriously interrupted his activities.

Notwithstanding his physical infirmities, the child "Teedie" showed an extraordinary zest for life. His affectionate and responsive parents were partly responsible; indeed, their affection for their sickly son was so strong that he might have developed abnormal attachments had he been an only child. But fortunately there were brothers and sisters— Anna, the eldest, then Elliott and Corinne, both born after Theodore. There was also direction and discipline, perhaps in excess, from the father. In his *Autobiography,* written when he was fifty-four years old, Roosevelt described his mother as "a sweet, gracious, beautiful Southern woman, a delightful companion . . . beloved by everybody" and "blessed with a strong sense of humor." But he lavished praise upon his father. "He combined strength and courage with gentleness, tenderness, and great unselfishness. . . . With great love and patience, and the most understanding sympathy and consideration, he combined insistence on discipline . . . he was the only man of whom I was ever really afraid."

Theodore's anguished diary entries following the senior Roosevelt's death in 1878, during Theodore's nineteenth year, offer even more insight into the unusual relationship between father and son. "I feel that if it were not for the certainty, that . . . 'he is not dead but gone before,' I should almost perish," he wrote five days after his father died. A month later he said that it seemed as if his heart would break when he thought of his terrible loss. He added that his father had "shared all my joys, and in sharing doubled them, and soothed all the few sorrows I ever had." A subsequent entry lamented the loss of "the only human being to whom I told *everything,* never failing to get loving advice and sweet sympathy in return; no one, but my wife, if ever I marry, will ever be able to take his place."

Although the number of references gradually declined, the intensity remained. "O, Father, Father how bitterly I miss you, mourn you and long for you!" Theodore exclaimed several months later. More significant still, he despaired that he could live up to his image of his father. "I realize more and more every day that I am as much inferior to Father morally and mentally as physically," he confided to the diary a full half year after the senior Roosevelt died. "But," he added in a display of fatalistic resilience that would lose its religious cast as he grew older, " 'Trust in the Lord and do good!' "

Theodore Roosevelt, Sr., had been a large-framed, athletic man with a leonine head, a striking beard, and a buoyant, dominant manner, born to the old Dutch mercantile tradition. He loved life and he regarded business as merely a means for supplying his own and his family's considerable wants. After his main interest, the import glass trade, collapsed some years before his death, he never took up another, absorbing himself instead in social life and the philanthropic and civic matters which had long excited his interest. His understanding of the festering social and economic problems of the times was delimited by his concern with individual character and morality; yet he felt obligated to aid the suffering and the oppressed, to work for reform without disturbing the existing social framework. He was a founder of the Orthopedic Hospital, the Children's Aid Society, and the State Charities Aid Association, and he actively supported the Newsboys' Lodging House and the Y.M.C.A. To Theodore, Jr., he transmitted his sense of moral duty and habit of *noblesse oblige*.

Whatever the psychological nuances of their relationship, this distinguished gentleman failed his eldest son in only one overt respect: He remained a civilian throughout the Civil War, probably in deference to his Southern-born wife. True, he gave abundantly of his energies and talents. With two other public-spirited men he drafted and pressed Congress to pass the bill establishing an Allotment Commission and then toured the camps in an exhaustive effort to persuade enlisted men to send home a portion of their monthly salaries. "I would never have felt satisfied with myself after this war is over if I had done nothing," he confided to his wife in a letter from the field, "and that I do feel now that I am only doing my duty." Yet it was the duty of the civilian rather than that of the soldier. Theodore, who boundlessly admired two maternal uncles who served the Confederate navy with distinction, was always sensitive about the fact that his father had not borne arms.

After the war the Roosevelt family again enjoyed the perquisites of moderate wealth and social position. For the parents there were gracious entertainments, dinner parties and balls, fine wines and small talk with relatives and friends, as well as continued civic activity. For the children there were exciting rides in the rig with their father, who loved to race; long hours reading with their mother, who was well read in a limited, genteel sense; most of the toys they chanced to want; and frequent visits with other youngsters of their background. On the whole, however, the children's activities centered in and around the four-story brownstone house and yard at 28 East 20th Street where Theodore had been born on October 27, 1858, and where the family lived until they moved into another brownstone on 57th Street.

Theodore's advantages softened the misery of his poor health somewhat, and his effort to conquer it remains a striking testament to his courage and determination. Yet to explain Roosevelt the man solely, or even largely, in terms of his sickly childhood and adolescence is to do injustice to other of his natural endowments. Even as a slender, almost spindly youngster, he possessed such surging physical and intellectual energy as left little time either to brood or to rest or, in a very real sense, to suffer. From the beginning he capitalized on his keen intelligence, gave vent to his insatiable curiosity, and sought outlets for his burning desire to be recognized.

Of the passions of Theodore's youth, nature was the most consuming. At the age of eight he started the practice of collecting live mice and reptiles which would be emulated by his own sons and would keep various Roosevelt family servants on edge for upward of forty years. By the age of fourteen he had grasped the main tenets of Darwin. And when he entered Harvard in the autumn of 1876 he probably could have passed an examination in the general works of the most renowned naturalists of the era. By then, too, he had built a collection of bird skins, writes the zoologist, Paul R. Cutright, "which for size, variety, and skill of preparation was doubtless unequalled by any boy his age in the United States." Based on that observation and study which always distinguished Roosevelt from the man of pure action, this interest later enabled him to discourse learnedly with eminent professional naturalists and to make modest personal contributions to the over-all body of scientific classification; it projected him into one of the most celebrated and unnecessary controversies of his presidential years—that over the "Nature Fakers" —and it formed the springboard for one of his greatest accomplishments, the vitalization of the conservation movement.

If nature was young Roosevelt's first great interest, books were his second. Even as a child he read omnivorously and with surprising catholicity. Works of maudlin sentimentality, pious morality, high adventure, and classical quality were all devoured by his restless mind. "I worshipped *Little Men* and *Little Women* and *An Old-Fashioned Girl,*" he nostalgically recalled. But "I disliked the Swiss Family Robinson because of the wholly impossible collection of animals met by that worthy family as they ambled inland from the wreck." On his first trip to Europe at the age of eleven, a trip that he professed not to enjoy though his letters indicate that he did, he and Elliott and Corinne reportedly read fifty or more novels!

Theodore's travels in Europe, his fascination with nature, his readings, and his vacations with his sisters, cousins, and robust brother Elliott, who for a while served as his protector—these and the passage of time wrought their influence upon his personality. From a rather shy, retiring child he changed into an outgoing, uninhibited adolescent with a developing sense of humor and a growing tendency toward mild exhibitionism.

"As a young girl," wrote one of the family friends, "I remember dreading to sit next him at any formal dinner lest I become so convulsed with laughter at his whispered sallies as to disgrace myself and be forced to leave the room." Or, as Theodore himself once wrote his mother, "I went to Miss Nelly Dean's wedding yesterday, and made myself so agreable (*sic*) that one old Lady paid me a compliment. She evidently had a great deal of discrimination." These traits did not escape his contemporaries. Theodore "always thought he could do things better than anyone else," his cousin, Maude Elliott, wrote during his second trip abroad when he was fourteen.

Maude Elliott's characterization of her ebullient cousin was not wholly accurate. Theodore only *tried* to do things better than everybody else. In spite of his formidable powers of rationalization, he had a realistic insight into his own abilities; neither as a boy nor as a man did he tend to overestimate them. If he too often indulged in self-praise, it was because of deserved pride in deeds performed and barriers surmounted. Life was an unrelieved, if mainly joyous, struggle, and false modesty was not among its virtues. As Theodore wrote his father that same year, "I then had several rounds with Johnie and Edward, in which I kept my own, as Johnie is smaller, though more used to fighting, and Edward, although much larger does not know so much about boxing." A few years later he would remark that of his five closest friends, two overestimated him, two undervalued him, and only one gauged his true worth.

Young Roosevelt also abounded in warmth, sympathy, and affection. His letters repeatedly reveal him inquiring solicitously of his parents' health, writing fondly of "cunning" young children, and pouring out his love for "My own darling little Motherling" and "My dear Papa." Nor were the diary entries of his college years less effusive: "Elliott is a noble fellow, wonderfully grown up in every way." "What a wonderful set of relations I have got—cousins and all, especially my own family." "I wonder if ever a man had two better sisters than I have!"

In maturity Roosevelt would lose little, if any, of those qualities. They would be modified or offset, however, by an extraordinary severity of judgment and by a strain of ruthlessness and a capacity for passing hatred which so often mars the competitive personality.

If there was anything in Theodore's boyhood, aside from the sense of duty and *noblesse oblige* that he got from his father, to suggest that he would someday become a social reformer it was only his strident moralizing. "Did you hear that Percy Cushion was a failure?" he once wrote his father from Dresden. "He swore like a trooper and used disreputable language, so I gave him some pretty strong hints, which he at last took, and we do not see much more of him." As a green college freshman a few years later Theodore would righteously report that of the eleven other boys at his table, "no less than seven do not smoke and four drink nothing stronger than beer." As a more sophisticated sophomore, however, he would concede that although he got rather bored with the drunken brothers of D.K.E. he found an occasional fraternity social "good enough fun." In one of the few intimations in his diary of repressed aggressions, he would also confess that "Wine makes me awfully fighting."

Roosevelt had entered Harvard in 1876 after two years of intensive preparation under a private tutor. Because of his lingering asthma he took private rooms, and in spite of membership in the best clubs, success in athletics and academics, and an active social life in Cambridge he remained always a little apart. William Roscoe Thayer remembered that he was "a good deal of a joke . . . active and enthusiastic and that was all." But another friend, Charles Washburn, who knew him more intimately, contended that he was "loved by many," was "in a class by himself," and was recognized as "a person *sui generis*" who was not to be judged by ordinary standards.

Whether Theodore, as he preferred to be called until his service in the Spanish-American War earned him the title of Colonel, got all that he should have from Harvard is problematical. Certainly he enjoyed himself. "What a royally good time I am having," he wrote in his diary as a junior. "I can't conceive of a fellow *possibly* enjoying himself more." Academically, he did well in those subjects which interested him, notably natural history, literature, and political economy; only passably in those which did not. But his over-all performance was sufficiently high—he finished "second among the gentlemen" and twenty-first in a class of 158—to win election to Phi Beta Kappa. And his writing was so well regarded that he was made an editor of *The Advocate,* one of the three undergraduate papers. He later complained, however, that "There was very little in my actual studies which helped me in after-life." In his *Autobiography,* written just after the Progressive campaign of 1912, he lamented that "there was almost no teaching of the need for collective action, and of the fact that in addition to, not as a substitute for, individual responsibility, there is a collective responsibility. Books such as Herbert Croly's *Promise of American Life* and Walter E. Weyl's *New Democracy* would generally at that time have been treated either as unintelligible or else as pure heresy."

Perhaps. Yet Roosevelt conceded that his readings at Harvard did reinforce that individual morality—that "self-reliance, energy, courage, the power of insisting on his own rights and the sympathy that makes him regardful of the rights of others"—which had been his father's teaching as well as the lesson of *Our Young Folks.* And in spite of his disappointment in some of his courses, he was obviously stimulated. As he wrote his mother in October, 1878, political economy and metaphysics "are even more interesting than my Natural History courses; and all the more so, from the fact that I radically disagree on many points with the men whose books we are reading (Mill and Ferrier)."

Roosevelt's extracurricular activities at Harvard further confirm his intellectual awakening. He became an active convert to the free-trade movement, probably from reading John Stuart Mill and other laissez-faire economists. He served as undergraduate head of the Natural History Society. He helped organize and for a time presided over the Finance Club, under the auspices of which two of the most celebrated economists in the country, Professor William Graham Sumner and Professor Francis A. Walker of Yale, delivered special lectures at Cambridge. And in the spring of 1880 he participated in a mock presidential election in which he cast his ballot for the Democrat, Senator Thomas Bayard, in a display of contempt for the Republican candidates—Grant, Sherman and Blaine. "The gentleman [Roosevelt] in charge of the polls is a proof that the movement is not one of idle curiosity, but of earnest purpose," *The Advocate* said editorially.

Roosevelt also belonged to a literary-political discussion group to which he submitted a paper, "The Machine in Politics"; was a member of the Art Club; and supported the Glee Club in a non-singing role. He was "forever at it," one of his classmates recalled, "and probably no man of his time read more extensively or deeply, especially in directions that did not count on the honor-list or marking-sheet. He had the happy power of abstraction, and nothing was more common than a noisy roomful of college mates with Roosevelt frowning with intense absorption over a book in the corner." Theodore himself was satisfied. Reviewing his life a few weeks after graduation, he wrote in his diary that there was nothing he would have cared to change. Indeed, he added, *"my career* (both in and out of college) *has been more successful than that of any man I have known."*

It was at Harvard, too, that Roosevelt's compulsion to exhort and admonish became evident. "He used to stop men in the Yard, or call them to him," a classmate remembered. "Then he would block the narrow gravel path and soon make sparks from an argument fly. He was so enthusiastic and had such a startling array of deeply rooted interests that we all thought he would make a great journalist." But it was preacher-at-large to the American people that he was to be. The future was vaguely foreshadowed in one of his few editorials in *The Advocate*. Commenting on an impending football game with Yale, he warned that "nothing but very hard work will enable our men to win to victory. . . . Last year we had good individual players, but they did not work together nearly as well as the Princeton team, and were not in as good condition as the Yale men. The football season is short; and while it does last, the men ought to work faithfully, if they expect to win for Harvard the position she held three years ago." Twenty years later, as President of the United States, Roosevelt would address the captain of the Harvard squad in the same vein.

Theodore also developed into a competent athlete at Harvard. After being soundly thrashed by a country bully as a youngster, he had characteristically resolved to learn to box well enough to defend himself. Long after he fulfilled that purpose (he had one fight, which he won, as an assemblyman and he threatened to fight in at least one other case) he continued to spar regularly, often with professionals. He became as proficient as his poor eyesight would permit—his right hand was said to have been powerful—and in his junior year he reached the finals in the lightweight class. He lost the championship bout, but won the plaudits of the spectators by commanding them to stop hissing his opponent for bloodying his nose after the referee had called the end of a round. "It's all right," he dramatically exclaimed with his arm upraised, "he didn't hear him." (He failed to mention the incident in his diaries.)

Roosevelt was too light for football; so besides rowing, tennis, and riding, he channeled his cascading energy into camping trips into the Maine wilderness, where he fused the qualities of the hunter and naturalist to the bewilderment of his latter-day critics. It was a long jump from high tea in Back Bay to boiled coffee in the Maine woods, but he easily made it both ways. As W. W. "Bill" Sewall, a brawny, bearded woodsman of thirty-three who was to serve Roosevelt as guide, counselor, and companion for several years thereafter, recalled, "He was different from anybody that I had ever met," especially in that "he was fair-minded."

> He and I agreed in our ideas of fair play and right and wrong. Besides, he was always good-natured and full of fun. I do not think I ever remember him being 'out of sorts.' He did not feel well sometimes, but he never would admit it. . . . Some folks said that he was headstrong and aggressive, but I never found him so except when necessary. . . . Of course he did not understand the woods, but on every other subject he was posted. The reason that he knew so much about everything, I found, was that wherever he went he got right in with the people . . . he was quick to find the real man

in very simple men. He didn't look for a brilliant man when he found me; he valued me for what I was worth.

Theodore's contact with Sewall and other woodsmen was the one broadening influence in his social development during his undergraduate years. He otherwise consorted with his social peers, and though he gradually lost his more blatant class-consciousness (as a freshman he had found the Yale undergraduates a "scrubby set" and had been reluctant to become intimate with the New York crowd at Harvard because he knew nothing of their "antecedents"), he always prided himself on his election to The Hasty Pudding and the Porcellian. As President of the United States, in fact, he was actually concerned lest his sons not receive the same distinctions. A letter to his "Darling Motherling" at the start of his senior year describes a normal round of social activities:

> Last Monday I drove Jack Tebbets over to call on the Miss Bacons, who are very nice girls. Wednesday I dined at the Lees, and spent the loveliest kind of an evening with Rosy, Alice and Rose. The two girls must come on to Boston next month if only to see Chestnut Hill; and, by Jove, I shall be awfully disappointed if they do'n't like it. Mamie Saltonstalls birthday was on Friday; I gave her a small silver fan-chain. Saturday I spent all the morning playing tennis with the two Miss Lanes. . . .
> . . . Wednesday Harry Shaw and I give a small opera party to Mr. and Mrs. Saltonstall, Rose and Alice.

One of the girls mentioned in that letter was Alice Hathaway Lee, a tall, graceful young lady of Brahmin lineage, classic features, and feminine demeanor, who resided on Chestnut Hill. Theodore had been "courting" her since early in his junior year and in February, 1880, their engagement was formally announced. "She is just the sweetest, prettiest sunniest little darling that ever lived, and with all her laughing, teasing ways, she is as loving and tender as she can be," Theodore wrote his sister Corinne. Everything had been "subordinate to winning her," he confided to a friend, Henry Minot, at the time of the engagement, "so you can perhaps understand a change in my ideas as regards science &c."

Not quite "everything" had been subordinated to romance during that final year. Although Roosevelt neglected his duties as an editor of *The Advocate* and failed to deliver the commencement "dissertation" to which his rank in the class entitled him ("I have always studied well . . . so I can afford to cut now," he commented in his diary shortly after his engagement) he won honor grades in four of his five courses, wrote a senior thesis on "The Practicability of Equalizing Men and Women Before the Law," and drafted the first two chapters of his *Naval War of 1812,* which was published two years after his graduation. A work of limited scope, high technical competence, and considerable dramatic power, *The Naval War* was to win favorable reviews in the United States and be so well received in Great Britain that Roosevelt would be invited to do the section on the War of 1812 for Clowes's *History of the Royal Navy.*

Alice Lee was only eighteen years old when she became engaged to Theodore after a frenetic courtship of eight months. "See that girl?" he is said to have exclaimed to a friend at one point. "I am going to marry her. She won't have me, but I am going to have her." Alice had resisted him, however, and during the fall of 1879 Theodore became so depressed that friends sent to New York for a relative to come and soothe him. "I have been pretty nearly crazy," he later confessed in his diary (night after night he had wandered through the woods). "But I do not think any outsider suspected it; I have not written a word about it in my diary since a year ago last Thanksgiving."

On January 25, 1880, however, Alice Lee had submitted. "I am so happy that I dare not trust in my own happiness," Theodore wrote in his diary that night. "How she, so pure and sweet and beautiful can think of marrying me I can not understand, but I praise and thank God it is so." He added that it was love at first sight. "Thank heaven I am absolutely pure," he wrote two weeks later. "I can tell Alice everything I have ever done."

Alice's parents had at first opposed an early marriage, but after what Theodore described as "a long but very peaceable argument," they acceded to his wishes. On October 27, 1880, his twenty-second birthday, Theodore and Alice Lee were married in the Unitarian Church of Brookline. A short honeymoon at Oyster Bay, Long Island, followed. "Our intense happiness is too sacred to be written about," was Theodore's terse diary entry. There were drives in the buggy, tennis games, walks in the woods, and reading aloud in the evenings from the *Pickwick Papers, Quentin Durward,* and Keats. Probably there was also excited planning of a future home in that then charm-

ingly rural country, for a few months later Roosevelt purchased the
first of three deeds totalling 155 acres and including the hilltop overlooking the Long Island Sound where Sagamore Mohannis and other
Indian chieftains had held their councils of war in years long past.

At the end of their brief honeymoon Theodore and Alice returned
to New York City to pass the winter in the house on West 57th Street
with Mrs. Roosevelt, Sr., preparatory to an extended tour of Europe
in the spring. Meanwhile Alice joined the Presbyterian Church. "Now
we are one in *everything,*" Theodore said in his diary. "My cup is
almost running over."

It was to the study of law rather than of nature that Theodore
turned during that first winter of his marriage. He had entered
Harvard determined to pursue a scientific career in the face of his
father's warning that the financial remuneration would be small.
Early in his sophomore year he and Henry Minot, with whom he
had gone camping in the Adirondacks the previous summer, published
a short paper, "Summer Birds of the Adirondacks in Franklin
County, N.Y.," which earned a commendation from the zoologist
C. H. Merriam, who would later term Roosevelt the "world's authority on big game mammals." And in his junior year Roosevelt
compiled and published on his own another small pamphlet, "Notes
on Some of the Birds of Oyster Bay." Meanwhile, his name was listed
in the *Naturalist's Directory.*

But as his letter informing Minot of his engagement suggests,
Roosevelt had decided to forego science by the time of that memorable event and possibly before. He later blamed Harvard's teaching
methods for the decision. "They treated biology as purely a science
of the laboratory and the microscope," he charged in his *Autobiography.* "There was a total failure to understand the great variety
of kinds of work that could be done by naturalists, including what
could be done by outdoor naturalists." There was truth in those
charges, but there is little evidence that Roosevelt thought so at the
time. In fact, his diary indicates that he enjoyed laboratory work but
was "perfectly blue" at the prospect of three years abroad completing
his professional training.

Roosevelt's interests were also widening. His growing fascination
with politics was part of his intellectual awakening at Harvard, and
it antedated his courtship of Alice Lee. A year before his engagement

he ended his habit of taking field notes. And at almost the same time he severed connections with the Harvard Natural History Society because of the "press of other duties (in my studies and in outside societies)." It was during this formative period, also, that Roosevelt besought the advice of the economist, J. Laurence Laughlin, then on the threshold of his long and distinguished career. Should he continue in biology or turn, perhaps, to economics? Laughlin's response, which may well have been an adjuration for the duty-conscious Roosevelt, was that the nation needed men who could think clearly on public questions.

However that may be, Roosevelt finally decided to study law. Following his honeymoon he read law in the offices of his uncle, Robert Barnhill Roosevelt, and attended the Columbia Law School, where he distinguished himself for his egotism and energetic questioning of the lecturers. He lacked the air of the professional student, one classmate remembered, but he was a "favorite" and was "one of the best men there, considered as a man." Theodore was already too much the moralist to give his heart to the law, however, and though he professed in his diary to "like the law school work very much," he soon abandoned it without genuine regret. "Many of the big corporation lawyers, to whom the ordinary members of the bar then as now looked up, held certain standards which were difficult to recognize as compatible with the idealism I supposed every high-minded young man is apt to feel," he wrote in his *Autobiography*. That statement has too much of the ring of the 1912 Progressive campaign to be taken literally; yet it probably reflected Roosevelt's views during 1880–81 in some degree. As Carleton Putnam cogently phrases it, "he aligned the moral law and the common law and was shocked at the discrepancy."

The event which changed the course of Roosevelt's career was his nomination as the Republican candidate for assemblyman from the twenty-first district in the fall of 1881. He had joined the district club the year before because "I intended to be one of the governing class." And he had joined the Republican club in particular because "a young man of my bringing-up and convictions could join only the Republican party." This was particularly true in cities such as New York and Boston, where the Tammany type pervaded Democratic ranks. In spite of the G.O.P.'s corruption and callous disdain for the needs of the masses, it still loomed large as the heroic preserver of national

union. To young Roosevelt, an uncompromising Unionist since boyhood—he had once prayed to "divine Providence to grind the Southern troops to powder"—and a strident nationalist from the time of his
matriculation in college, that was reason enough for joining it.

Roosevelt's baptism as a reformer occurred at one of the meetings
of the District Club during the winter of 1880–81 when he and a
handful of idealistic compatriots stood against close to a hundred
regulars in hopeless support of a movement for nonpartisan street
cleaning. He otherwise devoted his energies that year to breaking
down the barriers that separated him from the lower-class Republican
brethren. "I went around there often enough to have the men get
accustomed to me and to have me get accustomed to them, so that
we began to speak the same language, and so that each could begin
to live down, in the other's mind, what Bret Harte has called 'the
defective moral quality of being a stranger.' " In his way, he succeeded. Most of the professionals continued to regard Roosevelt as
unique, but many of them liked him. By the spring of 1881 he was on
fairly good terms with Jake Hess, the German-American district
leader, and on quite close terms with Joe Murray, an Irish-born
lieutenant who had been "raised as a barefoot boy on First Avenue,"
served in the Army of the Potomac, and would eventually be appointed Deputy Commissioner of Immigration for New York by
Roosevelt himself.

While Theodore and his bride of less than a year were leisurely
wandering through Europe in the summer of 1881, rumblings of
revolt were disturbing the harmony of the Twenty-first District Republican Club. Riled by the failure of Hess's man to support the
nonpartisan street-cleaning bill in the last legislative session, civic-
minded Republicans were threatening defection, or at least a tightening of the purse strings. Other, less civic-minded Republicans were
champing at Hess's inability to get a full measure of patronage from
President Chester A. Arthur.

In these circumstances Roosevelt's new-found friend, Joe Murray,
decided to break Hess's control by backing a candidate of his own
for the Assembly. Fastening upon Roosevelt as most likely to appeal
to the "better" elements—the Twenty-first ran from the pretentious
stone mansions of Fifth Avenue to the shabby brick tenements of the
West Side—Murray prepared his ground well. And when the nominating convention met on October 28 in the "large, barn-like room

over a saloon" that served as Club headquarters, he mustered a 16–9 majority for Roosevelt on the first ballot. Roosevelt, who had allowed his name to be entered with some reluctance, meanwhile announced that he was owned by no man, would go to Albany untrammeled and unpledged, and would vote independently on municipal and other public matters. He added, upon formal notification of his nomination, that he would vote with the Republican party on national issues.

Roosevelt's nomination struck a responsive chord except among a few close relatives. One Republican newspaper observed that the "substantial property owners" of the district needed a representative at Albany who could appreciate the "responsibility" of the situation. Roosevelt was ideal for that purpose because his "family has been long and honorably known as one of the foremost in this City." Another declared that "no better representative of the taxpayers of New York could have been selected." And a group of prominent Republicans, all of them gentlemen and some of them lawyers of the type against which Theodore would later inveigh, applauded him as "conspicuous for his honesty and integrity, and eminently qualified."

Meanwhile, Hess good-humoredly mustered the machine behind the young aristocrat who had been made the instrument of his own rebuke —but not until after he and Murray found it expedient to change tactics abruptly, following Roosevelt's first sally into the heart of the district.

"We started in a German lager-beer saloon on Sixth Avenue," Murray recalled:

> The saloon keeper's name was Carl Fischer. Hess was well acquainted with him. I knew him slightly. We had a small beer and Hess introduces T. R. to Fischer and Fischer says, "By the way, Mr. Roosevelt, I hope you will do something for us when you get to Albany. We are taxed much out of proportion to grocers, etc., and we have to pay $200 for the privilege."
>
> "Why that's not enough!" said T.R.
>
> After we got out on the sidewalk we came to the conclusion that we had better stop the canvass right then and there. I says, "Mr. Roosevelt, you go see your personal friends. Hess and I will look after this end. You can reach your personal friends, we can't."

Roosevelt heeded their advice; on election day he mounted a handsome majority and led the entire Republican ticket by 600 votes. "Too True! Too True! I have come a 'political hack. . . .'" he wrote Washburn the day after his election. "But do'n't think I am going to go into politics after this year, for I am not." A little less than two months later, on January 2, 1882, he presented himself in pince-nez, gold fob, and evening dress to the Republican caucus at the Delavan House in Albany.

What Roosevelt found in Albany was not encouraging. The Republicans were bad, he wrote in a diary he kept sporadically during the ensuing months. But, he added, at least they had numbers of lawyers and farmers among them. The Democrats included "six liquor sellers, two bricklayers, a butcher, a tobacconist, a pawn broker, a compositer (*sic*) and a typesetter . . ." Worse yet, twenty-five were Irish, and "the average catholic Irishman of the first generation as represented in this Assembly, is a low, venal, corrupt and unintelligent brute." The Tammany men were "managed entirely by the commands of some of John Kelly's lieutenants who are always in the Assembly chamber"; the County Democrats by the Commissioner of Public Works, Hubert O. Thompson, "a gross, enormously fleshy man, with a full face and thick, sensual lips . . ." Still, there were a few who seemed "to be pretty good men." Two Republican farmers, O'Neil and Sheehy, were "among the best members of the house."

Actually, Roosevelt's strictures against first-generation Irish Catholics were grounded more on observation than deep-seated bias; before the end of the five-months session he was to form strong friendships with several Irish Democrats of anti-Tammany persuasion. Nor did he even then sympathize with those of his class who tended "to trace all evils, from the absence of rain to the fight with Arabi Pascha, to the presence of Roman Catholics in America." He recognized Tammany Hall for what it was—a sink of corruption dominated by Irish Catholics—and he saw among Republicans a somewhat better class of citizen. As he confided to his diary, "if the worst elements of all, the twenty low Irishmen, were subtracted, the Republican average would still be higher than the Democratic." Roosevelt failed to realize, of course, that up-state Republicans of Protestant background could be as opposed to social justice in their avowedly moralistic way as Tammany Democrats in their blatantly unscrupulous way; that Democratic iniquity in low places had long been surpassed by Republican solicitude for private business interest in high places. But those were lessons of the future.

Roosevelt managed to contain within his diary most of his opinions of his associates, but he proved unable to suppress his views on public matters. Every fiber of his being compelled him to speak out, and he several times took positions that he later regretted during his three terms in the Assembly. "He was the most indiscreet guy I ever met. . . ." Isaac Hunt recalled. "George [Spinney], Billy O'Neil and I used to sit on his coat-tails. Billy O'Neil would say to him: 'What do you want to do that for, you damn fool; you will ruin yourself and everybody else!' . . . He was the most impulsive human being I ever knew."

Roosevelt's impulsiveness was to become tempered by age and responsibility; only rarely in later years would he act without deliberation on matters of high public policy. Even as he matured, however, he continued to seem impulsive, for he could phrase the most carefully balanced speech sensationally and make the most considered action appear spontaneous. To the end, moreover, he remained impulsive in his personal habits, especially his conversation; and to the end the quality constituted one of the mainsprings of his hold upon the American public. Men of conservative temperament were alienated and Roosevelt's friends often embarrassed by it. But the trust and devotion of the middle classes were inspired by it. They seemed to believe Roosevelt incapable of dissemblance, though in truth he had an artful side; and they expected that he would act invariably on his words, though in fact he often failed to do so.

Even before he had unloosed his attack on Judge Westbrook, Roosevelt had laid the foundation for a minor reputation as a reformer. His maiden speech had been undistinguished, indeed presumptuous and partisan. Delivered in a halting, almost lisping style, it was a protest against a movement to overcome the Democratic factionalism that had prevented the Assembly from being organized for more than three weeks by forming a coalition of Republicans and Democrats. "While in New York I talked with several gentlemen who have large commercial interests at stake," Theodore condescendingly remarked on January 24, 1882, "and they do not seem to care whether the deadlock is broken or not." Indeed, he concluded, "they felt rather relieved."

Within a few weeks, however, Roosevelt proved his real mettle. The Syracuse Ring, as one group of Republican spoilsmen were known, had agreed to support the Tammany legislative program in return for a division of appointive offices. The mechanics of the deal called for the transfer of a number of positions to the control of the Republican Clerk; and on February 21 the veteran war horses held a G.O.P. caucus preparatory to feeding at the Tammany trough. Roosevelt, Hunt, and a number of like-minded younger Republicans raised such a vigorous protest, however, that they carried the majority with them. "I did not believe the Republican party should degenerate and become a party scrambling for the spoils of office, and such action would certainly drive the best elements of the party from it," Roosevelt explained to a reporter just after the caucus ended. "Rarely in the history of legislation here has the moral force of individual honor and political honesty been more forcibly displayed," the New York *Herald* exuberantly declared the next morning. Theodore's diary entry was less high blown: "I firmly and sweetly declined" the preferments offered should he change his position, he wrote.

Ten days after that first minor triumph, Roosevelt spoke in support of a bill of his own to alter the procedure for electing aldermen in New York City. He contended that the nominating power was "largely divorced from the mass of voters of the same party" and that "every underhand expedient known to the lowest kind of trading politics" was thus called into play. He proposed to eradicate those evils by having each assembly district elect its own alderman. This would have reduced the number of seats held by his own party and would have weakened the influence of the professionals in both parties. The bill died aborning.

Theodore's attitude toward labor during that first formative year showed few signs of the obsession with justice which otherwise characterized him. His social philosophy still encompassed little more than the Republican predilection for low taxes and minimal social services, and when a measure to pay municipal laborers a minimum of two dollars a day was favorably reported, he had bolted from his seat to oppose it. "Why, Mr. Speaker, this bill will impose an expenditure of thousands of dollars upon the City of New York," he heatedly said. Nor was that all. He also spiritedly opposed salary increases for New York City's underpaid policemen and firemen.

Whatever the narrowness of his views, Roosevelt had not lacked courage during this baptismal year. He alone of the representatives from New York City had spoken out against the popular salary-increase measures. And he alone, reported the militantly Democratic

New York *World,* had "put a quietus upon a gigantic job which had
been quietly reported" to grant monopolistic powers over the construction of bonded warehouses and grain elevators along the water-
fronts to the Terminal Warehouse Elevated and Docking Company.
He had capped those signal actions by forcing the investigation of
Judge Westbrook.

The result was reward, and in certain places, approval. The New
York *Evening Post,* like Roosevelt a bull on morality and a bear on
social reform, asserted at the end of the session that he "accomplished
more good than any man of his age and experience has accomplished . . . in years." Carl Schurz, the German-American Civil
War general and civil service reformer who was then one of Roosevelt's political idols, declared that Roosevelt and two other assemblymen had "stemmed the tide of corruption in that fearful legislative
gathering." And a group of the young Assemblyman's personal
friends were so impressed by his services that they tendered him a
testimonial dinner at Delmonico's. But most important of all, Isaac
Hunt recollected, he was now "considered a full-fledged man worthy
of any one's esteem."

CHAPTER 2

A LEADER EMERGES

> But as yet I understood little of the effort which was already
> beginning . . . to secure a more genuine social and industrial
> justice.
>
> —Theodore Roosevelt, *An Autobiography*

Roosevelt's re-election was practically inevitable, so illustrious was
his reputation by the end of his first term. Nevertheless, a mild flurry
of activity marked his campaign in the fall of 1882. He was commended for his "fearless, honest, and independent action" by a group
of prominent constituents. Jake Hess and his regulars fell in behind
him because they were stuck with him. And the *New York Times,
Herald,* and *Evening Post* supported him on the grounds that he had
been "self-sacrificing," "the leader of the younger and better element,"
and opposed to "corrupt jobs of all kinds." On November 7 Roosevelt
led the entire ticket with a spectacular two-to-one majority even
though Grover Cleveland, the Democratic candidate for governor,
carried his district by 1,800 votes.

Roosevelt had made only one important campaign speech. On
October 28, to an overflow crowd of friends and party workers in
Lyric Hall, he had forthrightly stated his own policies, called for
party regularity, and lashed the Democrats with that partisan fury
which would almost always mar his campaign speeches.

"As long as the history . . . of our nation has lasted, the
Democrats have been one and the same," he asserted, as he con-
temptuously referred to Thomas Jefferson, "miscalled the Great," and
James Buchanan, "the Little." The Republicans? Were they not the

24

party of Hamilton, Webster, and Clay; the "great party which has
produced a Lincoln . . . the party within whose ranks we now hold
Schurz and Choate, and every other name almost that tends to make
this city illustrious"? If he were re-elected, Roosevelt declared, he
would endeavor to carry "honesty and courage" as well as "private
morality" into public office. He would also tackle the issue of "great
importance"—monopoly. ". . . there is no question that there is a
vital spirit underlying it; that we as a people are suffering from new
dangers; that as our fathers fought with slavery and crushed it, in
order that it would not seize and crush them, so we are called on to
fight new forces."

The young New Yorker kept well that faith. During his second term
he again stood out as a fearless foe of corruption and an unfailing
champion of governmental reform. And he also started a campaign
to control monopoly which was to carry into his governorship and on
through his presidency. His record was so striking, in fact, that halfway through the session he received national recognition in the pages
of *Harper's Weekly* and by the end of the session had emerged as
the leader of a faction openly known as "The Roosevelt Republicans."
In his third and final term, yet more honors befell him.

Roosevelt's near-meteoric rise was the result of a partial measure
of good fortune and a full measure of initiative and daring. It was his
fortune that those ignoble exemplars of easy political virtue, Roscoe
Conkling and Thomas C. Platt, were without great power during his
three years in the legislature. And it was probably his fortune, too,
that his last terms coincided with the governorship of Grover Cleveland. Several times during the sessions of 1883 and 1884 Cleveland and Roosevelt caught the public imagination by cooperating
against their party machines, and in one graphic cartoon the stolid
Democratic Governor and the ebullient Republican Assemblyman
were portrayed with arms linked surveying a disintegrated Tammany
tiger. But in the end the relationship between the two future Presidents, the one forty-six years old and increasingly conscious of his
destiny, the other twenty-four and still uncertain of his life's work,
was marred by recrimination.

The event that first joined the two men in common cause was
Cleveland's veto of a bill, twice supported by Roosevelt, to reduce
the fare on the elevated railways from ten to five cents. Always a
popular issue, it had special significance at the time because of a

public indignation against Jay Gould. Many of the most respected elements in the city regarded the bill as a means of dealing that haughty buccaneer a heavy blow, and the city's Republican delegation at Albany prepared to support it almost to a man.

Roosevelt would normally have opposed such a radical measure. The laissez-faire teachings of Harvard had held that the regulation of business was not a legislative function. The social milieu in which Theodore had been reared confirmed the tradional ordained rights of property. And the experience of the previous year had convinced him that "corporations are more sinned against than sinning." Yet the Westbrook investigation had given him an insight into the machinations of Jay Gould and people like him. He allowed himself to be carried along by the swelling tide.

The tide failed to engulf the ultra-conservative gentleman in the Executive Mansion, however. Convinced that the fare-reduction bill embodied a breach of contract, Governor Cleveland vetoed the measure in a magnificent display of courage. "The State should not only be strictly just," he solemnly affirmed, "but scrupulously fair."

Young Roosevelt took Cleveland's words to heart. No sooner was the veto message read to the Assembly on March 2, 1883, than he jumped to his feet (he had already been likened to a jack rabbit by Gould's New York *World*). He had risen to confess, he dramatically announced, that he had blundered grievously in supporting the bill originally. "I . . . weakly yielded, partly in a vindictive spirit toward the infernal thieves and conscienceless swindlers who have the elevated railroads in charge, and partly to the popular voice of New York." The measure "breaks the plighted faith of the state" and was therefore at root "a question of justice to ourselves." He would rather leave politics with the feeling "that I had done what was right than stay in with the approval of all men, knowing in my heart that I had acted as I ought not to."

Roosevelt's courageous sentiments were echoed less publicly by many of his colleagues, and on March 7 the veto was decisively sustained. Although the sensationalist press continued to berate him, many responsible newspapers commended his action warmly. Roosevelt was a gentleman "whose probity is as generally recognized as his ability," the New York *Tribune* said in a representative editorial; he had acted with "characteristic manliness" in reversing himself on the five-cent-fare bill.

Nor was that the only time that Roosevelt made a manly change of front that spring. For some months Theodore had been immaturely excoriating an aged assemblyman from Richmond, one Erastus Brooks. Finally, near the close of the session, Brooks delivered a full-dress defense of his actions, and he also attacked Roosevelt sharply. When the Richmond Assemblyman had finished, relates Putnam, Roosevelt strode forward with tears in his eyes to shake his adversary's hand. "Mr. Brooks, I surrender," he contritely exclaimed. "I beg your pardon."

In the meantime Roosevelt had mounted a new attack on Jay Gould. Within a week of his vote in support of Cleveland's veto, he introduced a resolution directing the Attorney General to bring suit for the dissolution of Gould's Manhattan Elevated Railway Company. And a few days after that he boldly charged that the New York *World* was "a local stock-jobbing sheet of limited circulation and versatile mendacity, owned by the arch thief of Wall Street, and edited by a rancorous kleptomaniac with a penchant for trousers."

The words were impetuous, but the theme was not. A year before, so Roosevelt's *Autobiography* suggests and his record seemingly confirms, Roosevelt had come to a personal crossroads. Some time after the Westbrook investigation an old family friend had taken Theodore to lunch. After remarking that it had been a good thing for Roosevelt to have made the "reform play," the friend advised him to leave politics and identify himself with "the right kind of people, the people who would always in the long run control others and obtain the real rewards." Theodore asked if this meant that he should yield to the "ring." The patronizing retort was that the so-called "ring" included "certain big business men, and the politicians, lawyers and judges who were in alliance with and to a certain extent dependent upon them, and that the successful man had to win his success by the backing of the same forces, whether in law, business, or politics."

Meanwhile, Roosevelt and Cleveland had come together in support of civil service reform, the bête noire of machine politicians in both parties. Early in the session Cleveland conferred in his office with Roosevelt and a few other Republicans in an effort to form such a coalition of antimachine Republicans and anti-Tammany Democrats as would prevent the machine politicians in both parties from thwarting his program. Roosevelt was amenable, and the coalition was formed. Several important measures were enacted in consequence, the most far-reaching of which created a Civil Service Commission. In addition, a large number of bills conferring special privileges on corporations were killed. The Roosevelt Republicans, the *New York Times* correspondent enthusiastically reported at the close of the session, had been "as effective as any minority the writer has ever seen in the Assembly."

Governor Cleveland's resolve to brook no compromise with Tammany had split the Democrats and provoked a Republican victory in the legislative elections of 1883. Roosevelt thereupon decided to bid for the speakership, for which post he had received his party's complimentary nomination at the start of his second term. Employing the techniques of the professional politician for the first time, he threw himself into the contest with remarkable vigor. He went into remote rural regions to seek out assemblymen-elect. He requested and authorized his friends to work for him. And he wrote numerous letters soliciting support. Yet he apparently made no deals. "I am a Republican, pure and simple, neither a 'half breed' nor a 'stalwart'; and certainly no man, nor yet any ring or clique, can do my thinking for me," he informed at least one correspondent:

> As you say, I believe in treating all our business interests equitably and alike; in favoring no one interest or set of interests at the expense of others. In making up the committees I should pay attention, first, to the absolute integrity of the men, second, to their capacity to deal intelligently with the matters likely to come before them—for . . . honesty and common sense are the two prime requisites for a legislator.

Roosevelt concluded that he was much stronger than he had dared hope, and on the eve of the contest he wrote that his chances were good even though the lobby and the politicians had raised the free-trade scarecrow against him. Had not the *New York Times* remarked that the only thing against him was "the curable defect of being a young man"? When the Republican caucus met on New Year's Eve, however, Titus Sheard, a reputable, self-made manufacturer from Herkimer County was elected by 42 votes to 30. Theodore had suffered his first political defeat, and he was, he conceded, "chagrined."

Roosevelt's strength was so great, however, that Sheard appointed him chairman of the Committee on Cities and then made him chairman of a special committee to investigate the Public Works Department. In spite of the personal burdens that I will describe in the next chapter, Roosevelt's special committee conducted one of the most sensational investigations of municipal government to that time. Day after day Theodore and his colleagues relentlessly grilled minor and major officeholders as they sought to unravel the interlocking hold of corruption on New York City. Finally, on March 14, the committee filed its report. "Appalling Condition of Affairs"; "Surrogate's Office a Place for Blackmailing"; "How the City is Robbed"; "Sweeping Changes Urged"; "Roosevelt's Blunderbuss"—so the newspapers heralded it.

The findings justified the headlines. The committee's report revealed that the county clerk had netted $250,000 through the fee system and that the register of deeds and mortgages had paid approximately $50,000 for his appointment. It showed that "a system of the grossest blackmail and extortion prevailed among the employees" in the surrogate's office. The Department of Taxes and Assessments was found to have "absolutely no system whatever in the assessing" of real estate, while the "grossest abuses" were discovered in the sheriff's office. Worse still, the investigation indicated that the real governing authorities of the City of New York were "outside parties who cannot be held responsible to the law."

Roosevelt proposed to eradicate these evils by a comprehensive program of reform legislation. Shortly after the special committee had reported he introduced nine bills, seven of which were eventually enacted into law. The most important substituted salaries for the fee system, deprived the board of aldermen of the authority to confirm the mayor's appointments, and empowered the mayor to appoint city department heads and other municipal officials as well as to remove them for cause with the governor's approval.

Meanwhile Roosevelt drew up a bill designed to force the removal of Commissioner of Public Works Hubert O. Thompson, the leader of the County Democrats. At the same time Roosevelt openly pressed Cleveland to investigate again Sheriff Alexander V. Davidson, who had been acquitted of extortion following a grand-jury indictment. Cleveland was thereby caught in a nightmarish dilemma. Both Thompson and Davidson had played important roles in his rise to the governorship; their cooperation would be urgently needed in the drive for his nomination for the presidency. He had already broken with Tammany. Could he now destroy Thompson and Davidson and yet himself survive?

For the first and perhaps the only time during his governorship Cleveland pursued an equivocal course. He vetoed the bill which would have effected Thompson's removal, and in spite of Roosevelt's presentation of evidence which the grand jury had not considered, he failed to move against Davidson.

Actually, Cleveland's veto was well founded. The bill had been so amended by Republican allies of Tammany that it probably could not have accomplished its purpose. As its original draftsman pointed out in a letter to the *New York Times,* the final version was "unfit to find a place in the statute book." Nevertheless, the veto and the dismissal of Roosevelt's charges against Davidson gave the Republicans, grown desperate for an issue against the popular Cleveland, what they had almost despaired of finding. "Now we had several bills that bore upon Tammany Hall," Roosevelt exclaimed in a campaign speech the following fall. "The Governor signed those most unflinchingly— with reckless heroism. Then we had several that affected the County Democracy, and the leader of the County Democracy—my esteemed fellow citizen, Mr. Hubert O. Thompson, and those measures came to an untimely end."

Although Roosevelt's legislative lodestar was political reform, his restless mind and compelling sense of duty impelled him to explore and speak out on a wide range of subjects. In 1883 he vigorously opposed a bill to tighten the newspaper libel law on the grounds that "it is a great deal better to err a little bit on the side of having too much discussion and having too virulent language used by the press, rather than to err on the side of having them not say what they ought to say, especially with reference to public men and measures." And in 1884 he spoke against a prohibition bill, arguing that it would play into the hands of the very elements it was designed to repress.

Roosevelt also took a firm position on the absolute separation of church and state. Catholic and Protestant charitable organizations periodically solicited financial support from the legislature, and during the 1883 session it was proposed that the Catholic Protectory at Elmira be granted $25,000 for the construction of a new sewerage plant. Roosevelt interposed a forceful objection, asserting that the connection of church and state was "wholly wrong," that it brought religion into politics, and that it violated the spirit of the Constitution. His brief was unavailing, however; the bill passed by 99 to 17. A few weeks later when a bill to grant funds to a Protestant organization came up he took a similar position and was again resoundingly defeated. Yet his consistency did not go unnoticed. "Mr. ROOSEVELT enjoys in the Assembly the distinction of having convictions and acting up to them," the *New York Times* said.

It was Roosevelt's attitudes toward labor which were most revealing of his development during these formative years. He was slow to comprehend the changes brought about by the industrial revolution— the growing impersonality of the relations between employer and employee, the wearying monotony of routine labor, the frequent intervals of unemployment, and the intense competition for jobs of the meanest sort. Nor did he then understand the function of unions. He attributed the deplorable conditions of labor to the workings of natural law rather than to the gross mismanagement of human resources; and natural law, in the prevailing view, was inviolable. As the Rev. Henry Ward Beecher, who was as convinced that God was on the side of the capitalists as he was certain that Satan was allied with the saloon-keepers and their workingmen customers, declaimed: "The things required for prosperous labor, prosperous manufactures, and prosperous commerce are three. First, liberty; second, liberty; and third, liberty."

It is a tribute to Roosevelt's capacity for growth that his labor views changed at all. Unlike Henry Cabot Lodge, Elihu Root and most leading Republicans of his generation, he gradually came to possess some comprehension of the labor problem. And though he failed to emerge of a sudden as an advanced labor reformer, his three years as an assemblyman saw his first cautious wandering from the hallowed highway of laissez faire.

True, his wanderings were inconsistent. Even in his final term Roosevelt opposed a bill to reduce the working time for some 15,000 streetcar conductors to twelve hours per day. He first argued that to oppose the law of supply and demand because it was unfeeling was like trying to repeal the law of gravity because its results were sometimes brutal; he then charged that the twelve-hour legislation would tie labor to the apron strings of the state. To offer a worker such protection, he exclaimed, was both un-American and insulting! Had not Speaker of the Assembly Titus Sheard risen from laborer to manufacturer without such aid? The statement was correct, Sheard acknowledged in reply. He added, however, that he had found working fourteen hours a day painful, brutalizing, and not in any way related to his subsequent success. Indeed, Sheard said, he believed that he would have been even more self-reliant if his hours of labor had been shorter and his wages higher!

Nevertheless, the still callow Roosevelt continued to oppose the bill. He raised the haunting specter of communism and socialism and he inveighed against the Knights of Labor, who were then approaching the peak of their power. Every man should stand on his own bottom, he self-righteously declared at one point, only to be reminded, in what should have been the most mortifying blow of his legislative career, that his own bottom was his inheritance from his father, the laboring man's nothing. It was not surprising that *John Swinton's Paper,* a militant labor journal edited by a fiery idealist, called him a "crested snob." Yet Roosevelt won his point; Grover Cleveland, who was to prove far less sympathetic to labor than Theodore Roosevelt in the summing up, vetoed the bill on the grounds that it was "class legislation."

John Swinton's bitter characterization of Roosevelt was animated by more than resentment of the young Assemblyman's opposition to the twelve-hour bill. By then Roosevelt had several times flaunted labor or its interests. He had recommended public whipping for certain crimes. He had dismissed with thinly veiled contempt labor's charge that the convict-labor system "was a vital cobra which was swamping [*sic*] the lives of laboring men." He had supported an anti-riot bill which labor quite realistically regarded as an antistrike measure. And he had once invited "a labor agitator from Brooklyn" to "step outside" to defend himself. The trouble with the working-men, he wrote in a patronizing magazine article the year after he retired from the Assembly, was that they had been instilled with false hopes by "professional agitators" who were "always promising to procure by legislation the advantages which can only come to work-ingmen . . . by their individual or united energy, intelligence, and forethought."

Years later Roosevelt regretted his manifest hostility toward unions and most labor legislation during this period. "One partial reason for my slowness in grasping the importance of action in these matters," he wrote in his *Autobiography,* "was the corrupt and unattractive

nature of so many of the men who championed popular reforms, their
insincerity, and the folly of so many of the actions which they
advocated."

Samuel Gompers, the convivial, dedicated, English-born Jew who
gave the American labor movement its pragmatic character, was
responsible for Roosevelt's first real insight into the degrading effects
of his vaunted natural law. For years humanitarians had been denouncing the manufacture of cigars in New York tenements by un-
organized immigrants who labored for wages that might have been
termed subsistence had not their death rate belied it. Finally, in 1882,
Gompers arranged the introduction of a bill to outlaw the manufacture
of cigars in tenements, and a three-man committee, including the
freshman Roosevelt, was appointed to investigate.

Roosevelt later believed that he was put on the committee in the
cynical expectation that he would perfunctorily report against the
tenement bill. Possibly he was. Neither the Democratic nor the
Republican leadership wanted to strike against the status quo; nor did
the two other members of the committee plan to act in full conscience. The Republican member confided to Roosevelt that he would
support the measure because of labor strength in his district, and the
Democrat, "a sporting Tammany man who afterward abandoned
politics for the race-track," as Theodore remembered, frankly
admitted that he had to oppose the bill because of certain powerful
interests. But he suggested that Roosevelt look into the situation,
adding that he believed Roosevelt would favor the labor proposal on
firsthand knowledge.

Impressed by Roosevelt's "aggressiveness and evident sincerity,"
Gompers meanwhile invited the young Assemblyman to tour the
tenement area with him. Roosvelt accepted, though he was then inclined to oppose the bill. As he afterward wrote: "The respectable
people I knew were against it; and it was contrary to the principles of
political economy of the *laissez-faire* kind; the businessmen who spoke
to me about it shook their heads and said that it was designed to
prevent a man doing as he wished and as he had a right to do with
what was his own." But his several inspections of tenements—he went
once with Gompers and several union officials, once with the other
members of the committee, and once or twice on his own—convinced
him of the need for the legislation. "I have always remembered one
room in which two families were living," he recalled. "There were

several children, three men, and two women in this room. The tobacco was stowed about everywhere, alongside the foul bedding, and in a corner where there were scraps of food. The men, women, and children in this room worked by day and far on into the evening, and they slept and ate there. They were Bohemians, unable to speak English, except that one of the children knew enough to act as interpreter."

When the tenement bill was brought out of committee late that winter, Roosevelt supported it on the floor. The measure got through the Assembly, but it failed to be considered by the Senate, the copy of the bill being stolen from the clerk's files by a member of the manufacturers' lobby. The following year, however, a similar measure passed both houses and was sent to the Governor for approval. Cleveland balked, fearing the bill was unconstitutional; but he did agree to hold a hearing on March 8. Roosevelt thereupon consented, as he phrased it, to act "as spokesman for the battered, undersized foreigners who represented the Union and the workers," and on the appointed day he argued convincingly for its adoption. After listening impassively to Roosevelt and other interested parties, the Governor surmounted his scruples and signed the measure into law.

Refusing to accept defeat, the manufacturers took the issue to the courts. Their able attorney, former Secretary of State William M. Evarts, argued that tobacco was "a disinfectant and a prophylactic," that socialism and communism were responsible for the bill's conception, and that home manufacture was actually conducive to "the proper culture of growing girls." Apparently convinced by Evarts's reasoning, the New York Court of Appeals ruled the tenement law unconstitutional within less than a year of the bill's passage.

Three months after that shocking decision, an indignant legislature overwhelmingly passed a slightly modified bill. Again, Roosevelt vigorously championed the measure in a speech in which he strayed far from the philosophical tenets of his youth. He conceded that the abolition of tenement workshops was not only a dangerous departure from prevailing doctrines, but was "in a certain sense a socialistic one." Nevertheless, he added in an understanding passage, the constantly increasing extremes of poverty and wealth demand that we "modify the principles or doctrines on which we manage our system of government." Otherwise, he continued, neither the cigar makers nor their children would ever be fit to perform the duties of American citizenship. He concluded that the bill merited passage as a "hygienic measure alone," and he emphasized that he was supporting the measure on the basis of his own findings rather than the union's recommendations.

Whatever his reservations about labor unions, the struggle over the tenement bill was a powerfully formative experience for Roosevelt. For the first time he had faced the bleak fact that the American economic system was cruelly denying social development to hundreds of thousands, and probably millions, of working people. Either their lot would be ameliorated or democratic capitalism would be destroyed. Those were the alternatives. Young Roosevelt was one of the few of his class or party to perceive them, however faintly.

Theodore's growth was evidenced by several other actions during his three years in Albany. He sponsored a bill to regulate the working conditions of women and children; he several times voted for bills instituting safety measures in factories and various trades; and he gave full support to the creation of a labor bureau. Only on the wage increases for firemen, policemen, and city laborers, which he regarded as politically inspired, did he stubbornly hold out.

After he left the legislature Roosevelt's insight into the character of American society, and especially of the judiciary, continued to deepen. In January, 1885, the New York State Court of Appeals found in the *In re Jacobs* case that the tenement law passed in 1884 was patently unconstitutional. How, the court asked, can the health and morals of the producer be improved "by forcing him from his home and its hallowed associations and beneficent influences, to ply his trade elsewhere?" The tenement law, the court continued, was an indisputable abridgment of the cigar makers' "fundamental rights of liberty."

Roosevelt's reaction to the *Jacobs* decision at the time is uncertain. Probably his autobiographical commentary is a fair statement of his attitude. "It was this case which first waked me to a dim and partial understanding of the fact that the courts were not necessarily the best judges of what should be done to better social and industrial conditions," he wrote. "Of course it took more than one experience such as this Tenement Cigar Case to shake me out of the attitude in which I was brought up." For the fact was "the people with whom I was most intimate were apt to praise the courts for just such decisions as this, and to speak of them as bulwarks against disorder and barriers against demagogic legislation." But as a result of numerous such decisions, he continued, "I grew to realize that all Abraham Lincoln had said about the Dred Scott decision could be said with equal truth and justice about the numerous decisions which in our own day were erected as bars across the path of social reform, and which brought to naught so much of the effort to secure justice and fair dealings for working men and working women, and for plain citizens generally."

Young Roosevelt's political horizons meanwhile broadened even more rapidly than his social insights deepened. Eighteen eighty-four was a presidential election year, and the Grand Old Party's controlling clique was determined to make James G. Blaine, of Maine and "Mulligan letters" fame, the Republican nominee. Repelled by Blaine's unsavory political character, George W. Curtis, Carl Schurz, Henry Cabot Lodge, and other reform-minded Republicans decided to oppose the "Plumed Knight" with Senator George F. Edmunds of Vermont, an honest, conservative Yankee of no particular distinction. Roosevelt, who was not less repelled by Blaine than Curtis and the others, joined them. He announced himself for Edmunds in mid-January, though the Twenty-first District machine was for President Arthur, and in mid-April his slate of Edmunds men defeated Jake Hess's in the contest for delegates to the Republican State Convention.

Thereafter the story blurs. The *World* later charged that Roosevelt had compromised with John J. O'Brien, the city Republican leader, in his battle against Hess. Contending that Roosevelt had needed O'Brien's support to defeat Hess, the *World* claimed that he failed to make a sufficiently strong effort to pass a reform bill—the Bureau of Elections Bill—which would have removed O'Brien as Chief of the Bureau of Elections. Had Roosevelt worked as hard for passage of that bill as he had for the Tenure-of-Office bill, the *World* wrote, it would have gone through.

No other evidence confirms those charges, and Putnam concludes that they are groundless. Yet Roosevelt makes the following admission in his *Autobiography:*

> I at one period began to believe that I had a future before me, and that it behooved me to be very far-sighted and scan each action carefully with a view to its possible effect on that future. This speedily made me useless to the public and an object of aversion to myself; and I then made up my mind that I would try not to think of the future at all, but would proceed on the assumption that

each office I held would be the last I ever should hold, and that I would confine myself to trying to do my work as well as possible while I held that office.

Whether that passage refers to the *World's* charges is unclear. It is certain, however, that except for an assertion by the *Evening Post* after the presidential election of 1884 that Roosevelt had "showered certificates of good character and promise of 'support' on candidates for all sorts of city offices," no other action of his legislative career remotely suggests such a compromise.

The New York Republican party was torn with dissension as it prepared to convene in Utica that spring. Most "stalwarts" lined up behind President Chester A. Arthur, who had drawn on theretofore untapped resources to give the country a competent administration. The "half-breeds" fell in behind Blaine, as did a faction of stalwarts headed by State Senator Thomas C. Platt, who had come out of seclusion and was soon to build the machine that made him the dominant power in New York politics for almost two decades. The Oswego druggist was for Blaine because he thought he would win; and also because he hated Arthur. Between the stalwarts and the half-breeds were the independents. Most were mildly for Edmunds, but all were vehemently against both Arthur and Blaine. They numbered perhaps a seventh of the convention delegates and they were led by the twenty-five-year-old Roosevelt. At stake was the selection of four delegates-at-large to the national convention, scheduled to convene in Chicago six weeks after the state meeting.

Fresh from his victory over Hess four days before, Roosevelt arrived in Utica on April 21. Perceiving the Arthur forces' implacable opposition to Blaine, he audaciously insisted that they support the entire Edmunds slate. The Arthur men bitterly resented his imperious demand, but they despised Blaine more. Reluctantly they submitted after a final conference in Roosevelt's hotel room at two A.M., April 22; and when the convention met in the Utica Opera House early that afternoon, Roosevelt and three other Independents, including Curtis and President Andrew D. White of Cornell University, were elected on the first ballot. In his youthful exuberance Roosevelt then turned to ex-Governor Warner Miller, who had spearheaded his defeat for Speaker in January, and expostulated, "There, damn you, we beat you for last winter." Meanwhile a great cry went up for

Roosevelt to appear on the platform. The *New York Times* described the scene:

> Mr. Roosevelt disregarded the call for a moment, and then, amid enthusiastic cheers, made his way to the stage. His slender, erect form, bright young face and active ways have made him familiar within a few days to almost every one who took part in the convention, and his legislative work had won admiration and a respect for his industry, capacity, and judgment. He wisely curbed any natural desire he may have had to make a speech. Simply and frankly he said: "I have nothing to say except to thank you for the honor you have conferred upon me. I shall try to so behave myself as to serve the best interests of the Republican Party, and to make you feel no regret in selecting me."

All through his life, even in moments of triumph, Theodore Roosevelt was wont to have forebodings of disaster; the aftermath of his victory at Utica was no exception. A week after the convention ended he unburdened himself to a friendly Utica newspaper editor:

> I have very little expectation of being able to keep on in politics; my success so far has only been won by absolute indifference to my future career; for I doubt if any man can realise [*sic*] the bitter and venomous hatred with which I am regarded by the very politicians who at Utica supported me, under dictation from masters who were influenced by political considerations that were national and not local in their scope. I realize very thoroughly the absolutely ephemeral nature of the hold I have upon the people, and a very real and positive hostility I have excited among the politicians. I will not stay in public life unless I can do so on my own terms; and my ideal, whether lived up to or not, is rather a high one.

What did he mean? That he had compromised once and was too conscience-ridden to do it again? That he sensed that he would have to support Blaine eventually or get out of Republican politics? That he was not yet ready to accept politics as the art of the possible?

Whatever he meant, he characteristically acted rather than brooded. During the interim between the state convention at Utica and the national convention at Chicago, Roosevelt worked feverishly to bind together the scattered Edmunds delegates, who never numbered a hundred. He hoped that they would again comprise the balance of power, though he was far from sanguine. "Unquestionably, Blaine is

our greatest danger," he warned Henry Cabot Lodge, who was working for Edmunds in Massachusetts, "for I fear lest, if he come too
near success, the bread-and-butter brigade from the south will leave
Arthur and go over to him. We who stand against both *must* be
organized . . ."

When the Republican convention convened the first week in June
in Chicago, however, the forces of emotionalism and materialism
proved overpowering. Blaine's magnetic personality inspired loyalty
and enthusiasm if not much else, and on the fourth ballot the Grand
Old Party gave him its nomination. There followed a wildly climactic
scene which saw William McKinley, then a relatively obscure Ohio
congressman, push his way through to Roosevelt on the floor and ask
him to make a unity speech for the "Plumed Knight." The New York
leader refused.

The first of a long succession of Gethsemanes was now at hand.
Roosevelt had been a center of attention throughout the convention.
The press, remarks Putnam, had treated him whimsically, commenting
on his "nobby straw" hat, "jaunty" attire, "nervously forcible" gestures and "pugnacious" nose. The New York *Sun* had described him
as "bubbling over with martial ardor" as he vainly sought to bolster
the dampened spirits of the Edmunds men. And another paper
related how "Roosevelt, Fish and Lodge applauded with the tips of
their fingers held immediately in front of their noses."

Yet, as Putnam also observes, Roosevelt's remarkable capacity for
leadership had come through. The *World* described his seconding
speech for Thomas R. Lynch, a Mississippi Negro nominated for
temporary chairman by Lodge in a successful maneuver against the
Blaine delegates, as blunt and manly. The *New York Times* reported
that though he "scrambled to his perch on the chair with juvenile
activity," he spoke with the authority of "a positive practical man"
rather than a youth. And Joseph B. Foraker, the Ohio spoilsman with
whom Roosevelt, when President, would clash bitterly, recalled that
his conferences with Roosevelt had been "so taxing upon the strength
and the mental operations . . . that I felt scarcely able to attend the
evening session . . ." Obviously, McKinley would not have sought
Roosevelt's support for Blaine had the convention as a whole regarded the young reformer as sensationalist reporters portrayed him.

Roosevelt and the other independent-minded New Yorkers had "sat
with troubled countenances biting their lips, crimson with vexation

and dismay" as Blaine's fourth-ballot nomination impended. Now, in the agonizing aftermath of the "Plumed Knight's" victory, they knew they would have to decide whether they would support him in the campaign that fall. "I was at the birth of the Republican party, and I fear I am to witness its death," Curtis exclaimed as he awaited the final tally. The *Harper's* editor refused, however, to comment once the final result was announced. Roosevelt was less self-contained. He was variously reported as declining comment, advising reporters to see him the next week, and attributing Blaine's nomination to "mistaken public enthusiasm." The *New York Times* quoted him most fully:

> To say that I am satisfied with the nomination of Mr. Blaine would be false. I have participated in a Republican convention, and by all the usages of the party, I would be expected to support its nominee. I could have given an earnest and enthusiastic support to a ticket headed by such a man as George F. Edmunds. . . . I should suppose, from what I have heard many independents say, that they would not give Mr. Blaine any support whatever; and I believe they will keep their promise.

Roosevelt's assertion was correct. Curtis, Carl Schurz, Henry Ward Beecher and a great host of reformers and plain, respectable citizens throughout the nation were going to bolt. That Roosevelt would fail to go along with them was unthinkable. William Roscoe Thayer, upon whom the nomination of Blaine weighed "like a nightmare," described the esteem in which he then held the young reformer. "I thought of him as of a paladin against whom the forces of evil would dash themselves to pieces," Thayer wrote. "I thought of him as the young and dauntless spokesman of righteousness whose words would silence the special pleaders of iniquity. I wrote him and besought him to stand firm." Others implored him to do the same.

When it became evident early in July that Roosevelt would "stand firm," but with the Republican party rather than with his reformer friends, it was as though a piece of Thayer's heart had been cut out. "I felt as Abolitionists felt after Webster's Seventh of March speech," he later recalled. "My old acquaintance, our trusted leader, whose career in the New York Assembly we had watched with an almost holy satisfaction, seemed to have strangely abandoned the fundamental principles which we and he had believed in, and he had so nobly upheld. Whittier's poem, 'Ichabod,' seemed to have been aimed at him."

Not all the fundamental principles had been on the side of the poet; nor were they now all aligned with the reformers. Roosevelt had gone to Chicago knowing that Blaine's nomination was probable. By the rules of politics he was bound to support the convention's choice. As his earlier speeches reveal, moreover, he regarded the Republican party as a principle itself. Much as he gloried in the heroic exploits of Confederate soldiers, he deplored the states-rights philosophy upon which secession had been based and to which the Democratic party still adhered. He would write the next year that Jefferson Davis "enjoys the unique distinction of being the only American with whose public character that of Benedict Arnold need not fear comparison"; and when he himself stormed out of the G.O.P. in 1912 it was partly to create a more nationalistic party than the one he was abandoning. If ever a reformer was foreordained to swallow the bitterness of personal contempt with the sweetness of party loyalty, it was Theodore Roosevelt in 1884.

Nevertheless, it is hard to explain the intensity of Roosevelt's activities that fall. He could have refused to issue a public statement, or he might have sat out the campaign on his ranch in Dakota, where he had sped at the close of the convention. Either course would have enabled him to retain his party standing. Either would have maintained his prized reputation for independence. But he chose instead to come out openly for the "decidedly mottled" Blaine, as he referred to his party's nominee, and to castigate the rock-ribbed Cleveland.

Roosevelt's public statement evoked a bitter outcry from the independents. The Boston banker, Colonel Henry Lee, is said to have growled to his cousin George, Roosevelt's father-in-law: "As for Cabot Lodge, nobody's surprised at *him;* but you can tell that young whippersnapper in New York from me that his independence was the only thing in him we cared for . . ." The New York *Evening Post* observed that "There is no ranch or other hiding place in the world in which a man can wait for Blaine and the Mulligan letters to 'blow over' . . ." And others spared Roosevelt no less.

Roosevelt never forgave the mugwumps for their failure to accept his decision to support the Republican ticket in 1884. As that astute English observer, James Bryce, perceived, they had "impeached his own righteousness and classed him with the politicians." They had, in addition, abandoned the party of Union for that of secession. "I am glad I am not at home," Roosevelt wrote Lodge from Dakota just before he decided to enter the campaign actively. "I get so angry with the 'mugwumps,' and get to have such a scorn and contempt for them, that I know I would soon be betrayed into taking some step against them, and in favor of Blaine, much more decided than I really ought to take." That fall he lashed them almost as ferociously as he whipped the Democrats.

Roosevelt had returned on October 9 to New York, where, in what was probably the most revealing of his statements on the matter, he told a reporter from the *Sun* that "It is altogether contrary to my character to occupy a neutral position in so important and exciting a struggle." Then, in a series of speeches delivered in Massachusetts, New Jersey, and New York, he revealed the depth of his Republican convictions, discreditably capitalized on Cleveland's moral laxness and conveniently dismissed Blaine's. "Now in 1864 nobody that I know of questioned the moral character of George B. McClellan, and yet no disaster . . . would have begun to equal in importance the terrible disaster that it would have been to have McClellan elected as President," he said at Malden, Massachusetts. Therefore, he continued, "everyone in his senses must recognize that the man is not everything, that the man is not even so much, but that the party is most of all." In Winchester, he warned that there was a chance that the next President would appoint as many as four new justices to the Supreme Court:

> Now I want to have a bench that will decide, should the question ever come before them, that the national banks are constitutional, that the law providing for the suppression of pleuro-pneumonia and of kindred [cattle] diseases by the National Government should be held constitutional. Issues like that are not decided in a day. They are not decided in 20 years. It is a question of national growth, and the same fight that has been going on for the last half century or more will continue to go on for some time longer.

Roosevelt was received well in Massachusetts. But it was his address to the Young Men's Republican Club in New York that evoked the most enthusiastic response. "A gentleman told me recently he doubted if I would vote for the Angel Gabriel if found at the head of the Democratic party, to which I responded that the Angel Gabriel would never be found in such company," he remarked at the outset. He then commented on his decision to remain with the G.O.P. "It may be right to bolt," he acknowledged, "but you must be certain that the time is right; that you are acting to reform, not to destroy the Republican party." He had opposed Blaine's nomination, he disingenuously added, "but then I saw, and every man who didn't view the scene with jaundiced eyes saw too that Mr. Blaine was nominated fairly and squarely because the bulk of Republicans in the Republican States wishes him to be their nominee." Adding that these were the men Abraham Lincoln used to call the "plain people," he concluded: "I am thankful that I am still, where by inheritance and education I feel that I belong, with the Republican party."

CHAPTER 3

THE WESTERNER: RANCHER,
HUNTER, AND HISTORIAN

> We knew toil and hardship and hunger and thirst; and we saw
> men die violent deaths as they worked among the horses and
> cattle; but we felt the best of hardy life in our veins, and ours
> was the glory of work and the joy of living.
> —Theodore Roosevelt, *An Autobiography*

Roosevelt's political and social life had merged only infrequently
during his three years in the legislature. His young bride, whom Isaac
Hunt remembered as "a very charming woman . . . tall and
willowy," had spent most of his first term and part of his second term
with him in a suite at the Delevan House in Albany. They had seen
little of his colleagues except at official functions, however, and when
Theodore's third term started in January, 1884, Alice stayed in New
York to wait for the birth of their first child.

Two or three weeks before Alice's baby was expected, she had
entertained three of her husband's colleagues, one of them an Irish-
American Democrat, at lunch. "All of the men were perfectly enchanted with their visit," Theodore wrote after he had returned to
Albany. "They could hardly believe that mother was really our
mother; and above all they praised my sweet little wife. I was very
much amused by Welch, who said that he had never seen anyone
look so pretty as you did when you were asking me not to tell the
'shaved lion' story; he said 'I would have felt just as badly as she
would have if you had gone on to tell it.' So I felt very glad we had
entertained the three 'pollys.' "

Seventeen days later the mother and the wife were dead.

Theodore and Alice's three years of marriage had been extraordinarily happy. Although she seems never to have matured—he deferred to her as to a child during the whole of their brief life together—he was as enamored of her at the end as he had been at the beginning. "How I did hate to leave my bright, sunny little love yesterday afternoon," he had written her from Albany the week before she died. "I love you and long for you all the time, and oh *so* tenderly; doubly tenderly now, my sweetest little wife."

Roosevelt's letters from Europe during a tour they had made the first year of their marriage are similarly illuminating. "Really, Alice is an excellent traveller," he informed his sister Corinne. "When I reach a station I leave her in a chair with the parcels, and there she stays, round eyed and solemn, but perfectly happy, till I have extricated my luggage, had it put on a hack and arranged everything." In other letters Theodore referred to Alice as "Baby," indulgently reported that she resented being addressed in any other language than "english" [*sic*], and described how she had been convulsed by seasickness on the voyage over and had "requested me to wear a mustard plaster *first,* to see if it hurts." Yet they also shared many pleasures maturely, including art, and Theodore freely conceded that her appreciation was "far keener" than his.

The idyl ended on February 14, 1884, the fourth anniversary of the announcement of their engagement. In Albany, the day before, Theodore had reported fourteen bills out of the Cities Committee and was planning to remain in the Chamber until the vote was taken that afternoon on his Aldermanic Bill, though he had received a telegram that morning reporting the birth of a daughter. "I shall never forget when the news came and we congratulated him . . . ," Hunt recalled. "He was full of life and happiness." But then, Hunt added, "the news came of a sudden turn and he took his departure."

After a depressingly slow trip through a dense fog then in its tenth day, Roosevelt reached his mother's house on West 57th Street shortly before midnight. He found Alice stricken by Bright's disease and barely able to recognize him. All that night he held her in his arms, leaving only to spend a few minutes with his mother who was dying of typhoid fever in another room. At about three o'clock that morning Martha Bulloch Roosevelt died. Theodore, standing by her bedside, repeated the words his brother Elliott had greeted him with a few hours earlier: "There *is* a curse on this house." He then returned to Alice. Dawn came, but not the sun. Alice continued to sink and at two o'clock that afternoon, February 14, she also died. She was twenty-two and one-half years old.

The senior Mrs. Roosevelt, the New York *Herald* reported the next day, was the "widow of the distinguished philanthropist" who had founded the Roosevelt (Orthopedic) Hospital. "The devotion of her four children to her person was akin to chivalrous loyalty, and was remarked by all who came under her roof and under the spell of her hospitable manner and brilliant powers as the leader of a *salon*." The junior Mrs. Roosevelt, the *Herald* continued, "was famed for her beauty as well as for many graces of the heart and head." The two ladies took an active interest in the late Mr. Roosevelt's many charities, the obituary concluded, and from "visiting hospital wards to dispensing ice cream at a newsboys' lodging house, both found pleasure in making this world less of a sorrow to the poor and more of a lesson to the rich."

In Albany, meanwhile, seven assemblymen, including two or three of Theodore's inveterate opponents, spoke movingly in support of a resolution to adjourn in the hope that Roosevelt might be fortified "in this moment of his agony and weakness." When finally the members arose to endorse the resolution unanimously, tears swelled many of their eyes. It was "an unusual compliment," the *New York Times* observed, one that reflected "the high position in the general esteem which Mr. Roosevelt has won by his straightforward and courageous course in the Legislature and in politics."

A little after ten o'clock the next morning, Saturday, February 16, Theodore entered a front pew of the Fifth Avenue Presbyterian Church. The choir chanted "Jesus, Lover of My Soul" and a quartet sang "Rock of Ages," after which his mother's friend and pastor, the Rev. Dr. John Hall, who was visibly moved, preached a short sermon. Following the benediction the choir sang "Angels of Jesus, Angels of Light." Two rosewood coffins covered with roses and lilies of the valley were then borne down the center aisle to the muted organ strains of the funeral march from Beethoven's Third Symphony as Theodore and the immediate family walked slowly behind. They entered waiting coaches and rode slowly behind twin hearses to Greenwood Cemetery.

Theodore was "in a dazed, stunned state" that day, his old tutor,

Arthur Cutler, wrote Bill Sewall. "He does not know what he does or says." Sometime that day, however, probably just before he went to bed, Roosevelt noted in his diary that "we spent three years of happiness greater and more unalloyed than I have ever known fall to the lot of others." He added that "For joy or for sorrow my life has now been lived out."

Yet in death there was life. The four-day-old baby, Alice Lee, survived; and within less than a week her twenty-five-year-old father had returned to Albany and immersed himself in the investigation of corruption in New York City, the struggle for his reform bills, and the organization of the Edmunds forces. By every law of nature that Roosevelt had studied and by most of those he had superimposed on human history, life went on. Resolutely, he summed up his philosophy in a letter to Sewall three weeks later: "It was a grim and evil fate, but I have never believed it did any good to flinch or yield for any blow, nor does it lighten the blow to cease from working."

Nevertheless, Theodore suffered. Alice seems hardly to have influenced his basic personality; but she had touched the depths of his sensitivity. "You could not talk to him about it," Hunt recalled. "You could see at once that it was a grief too deep. . . . There was a sadness about his face that he never had before. . . . He did not want anybody to sympathize with him."

In Dakota that summer Roosevelt penned a moving memorial to Alice Lee. "She was," her young widower wrote, "beautiful in face and form, and lovelier still in spirit; as a flower she grew, and as a fair young flower she died."

Her life had been always in the sunshine; there had never come to her a single great sorrow; and none ever knew her who did not love and revere her for her bright, sunny temper and her saintly unselfishness. Fair, pure, and joyous as a maiden; loving, tender, and happy as a young wife; when she had just become a mother, when her life seemed to be but just begun, and when the years seemed so bright before her—then, by a strange and terrible fate, death came to her.

"And when my heart's dearest died," the memorial, which he had printed and circulated among his friends and family, concluded, "the light went from my life forever."

Thereafter, as Henry Pringle observes, a door closed on Alice Lee.

Roosevelt maintained cordial relations with her relatives. But that was all. Within three years he had married again; and in the crowded years that followed he never again mentioned her, not even to their daughter Alice. His silence, Putnam concludes, "seems pathologically rigorous" and suggests a "discipline approaching cruelty."

Fortunately, Roosevelt had entered the cattle business in the Bad Lands of the Dakota Territory the autumn before his double bereavement. Following the Republican Convention in Chicago in June, 1884, he went directly West to lose himself in the challenge—of the round-up, of exploration, of man-killing animals, and of near total isolation. He found that and more. His years in Dakota constituted one of the great formative experiences of his life, and in passing moments he even considered making a full-time career of ranching, hunting, and writing.

The story of Roosevelt's Western adventures has been told many times—so often, in fact, that it has become a kind of national saga. Yet certain episodes must perforce be repeated, and of these, none is more revealing than that of his gradual acceptance by the leathery cowhands, guides, and ranchers with whom he associated.

The spurs were not easily won. As Roosevelt later half-seriously remarked, glasses were considered a sign of "defective moral character" in the Bad Lands; and when he first visited Dakota in 1883 he had been forced to use all his persuasive powers merely to hire a hunting guide, so contemptuous was the reaction to his appearance and manner. Only after he had several times proved his mettle did opinion change, and then but slowly.

Once, Roosevelt relates in his *Autobiography,* a drunken stranger accosted him in a hotel. "Four-eyes is going to treat," bellowed the drunk, who had already shot up the face of the barroom clock. Waving two cocked pistols, he strode over to Roosevelt, who had quietly taken to a chair behind the stove, and repeated his demands in a stream of profanity. Roosevelt rose from his chair as if to oblige, then suddenly struck, first with a short right and left, then with another right. The guns discharged aimlessly as the drunk fell to the floor.

On another occasion Roosevelt brought "Hell-Roaring" Bill Jones, the sheriff of Billings County, to bay. Primitive, shiftless, and quick-tempered, "Hell-Roaring" Bill was "a thorough frontiersman, excellent in all kinds of emergencies, and a very game man," or so Roosevelt wrote. He was also "a thoroughly good citizen when sober." The encounter occurred in the office of the *Bad Lands Cowboy,* a newspaper published and edited in Medora by A. T. Packard, a University of Michigan graduate who had drifted to the Bad Lands about the same time as Roosevelt. "Hell-Roaring" Bill had been passing the time telling off-color stories to a group of cowpunchers, and Roosevelt, who had no taste for obscenity, though he was given to mild profanity in later years, finally decided that he had heard enough.

"I can't tell why in the world I like you, for you're the nastiest-talking man I ever heard," he blurted out at the startled sheriff. Packard and the cowpunchers froze in their chairs, for "Hell-Roaring" Bill had been known to shoot on less provocation. By then, however, Jones had come to respect Roosevelt.

"I don't mind saying that mebbe I've been a little too free with my mouth," he sheepishly replied.

It was these and similar incidents that helped Roosevelt gain acceptance in the Bad Lands. Even after he had won it, however, he was regarded as a man apart, as a New Yorker turned Westerner, as a captain but never a private. Partly this was the result of his rancher status. But in the main it reflected his natural qualities of leadership.

Not that Roosevelt ceased to amuse, even to amaze, the hard-bitten Dakotans. They never forgot how once when some cattle broke loose on a roundup, he commanded a hand to "Hasten forward quickly there." His guides and hunting companions also long remembered his ecstatic outbursts and Indian dances over a successful kill (they were often climaxed by the presentation of a hundred dollars to his guide). Nor did they fail to enjoy Roosevelt's penchant for ostentatious dress. Whether stepping off the train at Little Missouri in a derby hat or riding the range in a tailored buckskin suit, Roosevelt created an effect not unlike that of his appearance in evening clothes at his first Republican caucus in 1882. Yet even this sartorial brilliance failed to enhance the gracefulness of his seat on a horse. "He was not a purty rider," one of his acquaintances recalled, "but a hell of a good rider."

Roosevelt's experiences as a hunter also enhanced his stature. Sooner or later his pluck and courage, his insistence on taking the hard way, and his perseverance under adverse conditions became known. He captured the flavor of one of his early bear hunts in the Big Horn Mountains in a letter to his sister Bamie:

> I shall not soon forget the first one I killed. . . . Cocking my rifle and stepping quickly forward, I found myself face to face with the great bear, who was less than twenty-five feet off—not eight steps. He had been roused from his sleep by our approach; he sat up in his lair, and turned his huge head slowly towards us. At that distance and in such a place it was very necessary to kill or disable him at the first fire; doubtless my face was pretty white, but the blue barrel was as steady as a rock as I glanced along it until I could see the top of the bead fairly between his two sinister looking eyes; as I pulled the trigger I jumped aside out of the smoke, to be ready if he charged; but it was needless, for the great brute was struggling in the death agony, and, as you will see when I bring home his skin, the bullet hole in his skull was as exactly between his eyes as if I had measured the distance with a carpenters rule. This bear was nearly nine feet long and weighed over a thousand pounds. Each of my other bears, which were smaller, needed two bullets apiece; Merrifield killed each of his with a single shot.

Drawing on the experiences of that and other hunting trips, Roosevelt in 1885 wrote *Hunting Trips of a Ranchman,* the first volume of a trilogy on hunting, ranching, and nature observation. Three years later the second, *Ranch Life and the Hunting Trail* was published, and in 1893 the last, *The Wilderness Hunter,* came out. The three volumes set a new style in hunting books, embracing, in Paul R. Cutright's words, "vivid pictures of windswept prairie and baldface mountain, of lovely, sweet-smelling flowers and endless virgin forests; thumbnail sketches of birds and small mammals; and fascinating biographies of large game animals, from buffalo to bighorn."

All three books were warmly praised by critics though they had serious deficiencies. They tended to be repetitious, to draw too heavily on unreliable sources, and to indulge in extravagant statements. Roosevelt himself was dissatisfied. "I wish I could make my writings touch a higher plane," he confided to the novelist Owen Wister, "but I don't well see how I can. . . . I go over them a good deal and recast, supply or omit, sentences and even paragraphs, but I don't make the reconstruction complete in the way that you do." Nevertheless, the chapter on the habits of the grizzly bear in *The Wilderness Hunter* was the most comprehensive to that time, while the essay on the Bighorn in *Ranch Life and the Hunting Trail* is still regarded as superb. As Brander Matthews, the Columbia professor and arbiter of Arts and Letters, wrote years later, Roosevelt's writings were invariably "Tinglingly alive, masculine and vascular."

Impressed with the natural beauty of the Bad Lands, desirous of a hunting base of his own, and pleased by a financial investment in which he could be genuinely interested, Roosevelt had meanwhile expanded his original stake of $14,000. Shortly after Alice died he invested $26,000 more; then, in April 1885, he poured in an additional $12,500. All this was done against the advice of his banker uncle, James Roosevelt, who not unreasonably regarded him as impetuous and visionary in financial matters.

Roosevelt's original contract was a "gentleman's agreement" with two young and sinewy Canadians, Sylvane Ferris and Bill Merrifield, wherein he gave them a check of $14,000 in the fall of 1883 to purchase cattle for him. They were to run them on government lands around their own ranch, the Maltese Cross. When Roosevelt returned to Dakota in June, 1884, however, he bought a thousand additional head and established his own ranch thirty miles down the Little Missouri River. It was called Elkhorn, and it was managed by Bill Sewall and his nephew Will Dow under a contract that gave them specified salaries and a percentage of the profits but no liability for losses. They constructed the log ranchhouse that summer which was to be Roosevelt's headquarters in Dakota until he sold out in 1897.

Having thus established his stake, Roosevelt soon plunged into the turbulent affairs of the region. The ranchers were ripe for organization. They were plagued by thieves, marauders, and inadequate range laws; and in November, after riding through blizzards in temperatures of twenty below to talk with other ranchers, Roosevelt issued a call for a meeting the next month. Out of it came the Little Missouri Stockmen's Association. Roosevelt was elected chairman and was reelected the next year. "The association can congratulate itself," the *Bad Lands Cowboy* commented. "Under his administration, everything moves quickly forward and there is none of that time-consuming, fruitless talk that so invariably characterizes a deliberative assembly without a good presiding officer."

Roosevelt also participated actively in the much larger Eastern Montana Stockgrowers Association, and in April, 1886 he attended a three-day convention in Miles City, a thriving frontier town, as he described it, "thronged with hundreds of rough-looking, broad-hatted men, numbering among them all the great cattle and horse raisers of the Northwest."

"I took my position very well in the convention," Roosevelt wrote shortly after, "and indeed these Westerners have now pretty well accepted me as one of themselves, and as a representative stockman." He was appointed a member of a committee charged to influence the establishment of stockyards in St. Paul, Minnesota, and in 1887 he persuaded the convention to modify a resolution criticizing the newly established Interstate Commerce Commission on the grounds that the criticism was premature. He also effected the discharge of the incompetent livestock inspector at Medora.

By then Roosevelt's interest in the Montana and Little Missouri Associations had already begun to wane. A prolonged drought in the summer of 1886 followed by a disastrously severe winter had wiped out a large part of his herd; and he had committed himself to the East for personal reasons anyway. Bill Sewall, who had viewed the cattle venture with pessimism from the outset, had returned with Dow to Maine in the late summer of 1886. A raging fire had destroyed the office and press of the *Bad Lands Cowboy*. And rancher after rancher had gone out of business in the aftermath of the disastrous winter of 1886–1887. A brief item in the Dickinson *Press* summed it up: "D. O. Sweet and family have moved from Medora to Dickinson. Mr. Sweet desired to reside where there was some life and prospect of growth."

Roosevelt returned to the Bad Lands on hunting trips in 1888, 1890, 1892, 1893, and 1896; but he never again took an active part in running his cattle. When he finally sold out in 1897 he had lost more than $20,000 plus interest. Yet the money had been well spent. In spite of arduous days in the saddle, almost sleepless nights on the roundup, and prolonged exposure to near intolerable heat and cold, his body had developed remarkably. "No longer was he the slight and somewhat delicate-looking young man whom we had entertained at the Cannonball camp less than two years before," one of his Western friends recalled. Roosevelt "got to be lookin' more like a rugged man," another added. Even more important, he had proved what he was constrained to prove again and again throughout his life—that he was a man among men. Not only had he held his own on the roundup, captured two thieves at gun point, and showed his mettle in dozens of other incidents, he had comported himself with dignity, discretion, and bravery when threatened with a duel. What most men sublimated, Theodore Roosevelt had experienced.

Meanwhile, the young rancher-hunter-historian had written and published a biography of Thomas Hart Benton, was writing a second on Gouverneur Morris, and was planning a multivolume history of the settlement of the West. Both the biographies were highly superficial. *The Life of Thomas Hart Benton* represented not more than three months of scholarship and three months of intense, but spasmodic, writing, much of it done in the ranchhouse at Elkhorn and some of it in a room over a store in Medora. Yet, as Putnam suggests, "To produce such a work in a few months, with all its faults, required both basic knowledge and prior deliberation to which few men of his age and varied activities could aspire."

However serious the academic deficiencies of the lives of Benton and Morris, the books are invaluable for the light they cast on the future President's political philosophy. Here Roosevelt was grappling with currency problems, public morality, and land policy—with the great questions of the American past and, indeed, of the American future. He was the politician justifying his own support of Blaine in 1884 and visiting his resentment on the mugwumps with broad indictments of extremist reformers and spirited defenses of party regularity. And he was also the young politician-intellectual forging an interpretation of American history which was to influence his own actions until the end of his life.

Of the two books, *Benton* was the most complex in subject and historical content. The magniloquent Senator from Missouri represented much that Roosevelt admired. He was at once a sectionalist and a nationalist, a spokesman of the West and a staunch defender of the Union. He disdained the abolitionists and proslavery extremists alike. He energetically championed the interests of individual Western settlers and he condemned out of hand the great land engrossers and speculators. He wanted no part of Mexico to the Southwest, but he wanted a large part of Canada to the Northwest. And he resisted at all times infringement by the states of the rights of the national government. Benton "had risen and grown steadily all through his long term of service," Roosevelt concluded near the end of his volume.

"Compare his stand against the slavery extremists and disunionists, such as Calhoun, with the position of Webster at the time of his famous 7th of March speech, or with that of Clay when he brought in his compromise bill! In fact, as the times grew more troublesome, he grew steadily better able to do good work in them."

Roosevelt's own comments on the issues were even more revealing than his favorable appraisal of the broad sweep of Benton's career. He viewed the Missouri Senator's fight to dispose of the public lands to actual settlers at low cost as "a move of enormous importance to the whole West," one which encountered intense opposition, "especially from the short-sighted selfishness of many of the northeastern-ers." The drive toward Mexico was a "belligerent, or, more properly speaking, piratical way of looking at neighboring territory." But the land claimed by Canada in the old Northwest, so Roosevelt agreed with the vain and swaggering Missourian, "was by right our heritage."

As for slavery, Roosevelt regarded it as "a grossly anachronistic and un-American form of evil." He believed, however, that it might have been better to have allowed it to continue a century longer, "its ultimate extinction being certain." And he was certain that non-abolitionist political leaders such as Lincoln and Seward "did more than all the professional Abolitionists combined really to bring about its destruction." The abolitionists "belonged to that class of men that is always engaged in some agitation or other," he sharply asserted; "only it happened that in this particular agitation they were right."

Roosevelt's contempt for the abolitionists was matched by his disapproval of Andrew Jackson's wholesale removal of officeholders and destructive attack on the Second Bank of the United States. The former was a change "for the worse"; the latter an appeal "to the vague fear with which the poorer and more ignorant voters regard a powerful institution whose workings they do not understand." Shifting back to the other extreme, Roosevelt then extolled Jackson and Benton for standing by hard money; he also foreshadowed his own castigation of the Populists and Free Silver Democrats in the 1890's:

> A craze for "soft," or dishonest, money—a greenback move-ment, or one for short-weight silver dollars—works more to the disadvantage of the whole mass of the people than even to that of the capitalists; it is a move directly in the interest of "the money power," which its loud-mouthed advocates are ostensibly opposing in the interests of democracy.

The biography of Gouverneur Morris was poorer history than the life of Benton, but it offered an even more penetrating insight into Roosevelt's thinking. Morris was a Federalist, one who "embodied to a peculiar degree both the qualities which made the Federalist party so brilliant and so useful, and those other qualities which finally brought about its downfall." He possessed those attributes "of generous daring and lofty disinterestedness which we like to associate with the name American. . . . He stood for order. He stood for the honest payment of debts." However—and here was Roosevelt's brief against the Federalists and eventually much of the Republican party as well—Morris "distrusted the mass of the people, and especially the mass of the people in other sections of the country."

Indeed, Roosevelt continued, "the force and subtlety of his reasoning were all marred by his incurable cynicism and deep-rooted distrust of mankind." At the Constitutional Convention Morris "throughout appears as *advocatus diaboli*," frankly avowing "his disbelief in all generous and unselfish motives." The New York financier "championed a strong national government, wherein he was right; but he also championed a system of class representation, leaning toward aristocracy, wherein he was wrong." Worse still, Morris "feared and dreaded the growth of the Union in the West," actually desiring the Convention "to commit the criminal folly of attempting to provide that the West should always be kept subordinate to the East." And most grievous of all, he urgently opposed the War of 1812, appearing as the "open champion of treason to the nation, of dishonesty to the nation's creditors, and of cringing subservience to a foreign power." Still, Roosevelt concluded, Morris's over-all contributions were impressive.

Roosevelt was not wont to brook intellectual confinement. In writing the work on Morris he had wandered through Hamilton to Abraham Lincoln, whose life he seems really to have wanted to write. Hamilton remained Roosevelt's intellectual hero, for he was the architect of the base. But Lincoln, who had both preserved and humanized the Federalist system, captured his heart.

Yet Roosevelt rarely acknowledged Lincoln's Jeffersonian strain. Nor could he willingly admit that his own views reflected Jefferson's influences, though throughout his life he exhorted the Republican party to espouse policies that by a humanistic construction were eminently Jeffersonian. Only after he had twice been President was

Roosevelt to conclude, and then but temporarily, that the marriage of government and business that Hamilton had fostered was beyond the power of high-minded men to direct in the public interest. Otherwise he never abandoned hope that the Republican leaders would rise above private interest and exert their great abilities for the good of all as they had, he believed, in Lincoln's time. The ennobled Civil War President, Roosevelt wrote, "was the first who showed how a strong people might have a strong government and yet remain the freest on earth."

He seized—half unwittingly—all that was best and wisest in the tradition of Federalism; he was the true successor of the Federalist leaders; but he grafted on their system a profound belief that the great heart of the nation beat for truth, honor, and liberty.

If the fame of the *Benton* and *Morris* rests largely on Roosevelt's political eminence, the four-volume *Winning of the West* endures for its merits. It stamped its author as a historian of genuine distinction: of brilliant, though uneven, literary power; of broad, and often acute, comprehension; and of extraordinary narrative force. As the foremost academic historian of the West, Frederick Jackson Turner, wrote in his review of the final volume, "Mr. Roosevelt has done a real service to our history" and "has rescued a whole movement in American development from the hands of unskillful annalists." With "graphic vigor," he continued, "he has portrayed the advance of the pioneer into the wastes of the continent" and yet "considered his subject broadly, in its relations to world-history." Roosevelt's work "will be to the general reader a revelation."

Nevertheless, *The Winning of the West* failed to fulfill Roosevelt's youthful ambition ("a mere dream," he called it) to write someday a book "that would really take rank as in the very first class." It lacked reflection and sobriety of judgment, and it was weak in analytical quality. It was also rife with partisanship and presentism. The failings were unfortunate, for Roosevelt could be forcefully objective. That later tendency, so disconcerting to his liberal critics, to offset the emphatic criticism with the emphatic commendation, was even then in evidence; and many of his appraisals of controversial issues were scrupulously fair. But he could not consistently hold the high ground. His obsessive contempt for the Jeffersonians and their political descendants colored *The Winning of the West* no less than his other

writings, and with grievous consequence. On the flimsiest circumstantial evidence he accused Jefferson of engaging in a "characteristic
. . . tortuous intrigue" against President Washington. He further
failed, as Turner pointed out, to make a "detailed study of the
incompatibility of temperament between Federalism and the West."

There were other shortcomings. Roosevelt drew on many theretofore
unexplored manuscripts, but his duties were so heavy (he wrote much
of the work while he was Civil Service Commissioner or Police Commissioner) that he was unable to exploit them properly. He also
neglected economic and institutional history, partly because, as he
revealingly confided to Turner, "I have always been more interested
in the men themselves than in the institutions through and under which
they worked." For all these and other faults, however, *The Winning
of the West* remains a pioneering account of the American people's
westward advance; one that justifies its author's reputation as a major
American historian of the narrative school.

Although the main focus of the work was on the quarter century
between 1765, when the intrepid Daniel Boone, "a tall, spare, sinewy
man with eyes like an eagle's and muscles that never tired," made his
first exploration, until roughly 1796, when the British, who were
"guilty of treachery to both friend and foe," at last recognized the
American conquest of the West, the introductory chapter ranks as one
of the classics of American historical literature in its tersely powerful
description of the spread of the English-speaking peoples. "They were
led by no one commander," Roosevelt wrote of those who thronged
across the Alleghenies:

> They acted under orders from neither king nor congress; they
> were not carrying out the plans of any farsighted leader. In obedi-
> ence to the instincts working half blindly within their breasts,
> spurred ever onward by the fierce desires of their eager hearts, they
> made in the wilderness homes for their children, and by so doing
> wrought out the destinies of a continental nation. They warred and
> settled from the high hill valleys of the French Broad and the upper
> Cumberland to the half-tropical basin of the Rio Grande, and to
> where the Golden Gate lets through the long-heaving waters of the
> Pacific. . . . The fathers followed Boone or fought at King's Moun-
> tain; the sons marched south with Jackson to overcome the Creeks
> and beat back the British; the grandsons died at the Alamo or
> charged to victory at San Jacinto. They were doing their share of

a work that began with the conquest of Britain, that entered on its second and wider period after the defeat of the Spanish Armada, that culminated in the marvelous growth of the United States.

Within those broad outlines Roosevelt wove his story, retracing the steps of the pioneers, superimposing chronology upon chronology, wallowing in tales of Indian massacres, taking swipes at the French, the British, the Indians—at all who stood in the way. Within that framework, too, he discoursed learnedly and perceptively on the character of the frontiersmen and the social customs of those who settled in their wake; he waxed eloquently on the courage of friend and foe alike; and he gloried, always, in the ceaseless and terrifying advance to the West.

Roosevelt saw that the British effort to forestall the colonists' occupation of the trans-Appalachian regions was one—he regarded it as the main—of the prime causes of the Revolution. Great Britain "wished the land to remain a wilderness, the home of the trapper and the fur trade, of the Indian hunter and the French *voyageur*," he asserted. "She desired it to be kept as a barrier against the growth of the seaboard colonies toward the interior. She regarded the new lands across the Atlantic as being won and settled, not for the benefit of the men who won and settled them, but for the benefit of the merchants and traders who stayed at home. It was this that rendered the Revolution inevitable." Roosevelt conceded that "the sins and shortcomings of the colonists had been many—but on the great underlying question they were wholly in the right, and their success was of vital consequence to the well-being of the race on this continent." It was no less true, he elsewhere acknowledged, that Americans might have stirred up the Indians themselves under different circumstances. But, he concluded, "We have to deal, not with what . . . the Americans might have done, but with what the British actually did; and for this there can be many apologies, but no sufficient excuse."

Roosevelt recognized no moral question in the engrossment of Indian lands by the American pioneers (his "courageous and virile" treatment, wrote Turner, "enables the reader to correct the . . . not altogether well-founded criticisms . . . by Eastern writers"):

> There were a dozen tribes, all of whom hunted in Kentucky and fought each other there, all of whom had equally good titles to the soil, and not one of whom acknowledged the right of any other

. . . save the right of the strongest. . . . The conquest and settlement by the Whites on the Indian lands was necessary to the greatness of the race and to the well-being of civilized mankind. It was
as ultimately beneficial as it was inevitable . . . all that can be
asked is that they shall be judged as other slayers and quellers of
savage people are judged.

And so Theodore Roosevelt judged them, extolling their intrepidity
and denouncing their regression to semibarbarity. The story of the
white man's triumph over the redman, he wrote,

> shows us a stern race of freemen who toiled hard, endured greatly,
> and fronted adversity bravely, who prized strength and courage and
> good faith, whose wives were chaste, who were generous and loyal
> to their friends. But it shows us also how they spurned at restraint,
> and fretted under it, how they would brook no wrong to themselves,
> and yet too often inflicted wrongs on others; their feats of terrible
> prowess are interspersed with deeds of the foulest and most wanton
> aggression, the darkest treachery, the most revolting cruelty . . .
> we see but little of such qualities as mercy for the fallen, the weak,
> and the helpless, or pity for a gallant and vanquished foe.

Roosevelt's sketches of frontier types were as sharp as his accounts
of the long hunt, of the pursuit of new lands, and of the Homeric
battles between Indians and whites. Among the best was that of the
great Iroquois warrior, Logan:

> He was a man of splendid appearance: over six feet high, straight
> as a spear-shaft, with a countenance as open as it was brave and
> manly, until the wrongs he endured stamped on it an expression of
> gloomy ferocity. He had always been the friend of the white man,
> and had been noted particularly for his kindness and gentleness to
> children. . . . A skilled marksman and mighty hunter, of com-
> manding dignity, who treated all men with a grave courtesy that
> exacted the same treatment in return, he was greatly liked and
> respected by all the white hunters and frontiersmen whose friend-
> ship and respect were worth having; they admired him for his
> dexterity and prowess, and they loved him for his straightforward
> honesty, and his noble loyalty to his friend.

Francis Parkman, to whom Roosevelt had admiringly dedicated
The Winning of the West, did not more graphically delineate the
backwoods French. "Three generations of isolated life in the wilder-

ness had greatly changed the characters of these groups of traders, bateau-men, and adventurous warriors," Roosevelt wrote:

> Hospitable, but bigoted to their old customs, ignorant, indolent, and given to drunkenness, they spoke a corrupt jargon of the French tongue; the common people were even beginning to give up reckoning time by months and years, and dated events, as the Indians did, with reference to the phenomena of nature, such as the time of the floods, the maturing of the green corn, or the ripening of the strawberries. All their attributes seemed alien to the polished army officers of old France; they had but little more in common with the latter than with the American backwoodsmen. But they had kept many valuable qualities, and, in especial, they were brave and hardy, and, after their own fashion, good soldiers.

Of all the frontiersmen, Roosevelt most admired the Scotch-Irish. "These Irish representatives of the Covenanters were in the West almost what the Puritans were in the Northeast, and more than the Cavaliers were in the South," he wrote. "Mingled with the descendants of many other races," he continued, "they nevertheless formed the kernel of the distinctively and intensely American stock who were the pioneers of our people in their march westward, the vanguard of the army of fighting settlers, who, with axe and rifle, won their way from the Alleghanies to the Rio Grande and the Pacific."

To be sure, there were great numbers of others—English, German, Huguenots, and some Dutch and Swedish. But a single generation "was enough to weld together into one people the representatives of these numerous and widely different races." Long before the Revolution they had "lost all remembrance of Europe and all sympathy with things European," Roosevelt wrote in a passage that anticipated many of Turner's formal conclusions. "Their iron surroundings made a mould which turned out all alike in the same shape. They resembled one another, and they differed from the rest of the world—even the world of America, and infinitely more, the world of Europe—in dress, in customs, and in mode of life." Furthermore, he concluded, "the influence of heredity was no more plainly perceptible than was the extent of individual variation. . . . All qualities, good and bad, are intensified and accentuated in the life of the wilderness."

Similarly, Roosevelt maintained his faith in the uplifting influence of the battle hard-won, of manly physical combat, of the near-animal struggle for existence. "The first lesson the backwoodsman learnt was the necessity of self-help; the next, that such a community could only thrive if all joined in helping one another. . . . Their lives were harsh and narrow, they gained their bread by their blood and sweat, in the unending struggle with the wild ruggedness of nature. . . . They were relentless, revengeful, suspicious, knowing neither truth nor pity"; but, he continued, "they were also upright, resolute, and fearless, loyal to their friends, and devoted to their country." And so, it might be said of those last words, was Theodore Roosevelt. But his perspective was deeper, his stage of action wider, and his values more complex.

Roosevelt repeated those generalizations many times in *The Winning of the West*. He also touched upon the democratizing influence of the frontier, a thesis Turner was already developing when the third and fourth volumes were published. And he particularly stressed the deterministic character of the mighty westward advance. Thus Boone was more interesting as a type than as a leader or an explorer, for the West was neither discovered, won, nor settled by any single man. Of George Rogers Clark alone, Roosevelt concluded, "can it be said that he did a particular piece of work which without him would have remained undone."

Such, then, was Theodore Roosevelt's literary and historical contribution to the epochal story of the American people. As the political leader of those people, he would soon project that epoch onto the world-wide stage.

The Winning of the West had been started shortly after, and been completed long after, Roosevelt had shifted his base of operations back to the East in 1886–1887. But his own experiences in the Bad Lands had made it the richer. (Even Turner contended that he had depicted the westward movement "as probably no other man of his time could have done.") Without those experiences he could not have written so perceptively of Boone and his like; nor could he have understood so acutely the frontier's tendency to barbarize the weak and to make superior men of those who were already strong. "All qualities, good and bad, are intensified and accentuated in the life of the wilderness," he had written in a passage as applicable to the Bad Lands in the 1880's as to the black forests of Kentucky in the 1770's.

That was as true, probably, of Roosevelt himself as of Boone, Clark, and the others. Two years in the West had converted Roosevelt's iron resolve to one of steel. They had reinforced his high code of personal morality. They had developed his natural qualities of leadership. And they had encouraged his growing tendency to judge men on their merits rather than their social backgrounds. They had also accentuated his intolerance of the weak, if not of the colorfully wicked. They had whetted his craving for hardship. And they had made his Darwinian concept of struggle more harsh and inclusive than ever.

With genuine regret Dakota had bade him what it knew was good-by when he went East in the fall of 1886. "Theodore is a Dakota cowboy, and has spent a large share of his time in the Territory for a couple of years," the Sioux Falls *Press* said.

He is one of the finest thoroughbreds you ever met—a whole-souled, clear-headed, high-minded gentleman. When he first went on the range, the cowboys took him for a dude, but soon they realized the stuff of which the youngster was built, and there is no man now who inspires such enthusiastic regard among them as he.

PART II

THE ROAD TO THE WHITE HOUSE

CHAPTER 4

FOR THE GOOD OF THE NATION

> He is a young man still, with all the impulsiveness char-
> acteristic of youth, and occasionally this leads him to say or do
> zealous things which seem to older men imprudent; but . . .
> he is so honest and so courageous that he does not make the
> serious blunders resulting from dishonesty or timidity.
>
> —The Philadelphia *Record*

Within two and one-half years of his return to New York in the fall
of 1886 Roosevelt had begun a flamboyantly creative six-year tenure
on the Civil Service Commission in Washington. Before assuming this
new charge, however, he had scored labor violence in a memorable
personal letter, engaged in a "bully" campaign for the mayorship of
New York, and made an eminently successful second marriage with
a childhood playmate.

TR's epistolary foray against labor actually occurred five months
before he left Dakota. On the evening of May 4, 1886, a seething
crowd of strikers, socialists, and anarchists had gathered in Haymarket
Square, Chicago to protest police violence in particular and managerial
repression in general. The meeting had been proceeding peaceably,
though passions were high and the words from the platform in-
cendiary, when suddenly, on an ill-considered command from their
captain, one hundred and eighty policemen had moved to disperse the
assemblage. Someone, identity unknown, had thereupon heaved a
bomb into the officers' serried ranks, and in the ensuing melee eight
policemen had been killed and sixty-seven wounded.

Eight known anarchists were subsequently arrested and tried. Although no one of them was ever proved to have thrown a bomb, all eight were found guilty: first by an inflamed and vengeful public opinion, then by courts of the law after one of the most injudicious trials in American legal annals. Seven were sentenced to death and one to life imprisonment.

Like most other vocal Americans, Roosevelt had been outraged when he read reports of the Haymarket tragedy at the Chimney Butte ranch in Dakota; and like numerous of his countrymen, he had reacted instinctively in terms of counterviolence. "My men are hard working, labouring men, who work longer hours for no greater wages than many of the strikers . . . ," he wrote his sister Bamie at the time. "I believe nothing would give them greater pleasure than a chance with their rifles at one of the mobs. . . . I wish I had them with me and a fair show at ten times our number of rioters; my men shoot well and fear very little."

To this day, that statement has haunted Roosevelt's reputation among men of reflection. It is possible that they have exaggerated its significance; that they have failed to weigh it against TR's signal services to the labor movement during his later career. He was only twenty-seven years old at the time, and his judgment had been formed by biased newspaper reports. Moreover, even Henry George approved the punishment meted out to the anarchists. And as Putnam writes, "When capitalists like Jay Gould broke the law, Roosevelt was [equally] rampant to correct and avenge."

Yet TR never altered the broad sense of that first violent reaction. Long after the evidence was in he continued to rail against the "murderous rioters"; long after thoughtful Chicagoans had soberly reconsidered their own emotional reactions Roosevelt remained impervious to the injustice of his attitude. And when, seven years after the Haymarket tragedy, Illinois's German-born governor, John Peter Altgeld, responded to the humane dictates of his Lincoln-like conscience by pardoning the three surviving victims of the law's miscarriage, TR angrily relegated him to the ranks of Robespierre and the Jacobins. The conclusion is inescapable: In the Haymarket affair and numerous similar cases down through the years, TR's compulsion for order and a Hebraic-like justice constrained him to give short shrift to the historic safeguards of the Anglo-American law.

Roosevelt's inability to fathom the wellsprings of industrial violence reflected in part his failure to frame the passing insights of his legislative years into a mature philosophy of labor. At times he perceived the near-controlling force of the external environment; but he could not, or would not, generalize rationally on his perceptions. His mayorality campaign in the fall of 1886 attests further to this.

TR had entered the race with reluctance. The real contest was between the Democratic industrialist-philanthropist, Abram S. Hewitt, and Henry George, who was running on the United Labor party's ticket. George's epochal work, *Progress and Poverty,* had terrorized defenders of the status quo with its classic indictment of poverty and not wholly visionary proposals for tax reform, and it was widely understood that thousands of conservative Republicans would vote Democratic to assure his defeat. In these circumstances no Republican of prominence wanted the G.O.P. nomination; and Tom Platt, the unsavory Republican boss, had turned in desperation to young Roosevelt in early October. "The simple fact is that I had to play Curtius and leap into the gulf that was yawning before the Republican party," TR explained. Had the party's chances of winning been better, he added, he would not have been asked.

During the whirling campaign that had followed Roosevelt's acceptance he had characteristically acted as though he thought he could win. He tried to forestall a mass defection of Republicans to Hewitt, whose intemperate and irrational attack on George did his own reputation no honor, by treating George's advanced views lightly and playing on the Republicans' traditional revulsion against Tammany. He charged that Hewitt would be unable to divorce himself from his unsavory Tammany supporters. And he repeatedly declared that he would, if elected, "go to City Hall unpledged to any one."

More significantly, Roosevelt reaffirmed the attitudes of his years in the Assembly by excoriating owners of slum properties. Then, in an apparent effort to redress a balance that had never been, he had exhorted labor to rise by its own exertions. Only through "steady, individual self-help" could industrial evils be eradicated, he admonished slum-imprisoned workers who were powerless even to form an effective union. Indeed, he continued, industrial evils could "no more be done away with by legislation than you could do away with the bruises which you receive when you tumble down, by passing an act to repeal the laws of gravitation." Not until after TR became President would he finally realize that the repressive force of capital was so powerful, the enervating effect of subsistence wages so pervasive, that for all but the very strongest "individual self-help" was woefully less than enough. Had he digested Henry George's penetrating analysis of society at the time, he would have known it then.

Young Roosevelt's vigorous campaigning had proved unavailing; he ran third, thirty thousand votes behind Hewitt and eight thousand behind George. As Jacob Riis reported, "in the wild dread of the disaster that was [supposedly] coming, men forsook party, principles, everything, and threw themselves into the arms of Tammany." TR was hurt. "Am badly defeated," he wired Henry Cabot Lodge. "Worse even than I feared."

A few days after the returns were in, Roosevelt sailed for England to be married again. For more than a year after Alice Lee's death in February, 1884, he had contrived to avoid meeting Edith Carow, whom he had known when they were children and escorted to dances and parties as a youth. Theodore and Edith's friends had assumed before he met Alice that they would be married after he was graduated from Harvard, but they had gradually drifted apart, perhaps, suggests Hermann Hagedorn, because "Her ladyship," as Roosevelt often referred to Edith, had her "bad days" as well as her "good days." (Edith would later hold that she several times rejected Theodore's proposals, but the evidence is lacking.)

There is no record of what Edith thought when she attended Theodore and Alice's wedding in 1880. During the next five years, however, her lifelong disposition to remain aloof from society was accentuated. "I believe you could live in the same house with Edith for fifty years and never really know her," a former classmate at Miss Comstock's school once remarked.* Nevertheless, Edith continued to visit Theodore's sister Bamie, and about eighteen months after Alice's death she accidentally encountered Theodore himself at Bamie's house. Theodore's romantic resolve to be true to the memory of his first wife thereupon began to weaken. For days the letter "E" was the only entry he made in his diary, and a few months later, on November 17, 1885, they became secretly engaged. Although Theodore was reportedly overheard murmuring fitfully to himself the following summer that he wished he could be constant to Alice, they were

---

* Although Edith Roosevelt's attitude toward scholars' use of her husband's papers was most enlightened, she destroyed the personal correspondence between him and her following his death in 1919.

married in London in December, 1886. Cecil Spring-Rice, an urbane and witty young English diplomat, was best man.

Edith Carow Roosevelt was a woman of many moods and some paradoxes. She was kind, considerate, and tactful; she was also shrewd, calculating, and at times ruthless. She suffered from neuralgia, and neither Theodore nor the children knew quite what to expect of her. Her tongue was sharp, and for all her genuine affection for her ebullient husband, she often silenced him with a rapier-like word or phrase. She is said to have been possessive and demanding; yet she tolerantly accepted her children as nature had variously endowed them. Her intelligence was wide-ranging and sensitive and her literary judgments were by all accounts penetrating. She read poetry aloud with quietly dramatic effect, and she was considered by her friends to be an authority on Shakespeare. She was also well read in philosophy and versed in current affairs. As Theodore observed many years after their marriage, Edith "is not only cultured but scholarly."

Down through the years Edith became as indispensable, probably, as any one person could become to her many-sided and resilient husband. She raised Alice Lee's daughter and bore four sons and a daughter of her own. She suffered Theodore's myriad political acquaintances and she tolerated some and enjoyed others of the legions of intellectuals who crossed her threshold on his invitation. When she was bored, which was not infrequent, she absented herself from lunch or retired early after dinner. And though she was invariably gracious at official functions, she was to the end of her life more a spectator than participant.

Edith wisely gave sparingly of her counsel on political affairs—she seems to have sensed intuitively when her advice would weigh and when it would not—and she resignedly accepted many of Theodore's most disruptive decisions in the realization that they "were best for him." TR was aware that he often piqued her, and when Ted Jr. became engaged in 1910 he commented revealingly on their quarter century together. "Greatly tho I loved Mother," he wrote his first-born son, "I was at times thoughtless and selfish, and if Mother had been a mere unhealthy Patient Griselda I might have grown set in selfish and inconsiderate ways." She was, he elaborated, "always tender, gentle and considerate, and always loving, yet, when necessary pointed out where I was thoughtless, instead of submitting to it."

Had she done otherwise, he concluded, her life would have been "very much harder, and mine very much less happy."

Nor was Edith uninfluenced by her gregarious husband. "One should not live to oneself," she warned Ted in her own congratulatory letter. "It was a temptation to me, only Father would not allow it. Since I have grown older and realize that it is a great opportunity when one has a house that one can make pleasant for younger—and also older—people to come to, I have done better."

Following their wedding on December 2, 1886, Theodore and Edith had taken a leisurely tour on the Continent. Theodore was captivated by Venice. ". . . the architecture has a certain florid barbarism about it—Byzantine, dashed with something stronger—that appeals to some streak in my nature," he wrote home. He was also enthusiastic about the Dying Gladiator, Raphael, Michael Angelo, and the Milan cathedral.

> The lofty aisle, with its rows of towering columns, white and shadowy, and the fretted, delicate work above, all seen in the dim half light that comes through the stained glass windows, really awes me; it gives me a feeling I have never had elsewhere except among very wild, chasm-rent mountains, or in the vast pine forests where the trees are very tall and not too close together. I think I care more for breadth, vastness, grandeur, strength, than for technique or mere grace or the qualities that need artistic sense or training to appreciate.

On March 19 after a short visit in Paris and an exciting whirl in high British social and intellectual circles, the Roosevelts embarked for the United States. They were to make their home at Sagamore Hill, the spacious gabled house which Theodore and Alice had planned and the architects Lamb and Rich had executed.

The house "was nothing to soothe the eye or melt the spirit with subtle harmonies of proportion or grace of line," Hagedorn writes in his engaging *Roosevelt Family of Sagamore Hill*. Roosevelt knew what he wanted in the interior—a library, great fireplaces, and a big parlor or drawing room—but he had slight conception of how the exterior should look. "So the architects gave him on the outside what self-respecting men of substance of the 1880's valued more than beauty, and what architects were summoned to express: solidity, first of all; dignity, hospitality, comfort, the social stability of the owner, and permanence. The foundations were twenty inches thick; joists, rafters and roof boards were in proportion. Long Island's gales were not going to shake this house, if Mr. Lamb and Mr. Rich could prevent it. Theodore's desires regarding fireplaces were fully covered, moreover, with four on the first floor, four on the second, and a dumbwaiter for firewood rising from the cellar to feed them. Apart from the satisfaction of crackling logs and dancing flames, Theodore was assuming—quite correctly, as the event proved—that even two hot-air furnaces in the cellar might need supplementing."

At Sagamore, Theodore soon immersed himself in the pleasures of family life. Alice is "too sweet and good for anything," he reported when his first wife's child was three and one-half years old. "Eleanor" —the shy and retiring niece who in 1905 married a distant cousin, Franklin Delano Roosevelt—"plays all the time with her." The baby —Theodore Jr., born to Edith on September 13, 1887—"crawls everywhere, does his best to stand and talk—but fails—and is too merry and happy for anything. I go in to play with them every morning; they are certainly the dearest children imaginable." And so it was over the years. Kermit came in 1889, Ethel in 1891, Archibald in 1894, and finally Quentin in 1897. Each was "the sweetest little fellow [or girl] in the world"; and each received a full measure of the father's time and attention.

Meanwhile Roosevelt published his biography of Thomas Hart Benton, wrote his *Gouverneur Morris,* and started *The Winning of the West.* He rode to the hounds and he helped organize a polo club. He took a perverse pleasure in falls—only the courageous rode hard enough to suffer mishap—and he once remounted with a broken arm and continued the chase to the kill. He talked glowingly of his triumphs and humorously of his foibles, especially in tennis, which he played with more energy than finesse. "I was given a first class partner who won in spite of me," he typically commented after a tournament victory. "I have turned my share of the 'cup' into a new Winchester rifle that I have been longing for." He also went West to hunt during these years; and partly to replenish his ranching losses, but mainly because of his compulsion to express himself, he wrote numerous articles on his experiences.

Gradually, TR's circle of friends became wider and more cosmopolitan, but it was with Henry Cabot Lodge, ten years his senior and his opposite in personality, that the deepest friendship developed. A moralist sans fervor, Lodge began his long career as a moderate reformer and ended it as the archpartisan of his age. He was more intellectually agile and polished than Roosevelt, yet he lacked his friend's breadth and flexibility. Nor was he warm and spontaneous. His letters reveal a man as calculating in the small things as in the large things, a man predisposed to read the meanest motives into others. From his adolescence to his old age, moreover, there was about him a supercilious quality that his drooping eyelids sharply accentuated; and though his very real abilities were widely recognized, he was respected but neither liked nor generally admired. Never, not even in the United States Senate where he held the seat of Webster and Sumner for thirty years, was Lodge a leader in the classic mold; and never, for all his eminence, was he seriously considered for the presidency, except by Roosevelt in 1916. Yet his intellectual power was considerable, and he had an element of high-mindedness. His contributions to the civil service movement, to administrative reform, and to national defense were substantial and meritorious.

Roosevelt and Lodge's relationship had been forged on the political crucible of the Blaine campaign and tempered by common interests uncovered thereafter. No less than Roosevelt, Lodge loved history; and even more than Roosevelt, belles-lettres. Both men had been long interested in civil service reform; both were strident nationalists and budding imperialists. Until Roosevelt espoused the humanism of Jefferson, or so he always insisted, of Lincoln, both were also conservative Hamiltonians. Notwithstanding his public hauteur, Lodge was affectionate and gracious in the security of his home. And though he lacked TR's bubbling zest, he was an impassioned horseman and polo player. His wife, Nannie, had a scintillating mind and surpassing charm as a hostess; Theodore admired and enjoyed her, and so, happily, did Edith.

From the outset Lodge recognized Roosevelt's extraordinary power and potential; through the three and one-half decades of their relationship he labored devotedly and at times almost selflessly to advance TR's political career. Roosevelt, who numbered few men among his friends although he had thousands of acquaintances, responded with his greatest gift. To Cabot Lodge more than to any other man, he gave his personal confidence. As TR confessed to him at one point, "I can't help writing you, for . . . there are only one or two people in the world, outside of my own family, whom I deem friends or for whom I really care." Such was the strength of the bond that bound them together that not even Roosevelt's bolt from the Grand Old Party in 1912 dissolved it completely.

Following his return from abroad in 1887, Roosevelt had maintained a passing interest in politics. He engaged in a vendetta with the mugwump editor, E. A. Godkin of *The Nation*. He unloosed a bitingly unfair attack on Henry George's theories, which he misrepresented. And he supported Benjamin Harrison for the presidency in 1888, though he had again steeled himself to accept Blaine on the grounds that "his name alone wakens enthusiasm, and . . . he would poll the most votes." Even as he stamped himself as a partisan Republican, however, he worked sincerely and energetically to reform the G.O.P. from within.

Two of the most agitated issues of the 1880's were tariff and civil service reform. On both the Republican leadership stood militantly for the status quo, and on both young Roosevelt took a position well in advance of his party. In private correspondence, on the fringes of the inner councils, and in public addresses, young Roosevelt urged the G.O.P. to rise to them. As the presidential campaign of 1888 impended, he even tried to beard the lion in its den. It would be a mistake, he told the Union League Club, "for the Republican party to announce that the inequalities and anomalies in the present tariff must not be touched, and to announce that the high tariff is a fetich, something to which every other issue must yield. . . ." There was needed, he boldly exclaimed, "a prudent and intelligent revision of the tariff" in order that the presidential campaign could be waged "on the broad ground of Republicanism, with all and not part merely of what the name implies." Thus were the unregenerate regulars, some of whom had feared Roosevelt's youthful enthusiasms more than Henry George's radicalism in the mayorality contest of 1886, confirmed in their judgment.

Following Benjamin Harrison's election, Roosevelt had sought to stay the victorious G.O.P.'s gathering assault on the merit system in a speech to the Federal Club of New York City. After conceding that there was "an immediate necessity to remove a great number of Mr. Cleveland's more vicious and incompetent appointees," he urged that the classified system be substantially extended "on the lines of the excellent bill introduced in Congress by my friend Cabot Lodge." He was speaking, he pointedly exclaimed, "on behalf of very many tens of thousands of Republicans who belong to the party because they believe in it, not for what they can make of it. . . ." A few months after that declaration Roosevelt commenced his notable labors on the Civil Service Commission.

For some time TR had yearned to play the larger role for which friends, newspapermen, and his own consciousness had told him he was destined. Neither his interests in the West nor his writing and diverse activities at Sagamore Hill had absorbed his vaulting energies. And he had begun to doubt that he could write a truly great book. Almost three years before, in August, 1886, he had rejected overtures to serve as president of the New York Board of Health. That same month visions of military glory—visions that would never die— had brightened momentarily when an incident along the Mexican border precipitated a flurry of war talk. Eagerly, Roosevelt had petitioned the Secretary of War for authority to raise an outfit of horse riflemen in the event of hostilities. "I haven't the least idea there will be any trouble," he explained to Lodge, "but as my chance of doing anything in the future worth doing seems to grow continually smaller I intend to grasp at every opportunity that turns up." Thereafter had come the mayoralty race, and following it, repeated protestations that he was through with politics.

As the Harrison administration took shape in the spring of 1889, TR's political ambition flared anew. He would, he now confided to Lodge, "like above all things to go into politics." He feared, however, that he was *persona non grata,* and he resignedly reconciled himself to a literary career, planning only to take the interest in politics "that a decent man should." That his fears were warranted is shown by the reaction of the new Secretary of State, the tainted James G. Blaine, to Mrs. Lodge's suggestion that he appoint Roosevelt Assistant Secretary of State. "I do somehow fear that my sleep at Augusta or Bar Harbor would not be quite so easy and refreshing if so brilliant and aggressive a man had hold of the helm," Blaine replied to Mrs. Lodge. "Matters are constantly occurring which require the most thoughtful concentration and the most stubborn inaction. Do *you* think that Mr. T.R.'s temperament would give guaranty of that course?"

Blaine knew his man. And so did Benjamin Harrison. The President was reluctant to give the thirty-year-old New Yorker *any* post in his administration; but under pressure from Lodge and others Harrison finally agreed to offer Roosevelt one of the four posts on the Civil Service Commission. To the President's subsequent dismay, Roosevelt accepted at once.

The civil service system was in a precarious state when Roosevelt breezed into office on May 13, 1889. Although Cleveland had strengthened the rules and extended the classified lists as he left Washington, he had made a virtually inclusive partisan sweep of all positions not covered by the law during the preceding four years. Partly in vengeance, but mainly because they also believed in the spoils system, thousands of Republicans had swarmed into the capital or beseeched their congressmen by letter for government positions in the weeks preceding Roosevelt's appointment. As one confirmed Republican newspaper blatantly proclaimed at the time: "Hundreds of Offices," "Places to Suit All Classes," "Take Your Choice."

In these circumstances, President Harrison decided to give the job-hunger of the party stalwarts precedence over the moral fervor of the reformers. Under the benign dispensation of Postmaster General John Wanamaker, pioneering merchant, Sunday school teacher, and G.O.P. "fat cat," 30,000 fourth-class postmasters were soon replaced by loyal, and presumably deserving, Republicans. Other cabinet officers were more restrained because their departments were smaller; but their comparative performances were as good, or bad. Harrison had been in office hardly a month before that paladin of civil service reform, *Harper's Weekly,* was in despair charging that "There was never in our history a grosser violation of distinct promises and pledges than the partisan devastation of the post offices under this administration."

The belated appointee of a skeptical President, Roosevelt was none-theless determined to enforce the law with accustomed zeal. "I am a great believer in practical politics," he wrote Lodge a little later, "but when my duty is to enforce a law, that law is surely going to be enforced, without fear or favor. I am perfectly willing to be turned out—or be legislated out—but while in I mean business." In truth, the waters ran deeper. Civil service reform was at once the most confirmed and most sustained cause of Roosevelt's career, and he read into it both the gospel of efficiency which is the conservative's creed and the open society which is the democrat's dream. As he and his colleagues wrote in their annual report of 1892–93, "a man enters the public service on his merits, after fair trial, in comparison with others of his fellow citizens, and is retained as long as he honorably serves the public." Roosevelt also regarded it as a prime preventive of moral degradation. The "spoils system," said that same report, "is a fruitful source of corruption in national life," one that prevents "decent men" from taking part in politics and that "degenerates into a mere corrupt scramble for plunder."

Young Roosevelt believed at first that President Harrison would approve his rigorous enforcement of the existing laws. "I have strengthened the administration by showing, in striking contrast to the facts under Cleveland, that there was no humbug in the law now," he wrote after six weeks in office. Two years later, however, he was not so sanguine; on count after count Harrison, who privately complained that TR "wanted to put an end to all the evil in the world between sunrise and sunset," had failed him. "The President actually refuses to consider the changes in the rules . . . necessary to enable us to do our work effectively," Roosevelt wrote Lodge. "He has never given us one ounce of real backing. He won't see us, or consider any method for improving the service, even when it in no way touches a politician. It is horribly disheartening to work under such a Chief."

Disillusioned though he was, Roosevelt and his colleagues had actually accomplished much during those first two years. They issued critical reports on examination procedures, they relentlessly pursued charges of fraud, and they made a well-publicized inspection tour of government offices in the West. "We have to do two things," Roosevelt, who soon became head of the Commission in title as well as in fact, told reporters on the eve of their departure. "One is to make the officials themselves understand that the law is obligatory, not optional, and the other is to get the same idea into the heads of the people."

Roosevelt's dynamic exertions continued throughout the Harrison administration though he privately complained of inactivity. The annual reports "revealed the presence of a new vigor and administrative power, and of a mind appreciative at once of ideal ends and practicable possibilities," one of the historians of the movement later wrote. Stories of Roosevelt's deeds "are handed down from generation to generation of Commission employees," the Chairman of the Commission reported sixty-two years after TR had resigned his post. And understandably so. Roosevelt lectured a recalcitrant Congress on means to improve the Pendleton Law. He called Southern Democratic congressmen into his office to explain how their constituents could win federal jobs by competitive examination. And he firmly refused to jump names on the lists. "You saw the . . . register when you were down here," he wrote a congressman who made inquiries for a constituent. "Her average was good . . . but it was not good enough." Or, as he bluntly admonished a job-seeker who had the temerity to discuss his connections: "No political influence will help you in the least. Not both your Senators and all your Representatives in Congress together could avail to have you certified from our registers."

That was not all. Roosevelt devised new and practical tests for applicants. "When we hold an examination for assistant statistician our aim is to get . . . an assistant statistician, not . . . a Civil Service Commissioner or Cabinet Officer," he explained to one correspondent. "We make the examinations as simple as the duties of the places to be filled admit," he informed another. He also placed women on the same competitive plane with men in many positions, the result being a notable increase in the number of women employed during his tenure. In addition, TR wrote numerous magazine articles, delivered uncounted speeches, and lobbied vigorously for increased appropriations for the Commission. "The last few years politically for me have been largely a balancing of evils," he revealingly confided to Brander Matthews, "and I am delighted to go in on a side where I have no doubt whatever."

One of the side effects of Roosevelt's relentless enforcement of the civil service laws was his restoration to grace by the mugwumps. The Old Guardsmen and their organs fumed over his refusal to play the party game, the Washington *Post* openly labeling him "The Rollicking Ranchman of Bogus Reform." But President Eliot of Harvard praised him as the "ideal citizen," and the New York *Evening Post* began again to refer to TR's "characteristic candor." Great numbers of Republican and Democratic newspapers also endorsed him warmly. He was, the Philadelphia *Record* said editorially, a man who "believes rather in the principles than the practices of his party."

His colleagues were quiet men, who supported him to a considerable extent, but he did the fighting in the newspapers, before congress and everywhere else, and of course bore the brunt of the consequent attack which by and by came largely to be personal to himself, as he became recognized as the leading spirit of the Commission.

TR professed to resent the encomiums of the mugwumps and Democrats on the grounds that they would "discredit me with well-meaning but narrow Republicans." But in reality it was his own actions that alienated him from the party warhorses. For he not only cut their feed bags, he impugned the integrity of a cabinet officer and spread the charges on the record in the election year 1892.

The main fight centered on the Post Office Department. John Wanamaker's talents were those of a near administrative genius. And although the most imaginative of his proposals—those for parcel-post deliveries, postal savings banks, and the decentralization of administration—were blocked by the indifference of Congress, he had nevertheless pushed through such a spate of reforms as made his tenure the most distinguished since the Civil War. On the other hand, Wanamaker had continued to promote the political interests of the Grand Old Party, partly because he hoped for congressional support of his legislative program, partly because he was a thoroughgoing partisan. As his sympathetic biographer admits and his 30,000 removals of fourth-class postmasters proves, he had "no profound objection to the theory that to the victors belong the spoils." Nor did Wanamaker have any "profound" respect for certain laws of the land.

In the spring of 1891 Roosevelt had investigated reports of maladministration in the Baltimore office. "We certainly struck pay gravel," he enthusiastically wrote Charles J. Bonaparte, the Baltimore patrician reformer who would later serve in his cabinet. Actually, Roosevelt had found that the Baltimore postmaster had arbitrarily removed about half the employees in the classified service and that he had allowed the law banning compulsory political assessments of classified employees to be flagrantly violated. Roosevelt had thereupon recommended to Wanamaker and the President that twenty-five Republican appointees in the Baltimore office be dismissed; but the report was pigeonholed. Unable long to endure the agony of inaction, TR had soon unburdened himself at a tempestuous meeting of the Civil Service Reform Association in New York. Then, following a melodramatic scene in which he exclaimed "damn John Wanamaker," he had returned to Washington on the advice of Carl Schurz and demanded an investigation by the House Civil Service Committee.

The Democratic-controlled committee readily obliged. For days charges and countercharges filled the air as Roosevelt and Wanamaker made separate appearances before the Committee and Roosevelt indirectly accused the Postmaster General of "slanderous falsehoods." The consequence was a boon to the civil service movement and a body blow to Harrison's chances of remaining in the presidency. And TR knew it. Contritely, and yet resolutely, he wrote the President that he had "used every effort to avoid a conflict with the Post Office Department" and explained that it "has now become merely a question of maintaining my own self-respect and upholding the civil service law."

By then the damage was done. The "little grey man in the White House," as Roosevelt referred to the cold and distant President, had to retain his maverick Civil Service Commissioner, for TR had so dramatized the merit system that his dismissal would have been construed as its overt repudiation. To be sure, Roosevelt oiled the surging waters by speaking energetically for Harrison's re-election in the campaign that fall. But the oil proved too thin or the waters too turbulent. The Wanamaker incident, the Populist movement, and a host of other factors combined to defeat the President and make Grover Cleveland the only man to serve two interrupted terms in the White House.

Roosevelt desired to continue as Commissioner under Cleveland in spite of his earlier insults to that sturdy gentleman, and with characteristic aggressiveness he encouraged Carl Schurz to intercede with the President-elect. He warned Schurz, however, that he would stay on only if Cleveland agreed to stand by him and appoint a strong commission. Schurz was of like mind. He advised Cleveland that he was in a unique position to "deal a blow to the spoils system from which it will never recover" and he pointed out that he could "hardly find a more faithful, courageous and effective aid than Mr. Roosevelt" for that purpose. Six weeks after his inauguration the President reappointed TR.

Many of the old problems now recurred, for the Democratic hosts proved as numerous and deserving as those of the Grand Old Party. Indeed, by an attorney general's opinion rendered in June, 1893, political parties were authorized to solicit contributions by mail from government employees. The result, reported the Commission, was that more solicitation occurred in the congressional campaign of 1894 than in any recent nonpresidential canvass. Nevertheless, the merit principle steadily advanced. President Cleveland cooperated wholeheartedly with Roosevelt and he encouraged high administration officials to do likewise. Early in his tenure he removed a Democratic commissioner who was out of sympathy with TR's policies, and in the one instance that Roosevelt quarreled publicly with a cabinet officer the President backed TR. So cordial was his support that in the summer of 1893 Roosevelt actually defended Cleveland against remonstrations by Schurz.

It was with deep satisfaction in the accomplishments of the preceding six years, therefore, that halfway through the Cleveland administration TR resigned to become a member of the Board of Police Commissioners of New York City. He had not, it is true, prevailed on Congress to place a sufficiently large number of high government positions under the civil service laws. Nor, for all the excellence of his administrative procedures, had he found a full solution to the perplexing problem of promotion for merit in a bureaucracy. Yet the classified lists had been more than doubled during his regime, while the Commission's position had become so firmly established that the future of the civil service movement was reasonably assured.

Others, of course, had shared in the achievement. The Civil Service Reform Association, major elements of the American press, and public-spirited citizens the country over had contributed to the climate of opinion that made reform possible. President Cleveland's cooperation had been vital. As TR wrote in a letter of resignation that warmly commended the Chief Executive for his courtesy and cooperation, Cleveland's "sweeping reduction . . . of excepted places . . . worked a most valuable reform in the execution of the law itself." Roosevelt's colleagues had also borne a share of the load; and TR rejoiced when one of them, the "high-minded and upright" John R. Proctor, ex-Confederate soldier and Democrat, was selected by the President to replace himself as head of the Commission. But more than any other individual, Roosevelt had been responsible for the Commission's rejuvenation and for the marshaling of public sentiment behind its program. His imaginative and energetic enforcement of the laws had virtually institutionalized the civil service system; and had he never performed another service for the American nation, that alone would have assured the perpetuation of his memory as a secondary figure of substantial accomplishment.

CHAPTER 5

THE FIGHT FOR THE RIGHT

> It may be truthfully said that Theodore Roosevelt at no time in his career fought more effectively for the basic principles of free government than he fought for them as New York Police Commissioner.
>
> —Former Commissioner Avery D. Andrews

When Roosevelt resigned his New York police commissionership two years after he left Washington he could also look back to reforms achieved and victories hard won. But the reforms would prove even more tangible, the battles yet more bitter and controversial, than those of his civil service years.

Not in all Roosevelt's career were the opponents of honest government more widely and deeply entrenched than those he faced when he accepted fusion Mayor William L. Strong's appointment in April, 1895. Their locus was Tammany Hall, or so it seemed to the uninitiated. But Lincoln Steffens later reported that they actually included "parts of the Republican machine, the saloons, gambling-houses, all vice interests, sportsmen generally, and to [Steffens'] . . . curious surprise many business men—the ablest, biggest, richest business men in local business; gas, transportation, banks, and the great financiers." Periodically sensational civic leaders like the fiery, bearded, Presbyterian minister, Dr. Charles H. Parkhurst, would bring corruption under the spotlight with such penetrating intensity that the citizenry would be aroused. But the "system" described by Steffens was too well organized, its tentacles too sharp and grasping, for reform waves to have enduring effect.

Roosevelt clearly understood the formidable nature of his new assignment. "I must make up my mind to much criticism and disappointment," he confided to Bamie as he decided to undertake it, for conditions make "it absolutely impossible to do what will be expected of me." He was nevertheless convinced that the reasons for accepting the charge were more compelling than those for rejecting it: to wit, his work on the Civil Service Commission was becoming routine; he deemed it wise to identify himself again as a Republican in his native state; and his competitive spirit was whetted by the challenge.

Having made his decision and expressed his forebodings, TR reported for duty on May 6 in high hopes, bounding up the steps of Police Headquarters on Mulberry Street and firing questions at his devoted friend Jacob Riis. "Where are our offices? Where is the board room? What do we do first?" he asked the Danish-born humanitarian and newspaperman. "It was all breathless and sudden," Steffens, whom Riis introduced to Roosevelt on the run, recalled. "It was just as if we three were the police board, T.R., Riis, and I, and as we got T.R. calmed down and made him promise to go a bit slow, to consult with his colleagues also. Then we went out into the hall, and there stood the three other commissioners together, waiting for us to go so that they could see T.R."

Roosevelt's fellow commissioners had at once elected him president of the Board. But only one of them, Major Avery D. Andrews, was destined to support him for long. A nominal Democrat and a West Pointer, class of 1886, Andrews had forsaken the Army for the law two years earlier. He was soft-spoken and unobtrusively efficient; and following his appointment a few months before, he had commenced the reform program TR would now expand. The other two, Colonel Frederick D. Grant and Andrew D. Parker, were soon to break with Roosevelt on personal or political—probably both—grounds. Grant was the son of the illustrious General and hapless President. He was slow-moving, kindly, and weak, and the press compared him to TR as "a freight train" to a "limited express." His politics were Republican. As his father had done before him, he also would seek to advance his own fortunes by joining a cabal against his superior. Parker was a handsome, strong-willed lawyer of considerable intellectual endowment. He had served three years as an assistant district attorney and he was affiliated with the County Democracy, though not because he opposed Tammany on ethical grounds. Steffens tolerantly described him as "the man that liked to sit back and pull wires just to see the puppets jump." But Andrews, who had more insight into Parker than that celebrated reporter, recalled simply that he "lacked the moral character . . . essential to the post."

Buoyed up by the apparent quality of his colleagues, TR again plunged into his new duties accompanied by the customary newspaper fanfare: "Roosevelt on Deck; Roosevelt on the Board for Business; He Wants to Know, and He Asks Some Pointed Questions; Trials are Trials Now; New Police Brooms Busy; Delinquent Policemen Get Short Shrift From Roosevelt."

Throughout the spring of 1895 TR's midnight prowls over patrolmen's beats, dramatic changes in personnel, and emphatic pronouncements combined to keep him favorably in the news. As he histrionically exclaimed at the end of his second month in office, "Two years and eight months left to me on this Board and that is time enough to make matters very unpleasant for policemen who shirk their duty."

Many of the police reporters—Steffens, Arthur Brisbane, and Joseph B. Bishop—meanwhile formed strong attachments to the effervescent Commissioner. They gravitated to TR because his nearly every move and offhand remark were lively with human interest; but they supported him because they believed in what he was doing. "We have a real Police Commissioner," Brisbane wrote in the usually hostile *World*. "His teeth are big and white, his eyes are small and piercing, his voice is rasping. He makes our policemen feel as the . . . little froggies . . ." However, Brisbane continued, "he looks like a man of strength . . . a determined man, a fighting man, an honest, conscientious man, and like the man to reform the force."

Bishop was not less perceptive. "The peculiarity about . . . [Roosevelt] is that he has what is essentially a boy's mind," he wrote in the *Evening Post*. "What he thinks he says at once, thinks alive. It is his distinguishing characteristic." However, Bishop added, "with it he has great qualities which make him an invaluable public servant—inflexible honesty, absolute fearlessness, and devotion to good government which amounts to religion. We must let him work in his own way for nobody can induce him to change it." Furthermore, he concluded, "he is talking to a purpose. He wishes the public to know what the Police Board is doing so that it will have popular support."

Unhappily, the "popular support" Roosevelt deemed so necessary to the reformation of the Police Department was not long sustained.

It began to diminish when he forced out Superintendent Tom Byrnes, an extraordinarily able and popular officer who had long collaborated with the politicians, vice men, and business men including Jay Gould, who comprised the grand *mésalliance*. And it suffered a body blow when he persisted in enforcing the law against the sale of intoxicating beverages on Sunday. Put on the statute books by the Tammany Democrats and kept there by the votes of well-meaning Protestant legislators from upstate, the Raines, or Sunday closing law, was an open sesame of graft. Saloonkeepers by the hundreds regularly paid off the police for the privilege of opening their doors in defiance of its provisions.

Roosevelt realized that the Raines Law should have been repealed; and at one point he publicly stated that he would have opposed its enactment. As he also explained, however, he had "to choose between closing all the saloons and violating my oath of office" as long as it remained on the books. More important still, for TR was never so committed to a literal interpretation of his duties as that remark implied, he had to enforce the Raines Law in order to attain his pre-eminent objective—the creation of an honest police force. Not until all the saloons were closed on Sundays could bribery be stamped out; and not until bribery was eliminated could the administrative reforms he and Andrews were fostering become truly meaningful.

Unfortunately, the Sunday closing law ran athwart the customs of New York's large and reputable German-American population which had long observed the Continental Sunday. The German-Americans bitterly resented the imputation that a Sunday afternoon in a beer garden with a string ensemble playing Strauss and children pattering around the tables was sordid. And all that summer they complained and grumbled over the forced closing of their neighborhood drinking places. Finally, in September, they vented their grievances in a protest parade which saw thousands of marchers, many bearing placards emblazoned with remarks such as "Good Morning, Have You Seen Roosevelt's Name in Print?" "Liberty, Priceless Gem, Where Hast Thou Flown? To Hoboken!" stream by a reviewing stand where TR, who had unabashedly accepted their invitation to witness the parade, comported himself with such high good humor that he drew cheers from the protesting paraders.

Roosevelt's troubles were compounded meanwhile by misrepresentations in unfriendly newspapers. As the protest of the German-

Americans and the complaints of the counsel for the Liquor Dealers' Association, who claimed that ninety per cent of the saloonkeepers had gone bankrupt from loss of revenue, attest, the Raines Law was broadly and effectively enforced. In an effort to discredit TR, however, newspapermen who trailed Roosevelt and Andrews when they made Sunday inspections reported that saloons were doing a flourishing business by means of side or rear doors. " 'East Side, West Side, all around the town,' yesterday went King Roosevelt I, ruler of New York and patron saint of dry Sundays," William Randolph Hearst's *Evening Journal* commented a month before the German-Americans organized their demonstration. Even Mayor Strong, who understood what Roosevelt was trying to do, succumbed to the popular urge and ridiculed his ubiquitous commissioner. "I found that the Dutchman whom I had appointed meant to turn all New Yorkers into Puritans," he laughingly said at a public dinner that fall.

Nor was all the criticism humorous. For a time the mail brought in anonymous denunciations, threats, and, at least once, a crudely designed bomb. TR was shadowed at night in a vain effort to blackmail him. And the chairman of the Republican County Committee angrily read Roosevelt out of the G.O.P. in a desperate attempt to hold the German-American vote. Unmoved by these and other pressures, including an implied threat by Strong that he would turn him out unless he relaxed his enforcement of the Raines law, TR resolutely held his ground. "We have no right to consider the [political] results," he righteously declaimed before the Republican Reform Club at the height of the campaign against enforcement.

The consequence was disaster for Roosevelt's party and vindication for his program. The Republicans suffered a crushing defeat at the polls that fall as 30,000 German-Americans reportedly bolted to the Democrats. But the Wine, Liquor and Beer Association resolved that it would expel any member who opened his shop on Sunday. "There has not been a more remarkable triumph of law in the municipal history of New York," the correspondent for the London *Times* reported. "The consensus is that to Theodore Roosevelt's courage and ability more than to any other single cause this victory is due."

Notwithstanding charges to the contrary, TR had enforced the law against the singing and drinking places of the rich as well as against the beer gardens and saloons of the middle and lower classes. One of the most sensational incidents of the enforcement campaign, in fact, had been the raiding of Sherry's restaurant during a dinner attended by many eminent New Yorkers. Partly to prevent such inconveniences to gentlemen, but largely to circumvent the Sunday closing law as a whole, a measure authorizing the sale of liquor with meals in hotels was put through the legislature the next year. The law was so loosely framed that it spawned a host of fake hotels and ramshackle brothel-saloons, and Roosevelt again took the offensive. As he reported when he left office, however, it proved impossible to close most of the places legally.

Roosevelt's second year in office was even more tumultuous than his first, the Board of Commissioners being virtually paralyzed by internal dissension and deadlock throughout most of it. Steffens later placed the blame on personalities.

> T.R. liked to lead cavalry charges with a whoop out in the open, Parker to direct his troops mysteriously from the rear unseen. He hated the way T.R. took command of the police from the first day and kept saying "I" and "my policy". . . . Parker enjoyed turning up at a meeting one day with Grant to block some proposition of the president. He tried to get Andrews, too, but the young West Pointer did not like the crafty conspirator; he did not approve of T.R.'s cowboy style either, but he stared Parker down and joined and stood by the president.

Steffens was partly right, for Roosevelt was dominating if not domineering. Yet Steffens' statement was also misleading. Parker was later tried for maladministration, and if his trial proved nothing else, it demonstrated that he would have fought anyone who opposed his drive for control of the force.

As it happened, Parker found an ally in Tom Platt. The "Easy Boss" was angered by Roosevelt's support of Thomas B. Reed's presidential aspirations (Platt was for McKinley), by TR's removal of many of "his men" from the police force for incompetency and worse, and especially by his enforcement of the Sunday closing law. Platt could not risk offending the upstate "drys" by repealing the law; yet he had to win back the German-Americans. He decided, therefore, to deadlock the Board of Commissioners in the hope that the enforcement campaign would thereby break down. He used Grant as his instrument.

Roosevelt's response to Platt's diabolical scheme set a pattern he was to follow during his governorship and on through his presidency.

He avoided a personal break with Platt and the other party leaders, and he continued to identify himself as a regular Republican. But on the main issue, the enforcement campaign, he held absolutely firm. "I work and fight from dawn until dark, almost"; he wearily wrote his sister, "and the difficulties, the opposition, the lukewarm support I encounter give me hours of profound depression; but at bottom I know the work has been well worth doing."

> It is a grimy struggle, but a vital one. . . . All day I strive to push matters along; to keep on good terms with the Mayor, while rejecting his advice and refusing to obey his orders; not to be drawn into a personal quarrel with Platt; not to let my colleagues split either among themselves or with me; to work with reformers like Dr. Parkhurst, and yet not let them run away with the Department; to keep weeding out the bad men; to attend to the thousand complaints, well and ill-founded, of citizens; to try to improve discipline, and to build up the detective bureau, and develop leaders; and so on and so on.

The deadlock continued on into the spring of 1896. "I cannot shoot . . . [Parker]," TR complained to Lodge, "or engage in a rough-and-tumble with him—I couldn't even as a private citizen, still less as the chief peace-officer of the city; and I hardly know what course to follow as he is utterly unabashed by exposure and repeats lie after lie with brazen effrontery." Finally, however, Roosevelt, Andrews, and Dr. Parkhurst and his followers forced Mayor Strong to hold the public hearing that exposed Parker's naked mendacity, after which Strong ordered Parker's dismissal. At the instance of "Boss" Platt, however, the Republican governor refused to approve the order. Parker was still in office when Roosevelt resigned, feuding anew with TR's successor.

The Parker hearing was highlighted by one illuminating colloquy. After Roosevelt had charged on the witness stand that Parker was "mendacious, treacherous, capable of double dealing and exercising a bad influence upon the force," he was asked whether he would refuse to go along with Parker even if he knew him to be right. TR forthwith replied:

"No sir. I would be glad to yield to him if he was right."

"You enjoy yielding to a man, don't you?"

"By George, I do, and that's a fact."

Roosevelt was understandably gratified to move gracefully out by accepting an appointment as Assistant Secretary of the Navy in the spring of 1897. Not until the last year of his presidency would he again be so frustrated; not until 1912 so embattled. The Rev. Dr. Parkhurst had stood by him until the end—he even blazed out at Platt, who attended his church, from the pulpit. Thousands of disinterested citizens and dozens of reporters and editors, especially from out of state, also continued to support him unreservedly. A reporter for the Chicago *Times-Herald* termed him "undeniably the biggest man in New York," and others boomed him for the presidency. Yet his enemies had proved even more numerous and powerful than he had expected. They included not only Tammany and the Republican machine, not only the German-Americans, the saloonkeepers and the vice lords generally, but clergymen who resented his refusal to ban a professional fight. ("I suffered a heavier punishment sparring at Harvard," he told newspapermen after witnessing the bout, "and I have been knocked out at polo twice for a ten times longer period.")

Roosevelt had also antagonized labor. Union leaders had lauded his enforcement of the Sunday law against the restaurants and hostelries of the rich. And they had warmly endorsed his condemnation of more than one hundred "wretched and crowded" tenements, as he described them. (Twice wrathful landlords had tried to sue TR.) But they deplored his terrifyingly extreme remarks about striking mobs, and they felt that he had thrown the weight of the police force on the side of capital by giving protection to strikebreakers.

The raging controversies of Roosevelt's two years as president of the Board have lent to easy sensationalism and facile generalization. As TR had foreseen at the start, he was unable to rid New York City of corruption; and as he had not wholly foreseen, the leaders of his own party had actively opposed him. Only the moral support of the decent elements had prevented the machine from turning him out; only his extraordinary courage and self-esteem had kept him from resigning after three or four months in office. Yet he had compiled a peerless record. Never in the department's history had the law been so effectively and dramatically enforced; never had two years seen so many basic and sweeping reforms. When Roosevelt took office the price of a captaincy was said to have been $10,000; when he left office it was nothing. When Roosevelt assumed his duties on May 5, 1895, the flow of dismissals from the force was but a trickle; when he resigned in April 1897 it had become a flood. Steffens graphically described the scene at the height of the turnover:

> "Hey, there," [Roosevelt] yelled to me from his window one day, "come up here." I ran upstairs to his outer office, which was filled with all sorts of respectable people, evidently business men, lawyers, doctors, women, and two priests. Waving his hand around the circle of them, he squeezed through his teeth aloud: "I just want you to see the kind of people that are coming here to intercede for proven crooks. Come on, come into my office and listen to the reasons they give for letting bribers, clubbers, and crime-protectors stay on the police force and go on grafting on the public."

There were other, more permanent reforms. Roosevelt had early announced that "We are going to have fitness, physically, mentally and morally, constitute the standard and basis of admission to and promotion in the Department . . . ;" and within a few months of his appointment he had largely achieved that objective. An examining board was created, religious and political affiliations were struck off the unwritten criteria for appointment, and examinations patterned on the federal service were instituted. The eligibility list for initial appointment was zealously observed, though TR often made spot promotions for heroism and other exceptional acts. A probationary period was also established. So effective were the merit aspects of the new system, indeed, that it was warmly commended by a committee of the Civil Service Reform Association headed by Carl Schurz, which inspected the department on Roosevelt's invitation.

Repeatedly and unavailingly, the politicians tried to break it down or circumvent it. An incident related by the novelist Owen Wister, who was visiting TR in his office when a surgeon named Marvin Palmer happened in bearing a letter of recommendation from the Surveyor of the Port, is typical. "I entirely agree that a republican appointment would be timely," Roosevelt said after perusing the letter. "And I am quite sure, Dr. Palmer, that you are qualified for the position." After a momentary pause, he added: "And here's the way you can get the position. . . . Stand first on the Civil Service list!"

Whereupon the physician strode out of the office, stopping at the door just long enough to say, "You can go to hell!"

Meanwhile the force was partially modernized. A bicycle squad was formed, a telephonic system of communications was established, and recruits were given fairly intensive training before being assigned to beats. The force as a whole was warned to be polite to the public ("That a citizen devoid of 'pull' has any rights that a policeman is bound to respect, . . . [is] a novel proposition," the *Herald* sardonically observed). And for the first time in decades election officials were honestly selected. ("If nothing but this one reform had been gained by it," the *Tribune* commented, "the political revolution of last year would not have been in vain.")

But above everything else, above the administrative reforms, the modernization program, the political accusations and counteraccusations, towered Roosevelt's inspirational power. As an unnamed patrolman exclaimed to Steffens when the press reported that TR was resigning in the spring of 1897, "It's tough on the force, for he was dead square, was Roosevelt, and we needed him in the business." Nor did it die with TR's passing. Years later veteran officers confirmed what the New York *Evening Post* had predicted when Roosevelt closed his desk in April: "The end of the reign of Mr. Roosevelt . . . is not the end of Rooseveltism. Mr. Roosevelt may disappear utterly . . . but his personality will persist as an active influence in the force for a generation at least, till the youngest 'reform cop' is retired, and then he will not 'go out of business' entirely. . . . He will furnish another example for the young policeman and though most of them may choose the majority ideal, all will remember Roosevelt."

CHAPTER 6

THE GREAT ADVENTURE

> No qualities called out by a purely peaceful life stand on a
> level with those stern and virile virtues which move the men of
> stout heart and strong hand who uphold the honor of their flag
> in battle.
>
> —Theodore Roosevelt*

Theodore Roosevelt "will bring with him to Washington all that
machinery of disturbance and upheaval which is as much a part of
his entourage as the very air he breathes," the Washington *Post* said
the day the Senate confirmed TR's appointment as Assistant
Secretary of the Navy. "He is inspired by a passionate hatred of
meanness, humbug, and cowardice. He is a fighter, a man of indomitable pluck and energy, a potent and forceful factor in any equation
into which he may be introduced. A field of immeasurable usefulness
awaits him—will he find it?"

The President of the United States had been reluctant to appoint
Roosevelt to the Navy Department post. William McKinley had been
eased into the White House to preserve the business civilization
against William Jennings Bryan and his rampant agrarian legions,
not to build up the battle fleet or to force Spain out of the New World.
Would there be a clash of interests if TR became a member of his
administration? "I hope he has no preconceived notion which he
would wish to drive through the moment he got in," McKinley had

* In a review of Captain Alfred Mahan's *Life of Nelson* in *The Bookman*,
June 1897.

91

remarked to Lodge when the Massachusetts Senator had pressed
Roosevelt's case upon him in the winter of 1897. Whereupon Lodge,
with what reservations we may never know, had assured him that he
"need not give himself the slightest uneasiness on that score."

It happened, too, that the President-elect owed a political debt to
the New York Police Commissioner. Roosevelt had at first opposed
McKinley's nomination for President in the belief that he would not
hold up in a crisis, whether "a soft-money craze, a gigantic labor
riot, or danger of foreign conflict." But the confluence of Roosevelt's
election-year regularity and his exaggerated fears of Bryan—he called
the convention that pressed its highest accolade upon the broad, un-
furrowed brow of the Boy Orator of the Platte a "Witches' Sab-
bath"—had altered his perspective. When Mark Hanna invited him
to join his multimillion-dollar crusade for McKinley and the gold
standard, TR had signed on with a vengeance; and during the late
summer and fall of 1896 he had campaigned furiously for the
Ohioan's election and the Great Commoner's defeat.

Furthermore, a number of other prominent Republicans including
Tom Platt had urged Roosevelt's appointment upon McKinley. Platt
had been hesitant when TR first asked him to use his influence. He
was eager to have the righteous Police Commissioner out of his hair,
however, and after concluding that TR would probably "do less harm
to the organization as Assistant Secretary of the Navy than in any
other office that could be named," he had submitted Roosevelt's name.
Under these pressures the President had finally given in, and on
April 6, 1897, a month and two days after his inauguration, he sent
in Roosevelt's appointment to the Senate.

TR's desire for the assistant secretaryship reflected more than his
wish to ease out of his untenable situation in New York. That quality
of destiny which the newspapers, his friends, and even his political
opponents read into his future was looming larger; and he could
hardly have remained long as Police Commissioner under any circumstances. More than a decade earlier A. T. Packard, the editor of
the *Bad Lands Cowboy,* had suggested to Roosevelt that he might
someday become President of the United States. TR had forthrightly
replied: "If your prophecy comes true, I will do my part to make a
good one." But that had been in Dakota where men were inclined to
be direct. Rarely again did Roosevelt admit such a lofty ambition, and
never quite so simply.

Once, during Roosevelt's police commissionership, Jacob Riis had asked him directly if he was working for the presidency. Angrily, TR had expostulated that no friend would ever suggest such an idea. Quickly, however, he had regained his composure, put his arm over his devoted friend's shoulder, screwed his face into a knot, and said softly: "I am going to do great things here, hard things that require all the courage, ability, work that I am capable of." Then, in a flash of self-revelation, he had added: "I must be wanting to be president. Every young man does. But I won't let myself think of it; I must not, because if I do, I will begin to work for it, I'll be careful, calculating, cautious in word and act, and so—I'll beat myself. See?"

Roosevelt also looked forward to his return to Washington because the Navy Department post gave him a seat on the fringe of power. While on the Civil Service Commission he had chafed under the restrictions of his bipartisan office. "I often have a regret that I am not in with you, Reed, and others in doing the *real* work," he had confessed to Lodge. During all the years of his political apprenticeship, moreover, TR had been actively interested in foreign policy and military preparedness. He had commented on those issues in the presidential elections of 1884 and 1888; and he had interjected them into his campaign for mayor in 1886. He had long fretted over Cleveland and Harrison's lack of interest in the Navy, but he had taken heart at such assertiveness toward Germany, Spain, and Great Britain as they had sometimes shown. Cleveland's belligerence toward the British in the Venezuelan boundary dispute had won Roosevelt's warm endorsement, while his emphatic refusal to annex Hawaii had provoked his unbridled contempt—"a colossal crime," he called it. Roosevelt had further deplored Cleveland's steady resistance to demands that he press the decadent Spanish government into granting independence to the Cubans. At times, also, Roosevelt had looked forward to American acquisition of Canada, half hoping for an incident with Great Britain as the means to effect that end. He was, in addition, disgusted by the apathy of a succession of presidential administrations toward construction of a canal across the Central American isthmus, for he had long foreseen the strategic and economic advantages of such an undertaking. TR had no illusions that his new post would give him a major voice in the formulation of such policies; but he did believe that it would give him access to some of the men who made the decisions.

As it turned out, Roosevelt was to exercise a far greater influence during his year's tenure as Assistant Secretary of the Navy than he had expected and probably even hoped. Secretary John D. Long, an indulgent gentleman of declining energy, was often away from the department; and in any event, he delegated considerable authority to his energetic assistant. Thus Roosevelt was able from the start of his service to establish and direct his energies toward the realization of three broad objectives: the improvement of morale, administration, and tactical efficiency; publicity of the case for increased naval power; and preparation of the battle fleet for war with Spain. Within the year Roosevelt had firmly impressed his character on all three.

Soon after assuming office, for example, Roosevelt was detailed to investigate an accident involving a torpedo boat. Dutifully, he stated in his official report that commanders should take proper safety precautions. However, he added, "it is more important that our officers should handle these boats with dash and daring than that the boats should be kept unscratched." Shortly thereafter the new Assistant Secretary visited Newport News where the battleships *Kentucky* and *Kearsarge* were then being built. He was enthusiastic about the quality of the ships, but he disapproved their double turrets on the well-founded grounds that they made it necessary to train both light and heavy-caliber guns on the same target. In June, while Secretary Long was on vacation, Roosevelt undertook to lighten the paper work assigned torpedo-boat commanders. And in August, with Long again away, he lightened the load for battleship and battle-cruiser captains.

Meanwhile Roosevelt zealously guarded the prerogatives of Navy Department employees under the civil service system, bombarded Secretary Long with advice, and made numerous personal inspections of naval installations. At the Cramp shipyard in Philadelphia, where he inspected the *Iowa,* it was reported that he "broke the record for asking questions" and that he surprised officers and shipbuilders by his "evident theoretical knowledge of the construction of ships of war down to the details of bolts and rivets."

During the fall of 1897 Roosevelt served as chairman of a board on naval personnel which recommended that the distinction between engineering and line officers be eliminated, that unfit officers be pensioned, and that the salaries of line officers be increased. Then, over the opposition of conservative and economy-minded critics, he drew up a bill incorporating those recommendations. The measure was passed in 1899. The Assistant Secretary continued meanwhile to rail against the advancement of officers on the basis of tenure rather than ability.

Roosevelt's administrative reforms were usually made in cooperation with Secretary Long, whom he regularly posted when the latter was away from Washington. Nevertheless, TR's tendency to exert even more authority than Long had granted him and, especially, his disposition to make public statements on policy matters made conflict inevitable. The first major difference occurred in August, 1897, when Roosevelt told a meeting of naval reservists in Ohio that the United States ought to decide whether it should annex Hawaii without regard to the attitude of Japan or any other power. The headlines, TR confided to Lodge, "nearly threw the Secretary into a fit, and he gave me as heavy a wigging as his invariable courtesy and kindness would permit." A few weeks after that Long deleted a passage urging an increase in the size of the Navy from an article the Assistant Secretary was preparing for publication. Other incidents followed. And although the two men were still on good terms when Roosevelt resigned, it was mainly because of the Secretary's easygoing temperament and his personal affection for his irrepressible subordinate. Assuredly, TR had transgressed. "My chief usefulness has arisen from the fact that when I was Acting Secretary I did not hesitate to take responsibilities," he confided to Lodge shortly before he resigned in the spring of 1898, "and from the further fact that I have continually meddled with what was not my business, because I was willing to jeopardize my position in a way that a naval officer could not." Nor did Roosevelt overestimate his services. During the years from 1897 to 1909, writes a recent naval historian, William R. Braisted, Roosevelt "was perhaps more responsible than any other individual . . . for the shaping of the Navy into an effective instrument of war and diplomacy."

Roosevelt was particularly exercised by Long's sensitivity to the economy bloc in Congress, and though he hammered at the Secretary to request funds for six battleships—four for the Atlantic, where he foresaw ultimate trouble with Germany, and two for the Pacific, where Japan's growing power was the catalyst—the best he could get from Long was a recommendation in December, 1897, for the construction of one new battleship. The result, concludes Braisted, was that "American naval strategists, with but a one-ocean navy, were still studying the means to defend American possessions against Japan

without opening the way for a German assault in the Atlantic" a
decade later. Indeed, as early as May, 1897, Roosevelt had assigned
the Naval War College the following problem:

Japan makes demands on Hawaiian Islands.
This country intervenes.
What force will be necessary to uphold the intervention and how
shall it be employed?
Keeping in mind possible complications with another Power on
the Atlantic Coast (Cuba).

Meanwhile, as the war clouds over Cuba continued to darken,
Roosevelt tried to convince his superior that he should dispose the
fleet in a way that would give it the greatest possible striking power
in the shortest time span should war break out. But Long, who apparently lacked the power of bold decision, refused to act. Indeed, he
even failed to act following the destruction of the *Maine* in Havana
Harbor on February 15, 1898. Ten days after that epochal event he
unwittingly gave Roosevelt his opportunity by absenting himself from
the Department for the day. He warned his ebullient subordinate not
to take "any step affecting the policy of the administration without
consulting the President or me"; but Roosevelt, in a characteristic
disregard of authority, ignored his instructions. That very afternoon
he dispatched to Commodore Dewey that fateful telegram which
prepared the way for the defeat of the Spanish fleet at Manila Bay
and the acquisition of the Philippines:

Dewey, Hong Kong: Order the squadron, except the *Monocacy* to
Hong Kong. Keep full of coal. In the event of declaration of war
Spain, your duty will be to see that the Spanish squadron does not
leave the Asiatic coast, and then offensive operations in Philippine
Islands. Keep *Olympia* until further orders.

Secretary Long was furious when apprised of Roosevelt's action.
TR had "gone at things like a bull in a china closet"; he lacked "a
cool head and discrimination." Significantly, however, Long failed to
countermand the order, perhaps because he was relieved that the
Assistant Secretary had made the decision for him. And when war
was declared on April 19, Dewey set off in full steam for his
rendezvous with destiny.

However unpardonable Roosevelt's breach of personal faith, it was
a right move from an internal point of view; nor was it lightly made,

though the act of sending the telegram may have been impulsive. The plan, which had been conceived by Mahan, was one that Roosevelt had long pressed upon his chief, and a case can be made that the authority to issue the order was technically, if not morally, Roosevelt's. As TR had written Secretary Long six weeks earlier, the nation might suffer "one or two bitter humiliations" and would "certainly be forced to spend the first three or four most important weeks not in striking, but in making those preparations to strike which we should have made long before."

The tactical wisdom of Assistant Secretary of the Navy Roosevelt's order to Dewey is not be confused with his unofficial war-mongering as war impended in the spring of 1898. For many years Roosevelt had been extolling the warlike virtues, writing contemptuously of those who opposed military preparedness, and advocating American expansion as the manifest right of a superior people. Three years after he sought in 1886 to raise a troop of "as utterly reckless a set of desperadoes as ever sat in the saddle" for possible conflict with Mexico, TR was hoping for "a bit of a spar with Germany." To Spring-Rice he confided that "the burning of New York and a few other seacoast cities would be a good object lesson on the need of an adequate system of coast defences; and I think it would have a good effect on our large german [sic] population to force them to an ostentatiously patriotic display of anger against Germany." By 1895 he was requesting Governor Levi P. Morton of New York for a captaincy should war break out with Spain over Cuba. And late in the same year he was scorning "the bankers, brokers and Anglo-maniacs generally" who opposed Cleveland's truculence toward the British in the Venezuelan crisis. Then, in the spring of 1897, less than two months after he became Assistant Secretary of the Navy, he declared in a prepared address at the Naval War College that "No triumph of peace is quite so great as the supreme triumph of war." Unquestionably, as Howard K. Beale concludes in his authoritative work on Roosevelt's foreign policies, TR "came close to seeking war for its own sake."

It is difficult and probably impossible to square many of Roosevelt's statements on war with Roosevelt the moral man. Doubtless, as many students of Roosevelt's life have concluded, his aggressiveness derived in some part from his boyhood struggle against illness. It is unlikely, however, that the experience of his youth did more than determine the degree of his belligerence, for thousands of men of divergent psychological make-up subscribed to the same general theories. Cabot Lodge and John Hay shared TR's attitude toward war, though they were more circumspect in expressing it. Henry Adams's brilliant, introspective younger brother, Brooks, was a philosophical militarist. And Oliver Wendell Holmes, Jr., whose militarism has curiously escaped the obloquy of historians, was quite convinced that war "was divine" and that "this snug, over-safe corner of the world" needed one in order that the people might "realize that our comfortable routine is no eternal necessity of things . . . and . . . that we may be ready for danger." Furthermore, the cult of military valor was world-wide. Lord Wolseley, the commander in chief of the British forces, merely expressed what hosts of Englishmen believed when he wrote in 1889 that "All other pleasures pale before the intense, the maddening delight of leading men into the midst of an enemy, or to the assault of some well-defended place." The generation that thrilled to Alfred Lord Tennyson's "Charge of the Light Brigade" was followed by one that took Rudyard Kipling's *Barrack-Room Ballads* to its heart; and the reception accorded the poet laureate of imperialism was even more uncritical in Great Britain than in the United States.

Had Roosevelt been born in a later era he might have vented his primordial instincts on the athletic field. As it was, he thought of war in terms of man-to-man combat, dashing cavalry charges, and brilliant tactical maneuvers; not of mass carnage, germ-infested prison camps, and endless, stultifying boredom. Perhaps his heroic visions should not have been. There were many, even in Roosevelt's time, who cried out against them; among them his quondam friend, Carl Schurz, most of the other mugwumps, and tough-minded William James. It was James, in fact, who stripped the veneer of moral purpose from Roosevelt's exhortations. Not only is he "still mentally in the *Sturm und Drang* period of early adolescence," the Harvard philosopher wrote of his former student, he regards "one foe . . . as good as another," and "swamps everything together in one flood of abstract bellicose emotion."

For all who had eyes to see, moreover, the Civil War had been the first of the great modern holocausts. But for reasons that cut to the core of the human experience, a generation of politicians, participants, and propagandists of a lost cause had endowed it with an

ultraromantic aura before Roosevelt was yet an adolescent, and to
this day their creation survives. TR matured in that milieu. He
despised Jefferson Davis, whom he once subjected to personal insult,
as the symbol of disunion; but he esteemed Robert E. Lee, whose
services to the Confederacy were far greater, as the exemplar of the
soldierly virtues.

The views of Roosevelt, Holmes, and the rest did not lack an intellectual rationale. Their emphasis on preparedness and the will to fight
reflected a reading of the grand sweep of human history from a social-
Darwinian frame of reference. And if Roosevelt did not necessarily
regard the race among individuals as invariably to the swift, he nevertheless believed that it was almost always so among nations. A country had either to expand its influence by peaceful means if possible or
by war if not. Otherwise it would lose place, power, and prestige; or
at the least it would fail to fulfill its potential, of which failing there
was none greater, whether for individual or nation, in Roosevelt's
system of values. This required strength, determination, and sacrifice.
It presumed the development of the soldierly virtues and the will to
use them when challenged. "If our population decreases; if we lose
the virile, manly qualities, and sink into a nation of mere hucksters,
putting gain above national honor, and subordinating everything to
mere ease of life; then we shall indeed reach a condition worse than
that of the ancient civilizations in the years of their decay," Roosevelt
wrote in his review of Brooks Adams's *The Law of Civilization and
Decay*. Rome began to decline, he declared in one of those classic
half truths of which he was sometimes a master, when the "Roman
army became an army no longer of Roman citizens, but of barbarians
trained in the Roman manner . . ."

Yet, there were qualifications. TR was too buoyant, too much in
love with life, to imbibe of the Adams brothers' pessimism. And
even as he regretted with Brooks the passing of the military man, he
read his values into the new economic man. There were in the
American capitalistic system, he also said in his review of *The Law
of Civilization and Decay*, "great branches of industry which call
forth in those that follow them more hardihood, manliness, and courage than any industry of ancient times. . . . As yet, while men are
more gentle and more honest than before, it cannot be said that they
are less brave." In 1917, when it seemed to Roosevelt that Western
civilization stood on the brink of disaster, he earnestly sent forth his

sons to war. But some years before, when it had been time for his first-born to choose a career, he urgently advised him against West Point and the enervating life of a regular army officer.

Meanwhile there was a war at hand. Two generations of American historians have deprecated McKinley's submission to the hysteria generated by the "yellow journalists," Hearst, Pulitzer and their imitators, to a Protestant clergy irrational with compassion for the oppressed Cubans, to statesmen obsessed with illusions of national grandeur, and to a public opinion bursting with ultrapatriotism. James Ford Rhodes, friend of McKinley, brother-in-law of Mark Hanna, and judicious defender of Republican policies, called the conflict with Spain "a needless war." The distinguished student of American diplomacy, Samuel Flagg Bemis, termed its aftermath the "great aberration." And a long list of others have poured forth condemnations that are harsher still. Not even the relatively exemplary administration of the colonial empire which arose in its wake and the perspective afforded by two world wars have substantially changed those judgments. The most that has been said in extenuation is that resort to the sword was perhaps the only way to cut the Gordian Knot of Spanish barbarities in Cuba and to heed the American people's humanistic demand that they be ended; and that is hardly a tenable thesis. For Theodore Roosevelt, however, the war represented intellectual and emotional fulfillment.

Roosevelt believed that "every foot of American soil, including the nearest islands in both the Pacific and Atlantic, should be in the hands of independent American states," and he regarded the liberation of Cuba as a first step toward that end. He also believed that war with undermatched Spain would prove a rewarding tactical exercise for the fleet and that it would spur sentiment for a more powerful Navy, without which, he argued, the United States had no justification for retaining Alaska and annexing Hawaii and little possibility of building up its Far Eastern trade. Repeatedly during 1897 and early 1898 he pointed out to Secretary of the Navy Long and others that Japan was threatening to surpass the United States as a naval power and that the Imperial German government showed a tendency "to stretch out for colonial possessions which may at any moment cause a conflict with us." We should beware, he warned, "of letting a foolish hatred of England blind us to our honor and interest." Germany, not England, was the power most likely to conflict with the United States over the Monroe Doctrine.

As war actually impended in the winter and early spring of 1898 Roosevelt's emotions came to rule him. Fearful that a joint inquiry with Spain into the causes of the *Maine* disaster would fail to impose responsibility on Spain, he urged Secretary Long to advise the President against such an investigation. Meanwhile, in a ratiocination that gives point to Arnold Toynbee's aphorism that patriotism is the last infirmity of noble minds, he concluded that Spain was in fact culpable, that the ill-fated battleship "was sunk by an act of dirty treachery on the part of the Spaniards." And again and again as the crisis heightened he pleaded for war. On the eve of conflict he revealed his frustrations to Brooks Adams, whose courageous great-grandfather, John, had won historical fame and contemporary condemnation by preventing another needless war just one hundred years before:

> The blood of the Cubans, the blood of women and children who have perished by the hundred thousand in hideous misery, lies at our door; and the blood of the murdered men of the *Maine* calls not for indemnity but for the full measure of atonement which can only come by driving the Spaniard from the New World. I have said this to the President before his Cabinet; I have said it to Judge Day, the real head of the State Department; and to my own chief. I cannot say it publicly, for I am . . . merely a minor official in the administration.

Finally, on March 21, the naval court of inquiry reported that the *Maine* had been destroyed by the explosion of a submarine mine, but that it had been "unable to obtain evidence fixing the responsibility. . . ." Nor has that responsibility ever been determined. Three weeks later, despite the Spanish government's last-minute capitulation to McKinley's demand that it agree to an armistice in Cuba, the President submitted a militant war message to an aroused Congress. His action, write three recent historians, was "one of the most disastrous failures in the history of presidential leadership."

The pressures had been too overwhelming for McKinley, whom Roosevelt had characterized as having the backbone of a "chocolate eclair," to surmount. So great was the demand for war on all sides that there had been talk of Congress passing a war resolution over the President's veto. The talk was probably idle; but speculation that McKinley and the Republican party would be defeated in 1900 if he failed to take the country into the war may have been well founded. In any event, it was the latter threat that apparently caused Mark Hanna, business leaders, and finally the President to decide for war in the face of their own reluctance and Spain's near total submission. Elihu Root's warning that "Fruitless attempts to hold back or retard the enormous momentum of the people bent upon war would result in the destruction of the President's power and influence, in depriving the country of its natural leader, in the elevation of the Silver Democracy to power" was but one of several such counsels. In the face of them McKinley lost the will to resist. "I think . . . possibly the President could have worked out the business without war," his friend and confidant, Senator John C. Spooner of Wisconsin, mused three weeks later, "but the current was too strong, the demagogues too numerous, the fall elections too near."

Theodore Roosevelt was not thinking of the congressional elections of 1898 nor of the presidential campaign of 1900. He was consumed as few men have ever been consumed by concern with the role he would play in the war that at last had come, and he at once made plans to resign from the Navy Department and organize a regiment of volunteer cavalry. His family, his friends, and his superiors wanted him to continue as Assistant Secretary. Edith had given birth to her fifth child, Quentin, the previous fall and was even then convalescing after a major operation. She hoped that her husband would not go, though she knew that he must. President McKinley twice asked him to stay on. And Secretary Long, who continued to treat TR with fatherly indulgence, implored him not to go. "His heart is right, and he means well," he wrote of Roosevelt in his diary, "but it is one of those cases of aberration-desertion-vain-glory; of which he is utterly unaware."

But the most ironic pressure came from Roosevelt's fellow war-hawk, Cabot Lodge. A few years earlier Lodge had collaborated with TR on a book entitled *Hero Tales of American History*. Now, in the hour of trial, he sought to dissuade both his own spirited son and his dearest friend from volunteering. There was, he said, no need for them to go to war. Furthermore, he warned Roosevelt, his resignation would spell the end of his political career.

Roosevelt himself professed to be torn by conflicting emotions. He claimed that he was not going to war "with any undue exhilarations of spirits or . . . recklessness or levity." And he several times protested that he was not seeking military glory. Yet, as he must surely have realized, all his life had been a preparation for the test that was then to come. Few men ever went forth to war with greater zest and higher resolve to act gallantly than TR did in that turbulent spring of 1898; and when he wrote from the battlefield outside Santiago three months later that the charge up the heights had been his "crowded hour," he wrote in total emotional satisfaction. No other episode in Roosevelt's career, not even his election to the presidency in his own right in 1904, quite compared. As he confided to his military aide several years afterward, "I know now that I would have turned from my wife's deathbed to have answered that call." It was, he said, "my chance to cut my little notch on the stick that stands as a measuring rod in every family."

Roosevelt's sense of duty was so compelling, however, it is probable that he would have volunteered even if he had been unmoved by the call of glory. "I want to go because I wouldn't feel that I had been entirely true to my beliefs and convictions, and to the ideal I had set for myself if I didn't go," he wrote Paul Dana of the New York *Sun* at the time:

> I don't want you to think that I am talking like a prig, for I know perfectly well that one never is able to analyze with entire accuracy all of one's motives. . . . For two years I have consistently preached the doctrine of a resolute foreign policy, and of readiness to accept the arbitrament of the sword if necessary; and I have always intended to act up to my preaching if occasion arose. Now the occasion has arisen, and I ought to meet it . . . if we who have preached the doctrine fail to put our words into effect when the time comes, our preaching will lose much of its force.

The announcement that Theodore Roosevelt had resigned as Assistant Secretary of the Navy on May 6, 1898, to organize the First Volunteer Cavalry Regiment reverberated throughout the United States. A flood of applications for service—twenty-three thousand all told—poured in from men in all walks of life and from all sections of the country. Several hundred cowboys, a score of Indians, a handful of New York policemen, and a sizable number of athletes from the Ivy League were finally accepted. The selection process was erratic and personal, yet nonetheless effective, as the following incident suggests:

"My name is Dudley Deane," said a fine, athletic young man to Col. Theodore Roosevelt yesterday afternoon.

A broad and cordial smile of welcome beamed on Col. Roosevelt's face. "Yes," he said, "I know you. You are the man who saved the day for Harvard in the great football game with Yale. You are one of the kind of men we want."

More of that "kind" were taken—even the chaplain had played three years of varsity football at Wesleyan, so TR, with no little earnestness, pointed out. "You've got to perform without flinching whatever duty is assigned you regardless of the difficulty or danger attending it," Lieutenant Colonel Roosevelt told a batch of recruits in Washington. "If it is the closest kind of fighting you must be anxious for it. . . . No matter what comes you mustn't squeal."

At San Antonio, Texas, that spring, Roosevelt and the regiment's actual commander, Colonel Leonard Wood, an extraordinarily able officer who had won the Medal of Honor for his pursuit of the great Apache chief, Geronimo, quickly molded their troops into a surprisingly efficient fighting force. There were, inevitably, minor problems. TR never mastered the regular army formalities though he maintained a rough dignity, and when he detrained in San Antonio late in April he responded warmly to the uproarious cheers of troops who should have received him in a formal ceremony. A few weeks later Wood was forced to rebuke him for buying his men all the beer they could drink after a hot march in the saddle. "Sir, I consider myself the damnedest ass within ten miles of this camp," he contritely replied. And in Tampa, Florida, shortly before the Rough Riders, as the First Volunteer Cavalry Regiment had been affectionately dubbed by the press, sailed in mid-June for Cuba, Roosevelt took two of his sergeants to dinner in a hotel where Wood was dining with the commanding general of the Army.

The Rough Riders' first engagement occurred at Las Guasimas, a small Cuban village, on June 24. Their point, which was led by Sergeant Hamilton Fish, Jr., who was killed on the spot, ran into a force of Spaniards, and a sharp action ensued. The enemy mounted a strong resistance, but they eventually gave way. By the time American reinforcements arrived the fight was ended. Sixteen Rough Riders lay dead.

The supreme test came one week later after Wood had been advanced to brigade commander and Roosevelt had replaced him as commanding officer of the First Volunteers. On June 30 TR was ordered to move his regiment, which was without mounts, into position for an attack on the Spanish stronghold of Santiago. By nightfall the Rough Riders were bivouacked in a jungle at the foot of a series of hills flanking the east side of the city. The most prominent hill was San Juan, but there were entrenchments on all.

Morning came, but no further orders. Roosevelt champed, and when the regulars moved out from cover to attack he was about to order his men to advance to the sound of the gunfire. Before he could give the command, a message came directing him to advance through the bush toward the hill directly in front of his bivouac. It was the one next to San Juan, and it was called Kettle Hill. "The instant I received the order I sprang on my horse," TR later wrote, "and then my 'crowded hour' began."

It lasted most of the day. Through the whole time Roosevelt was a conspicuous figure as he exhorted his Rough Riders to charge against the enemy who maintained a destructive fire from behind their fortifications. "Are you afraid to stand up when I am on horseback?" he shouted at one terrified trooper. He said worse to others. His elbow was nicked by a bullet, a trooper was killed at his feet, and he had several other calls as close. Early that afternoon the Rough Riders and fragments of other regiments took the hill and held it under fire from the Spanish on San Juan. That night they dug in. More fights followed, but none matched the intensity of that charge. It was remarkable, wrote Richard Harding Davis, one of a coterie of newspaper man whose friendship with TR assured him a favorable press, that anyone had survived.

The campaign had brought out Roosevelt's best and some of his worst. He took pride in his regiment's heavy casualties, since they had proved that he and his troops had been in the thick of action. He gloated that he had personally "doubled-up" a Spaniard. And in one of those desecrations of the human spirit that will forever bar him from attaining the immortality of Jefferson, Lincoln, and Wilson, he invited post-battle visitors to "look at those damned Spanish dead." He had been as foolhardy as he had been brave and daring. And beyond a doubt he was boastful. "I do not want to be vain, but I do not think anyone else could have handled this regiment quite as I have," he wrote Lodge. "I rose over those regular army officers like a balloon," he said to Hermann Hagedorn many years later. He also wrote as much in a book, *The Rough Riders,* the title of which Finley Peter Dunne's Mr. Dooley found misleading. "If I was him," said Dooley, "I'd call th' book 'Alone in Cubia!' or 'Th' Darin' Exploits iv a Brave Man be an Actual Eye-Witness.' "

The campaign had also proved what there had been no need to prove—Theodore Roosevelt was an inspiring leader of men. He had, Leonard Wood later wrote, the all-important virtues of the soldier. He was courageous, solicitous of his troops' welfare, and accessible to those who bore complaints; and he commanded in consequence the respect of both his men and his officers. Stephen Crane, who observed TR in the field hospitals between engagements, wrote at the time that he "worked like a cider press . . . let him be a politician if he likes, he was a gentleman down here."

It was perhaps inevitable that even in Roosevelt's hour of greatest glory he should thrust his bull neck into controversy with those who had it in their power to do him honor. Yellow fever raged through the camps after Santiago fell, and when a group of ranking regular officers asked TR, who was by then a brigade commander, to request Secretary of War Russell A. Alger to expedite the army's transfer north, the Rough Rider consented. With the tacit approval of the commanding general, W. R. Shafter, he wrote a letter that was given out to the press before it reached Washington.

President McKinley and Secretary Alger were understandably outraged. Roosevelt's letter, together with one which the regular officers had drawn up on reconsideration, was an indirect, but damning indictment of the administration's conduct of the war. It also advertised to the Spaniards, who were then negotiating peace, that the American Army in Cuba was no longer a disciplined and effective fighting force. Furthermore, Alger had made the decision to evacuate just the day before.

On August 15, 1898, the disease-ridden but all-conquering Rough Riders disembarked from the transport *Miami* at Montauk Point, Long Island. A month later Roosevelt was called from his tent on the sands. The First Volunteer Cavalry Regiment was formed in a hollow square with the officers and color sergeant in the center. Roosevelt strode into the square and one of the troopers stepped forward and presented him with a reproduction of Frederick Remington's famed bronze, "The Bronco-Buster." It was a gift from the enlisted men. TR was visibly moved as he now addressed his troops for the last time. "I am proud of this regiment beyond measure," he declared. "It is primarily an American regiment, and it is American because it is composed of all the races which have made America their country by adoption and those who have claimed it as their country by inheritance." He closed with a tribute to the Negro soldiers who had fought with distinction beside the Rough Riders. Then, as the entire regiment, many of its members in tears, filed by him, he shook hands with each man and officer. The great adventure had ended.

There was an epilogue. Roosevelt had been recommended for the Medal of Honor. He wanted it painfully, partly because he believed it would help him in his political career, mainly because he needed throughout his life to surround himself with the outward symbols of achievement. After the original recommendation had been made, TR had written numerous letters on his own behalf, sought affidavits from those who had been with him in battle, and beseeched Lodge to obtain the War Department's endorsement. But Secretary Alger refused to make the recommendation to Congress.

There was a pathetic quality about it, for most of the nation knew anyway that Colonel Theodore Roosevelt had been a hero. The medal finally came, forty-six years late, and to TR's oldest son, who by all accounts had kept his father's faith on a beachhead in Normandy where he died in 1944. For his own bravery under fire Congress posthumously awarded to Brigadier General Theodore Roosevelt, Jr., the medal which Colonel Theodore Roosevelt, Sr., had also earned but never received.

CHAPTER 7

THE FINAL PREPARATION

> An honest and fearless Governor—a combination of conscience and backbone—is a mighty good thing to have at Albany!
> —The New York *World*

The Rough Riders were still convalescing or frolicking on the windswept sands of Long Island when their Colonel was plunged bodily into politics. At issue was the governorship of New York.

The administration of the incumbent, the Republican Frank S. Black, was proving grievously lacking. Black had antagonized Tom Platt by exerting a calculated independence and he had offended decent opinion by weakening the civil service system and by failing to act decisively to rid the administration of the Erie Canal of graft and corruption. So Platt, who was no sentimentalist, began casting about for a gubernatorial candidate. He wanted a man whom the people would elect and he could control.

Theodore Roosevelt fitted the first particular. His emergence as a military hero, coupled with his sustained reputation as a reformer, gave him such a luster that he was commonly recognized as the only Republican who could possibly stave off the threatening Democratic landslide in the November elections. Even before his transport anchored off Montauk Point many Republican newspapers had nominated him, and some all but elected him.

Senator Platt sensed that Roosevelt, who had been a minor irritant as police commissioner, would prove a major sufferance as governor. He also had forebodings that the Colonel would move from the governorship to the presidency. As an anti-imperialist, the "Easy

Boss" was reluctant to place Roosevelt in a position that might enable him to resolve the colonial problems growing out of the war with Spain. Yet Thomas Collier Platt was a practical politician to the marrow. As Chauncey M. Depew, the witty and jaded president of the New York Central Railroad, pointed out, the G.O.P.'s one chance of retaining the governorship lay in diverting attention from the Black administration's shortcomings. When questioned about the canal frauds during the campaign, Depew cynically remarked, he could say with conviction:

> We have nominated for governor a man who has demonstrated in public office and on the battlefield that he is a fighter for the right, and always victorious. If he is selected, you know and we all know from his demonstrated characteristics, courage and ability, that every thief will be caught and punished. . . . Then I will follow the colonel leading his Rough Riders up San Juan Hill and ask the band to play the "Star-Spangled Banner."

Platt saw Depew's point. He feared, however, that Roosevelt would break with him once he had galloped triumphantly into office; so he refused to endorse the Colonel until he received assurances of co-operation. Following a protracted negotiation, Roosevelt finally thrashed matters out with Platt at the latter's apartment in the Fifth Avenue Hotel on September 17. "We buried past differences," Platt wrote in his autobiography. The Colonel agreed to "consult with me and other party leaders about appointments and legislation in case he were elected."

The announcement that Roosevelt had visited Tom Platt provoked howls of anguish from reformers, who had naïvely hoped that Roosevelt would head up an Independent party ticket. "By accepting Platt he becomes the standard bearer of corruption and demoralization," Fulton Cutting charged in the New York *Evening Post.* "The matter is a question of honor," John Jay Chapman, who seemed to have convinced himself that Roosevelt had committed himself to their project, confided to his wife. "I do not believe that Teddy Roosevelt . . . has so far humbled himself as to go to Mr. Platt," TR's old ally, the Rev. Dr. Parkhurst, protested. It was 1884 and the fateful decision to support Blaine all over again, or so they believed.

The reformers might have known better. For all his dedication to good government, Roosevelt was too wise in the ways of politics to be anything but a Republican "regular." Prepared though he may have been to make the supreme sacrifice, he determined that it should be as a lion and not as a lamb. His flaunting of Jay Gould, Benjamin Harrison and even Tom Platt had proved that before, and his leadership of the Progressive hosts would prove it again. He well knew, however, that he had to match power with power; that he had to possess office before he could act constructively. He resigned himself accordingly to accepting the thorns with the roses.

The decision hurt. Had Roosevelt's ideals been lower, his contemporary reputation might have been higher; independent reformers would not have expected so much of him. But he had repeatedly proved that he was one of them at heart; and when, because he was in action a realist rather than a doctrinaire, he failed to fulfill their every ideal, they invariably vented upon him the self-righteous indignation of the true believer for the heretic.

The Colonel naturally returned their venom. Only rarely thereafter would he concede that the ferment whipped up by these and other men of good hope—the mugwumps, the muckrakers, the social theorists Henry George and Edward Bellamy, the social reformers Jane Addams and Ben Lindsey, and the humanistic politicians Bryan and La Follette—was all that prevented America from being swallowed whole by the voracious materialism he himself so deplored. It was an irony that history long afterward crowned. Notwithstanding his far-reaching legislative achievements, Theodore Roosevelt's most dramatic contribution to American life, most historians now agree, was the arousal of the public conscience to the need for even further reform.

Roosevelt's attitude toward his compromise with the machine is set forth in a letter to the civil service reformer, Francis E. Leupp, written before TR conferred with Platt on September 17. "I should be one of the big party leaders if I should take it," he wrote, and "I should have to treat with and work with the organization."

> I should see and consult the leaders—not once, but continuously —and earnestly try to come to an agreement on all important questions with them; and of course the mere fact of my doing so would alienate many of my friends whose friendship I value. On the other hand, when we come to a matter like the Canal, or Life Insurance, or anything touching the Eighth Commandment and general decency, I could not allow any consideration of party to come in. And this would alienate those who, if not friends, were supporters.

A few reformers accepted the logic of Roosevelt's necessity. "Nobody who has followed his career can doubt that in him, as Governor, civil-service reform would have a champion whom nothing could intimidate or seduce," the *Nation* wrote editorially. But others, whom Roosevelt termed "the idiot variety of 'Goo-Goos,' " viewed his fall from grace with less tolerance ("That goose Parkhurst is giving me some trouble," the Colonel would soon complain). And some, including Carl Schurz, now opposed him because of their still-seething resentment of his imperialism.

The campaign that autumn confirmed the prescience of Chauncey Depew. The cheers at the Republican state convention had been louder for Platt than for Roosevelt; but it was the Colonel's show on the hustings. The canal frauds were all but ignored, certainly by Roosevelt, who promised only further investigations, and presumably by the crowds, which partook of the Rough Rider's hard-won fame and succumbed to his vibrant personality. "Seven Rough Riders, wearing their uniforms of glory, were on the special train on which Roosevelt began a tour on October 17," writes Pringle. A bugler would sound the cavalry charge at each stop, and as the notes died the candidate would begin his address. " 'You have heard the trumpet that sounded to bring you here,' he exclaimed at Fort Henry. 'I have heard it tear the tropic dawn when it summoned us to fight at Santiago.' " Roosevelt would then urge his listeners to affirm the results of the war by electing a Republican Congress (also a Republican governor). The ultimate came at Port Jervis when ex-Sergeant Buck Taylor, one of the seven glorious props, was allowed to speak. "I want to talk to you about mah Colonel," Taylor told the crowd. "He kept ev'y promise he made to us and he will to you. When he took us to Cuba he told us . . . we would have to lie out in the trenches with the rifle bullets climbing over us, and we done it. . . . He told us we might meet wounds and death and we done it, but he was thar in the midst of us, and when it came to the great day he led us up San Juan Hill like sheep to the slaughter and so he will lead you."

It was a remarkable performance; and neither the Colonel's infectious pride in his own and his Rough Riders' heroics, nor the need to create a diversionary political issue, quite explains it.

A possible explanation is that Roosevelt had no program. As he wrote James Bryce shortly after the returns came in, he planned only to conduct an "honest administration." Another consideration was the Colonel's concern with the impending peace. He had already come out for annexation of the Philippines, and he was devoutly convinced that the anti-imperialistic Democrats constituted the gravest possible threat to national greatness. "Do you wish to keep or throw away the fruits of what we won in the war?" he admonished the crowds that swarmed about the rear platform of his campaign train: "We cannot avoid facing the fact that we occupy a new place among the people of the world . . . Greatness means strife for nation and man alike. . . . We must dare to be great . . . We are face to face with our destiny and we must meet it with high and resolute courage."

But the most compelling explanation is Roosevelt's desperate desire to win. Even John Jay Chapman was willing to overlook the Fourth of July aura which characterized the Colonel's canvass on the ground that he "really believes that he is the American flag." As Chapman confided to his wife, however, when Roosevelt "endorses the administration of McKinley in words that are intended to cover and do cover Alger, I despise him, for I know him to be dishonest."

Certainly the Colonel's deft glossing over of Republican corruption contrasted sharply with his full-bodied criticisms of Democratic malfeasance; and though he was confined at first to generalizations about Tammany, the revelation late in the campaign that Croker had refused to permit a state supreme court justice to be renominated because he would not appoint a Tammany hack as clerk of the court unexpectedly gave him the issue he needed. Croker's action, Roosevelt wrote in his *Autobiography,* enabled me to "fix the contest in the public mind as one between himself and myself." It paid off; and so probably did $60,000—$10,000 of it reportedly from J. P. Morgan—which Platt is said to have poured into Roosevelt's cause the last week or ten days. In any event, TR defeated his opponent, Augustus Van Wyck of Brooklyn, by 17,794 votes. He ran well ahead of his ticket, and for the first time, perhaps, became fully conscious of his extraordinary power to move great masses of people.

Billy O'Neil, Roosevelt's compatriot in reform during TR's three terms in the Assembly, described that power in a letter to Jonas S. Van Duzer, another of the old group. "Just before I met him [TR] I received a letter from a friend in Albany saying 'For God's sake tell Roosevelt to stop his self-adulation and talking about himself so much,' " O'Neil wrote. After listening to the Colonel's speeches, how-

ever, O'Neil advised him to follow "his own instincts and inspiration."
He continued:

> At Carthage, in Jeff. County, there were three thousand people
> standing in the mud and rain. He spoke about ten minutes—the
> speech was nothing, but the man's presence was everything. It was
> electrical, magnetic. . . .
> Some Democrats say it was only the idle curiosity of the crowd
> that always attends the entrance of a circus with a country town.
> I thought it something else, perhaps my own love and admiration
> for the man blinded me to the real facts. Perhaps I measured others
> by my own feelings, for as the train faded away and I saw him
> smiling, and waving his hat at the people, they in turn giving
> abundant evidence of their enthusiastic affection, my eyes filled
> with tears, I couldn't help it though I am ordinarily a cold-blooded
> fish not easily stirred like that.

"Senator Platt," wrote Roosevelt when he was still Governor-elect,
"is to all intents and purposes a majority of the Legislature." The
statement was accurate. Yet Roosevelt, armed with his own righteous
enthusiasm and supported by a public opinion which he both formed
and reflected, was soon to prove that Platt was not always an intractable "majority." By the end of Roosevelt's administration the "Easy
Boss" had deferred more to the Colonel on major matters than Roosevelt had to him. The Governor had regularly consulted him, after
which he "frequently did just what he pleased," Platt ruefully recalled years later. "My desire was to achieve results, and not merely
to issue manifestoes of virtue," Roosevelt explained in his *Autobiography*. "I had to work with the tools at hand. . . . It was only
after I had exhausted all the resources of my patience that I would
finally, if he still proved obstinate, tell him that I intended to make
the fight anyhow."

Tom Platt's first insight into the Governor's independence came
shortly after Roosevelt's inauguration on January 1, 1899. Roosevelt
was determined that the state canal system would be administered
with efficiency and honesty, and he accordingly proposed the appointment of former Comptroller James A. Roberts of Buffalo, who had
clashed with the "canal ring" in the past; however, as Roberts rejected Roosevelt's overtures for personal reasons, Platt thereupon
seized the initiative by offering the post to Francis J. Hendricks of
Syracuse. A machine politician of integrity and ability, Hendricks'

acceptability was compromised by the fact that he came from a canal county. Nevertheless, Hendricks accepted Platt's offer, and when Platt next saw the Governor in New York City he presented him with his *fait accompli*.

Roosevelt was invariably polite and sometimes deferential to Platt; he replied simply that he was "sorry," but that he could not appoint the Senator's man. Platt then lost his temper. Finally, however, he realized that the Governor would not yield, and the matter was settled when Roosevelt drew up a list of four names, one of which they both agreed upon. A master at playing on men's weaknesses, Platt seems not to have understood their strength. As William Allen White long afterward wrote, he "underestimated Roosevelt . . . because he had no sort of conception of that part of a man which is called the moral nature."

Thereafter Roosevelt usually pursued the course followed in the Hendricks case. The result was a minimum of friction and a generally, though not invariably, high level of major appointments. On minor offices, it is true, the Governor gave the machine a relatively free choice, partly out of physical necessity, partly because he understood the system. Only when he had special knowledge or desired to appoint a personal friend would he intervene. Joe Murray, his original sponsor in the Twenty-first District Republican Club, received a minor post, as did an occasional former Rough Rider. But in most instances Roosevelt refused even his friends, often giving needy acquaintances money from his own pocket—roughly a thousand dollars during his two years in office—rather than put them on the public payroll.

It was in the legislative arena, however, that Roosevelt most forcefully threw down the gauntlet to Platt. Cynical and contemptuous of the democratic process though he was, the Senator possessed a carefully considered socio-economic frame of reference. He believed that the function of government was to serve business, especially big business, and he was intolerant of all tampering with the foundations, and even the superstructure, of economic power. His machine was largely financed by the contributions of businessmen, and he openly prided himself on his ability to elicit contributions from J. P. Morgan and other titans. When, therefore, Roosevelt threw his influence behind measures designed to curtail corporate privileges in the spring of 1899, Platt became thoroughly alarmed.

I had heard from a good many sources that you were a little loose on the relations of capital and labor, on trusts and combination . . . on those numerous questions . . . affecting the security of earnings and the right of a man to run his business in his own way, with due respect, of course, to the Ten Commandments and the Penal Code.

Actually, Roosevelt's first message to the legislature had given the defenders of the status quo slight cause for uneasiness. Many of its points had been well taken, particularly those on the civil service and the labor welfare laws; but they portended little major economic reform. Within a few months, however, the Governor had become engaged in a full-scale battle over a series of bills designed to establish stricter controls on the operations of gas and transportation companies and to impose taxes on their franchises or earnings. None of the measures was conceived by Roosevelt; yet all received his considered support once he decided they were efficacious.

The most significant was a bill for the taxation of the value and the tangible assets of all street railway, gas, electric, and water franchises. The measure had been introduced by Senator John Ford, a Democratic lawyer and economist, and it was brought out of committee in March, 1899. Roosevelt approved the Ford bill in principle; and over the remonstrations of Elihu Root, who was lobbying for the Astoria Gas Company and had written a bill responsive to that company's interests, he also favored proposals to level a specific tax on the earnings of the franchises. "Ought there not be some arrangement by which, if the franchises prove very valuable, a portion of the gross earnings should be paid to the public treasury?" the Governor wrote Platt at the time. "I have no sympathy whatsoever with the demagogic cry against corporations when those corporations render public service," he told a state senator the same day. "But where, by act of the legislature, and through taking possession of a part of the public domain, state or municipal, the corporation gets advantages, it should be taxed for them in some intelligent way."

Jolted by this threat to their privileged position, the corporations raised a tremendous outcry through their retainers in the legislature and elsewhere. But small property holders all over the state stood to gain relief in the amount the utilities corporations were taxed; they exerted such an effective counterpressure on members of the legislature that passage of a token tax bill became virtually inevitable.

Meanwhile, Governor Roosevelt pondered over the larger question of the state's over-all tax structure. His own knowledge was deficient, so he characteristically consulted the experts—Professor Richard T. Ely of the University of Wisconsin, George Gunton an independent labor economist, and Professor E. R. A. Seligman of Columbia University, the nation's foremost authority on public finance. Impressed further by the complexity of their responses, Roosevelt on March 27 sent a special message to the legislature recommending the creation of a joint committee to study the situation and report to the next legislature. The message pointed out that farmers, mechanics, and tradesmen bore a disproportionate share of the tax burden, and it pronounced the light taxation of corporations an "evident injustice."

The supporters of Senator Ford were struck dumb by the Governor's action. Angrily, they interpreted Roosevelt's proposal as a shrewd maneuver to evade a showdown with the corporations and the Platt machine. Roosevelt vehemently denied that it was; yet he argued that the Ford bill might prove "so crude a measure as to provoke a revolt, or else be inoperative." In spite of an admission that special taxes might be advisable, moreover, he strongly urged consideration of a broader and more inclusive program than that offered by Ford. Whatever the political import of these subterfuges, it is nevertheless clear that Roosevelt's belief that corporations should bear a tax burden more commensurate with their resources placed him at an opposite economic pole from Tom Platt, Benjamin Odell, Chauncey Depew, Elihu Root, and most of the other leaders of his party.

During the next month the Governor reversed himself by coming out again for the Ford bill, and as the session drew to a close he threw the full force of his office and powerful personality behind it. To ease the way for legislators beholden to the corporations—one such blandly explained that he had "received orders not to pass it"—Roosevelt agreed to send a special, emergency message to the Assembly. He submitted it the night before adjournment, but Speaker Fred Nixon, a Platt man, refused to read it for fear of offending the "Easy Boss." Meanwhile the Governor was warned that he could not expect to run for office again "as no corporation would subscribe to a campaign fund if I was on the ticket." The result, Platt later affirmed, was that Roosevelt "clinched his fist and gritted his teeth, and drove the franchise tax-law through the legislature."

Enraged by this frontal assault on his power base, Platt on May 6 wrote the letter in which he questioned Roosevelt's concept of the relations between capital and the public. "At the last moment, and to my very great surprise, you did a thing which has caused the business community of New York to wonder how far the notions of Populism, as laid down in Kansas and Nebraska, have taken hold upon the Republican party of the State of New York," the irate, sixty-five-year-old boss added. Platt concluded by predicting that the Democrats would capture control of the state in 1900 unless Roosevelt changed his ways.

The Governor was now in command, the bill being his to sign or veto. He was alternately ingenuous and disingenuous. He wrote Platt that he would have preferred to take no action and that the bill was "forced upon" him. But he also wrote that his study of the problem had convinced him that the bill "was along the right" lines, and he responded directly to Platt's charge that he was fostering Populism:

> I do not believe that it is wise . . . for us as a party to take refuge in mere negation and to say that there are no evils to be corrected. It seems to me that our attitude should be one of correcting the evils and thereby showing that . . . the Republicans hold the just balance and set our faces as resolutely against improper corporate influence on the one hand as against demagogy and mob rule on the other.

Until 1912 that remained Roosevelt's abiding hope.

Roosevelt was of no mind to veto the measure—he later termed it "the most important law passed in recent times by any American state legislature"—yet he wanted to remedy its imperfections. He consequently decided to call immediately a special session to amend the bill. Platt and his cohorts would then have to accept his constructive amendments or suffer the original measure's being signed into law during the thirty-day period authorized for that purpose. The machine was thus cornered. As Roosevelt confided to Lodge, many corporations preferred in the showdown "to be blackmailed by Tammany rather than to pay their just dues to an honest Board of Assessors." Meanwhile, so Roosevelt wrote, Platt's son, Frank, and the corporation attorneys tried to sell him "a gold brick, by putting in seemingly innocent provisions which would have made the taxation a nullity." He refused, however, to yield. "I told them that unless they passed the bill exactly as I wished it, I should sign the Ford bill," he reported to Lodge.

Cowed by Roosevelt's threat, the machine reluctantly swung behind the Governor's amendments. These authorized state officials to make the assessments and provided for evaluation of corporate property as realty rather than in terms of securities which could easily be undervalued.

The conservatives' wrath at the Governor's triumph was almost boundless. The *New York Times* called the franchise tax "the robber baron science of taxation ruthlessly applied." Chauncey Depew, solicitous of the small interests for perhaps the only time in his career, mournfully predicted that every country trolley line in the state would be driven out of business. And the Brooklyn *Daily Eagle* first labeled the bill "communistic," then castigated it as an "invasion of Bryan's vocabulary or an infringement of geographical rights of use and sale in Bryan's territory."

That the franchise tax was as significant economically as Roosevelt thought is questionable. There is no doubt, however, that it was a first major thrust at corporative privilege and as such was a milestone in the development of economic justice in New York State. Even more important, it nurtured the Governor's growing realization that many industrial problems were beyond the capacity of local authorities to resolve. Laissez-faire, Roosevelt came more and more to see, would have to be abandoned if the corporations were to be made responsible to the society that sustained them.

Several other episodes also contributed to the views on trusts that later characterized Roosevelt's presidency. When, during his third month in office, Armour & Company offered to settle for $20,000 fines totaling $1,500,000 for violations of the law against the sale of oleomargarine as butter, he indignantly refused (Platt's son termed Roosevelt's action "admirable, even if it was not what I wanted"). And when, again, he learned that unsound insurance companies were defaulting in their obligations to the public, he gave his signature to a measure requiring all fire or marine insurance companies to have a minimum capitalization of $200,000. He also signed a bill designed to strengthen the resources of savings banks by limiting their investments in real estate mortgage and railroad bonds though it encouraged investment in the large, financially sound corporations at the expense of smaller and less stable companies and served the railroads' interests as well. Finally, he approved a bill authorizing the State Supreme Court or its agents to inspect the books and vouchers of corporations. Then, in the special session, he endorsed antimonopoly legislation bearing on transportation rates. His first year in office was further highlighted by the passage of several bills designed to improve the election and civil service laws.

Roosevelt had not won every issue; nor had he always been as independent of Platt as he later remembered. His most crushing defeat was on a bill to place the New York City police department under state control. Partly in order to stamp out election frauds by Tammany, Tom Platt had pressed a bill to establish a single police commissioner for the city, said commissioner to be appointed by the governor. Because of the opposition of upstate Republicans and Tammany Democrats, however, the measure failed. Platt thereupon had a group of attorneys draw up a new bill, the so-called Constabulary Bill, which would have created a state police commissioner empowered to appoint and supervise the chiefs in all major cities.

Roosevelt was thereby impaled on the horns of a dilemma. He had bitterly opposed Platt's effort to dominate the police department when he headed the Board of Commissioners; yet the New York force had regressed considerably in the three years since he left office. Platt's bill embodied much that Roosevelt approved, especially in its provisions for civil service examinations in all the cities affected, and he further believed that it was probably the only way to assure honest elections. After much soul-searching, he decided to give the Constabulary Bill his endorsement. But in the end he was forced to abandon it, so concerted and vehement was the opposition to it. He was similarly forced to give up such faint hope as he had of amending the Raines Law, the noxious liquor law which had proved such a challenge to law enforcement during his term as police commissioner.

The Governor's labor record proved no less controversial. Although his insight into the causes of labor strife was surely deeper than in earlier years, the memory of the Haymarket Riot, the Homestead, the Pullman, and other violent strikes lingered on; and even as he made measured contributions to the workingmen's welfare the fear of labor on the march was always close to the surface.

Thus Roosevelt once accepted uncritically a report of the Board of Mediation which wrongly exonerated a traction company from

charges that it was violating the ten-hour law. On another occasion
he alerted the state militia for strike duty without real cause. And on
a third he called out the National Guard to prevent rioting by grossly
underpaid Italian workmen on the Croton Dam project. A riot, one
death, and suppression of a valid strike resulted. Roosevelt's precipitate action, like that of President Cleveland's in the Pullman strike
five years before, was partly instinctive, but fundamentally it reflected
the fact that society, and especially responsible government officials,
were so biased that objective information was difficult to obtain.
Unlike Cleveland, however, Roosevelt perceived that something was
basically wrong. He characteristically sought remedial action.

Roosevelt's first message as governor had given more space to labor
relations than to any other subject. The problem was not too few
laws, he asserted, but rather "the lack of proper means of enforcing
them." He consequently recommended that their enforcement be
placed under the board of factory inspectors, that the number of inspectors be raised to fifty, and that the governor be authorized to
appoint ten unsalaried workers, presumably interested social workers.
These proposals had been widely endorsed by union leaders, though
radicals complained that the program was not comprehensive enough.

As the session unfolded, the labor question continued to absorb
much of the Governor's energy. He counseled with union officials far
more than any of his predecessors had done. And within the limits of
his philanthropic point of view, he made several modest advances in
redressing the balance against labor. His first concrete achievement
came on April 1, 1899, when, over the concerted opposition of
employer representatives, he signed bills providing for more stringent
regulation of tenement working conditions, for increases in the number
and authority of factory inspectors, and for limitations on the hours
of women and minors.

The Governor also won labor's approval by supporting a bill that
strengthened the eight-hour-day law for state employees. It was the
duty of the state, he said in a memorandum released to the press as
he signed the bill, "to set a good example as an employer of labor,
both as to the number of hours of labor exacted and as to paying a
just and reasonable wage." Conversely, Roosevelt aroused labor's ire
by vetoing a bill to reduce the long hours of drug clerks. "I am very
much puzzled," he explained to Jacob Riis:

. . . You and Seth Low and Reynolds are for it and I have had some touching letters from drug clerks . . . while the smaller east and west side druggists who keep but one clerk say it would mean absolute ruin. . . . What I am anxious to do is whatever will really benefit the druggist clerks in the smaller shops. . . .

I wish you would take the bill . . . and . . . go to some small druggists anywhere . . . on the East Side, and find out if you can what some of the clerks and some of the small druggists really think about it, and what they believe its effects really would be.

But the labor issue which most excited Roosevelt was the bitter struggle of New York City's schoolteachers for a minimum salary schedule. A bill embodying their demands had been vetoed by Roosevelt's predecessor on the grounds that teachers' salaries should be fixed by city officials. Roosevelt entertained similar views at first; but after conferring with Nicholas Murray Butler and the New York City Superintendent of Schools he came out for state action in a ringing public statement. The prevailing level of salaries inflicts "grinding injury on people who are more than any others responsible for the upbringing of the citizens of the next generation," he declared. The level must be raised.

Roosevelt was too firm an advocate of the merit principle to endorse increases based solely on length of service, however; on that account he opposed the bill then pending. But the measure sailed through both houses of the legislature over his objections. Caught thus between his conviction that a general increase was desirable and that superiority rather than mediocrity should be rewarded, Roosevelt finally compromised. He accepted the minimum-salary feature after persuading the teachers' representatives to agree to inclusion of a partial merit clause. He then combined "pleasure with duty," and signed the bill.

The action was characteristic of the mature Roosevelt. He deplored waste, and he relentlessly moved against it whenever feasible. But he no longer was obsessed, as he had been fifteen years before, with the need for low taxes. Only infrequently during his later career did he permit short-term considerations of economy to thwart programs he deemed in the public interest.

Those first four and one-half months in Albany had been the most sustained effort of all. From the colorful inaugural parade in near zero weather and the reception for six thousand people on New Year's Day until the last bill was studied and signed into law in May, Roosevelt had been immersed in his duties. Veteran newspapermen were amazed at his energy and work habits. He maintained a rigorous schedule, conferred with numberless visitors—corporation lawyers, labor leaders, politicians, social workers, college professors—and usually held two press conferences a day. "With a disregard of precedent that puzzles the politicians," the *New York Times* observed, "he has torn down the curtain that shut in the Governor and taken the public into his confidence . . . beyond what was ever known before."

It was during the governorship, also, that TR became friendly with Finley Peter Dunne. "I regret to state that my family and intimate friends are delighted with your review of my book," he wrote Dunne shortly after his "Mr. Dooley" had retitled Roosevelt's *The Rough Riders* "Alone in Cubia." What's more, he informed Dunne, your work is full of "profound philosophy," even on our points of disagreement. "I am an Expansionist, but your delicious phrase about 'take up the white man's burden and put it on the coon,' exactly hit off the weak spot in my own theory; though mind you, I am by no means willing to give up the theory yet."

One regrettable incident marred the Governor's satisfaction with his first year's achievements. About a month after he took office he had been forced to decide whether a Brooklyn woman who had killed her stepdaughter and assaulted her husband with an ax in a jealous frenzy should be executed. Humanitarians, women's organizations, and sensational newspapers subjected him to heavy pressure to commute the sentence. He was also warned that no governor who approved the execution of a woman could possibly be elected President (such a threat, he wrote, was "the last thing that will influence me"). Even his own Victorian consideration for the gentler sex pointed toward commutation. But his compulsion for justice and his advanced intellectual views toward women pulled him the other way. Roosevelt had never abandoned the partially feminist attitudes of his Harvard years and had, in fact, won the plaudits of feminists by advocating woman suffrage for school board elections in his first annual message. After studying the case and receiving medical reports that the murderess was sane, he approved the death sentence, explaining at a press conference that he could not accept sex as a valid reason for clemency. The murderess was executed on March 20, the first woman to die in the electric chair in New York State.

The unpleasantness of that episode was soon forgotten. In April and May had come the legislative victories, and in June a triumphal trip by special train to Las Vegas for the Rough Riders' first reunion. Roosevelt was greeted warmly all through the Middle West and from Kansas onward to his destination he received one thunderous ovation after another. Again and again local newspapers boomed him for the vice-presidency in 1900 and the presidency in 1904, and many small-town editors even proposed that he supplant McKinley on the Republican ticket in 1900. He repeatedly sought to steer them off by declaring emphatically for the President's re-election, and after he returned home he visited Washington to affirm his loyalty to the President. Nevertheless, he could no longer dismiss the presidency from his mind.

Roosevelt's second year in office was in substantially the same pattern as his first. In December Platt's lieutenant, Benjamin Odell, undertook to advise Roosevelt on his annual message, urging him to abandon his campaign for stronger employers' liability legislation and to modify his recommendations for increased publicity of corporate earnings. He also requested the Governor to tone down his remarks on the canal frauds. But the Governor was too far committed to a constructive approach to these problems to heed his advice.

In compliance with his original agreement to consult with the machine, however, Roosevelt submitted a proof of his message to Platt before it was delivered on January 3, 1900. "All the important parts I had gone over by various experts," he disarmingly explained. That was precisely the point. The Platt forces bitterly resented his association with intellectuals or, as they called them, "visionary reformers"; but to little avail. Roosevelt was too astute to adopt Platt's ways as his own and he was too aware of the profundity of the problems he faced to attempt to devise a program without aid from specialists. "I have come to the conclusion that I have mighty little originality of my own," he wrote President Andrew White of Cornell at the time. "What I do is to try to get ideas from men whom I regard as experts along certain lines, and then try to work out those ideas." To Lemuel Quigg, another Platt lieutenant, he tried further to explain himself:

As for my impulsiveness and my alliance with labor agitators, social philosophers, taxation reformers and the like, I will also go over all these questions with you when we meet. I want to be perfectly sane in all of these matters, but I do have a good deal of fellow feeling for our less fortunate brother, and I am a good deal puzzled over some of the inequalities in life, as life now exists. I have a horror of hysterics or sentimentality, and I am about the last man in the world who sympathizes with revolutionary tactics, or with the effort to make the thrifty, the wise and the brave go down to the level of the unthrifty, the slothful and the cowardly. I would a great deal rather have no change than a change that would put a premium upon idleness and folly. All I want to do is cautiously to feel my way to see if we cannot make the general conditions of life a little easier,—a little better.

And so Roosevelt continued to govern by consultation with experts. It was a technique that Robert M. La Follette was to use more intensively, more creatively, and more dramatically the next year as governor of Wisconsin, and it has come down in history as the Wisconsin Idea.

For example, the trust section of Roosevelt's second annual message was written in collaboration with President Arthur T. Hadley of Yale, Professor Jeremiah W. Jenks of Cornell, and Professor Seligman as well as Elihu Root and James B. Dill, who had recently drafted the New Jersey statute on holding companies. It reflected Roosevelt's acceptance of the inevitability of corporate growth and his moral revulsion against corporate malpractices. And it came out forthrightly for government regulation. It advocated publicity of corporate earnings, proclaimed the right of the state to intervene against monopoly, and asserted that corporations should not be exempted from taxation because of their own mismanagement of resources. "Our laws," the message stated in words that would become increasingly familiar during Roosevelt's presidential and Bull Moose years, "should be so drawn as to protect and encourage corporations which do their honest duty by the public; and to discriminate sharply against those organized in a spirit of mere greed, for improper speculative purposes."

The legislature failed to act on the proposals, however, and Roosevelt went out of office with his program unfulfilled. Aside from bringing the trust problem into political focus, their chief value, as Wallace Chessman, the historian of Roosevelt's governorship, concludes, was in the definition they gave Roosevelt's own thought.

The Governor's attitude toward public utilities was similarly revealing of his nondoctrinaire quality of mind. "There is grave danger in attempting to establish invariable rules," he said in a passage defending public ownership of the New York City water supply. "In one instance a private corporation may be able to do the work best. In another the State or city may do it best. In yet a third, it may be to the advantage of everybody to give free scope to the power of some individual captain of industry."

The Governor's handling of the canal frauds likewise foreshadowed the attitudes of his presidency. Early in his first year he had appointed two anti-Tammany Democrats of high repute, Austen G. Fox and Wallace MacFarlane, to serve as special counsel. After an exhaustive investigation, Fox and MacFarlane reported that criminal prosecution of the former officials charged with fraud was inadvisable and impracticable. During the first week in April, 1899, however, a coalition of Tammany Democrats and Platt Republicans decided to refrain from appropriating $20,000 needed to complete the investigation. When he heard the reports, Roosevelt flew into a rage. With flashing eyes and gleaming teeth he vowed that the investigation would go on if he had to pay for it out of his own pocket or raise a public subscription. "Governor's Ire Kindles"; "Roosevelt In Fighting Mood"; "Governor Indignant!", the papers reported. Four days later Roosevelt sent in a special message urging passage of the appropriation. Reluctantly, the Democratic and Republican machines bowed to the public outcry set off by the Governor's outburst.

Many were immune under the terms of the statute of limitations; others were safe because they had acted within the letter of a badly drawn law. Reviewing the findings in his message of January 3, 1900, Roosevelt concluded, just a little ingenuously, that "the one remedy was a thorough change in the methods and management." This had been accomplished, he reported, by enactment of a law during the previous session and by improved administrative techniques which had decreased the cost of operating the canals 25 per cent in spite of an increase in traffic.

As the new session advanced Roosevelt's cold war with Platt again became momentarily hot. This time conflict centered on the reappointment of Superintendent of Insurance Louis F. Payn, an upstate spoilsman and one-time lobbyist for Jay Gould who had earlier abused civil service procedures and originally opposed Roosevelt's nomination as governor. By October, 1899, Roosevelt had decided not to reappoint Payn when his term expired in February. Payn's standing with Platt was reinforced by the support of the insurance industry's responsible and irresponsible elements alike, however, and the Governor was not sanguine that he could name a successor acceptable to the machine.

The conflict was still in the formative stage when a new scandal involving Payn was aired. Newspapers reported that the State Trust Company had made an unsupported loan of $435,000 to Payn, whose salary was $7,000, presumably because several of the bank's directors also served on the boards of insurance companies under Payn's supervision. The Governor's resolve to displace Payn was strengthened by these charges, and he now reaffirmed his intent to Platt. The Senator was amenable at first, but when Payn indicated that he would fight for his job, Platt changed his mind. An impasse then threatened: Roosevelt could refuse to make the reappointment; and Platt could prevent the confirmation of his successor. In these circumstances, the Governor reluctantly prevailed on Platt's close friend, Francis J. Hendricks of Syracuse, to accept the appointment.

To Roosevelt the displacement of Payn was another hard-won victory for good government. But to many reformers the selection of Hendricks was a sellout to Platt, and they indignantly labeled it such. Hurt and irritated, Roosevelt unburdened himself to his friend Louisa Lee Schuyler. "I can say with all sincerity," he wrote, "that I do not believe that any Governor but myself could have put Mr. Payn out, backed as he was by the strongest political influences in the State, and in addition the entire enormous money power of the big insurance companies."

> You can have no conception of the pressure, political, financial, and every other kind that has been brought to bear upon me to keep him in. . . . If I had done what the *Evening Post* and Dr. Parkhurst and Mr. Godkin and the smaller fry like Jack Chapman advised, I would not have had ten votes in the Senate to confirm my man and Payn would have stayed in permanently.

One other awkward incident marred the Payn affair. The banking superintendent's report criticized Elihu Root, the State Trust Company's legal counselor and one of its directors, for countenancing the near half-million-dollar loan to Payn. Roosevelt responded uncharacteristically. He buried the report, ostensibly to avert a run on the Trust Company, but also, one suspects, to protect Root, who was by then

Secretary of War, from unfavorable publicity (Root and the other directors' action was legally, if not morally, defensible). So at least contended the *World*, which disclosed Root's involvement and charged that the Governor had wanted "to shield a personal friend."

It might be argued, though surely crudely, that Roosevelt was re-paying a favor (when a technicality had threatened his eligibility to serve as governor, Root had devised an argument to offset it), or that he was reluctant to place the McKinley administration under new embarrassment. It seems more likely, however, that Roosevelt's un-critical admiration for Root was in this case his controlling motive.

Incapable of panic, loyal yet curiously detached, a constructive adviser on programs that he would not himself have initiated, Elihu Root was to his intimates, and to many who were not, the embodiment of wise and incisive judgment. He was—and the comparison is not invidious—more analytical than creative, though his organizing intelli-gence was perhaps the finest of his era; and his mental cast was both sharpened and narrowed by a hard-tempered realism that blunted his resentments even as it dulled his enthusiasms. He was, as Morison with his usual acuteness puts it, "without illusion in his calculation of what had to be done or could be done by the human agency," and he had no conviction that "he or anyone else could remold the con-dition of things much closer to the heart's desire." Lacking the moral fervor that inspires men to supreme acts of the spirit, Root's appeal was to their instinct for the ordered conditions that ease the imperfect path of progress as Roosevelt's, for all his own similar commitment, was to their puissant ideals and unfulfilled emotions. Such, indubitably, was Root's pull on Roosevelt himself.

Understanding intuitively the need to contain his rawer impulses as well as to refine his nobler ones, Roosevelt sought in this confident, matter-of-fact counselor, thirteen years his senior, the means of re-straint. And Root, standing almost always firm in the turbulent back-wash of Roosevelt's surging force, supplied the want. He saw as few men did the throbbing tension induced by Roosevelt's unconscious urge to love or to hate and even, at times, to rule or to ruin, and he strove in his quietly self-assured way to reduce it; and also, because he was at heart conservative, to keep Roosevelt's creative drives within bounds. Repeatedly, Root turned his biting, sardonic humor on his ebullient friend, and Roosevelt, seemingly sensing the need for his own deflation, delighted in its edge.

Even so, the relationship was not without impact on Root. What this eminent public servant possessed in administrative ability, he lacked in boldness of imagination. More administrator than social philosopher, he recoiled from the possible ill consequences of change as other men were attracted by its potential liberating effect. He suffered especially the conservative's dependence on convention, and he actually opposed Roosevelt's corporate tax program with the classic half-truth that "the vast preponderance of the grand fortunes" had conferred "great benefits on the community." Yet Root was never a reactionary. His brief was for a moderate, ordered, and closely controlled progress. And in the daily rub of minds with Roosevelt during the presidential years, his conservatism became reasonably viable. For one brief decade, indeed, he unenthusiastically accepted the moral imperative of Roosevelt's thrust for social and economic justice.

The publicity over Payn and Root, coupled with increasing speculation about the Governor's political future, detracted from the otherwise substantial enactments of Roosevelt's second year in office. The law of 1899 opening corporation's books to agents of the supreme court was amended to open them to stockholders and creditors. A law granting a monopoly to a carriage company was supplanted by one designed to preserve competition in the automotive carriage industry. And a bill forbidding interest charges of more than 6 per cent a year was passed and signed.

On the other hand, the Governor did lose or concede one important round to the machine. Pursuant to the recommendation of the tax commission appointed in the spring of 1899, a measure instituting a one per cent tax on all mortgages and banking capital was introduced in 1900. At the request of J. P. Morgan and other finance capitalists, however, the Platt men amended it so as to exempt the New York Central Railroad and large corporations in general from its provisions. In consequence, the state lost six or seven million dollars in tax revenue. Although Roosevelt refused to support the Morgan-Platt amendments because of their discriminatory nature, he inexplicably failed to fight them forcefully.

Several other important measures were enacted in 1900 with Roosevelt's active support. These improved the civil service laws, standardized the labels on linen cloth, and prohibited newspapers from soliciting funds from candidates for political office. They instituted safeguards on the letting of contracts for the New York City water supply, and they prevented the traction companies from laying four sets of car tracks on Bedford Avenue in Brooklyn. They rounded out the Governor's conservation program by projecting a public park on the Palisades and reorganizing and expanding the state forest, fish, and game program. And they obliged both labor and the farmers by limiting the working hours of drug clerks and authorizing bounties for the production of beet sugar. Rejecting most, though regrettably not all, bills he believed inimical to the public interest, Roosevelt also vetoed or returned to the legislature some five hundred measures during his two-year term.

Among the approximately one thousand bills Roosevelt signed into law were two that strongly affected the public school system. The first, which he spurred on with an emergency message, banned race discrimination and repealed a previous authorization of separate schools for Negroes on a local-option basis. In common with most white Americans of the period, the Governor did not regard Negroes in general as the equals of whites. But he did believe that many individual Negroes were superior to individual whites, and he felt deeply that they should have full opportunity to prove their merit. "My children sit in the same school with colored children," he righteously remarked when the bill came up.

The second school measure carried over from the fight for higher salaries for teachers. For three months during the fall of 1899 the Tammany-dominated Board of Estimate had refused to pay teachers their salaries in Brooklyn and Queens. Roosevelt responded by pushing through an emergency bill in February, 1900, that directed city officials to transfer funds to meet their obligations to the teachers. Then in May he approved a measure designed to prevent a recurrence of the situation. "The difference between the attitude of Tammany and the republicans," he angrily wrote at the time, "is . . . that Tammany increased the salaries of all the useless offices but reduced the teachers almost to bankruptcy; whereas the republican party which is pre-eminently the party of the public schools has stood by these schools and teachers."

Reviewing his record at the end of the second regular session in the spring of 1900, Roosevelt was keenly satisfied. "I think I have been the best Governor within my time," he confided to his uncle, James Bulloch, "better either than Cleveland or Tilden."

The Governor's estimate of his relative worth was probably accurate. Within the shifting limits of such comparisons, he had excelled both Tilden and Cleveland. All three were men of estimable integrity and ability; each had battled corruption, driven through important administrative reforms, and yet maintained a working relationship with elements of his party machine. But by temperament and philosophy Tilden and Cleveland had been more passive than positive, and their administrations had suffered for it. Where they had refused to tread, Roosevelt had willingly broken new ground. They had been conservative of the power of the state; but Roosevelt, conscientiously seeking solutions to the problems forged by the rampant industrial order, had broken sharply with the laissez-faire theory and existing concepts of state and local relations. They had been solicitous of the traditional prerogatives of corporations; but Roosevelt, revealing himself receptive to the moderate progressive thought of the times, had begun to believe that public responsibilities, including tax payments, were correlative to the possession of enormous wealth and power. And they had been oblivious to the plight of labor, while Roosevelt had commenced to redress its prevailing imbalance with capital.

Besides all that, Roosevelt had taken major steps to preserve the wild life, forests, and natural beauty of his state. He had made a stab at arresting the spreading curse of the tenements. And he had imbued many officials with a sense of the public trust and instilled in others the fear of dismissal. Even the *World,* implying in an editorial that it might have crossed party lines to support him had he run for re-election, conceded that "the controlling purpose and general course of his administration have been high and good."

It would be an exaggeration to say, as an upstate editor did say shortly before Roosevelt was nominated for Vice President, that his "only qualification . . . for the office of Vice President is fitness for the office of President." But it would not be extreme to suggest that he had several critical qualifications for the higher office. Of these, none was more significant than his manifest capacity for growth and his signal ability to influence the flow of events by seizing the initiative at the strategic moment—the sure measures of a superior leader. In only one important province, and that, ironically, the one he regarded himself as strongest in—foreign affairs—were Roosevelt's qualifications suspect on the record. Time alone would reveal whether he also possessed the strength to conquer the *"Sturm und Drang"* impulses of his early manhood.

CHAPTER 8

THE PEOPLE'S CHOICE

"'Tis Teddy alone that's runnin', and he ain't r'runnin', he's gallopin'."

—Mr. Dooley

Roosevelt had reached the fork in the road. From June, 1899, when Westerners had hailed him as a presidential candidate as he went out to the Rough Riders' reunion in Las Vegas, until June of the following year, when the Republican convention met at Philadelphia, his political future evoked recurrent speculation. And by the time the convention delegates detrained in the Quaker City discussion of whether he would run for a second term as governor or would be forced up and out to the vice-presidency overshadowed all other questions.

Roosevelt most wanted to return to Albany, although he would have settled for the civil governorship of the Philippines. But he had no desire to accept the then empty honor of the vice-presidency. "I am a comparatively young man . . . and I like to work," he wrote Lodge in February, 1900. "I do not like to be a figurehead." Nor did the prospect of presiding over the Senate hold any appeal. "I should be in a cold shiver of rage at inability to answer hounds like Pettigrew and the scarcely more admirable Mason and Hale," he continued uninhibitedly. "I would be seeing continually things that I would like to do, and very possibly would like to do differently from the way in which they were being done." Nevertheless, a number of factors militated in favor of the vice-presidential nomination. Some were within his control, most were beyond it.

On January 20, shortly after Roosevelt's refusal to reappoint Louis Payn had embarrassed the Platt machine anew, the "Easy Boss" had urged the vice-presidential nomination upon the Governor during one of their regular meetings. "Platt is afraid," Roosevelt explained to Lodge, that "unless I take it nobody will be made Vice-President from New York, and that this would be a pity."

The Colonel's naïveté was characteristic. He almost always tended to believe well of those he was thrown in with, and generally with good result. His confidence brought out the best in men and often inspired near-fanatical loyalty and devotion. Sometimes, however, it backfired. When men's moral sensibilities were perverted or their material stakes were great, as with Tom Platt and later the managers of the United States Steel Corporation, Roosevelt could be deceived. Furthermore, TR never quite realized the overpowering impact of his own vibrant personality. Even such strong characters as Elihu Root and Cabot Lodge sometimes succumbed to it; and too often Roosevelt assumed that failure to challenge his enthusiastically expressed ideas implied agreement. On the whole, however, the advantages heavily outweighed the disadvantages.

Roosevelt had left Platt's apartment without committing himself on the vice-presidency. Although Lodge's counsel was that it was the "better" and "safer" road to the presidency, he soon decided against it. "I was eager to have a regiment in the war and if there was another war I should try to have a brigade," he wrote Benjamin Odell, "but nothing would hire me to continue as a colonel or brigadier general in time of peace." To Platt he added that since he had failed to amass a fortune, he felt honor bound to leave his children a record of achievement in politics or letters. "Now, as Governor, I can achieve something," he concluded, "but as Vice-President I should achieve nothing."

Both Platt and Odell were unimpressed by the Governor's protests; nor did they change their attitude when TR told them in a second conference on February 10 that he would "a great deal rather be anything, say professor of history, than Vice-President." Roosevelt's whole program as governor—civil service reform, corporate publicity and taxation, and enforcement of the factory laws—had constituted a near frontal assault on the Republican machine's foundations, and Platt was determined to avoid a second and possibly more sustained attack. Roosevelt's gradual realization of Platt's real motives is set forth in a letter to Lodge:

> I have found out one reason why Senator Platt wants me nominated . . . the big-monied men with whom he is in close touch and whose campaign contributions have certainly been no inconsiderable factor in his strength, have been pressing him very strongly to get me put in the Vice-Presidency, so as to get me out of the State. It was the big insurance companies, possessing enormous wealth, that gave Payn his formidable strength, and they to a man want me out. The great corporations affected by the franchise tax have also been at the Senator. In fact, all the big-monied interests that make campaign contributions of large size and feel that they should have favors in return, are extremely anxious to get me out of the State. I find that they have been at Platt for the last two or three months and he has finally begun to yield to them and to take their view.

Roosevelt's resolve to serve a second term as governor was sharpened by his insight into Platt's design and especially, one suspects, by his desire to dissipate the lingering suspicions of cowardice left by his resignation from the police commissionership four years before. As he also wrote Lodge, "I should feel like a coward if I went away from this work, because I ran the risk of incurring disaster and took a position where I could not fail, for the simple reason that I could not succeed." Throughout the spring of 1900, therefore, TR sought diligently to suppress the developing boom for his nomination as McKinley's running mate. In Chicago on April 26 he told reporters that the governorship of New York was next to the presidency in importance and that he would return to private life before accepting the vice-presidential nomination; and in a formal address that night he refused to comment though his audience gave him a standing, fifteen-minute ovation and chanted, "We want you, Teddy, yes we do." Two weeks later the Governor went to Washington to assure McKinley and Hanna that he intended to stand for re-election in New York. Roosevelt also reiterated his opposition to the vice-presidency to Secretary of War Elihu Root, who is said to have smiled disarmingly and replied: "Of course not, Theodore, you're not fit for it."

Meanwhile Roosevelt wrote numerous letters to his Western friends in an unavailing effort to repress their mounting enthusiasm. He thought for a while that he had contained the boom, but he was never overly sanguine. "If I were actually nominated; and if I were unable to stem the convention's desire to nominate me, it might be impossible to refuse," he confided to Joseph B. Bishop in April. "Still, maybe I could refuse anyhow. And I am almost sure I can prevent the nomination."

Tom Platt viewed the Governor's efforts with tongue in cheek, for the "Easy Boss" held both an ace and a trump. The ace was Senator Joseph Foraker of Ohio, a number of lesser anti-Hanna men, and Matthew Quay and his formidable Pennsylvania machine. All resented Mark Hanna's friendship with President McKinley and his hold on the Republican National Committee; all welcomed the opportunity to cross Hanna's will by nominating Roosevelt for the vice-presidency.

Platt's trump was the former Rough Rider's irresistible appeal to the Republican rank and file in the West. During the sixteen years that had passed since young Roosevelt had staked his claim in the hearts of Westerners they had followed his career as though he had been a native son. They had applauded his energetic enforcement of the civil service laws and his battles against vice and crime in New York City, and they had thrilled to his heroics in Cuba. This last circumstance was regrettable, perhaps. It clouded the fact that TR's hold upon Westerners was actually formed by his prewar record. The Kansas City *Star* pointed this out editorially: "Beneath Roosevelt's chivalry and the picturesque style which has aroused the enthusiasm of the Nation there is an intense sense of duty and a moral courage that is invincible."

> The record of Roosevelt as a civil officer is a quite sufficient plea upon which to go before the people. It is of a character to make plain his enmity toward corruption and his devotion to public morality. . . .

The Governor's popularity was not confined to the West. The Eastern reformers had sometimes recoiled and the party leaders had frequently squirmed, but TR had again and again captured the imagination of the great middle classes. More than any young national leader of his era, Roosevelt exemplified the perennial personal virtues—honor, courage, and duty—and he quickened America's conscience because of it. Even the New York *Sun,* which was always suspicious of TR's economics, conceded as much just after the Republican Convention of 1900 ended:

People got to saying, "This man ROOSEVELT seems to do about what he thinks is right and doesn't care a rap for the consequences. He must be all right."

When, against that background, Roosevelt refused to say that he would not accept if chosen and insisted on going to Philadelphia as a delegate on the grounds that it would be cowardly not to go, his nomination for the vice-presidency was virtually foreordained. As Platt was reported to have said, "Roosevelt might as well stand under Niagara Falls and try to spit water back as to stop his nomination by this convention."

The New York boss had hardly exaggerated. Roosevelt tried for a while to hold back the flood. And when Platt told him the night the convention opened in Philadelphia on June 19 that he would prevent his renomination for governor if he turned down the vice-presidential nomination, TR reportedly replied "that this was a threat, which simply rendered it impossible for me to accept, that if there was to be war there would be war, and that that was all there was to it." Thereupon, Roosevelt added, "I bowed and left the room." Platt's account differs; but it is clear that there had been a tense scene.

Even as Roosevelt resisted Platt, however, the waters were surging over. Roosevelt himself had earlier sparked a spontaneous demonstration on the convention floor by striding briskly to his seat in a black civilian version of the Rough Rider's slouch campaign hat—"an acceptance hat," so one delegate dubbed it. And for hours that night scores of Western delegates noisily paraded up and down the corridors outside Hanna's suite shouting "We want Teddy." Meanwhile Quay's Pennsylvania forces announced their endorsement of the New York Governor while Platt, Quay, and Foraker pressed his nomination on various convention leaders.

All through the next day, the demands for Roosevelt's nomination continued to mount. The Colonel was told that his political future hung in the balance; he was warned that the West might go to Bryan if he rejected the nomination; and he was admonished that it was his duty to honor the wishes of his legions of admirers. He may also have been threatened with elimination from politics. Succumbing finally to these enormous pressures, he agreed to accept the nomination if the delegates willed it. Late that night Mark Hanna, who had earlier received a wire from McKinley stating that he did not intend to stand in Roosevelt's way if the convention wanted to nominate him, also submitted.

The next day, after McKinley was renominated, a portentous hush fell over the convention as LaFayette Young, head of the Iowa delegation, rose to his feet to withdraw the name of Jonathan Dolliver, Iowa's favorite son, and place Theodore Roosevelt's in nomination. It was the moment the rank and file had been waiting for. Hats flew into the air, state standards were raised from the floor, and pictures and banners appeared out of nowhere while the vast assemblage sprang to its feet in one great instinctive movement. The band struck up "There'll Be a Hot Time in the Old Town Tonight." And the delegations roared their congratulations at the Governor as they marched exuberantly past the New York section where Roosevelt sat grimly in his seat, expressionless except for a tightening of lines around his mouth. In her box up above, Edith Roosevelt gasped momentarily, then flashed a smile.

Finally the convention quieted for the seconding speeches. The most eloquent was by Chauncey Depew, whose Republicanism was the antithesis of Theodore Roosevelt's. The balloting followed, and when Lodge announced the near-unanimous result, the rank and file gave forth the mightiest and most sustained cheer of the entire convention. Roosevelt was nominated, reported an obscure country weekly, not because of the bosses, "but because the convention recognized Theodore Roosevelt as that which Henry C. Payne of Wisconsin had called him—'not New York's son, but the nation's son.' "

Even as they had been all along, however, the Governor's emotions were mixed. Roosevelt's "tail-feathers were all down," Nicholas Murray Butler, who saw him an hour after he had made his decision to submit the night before, remembered. "The fight had gone out of him and he had changed his former tune to that of 'I cannot disappoint my Western friends if they insist. . . . I cannot seem to be bigger than the party.' "

Roosevelt's personal letters say much the same. They also reveal that he was reconciled to his lot: "It was simply impossible to resist so spontaneous a feeling." "I would be a fool not to appreciate and be deeply touched by the way I was nominated." "I believe it all for the best as regards my personal interests." ". . . had I been running for re-election as Governor I could not have helped feeling an uneasiness of mind as to my own fate." "Mrs. Roosevelt has begun to look at the matter our way now." And finally:

> Every real friend of mine . . . will speak of me as exactly what I am—the man chosen because it is believed he will add strength to a cause which however is already infinitely stronger than any strength of his—a man absolutely and entirely in the second place whom it is grossly absurd and unjust to speak of in any other capacity.

The cause was Republicanism. It was the gold standard, the protective tariff, and the supremacy of the nation over state and region. It was the unrestricted development of big business and the casting aside of the old isolation. It was integrity, efficiency, and high-mindedness, the skullduggery of the bosses, the maladministration of the Army, and the McKinley administration's assault on the civil service notwithstanding. It was anti-Bryanism, anti-Populism, and anti almost everything else that threatened the party's success. It was, in a word, whatever the Republican orators chose to make it.

Roosevelt chose to make the coming campaign a moral crusade for good government and a referendum on the new foreign policy. He had virtually a free rein in so doing, for the President again confined himself to nebulous pronouncements from his front porch in Canton, Ohio.

Mindful of the dignity of his new situation, Roosevelt told Hanna at the outset that he was emphatically opposed to appearing "like a second-class Bryan." He tried to nip in the bud a plan to form Rough Riders' marching units all over the country, and he announced that he intended to campaign on his accomplishments as governor, not on his military record. But he also declared that he felt "strong as a bull moose."

That summer and fall Roosevelt canvassed the nation with a thoroughness no vice-presidential candidate had theretofore matched and only one presidential candidate, Bryan, had surpassed. Besides a trip to Oklahoma, where he fired his opening volley from the camp grounds of the Rough Riders' reunion, he made a quick excursion into the Middle West and an extended tour through the Rocky Mountain states, where he experienced one long triumphal homecoming: "RANGE GREETS ROOSEVELT"; "WYOMING IS STIRRED UP"; "ROOSEVELT ROUSES BUTTE."

All told, Roosevelt covered 21,000 miles in twenty-four states, spent eight weeks on the road, and made several hundred speeches. Everywhere he preached his four-square gospel of duty, responsibility, Republicanism, and Americanism; and the curious, excited, and adulatory crowds that came out of the hinterland to swarm about the rear platform of his special train at every whistle stop could no more contain their enthusiasm than he could suppress his moralistic exhortations. "Tis Teddy alone that's runnin'," exclaimed the inimitable Mr. Dooley, "and he ain't r'runnin', he's gallopin'."

Roosevelt's nominal opponent was the Democratic vice-presidential candidate, Adlai E. Stevenson of Illinois; but his real adversary was William Jennings Bryan. Few pulses ever beat more quickly for the plain people everywhere than did that of the Great Commoner from Nebraska. For three decades the farmers and small townspeople of the South and the Middle West basked in his prairie-like simplicity and whole-souled sentimentality, and three times they bestowed upon him their highest accolade—the Democratic presidential nomination. Nor did he ever fail them in eloquence and devotion. Nineteen years after they first gave him their charge he selflessly resigned as Secretary of State to serve better by his lights the cause of peace that he and they loved, and as he neared death a decade after that he fought unabashedly to uphold their fundamentalist faith against an evolutionary doctrine that Roosevelt had mastered as an adolescent a half century before. Again and again this great-hearted Christian phrased with poetic insight and preached with evangelical passion their swelling protest against the cruel maladjustments wrought by the new industrial order; and it was for his broad understanding of the economic nature of their problems, even more than for his abiding compassion for all mankind, that he was truly distinguished.

As Henry Steele Commager, one of the few modern historians to see Bryan whole, asserts, he was the link between the agrarian progressivism of the Populists and the sophisticated urban progressivism of the later Roosevelt. And if he did not conceive, he did pioneer in the advocacy of "more important legislation than any other politician of his generation." For what Bryan lacked in profundity, he possessed to overflowing in instinct. He had a firmer grasp of the public essentials, if not of the technical details, of the money and tariff questions than Mark Hanna, McKinley, and their Wall Street compatriots, and until Roosevelt came into his own in his second term, Bryan's social thought was

the more advanced. His one great failing—and a critical one it was—
was his lack of the scientific spirit and his resultant inability to refine
his arguments. He was to the end more descriptive than analytical.
A born generalizer, it was enough for Bryan that he should conceive
his mission as the liberation of the government from the hands of the
plutocrats; and when in 1896 he first burst upon the national scene,
he proclaimed of the cause he led:

> On the one hand stand the corporate interests of the United
> States, the moneyed interests, aggregated wealth and capital, im-
> perious, arrogant, compassionless. . . . On the other side stand
> an unnumbered throng, those who gave to the Democratic party a
> name and for whom it has assumed to speak. Work-worn and dust-
> begrimed, they made their mute appeal, and too often find their
> cry for help beat in vain against the outer walls, while others, less
> deserving, gain ready access to legislative halls.

That had been in 1896. Now, four years later, the cause was
essentially the same, though Bryan's early campaign speeches focused
on the imperialism issue. "Imperialism finds no warrant in the Bible,"
the Great Commoner thundered up and down the land. "The command, 'Go ye into all the world and preach the gospel to every creature,' has no gatling gun attachment," he declaimed. "Love, not force,
was the weapon of the Nazarene; sacrifice for others, not the exploitation of them, was His method of reaching the human heart"—
so he exclaimed to the tens of thousands of Baptists, Methodists, and
Presbyterians who made his campaign even more revivalist-like than
Roosevelt's.

In effect, Bryan was asking the American people to deny the
righteousness of a war they had heroically won and of a world
prestige they had suddenly acquired. This was an underestimation of
human passion. The emotions that had carried the nation exuberantly
to war two years before were still potent; the zealous pride in the
national achievement was still swollen. The colonial empire was a
fait accompli rather than a debatable political issue; and the United
States was now a major power in a world of great powers, not of
Nazarenes. The insurrection of the Filipino patriot, Aguinaldo, invoked the application of force rather than Christian charity; and even
as Bryan's impassioned phrases poured forth, American troops were
relentlessly applying that force. Not even the editorial spokesmen of

American Protestantism succumbed to the Great Commoner's rolling periods. "God's hand," said the Methodist Episcopal *Zion's Herald,* was behind the circumstance "that those most beautiful islands of the Pacific, named for one of the worst monarchs that ever sat on the throne of Spain, should come into the possession of the most Protestant nation of the nineteenth century. . . . The present year of grace is 1900, and not 1800."

Roosevelt's reactions to Bryan's indictment of the colonial aftermath of the war with Spain embodied his cascading fervor for honor, duty, and the flag. They embraced his Social Darwinian conception of the evolutionary stages of the races. And they reflected his continuing grasp of many of the hard facts of the international struggle for position. Thus he deprecated the suggestion that the Philippines be abandoned, invoking the same strategic, commercial, and chauvinistic rationale which had actuated him, Lodge, and Mahan to press for their acquisition in the first place. We would have "to pledge ourselves to perpetual war with them and for them," he argued. He declared that the American guardianship was a sacred trust deriving from "the most righteous foreign war that has been waged within the memory of the present generation." And he repeatedly drew a specious parallel between Jefferson's administration of the Louisiana Territory and the projected Republican administration of the Philippine Islands.

But Roosevelt's main theme was that the United States stood on the threshold of greatness. "It rests with us now to decide whether . . . we shall march forward to fresh triumphs or whether at the outset we shall cripple ourselves for the contest," he admonished the Republican convention in his speech seconding McKinley's renomination. "We challenge the proud privilege of doing the work that Providence allots us, and we face the coming years high of heart and resolute of faith that to our people is given the right to win honor and renown as has never yet been vouchsafed to the nations of mankind."

Roosevelt's rhetoric, romanticism, and egocentric nationalism to the contrary, his remarks at least touched the periphery of those momentous questions that have been a half century in the settling: Was the United States to play an assertive role commensurate with its emerging power in the affairs of the world? Was it to bury itself in an ostrich-like isolationism? Or was it to indulge in a nebulous internationalism unsupported by military force. Roosevelt and the other imperialists believed that there was no real choice. They sensed that the revolution in communications had so altered traditional concepts of time and space that the old isolationism was as anachronistic by the turn of the century as the pony express. They recognized that the sheer fact of industrial might made America a *de facto* member of the community of powers. And they clearly understood what the anti-imperialists, and especially Bryan, would not concede—to abandon the Philippines was to invite a scramble by England, Germany, Japan, and Russia, and possibly to precipitate world war.

Nevertheless, the Colonel's armor was penetrable. The Philippines were militarily indefensible, and within the decade Roosevelt himself would pronounce them an "Achilles' heel"—a tacit admission that the overextension of lines was not necessarily synonymous with the emergence from isolationism. Nor would the imperialists' loose expectations of a burgeoning Far Eastern trade be realized in Roosevelt's generation, or even in the two that followed. But the most glaring flaw was moral. In the opinion of sensitive men then and since, the "honor and renown" that Roosevelt read into the Philippine venture came not with the brutal subjugation of Aguinaldo's partisans, but rather with the enlightened administrative policies that culminated in Philippine independence in 1946. It is a tribute to Bryan's rightmindedness, if not to his tactical wisdom, that he worked to that end from the beginning.

If Roosevelt's insight into foreign affairs was at once more romantic and more realistic than the Great Commoner's, his comprehension of domestic issues was in all but a few respects far shallower. Like William Allen White, whose stirringly vacuous editorial, "What's the Matter with Kansas," had catapulted him to fame in the summer of 1896, TR was deluded by fear of free silver. Neither in 1896 nor in 1900 did Roosevelt understand that the Westerners and Southerners' grievances derived from more than moral laxity, wool-hat demagoguery, or a bad turn in the weather. Neither in 1896 nor in 1900 did he concede that the underlying issue involved more than "decent government and the honest payment of debts." He wildly charged in 1896 that Bryan and the Democrats represented the "spirit of lawless mob violence"; and he repeated and embellished the indictment in 1900. As White, in a passage as applicable to Roosevelt as to himself, wrote long afterward: "How intellectually snobbish I was

about 'sound economics.' . . . Being what I was, a child of the
governing classes, I was blinded by my birthright. . . . It seemed
to me that rude hands were trying to tear down the tabernacle of our
national life, to taint our currency with fiat." And so, White continued,
"swallowing protection as a necessary evil and McKinley's candidacy
as the price of national security, I went into the campaign with more
zeal than intelligence, with more ardor than wisdom."

Roosevelt's delusion both in 1896 and 1900 was made the easier
by the character of Bryan's impassioned hosts. One major element
included the remnants of the Populist party. And though TR himself
would later espouse that part of the Populist manifesto of 1892 which
read, "We believe that the powers of government . . . should be
expanded . . . to the end that oppression, injustice, and poverty
shall eventually cease in the land," he gave little evidence of his future
beliefs in 1900 and even less in 1896.

Another great division of Bryan's forces was spearheaded by John
Peter Altgeld, who had compounded his "crime" in pardoning the
surviving Haymarket anarchists by courageously attacking Cleveland's
handling of the Pullman strike of 1894. Roosevelt seemed not to
realize that Altgeld was actually a sensitive and responsible spokesman for the submerged urban masses; and in both campaigns he pum-
meled the Illinois Governor unmercifully and unjustifiably, expos-
tulating at one point that Altgeld "would connive at wholesale murder
and would justify it by elaborate and cunning sophistry for reasons
known only to his own tortuous soul." So sweeping were TR's
charges, in fact, that Hanna worriedly consulted him about them after
an especially unbalanced speech in St. Paul in the fall of 1900.

Hanna failed, of course, to dampen Roosevelt's ardor; nor did
anyone else. Neither age nor experience brought moderation, mellow-
ing, or development, and until the day of his death TR remained an
extremist in speech when the battle was on.

Yet, for all Roosevelt's irresponsible assertions, for all his failure
to speak fairly to Bryan's proposals for an inheritance tax, graduated
income tax, reduced tariff, and expanded money supply, TR did
come out with one constructive proposal in 1900—the regulation
of big business. Drawing on his experience as governor, he recommended publicity of capitalization and profits, taxation of corporations, and "the unsparing excision of all unhealthy, destructive and
anti-social elements." This program was indefensibly vague—it failed,

for example, to specify whether the states or the federal government should assume responsibility for its enactment, and it was a pale shadow compared to Bryan's comprehensive, if also inadequate, program. Yet its emphasis on the regulation rather than the dissolution of the great corporations dimly foreshadowed the future.

In spite of McKinley's front-porch circumlocutions, and Bryan's perfervid oratory, the President's re-election was never in doubt. On Election Day his popular vote soared several hundred thousands above his total of 1896, and his majority reached the highest level since Grant's re-election in 1872. Roosevelt's contribution to this impressive victory cannot be measured with accuracy; but by common agreement, it was considerable. He had borne the brunt of the canvass, speaking, however egregiously at times, to the issues as no other Republican of prominence had done, and he had carried into the campaign the most devoted personal following ever rallied by a vice-presidential candidate. As Margaret Leech, McKinley's sympathetic biographer, acknowledges, Roosevelt's "forthright censure of the trusts did much to counterbalance the deference to business which paralyzed Republican leadership on economic questions, and to attract the enthusiastic support of younger and more progressive elements of the party." Although TR claimed that he had dug his own political grave, the testimony of the rank and file was that he had laid the foundations for his elevation to the presidency in 1904.

The special session of Congress following the inaugural ceremonies four months later lasted only four days, so Vice-President Roosevelt never had a chance to prove that he could have presided over the Senate with equanimity; and it is of no moment. He tarried in Washington less than a week after Congress adjourned, then returned to Sagamore Hill for the spring and early summer.

Unburdened by pressing duties for the first time since the winter of 1889, TR there experienced perhaps the most pleasant vacation of his life. His seven children were still bound to the family's bosom, though Alice, witty, contrary, and worldly beyond her seventeen years, was straining to break away. TR enjoyed her immensely for she shared his lust for life. But she was already enamored by the superficially unconventional, and he could only with difficulty contain her. She eventually married a stand-pat Republican politician, Nicholas Longworth, who became Speaker of the House when the business civilization reached its apogee under Calvin Coolidge.

Ted, who would become thoroughly imbued with his father's military values and moderately imbued with his social attitudes (he governed Puerto Rico and the Philippines with enlightenment and compassion in the 1920's and early 1930's), was then just short of fourteen. He was in his first year at Groton and was already able to best TR in tennis. The others, ranging down to chubby and effusive Quentin, who at three and one-half wanted and often got in on the fun, all had interests their father enjoyed. They rowed, hiked, waded, and swam together on fair days; romped, read, and recited poetry on rainy days. Inevitably, TR pushed the boys too hard because of his obsession that they should prove their manliness—"I would rather one of them should die than have them grow up weaklings," he once growled at a woman who criticized their playing football. And he apparently drove Ted to a minor nervous breakdown at one point. Yet he had flashes of understanding for the limitations of the mind, if not of the will. He rarely demanded more than an individual could give, and as Wagenknecht points out, he resignedly accepted the fact that most men's best is not very good. "If Archie, through sheer inability, failed in mathematics," he wrote a few days later, "I should not in the least hold it against him; but where Ted gets on probation because he has been such an utter goose as pointlessly to cut his recitations I am not only much irritated but I also become apprehensive as to how Ted will do in after life."

The new Vice President continued to make occasional speeches during the spring and summer of 1901. In April he spoke at the Newsboys' Lodging House. In May, with no sense of foreboding, he opened the Pan-American Exposition in Buffalo. And in June he addressed the Long Island Bible Society at Sagamore Hill and his Harvard class dinner at Cambridge. Then in July on the piazza at Sagamore he conducted an informal seminar for a selected group of Harvard and Yale undergraduates who stayed far into the evening listening to him and a few other idealistic Republicans urge upon them the compelling need for men of character to enter politics. In August Roosevelt participated in the observance of Colorado's twenty-fifth year of statehood, and on September 6 he spoke at the annual outing of the Fish and Game League on Isle la Motte in Lake Champlain.

The afternoon that the Vice President addressed the Fish and Game League on Isle la Motte, President McKinley was mortally wounded in Buffalo. For the next five days McKinley hovered between life and death, but on the sixth day, Friday, September 13, he sank rapidly. Repeating the title of his favorite hymn, "Nearer, My God, to Thee," he murmured finally "It is God's way," then sank into semi-consciousness. At 2:15 in the morning of September 14 the President died.

William McKinley had been a well-intentioned man, uncertain as to the staggering challenges of his times, but striving slowly and as conscientiously as he could to rise to them. His last public address, delivered the day before he was shot, had been his finest. He had declared that the old isolationism was dead and he had counseled the modification of that tariff system of which he himself was the symbol. A transitional President at best, his election in 1896 had marked the end of the old order, his passing in 1901 the ushering in of the new.

McKinley and Roosevelt had never been close; nor had either's opinion of the other ever been high. To the end, McKinley had been unnerved as well as amused by Roosevelt's shrill bellicosity and flagrant disrespect for the established forms. From the beginning, Roosevelt had been contemptuous of McKinley's caution and indecisiveness, his lack of conviction and his failure to respond to the moral imperatives of his office. Yet Roosevelt, like many strong-minded men whose lives touched McKinley's, was not unmoved by the President's homely virtues—by his personal honesty, devotion to his invalid wife, unswerving loyalty to friends, and reluctance to give hurt even to those, like Roosevelt, who themselves had hurt him. He seemed genuinely saddened by his death. "He comes from the typical hard-working farmer stock of our country," Roosevelt wrote Lodge in a letter that unwittingly played on McKinley's tragic belief that it was a President's function to reflect rather than to lead. "In every instinct and feeling he is closely in touch with . . . the men who make up the immense bulk of our Nation. . . . His one great anxiety while President has been to keep in touch with this body of people and to give expression to their sentiments and desires."

Roosevelt had rushed by special train from Burlington, Vermont, to Buffalo upon being informed of the President's misfortune. There, so his most critical biographer concedes, he comported himself with dignity and restraint for three days. On September 10, the physician's reports being encouraging, he left to join his wife and the children in the Adirondacks on the theory that his withdrawal would reassure the country. He reached the Adirondacks, Mrs. Roosevelt wrote Bamie, "naturally much relieved at the rapid recovery of the President." On Friday morning, as the President's physician in Buffalo abandoned hope, Roosevelt and a party climbed Mount Marcy. They had descended as far as Lake Tear of the Cloud and were having lunch beside a brook at two o'clock in the afternoon when a man came puffing up the trail with a message from Elihu Root: "The President appears to be dying, and members of the Cabinet in Buffalo think you should lose no time in coming."

Roosevelt reached his base at six that night. After sending a messenger six miles ahead to the nearest telephone, he retired at nine, to be awakened at eleven by the same messenger. The President was dying; a special train had been arranged to pick up the Vice-President at North Creek, thirty-five miles distant. All that night Roosevelt sat on a buckboard as relays of horses and drivers rushed him over the gutted roads where in places a wrong turn meant a drop over a precipice. He arrived at North Creek at 5:30 Saturday morning, and he reached Buffalo at 1:30 that afternoon.

The new President went at once to the house where the old President lay dead. After paying his respects to the bereaved widow, he was driven to the home of a friend, Ansley Wilcox, where all of the McKinley Cabinet except John Hay and Secretary of the Treasury Lyman J. Gage solemnly awaited him. Root suggested that the oath be taken at once, whereupon Roosevelt bowed slightly and addressed the group. "I wish to say that it shall be my aim to continue, absolutely unbroken, the policy of President McKinley for the peace, the prosperity, and the honor of our beloved country." The oath followed, Roosevelt adding his own redundant touch: "And so I swear."

Following the ceremony Roosevelt took a brief walk with Elihu Root. They returned just before Mark Hanna drove up to the Wilcox house. When the President saw Hanna appear, he rushed out to meet him. It was a tense moment. Hanna had loved McKinley like a brother; he seems also to have aspired to the office Roosevelt now held. Yet Hanna, like Roosevelt, had large habits of mind. When the President repeated the assurances he had given the Cabinet, he replied that although he would not then commit himself to Roosevelt's nomination in 1904, he would do all in his power to make the administration a success during the next three years. "I trust," he concluded, "that you will command me if I can be of any service."

The date was September 14, 1901, six weeks before Roosevelt's forty-third birthday. He was the youngest President in the nation's history.

PART III

THE SQUARE DEAL BEGINS

CHAPTER 9

THE FIRST FELL BLOWS

> When I became President, the question as to the *method* by which the United States Government was to control the corporations was not yet important. The absolutely vital question was whether the government had power to control them at all.
> —Theodore Roosevelt, *An Autobiography*

For five months after Theodore Roosevelt took the presidential oath in the simple ceremony at Buffalo an uneasy calm hung over the American business community. The mighty masters of industry and finance understood that Roosevelt was no Eugene V. Debs, nor even a William Jennings Bryan. They knew, however, that he lacked reverence for the "system" their constructive labor and political influence had created. They remembered how he had struck out at monopoly as a fledgling legislator two decades before. They recalled how as Civil Service Commissioner he had flaunted the "system's" Grand Old Protector—the Republican party. And they could not forget, for they were still challenging the legislation in the courts, how he had imposed a tax on corporations while governor. Nevertheless, they hoped that he would prove himself in the image of McKinley— their "very supple and highly paid agent," as Henry Adams regarded the late President—though by what process of alchemy they were not quite sure. Until Roosevelt destroyed their forced optimism by striking out boldly on his own, their editorial spokesmen worked heroically to imbue him with his lamented predecessor's heritage.

President Roosevelt is "in perfect sympathy with the triumphant policies of Mr. McKinley," the New York *Tribune* said. It would be wrong to think, warned the *New York Times,* "that the temper of President Roosevelt's mind will incline him to seek for himself some more shining glory than that which has crowned the administration of his predecessor." The new President, the New York *Sun* added in a series of urgent editorials obviously designed for Roosevelt's eye, "is a man on whom the American people can rely as a prudent and a safe and sagacious successor to William McKinley."

He represents the same political party and spirit and policies which were represented by Mr. McKinley; his political future, his whole reputation, depends on his fidelity to the sentiment of his party. President Roosevelt's career has been as a strict party man, happily for the public. His policy as President can be assumed from the policy of his party. It will not depend on the possible vagaries of an individual judgment.

Yet Wall Street half sensed that these statements would prove more wishful than realistic. It assumed, however, that the President would at least take it into his confidence when and if he decided to alter McKinley's policies. Great was its consternation, therefore, when late in the afternoon of February 18, 1902, Attorney General Philander C. Knox announced that the President had directed him to invoke the Sherman Antitrust Law against J. P. Morgan's latest paper creation, the Northern Securities Company. There had been no warning save the logic of Theodore Roosevelt's career.

The first memorable event of the Roosevelt era, the resurrection of the Sherman Law, struck financial circles like a shattering shaft of lightning. In New York City, where he was giving a small dinner, Pierpont Morgan received the news with stunned dismay. Roosevelt had not acted as a "gentleman," he plaintively remarked to his guests. Morgan's partner in the Northern Securities venture, the railroad magnate James J. Hill, was yet more bitter. "It really seems hard," he indignantly wrote a friend, "that we should be compelled to fight for our lives against the political adventurers who have never done anything but pose and draw a salary."

The lesser men of the business world mirrored these two Goliaths' reactions. As the uninhibited Detroit *Free Press* sardonically observed, "Wall Street is paralyzed at the thought that a President of the United States would sink so low as to try to enforce the law." When the Exchange opened the next day, the listings dropped markedly across the board. "Not since the assassination of President McKinley has the stock market had such a sudden shock," the *Tribune* reported.

What was behind Roosevelt's sensational action? Years later when Roosevelt wrote in his *Autobiography* that he had not "entered the Presidency with any deliberately planned and far reaching scheme of social betterment," he did himself a partial injustice. In actual fact, the whole body of his ethical beliefs was bound up in the question. The lineage of the presidential Square Deal traced directly to the antimonopoly and good-government platforms Roosevelt had expounded when he first entered politics; and so, indeed, did the New Nationalism of 1912.

Assuredly, the details differed. The problems Roosevelt now confronted were both similar to and more complex than those he had earlier faced. Urban slums were multiplying, and crime and corruption were growing apace. The political machines, whether based on the frustrations of the repressed lower classes or grounded on the greed and fear of the high business order, were tightening their grasp on the body politic. Nature's heritage was being ruthlessly squandered out of apathy, ignorance, and avarice. And worse, even, than that, there was rising such a concentration of business power as made a mockery of the democratic process and threatened the very foundations of the American republic. The Northern Securities Company, by no means the hub of Morgan's empire, was but the most recent example of monopoly's arrant growth. So long as these freebooting activities continued, so long did the corrosive trends that accompanied them promise to flourish.

In the face of these foreboding realities, Theodore Roosevelt stood in September, 1901, as the accidental head of a political party whose leadership was openly hostile toward moves for their reformation. The most powerful brake on the new President's action was the United States Senate. By the turn of the century that body had arrogated to itself much of the authority that Jefferson, Jackson, and Lincoln had vested in the executive office. Most of its members owed their seats to machine-dominated state legislatures, and the ablest among them were long in the habit of flaunting major elements of public opinion. Only such a unique concatenation of events as was to mark the Roosevelt era would force them to compromise; and no force or event would compel many of them to submit.

The Republican leaders of the Senate were at once more ideological and more effective than their counterparts in New York. Many were men of personal wealth, the fruit of earlier careers in business or of continuing, and not wholly disinterested, investment. They were often leaders of their state machines. And they frequently radiated charm and graciousness. With some exceptions, such as Matthew Quay of Pennsylvania, who narrowly escaped the penitentiary, their private morality was high. And even their public morality was estimable by prevailing standards. The powerful "Four," Nelson W. Aldrich of Rhode Island, John C. Spooner of Wisconsin, Orville H. Platt of Connecticut, and William B. Allison of Iowa were cut of fine, if purely conventional cloth; and so also were Mark Hanna and numbers of others. They were not to be compared with Quay or to Boise Penrose, the Pennsylvania aristocrat whose entire political career was virtually an unrelieved stench.

Yet even the best of these men were unable to divorce themselves from their backgrounds. The modern concept of conflict of interest was foreign to their make-up, and they freely promoted their own business interests in the United States Senate. They were generally purblind to the most elementary considerations of social or economic justice. And they were supremely confident that the arrogant business society they so faithfully represented was an unexampled blessing to the American people. Intelligent, and in some instances even learned, they were undistinguished in either intellectual depth or consistency. They fixed upon those theories of John Stuart Mill and William Graham Sumner which subserved their purposes, and they contemptuously dismissed those that confuted them. They supported government subsidies for business both overtly and covertly (through the protective tariff and in earlier years railroad grants); but they self-righteously invoked the doctrine of laissez faire against reformist efforts to regulate and tax either corporate or individual wealth. Calvin Coolidge's dictum that "the business of the United States is business" well stated the G.O.P.'s dominant philosophy in the 1920's; but it applied even more pertinently to the Republican oligarchy Theodore Roosevelt inherited from William McKinley in 1901. "These men still from force of habit applauded what Lincoln had done in the way of radical dealing with the abuses of his day; but they did not apply the spirit in which Lincoln worked to the abuses of their own day," Roosevelt wrote in his autobiography.

So it was that party leaders gasped and outside observers chuckled when the President unloosed his bolt at J. Pierpont Morgan's Northern Securities Company five months after he took office. Symbolically, at least, Roosevelt had crashed headlong into the "system" that made business, through its ideological partners or political hirelings in the House and the Senate, the *de facto* governing body of the nation.

From the start of his administration Roosevelt had seen the difficulties of his position. He also realized, and doubtless enjoyed, the irony of his sudden rise to eminence. But whether he at first comprehended the power and latitude that lay dormant in his new office is debatable. Possibly he did, given his experience as Governor of New York. Yet he also knew that he would have to compromise in order to get legislation passed. Accordingly, he had at once entered into warm, seemingly deferential, relations with the men of power.

In spite of the editorial assurances of Roosevelt's basic conservatism, McKinley's assassination in September had been a devastating blow to the high priests of the market place. Stock prices had declined when news of the shooting had first come through, and they had fallen again when the President died. The volcanic Morgan was variously reported to have been enraged and stupified, to have cursed wildly and to have muttered soulfully. And from the depths of a seemingly boundless despair, Charles M. Schwab of the United States Steel Corporation had even violated the unwritten code by predicting as McKinley lay on his deathbed that business would surely suffer if he failed to recover.

Business leaders had been unwilling to let events run their own course, however. Their editorial spokesmen had yet to publish their wishful affirmations of Roosevelt's conservatism when they tried to exert personal pressure upon the new President through his brother-in-law, Douglas Robinson. He had been urged, Robinson wrote Roosevelt in a letter dispatched to Buffalo by special messenger, "to impress upon you the fact that you must . . . be as close-mouthed and conservative as you were before your nomination for Governor" and that you should "assure the country that you intend to carry out the administration policy."

I must frankly tell you that there is a feeling in financial circles here that in case you become President you may change matters so as to upset the confidence . . . of the business world, which would be an awful blow to everybody—the West as well as the East—as that means tight money.

The advice had been superfluous. By the time he received Robinson's entreaty, Roosevelt had already announced his intention of continuing the McKinley policies in a statement that even Democratic and independent newspapers had heartily applauded. You have, wrote Lodge from England soon afterward, done "admirably, splendidly," and have not "made a single mistake."

Nevertheless, there was an infectious change of pace in the White House. "Every day or two . . . [Roosevelt] rattles the dry bones of precedent and causes sedate Senators and heads of departments to look over their spectacles in consternation," the Detroit *News* observed. "Mr. Roosevelt talks to every one alike," a British embassy official reported to his government, "and apparently in President McKinley's time Senators were accustomed to have their views received with a certain deference." The President was receiving scores of people such as had rarely crossed the White House threshold in the past and would rarely do so in the future—writers, reformers, scientists, professional social workers, and labor leaders. He was walking regularly to the little Grace Reformed Chapel on 15th and O Streets where he attended services almost every Sunday he was in Washington. And he was beginning, with results that would prove both salutary and unsalutary, to conduct diplomacy on horseback or while scrambling among the wilds of Rock Creek Park. Even crabbed Henry Adams admitted to mild exhilaration. "Theodore helps us by his gaiety, and delights Hay by his sense of fun," Adams wrote. " 'Cabot didn't mind having the newspapers say that he was head of the kitchen-cabinet,' said Theodore, 'but he was frantic with fury when they said he was learning to ride, so as to go out with me.' " In numerous other ways also, including the borrowing of books from the Library of Congress, Roosevelt was giving his administration a uniquely personal distinction. Mark Sullivan captured its essense in his *Our Times*:

Roosevelt's first three months in the Presidency were interesting, even spectacular. . . . His high spirits, his enormous capacity for work, his tirelessness, his forthrightness, his many striking qualities, gave a lift of the spirits to millions of average men, stimulated them to higher use of their own powers, gave them a new zest for life. 'He brought in,' said Harry Thurston Peck, 'a stream of fresh, pure, bracing air from the mountains, to clear the fetid atmosphere of the national capital.'

There was still no word, however, on the key question. Would Roosevelt continue McKinley's benevolent policy toward big business?

The first insight into Roosevelt's state of mind came with the release of his first annual message on December 3, 1901. A verbose and lengthy report, that message was well designed to allay the fears of business while yet suggesting a program of moderately positive action. Paragraph balanced paragraph, and sentence balanced sentence as Roosevelt made countless mental reservations of the "on the one hand" and "on the other hand" variety. Finley Peter Dunne's Mr. Dooley well summed up its apparent spirit:

> "Th' trusts," says he, "are heejous monsthers built up be th' inlightened intherprise iv th' men that have done so much to advance progress in our beloved counthry," he says. "On wan hand I wud stamp thim undher fut; on th' other hand not so fast."

What Mr. Dooley and other contemporary observers did not know was that the President had earlier rejected suggestions by the House of Morgan that he revise drastically his measured call for business reform. While the message was being drafted, Morgan had sent two associates, George W. Perkins and Robert Bacon, to Washington to persuade the President to stand pat. Roosevelt had received them courteously though they argued, he informed Douglas Robinson, "like attorneys for a bad case." They would not have done so, he continued, were they not representatives "of a man so strong and dominant a character as Pierpont Morgan." The President added that they wanted him "to go back on my messages to the New York Legislature and on my letter of acceptance for the Vice-Presidency."

> I intend to be most conservative, but in the interests of the big corporations themselves and above all in the interest of the country I intend to pursue, cautiously but steadily, the course to which I have been publicly committed again and again, and which I am certain is the right course.

The President had also had trouble with Mark Hanna. " 'Go slow,' " McKinley's former confidant had warned Roosevelt on October 12. Soon afterward Hanna had taken exception to the President's criticism of overcapitalization in the draft of his message. Not even labor wanted corporation control "made a political issue," he admonished Roosevelt, whereupon the President had agreed to delete the questionable passage. In the message as sent to Congress, however, Roosevelt stated that "one of the chief" of the "real and grave evils" threatening the nation was "overcapitalization."

Granting the indecisive tone of that first message, the section on corporations was still a reasoned statement of the President's views. Roosevelt never had taken anything but a Darwinian view of big business growth; he therein reaffirmed it. The corporations' development "has not been due to the tariff nor to any other government action," he noted, "but to natural causes in the business world, operating in other countries as they operate in our own." Furthermore, he continued, "concerns which have the largest means at their disposal and are managed by the ablest men are naturally those who take the lead in the strife for commercial supremacy among the nations of the world." Foreign markets are "essential," and it would "be unwise to cramp or to fetter the youthful strength of our nation."

Roosevelt also realized, however, that there were abuses, many of them grave and ominous. These should be eradicated by federal regulation. "It is no limitation upon property rights or freedom of contract to require that when men receive from government the privilege of doing business under corporate form . . . they shall do so upon absolute truthful representations as to the value of the property in which the capital is to be invested," the President asserted. As a first remedial step he proposed a law providing for compulsory publicity on the theory that a specific program of regulation and taxation could not be rationally devised until after the facts were known.

Conscious that his proposals for national regulation would affront the numerous and vociferous defenders of states' rights, the President attempted to outflank them with historical reasoning. "When the Constitution was adopted, at the end of the eighteenth century," he wrote in a passage that graphically revealed his evolutionary approach to constitutional law, "no human wisdom could foretell the sweeping changes, alike in industrial and political conditions, which were to take place at the beginning of the twentieth century":

> At that time it was accepted as a matter of course that the several States were the proper authorities to regulate, so far as was then necessary, the comparatively insignificant and strictly localized

corporate bodies of the day. The conditions are now wholly different and wholly different action is called for. I believe that a law can be framed which will enable the National Government to exercise control along the lines above indicated. . . . If, however, the judgment of the Congress is that it lacks the constitutional power to pass such an act, then a constitutional amendment should be submitted to confer the power.

The real portent of these recommendations was largely unrecognized, and the President's message had stirred scarcely a ripple of excitement on Wall Street and among conservatives in general. Here and there, it is true, an isolated outcry was heard. In conservative Connecticut the Hartford *Courant* unloosed the first of a stream of editorial criticisms of the new President, exclaiming that federal control "is a few steps ahead of government ownership, and is in the same path." But on the whole the reaction was favorable. Many conservative newspapers heaved a great sigh of relief that the President's recommendations had been relatively restrained; some, including the *Wall Street Journal,* endorsed them openly; and others, viewing them with a cynicism born of realism, suggested that Congress could readily ignore them.

Why this mild reaction? One explanation is that big business and its defenders had feared the worst—an explosive, single-minded assault on the iniquities of "the criminal rich" and the "malefactors of great wealth." Another is that they were confident that the President's proposals would be buried by Congress. William McKinley was no longer in the White House, but God was in his heaven and Aldrich, Hanna, Spooner, and those who thought like them were still in control of the United States Senate. Did they not stand unalterably for the status quo, or at least for change in only the slightest degree?

If more assurance were needed, the conservative Cabinet that came down from McKinley must have given it. The member most directly involved, Attorney General Philander C. Knox, was able and public-spirited. But he was conservative in temperament and a corporation lawyer in background. He might be expected, also, to be dwarfed in influence by Elihu Root, whose imposing talents, forceful personality, and intimate friendship with Roosevelt lent credence to reports that his hand would extend far beyond the War Department where he was already performing with brilliance. Root's attitude toward corporation control was no secret; he largely opposed it.

Had Pierpont Morgan, E. H. Harriman, and their minions been closer students of human nature, they might have been more apprehensive. For Roosevelt had at his command the means for independent executive action. Eleven years earlier a Republican Congress had responded to the demands of social critics by enacting the Sherman Antitrust Law. Modern scholarship indicates that the measure had been passed in relatively good faith despite contemporaneous assertions that although no one knew what it would do to the trusts, almost everyone agreed that "something must be flung out to appease the restive masses." Nevertheless, a succession of presidential administrations had invoked it sparingly, when at all. Harrison instituted seven suits, Cleveland eight, and McKinley, under whom more trusts were formed than ever before, a total of three. Indeed, the most notable effective prosecution under the Sherman Law had been against the benighted labor leader, Eugene V. Debs; and this despite Congress' apparent conviction that labor unions were exempted from its provisions. Of at least comparable significance, so the historian Hans Thorelli suggests, is the fact that until 1902 not a single action against a business combine had been instituted on the initiative of the Department of Justice headquarters in Washington; excepting only the four labor cases growing out of the Pullman strike of 1894, every one of the suits under Harrison, Cleveland, and McKinley had been originated by zealous district attorneys in the field. Indubitably, the utilization of the Sherman Law as a broad instrument of national policy awaited the application of a bold and imaginative intelligence.

Just five weeks after Theodore Roosevelt took the presidential oath the spawning of new trusts had come to a temporary climax as incorporation papers for the Northern Securities Company were filed in Trenton, New Jersey, at the instance of J. Pierpont Morgan.

"What a whale of a man!" was the way one of his contemporaries described the imperious Morgan. "There seemed to radiate something that forced the complex of inferiority . . . upon all around him, in spite of themselves," he continued. "The boldest man was likely to become timid under his piercing gaze. The most impudent or recalcitrant were ground to humility as he chewed truculently at his huge black cigar." In the parlance of the "Street," wrote James Ford Rhodes, he was known as "Jupiter." The appellation "was properly bestowed," Rhodes added, "for his word was 'I command.' "

This First Lord of American Finance was no more committed to the pure theory of capitalism, however, than the propagandists who fashioned its folklore. He too idealized the concept of an economy unfettered by governmental restraints. But on the critical abstraction—that of a genuinely open market—he was from the beginning a radical deviant. Like Aldrich and the other senators whose views reflected or paralleled his own, Morgan did not believe in free competition. Always, he yearned for the stability and security of an economy ordered by gentlemen bankers and corporation managers; always, he feared the instability of the hard and creative clash of undisciplined economic units.

Firm in the conviction that competition was wasteful, destructive of confidence, and erratic in impact, Morgan had been striving since 1885 to regularize the organization of the railroads in particular. By Roosevelt's accession he had already reorganized thousands of miles of Eastern lines with results that graphically bore out the injurious, no less than the beneficial, effects of finance-capitalist control. He had also acquired a major interest in James J. Hill's Northern Pacific and Great Northern lines. Striking out from there in partnership with Hill, he had masterfully extended his interests over the Burlington road into Chicago.

The acquisition of the Burlington line by the Morgan-Hill interests had been a bitter blow to the intrepid E. H. Harriman, long-time antagonist of Hill and dominant figure in the Union Pacific Railroad. Harriman believed that the conjunction of the Burlington and the Northern Pacific threatened his own "empire" to the south; and he boldly demanded permission to buy a one-third interest in the Burlington. Morgan and Hill had peremptorily refused, whereupon Harriman started an all-out fight for control of Morgan and Hill's Northern Pacific road. For a few frenzied hours the battle of the railroad and financial titans caused Northern Pacific shares to soar to more than $1,000 a share; but finally Harriman failed of his objective by a narrow margin. He had provoked such a disturbance and made such heavy inroads in the Northern Pacific, however, that Morgan and Hill retreated. The order to combine rather than compete was given out, and the Northern Securities Company was organized to implement it. The new corporation brought together the stock of all three roads, the Northern Pacific, Union Pacific, and Burlington, under a board composed of the Morgan, Hill, and Harriman interests and the latter's bankers, Kuhn, Loeb & Company. One-third of the

Northern Securities Company's stock was "water"; even more important, shippers through the entire upper West had no recourse but to pay such charges as the new combine fixed.

President Roosevelt had given no intimation of his feelings when the Northern Securities Company was formed in the fall of 1901; nor had he mentioned the company in his December message. Some time during the early winter of 1901–1902, however, perhaps when he learned that Minnesota had instituted proceedings against it, he decided to investigate. Only to Attorney General Knox, who was soon to be castigated as a "country lawyer" by irate Wall Street men, did Roosevelt give his confidence.

Pierpont Morgan's concern encompassed more than the President's violation of the "gentlemen's code" when the suit against the Northern Securities Company was announced on February 19. He feared that the government's action presaged a broadside attack on his other interests, several of which were closer to his leonine heart than the Western railroads; and soon after the suit was instituted he sped to Washington to impress Roosevelt with the gravity of his action and, particularly, to ascertain his future intentions.

"If we have done anything wrong," the lordly financier exclaimed to the President of the United States, "send your man [the Attorney General] to my man [one of Morgan's lawyers] and they can fix it up." Roosevelt, who seems to have been somewhat awed by Morgan's commanding presence (though not enough so to alter his policy), replied simply, "That can't be done." And Knox added that the administration wanted to stop such combinations rather than destroy them. Morgan then came to the main point. "Are you going to attack my other interests, the Steel Trust and the others?" he asked. "Certainly not," the President responded, "unless we find out that in any case they have done something we regard as wrong."

"That is a most illuminating illustration of the Wall Street point of view," Roosevelt remarked after Morgan left the White House. "Mr. Morgan could not help regarding me as a big rival operator, who either intended to ruin all his interests or else could be induced to come to an agreement to ruin none."

Morgan was not alone in resenting the President's failure to reveal his confidence. Elihu Root felt that he too should have been informed, and he vented his irritation on Knox in the erroneous belief that he was responsible for the President's closemouthedness. Mark

Hanna must also have been irritated, though he failed to show it. He had accompanied Morgan on one of his two visits to the White House, but had refused to urge Roosevelt to change his policy. "I warned Hill that McKinley might have to act against his company," the large-minded Ohioan said. "Mr. Roosevelt's done it."

The reasons for Roosevelt's cloak-and-dagger attitude are unclear. His only recorded comment suggests that he feared the stock market would have been upset had word got out. It is more likely, however, that he simply decided that an independent assertion of executive power would best serve his interests. More effectively than any words he might write or utter, such action would demonstrate that he was President in fact as well as in name; that he had finally broken free of the McKinley nexus. It would also signify the weakening of that business-government partnership which Roosevelt was compelled by his own inner necessity to attack. And most important of all, for Roosevelt could suppress his moral compulsions temporarily, it would win the support of the middle classes while impressing Congress with the need to compromise its opposition to his legislation program or suffer the consequences in the executive arena. As Mowry concludes, "With the path to effective regulation blocked by a stubborn, conservative Congress, the only way for Roosevelt to bring the arrogant capitalists to heel was through the judicious use of the anti-trust laws." Thus the President would have seriously weakened his position or, at the least, subjected himself to agonizing intellectual turmoil, had he consulted with Root, the Senate Four, or the Morgan group.

For nearly two years after suit was instituted in the winter of 1902, the Northern Securities case wended its way through the lower courts. The feeling was strong that the Supreme Court would reaffirm its opinion in the Knight Case of 1895—to wit, a mere stock transaction was not in itself an act of commerce—and upon that reasoning the combine's able lawyers based the burden of their arguments. When the Northern Securities decision was finally rendered on March 14, 1904, however, the government's action was upheld by a five to four majority. John Marshall Harlan, one of the strongest (and paradoxical) minds to grace the High Tribunal in the late nineteenth century and the author of the dissenting opinion in 1895, this time spoke for the majority.

For the Court to accept the contention that the act violated state sovereignty, Justice Harlan declared, would mean "nothing less than that Congress, in regulating interstate commerce, must act in subordination to the will of the states when exerting their power to create corporations." And such a view, the tough-minded jurist concluded, could not "be entertained for a moment." Thus was laid another major section of the legal roadbed for a broad extension of federal regulatory powers during the next half century.

President Roosevelt's pleasure in the Court's ruling was tempered by the fact that Oliver Wendell Holmes, the first and most eminent of his appointees to the Supreme Court, cast his vote with the minority. Harlan's was an interpretation of the law, said Holmes in his dissenting opinion, that would "disintegrate society so far as it could into individual atoms." The tremendous size of the railroad combination was but "an inevitable incident" in their development and was hardly a legitimate reason for ordering their dissolution.

Roosevelt was exacerbated by Holmes's dissent, which he characteristically blamed on lack of courage. "I could carve out of a banana a judge with more backbone than that," he reportedly exclaimed. Always thereafter Holmes and Roosevelt's relationship was subtly hedged in though they continued to see each other. "Holmes should have been an ideal man on the bench," Roosevelt unforgivingly complained to Lodge two years later. "As a matter of fact he has been a bitter disappointment." The great jurist carried his resentment beyond Roosevelt's grave. Refusing to read a laudatory biography of the late President in 1921, he mused about the incident: "[The affair] . . . broke up our incipient friendship. . . . [Roosevelt] looked on my dissent to the *Northern Securities case* as a political departure (or, I suspect, more truly, couldn't forgive anyone who stood in his way). We talked freely later but it was never the same. . . ." Holmes added a characterization not unlike the one he would make of Franklin D. Roosevelt a decade hence. "[Theodore] . . . was very likeable, a big figure, a rather ordinary intellect, with extraordinary gifts, a shrewd and I think pretty unscrupulous politician. He played all his cards—if not more. *R.i.p.*"

The incident was regrettable, for the President's conception of the law roughly paralleled the evolutionary interpretation Holmes had written into his epochal *Common Law* more than twenty years earlier. (Holmes never acknowledged the coincidence, preferring the formulation of one of Roosevelt's senatorial contemporaries: "What the boys like about Roosevelt is that he doesn't care a damn for the law.")

Indeed, the President had offered Holmes the seat in 1902 partly in the belief that he would bring breadth and balance to the corporation-oriented High Tribunal—Holmes's prolabor opinions in Massachusetts had especially impressed him. And though, as Holmes complained, Roosevelt's irritation over the Northern Securities dissent was both personal and political, it was also ideological. Too perceptive a student of history to accept the fiction that legal decisions are made in a social and political vacuum, Roosevelt had sought a jurist of stature whose philosophy was consonant with his own; who was, as he apparently told Holmes before he appointed him, a party man in the tradition of Marshall. "The ablest lawyers and greatest judges are men whose past has naturally brought them into close relationship with the wealthiest and most powerful clients," the President wrote shortly before he announced the appointment of Holmes, "and I am glad when I can find a judge who has been able to preserve his aloofness of mind so as to keep his broad humanity of feeling and his sympathy for the class from which he has not drawn his clients. I think it eminently desirable that our Supreme Court should show in unmistakable fashion their entire sympathy with all proper effort to secure the most favorable possible consideration for the men who most need that consideration. . . ."

Even more ironic was the actual coincidence of Holmes's and Roosevelt's views on business combinations. The President perceived that monopoly was in some instances as advantageous as it was inevitable; and his economic brief against the giant trusts, as distinguished from his political brief, was that they were free to exploit the shippers or consumers. His much lampooned distinction between "good" and "bad" trusts was a partial manifestation of this; and his sustained interest in regulation, which contrasted sharply with his erratic interest in dissolving the trusts, was a clear manifestation of it. To the end he regarded the Sherman Law as a special, rather than a general, weapon.

The administration's prosecution of the Northern Securities Company, which was followed shortly by a successful suit against Swift & Company, heartened social critics everywhere, the more so because of Congress' hostility to comprehensive regulatory legislation. The Republican leaders in both the Senate and House had treated the President's moderate recommendations in December, 1901, with the indifference they habitually reserved for such "visionary" proposals;

and during the summer of 1902 Roosevelt had taken the issue to the people, who gave warm approval to his fighting, yet balanced, speeches. When the new Congress convened in December, 1902, the President pressed for legislation with considerably more forcefulness than he had done the year before.

"This country cannot afford to sit supine on the plea that under our peculiar system of government we are helpless in the presence of the new conditions," Roosevelt declared in his second annual message. "The power of the Congress to regulate interstate commerce is an absolute and unqualified grant, and without limitations other than those prescribed by the Constitution." Should the proposed laws transgress the authority granted to Congress, the Chief Executive asserted, "we should not shrink from amending the Constitution so as to secure beyond peradventure the power sought."

These were forceful generalizations; however, Roosevelt finally accepted a modest program embracing inspection and publicity of corporate earnings. He would undoubtedly have welcomed more; and for a short period he supported a sweeping measure offered by Representative Charles E. Littlefield of Maine. But when Aldrich threatened to withdraw support of the administration and Senator Hoar of Massachusetts blunderingly appended an even more radical bill of Littlefield's to the pending measure to create a Department of Commerce and Labor, Roosevelt backed down. He had no alternative, given Aldrich's position. Nevertheless, the President characteristically deluded himself. It was, he wrote William Howard Taft, "far more satisfactory to work" with Aldrich, Hanna, Spooner and the rest— "the most powerful factors in Congress"—than with "the radical 'reformers,' like Littlefield."

Roosevelt's pique was understandable, for he had already artfully threatened to call a special session if Congress failed to give him a Bureau of Corporations within the Department of Commerce and Labor (he ingeniously told the press that John D. Rockefeller was secretly influencing Congress against the measure). He had also made arrangements by then to enact the Elkins anti-rebate measure and to pass a law increasing the Attorney General's power to expedite antitrust proceedings.

Viewed as a whole, and including the epochal Supreme Court cases which Roosevelt initiated, the President's corporation program was a profoundly creative undertaking. The new Department of Commerce and Labor possessed obvious merits. The Bureau of Corporation's provisions for inspection and partial publicity of corporative activities were a long stride forward. The Elkins Act's intended elimination of long-standing abuses by powerful shippers was a major, if still inadequate, reform. And the legislation strengthening the Attorney General's authority to expedite cases under the Sherman Law was by any criterion salutary.

The trust problem was still far from resolved. Yet the way was prepared for an expansion of the executive power by Roosevelt and those of his successors who were sensitive to the increasingly complex demands of the twentieth-century industrial and financial order. At a time when the American people's government was perilously close to becoming a mere satellite of big business, Theodore Roosevelt, by a masterful assertion of both his moral and political authority, had reaffirmed the people's right to control their affairs through their elected representatives.

Ironically, it was a devoted Democrat with little taste for the President's personality who most trenchantly stated this overriding fact. Recoiling from his own editor's constant "nagging" of Roosevelt, Joseph Pulitzer in the spring and summer of 1907 privately enjoined them to stop. "Support him on the main line—no hypercriticism of his minor faults," the brilliant publisher advised the *World's* leading editorial writer, Frank Cobb:

> If Roosevelt had never done anything else, and if he had committed a hundred times more mistakes, and if he were one hundred times more impulsive, changeable, unpresidential in dignity, loud and vociferating in manner and speech—. . . if he had done nothing else except to start the great machinery of the government and the most powerful force and majesty of the law in the direction of prosecuting these great offenders, he would be entitled to the greatest credit for the greatest service to the nation. This one initiative impulse and persevering instinct must be held as offsetting a hundred wrong impulses of a minor character. The greatest breeder of discontent and socialism is lack of confidence in the justice of the law, popular belief that the law is one thing for the rich and another for the poor.

Theodore Roosevelt, wrote the man whose newspaper had opposed his election as Governor in 1898, as Vice President in 1900, and as President in 1904, "has subjugated Wall Street."

CHAPTER 10

A HISTORIC DEPARTURE

> I could no more see misery and death come to the great masses of the people in our large cities and sit by idly, because under ordinary conditions a strike is not a subject of interference by the President, than I could sit by idly and see one man kill another without interference because there is no statutory duty imposed upon the President to interfere in such cases.
> —Roosevelt to Mrs. W. S. Cowles

"[The] turbulence and violence you dread is just as apt to come from an attitude of arrogance on the part of the owners of property and of unwillingness to recognize their duty to the public as from any improper encouragement of labor unions," the President warned Robert Bacon in the fall of 1902 as a summer-long coal strike threatened to set off an outbreak of mass strife in the great urban centers of the East. "Do you think you are fully alive to the gross blindness of the operators?" Roosevelt asked his old friend Bishop of the New York *Evening Post.* "Do you realize that they are putting a heavy burden on us who stand against socialism; against anarchic disorder?"

What sophisticated Mark Hanna had averted in 1900 had come to pass in 1902. On May 12, 1902, virtually the entire anthracite industry in the gloomy, cavernous regions of eastern Pennsylvania had been struck. Two years before, the operators had made a 10 per cent wage concession to the mine workers in response to Hanna's earnest entreaties. But that had been an election year, and almost no price had seemed too high for William Jennings Bryan's defeat.

With the Great Commoner safely consigned to the Chautauqua

circuit in 1902, the operators felt free to follow their normal pre-dispositions. When John Mitchell, the United Mine Workers' articulate president, invited them to discuss a new wage scale in February, they rebuffed him on the contention that he did not really represent the mine workers. They resented their strategic retreat of 1900, and they resolved to make last-ditch resistance their new battle order.

Two months after the operators thus manned the ramparts, the UMW appealed to the National Civic Federation, a recently organized group of labor, industrial, and political leaders under Mark Hanna's chairmanship. Hanna obligingly arranged for the UMW officers and the presidents of the major coal companies to meet with the leaders of the Civic Federation in New York City.

The ensuing conference proved barren of results, the operators refusing both to recognize the miners' union and to treat their grievances on an industry-wide basis. The operators' attitude seemed reasonable. The right-of-the-employer concept was deeply ingrained in the public consciousness, and there were few in America aside from labor leaders and a coterie of intellectuals who perceived how anachronistic the rise of large-scale industry had made it. Clinging to the historic, agrarian-molded conception of individual liberty, the middle classes refused to regard mass unionism as the logical counterweight to mass industrialism; and though they often conceded that workers should be free to join a union, they firmly believed that the employer should suffer no compulsion to recognize it. Not even in the darkest days of this bitter strike, therefore, was the miners' demand for recognition of their union given broad popular support.

The fact was, however, that the average coal company's holdings were so varied and its financial resources so great—six railroad corporations owned upward of 70 per cent of the anthracite mines—that big unionism offered the only possibility of relief for the mine workers. That was the crux of the recognition issue, and the operators, who were far from novices in the field of labor relations, knew it. As Pulitzer's *World* argued editorially a few months later, "It is preposterous to put the coal trust in the position of a champion of free labor, or any sort of freedom except the freedom to mine coal or to stop mining as it pleases—to raise prices arbitrarily at will—to pay the wages it shall decide upon and exact any hours or conditions of work that it may decree without regard to the public, to its miners, or to the law."

The mine workers' decision to strike on May 12 had not been hastily made. Mitchell had persuaded them to refrain from issuing an immediate strike call in April; and at the final meeting sponsored by the Civic Federation he offered to accept a 5 per cent wage increase though the rank and file were demanding twenty. But in the face of Mitchell's moderation, the operators remained intransigent. Even Mark Hanna, who had been burning the long-distance wires and cabling American business leaders in Europe in a desperate effort to effect a compromise, finally threw up his hands in disgust. "Well! they will not only strike," he angrily exploded, "but they will get ten per cent increase before they settle."

The wage issue, at least, was more complex than later appeared. The anthracite industry was even then "sick," and the operators were probably correct in arguing that an increase in wages would necessitate a rise in prices. To prove their point, they actually offered to open their books to Mitchell, who countered by suggesting that they raise prices if necessary. Their reply was that they would then be subjected to inroads by bituminous coal dealers, already a source of stiff competition. "Anthracite mining is a business, and not a religious, sentimental, or academic proposition," George F. Baer, President of the Philadelphia and Reading Coal and Iron Company and the industry's chief spokesman, remarked a week before the strike started. Later, Baer would take an even more theological view of management's right to direct the industry's affairs.

Contrariwise, the operators failed to appreciate the psychology of the miners' drive for an ever higher standard of living—the only tenable excuse for their beastlike sweat and toil. As Roosevelt reflected a decade later, "The majority of the men . . . if they wished to progress at all, were compelled to progress not by ceasing to be wage-earners, but by improving the conditions under which all the wage-earners in all the industries of the country lived and worked, as well, of course, as improving their own individual efficiency." In the face of a dramatic increase in the cost of living that almost wiped out the miners' wage increases of two years before, however, the operators persisted in holding out.

The operators were not disposed to treat with the miners' other grievances. Hours were long and in some jobs extreme. Machinery for a fair evaluation of the individual miner's daily output was deficient, ton weight varying between 2,740 and 3,190 pounds, and the men often spent many hours underground without compensation because of a shortage of cars. They were also subjected to a paternalism that belied the American dream. Even worse was the destruction of life, limb, and health. As Irving Stone writes in his passionate biography of Clarence Darrow, "Six men out of a thousand were killed every year; hundreds were maimed by explosions and cave-ins; few escaped the ravages of asthma, bronchitis, chronic rheumatism, consumption, heart trouble. By the age of fifty the miners were worn out and broken, good for little but the human slag heap."

When, against this background, the operators turned a deaf ear to Mitchell and Hanna's pleas for compromise—"[The miners] don't suffer," exclaimed George Baer, "why, they can't even speak English"—the coal workers had little recourse but to strike. Less than three weeks after they went out on May 12, an undetermined but substantial number of engineers, firemen, and pumpmen joined them. It was the greatest work stoppage up to that time.

In Washington that spring President Roosevelt followed the strike with increasing alarm. There was little violence in the coal fields at first; and at the outset the press generally sympathized with the miners. Until well into the summer, moreover, the stockpiles held up. Yet the strike was not two weeks old before the price of coal began to rise sharply. Meanwhile accounts of clashes between strikers and nonstrikers began to appear beside reports that the independent operators were prevented from coming to terms by the six great railroads which controlled the means of distributing the coal. Nor, apparently, were the operators disposed to tighten their own belts. "Official after official has had his salary increased," the *United Mine Workers' Journal* irately charged, and "President Truesdale, of the Lackawanna, got an increase of $10,000 per year."

Of all the charges and countercharges, that which most interested the President was one that the anthracite industry was a powerful, closely knit trust. Late in May the Springfield *Republican* pointed out that to the dealer and consumer there was but one seller of coal and that they must meet his terms or go without. "It would be difficult to conceive of a monopoly more perfectly established or operated than this monopoly which holds complete possession of a great store of nature most necessary to the life of the day," the *Republican* contended. "There is but one way to deal with [it] . . . public control or ownership."

Roosevelt's response was to direct Commissioner of Labor Carroll Wright to investigate the strike. But on the advice of the President's conservative intimates, he withheld publication of Wright's report. Nevertheless, Roosevelt became increasingly piqued at the operators as the summer wore on, and in August he seriously considered instituting antitrust proceedings against the coal companies. After Attorney General Knox advised him that suit would fail for want of evidence under the Sherman Law, however, he dropped the proposal. "There is literally nothing, so far as I have yet been able to find out, which the national government has any power to do in the matter," he wrote Lodge, who was fretting over the strike's probable impact on the congressional elections in November. "Nor can I imagine any remedial measure of immediate benefit that could be taken in Congress," Roosevelt continued. "That it would be a good thing to have national control, or at least supervision, over these big coal corporations, I am sure; but that would simply have to come as an incident of the general movement to exercise control over such corporations."

The President's reflections were to the point, given the conservative complexion of Congress. Yet the public temper was rising daily and would obviously continue to rise until the strike was settled. By early August pea coal had soared from $2.40 a ton to $6 in the New York area, while coal prices as a whole had increased 50 per cent or more. By October schools in New York and many New England towns would be forced to shut down for lack of fuel, while available stocks, which were almost everywhere low, would be commanding from $30 to $35 per ton.

To compound the problem, conservative allies of the operators were mounting a rising attack on Mitchell and the miners. Late in the summer Abram S. Hewitt, Roosevelt's erstwhile mayoralty opponent, charged that mild-mannered John Mitchell was trying to make himself "the dictator of the coal business" and extolled the operators for fighting for "the right of every man to sell his labor in a free market." Although Hewitt's contention was forcefully denied by many moderate editorial voices, that broad prejudice against labor which had been theretofore tempered by the manifest arrogance of the operators was beginning to come through. And when reports of growing violence—on-the-spot observers claimed they were exaggerated by metropolitan newspapers—received new prominence in late September, many conservatives accepted Hewitt's assertions as conclusive. The real issue, said the new president of Princeton University, Woodrow Wilson, was the union's drive "to win more power."

Whether the nation as a whole would have also turned against the miners is an open question. The UMW's resolve to prevent nonunion men from returning to the pits, the violence that must inevitably have ensued, and the costly discomfort to the public from the shortage of coal all suggest that the middle classes would have eventually shifted their sympathies; the unrelieved arrogance of the operators, together with the popular resentment of business malpractices in general, suggest that support of the mine workers would have continued. It is virtually certain, however, that Roosevelt could have swung them either way had he elected to take a one-sided stand.

The President's personal intervention came only after all possibilities except federal seizure of the mines had been seemingly exhausted. During the summer effort after effort had failed to bring the operators to terms. Even Hanna proved powerless to move them. He succeeded in persuading the bituminous miners from going out in sympathy. "It is one of the proudest moments of my life that I can state . . . that the men stood by their word," Hanna told a Chautauqua audience after the bituminous convention voted against a sympathy strike on July 17. And he prevailed on J. Pierpont Morgan and John Mitchell to formulate a compromise plan to end the anthracite stoppage. But as he despairingly wrote Roosevelt on September 29, George Baer rejected it outright.

Meanwhile Cabot Lodge importuned Roosevelt to act. "By the first week in November if the strike does not stop and coal begins to go down we shall have [a political] . . . overturn," he warned. "Is there any form of pressure we can put on the operators who are driving us to ruin? The unions are just as obstinate but the rising public wrath makes for them and they stand all the firmer."

Roosevelt was too astute a politician to be insensitive to the politics of the situation. Yet he felt helpless to act. "I am genuinely independent of the big monied men in all matters where I think the interests of the public are concerned," he replied to Lodge, "and probably I am the first President of recent times of whom this could be truthfully said. . . . But where I do not grant any favors to these big monied men which I do not think the country requires that they should have, it is out of the question for me to expect them to grant favors to me in return. . . . I am," he concluded, "at my wits' end how to proceed."

Nevertheless, the President continued to grope for a practical solution. After conferring with Root, Knox, Quay, and Governor Murray Crane of Massachusetts, he decided to invite the operators to confer with him. He contemplated telling them that he would "advise action [presumably to Congress] along the lines I have explained in my speeches but of a much more radical type in reference to their business unless they wake up." The same day he made that decision, however, Crane publicly called for him to meet with both the operators and miners. Roosevelt thereupon abandoned the idea of negotiating with the operators alone. On October 1 he requested the leaders of both groups to confer with him. There would have been no warrant in interfering in a strike of iron workers, he wrote his sister Bamie two weeks later, for iron was not a necessity. But, he continued, "I could . . . [not] see misery and death come to the great masses of the people in our large cities and sit by idly. . . ."

The presidential summonses were duly honored, though not in good grace by the operators. A little before eleven in the morning of the appointed day, October 3, the leaders of the operators and the coal miners entered the Blair House to await the President. For a few minutes they stood in knots at opposite ends of a long, second-floor room talking self-consciously. Shortly the President, who had been painfully injured in an automobile accident three weeks before, was wheeled in.

Roosevelt opened the meeting by disclaiming either the right or the duty to intervene. He presumed, instead, on the conferees' good will. "With all the earnestness there is in me," he solemnly declared, "I ask that there be an immediate resumption of operations in the coal mines in some such way as will, without a day's unnecessary delay, meet the crying needs of the people. I appeal to your patriotism, to the spirit that sinks personal consideration and makes individual sacrifices for the general good."

John Mitchell then rose to speak. Never, wrote Mark Sullivan in his dramatic account of the conference, did the swarthy, ex-breaker boy appear to greater advantage. "His natural distinction of person and manner was accentuated by his affecting the sober garb and the 'reversed' collar of the clergyman," and though the gathering was of the strongest men, "he stood out easily as the most intelligent force of all, save Roosevelt." Eschewing recrimination—for many weeks the operators had been abusing Mitchell vilely—he spoke simply and directly:

I am much pleased, Mr. President, with what you say. We are willing that you shall name a tribunal which shall determine the issues that have resulted in the strike; and if the gentlemen representing the operators will accept the award or decision of such a tribunal, the miners will willingly accept it, even if it be against our claims.

George Baer, the operators' spokesman, was outraged by Mitchell's measured remarks. Two and one-half months before the Reading President had invoked the divine right of plutocracy against suggestions that he agree to mediate the strike. "The rights and interests of the laboring man will be protected and cared for," he had then written, "not by the labor agitators, but by the Christian men to whom God in His infinite wisdom has given the control of the property interests of the country, and upon the successful Management of which so much depends." Though no longer blasphemous, he now stood just as firmly on business' right to conduct its own affairs. His flintlike eyes flashed fire at the President no less than at Mitchell as he referred to the "crimes inaugurated by the United Mine Workers, over whom John Mitchell, whom you invited to meet you, is chief," and admonished Roosevelt that "the duty of the hour is not to waste time negotiating with the fomenters of this anarchy." Baer added that there should be no governmental interference except through the Courts of Common Pleas in the mining districts (the established bulwarks of the status quo).

Throughout the long day, broken only by an adjournment for lunch, the operators continued to castigate Mitchell, the mineworkers, and the President. Roosevelt, the chief of the White House telegraphers later said, would have been justified in heaving chairs at the operators. They dismissed the union members as anarchists and criminals; they asked the President if he was not suggesting they "deal with a set of outlaws"; and they openly accused him of making "a grandstand play." There was "only one man in that conference who behaved like a gentleman," Roosevelt was afterward quoted as exclaiming, "and that man was not I."

Between expletives, the operators made three concrete proposals:

(1) The government should send federal troops into the anthracite regions. (2) The United Mine Workers should be prosecuted under the terms of the Sherman Antitrust Law. And (3), the miners should be forced to return to work at once, their grievances to be adjudicated by the local courts. Mitchell, who comported himself with stoic dignity during the entire proceedings, rejected all three proposals, and, late in the afternoon, the conference terminated.

That night Roosevelt was gripped by the depression that so often overcame him momentarily. "I have tried and failed," he wrote Mark Hanna. Mitchell's proposition was "entirely fair and reasonable," he continued. "I felt he did very well to keep his temper. Between times they insulted me for not preserving order." Nor did he know what his next move would be. "I feel most strongly that the attitude of the operators is one which accentuates the need of the Government having some power of supervision and regulation over such corporations. I would like to make a fairly radical experiment on the anthracite coal business to start with!"

To Roosevelt's credit, he resisted the step that would have at once resolved his political and economic, if not his ideological, dilemma. He could have broken the strike with a stroke of his pen by calling out federal troops as the operators requested and President Cleveland had done during the Pullman strike of 1894. Coal would then have been mined, prices would have dropped in time for the November elections, and he would have received the acclaim that is the man of action's desideratum. So acute was the public distress and so widespread the exaggerated reports of union violence, that he conceivably would have won overwhelming support from all but labor men had he pursued such a decisive course. Even newspapers which had been sympathetic to the United Mine Workers were demanding an end to conflict between strikers and nonstrikers. The union men "can not expect, and we believe do not ask, for public support of a strike that threatens to degenerate into a murderous plot," the Philadelphia *North American* remarked. "It is not a coal strike, but an insurrection," the New York *Journal of Commerce* contended.

Notwithstanding the rising hysteria, the President maintained his balance. "Have you ever read Hay and Nicolay's *Lincoln?*" he wrote Robert Bacon. "Just as Lincoln got contradictory advice from the extremists of both sides at every phase of the struggle for unity and freedom, so I now have carefully to guard myself against the extremists of both sides. The men who wish me to proceed under the Sherman antitrust law against the miners' union are if possible one shade more foolish than the others who wish me to proceed under the same law against the coal operators as such." And the same was true, he added, of those who wanted him to call out the troops "on the present state of facts and without further investigation."

In the midst of this worst crisis of his first administration, Roosevelt stole a few fleeting hours for his life's most consuming passion; reading. "I owe you much!" he wrote Librarian of Congress Herbert Putnam, who had recently sent him a shipment of books. "I am now reveling in Maspero and occasionally make a deviation into Sergis' theories about the Mediterranean races."

> It has been such a delight to drop everything useful—everything that referred to my duty—. . . and to spend an afternoon in reading about the relations between Assyria and Egypt; which could not possibly do me any good and in which I reveled accordingly; while my wife, who prefers belles-lettres, has read Shakespeare, which she brought down, and Tennyson which Ethel brought down. I have been reading Thackeray, Dickens, and Scott myself recently, and felt as if I simply *had* to enjoy a few days of history.

The President did not know it, but he had come almost to the crossroads. Shortly after the failure of the conference in the Blair House, he sent Carroll Wright to Mitchell with a proposal that the strikers return to work pending an investigation by a presidential commission, the findings of which he pledged himself to do all that he could to implement. But as Mitchell explained in turning it down, the miners had already gone halfway and had no reason to believe the operators would "do us justice in the future."

At this juncture there occurred an event which served powerfully to make the operators more tractable. For some time the operators had claimed that great numbers of miners would go back to work if protected from reprisals by the more zealous union members. There was a grain of truth in their contention, for a small minority of miners did desire to end the strike. When, accordingly, Governor William A. Stone of Pennsylvania called out the entire state militia to maintain order, moderate observers sensed that the critical test had come. Let the operators now "put 100,000 men to work" under the protection of the militia, the *New York Times* asserted, or else "send for

Mitchell and settle the strike on the best terms they can make."

The operators' worst fears were soon realized, for the great majority of strikers continued to stay out. Baer and his imperious associates were almost trapped. Just one alternative, short of concessions to the miners, remained. The government might still be persuaded to break the strike with federal troops. It was a thin reed, but the New York *Sun* waved it as if it had been a battle standard. "Pennsylvania is in a state of anarchy beyond the power of her entire Guard to control," the *Sun* proclaimed. The public demand for suppression of the Filipino guerillas had been fulfilled. "Why is not the same far-seeing patriotism and resolute loyalty to the flag and to the preservation of the rights it guarantees to its citizens now guiding those concerned with the coal strike, officially or otherwise?"

While the editors of the *Sun* and other conservatives were blasting Roosevelt for his decision to bring the operators and strike leaders together, another conservative was endorsing the President's conduct. "I am especially disturbed and vexed by the tone and substance of the operators' deliverances," Grover Cleveland wrote Roosevelt. Could not the operators and miners be persuaded to make a truce until the country's most pressing needs were fulfilled? Cleveland's proposal was even more impractical than the one Roosevelt had pressed upon Mitchell after the failure of the conference; yet it assured the President of Cleveland's good will.

Impressed by the failure of the strikers to return to work under the protection of the Pennsylvania troops, and emboldened by the moral support of the nation's most eminent living conservative, Roosevelt now evolved a plan as drastic as any he ever formulated. Unless conditions soon changed for the better, he would send federal troops into the anthracite fields to seize the mines and run them as a receivership.

The President had not come lightly to this momentous decision. "You were no alarmist," he wrote Murray Crane shortly afterward, "and when you saw the coal famine impending, with untold misery as the result, with the certainty of riots which might develop into social war to follow, I did not feel like longer delaying."

> The position of the operators, that the public had no rights in the case, was not tenable for a moment, and what most astounded me therein was their . . . ignorance of the fact that their violence and unreason and their inability or refusal to consider the terrible nature of the catastrophe impending over the poor were all combin-

ing to produce a most dangerous feeling in the country at large—a feeling which might have effect in great social disturbance. . . . Even without such a crisis the first long-continued spell of bitter weather meant misery and violence in acute form in our big cities.

Having made his decision, Roosevelt apparently called in Knox and Root. "I explained that I knew this action would form an evil precedent . . . and that they should both write letters of protest against it if they wished." Reportedly, Knox challenged the President's authority to act in the manner he proposed, but then submitted. ("Ah, Mr. President," Knox is supposed to have remarked when Roosevelt sought his advice on a subsequent occasion, "why have such a beautiful action marred by any taint of legality?") Root seems reluctantly to have acquiesced, partly, he later contended, because he was not sure the President would act. "Theodore was a bit of a bluffer occasionally," he recalled, "and at the same time he had nerve to go on—to take a chance his statements would have the deciding effect and, if not, to go on and trust the country would back him up."

Actually, Roosevelt's rationale was the broad construction principle he had always espoused. Representative James E. Watson recalled raising the issue at the time. " 'But,' I said to [the President] '. . . what about the Constitution of the United States? What about seizing private property for public purposes without due process of law?' I recall very vividly. He stopped suddenly, took hold of my shoulder and turned me about facing him and looked squarely into my eyes as he fairly shouted, 'The Constitution was made for the people and not the people for the Constitution.' "

Like so many other "Roosevelt" stories, Watson's may have been apocryphal. Surely, however, its point was accurate. He could not, the President wrote Murray Crane at the time, act "on the Buchanan principle of striving to find some constitutional reason for inaction." He added in his *Autobiography* that it illustrated what "I have called the Jackson-Lincoln theory of the presidency!"

> —that is, that occasionally great national crises arise which call for immediate and vigorous executive action, and that in such cases it is the duty of the President to act upon the theory that he is the steward of the people, and that the proper attitude for him to take is that he is bound to assume that he has the legal right to do whatever the needs of the people demand, unless the Constitution or the laws explicitly forbid him to do it.

To put through his bold and imaginative plan, the President sought out a general who "possessed the necessary good sense, judgment, and nerve to act." He found him in Major General J. M. Schofield, "a most respectable looking old boy, with side-whiskers and a black skull-cap, without any of the outward aspect of the conventional military dictator." Roosevelt told Schofield that if forced to move it would be only because the crisis was almost as serious as the Civil War. He added that the general was to obey only his orders (the Commander in Chief's) and that if served with a writ he was to send it to the President as had been done under Lincoln. Roosevelt had then given his plan an aura of constitutionality by secretly arranging for Governor Stone of Pennsylvania to request federal troops on signal. He did not, however, take Stone into his confidence; nor did he really delude himself that he was acting on a literal interpretation of the Constitution.* (A half century later Roosevelt's "stewardship" theory was ringingly denounced in the federal courts when a government attorney invoked it in support of President Truman's seizure of the steel industry in 1952. "With all due deference and respect for that great President [Roosevelt] . . . ," declared Judge David A. Pine of the District of Columbia Federal Court, "I am obliged to say that his statements do not comport with our recognized theory of government, but with a theory with which our government of laws and not of men is constantly at war.")

Meanwhile, in a move that subtly testified to the extraordinary power Pierpont Morgan wielded over American life, Root visited the financier in New York. Root had asked for and been granted permission to act as a private citizen. Morgan had no especial sympathy for the miners or their grievances; but he was incensed at the operators for botching their affairs and was fearful that the strike would have serious social consequences. He must also have been agitated by Roosevelt's plan for a government receivership. Accordingly, when Root suggested that the President appoint an independent arbitration commission, Morgan heartily endorsed the idea.

On Sunday, October 12, Morgan pressed Root's proposal on George Baer, who came up from Philadelphia. Then, two days later,

---

* Article IV, *Section* 4 specifies that federal troops may be called out "on application of the legislature, or of the executive (when the legislature cannot be convened) against domestic violence." At the time Roosevelt contemplated action there was no evidence that the state militia was unable to control violence.

Morgan and Robert Bacon speeded to Washington to present the operators' tentative approval to the President. "It was a strange experience for Morgan," Frederick Lewis Allen wrote in his friendly biography of the financier. "Only a few months before he had faced Roosevelt as a man accused of the offense of setting up machinery to bring peace among warring railroad companies; this time he faced him as an ally in setting up machinery to bring peace between railroad companies and organized labor."

There now unfolded a high drama, or, as Roosevelt more fittingly dubbed it, "a ludicrous comedy." The agreement Morgan wrought from the operators provided that the arbitration commission should include "a man who by active participation in mining and selling coal is familiar with the physical and commercial features of the business," but it failed to allow for a labor representative. The mine workers resented the omission; and though they agreed to the general plan, they requested a fairer representation, specifically the addition of a union man and of a Roman Catholic cleric. The operators demurred; nor would they accept former President Cleveland, whom Roosevelt wanted to appoint in place of the army engineer called for in the agreement. An impasse again threatened.

Root resolved it temporarily by telegraphing Morgan, who had returned to New York, to send down a member of his firm for consultation. "That night Bob Bacon and Perkins came on from Morgan, both of them nearly wild," Roosevelt wrote a few days later. "The operators were balking. They refused positively to accept the two extra men, and Morgan said he could not get them to accept. It appeared," the President continued, "that the men who were back of them, who were in the narrow, bourgeois, commercial world, were still in a condition of wooden-headed obstinacy and stupidity."

For two hours the President argued with Morgan's emissaries, who kept an open line to the financier and the uncompromising Baer in New York. The operators were anxious to settle—they had undoubtedly learned that drastic action was in the offing—and they were willing to accept a Catholic prelate, even a liberal one. But they would not agree to the naming of a labor leader, for they continued to regard union recognition as the pre-eminent issue.

Such, then, was the state of affairs when the President suddenly conceived a solution. He would appoint a union man to the sociologist's post, but would call him a sociologist. "I at last grasped the fact," Roosevelt explained to Lodge, "that the mighty brains of these captains of industry had formulated the theory that they would rather have anarchy than tweedledum, but if I would use the word tweedle-dee they would hail it as meaning peace."

With that brilliant stroke, the President cut the Gordian knot. The operators saved face, among themselves if no one else. The miners won a fair representation, Roosevelt naming E. E. Clark, Grand Chief of the Order of Railway Conductors, as the sociologist. And the President avoided an action that was clearly extraconstitutional and probably unconstitutional. The infant discipline of sociology was also given a new distinction. "Sociologist," wrote Roosevelt after Clark's name on the list handed the press, "means a man who has thought and studied deeply on social questions and has practically applied his knowledge."

The miners returned to the pits almost at once, and five months later the arbitration commission submitted a report moderately favorable to the workers. Wages were broadly increased by 10 per cent, and hours were generally reduced to nine, and in a few jobs to eight per day. Many of management's more flagrant abuses were corrected, though the old method of weighing coal continued. And the Anthracite Board of Conciliation was created to settle future differences. The operators won their point on nonrecognition, but only formally, for the representatives of the United Mine Workers were granted a seat on the new Board of Conciliation. The operators were also granted a 10 per cent increase in the price of coal. Peace had come to the anthracite fields.

The passing of a half century has failed to diminish the historical significance of the President's achievement. It is probably true, as his detractors assert, that he was more animated by fear of social up-heaval than genuine sympathy for the mine workers' plight, that his plan to use federal troops reflected an authoritarian disregard of legal restraint, and that Lodge's hysterical pleas for action in the interest of everyday Republican politics probably hastened his decision to act. But it is also true, as the Springfield *Republican* declared at the time, that he had thwarted the operators' drive to crush the United Mine Workers:

> This is the great distinguishing fact of what is to be the memo-rable coal strike of 1902; for while the operators still nominally

refuse to recognize the mine workers' union, that union nevertheless is a party to the President's plan of arbitration and is so recognized by him. What the operators said they never would concede has been conceded, and hence, and hence only, does the strike draw rapidly to an end.

Perhaps labor could have got even more than it did. The impassioned agitator, Mother Jones, thought that it could have; and she so informed John Mitchell. But Samuel Gompers believed otherwise; he congratulated Mitchell on the UMW's "splendid" achievement. Clarence Darrow, who served as counsel to the mine workers, was similarly pleased.

The personal significance of the President's action was not that he ended the strike, though he prided himself that he had. Nor was it in the great service he incidentally rendered the American labor movement, though he also took satisfaction in that. It was, rather, that in both his contemplated use of federal troops and in his actual success in winning an arbitration agreement, he had by his own lights acted in fairness. The precedents were overwhelmingly for government intervention in management's interest. By refusing to follow them, by making the government, as Mowry phrases it, "a third force and partner in major labor disputes," Roosevelt gave meaning to what he was to call his "Square Deal." His comportment in the anthracite strike, coupled with his blows against the trusts, indelibly stamped him within a year of his accession as the first President of the modern era who was not indissolubly wedded to the business point of view.

CHAPTER 11

AFFAIRS OF STATE

> "When I left the presidency, I finished seven and a half years
> of administration, during which not one shot had been fired
> against a foreign foe. We were at absolute peace, and there was
> no nation in the world . . . whom we had wronged, or from
> whom we had anything to fear."
> —Theodore Roosevelt, *An Autobiography*

Of all the functions of executive leadership, none more fascinated
Roosevelt nor more graphically revealed his versatility than the conduct of foreign affairs. He was zestfully absorbed by the responsibilities that were thrust upon him and went out of his way to shoulder
others that were not. He gloried in the unfolding opportunities for
national expression afforded by a world in flux. And he viewed with
impatience and at times forebodings his countrymen's slowness to face
the realities of the world struggle for power. He acted with impetu-
osity and restraint, with bluster and sensitivity, with belligerence and
accommodation. And he acted always to promote the American
national interest as he conceived it. Neither the idealistic peace movement of the Bryans and the Carnegies nor the gathering internationalism of the era diverted him from that course, though he often used
the internationalist vocabulary and eventually supported arbitration
agreements not affecting the nation's vital interests.

During Theodore Roosevelt's presidency the United States established a proprietary interest in Latin America. It self-consciously interjected itself into European power politics. It took an assertive interest
in the Pacific and parts of the Far East. It modernized its army and

expanded its battle fleet. It helped negotiate peace between the Tsar-wearied Russians and the empire-minded Japanese. And it pursued a generally enlightened policy toward its newly acquired colonial dependencies.

Roosevelt was not the sole architect of these momentous policies and events. Some were inherited from the McKinley administration, some were conceived by the President's able subordinates, and many grew logically out of the stresses and strains of the changing world situation. Still others reflected the influence of Admiral Mahan, with whom Roosevelt continued to maintain his stimulating relationship. Yet the controlling hand was Roosevelt's. Concluding that there was no retreat from a world power position that the Spanish-American War had dramatized and accentuated but which the revolution in communications and the rise of America as an industrial power had forged, he stamped his imprint upon American foreign policy with a force exceeded by only a few wartime Presidents and equaled, prob-ably, by no peacetime President. So decisive was the personal equa-tion, in fact, that the unfolding drama of American foreign relations from 1902 through early 1909 is essentially the story of the vigorous interplay of Roosevelt's personality and the surging mainstream of events.

Roosevelt had not been in office two weeks before he interjected himself into the administration of the colonial dependencies. His habit of noblesse oblige, his belief that the United States was obli-gated to impose a better order on the ruins of the one it had destroyed, and his conviction that despotism was the high road to disaster all impelled him to take an active and enlightened interest in the adminis-tration of the empire; and so in no small degree did his urge to spread American culture in the manner of the great nations of the past. As he had explained to Frederic Coudert while still Vice President:

Rome expanded and passed away, but all western Europe, both Americas, Australia and large parts of Asia and Africa to this day continue the history of Rome. . . . Spain expanded and fell, but a whole continent to this day speaks Spanish and is covered with commonwealths of the Spanish tongue and culture. . . . Eng-land expanded and England will fall. But think of what she will leave behind her . . ."

Accepting literally, therefore, Rudyard Kipling's charge to

"Take up the White Man's burden—
Send forth the best ye breed—"

Roosevelt announced in late September, 1901, that "absolutely no appointments in the insular possessions will be dictated or controlled by political considerations" lest the United States tread the path that had led to the decay of Spanish rule. And to that dictum he adhered with slight deviation during the next seven years. At almost the same time he urged, as he had been doing from the time of the great imperialism debate, that the United States make the Filipinos "fit for self-government after the fashion of the really free nations." To this estimable goal he also strove during the whole of his presidency, acting always, however, within the limits prescribed by his conception of America's vital interests.

The administration of the insular empire under Roosevelt was neither without controversy nor frustration. One of the earliest and most revealing incidents involved the President's effort to work out a rational solution to a long quarrel between the Filipinos and the Spanish Dominicans who had acquired tremendous holdings of choice farmlands during the three centuries of Spanish rule. When the Filipino patriots had risen against Spain in 1896, two years before Dewey's victory in Manila Bay, the fiery Emilio Aguinaldo had confiscated the church lands by executive decree; and by the time the Americans encamped on the archipelago the Filipinos were working them as their own.

Shortly before Roosevelt became President, William Howard Taft had proposed that the United States purchase title to the disputed lands and then restore them to the Filipino farmers. But the McKinley administration had shown little desire to press the issue. Late in February, 1902, however, after conferring with Taft, Root, and Archbishop Ireland, Roosevelt decided to send Taft to the Vatican to make the necessary arrangements. Three months later the gargantuan Taft was received with gracious circumspection by the venerable Leo XIII. The Vatican consented to sell the friar's lands, but the negotiations broke down when it refused to withdraw the obnoxious monastic orders as the Filipinos and the American hierarchy, which wanted to send over American priests, desired. Taft reopened the negotiations a year later. "The matter assumed all the aspects of a New England horse trade," Henry Pringle later wrote; and not until November, 1903, when the United States agreed to pay approximately 50 per cent more than the appraised value of the lands and to abandon the demand that the Vatican withdraw the Spanish friars, was it finally settled.

Superficially, the Vatican had won its case. But in reality the Roosevelt administration had won a memorable victory. The Spanish friars failed to regain their power—only two hundred stayed on in the Islands—while the former church lands became the basis of a native yeoman class. By 1912, fifty thousand Filipinos worked small farms which they had purchased on generous terms from the American government.

Ironically, this enlightened diplomacy was bitterly criticized by some American Catholics who refused to credit the charges against the friars and bitterly resented the establishment of a secular school system on the islands. The President refused, however, to yield to their protests. Indeed, he heartily endorsed Taft's effort to create an educational system on the American model and he several times warned that it should be completely nonsectarian. "The teachers must not only be careful to abstain from taking sides for or against Catholicism or any other creed," he warned Taft in July, 1902, "but they must be careful to abstain from action which gives the impression that they are thus taking sides."

To compound the religious problem, an articulate minority of American Catholics tried frenetically to enlist Roosevelt's support in crushing a group of Filipinos who had severed ties with Rome—the Aglipayans. Roosevelt bitterly resented this high-handed proposal, and on June 22, 1904 he wrote Bishop Frederick Z. Rooker of Jaro in the Philippines one of the angriest letters he ever penned to a member of the Roman Catholic hierarchy. He said in part:

> Now, my dear Bishop Rooker, to be frank with you, your letter makes it evident that what you in your heart desire is to take the place of the friars, and have American troops take the place of the Spanish troops in upholding a clerical and political despotism in the islands, without regard to the wishes of the islanders. You say that you wish the civil government to come to an end, the power to be taken out of the hands of the natives, and a military government established under some general like my good friend Wood, with instructions instantly and without regard to law to give you and your colleagues possession of all the churches and other property which the Aglipayans claim. In other words, you desire us to

establish a military despotism in the interests of the Catholic Church. I think you must be singularly ignorant of the temper of the American people if you believe such a proposition feasible.

Meanwhile, the President sought to endow the island dependencies, both in the Caribbean and the Pacific, with modest economic advantages. As John Blum writes, "he defied the sugar lobby, the Democrats, and a considerable fraction of Republicans to obtain for Cuba a tariff advantage essential for the economic stability of the government he had helped to establish there"; and he would have done likewise for the Philippines had the Republican Old Guard permitted him. But it would not. If the President had not known it before, he knew thereafter that no consideration of rational economics, of the general welfare, and assuredly not of the "White Man's burden" could touch the Grand Old Party's most sacred of cows.

Fortunately, other areas of executive action remained open. Both before and after Roosevelt's inauguration in 1905 the economic, political, and social uplifting of the new colonials advanced markedly. Railroads were built, sanitation facilities were introduced, and schools were constructed and staffed by the hundreds. Meanwhile Roosevelt cautiously, yet consistently, urged the colonial administrators to give the islanders greater participation in the conduct of their affairs. "I shall endeavor," he said more than once, "progressively to increase the share which the Filipinos themselves take in the government of the islands, letting the advance in this direction be rapid or slow precisely in accordance with the capacity which the Filipinos themselves develop for self-restraint, moderation, and ability to combine the enjoyment of liberty with the enforcement of order." Failing finally to provide enough self-government to satisfy the anti-imperialists, and giving too much to please the unregenerate Old Guard, he yet managed to turn over to his successor a colonial empire that was the most progressively governed of any in the world.

On one count only, aside from his failure to strike down the tariff barrier and otherwise build up the economy of the archipelago, did Roosevelt's administration of the Philippines fail. He steadfastly refused to make a categorical promise of independence. He feared, for one thing, that Japan or Germany would move in if the United States moved out; he believed, for another, that the Filipinos were not then capable of self-government. In a moving letter in June, 1902, to the high-minded anti-imperialist, Senator Hoar of Massachusetts, he emphasized the latter:

I am encouraging in every way the growth of the conditions which now make for self-government in the Philippines and which, if the Filipino people can take advantage of them, will assuredly put them where some day we shall say that if they desire independence they shall have it. But I cannot be certain when that day will be, and of course there is always the possibility that they may themselves behave in such fashion as to put it off indefinitely. Now I do not want to make a promise which may not be kept. Above all things, I want for myself and for the nation that there shall be good faith. Senator Hoar, I honor you and revere you. I think you are animated by as lofty a spirit of patriotism and of devotion to and belief in mankind as any man I have ever met in public life. I hate to seem in your eyes to be falling short of my duty on a great question. I ask you to believe that after much painful thought, after much groping and some uncertainty as to where my duty lay, I am now doing it as light has been given me to see it.

The President's attitude might have been more favorably reviewed before the bar of history had he always expressed himself on that high plane. But he had not. Critics have never forgotten that during the campaign of 1900 he had called Aguinaldo's beleagured patriots "Talgal bandits," "Chinese halfbreeds," and worse; that he had refused to concede the legitimacy (whatever the practicality) of the native independence movement; and that he had defended the American troops' cruel repression of Aguinaldo.

The organization and administration of the new possessions and the Cuban protectorate had been a collective enterprise. Besides Roosevelt and Taft, the late President McKinley, Elihu Root, Leonard Wood and three physicians—Majors Walter Reed, William C. Gorgas, and Dr. Jesse W. Lazear, had all made contributions which radically affected the character of the American empire.

But it was Roosevelt who was responsible for the more strictly diplomatic accomplishments of his administrations. One of the earliest of these was the settlement of the long-standing Alaskan boundary dispute.

Thirty-seven years before Secretary of State William H. Seward arranged the purchase of Alaska, the British and Russian governments had ratified a treaty which loosely defined the line between British Columbia and the Alaskan Panhandle as running thirty miles inland from the head of tidewater. Following the discovery of gold in the Canadian Klondike in 1896, however, Canadians sought to have the boundary redefined so as to give them access to the gold fields. National passions had momentarily flared as Whitehall found itself caught between the Scylla of American enmity and the Charybdis of Canadian resentment against imperial rule. In October, 1899, however, Secretary of State Hay arranged to give the Canadians temporary control of the area they most desired. This *modus vivendi* was in force when Roosevelt became President.

Roosevelt never had believed that the Canadian claim was valid. "If we suddenly claimed a part of Nova Scotia you would not arbitrate," he wrote Sir Arthur Lee while he was still Vice-President. "This Canadian claim . . . is entirely modern. Twenty years ago the Canadian maps showed the lines just as ours did." For several months after he took the presidential oath, however, Roosevelt was content to "let sleeping dogs lie." Not until March, 1902, when he learned that gold might be discovered in the disputed territory, did he act. Then, in a first display of "Big Stick" diplomacy, he brought the full force of his powerful personality to bear upon the British and Canadians. If gold is discovered, the President pointedly told a London *Times* correspondent in a White House interview, "I shall send up engineers to run our line as we assert it and I shall send troops to guard and hold it." A few weeks later, after discussing the matter with Lodge, he ordered Root to move "additional troops . . . as quietly and unostentatiously as possible to Southern Alaska, so as to be able promptly to prevent any possible disturbance." Then, as Howard K. Beale points out, he and other Americans repeatedly "made it clear to the British Government that America would never yield."

In order, so he admitted, "to save his face," Sir Wilfrid Laurier, the Canadian Prime Minister, finally suggested the creation of an arbitration commission. Roosevelt was at first unsympathetic to Laurier's proposal, for he was absolutely convinced of the righteousness of the American case. Only after he realized that the presence of three Americans on the proposed six man commission portended no worse than a deadlock did he consent; and even then he took pains to let it out that he would instruct the American commissions "in no case to yield any of our claim." As he informed Hay, who was probably the decisive factor in his decision to agree to a form of arbitration, "The fact that they have set up an outrageous and indefensible claim and in consequence are likely to be in hot water with their constituents when they back down, does not seem to me to give us any excuse for paying them money or territory. To pay them anything where they are entitled to nothing would . . . come dangerously near blackmail."

During the summer and fall of 1902 negotiations continued, though the President diverted much of his energy to the settlement of the anthracite strike and the Panama Canal controversy with Colombia. Finally, in January, 1903, Hay and Sir Michael Herbert, the British Ambassador, signed a treaty providing for an arbitration tribunal of six "impartial jurists of repute" who would "consider judicially the question submitted to them." Three were to be selected by the President of the United States; three by His Britannic Majesty.

The treaty received a rough reception in the Senate, so firm was the conviction that Canada was completely in the wrong. At one point the President was forced to withdraw it temporarily in order to make its wording more palatable, and for a while it was doubtful that the Senate would ratify it under any circumstances. Finally, however, after two members of the Supreme Court refused to serve on the proposed commission, Roosevelt confided to Lodge that he would appoint Root, Senator George Turner of Washington, and Lodge himself if the Senate approved the treaty. Lodge thereupon whispered the President's intentions about the Senate chamber, and opposition vanished.

The formal announcement of the President's appointments provoked a resoundingly hostile reaction. "All my illusions are gone," Sir Michael Herbert exclaimed. Roosevelt "is obstinate and unreasonable." Laurier was no less outraged; he even talked of breaking off further negotiations. Nor did the American press spare the President. "President Roosevelt ought not to appoint . . . [Lodge] to the place," the Springfield *Republican* declared. "[Lodge] has been playing for years to the gallery where the England-haters sit," the Hartford *Courant* added, "and to the determination of this boundary question he does not bring the judicial mind." (The Senator confirmed those judgments by delivering a violently anti-Canadian speech in Boston shortly after his appointment was announced.)

The President must have known that his nonjudicial appointments would evoke a thunderous protest. Neither in his correspondence nor in his *Autobiography,* however, does he offer an explanation. The most plausible theory, and the one Beale advances, is that Lodge convinced Roosevelt that his own and Turner's appointments were necessary to see the treaty through the Senate. Certainly the opposition in that body had collapsed like an accordion when word that Roosevelt would appoint Lodge and Turner was passed about the Senate cloakroom.

Roosevelt did not regard his selections as a breach of faith. Notwithstanding the judicial phraseology of the treaty, he had consistently made clear his determination to secure a decision favorable to the United States. Even after the commissioners had been selected, he continued to press the validity of the American case on the British Foreign Office. Lord Alverstone, the British appointee, was wined, dined, and politely badgered. And when Justice Holmes went to England for a vacation that summer, he carried with him a letter from the President revealing his intense belief in the righteousness of the American cause. For a time, also, Roosevelt considered terminating negotiations under Lodge's insistent urgings. Taking counsel from Hay and Ambassador Choate, however, he finally repudiated that unseemly suggestion. The Alaskan controversy is "altogether too important a matter to take a snap judgment or to forfeit a single chance of bringing it to a successful conclusion," Roosevelt cabled Lodge. "There is not at present one single act which would justify so much as considering the breaking off of the negotiations."

Nevertheless, Roosevelt refused to relax his resolve to run the boundary line with American troops should a settlement fail. In this he was supported by Hay, Choate, and Root, all of whom were conservative by temperament, and two of whom, Hay and Choate, were extraordinarily cordial toward the British. Indeed, this threat may have been responsible for Lord Alverstone's support of the burden of the United States' demands, for it served as mute testimony of the depth of American feelings. Thus, Beale concludes, "The plan to use troops resulted not just from the desire of an impetuous President to bully or to have his own way; it grew in part at least out of a calm decision of cautious advisers, who feared growing frontier tension created by a lawless population might blow up into a dangerous international incident if uncontrolled."

The Alaskan boundary dispute was neither the first nor the last time Roosevelt "spoke softly" and waved a "big stick" behind the scenes to impress upon the world powers the righteousness, or dominance, of American claims. During the winter of 1902–03 he had pressed Kaiser Wilhelm II's Imperial Germany hard; and in 1904 he waved his "stick" clear around as he openly informed all Europe that the United States was assuming the time-worn custom of policing the financial affairs of the more impecunious Latin American nations.

The origins of the Venezuelan crisis and the Roosevelt Corollary to the Monroe Doctrine were deep-rooted and tangled. Both grew out of the perennial instability of Latin American governments. Both revealed Roosevelt's growing concern for the United States' strategic interests in the Caribbean. And both reflected America's new power position vis-à-vis Europe. Of the two, the Venezuelan affair was the more immediately serious; the announcement of the Roosevelt Corollary the more far-reaching. Out of the one grew the other.

The Venezuelan crisis had come to a head in early December, 1902, when Germany and Great Britain, despairing of diplomatic efforts to collect debts due their nationals, attempted to coerce the Venezuelan government by blockading that nation's coastline and seizing or sinking such gunboats as comprised its navy. The American government had first learned of German intentions to move against Venezuela in December, 1901. Hay seemingly acquiesced in the German design, warning only that the United States would tolerate no territorial aggrandizement; but the administration was in fact gravely alarmed. On December 17 Roosevelt ordered Culebra, off Puerto Rico, to be transferred to the Navy Department in order that a base might be established "in case of sudden war." Further precautionary measures followed. Arrangements were made to mobilize the fleet in the Caribbean at the end of the year, and in the early summer the General Board of the Navy ordered "a careful reconnaissance of the terrain most likely to be occupied by German forces as well as a detailed examination of all localities where landing operations might be affected." These moves were climaxed by the appointment of Admiral Dewey to the command of the Caribbean fleet, an unprecedented assignment for a four-star admiral.

On December 8, 1902, the day the hero of Manila Bay raised his flag on the gunboat *Mayflower,* Germany and Great Britain severed relations with Venezuela. Within a fortnight they seized several Venezuelan naval vessels, bombarded two forts at Puerto Cabello, and established a formal blockade of the Venezuelan coast. Roosevelt responded by confirming existing orders to move the battle fleet to Trinidad, five hundred miles closer to Venezuela, and by apparently talking pointedly to the German ambassador.

Results were soon forthcoming. The day the order to move the fleet was announced, the German chargé d'affaires hustled over to the State Department where Hay raised the specter of a congressional resolution calling on the President to act to uphold the Monroe Doctrine. Meanwhile, Ambassador Theodor von Holleben sent two urgent warnings to Berlin. By then, it appears, the self-centered Wilhelm II had begun to realize that he could not capitalize indefinitely on the good will created by his younger brother's recent visit to the United States, and on December 10 Speck von Sternburg, an old friend of the President's, who had talked with Roosevelt earlier that fall, was called to Berlin to give his impressions to high German officials. He stunned them, if the account he wrote Roosevelt is correct. "Nothing could have pleased me more," he confided to the President, "because it gave me a chance to tell them the truth. I've told them every bit of it and I have used rather plain talk. . . . Fear I've knocked them down rather roughly, but should consider myself a cowardly weakling if I had let things stand as they were." Against this background Germany agreed to arbitration; it also decided to replace Ambassador von Holleben with von Sternburg, a change Roosevelt had long urged.

The Venezuelan affair was a watershed in the President's thinking on the Monroe Doctrine. At the start of the crisis he had believed that European intervention in Latin American affairs was tolerable if it did not lead to territorial aggrandizement. By its end, however, he had begun to see the potentialities of such a policy; and less than a month afterward he had taken the first tentative step toward formulation of the "Roosevelt Corollary" to the Monroe Doctrine. The catalytic agent was a talk with von Sternburg in mid-March. Thus Roosevelt wrote Hay in confidence: "Speck was in today, evidently inspired from Berlin, to propose for our consideration in the future the advisability of having the great Powers collectively stand back of some syndicate which should take possession of the finances of Venezuela."

The German proposal had an abstract appeal, for there was no assurance that the Venezuelan dictator, Castro, who clung to his shaken authority, had reformed permanently. Nor was there any guarantee that similar crises would not occur in any of a dozen or more Latin American nations. Yet the plan implied compromise of the substance, if not the form, of the Monroe Doctrine; and Roosevelt was quick to sense it. His "first blush" judgment, he told the new German Ambassador, was that it "would pave the way for reducing Venezuela to a condition like that of Europe, and that the American people interpreted the Monroe Doctrine as meaning of course that no European power should gain *control* of any American republic." The whole debt-collection process, he realistically observed to Hay, could prove a "subterfuge" for exercising control.

It was conditions in debt-ridden and revolution-wracked Santo Domingo that finally impelled Roosevelt to decisive action. The affairs of that island republic differed from those of a number of other Latin American nations only in their particulars; and in July, 1903, four months after the Venezuelan crisis had ended, the German, Italian, and Spanish governments had forced the Dominican authorities to sign protocols for the payment of monthly installments on the debts owed their nationals. Thereafter matters had moved from bad to worse. Finally, in January, 1904, the harried Dominican Minister of Foreign Affairs made a special trip to Washington to prevail upon the American government, in Roosevelt's words, "to establish some kind of protectorate over the islands, and take charge of their finances."

The President would have preferred to avoid involvement completely—he had, he said at the time, "about the same desire to annex it as a gorged boa constrictor might have to swallow a porcupine wrong-end-to"—but he agreed to send down an informal mission. Then, on February 1, insurrectionists fired on an American cruiser, the *Yankee,* and a few days later new disturbances occurred. American plantation owners and investors now implored the government to act, and on February 5 Roosevelt cabled Rear Admiral Wise to take "immediate steps for protection of United States citizens and property." Two weeks later he directed Admiral Dewey to go to Santo Domingo and give him "a full, impartial searching account of the situation as it now presents itself to your eyes." He was still reluctant, however, to undertake a major intervention. "I hope it will be a good while before I have to go further," he wrote Ted, who was then an undergraduate at Harvard. "But sooner or later it seems to me inevitable that the United States should assume an attitude of protection and regulation in regard to all these little states in the neighborhood of the Caribbean."

Fearful of another ugly crisis like that over Venezuela and predisposed in any event to resolve the larger problem, Roosevelt took a decisive step: On May 20, in a letter to Root which the latter read at a Cuban anniversary dinner in New York, the President set forth the principles of what became known as the Roosevelt Corollary to the Monroe Doctrine. "If a nation shows that it knows how to act with decency in industrial and political matters, if it keeps order and pays its obligations, then it need fear no interference from the United States," he wrote in part. "Brutal wrongdoing, or an impotence which results in a general loosening of the ties of civilizing society, may finally require intervention by some civilized nation; and in the Western Hemisphere the United States cannot ignore this duty."

A violent, and mixed, reaction ensued; and though Roosevelt professed to be "amused at the yell," he was actually irritated at his critics' refusal to face reality. It was "the simplest common sense, and only the fool or the coward can treat it as aught else," he angrily charged. "If we are willing to let Germany or England act as the policemen of the Caribbean, then we can afford not to interfere when gross wrong-doing occurs. But if we intend to say 'Hands off' to the powers of Europe, sooner or later we must keep order ourselves."

Roosevelt never backed down from that position. Emphasizing in his annual message six months later that the United States entertained neither "land hunger" nor other ulterior ambitions toward the "other nations of the western hemisphere save such as are for their welfare," he underlined his profound reluctance at having to undertake the policeman's role. "We have plenty of sins of our own to war against," the President observed, "and under ordinary circumstances we can do more for the general uplifting of humanity by striving with heart and soul to put a stop to civic corruption, to brutal lawlessness, and violent race prejudices here at home than by passing resolutions about wrong-doing elsewhere."

The ink was barely dry on Roosevelt's "Corollary" message to Congress before he found it necessary to act under its terms. During the summer and autumn of 1904 conditions in Santo Domingo had steadily deteriorated. The national debt had soared to $32,000,000 and was still rising. One of the main customs houses had been turned over to an agent of a New York corporation which claimed an unpaid debt of $4,500,000. The Italians, French, and Belgians were angrily protesting that Santo Domingo was violating the protocols of 1905. And the Morales administration was suffering attack from within. It was Venezuela all over again, or so it seemed; and Roosevelt and Hay were determined to prevent a repetition of the final chapter. On December 30, accordingly, the Secretary of State directed the American minister to Santo Domingo to ascertain "discreetly but earnestly" whether President Morales "would be disposed to request the United States to take charge of the collection of duties." Morales proved amenable, and on February 7, 1905, a protocol providing for American control of the republic's customs houses was finally arranged. One of the stormiest and most prolonged controversies of Roosevelt's presidential career followed.

From the start, many senators had viewed the President's proceedings with grave misgivings. Led by Roosevelt's standing enemies, Senators John Morgan of Alabama and Augustus O. Bacon of Georgia, but including a handful of Republican anti-imperialists as well, they charged that the protocol would lead to an American protectorate over the island republic and they accordingly refused to vote approval when the President submitted it for ratification on February 15. While Roosevelt fumed—"Bacon is a man of meticulous mind, a violent partisan, with no real public spirit"—and conditions in Santo Domingo daily grew more precarious, the Senate sat tight. Both the regular and special sessions of Congress expired without the protocol coming to a vote on the floor, although the Foreign Relations Committee finally reported it favorably.

Whether the President would have allowed matters to drift until Congress met in December, had affairs not taken a turn for the worse, is conjectural. Possibly he would have. On March 14, however, an Italian cruiser appeared off the coast of Santo Domingo, while at almost the same time the French and Belgians renewed pressure for payment of their debts. The crisis Roosevelt had urgently sought to avert was thus upon him. Either the United States moved in, or the three European nations took action on their own. Even Senator Morgan recognized that something had to be done. And to the

President's unmitigated disgust, the Alabama legislator proposed that the great powers be encouraged to act in concert—the very action that Roosevelt's diplomacy, which was predicated on opposition to the spread of European influence in Latin America, was designed to forestall.

The President held off for a few more days in the hope that the crisis would fail to jell. On March 28, however, the American minister cabled that the Dominican government was in "domestic peril," that a *modus vivendi* was "absolutely necessary," and that the European powers awaited an American decision to appoint a collector of customs. Roosevelt thereupon turned to individual senators for advice. He first called in the Republicans, Spooner, Foraker, Lodge, and Knox, to discuss the situation with him and Taft, who had replaced Root as Secretary of War. All "heartily" agreed that he should take over the Dominican customs as President Morales wanted, Minister Dawson recommended, and the European nations approved; and all submitted to Taft's genial chaffing for their surrender to "usurption of the executive." The President then consulted with the Democratic minority leader, Senator Arthur Pue Gorman of Maryland, an old foe. Gorman also agreed that the President should appoint a customs collector in spite of the Senate's earlier failure to ratify the protocol. Thus fortified by the support of the leaders of both parties, Roosevelt directed Acting Secretary of State Alvey A. Adee to make the necessary arrangements for the collectorship.

An American was appointed general receiver and collector of Santo Domingo's customs in due course, and for some years thereafter the islanders enjoyed such a financial stability as they had never before experienced. Roads were built, schools established, and a revenue service created. The foreign debt was drastically scaled down, and the Dominican share of customs collections soared beyond all previous totals. Moreover, the threat of European intervention was dissipated. On the other hand, as Mowry points out, the seeds of the later "Dollar Diplomacy" were sown when it was proposed in 1906 that the European-held debt be taken over by a private American bank.

The success of the experiment in Santo Domingo failed to cool the tempers of the anti-Roosevelt forces in the United States Senate. So sustained was their resentment of the President that when the protocol again came to a vote in 1906 it failed for a second time to win the necessary two-thirds majority. Not until February, 1907, was the arrangement formalized; and then it was Root's conciliatory influence that carried the day. The whole affair was unfortunate. The measured, reluctant, and extraconstitutional action of a responsible chief executive, it gave superficial credence to the charges that he aspired to powers that were not lawfully his. It enlarged the partial truth that his diplomacy possessed the sensitivity of a blunderbuss. And it deepened Latin American hostility toward the powerful neighbor to the north.

The Santo Dominican incident sharply points up both the strength and weakness of Roosevelt's Latin American diplomacy. The President's intervention broke the crisis, gave relief to the Santo Dominicans, and made the eighty-three-year-old Monroe Doctrine a viable instrument of national policy. By using the crisis to enunciate the general principle of American obligation to intervene in future crises —the so-called "Roosevelt Corollary"—however, Roosevelt incited resentment throughout Latin America and cost the United States the good will of European idealists. Furthermore, as Dexter Perkins and other scholars have pointed out, the public declaration was largely unnecessary. When President Monroe pronounced his memorable doctrine in 1823 the United States was a third-class power dependent upon moral suasion and the British Royal Navy; when President Roosevelt elaborated his corollary in 1904 the United States was a first-class power, one that had already brought Imperial Germany to bay by a display of strength and determination. Had the President stood on his own maxim—"actions speak louder than words"—and confined his intention to prevent further European intervention to diplomats alone, he might have served his country's purposes more fully. But by speaking out publicly, he converted a triumph of action into a near tragedy of words.

CHAPTER 12

NOBLE ENDS AND LESS NOBLE MEANS

> By far the most important action I took in foreign affairs
> . . . related to the Panama Canal. Here again there was much
> accusation about my having acted in an "unconstitutional"
> manner— . . . and at different stages of the affair believers in a
> do-nothing policy denounced me as having "usurped authority"—
> which meant, that when nobody else could or would exercise
> efficient authority, I exercised it.
> —Theodore Roosevelt, *An Autobiography*

From that September day in 1513 when Vasco Núñez de Balboa first gazed upon the placid blue waters that led to the fabled East, men of imagination had dreamed of linking the Atlantic and the Pacific Oceans with a canal across the Central American isthmus. For four centuries, however, their vision had been thwarted by the formidable engineering obstacles that weighed upon it. Not even the genius of Ferdinand De Lesseps had been able to give it substance; and only after Theodore Roosevelt marshaled the political, financial, and scientific resources of the United States behind it in a sustained assertion of power was it finally realized.

A half century before Roosevelt became President the United States and Great Britain had agreed through the Clayton-Bulwer Treaty of 1850 to facilitate construction of an unfortified canal open to the commerce of all nations in times of war as well as of peace. As the United States grew mighty in the aftermath of the Civil War, however, the treaty was persistently denounced by American nationalists; and when the battleship *Oregon* was forced to steam around

South America to reinforce the fleet off Cuba in 1898, demands for repudiation of the treaty and for construction of an American-owned and fortified canal reached a crescendo. The result was the drawing up of a new treaty early in 1900—the First Hay-Pauncefote Treaty. Under its terms the United States was authorized to construct and administer the proposed canal, but not to fortify it or close it in time of war. This arrangement was poorly calculated to appease a body politic already pressing for unilateral action. And though it was received with moderate favor in conservative circles, it met a thunderous opposition by the jingo press, partisan Democrats, Irish-Americans and German-Americans, and professional twisters of the British lion's tail. It also incited the measured and articulate opposition of Theodore Roosevelt, who was then governor of New York.

Roosevelt was hesitant to offend his old friend, Secretary of State John Hay. At the urging of friends in New York, however, he reluctantly came out against the treaty in February, 1900. "I most earnestly hope that the pending treaty . . . will not be satisfied unless amended so as to provide that the canal, when built, shall be wholly under the control of the United States, alike in peace and war," he declared in a public statement. "This seems to me vital, from the standpoint of our seapower, no less than from the standpoint of the Monroe Doctrine."

Hay was hurt and irritated by Roosevelt's statement, for he believed that defeat of the treaty would prove a heavy blow to the Anglo-American entente he was then cultivating. "Cannot you leave a few things to the President and the Senate who are charged with them by the Constitution?" he angrily wrote the Governor. "Do you really think the Clayton-Bulwer Treaty preferable to the one now before the Senate? There is no third issue, except dishonor."

Roosevelt's reply had been tender yet firm. "I hesitated long before I said anything about the treaty through sheer dread of two moments —that in which I should receive your note, and that in which I should receive Cabot's," he wrote. "You have been the greatest Secretary of State I have seen in my time, but at this moment I can not, try as I may, see that you are right." He then argued that a canal constructed under the treaty terms would be a military liability on the grounds that the fleet would be tied up in its defense. He also contended that it would vitiate the Monroe Doctrine:

If we invite foreign powers to a joint ownership, a joint guarantee, of what so vitally concerns us but a little way from our
borders, how can we possibly object to similar joint action say in
Southern Brazil, or Argentina, where our interests are so much less
evident? If Germany has the same right we have in the canal across
Central America, why not in the partition of any part of Southern
America? To my mind, we should consistently refuse to all European powers the right to control, in any shape, any territory in the
Western Hemisphere which they do not already hold.

Meanwhile Lodge, who was then emerging as the most powerful
member of the Foreign Relations Committee, supported amendments
which reserved the right of fortification to the United States and
excised an article inviting interested powers to concur in the treaty.
As thus altered the First Hay-Pauncefote Treaty was approved by the
Senate on December 20, 1900. "Now the onus is on England," the
Massachusetts Senator triumphantly wrote in his personal journal.
"If she accepts well. If she, out of infinite stupidity, refuses, then we
can honorably go on, & abrogate the treaty and build the canal." The
way was now opened for Theodore Roosevelt to fulfill the dream of
four centuries. For although Great Britain rejected the amended
treaty, she eventually ratified a second treaty virtually incorporating
the Senate amendments.

Except for his public statement in February, Roosevelt had taken
no part in the proceedings. When he became President in September,
1901, however, the Second Hay-Pauncefote Treaty had not yet been
laid before the Senate. He accordingly urged its ratification in his first
annual message on December 3, and thirteen days later the Senate
so acted. The United States had only to choose a route and start construction, or so it appeared.

Before a route was selected and work on the canal begun, however,
the Roosevelt administration became involved in such a stage play of
high and low comedy as the American people had seldom before
witnessed. When the curtain crashed down at the end the pockets of
a mésalliance of American, Colombian, and French adventurers were
filled to overflowing, Ferdinand De Lesseps's vivid imagination and
bold daring were vindicated, and the United States was endowed with
a legacy of ill-will which the Good Neighbor policies of later Presidents to this day have failed to dissipate entirely. In addition, Roosevelt's desire for achievement was gratified, his engineering judgment

affirmed, and the strategic interests of the United States well served.

The bizarre events preceding the final curtain call have been many times related, often with a fine sense of drama, occasionally with an informed appreciation of their complexity, and almost always with an anti-Roosevelt bias. Biographical unity requires that they be retold once more.

When Ferdinand De Lesseps's grandiose project collapsed in 1889 with a boom that reverberated around the world, American interest in an isthmian canal shifted to Nicaragua where engineering difficulties seemed less imposing and the political climate more favorable. In 1899 a commission headed by Rear Admiral John G. Walker recommended in a preliminary report based largely on administrative considerations that the Nicaraguan route be used. This recommendation had been well received in the Senate; but it failed to win support in the House, which demanded that a new commission be formed to explore all possible routes. Nor did the Walker Commission's preliminary report evoke favorable response in scientific circles. By the late 1890's a growing body of technical opinion favored resumption of work on De Lesseps's uncompleted project, partly on the grounds that the increasing size of ocean-going ships would soon make a Nicaraguan canal obsolete because of its dependence on narrow and shallow rivers. As the Philadelphia *Times* observed:

> The preference for the Nicaraguan route is determined by other than purely scientific considerations, and it leaves a doubt in the unprejudiced mind whether the commerce of the world might not be better served, after all, by encouraging the completion of the Panama canal than by undertaking a competitive canal by a less advantageous route.

Over these measured objections, the Nicaraguan route might still have been selected had it not been for the sensational lobbying campaign waged by the De Lesseps company's receivers. Organized as the New Panama (Canal) Company, they conspired to influence a decision favorable to Panama and to unload their franchise on the American government for the princely sum of $109 million. To these ends an enterprising New York attorney, William N. Cromwell, was retained to press the company's case in high places. A $60,000 contribution was made to the Republican campaign fund in 1900.

And a comic-opera revolution was instigated in the long restive state of Panama.

The manipulations of Cromwell and his unfriendly ally, a flamboyantly imaginative Frenchman named Philippe Jean Bunau-Varilla, defy complete reconstruction. It is clear, however, that Cromwell was responsible in some part for the omission in the Republican platform of 1900 of a preferential statement for the Nicaraguan route; that he was responsible in large part for Mark Hanna's decision to carry the fight for a Panamanian route to the floor of the Senate; and that he probably reinforced Roosevelt's interest in the Panamanian route. It is similarly clear that the versatile Bunau-Varilla capitalized on every opportunity, the most notable a gift from nature, to win his case. Thus when Mt. Momotombo in Nicaragua spewed forth a molten stream of lava just as debate on Senator Spooner's bill for the Panama route was coming to a head in June, 1902, Bunau-Varilla hastily purchased ninety Nicaraguan stamps portraying the majestic mountain and a great cloud of smoke at its summit. These he had placed on each Senator's desk accompanied by an appropriate inscription: "An official witness of the volcanic activity of Nicaragua." Three days after that byplay, the Panama faction won a key test by a 42-to-34 vote.

In consequence of these happenings, a wrong inference about the administration's decision to choose the Panama route has often been drawn. It is undeniable that Cromwell exerted a powerful influence on Hanna, Hay, and the President. Again and again they reflected his point of view, and in the end they accepted a settlement consonant with his recommendations. Yet there is not a scrap of evidence to indicate that they were animated by ulterior considerations, as Cromwell assuredly was. Even more in 1902 than in 1900, the overwhelming burden of engineering opinion, including that of the Walker Commission, was for the Panama route; and as the editors of Roosevelt's *Letters* emphasize in a suggestive note, the President was fully informed of and in agreement with that opinion.

If the President's decision to press the Panama route on Congress was measured and responsible, his negotiations with Colombia for permission to construct the canal through the isthmus is one of the ineradicable blots on his record. It is the measure of his arrogance toward smaller and less highly developed states, in fact, that in selecting the Panama route he seems not even to have considered treating

Colombia as a truly sovereign power. As he wrote Hay in the summer of 1902 when apprised that preliminary negotiations were proceeding unsatisfactorily, "I think they [the Colombians] would change their constitution if we offered enough."

To be sure, there were extenuating circumstances. The most important of these grew out of the unsettled state of affairs in Colombia, where the harassed and high-minded dictator, José Manuel Marroquín, sat veritably on another volcano—one compounded of greed, nationalism, and political intrigue. Unfortunately for Roosevelt and his country, it also erupted.

Colombia had been on the threshold of revolution since 1899, and in the fall of 1902 fighting actually broke out. By November the Colombian minister to the United States had been discredited by his own government's minister of foreign affairs. Meanwhile Secretary of State Hay, who was to prove as impervious of Colombian sensibilities as he had been deferential to those of the British, wrung an agreement satisfactory to American interests from the new Colombian minister, one Dr. Tomás Herrán. On January 22 that harried gentleman and the overbearing American Secretary of State affixed their signatures to the Hay-Herrán Treaty, and a little less than two months later the United States Senate ratified it by a vote of 73 to 5.

Three days after Dr. Herrán signed the treaty he had received a cable from Bogotá instructing him to withhold his signature. The proposed arrangements were substantially unsatisfactory to the Colombian government, the Colombian senate, and the Colombian people. The treaty provided for the payment of $40 million to the New Panama Canal Company and but $10 million plus $250,000 a year to the Colombian government. It granted the United States perpetual control of a five-kilometers-wide zone across the isthmus. And it provided for the establishment of a system of mixed courts that would further have compromised Colombia's sovereignty. So vehement was the reaction against these arrangements that Marroquín, whose dictatorship was neither as total nor as stable as Washington assumed, refused to identify himself with the treaty; he forwarded it to the Colombian senate without his signature or an affirmative recommendation.

Roosevelt and Hay were infuriated by Colombia's reaction. Had not the Colombian government initiated talks in December, 1900, out of fear that the United States would choose the Nicaraguan route?

Why should it now oppose terms which were absolutely necessary to American construction and operation of the canal?—terms which Colombia's own accredited envoy had approved.

The fault was partly Herrán's. He had made no effort to withdraw his signature upon receipt of his belated instructions; nor had he informed Hay of their import. Furthermore, American intelligence was poor and misleading. The American minister to Colombia, Charles B. Hart, failed to report accurately the gathering opposition at Bogotá. And neither he nor his successor, Arthur M. Beaupré, ever fully informed the administration of the importance high principled Colombians attached to the sovereignty features of the treaty. Dismissing such protests as "unimportant and largely hypocritical," Beaupré gave Hay and Roosevelt the impression that the Colombian government placed gold above honor, as in actual fact, many, though by no means all, Colombian officials did.

There was no possibility that the United States would modify its demands for control over the projected canal zone, given the dictates of military security. Even President Marroquín recognized this. "I find myself in a horrible perplexity," he pathetically wrote one of his generals, ". . . in order that the North Americans may complete the work by virtue of a convention with the Government of Colombia, it is necessary to make concessions of territory, of sovereignty and of jurisdiction, which the Executive Power has not the power of yielding; and if we do not yield them . . . we will lose more sovereignty than we should lose by making the concessions they seek." "History will say of me," the distraught dictator continued, "that I ruined the Isthmus and all Colombia, by not permitting the opening of the Panama Canal, or that I permitted it to be done, scandalously injuring the rights of my country."

Other Colombian leaders also recognized their government's dilemma; and in a desperate effort to salvage something, they sought to place what amounted to a lien on the $40 million the United States was prepared to pay the New Panama Canal Company. Whether Colombia would have then ratified the treaty is a moot question; but there is no doubt that American acquiescence would have dispelled the shadowy charges of collusion to which Cromwell's backstage maneuvering later gave birth.

Cromwell's main design was to protect the impending $40 million settlement. Arguing that it would be immoral for the United States to accept an amendment that would allow the Colombian government to expropriate any of the $40 million slated for the New Panama Canal Company, he persuaded Hay to send the American minister in Bogotá a long memorandum that in effect committed the United States "to the complete support of the New Company's financial interests." This was a staggering diplomatic blunder. Nothing short of an ulti-matum to sign or submit to force could have had a more deleterious impact on the treaty's prospects; and if any single action constituted its death blow, it was that note, a copy of which was sent to the New Panama Canal Company's office in Paris.

In reality, no single action was responsible. President Marroquín had long known that his political opposition was determined to pre-vent final disposition of the question while he was in office regardless of the terms. And Hay's blunders—the note of April 28 was but one of several—served more to accentuate than to cause the Colombian's determination to reject the Hay-Herrán Treaty.

When, therefore, the Colombian senate decisively rejected the Hay-Herrán Treaty on August 12, 1903, Roosevelt vented his indignation. The "Dagos" had acted "exactly as if a road agent had tried to hold up a man," he privately wrote. "They are mad to get hold of the $40,000,000 of the Frenchmen." "I do not think that the Bogota lot of jack rabbits should be allowed permanently to bar one of the future highways of civilization."

Unwisely influenced by Cromwell, misinformed by diplomatic dis-patches from Bogotá, and victimized by Hay's obtuseness, Roosevelt's reaction was understandable, if not excusable. He backtracked just a little in his autobiographical account of the episode:

> I am well aware that the Colombian people have many fine traits; that there is among them a circle of high-bred men and women which would reflect honor on the social life of any country; and that there has been an intellectual and literary development within this small circle which partially atones for the stagnation and illiteracy of the mass of the people; and I also know that even the illiterate mass possesses many sterling qualities. But unfortunately in international matters every nation must be judged by the action of its government. The good people in Colombia apparently made no effort, certainly no successful effort, to cause the government to act with reasonable good faith toward the United States; and Colombia had to take the consequences.

Meanwhile, Roosevelt pondered a course of action. The United States could seize Panama under the so-called right of "international domain," as a militant minority of newspapers were demanding. It could construct the canal under an attenuated interpretation of an 1846 "right of transit" treaty as Professor John Bassett Moore, of Columbia University, was urging. It could support a revolution in Panama, which had revolted against Colombia (New Granada) many times in the past, and where discontent was again rife. Or it could return to the Nicaraguan route as many Southern Democrats were suggesting. In any case, the decision was Roosevelt's to make.

By the time the President made his decision he had also emerged as his own Secretary of State. He never doubted that the canal would be constructed, and he doubted very little that it would be routed through Panama. As he wrote Hay at the time, "the great bulk of the best engineers are agreed that that route is best . . . [and] what we do now will be of consequence, not merely decades, but centuries hence, and we must be sure we are taking the right step before we act."

The "right step" was a hard one to choose. Roosevelt's first inclination was to act on the basis of Professor Moore's sophistic report. "If under the treaty of 1846 we have a color of right to start in and build the canal," he wrote Hay after reading Moore's memorandum at Sagamore Hill, "my offhand judgment would favor such proceeding." By early autumn Roosevelt had prepared a rough draft of a message to Congress requesting authority to proceed independently of Colombia on the grounds that it was "out of the question to submit to extortion." The interests of the United States and of world commerce demanded "that the canal should be begun with no needless delay," the proposed message stated. It added that the "testimony of the experts is very strong, not only that the Panama route is feasible, but that in the Nicaraguan route we may encounter some unpleasant surprises."

In the meantime the President had rejected suggestions that the United States foment a revolt by the Panamanians, or that he make a militant public statement. TR unburdened himself on October 10 to Albert Shaw, always something of a jingoist, who was on the point of coming out editorially in his *Review of Reviews* for a revolution:

> I cast aside the proposition made at this time to foment the secession of Panama. Whatever other governments can do, the

United States cannot go into securing by such underhand means, the secession. Privately, I freely say to you that I should be delighted if Panama were an independent State, or if it made itself so at this moment; but for me to say so publicly would amount to an instigation of a revolt, and therefore I cannot say it.

Fortunately, the President neither had to "say it," nor to submit his proposed message to Congress. On November 5 a revolutionary junta declared Panama's independence of Colombia, and four days later the United States extended *de facto* recognition to the new republic.

Of all the events in the Panama story, the most extraordinary were those encompassing that revolution. They revealed Cromwell and Bunau-Varilla at the high tide of their resourcefulness and influence; they showed Roosevelt and Hay at their circumspect best; and they displayed the Colombian government at its confused and disorganized worst. They also saw the Panamanians fulfill aspirations a half century old. It was these very aspirations, in fact, that formed the springboard for Cromwell and Bunau-Varilla's activities and which allowed Roosevelt to acquiesce silently, yet in reasonably good conscience, to what he could not advocate publicly.

Panama had long lacked both the capital and political climate essential to material and cultural progress. Separated from Bogotá by a near impenetrable tropical jungle and a lofty mountain range, she was fifteen days' traveling time from the capital city, where the ruling gentry regarded her alternately with disdainful indifference or avaricious curiosity. Neither by "community of interest nor racial sympathy" were the Panamanians drawn to their Colombian overlords. They had repeatedly demonstrated by armed rebellion their dissatisfaction with absentee rule over the years; but always they had been beaten down, sometimes by American troops. Six times during the fifty-three years prior to the climactic revolution of 1903 American sailors or marines had gone ashore to restore that order necessary to the open transit across the isthmus guaranteed by the Treaty of 1846; and four times—in 1861, 1862, 1885, and 1900—the impotent Colombian government had itself requested American military intervention. As Roosevelt contended in his *Autobiography,* Colombia's "connection with the Isthmus would have been sundered long before it was" had it not been for American intervention.

Against such a background, those masters of intrigue and persuasion, Cromwell and Bunau-Varilla, had little trouble in finding Panamanians whose revolutionary fervor burned more fiercely than ever when confronted with the prospect of an independent Republic of Panama endowed with the $10 million the United States had been prepared to pay Colombia. During the summer of 1903 Cromwell and Bunau-Varilla sustained the hopes of a small band of Panamanian conspirators and in the early autumn of 1903, when the conspirators were on the point of abandoning the project for want of funds and encouragement, Bunau-Varilla gave them both. The result was revolution.

Roosevelt and Hay knew from reports of special observers and from conversations with Cromwell and Bunau-Varilla that a revolution was in the making. The President could readily have suppressed it; but in accordance with his interpretation of American interest, he gave it silent approval, Hay advising him that the United States should act "to keep the transit clear" and warning that American intervention "should not be haphazard nor, this time should it be to the profit, as heretofore of Bogota." Hay also gave Bunau-Varilla the information he most needed by confiding to the flamboyant Frenchman on October 16 that American naval forces had been ordered "to sail towards the Pacific." Coming after an earlier interview with Roosevelt which Bunau-Varilla construed as favorable although the President failed to give explicit approval to his design, Bunau-Varilla hardly needed to know more. The stage was set for the final act.

On November 2 the captains of United States warships already dispatched to isthmian waters were ordered to "maintain free and uninterrupted transit" and to "prevent landing of any armed force, either government or insurgent at any point within fifty miles of Panama." This meant that Colombia would be unable to reinforce its tiny garrison in Panama. Then, at 5:49 A.M. on November 3, exactly forty-nine minutes after the Panama City fire brigade started to distribute weapons to crowds in the streets, the revolution against Colombia was accomplished. Except for a brief shelling by a Colombian gunboat which killed an innocent bystander and mortally wounded an ass, there was no violence. For the Colombian governor of Panama, José Domingo de Obaldía, participated in the conspiracy, and the Colombian army detachment in Panama City sold its services to the revolutionary cause, as financed by the New Panama Canal Company.

The next day the Panamanians celebrated their independence with a formal ceremony. The Colombian general was presented with $30,000, most of his officers with $10,000 each, and every soldier in the ranks with fifty gold dollars. The American consul, Felix Ehrman, joined in a gala parade, and the President-to-be, Dr. Manuel Amador Guerrero, delivered an oration:

> The world is astounded at our heroism! Yesterday we were but the slaves of Colombia; today we are free. . . . President Roosevelt has made good. . . . Free sons of Panama, I salute you! Long live the Republic of Panama! Long live President Roosevelt! Long live the American Government!

Dr. Amador was almost premature. The same day he was proclaiming long life to the new republic and its North American friends, the commandant of the five hundred Colombian regulars in Colón was threatening to kill every Yankee in the city unless his force received rail passage to Panama City. Before he summoned the necessary nerve, however, a detachment of United States marines was landed under orders to prevent the Colombians from using the railroad. The success of the revolution was assured.

Washington learned of the revolution's success the morning after this last threat was dissipated. Within an hour and a half Secretary Hay, in conformance with instructions from Roosevelt, directed the American consul at Panama City to recognize Dr. Amador's *de facto* government. Within five days the President received the ubiquitous Bunau-Varilla, who entered the White House as Minister Plenipotentiary of the Republic of Panama.

Less than a week later, Bunau-Varilla signed for the Republic of Panama a treaty which enabled the Panama Canal to be constructed on terms favorable to Panama, the United States, the New Panama Canal Company, and probably civilization as a whole. Written partly by Bunau-Varilla and partly by Hay, who consulted with Roosevelt, Root, Knox, and Albert Shaw, it made Panama a virtual protectorate of the United States. The treaty granted the United States perpetual "use, occupation, and control" of a strip across the Isthmus ten miles wide, and it authorized the United States to fortify the canal and safeguard the independence of Panama. Panama was awarded $10 million and a $250,000 annual payment to begin nine years later.

The New Panama Canal Company received $40 million; Colombia nothing.

For Roosevelt, the sword of righteousness had again thrust through the shield of iniquity. Just as the American colonies "had revolted from England because England declined to treat them as free men with equal rights," so had "Panama revolted from Colombia because Colombia, for corrupt and evil purposes or else from complete governmental incompetency, declined to permit the building of the great work which meant everything to Panama." Nor need the Colombians, who offered to ratify the Hay-Herrán Treaty by executive decree, now expect the United States to respond to their change of front. "In their silly efforts to damage us they cut their own throats," the President charged. "They tried to hold us up; and too late they have discovered their criminal error." Furthermore, their belated offer proves beyond cavil that when the same government said earlier that it had no power to take that step "it was guilty of deliberate bad faith." Consequently, the President concluded, "nothing could be more wicked than to ask us to surrender the Panama people, who are our friends, to the Colombian people, who have shown themselves our foes."

Roosevelt held in the main to that analysis over the years. True, he allowed his boundless pride in the achievement to overrule his discretion by declaring in an address at the University of California in 1911, "I took the canal zone and let Congress debate, and while the debate goes on the canal does also." And in his *Autobiography* he asserted that "From the beginning to the end our course was straightforward and in absolute accord with the highest standards of international morality." But other statements in his *Autobiography* were more representative:

> I did not lift my finger to incite the revolutionists. . . . I simply ceased to stamp out the different revolutionary fuses that were already burning. . . . I deeply regretted, and now deeply regret, the fact that the Colombian Government rendered it imperative for me to take the action I took; but I had no alternative, consistent with the full performance of my duty to my own people, and to the nations of mankind.

It is doubtful that the case for and against Roosevelt's conduct will ever die. The story is too dramatic, the characters too romantic, the maneuverings too intricate. This much, however, is clear: Roosevelt's controlling motive was his conviction of the United States' vital interest in constructing a canal through Panama under conditions favorable to the national security. Had he not been so compulsively eager to act; had he not been so quick to rise to the challenge thrown up by Colombia's rejection of the Hay-Herrán Treaty; and had he been more accurately and broadly informed, he might have realized that great objective without leaving a heritage of ill-will. Indeed, he might even have assuaged the Colombians by paying them a sum equal to that paid Cromwell's group. But because he persisted in regarding the Colombians as blackmailers, and because delay was foreign to his nature and possibly subversive of his presidential ambitions in 1904, he allowed himself to pursue a blameworthy course. His autobiographical explanation is illuminating but certainly not convincing:

My belief then was, and the events that have occurred since have more than justified it, that from the standpoint of the United States it was imperative, not only for civil but for military reasons, that there should be the immediate establishment of easy and speedy communication by sea between the Atlantic and the Pacific. These reasons were not of convenience only, but of vital necessity, and do not admit of indefinite delay. . . . Colombia proposed to wait a year, and then enforce a forfeiture of the rights and property of the French Panama Company, so as to secure the forty million dollars our government had authorized as payment to this company. If we had sat supine, this would doubtless have meant that France would have interfered to protect the company, and we should then have had on the Isthmus, not the company, but France; and the gravest international complications might have ensued.

CHAPTER 13

IN HIS OWN RIGHT

> In politics we have to do a great many things we ought not
> to do.
>
> —Theodore Roosevelt

March 4, 1905, dawned clear and brisk. The wind was fair for the season, and the sky was blue and almost cloudless. To the East, where the oversized dome of the Capitol broke the horizon, a tuft of storm clouds hovered; but they were political, and from noon on, invisible. Two years were to pass before they would burst in full fury. This was Theodore Roosevelt's day of glory, even greater perhaps than that day seven years before when he and his Rough Riders had braved the withering Spanish fire in Cuba.

A few minutes after noon Roosevelt stepped forward on the east portico of the Capitol to face Chief Justice Melville E. Fuller. In the background stood an honor guard of Rough Riders, high government officials, foreign diplomats and their ladies, personal friends of many years past, and the ubiquitous Roosevelt family. Slowly and deliberately, his eyes fastened on the Chief Justice, Roosevelt placed his left hand on an open Bible, raised his right hand, and repeated the measured phrases of the presidential oath.

The President was heavier and more deeply lined, especially around the eyes, than he had been four years before when he was sworn in as Vice-President. His face was wider, his shoulders broader, his neck thicker. He was much larger through the midriff, and he seemed stronger than he had as a young man, when his square face alone conveyed the impression of physical strength. His power and confidence were evident, and his voice, always imperfect and too high in pitch, had the timbre of a man proven; proven in battle in another era, and proven in office in the years just gone by. Roosevelt on March 4, 1905, was in command. As he repeated the last words of the presidential oath, the throng that milled about the plaza between the Capitol and the Library of Congress gave forth an approving roar —the first display of an enthusiasm that was to eclipse that of all previous inaugurations save Andrew Jackson's first.

The President's inaugural address was undistinguished in form and, on first reading, in substance. Its theme was the familiar one of duty, responsibility, and courage, and its locus was the relationship of those values to a changing society. Its generalizations were broad enough to be trite while its peroration lacked little in grandiosity. Yet when that address is reread against what had already transpired and what was soon to transpire, its relevance as a testament of Roosevelt's faith and intent becomes apparent. The "Giver of Good," said the President, had blessed mightily the American people. "We are the heirs of the ages, and yet we have had to pay few of the penalties which in old countries are exacted by the dead hand of a bygone civilization." Still, we had faced perils which "called for the vigor and effort without which the manlier and hardier virtues wither away." And so now did we continue to face these, the perils of an advanced industrial civilization. "The conditions which have told for our marvelous material wellbeing, which have developed to a very high degree our energy, self-reliance, and individual initiative, have also brought the care and anxiety inseparable from the accumulation of great wealth in industrial centers." Upon the resolution of these problems, exclaimed this first major statesman of the new order, depended the welfare of the American people, and perhaps of mankind itself. "If we fail, the cause of free self-government throughout the world will rock to its foundations." But, he added, we need not fail. For the qualities now needed were not different from what they had ever been. They were those "of practical intelligence, of courage, of hardihood, and endurance, and above all the power of devotion to a lofty ideal." They had made great the men who founded the Republic under Washington, and they had made great the men who preserved it under Lincoln. They could also, he concluded, make great the present generation.

Through the remainder of that March afternoon Roosevelt was zestful, ebullient, and even prideful. On the reviewing stand an hour or two later, he alternately sat and stood, grinned and laughed, waved and applauded. He stamped his feet and bent his knees to the rhythm of "There'll Be a Hot Time in the Old Town Tonight." He glowed when a troop of Rough Riders, fortified by three days of liquid preparation for the indignity of riding artillery rather than cavalry mounts, rode uproariously by. And he chatted freely, almost constantly, with members of the presidential party.

The President was also mindful of the charges that he had usurped congressional power and exploited colonial peoples, or so the newspapers, with perhaps more license than veracity, reported him as being. "I really shuddered today as I swore to obey the Constitution," the President supposedly joked at the outset of the parade. Later, as the Puerto Rican contingent passed in review, he turned to Senator Bacon, the anti-imperialist from Georgia, and remarked with a chuckle: "They look pretty well for an oppressed people, eh, Senator?" Roosevelt again fixed his gaze on the discomfited Georgian when a finely drilled body of Filipino Scouts swung past the reviewing stand to the buoyant strains of "Gary Owen." "The wretched serfs disguised their feelings admirably," he shouted as Bacon turned his face from the scene.

The President's high spirits were warranted. He was acutely aware that his effectiveness during his first term had been circumscribed by the accidental nature of his elevation to power; that Congress had tolerated him and at times angrily compromised with him, but had supported him only when his recommendations had coincided with its own views. Now, however, he was President by popular mandate rather than by assassin's hand. He had swept scores of Republicans into office with him. And he had already indicated by messages, speeches, and informal maneuvers that he would no longer pay lip service to the dead hand of McKinley or be again so deferential to the will of the Senate oligarchy. "Tomorrow I shall come into my office in my own right," he is said to have exclaimed on the eve of his inauguration. "Then watch out for me."

If the President's inaugural address exemplified those high and statesman-like ideals to which Roosevelt so urgently aspired, the events preceding the election had revealed that ruthlessness and low cunning that made him the master politician of his own age and one of the masters of all ages. During the three years the President was serving the nation and incidentally enhancing his prestige by battling the trusts, intervening in the coal strike, and acquiring the Panama Canal Zone, he had also been waging a fiercely single-minded campaign for his nomination and election in 1904. He manipulated the patronage with cold disingenuousness. He signed a controversial pension bill. And during the third of those years he slowed the momentum of his antitrust campaign and temporarily reaffirmed that historic alliance between the Republican party and big business that his earlier policies had begun to weaken.

Roosevelt's triumphal election in November, 1904, had actually been an anticlimax. The real contest had been for the nomination, and it had been won more than a full year before—won, ironically, against Mark Hanna, the man who symbolized the McKinley policies Roosevelt had so spontaneously promised to continue upon assuming office.

Marcus Alonzo Hanna was no Joseph G. Cannon committed to the preservation of the status quo at any cost but the political; nor was he a Nelson W. Aldrich dedicated to its preservation at almost all costs including the political. Rather, the portly, convivial Ohioan was a genuinely sophisticated conservative. An eminently successful businessman in his own right, he is said to have tried most of the customary means of suppressing labor during his early career only to have concluded that an open-handed policy was more profitable in the long run than recurrent strife. Although he had coined the slogan "Stand pat" for the campaign of 1900, Hanna understood that the predatory ways of capital would have to be reformed, the rights of labor more generally affirmed, if social upheaval was to be averted. And he had, consequently, little sympathy with those of his Republican colleagues in the Senate who sought to convert his campaign slogan of 1900 into a political philosophy. Why, then, did Roosevelt choose to move against him?

The reason was power. Hanna had it and Roosevelt wanted it. The President wanted it, assuredly, to satisfy his ego. He was in that sense not basically different from Jackson and Lincoln, Wilson and Franklin D. Roosevelt, nor even Washington and Jefferson. Like several of those storied figures, also, he took an extraordinary, almost primitive satisfaction, in the free-wheeling exercise of power. Yet, as Abraham Lincoln was distinguished from Stephen A. Douglas by the depths of his idealism rather than his ambition, so was Theodore Roosevelt set apart from the overwhelming number of his political contemporaries by his dedication to the public interest. Had Roosevelt's moral sensibilities been less acute he might have been likened to Hanna himself, a good and well-intentioned man, but hardly a great man; and had they been genuinely dull he might have been compared to Platt, or Quay, or Penrose, men to whom power was the consuming end of life. Roosevelt might even have emerged as a violent demagogue, for he had not a few of the attributes, among them the ability to oversimplify, smear his opponents, and stir the masses.

If Roosevelt wanted Hanna's power to gratify his baser urges—and it bears underlining that he did—he also wanted it to assure the success of those high public purposes to which his vaulting ambition and love of power had long been dedicated. For all his sophistication, Hanna was hardly prepared to rally the Grand Old Party behind those parts of the President's program which were too advanced for his own tastes. The question of whether Roosevelt's maturing progressivism, a progressivism that was even then dimly pointing toward basic changes in the distribution of power in American society, or Hanna's program of piecemeal concessions that failed to modify the capitalists' control of the body politic, was far from idle. And since Hanna wanted at the least to continue the role of Warwick and at the most to become President himself, Roosevelt believed he had either to crush him or suffer the constriction of most of the policies he himself represented.

Whatever the baseness or loftiness of Roosevelt's motives, however groundless some of his rationalizations and praiseworthy other of his justifications, his drive to unseat the man who had made McKinley was at once subtle, open, and pitiless. It saw the President ally himself with, and even be obsequious to, the unsavory bosses Quay and Penrose and the archconservative Foraker of Ohio. It saw him appoint a great host of Quay, Penrose, and Foraker's friends, not a few of them the "low morality" types Civil Service Commissioner Roosevelt had so despised, to the government service. And finally, after Foraker had boxed in Hanna by calling on the Ohio Republican Convention to endorse the President in the spring of 1903, it saw Roosevelt force Hanna's hand by publishing a private telegram from the Senator, a low blow that left Hanna little alternative but to allow the Convention to endorse the President. From that point on, in fact, Roosevelt was the head of the Republican party outside Congress. "It simplified things all around," he exulted to Lodge. "Hanna was my only formidable opponent so far as the nomination . . . [was] concerned."

Nine months later Mark Hanna lay dead of typhoid fever. To the end he had maintained cordial relations with the President, and Roosevelt had visited him during his final illness; and fittingly so. More than any man in the United States, Hanna could have ruined Roosevelt in the formative years, 1901–1902. But in spite of his own ambition and his contempt of Roosevelt's flamboyance and distaste for many of his policies, Hanna had chosen to place public and party interests above his own political fortunes. Roosevelt acknowledged as much in a moving letter to Elihu Root the day after his Olympian adversary died:

> I think that not merely I myself, but the whole party and the whole country have reason to be grateful to him for the way in which, after I came into office, under circumstances which were very hard for him, he resolutely declined to be drawn into the position which a smaller man of meaner cast would inevitably have taken; that is, the position of antagonizing public policies if I was identified with them. He could have caused the widest disaster to the country and the public if he had attacked and opposed the policies referring to Panama, the Philippines, Cuban reciprocity, army reform, the navy and the legislation for regulating corporations. But he stood by them just as loyally as if I had been McKinley.

Hardly less than his obsession with power, Roosevelt's dextrous manipulation of the patronage in his campaign against Hanna had been disillusioning to the President's defenders. Actually, Roosevelt was incomparably more restrained than Lincoln, who appointed a string of inferior men to high civilian and military offices in order to secure the success and promote the great objects of his administration. But because Roosevelt was so emphatically on the record, and especially because he was so boorishly self-righteous, his compromises have subjected him to a heavy burden of censure.

The most flagrant violation of Roosevelt's principles was the appointment of James S. Clarkson of Iowa, the archspoilsman who had led the Republican hosts in their assault on the fourth-class postmasterships under Wanamaker, to a non-policy-making plum in New

York in 1902. Clarkson, the President explained to the numerous and vociferous critics of his startling appointment, was "in no way to be criticized" for his "occasional" removals of Democratic postmasters in years gone by. He was, indeed, "an honorable and capable man." To some, however, Roosevelt was more candid. "In politics," he confessed, "we have to do a great many things we ought not do."

Although the President thus lowered the bars on minor offices, he stood firm for the most part on major appointments. His attitude toward the Isthmian Canal Commission was a case in point. As Alfred D. Chandler, Jr. has written, the construction of the Panama Canal by the first great government corporation in American history was a worthy tribute to the President's pragmatic, trial and error administrative techniques. He took more pride in it than any other of his concrete achievements. And it was his personal decision to support Dr. William C. Gorgas, who insisted on pursuing Walter Reed's theories on yellow fever, that made the undertaking possible. When, accordingly, Senator Quay asked Roosevelt to appoint one of his constituents to the Isthmian Commission in 1904, the President forthrightly turned him down. "I hate to be in any way unreciprocative," he wrote the powerful Pennsylvanian. "But it does seem to me that in handling this Commission I should do nothing on the ground of locality."

> I have had to refuse to appoint an admirable young fellow in whom Lodge was intensely interested, though I was able to place him on the Philippine Commission. Senator Platt has been interested in a first-class man, Burr, who is entirely fit for the position; yet I am inclined to think . . . that Parsons is the better man. . . . In any ordinary appointments I am only too glad to consider political recommendations and the recommendations of my friends, and I should do the same even on extraordinary occasions where so much was not involved. But when we come to a position like this I feel as I do when I am choosing a judge for the Supreme Court, that I must have an eye single to the way the work will be done.

Nor was that the only instance of Roosevelt's reaffirmation of the faith of his civil service, police commissionership, and governorship years. The undeniable fact is that even as he used the patronage to create a personal political machine, he advanced efficiency, integrity, nonpartisanship at an unprecedented rate. The year before he came up for election he had indictments brought against an imposing array of Republicans for defrauding the Post Office Department and he also pushed an investigation of land corruptionists in Oregon, one of whom was a Republican congressman. He instituted a rigid civil service system in the Philippines, backed a measure sponsored by Lodge and Root for the improvement of the consular service, and gave forceful and informed support to Root's reorganization of the Army. He also added 50,000 positions to the classified civil service lists during his seven and one-half years in office. Notwithstanding Roosevelt's minor concessions to the bosses and paternal solicitude for unemployed ex-Rough Riders, the general level of his appointments was the highest since the halcyon days before Jackson. Never, said Lord Bryce, had he seen a more eager, high-minded, and efficient set of public servants, men more useful and more creditable to their country, than the men Theodore Roosevelt placed in positions of high responsibility.

In selecting men of character and ability for government office, Roosevelt went beyond the customary geographical considerations. Before he appointed Oscar Straus, the first Jew to serve in a Cabinet post, Secretary of Commerce and Labor in 1906, for example, he besought the advice of the respected banker and pillar of New York's civic-minded German-Jewish community, Jacob Schiff. Later, at a banquet of prominent Jews in honor of Straus, Roosevelt emphatically exclaimed that he had not even thought about Straus's religion when contemplating his appointment. But Schiff, whose hearing was failing, bungled the cue. "Dot's right, Mr. President," he exclaimed. "You came to me and said, 'Chake, who is der best Jew I can appoint Segretary of Commerce.' "

There is, regrettably, reason to suspect that the Schiff story is apocryphal. But there is no evidence to indicate that its larger sense is misleading. In similar vein, Roosevelt sometimes appointed a Roman Catholic, a labor union man, a white Southern Democrat or a Negro Southern Republican as he strove to make his administration reflect the rich ethnic diversity of American society. Invariably, he did so with an eye for the immediate political advantage. He consorted with Booker T. Washington, the first American Negro ever invited to break bread in the White House, because Washington was supporting him in his fight to wrest control of the party machinery from Mark Hanna; and he gave high place to other qualified Negroes for the same reason. Yet he also recognized Negroes and members of other suppressed ethnic and religious groups in ways that clearly transcended his political interests.

Roosevelt was too sophisticated a Reform Darwinist to believe blatantly in racial supremacy though a mild undercurrent of racism seems to have lingered in his unconsciousness. His thought coincided roughly with the moderate, informed opinion of the times; and it was in fact more advanced than that of reformer-economists like John R. Commons and politician-intellectuals like Cabot Lodge and Woodrow Wilson. Yet Roosevelt was never enthusiastic about the mass immigration of Irish, Slavs, and Southern Europeans—of Jews and Greeks and Roman Catholics. He believed that their numbers were too great, their conditions of life too impoverished, and their cultural backgrounds too different for easy assimilation. And he erroneously concluded that they were easy prey to political radicalism as well as to social and moral degradation. Unable to slow their influx—he unsuccessfully recommended immigration restriction and then appointed a commission of exports which submitted a racist report—he characteristically reacted by promoting their assimilation. To this end he fulminated against discrimination and sought actively to open the channels of advancement and opportunity to the more distinguished among them. "I grow extremely indignant at the attitude of coarse hostility to the immigrant," Roosevelt wrote the Rev. Lyman Abbott, publisher of the influential, Protestant-oriented *Outlook,* after he had renounced further political ambition:

> I have tried to . . . appeal to their self-respect and make it easy for them to become enthusiastically loyal Americans as well as good citizens. I have one Catholic in my Cabinet and have had another, and I now have a Jew in the Cabinet; and part of my object in each appointment was to implant in the minds of of our fellow-Americans of Catholic or of Jewish faith, or of foreign ancestry or birth, the knowledge that they have in this country just the same rights and opportunities as every one else . . . just the same ideals as a standard toward which to strive. I want the Jewish young man who is born in this country to feel that Straus stands for his ideal of the successful man.

Roosevelt's attitude toward the declining birth rate offers additional insight into his final acceptance of the "American Dream" and its implicit repudiation of racial, as distinct from national or cultural superiority. "The American stock is being cursed with the curse of sterility, and it is earning the curse, because the sterility is wilful," he said in an article in the *Outlook* in 1911. "If it were confined to Americans of old stock . . . we could at least feel that the traditions and principles and purposes of the founders of the Republic would find their believers and exponents among their descendants by adoption." And in that case, he wrote, "I, for one, would heartily throw in my fate with the men of alien stock who were true to the old American principles rather than with the men of the old American stock who were traitors to the old American principles." But unfortunately, he lamented, "the children of the immigrants show the same wilful sterility that is shown by the people of the old stock."

Roosevelt's intense preoccupation with Americanism, an Americanism that embraced personal morality as well as national loyalty and unity, pervaded his views on religion. Throughout his life he was a regular churchgoer, and by the testimony of some of his intimates, a devoutly religious man as well. "When a man believes a thing, is it not his duty to say so?" he said to the pastor of the St. Nicholas Dutch Reformed Church in New York at the age of seventeen. "If I joined the church, wouldn't that be the best way for me to say to the world that I believed in God?"

Over the years Roosevelt never wavered in his formal commitment to the church, nor to the Bible as a source of inspiration. Bill Sewall remembered that he took the Bible with him on trips into the North Woods as a Harvard undergraduate and that he would slip away to peruse it by himself. "Some folks read the Bible to find an easier way into Heaven," Sewall once said. But, "Theodore reads it to find the right way and how to pursue it." Nevertheless, Roosevelt's innermost convictions are unclear even to this day. As Hagedorn writes, "He trumpeted his moral convictions from the housetops and up and down the land, until even his friends begged for mercy. But his relation to the unseen was something else." Only three or four times in the near forty years of his maturity is he reported to have spoken freely of his faith; and in most of those instances the report is suspect or deficient.

Curiously, Roosevelt had been even more dependent on religion than most young men during his adolescence and early manhood—a reflection, perhaps, of what Elting Morison characterized "his capacity for total investment." At Harvard he taught an Episcopal Sunday school class until forced to resign because of his refusal to abandon

his Dutch Reformed affiliation; and he prayed regularly each morning
during his college years. It was to religion, moreover, that he had
turned for solace in the traumatic aftermath of his father's death. "It
is lovely to think of our meeting in heaven. . . ." "Lord, I believe;
help thou mine unbelief." "Nothing but my faith in the Lord Jesus
Christ could have carried me through this, my terrible time of trouble
and sorrow." These were his diary entries at the time. During Roosevelt's twenty-first year, however, the evidences of deep religious feeling had begun to abate; nor do they seem to have resurged in the
double tragedy of his mother's and his first wife's death when he was
twenty-five.

It is true that Roosevelt continued to pay formal obeisance to the
Judeo-Christian God, and occasionally to the Trinity as well. But
nowhere in the published addresses and writings of his later years is
there anything resembling a movingly spiritual confession of faith.
Nor was he ever, so far as is known, disturbed by the Darwinian
findings which were rocking the very substance of traditional theology
as he came into manhood. "I know not how philosophers may ultimately define religion," he wrote, "but from Micah to James it has
been defined as service to one's fellowmen rendered by following the
great rule of justice and mercy, of wisdom and righteousness." And
that, for Theodore Roosevelt, who lacked even Lincoln's mysticism,
was enough. As Gamaliel Bradford, in a dozen lines that atomize the
volume and more of essays designed to prove Roosevelt's spirituality,
concludes: "I cannot find God insistent or palpable anywhere in the
writings or the life of Theodore Roosevelt. He had no need of him
and no longing, because he really had no need of anything but his
own immensely sufficient self. And the abundant, crowding, magnificent presence of this world left no room for another. Bishop's *Life
of Roosevelt* ends with a quotation [from Roosevelt] which seems to
sum up the whole story: 'It is idle to complain or to rail at the
inevitable; serene and high of heart we must face our fate and go
down into the darkness.' I do not see God here anywhere at all."

If Roosevelt's rejection of both dogma and spirituality made for a
broad tolerance of religious diversity, his overwhelming commitment
to religion as a social and ethical force nevertheless imposed limits
on that tolerance. His ultimate test was whether a religion transgressed
the moral code that comprised the warp of the Judeo-Christian heritage. He was chary, accordingly, of the Church of the Latter-day

Saints. Yet, with uncharacteristic restraint, he opposed a proposed constitutional amendment against polygamy partly on the grounds "that there is less polygamy among the Mormons . . . than there have been bigamous marriages among an equal number of Christians." Roosevelt knew, it is perhaps no exaggeration to conclude, that the history of mankind is writ large with foolish and futile religious persecutions.

Roosevelt's dedication to the moral law coupled with his insight into the steady pressure of environment forces made him more sympathetic to Catholicism than most middle-class Americans of his times. He had little patience with the doctrine of papal infallibility and he especially resented the Roman Church's authoritarian structure. His frequent endorsements of the separation of church and state, his emphatic support of the free public school system, and his implied criticisms of parochial education even suggest a latent anti-Catholicism. But in the final analysis he was most impressed with Rome's beneficial influences—with its potential ability to impress upon the immigrants those Judeo-Christian ethical values which were the fount of his own inspiration and out of which Protestantism itself had sprung.

Nor was Roosevelt daunted by the prospect of a Catholic residing in the White House at some future date. Indeed, he welcomed it, for it implied a complete assimilation. Too pragmatic to be bound by doctrinaire principles himself, he was confident that other men of responsibility and patriotism would prove similarly chainless. He accordingly took pleasure in striking out at Protestant bigots and asserting that he would happily support a Roman Catholic for the presidency if he happened to be the best qualified man. Predicting in September, 1904 (a most politic timing, it is true), that there would be many Catholic Presidents in the years to come, he expressed the hope that if any one of them know "anything of me or my conduct, he will feel that I have acted along just the lines that he can afford to act." Over the years Roosevelt could, and did, consort in good conscience with Catholic and Episcopalian bishops, with Jewish rabbis and Methodist ministers, and with laymen of all denominations, including the Unitarian Taft.

Against this background, Roosevelt's ceaseless cultivation of political support by minority groups becomes more morally defensible. Had he been a religious bigot or an Anglo-Saxon supremacist dedicated to purity of the so-called race, his activities might have stamped him as a sheer political opportunist. But his commitment was to the preservation of American institutions, not to the privileged position of a particular in-group, and it was more intellectual than political in origin. To discriminate against an American citizen because of his own or his father's birthplace was to the mature Roosevelt, "a base infamy—utterly un-American and profoundly unpatriotic."

Had Roosevelt never faced an electorate he would probably have been as deeply involved in the Americanization of the newer immigrants as he was as an active politician. But since he had to face the electorate, and since he believed "in being thoroughly practical in politics," he spared no effort to win every last vote in every last minority group or organization that he had served during his twenty-year political career. During the presidential campaign of 1904 the word went out in a dozen different tongues from the professional ward heelers and precinct leaders that the President had appointed Jews and Catholics to high office; that he had defended immigrant working men against exploitation by the great coal barons; and that he had represented the little man against the privileged few in his strike against the trusts.

The whole man in 1904 was not only one of ideals, courage, and forthrightness; he was a man of surprising fear and no little expediency. If the appointment of Clarkson in 1902 had been designed to promote Roosevelt's cause at the nominating convention of 1904, a decision the President made to broaden the pension base for Union veterans in the late winter of 1904 by executive decree was calculated, at least in part, to advance his fortunes in the election that followed that convention. The President's unilateral action, roared W. Bourke Cochran, grandiloquent orator, Tammany chieftain, and spoilsman of the first order, was a clear-cut case of executive usurpation of congressional authority. The *New York Times* claimed that the American nation had rarely witnessed such a "remarkable" and "impudent" assertion of executive power. "There is an impression that we are to elect a President next November," was the New York *World*'s comment. "It is a mistake. Unless Mr. Roosevelt be totally at sea regarding the nature of his office, we are to elect a czar."

The Republicans in Congress had discreetly held their tongues. They had paid higher prices than "executive usurpation" for the political favors of the Grand Army of the Republic in the past. As for Roosevelt, he was as eager as they to reap the harvest of G.A.R. votes in November though he undoubtedly knew that his order would rub Congress the wrong way. "I came to the conclusion," he later explained, that if we waited on Congress "we would either have no legislation or else improper legislation." Yet he also had no doubt that he was morally right; that the pensions were deserved. The men who were to receive them were not former contractors who had waxed rich at the government trough during the war, or tariff protected manufacturers seeking just one more favor. They were, as Roosevelt, who honored them years before he became a politician, appropriately said, "the men who fought for union and liberty" and "not only saved this Nation from ruin, but rendered an inestimable service to all mankind."

Roosevelt well knew that during the four years the "plain people" had been at war Elihu Root took his degree at Hamilton College and Robert Lincoln finished his studies at Harvard. J. P. Morgan, a widower without children at twenty-four, procured a substitute to serve in the Army and began the career that was to make him the most powerful man in the nation by the time Roosevelt became President. John D. Rockefeller, who also hired a substitute, bent over his books in the produce commission business in Cleveland, invested in oil, and watched his annual income rise to $17,000 by the end of the conflict. Philip D. Armour made his first great "killing" by selling pork "short" as Grant marched through the Wilderness to Richmond. And Jay Gould, Jay Cooke, Andrew Carnegie, Colis P. Huntington, Jim Fisk, and dozens of others who preferred the emoluments of the market place to the miseries (or glories) of the battlefield either launched their careers or embellished their already sizable fortunes while the muskets rattled and the cannon roared. When the silence finally fell on Appomattox their futures were secure, or as nearly so as money could make them.

It was for "the plain people" who managed to survive the holocaust of Civil War that Roosevelt's pension order was designed. Whatever the political nuances of his decision to sign it (he self-righteously refused to admit any) the justification he offered was plausible. Admitting that there was an "unreasoning or demagogic demand for excessive and improper amounts" and claiming that he had prevented Congress from submitting to it, he reminded Jacob Riis that "there are very many excellent people who have lived softly, and who have no idea of what it is all one's life to earn one's living by toil, and then, without having been able to save, to face failing strength at the end of one's days." The age of sixty-two had been selected, he added in a passage that presaged the later, more socially conscious Roosevelt, "not at random, but after careful inquiry which satisfied us that in most great manufacturing and railroad establishments new men of the age of 62 who might apply for work were peremptorily refused. . . . There are exceptions, of course, but the average toiler, the average wageworker, whose work is physical, has at 62 lost half his capacity to do his work. In New Zealand, at 65 such a man, even if a civilian, is given an old-age pension, larger in amount by over one-half than the amount we thus allow." The Civil War veteran shall have such a pension, TR emphatically concluded, "because the presumption is that he needs it."

In a world that was beginning to become aware of the need for industrial societies to take care of the aged, the President's ruling was socially meaningful, however inadequate, exclusive, and political its application. Thirty-one years were to go by, and five Presidents were to pass in and out of the White House, before Roosevelt's reasoning would be applied to civilians as well as veterans; and then it would be in the first administration of his distant cousin and sometime disciple.

Just as Roosevelt sought the support of the minority groups and Union veterans for his campaign in 1904, he welcomed the backing of big business in general and of Wall Street in particular. In a maneuver that had further confused the distinctions between the parties, the Cleveland wing of the Democratic party had beaten down attempts to include free silver and income tax planks in the party platform in 1904 and then named Judge Alton B. Parker of New York to carry the once progressive Democratic standard. A confirmed Gold Democrat, and a colorless campaigner, Parker was a moderate states' rights adherent and a strong anti-imperialist. He was the antithesis of Bryan in personality, and he differed radically from the Great Commoner in social philosophy. He also offered a striking contrast to Roosevelt, "The Republican Bryan," as embittered members of the Old Guard were by 1904 calling the President.

Although Democratic newspapers had received Parker's nomination with diverse enthusiasm, they had quickly closed ranks, announcing from one end of the country to the other that the campaign would be waged on the issue of personalities. Theodore Roosevelt, declared Colonel Henry Watterson's Louisville *Courier-Journal,* embodies "absolutism" and the "Gospel of Force"; Alton B. Parker, said Pulitzer's editors on the *World,* stands for "conservative and constitutional Democracy."

Wall Street leaders sulked. There was enough truth in these assertions to challenge the wisdom of their supporting Roosevelt over the conservative Parker. Until the day of Hanna's death the Morgan, Harriman, Rockefeller and similar interests had hoped that the Ohio Senator would somehow wrest the nomination from the Rough Rider in the White House. As a meeting of railroad executives had urged Hanna in January, 1904: "Stop making presidents and become one yourself." But with the passing of that monumental symbol of "McKinleyism" in February, they had resigned themselves to the inevitable. Six weeks before Roosevelt's power-packed steamroller forced his unanimous nomination at Chicago before mechanically cheering delegates (the galleries were wildly enthusiastic), even the New York *Sun* had leaped atop the boiler:

> RESOLVED: That we emphatically endorse and affirm Theodore Roosevelt. Whatever Theodore Roosevelt thinks, says, does, or wants is right. Roosevelt and Stir 'Em Up. Now and Forever; One and Inseparable!

The rest of the Old Guard had gone along, or were soon to do so. Henry Adams had thought that they would not. "Roosevelt has no friends," he wrote in January with characteristic effort at effect. "I doubt whether he has in all Washington, including his own Cabinet, a single devoted follower; for even Cabot can hardly be called a devoted follower of anyone, except as a kitten follows its own tail . . . every man in the organization will dread his re-election. Half of them, and all the money, will sell him out."

That summer money flowed into Republican headquarters like a great tidal wave. J. P. Morgan contributed $150,000; H. H. Rodgers and John D. Archbold of the Standard Oil Company, $100,000; C. S. Mellon, $50,000; E. H. Harriman, $50,000; and William Nelson Cromwell, $5,000. All told, $2,195,000 swelled the Republican war chest, 72½ per cent the gift of corporations.

Historians still differ over the meaning of Wall Street's munificent support of Roosevelt's campaign in 1904. Some contend that it proved

the real issue was one of parties rather than of men; that a Democratic Congress was a more potent threat to the established order than
a Republican Congress, even with Roosevelt in the White House.
The editors of the New York *Sun* so believed: "We prefer the impulsive candidate of the party of conservatism to the conservative
candidate of the party which the business interests regard as permanently and dangerously impulsive." Others claim that the lords of
the market place and the heads of the counting houses were too
astute to fear Roosevelt; that they were persuaded by Elihu Root's
logic: "You say Roosevelt is an unsafe man. I tell you he is a great
conservator of property and rights." And many, of course, interpret
it both ways.

Roosevelt himself badly wanted Wall Street's support. But he
wanted it, or so he wanted to believe, on his own terms. And though
he had been consistently more temperate in his criticism of businessmen and their policies throughout 1904, he righteously directed the
chairman of the Republican National Committee to return the contributions of officials of the Standard Oil Company, which was then
under investigation. He further warned the chairman that there should
be no intimation to businessmen that the administration would become
conservative in return for their financial aid. "I should hate to be
beaten in this contest," he wrote, but I should not merely hate, I
should not be able to bear being beaten under circumstances which
implied ignominy. To give any color for misrepresentation to the
effect that we are now weakening . . . would be ruinous."

The force of the President's renouncement of Standard Oil money
is mitigated, however, by his failure to attempt to stay the main stream
of contributions from other corporations. It is further weakened by his
remonstrations to Root to spread through the financial community the
gospel that he was really protecting business from revolution. Root's
text bears reading:

> There is a better way to protect property, to protect capital, to
> protect . . . enterprises, than by buying legislatures. There is a bet-
> ter way to deal with labor, and to keep it from rising into the tumult
> of the unregulated and resistless mob than by starving it or by
> corrupting its leaders. . . . That way is, that capital shall be fair
> . . . fair to the consumer, fair to the laborer, fair to the investor;
> that it shall concede that the laws shall be executed. . . . Never
> forget that the men who labor cast the votes, set up and pull down

governments, and that our government is possible . . . the continued opportunity for enterprise, for the enjoyment of wealth, for individual liberty, is possible, only so long as the men who labor with
their hands believe in American liberty and American laws.

Those remarks had laid bare the essence of Roosevelt's policies.
No competent observer or biographer has challenged them as a statement of what Roosevelt was actually doing. But many historians have
used Roosevelt's endorsement of them as the point of departure for
a cynical appraisal of his motives and personality. It proves, they
suggest or declare, that he was at heart a sophisticated conservative
rather than a genuine progressive, that he hated the "malefactors of
great wealth" because he feared their excesses would provoke revolutionary violence, not because they were fundamentally unjust.

There is surely a large measure of truth in that analysis. One need
but recall Roosevelt's harangues against the Haymarket anarchists,
against Altgeld, Bryan, and the Silver Democrats, to realize how
obsessive was his fear of what he believed was upheaval from below.
"We shall have to do this in order to prevent that," is the suggestive
comment of Richard Hofstadter. Obviously, many of the sophisticated
conservatives with whom Roosevelt associated—Lodge, Hanna, Root
—were drawn to him because of this phase of his political personality,
though none was willing to go as far down the reform path as he.
Moreover, Roosevelt himself conceived his role in much the same
light. As he explained to the British historian, Sir George Trevelyan,
"Somehow or other we shall have to work out methods of controlling
the big corporations without paralyzing the energies of the business
community."

There were, nonetheless, significant differences between the President and his conservative friends. Roosevelt was temperamentally
disposed to act; they were inclined to stand pat until the external
pressures became overwhelming. Roosevelt became morally indignant
when confronted with injustice; they remained largely indifferent.
Roosevelt would become intellectually involved in the reform itself—
in its social and economic merit—and would make it part of his body
of affirmative beliefs; they would view it as a necessary evil. Above
all else, it was this positive accent that distinguished Roosevelt from
his sophisticated conservative consorts, the real proponents of strategic retreat. The President's goal was a better, a more just and less

privileged America; theirs a more ordered America. This had been evidenced by Roosevelt's actions during his legislature years, by the reforms of his governorship, most notably the franchise tax, and by several, if hardly all, of the policies of his first term as President. It would be further evidenced by the policies of his second term.

It is one of the regrettable ironies of Roosevelt's career that there had been no need for him to compromise himself as he did during the campaign of 1904. Having wrested control of the party machinery from Hanna, his election was a foregone conclusion, so firm was his hold upon the affections of the American people. That hold had already been demonstrated by a thousand and more incidents, and none more moving than by the reception accorded him on an extended whistle-stop tour through the West in the spring of 1903. Roosevelt, as always, had been profoundly, even mystically, stimulated. "Wherever I stopped at a small city or country town," he wrote John Hay, "I was greeted by the usual shy, self-conscious, awkward body of local committeemen, and spoke to the usual audience of thoroughly good American citizens—a term I can use in a private letter to you without being thought demagogic!"

That is the audience consisted of . . . gaunt, sinewy farmers and hired hands from all the neighborhood, who had driven in with their wives and daughters and often with their children, from ten or twenty or even thirty miles round about. For all the superficial differences between us, down at bottom these men and I think a good deal alike, or at least have the same ideals, and I am always sure of reaching them in speeches which many of my Harvard friends would think not only homely, but commonplace. There were two bodies which were always gathered to greet me—the veterans and the school children. The veterans felt that I had fought too, and they claimed a certain right of comradeship with me which really touched me deeply; and to them I could invariably appeal with the certainty of meeting an instant response. Whatever their faults and shortcomings, and however much in practise they had failed to come up to their ideal, yet they had this ideal, and they had fought for it in their youth of long ago. . . .

The President had also been amused—by the gifts of two bears, a lizard, a horned toad, and a horse; and by the undiluted democracy of the mayor of Butte, Montana:

. . . As soon as we got in the banquet hall and sat at the head of the table the mayor hammered lustily with the handle of his knife and announced, "Waiter, bring on the feed." Then in a spirit of pure kindliness he added, "Waiter, pull up the curtains and let the people see the President eat!"—but to this I objected. . . . Of the hundred men who were my hosts I suppose at least half had killed their man in private war. . . . As they drank great goblets of wine the sweat glistened on their hard, strong, crafty faces. They looked as if they had come out of the pictures in Aubrey Beardslee's [sic] Yellow Book.

On November 8, 1904 the people whose ideals Theodore Roosevelt exemplified had turned out by the millions to give him the greatest popular majority to that time. Judge Parker's campaign had fallen flat, as it had been foredoomed to do, and not even the revelation of the President's munificent support by Wall Street did more than create a mild flurry of excitement. Roosevelt's adroit and self-righteous handling of the issue, suggests Mowry—the President dismissed the exaggerated implications of Parker's charges as "unqualifiedly and atrociously false," but ignored the objective portions—may even have redounded to his advantage.

In any event, the returns gave the President a popular majority of more than 2,500,000 and an electoral majority of 196. Roosevelt swept every state in the North, including Missouri, and he was undoubtedly responsible for much of the Republicans' near one-hundred-seat majority in the House. It was, the New York Sun conceded, "one of the most illustrious personal triumphs in all political history."

On the state level, however, the President's personal popularity failed to offset completely the growing disenchantment with his party; five of the states he carried elected Democratic governors. Yet there were elements of vindication even in that circumstance; also of irony. For in spite of Roosevelt's baleful campaign compromises, the fact was, as the British Ambassador reported to Whitehall, the President's long-standing criticisms of "political machines and party government by 'bosses' has encouraged . . . the principle of independent judgment."

Roosevelt was astonished and elated by the magnitude of his victory. He was also sobered. On Election night, in accordance with a decision he had made some time before, he issued a statement of future intentions. "I am deeply sensible of the honor done me by the

American people . . . ," he said. "I appreciate to the full the solemn responsibilities this confidence imposes upon me, and I shall do all that in my power lies not to forfeit it."

> On the fourth of March next I shall have served three and a half years, and this three and a half years constitutes my first term. The wise custom which limits the President to two terms regards the substance and not the form. Under no circumstances will I be a candidate for or accept another nomination.

A sincere and high purposed affirmation of the national tradition, that statement was nevertheless the worst political blunder of Theodore Roosevelt's career.

PART **IV**

THE SQUARE DEAL MATURES

CHAPTER 14

ANOTHER MEASURED ADVANCE

> Three of the most cherished powers of private business had
> been the right to set its own prices for services, the right to main-
> tain its books and records in secrecy, and the right to negotiate
> with labor without interference by a third party. The President's
> 1905 message challenged . . . all these rights. . . .
> —George E. Mowry, *The Era of Theodore Roosevelt*

Roosevelt's majestic triumph at the polls in November, 1904, had not
altered the Old Guard's sentiments toward him. To the leaders of his
own party this greatest popular hero since Andrew Jackson was still
a maverick who must be contained and even repressed; and as they
detrained in Washington early in December for the lame-duck session
of the Fifty-eighth Congress, the Republicans had breathed defiance.
"Congress," growled Joseph G. Cannon, the grizzled, tobacco-chew-
ing Speaker of the House, "will pass the appropriation bills and mark
time."

Cannon's forecast had proved substantially correct. By Roosevelt's
inauguration on March 4 Congress had pigeonholed or rejected most
of the recommendations—railroad regulation, employers' liability
legislation, tariff relief for the Philippines, and a child labor law for
the District of Columbia—the President had made in his annual
message on December 6. Nor had it acted on the President's special
message urging ratification of the critical Santo Domingo treaty. There
had been, decidedly, an aura of resentment, of studied insolence about
that final session of the Fifty-eighth Congress.

The President had not really expected more. "Congress does from

235

a third to a half of what I think is the minimum that it ought to do, and I am profoundly grateful that I get as much," he confessed to Leonard Wood shortly after the inauguration. He was, it is true, exasperated by the Senate's cavalier treatment of the Santo Domingo treaty. "The Senate adjourns. I am then left to shoulder all the responsibility due to their failure . . . and have to spend an industrious summer engaged in the pleasant task of making diplomatic bricks without straw." Yet he was delighted that the lame-duck session had voted funds for the construction of two more battleships. "This navy puts us a good second to France and about on a par with Germany. . . . For some years now we can afford to rest and merely replace the ships that are worn out or become obsolete, while we bring up the personnel." And he was quietly confident that he had won the first skirmish in the looming battle for railroad rate regulation.

Roosevelt had originally hailed the Elkins Anti-rebate Act of 1903 as one of his administration's signal accomplishments. Within a year of its enactment, however, he had concluded that a more comprehensive system of regulation would have to be instituted. But he had waited until the people gave him their mandate in November, 1904, before pressing the case. Then, in his most unequivocal annual message to that time, he had forcefully delineated the lines of advance.

The President's paramount objective was the winning of authority for the Interstate Commerce Commission or a similar body to set "maximum" railroad rates. This was necessary, he told Congress, because "as the law now stands the commission simply possess the bare power to denounce a particular rate as unreasonable." The Commission's ruling should take effect immediately after it had been made (instead of after prolonged and immobilizing litigation), and it should remain in effect unless reversed by the courts. Otherwise the great highways of commerce could not be kept "open to all on equal terms." Nor should Congress be deterred by philosophical objections to big government. The question was empirical. National supervision, Roosevelt asserted, was the only means by which "an increase of the present evils . . . or a still more radical policy" could be prevented.

The President had struck at the opportune moment. The Elkins Act had diminished the rebate evil, but many powerful shippers were defying or circumventing its provisions. Other discriminatory practices, including freight differentials that wrought hardship on whole sections of the country, were rampant, while the consolidation of lines for purposes of efficiency was threatening great numbers of farmers and small manufacturers with the loss or drastic reduction of service. It was also widely, and exaggeratedly, believed that rates in general were excessive. The result was such a broadly based demand for reform as the nation had not theretofore witnessed.

Militant farmers and their organizations were bitterly prescribing the old Populist remedy, government ownership of the roads. Southern and Western state legislatures were memorializing Congress for relief from the "iniquities" of the railroad operators or were threatening to act on their own as they had done during the Granger era. And more important still, for the farmers had tried and failed with William Jennings Bryan, the small-town middle classes were swelling the mighty protest. Business and professional men who had cast Democratic ballots only when Blaine had run against Cleveland, men who had equated Bryanism with social revolution and financial madness— these and many, many more were furiously decrying the abuses of the railroads. Even conservative churchmen were indignantly viewing the rate issue as a moral problem. The sensational revelations of the muckrakers, spread broadcast on the pages of the magazines and newspapers, had finally aroused their consciences.

The Old Guard was visibly shaken. Repeatedly in the past it had dismissed or deflected mass pressures for reform; there were some who now argued that it could do so again. There were others, however, who painfully concluded that it could no longer hold the weakening line. These realists knew that the corporations' spokesmen in the Senate could still turn a deaf ear to the outcries of the agrarians and ignore with impunity the feeble demands of labor. But they were not so confident that they could resist the combined pressure of the agrarians and the urban middle classes and yet remain indefinitely in power. From Joseph G. Cannon and Nelson W. Aldrich on down, therefore, the leaders of the Old Guard reluctantly decided to give the President and the reformers the shadow of their program. They or their predecessors had done this before—with the original Interstate Commerce Act of 1887, the Sherman Antitrust Act of 1890, and even the Elkins Act of 1903. They would now do it again, this time by endowing the courts with such broad powers of review that the Commission's decisions would become virtually impossible to implement. Yet even this devious strategy was formulated under duress, for at heart many preferred inaction. Had it not been for the sustained and commanding influence of Theodore Roosevelt, they might well have done nothing, the political consequences notwithstanding.

The struggle that marked the Old Guard's decision to hoist the white flag proved bitter and dramatic. Waged when the President's power was at its very apex, it saw him abandon hope of tariff reform, submit to artful insult by Aldrich and his lieutenants, and back down from an advanced position. Yet it also saw him drive the Old Guard from its bastions, hold together a political party that a wrong move might have split asunder, and give the American people meaningful railroad legislation for the first time in the nation's history.

The first skirmish had been handily won by the President. Flushed by his stunning victory in November, Roosevelt had considered urging tariff revision as well as railroad reform when he drafted his annual message. Had not the Republicans beaten "the Democrats on the issue that protection was robbery, and that when necessary we would amend or revise the tariff ourselves"? He would take action, if only because the existing schedules threatened the very fabric of the enlightened colonial policy to which he was so firmly committed. Privately and discreetly, he revealed his feelings to the party faithful. He might call a special session of Congress in September to revise the tariff, he wrote Nicholas Murray Butler. It was possible that he would send in a special tariff message early in the new year, he confided to Cannon. Indeed, he had composed a draft of his proposed remarks; perhaps the Speaker would be interested in reviewing them!

The President neither sent in a special message nor called an extra session. Hardly had he made those first, perhaps impulsive gestures toward revision, in fact, than he began to draw back. The obstacles were too imposing. A minority of Republicans, mainly from the Middle West, favored revision. They could be counted on for informed, vociferous support; but their numbers were inconsequential. In opposition was a solid phalanx of stand-patters. They were headed by Cannon in the House and Orville H. Platt in the Senate, and they included virtually the entire Republican leadership. Committed by interest and conviction to the protectionist principle, they were unalterably opposed to a major reduction in schedules. For reasons of political expediency, they were also opposed to minor adjustments even on those schedules which no longer served a protectionist purpose. As Speaker Cannon candidly explained years later, "We know from long experience that no matter how great an improvement the new tariff may be, it almost always results in the party in power losing the following election."

Roosevelt nevertheless made measured soundings throughout November, 1904. They were not encouraging. "I am having great difficulty," he reported to Butler in early December. "The trouble is that there are large parts of the country which want no tariff revision. . . . They say, with entire truth, that neither in the platform nor in any communication of mine is there any promise whatever that there shall be tariff revision. . . . My argument in response is that I am meeting not a material need but a mental attitude. . . . What I am concerned about is to meet the expectation of people that we shall consider the tariff question, and the need of showing that the Republican party is not powerless to take up the subject."

Nine days later the President despaired of the chances of tariff revision, at least by the lame-duck Congress. There was, he informed Butler, "a strong majority against it—a majority due partly to self-interest, partly to inertia, partly to timidity, partly to genuine conviction. . . ." Nor was there anyone among the small minority of revisionists who possessed the "remarkable ability" needed to frame the law and steer its passage through Congress. A month later he privately conceded defeat. "On the interstate commerce business, which I regard as a matter of principle, I shall fight," he wrote Lyman Abbott, the editor and publisher of the *Outlook*. "On the tariff, which I regard as a matter of expediency, I shall endeavor to get the best results I can, but I shall not break with my party."

The President's statements were partly rationalizations. He recognized the need for tariff revision and he would have liked to effect it; his letters leave no doubt of that. Yet his decision to subordinate, and possibly to abandon, the issue did little real violence to his principles. Roosevelt's views on the tariff had paralleled the change in his attitude toward government regulation of industry and his repudiation of laissez-faire in general. By the mid-1890's and possibly before, he had come to believe that protectionism was a necessary instrument of national policy, one consonant with the obligation of the state to regulate in the interests of the whole. The mature Roosevelt could no more have weakened American industry's competitive advantage over foreign manufacturers by promoting free trade than he could have jeopardized America's world power position by jettisoning the battle fleet. The issue was urgent, not open to compromise, and only inadvertently Republican. Not even the bitter protests of his Western followers would move Roosevelt from his protectionist commitment when, in 1912, he emerged as the knight errant of the long-gathering progressive movement.

Still, Roosevelt was acutely aware that there were abuses, that the schedules on some products were so high that the term "competitive concept" was a mere play on words. Except in their impact upon colonial policy, however, he hardly regarded these abuses as critical. As he explained to Butler, "I think there are certain schedules that should be reduced, but I do not think it at all a vital matter to reduce them, so far as the welfare of the people is concerned." Hence his willingness to exchange the threat of tariff reform for rate regulation. This was regrettable, for Roosevelt's inability to alter the tariff stands as one of the signal failures of his presidency. Yet it had to be, so numerous and powerful were the high priests of protectionism within his party. Had he made a genuine effort to revise the tariff at any time during his seven and one-half years in office, he would have destroyed his effectiveness. Even as he virtually threw in the sponge, however, he decided to use the threat of action on the tariff to cajole and soften the Old Guard. Thus, as Blum shrewdly points out, he raised the dreaded specter at the outset of the fight for rate regulation and revived it at strategic moments thereafter until his offensive was fairly organized.

Of all the agitations then current, that for tariff reform was the most baleful to "Uncle Joe" Cannon. Railroad reform promised to alienate some important Republicans; but it bid to appease many more, notably the farmers and small shippers. Tariff reform, however, threatened to antagonize tens of thousands of party stalwarts—the small manufacturers who comprised the very sinews of the Republican party. In spite of his plan to have the lame-duck session "mark time," therefore, Cannon came quickly to terms in the winter of 1904–05. In return for inaction on the tariff, he allowed the President's railroad program as embodied in the Esch-Townshend bill to roll through the House by a staggering majority of 356 to 17. The Senate, of course, then refused to consider the measure; but it did provide for committee hearings following the adjournment of Congress. Hence the President's quiet confidence following his inauguration in March.

Meanwhile Roosevelt prepared to take the issue to the people—and to the enemy. He went to the enemy first, addressing the Union League Club of Philadelphia late in January, 1905. He had drawn his ground well. Philadelphia was long notorious for its craven politics, its corrupt business leaders, its complacent "nice people"; it was the financial capital of the state that regularly sent Quay and Penrose to the United States Senate; and it was one of the great railroad centers of the nation. Like the Old Guard it indifferently commissioned to represent it, the City of Brotherly Love stood immovably for the status quo.

The President said little in Philadelphia, or anywhere else, that he had not said before. But he did speak more emphatically, more effectively, and more authoritatively. His listeners could not but perceive what the leaders of the Senate were still unwilling to concede—that Roosevelt was President in his own right. He reminded the Union Leaguers, as he was shortly to remind the nation in his inaugural address, that "the great development of industrialism means that there must be an increase in the supervision exercised by the Government over business-enterprise." He observed, as he had done in his first message to Congress three years before, that the framers of the Constitution could not possibly have foreseen present-day developments, that state regulation was impractical and national regulation mandatory. And he called again for amendment of the Constitution if necessary. His peroration nailed down his conservative-progressive Square Deal:

. . . there must be lodged in some tribunal the power over rates, and especially over rebates . . . which will protect alike the railroad and the shipper on an equal footing. . . . We do not intend that this Republic shall ever fail as those republics of olden times failed, in which there finally came to be a government by classes, which resulted either in the poor plundering the rich or in the rich . . . exploiting the poor.

From then until the rate issue was finally settled eighteen months later, Roosevelt maintained his fire. After the lame-duck session ended without Senate action on the day of his inauguration, he again feinted with the tariff. In April and May, he campaigned through the Middle West and Southwest while en route to the annual Rough Riders' reunion at San Antonio. And during the summer of 1905 he again warned the Old Guard that tariff reform was still a possibility. Early in the fall he even went into the Southeast where he repeatedly praised the Confederate military leaders, commented pridefully on his own Southern blood, and declaimed on the need for railroad legislation. It was as though he "himself fired the last two shots from the *Alabama* instead of his uncle," the incredulous correspondent for the Washington *Star* reported. "Wherever the President's visit is discussed you will hear men who believed in and fought for the Confederate cause speak of him with the affection of a comrade."

It was well that Roosevelt thus mobilized his forces, for the railroads, abetted by the National Association of Manufacturers, had already organized theirs. While the President was warning that his program was the only alternative to socialism, an imposing battery of railroad lawyers was arguing before the Senate Committee on Interstate Commerce that it constituted a one way track to the destruction of private property. Nor did the railroads confine their fire to the Senate committee room. The distinguished scholar, William Z. Ripley, described their activities:

> Bogus conventions, packed for the purpose . . . passed resolutions unanimously, to be scattered broadcast by free telegraphic dispatches all over the country. "Associations for the Maintenance of Property" held conventions; the fact being duly advertised. Palpably garbled news items from Washington were distributed without cost. . . . An elaborate card catalogue of small newspapers through the United States was made; in which was noted all the hobbies, prejudices, and even the personal weakness of the editors. . . . Dakota farmers got suggestions as to the danger of the proposed legislation affecting their rates. Kentucky planters were warned of the probable effect upon tobacco prices.

This powerful propaganda barrage yet failed of its target, mainly because the public recognized it for what it was even as it was born. The deep-seated grievances of the farmers and small shippers, the rising indignation of professional men, the continued revelations of the muckrakers, and the relentless pounding of the President of the United States—all these combined to make the movement for regulation politically irresistible. Observer after observer recognized this at the time. As the Chicago *Tribune* reported, "Many Senators are willing to serve the railroads and big shippers, but they have no desire to arouse a popular sentiment which might deprive them of their seats." By December, 1905, when the Fifty-ninth Congress finally convened, the reform wave was so engulfing that such stalwart Old Guardsmen as William B. Allison of Iowa and John Spooner of Wisconsin had been swept onto its crest. One question, and one question alone, remained: What shape would the impending legislation take?

The events which answered that question afford as much insight into Roosevelt as any in his presidential career. They reveal especially his extraordinary skill and balance. The President insisted from the start that the attack be organized and disciplined, that it encompass the enemy's defeat, but not its annihilation. His order of battle, written into his annual message to Congress in December, 1905, was a model of calculated restraint. The President counseled that the railroads, for all their faults, "had done well and not ill" to American society. He warned that rate regulation was "a complicated and delicate problem." And he declared that because of the "extraordinary development of industrialism along new lines . . . which the lawmakers of old could not foresee and therefore could not provide against," the well-meaning corporations had been driven into malpractices by the compulsions of the struggle for survival.

Having recognized the railroads' constructive services, Roosevelt then revealed the idealism that caused him always to reject the business civilization's ultimate values. "There can be no delusion more fatal to the nation," he warned, "than the delusion that the standard of profits, of business prosperity, is sufficient in judging any business or political question—from rate legislation to municipal government." He would, accordingly, set up a moral and legal standard that would free "the corporation that wishes to do well from being driven into doing ill, in order to compete with its rival, which prefers to do ill." The rebate evil should be eliminated completely, the Interstate Commerce Commission should be empowered to fix maximum rates after appeal and investigation, and delay in implementing the Commission's findings should be drastically reduced. Those were his objectives. He would go a little beyond them; but he would not stop short of them.

As incorporated in the Hepburn bill, Roosevelt's rate recommendations passed the House early in 1906 by a majority even more imposing than that mounted on the Esch-Townshend bill the previous year. The Hepburn bill then went to the Senate, where progressives sought vainly to correct its inadequacies and the Old Guard tried urgently to compound them.

The problem in part was that the Hepburn bill failed to provide a means for determining rates realistically. Roosevelt had called for uniform accounting procedures and for government inspection similar to that exercised over the national banks. This was a first, and important, step toward a full solution; but it was inconclusive. Without authority for the Interstate Commerce Commission to evaluate the worth of the railroads, it was impossible to fix a fair rate. This was widely recognized at the time. But it was Senator La Follette who most forcibly impressed it upon the President.

Robert Marion La Follette had stormed out of Wisconsin, which he had given a gubernatorial administration that serves to this day as a prototype of enlightenment while building a political machine that survived until the rise of McCarthy, to be sworn in at the opening session of the Fifty-ninth Congress in March, 1905. A radical in the traditional sense—he was a root thinker to the point of single-mindedness—he would brook neither intellectual nor political compromise. Again and again during the twenty years he sat in the United States Senate this humorless, fiercely intense tribune of the upper Mississippi Valley championed unpopular causes, often with grave risk to his influence and not inconsiderable ambition, but almost always with honor to his convictions. Historians who shared his isolationist sympathies, and many who did not, would eventually set him down as the greatest twentieth-century senator of the progressive persuasion, excepting only, perhaps, George W. Norris of Nebraska.

La Follette had come to Washington in the high hope that the second Roosevelt administration would herald the full flowering of the national progressive movement. And though he brought reservations about the President—there was, he suspected, too much of the trimmer in his make-up—he yet knew that Roosevelt had an intelligent regard for the opinion of experts and that he was reputedly open to advice.

The redoubtable Wisconsin freshman's hopes had begun to sink when Roosevelt failed to come out for evaluation of railroad properties in his annual message. They sank further when it became apparent that the Hepburn bill would go to a final vote in the Senate without that important provision. Rebelling inwardly against the tradition that kept freshmen senators out of debate, La Follette maintained his silence for week after week. Nor did he discuss his views with the President. In accordance with his habit of working with those in whom the real power was vested, Roosevelt was not confiding in La Follette and others of his stamp. In February, 1906, however, the Wisconsin Senator's hopes were momentarily revived when Lincoln Steffens arranged for him and the President to meet.

For two hours late one Sunday night these two embattled leaders of the American social-justice movement discussed the rate problem in the privacy of the White House. Conceding the logic of La Follette's economic analysis, Roosevelt rejected its politics. "But you can't get any such bill as that through this Congress," he exclaimed as the Wisconsin Senator finished. "I want to get something through."

La Follette had characteristically replied that Roosevelt should capitalize on the popular sentiment for rate reform by sending a special message to Congress. Failing in that, he should take the issue to the next Congress. And even if that should also fail, the President would have at least familiarized the public with the only truly effective course of action; and that, concluded the unyielding Senator, would be a monumental achievement.

Both men were proved right. Roosevelt went on to win his immediate, and limited, objective, then took the more advanced issue to Congress and the people in succeeding years. La Follette, meanwhile, contributed to the general enlightenment, or, so Roosevelt complained, confusion, by raising the basic question. "I became utterly out of patience with his attitude. . . ." he wrote of La Follette a year later, "for . . . had it been effective, [it] would have meant the loss of the bill with absolutely no compensating gain." Still, the President added, he "often serves a very useful purpose in making the Senators go on record, and his fearlessness is the prime cause of his being able to render this service."

The futility of the course La Follette wanted Roosevelt to pursue was decisively demonstrated in April, 1906, when the Wisconsin freshman resolutely broke with tradition and took the floor of the Senate chamber, a 148-page manuscript clutched in his hand. As he started to speak senator after senator stalked off the floor, but before he had completed his presentation two days later most had returned— some out of idle curiosity, some to engage him in open debate, and some, like Jonathan Dolliver of Iowa, the President's floor leader of the moment, to become converts to his point of view. For to those whose minds were open, La Follette's logic was irrefutable. As Roosevelt well knew, however, the majority of the Old Guard's minds were closed. Their design was to mitigate the popular pressure, not to resolve the railroad problem. When La Follette's ideas were put to the roll-call test, only six Republicans supported them. By a vote of 40 to 27 the proposal for physical evaluation of the railroad's assets was defeated.

While La Follette was striving for the impossible, Roosevelt was earnestly mustering votes for the possible, and for a little that was not. The formidable character of his carefully defined task had again been driven home when Cabot Lodge declared on February 12 that freight rates were not generally excessive. "I have the gravest doubts," the Massachusetts Brahmin exclaimed in the Senate Chamber, "as to the wisdom of government rate-making even in the most limited form." Lodge's opposition must have hurt the President. So highly did he esteem his friend's purposes and affection, however, that it failed to affect their relationship. "I say deliberately," Roosevelt wrote Lyman Abbott soon afterward, "that during the twenty years [Lodge] has been in Washington he has been on the whole the best and most useful servant of the public to be found in either house of Congress. . . . Lodge is a man of very strong convictions." And this means, he continued in a flash of self-revelation, "that when his convictions differ from mine I am apt to substitute the words 'narrow' and 'obstinate' for 'strong'; and he has a certain aloofness and coldness of manner that irritate people who don't live in New England. But he is an eminently fit successor of Webster and Sumner." Roosevelt never really changed that judgment of his closest friend.

Even as Lodge flailed the heart of the President's program, the Old Guard leadership concluded that Roosevelt had the votes to win the right to fix maximum rates. It decided, therefore, to attack the flank by amending the Hepburn bill with such broad provisions for judicial review that the I.C.C.'s rate-making power would be dissipated. The architect of this strategy was Nelson W. Aldrich of Rhode Island.

A natural aristocrat of modest birth, Aldrich was by some estimates the ablest senatorial conservative of his times. He had been educated in the common schools of the mill town, East Killingly, Connecticut, gone into the wholesale grocery business in Providence as a youth, and been mobilized into the federal military service in 1862 at the age of twenty. Stricken by typhoid fever after six months of war, he had returned to Providence to move up the business and social ladder. By his middle twenties he had been made junior partner in the grocery firm, and by his middle thirties he had become president of the First

National Bank and of the Providence Board of Trade. He had meanwhile married well.

A boyhood interest in debate (he later eschewed oratory) and a
mature concern with civic affairs had caused Aldrich to gravitate to
politics. He became head of the City Council in Providence, served
one term in Congress in the late 1870's, and was made a United
States senator by the Republican organization in the early 1880's. In
Washington, where the irreverent dubbed him "Morgan's floor broker
in the Senate," Aldrich's impressive talents soon won him recognition
as one of the most persuasive young spokesmen of the burgeoning industrial and financial order. Witty, urbane, and gracious to his peers,
a connoisseur and patron of painting, Aldrich was intellectually facile
if not profound. He was imperious by nature, and he was both more
arrogant and less flexible than Elihu Root. Aldrich had always been
vaguely contemptuous of his inferiors, and as he grew older he became increasingly aloof, disdaining the intimacy of most other senators, yet wielding greater influence perhaps than anyone else in the
Senate.

Aldrich's failing was the common one of the self-made man: He
was insensitive to the inequities in the economic system that had
yielded undue preferment to his own superior abilities. The welfare of
labor, the farmers, and the consumers fell not within his compass
except incidentally, and in the classic manner of his type he believed
that government should subsidize and otherwise foster the ends of
business while desisting from regulatory action. A millionaire several
times over, the father-in-law of John D. Rockefeller, Jr., the holder of
vast oil and railroad securities, Aldrich nevertheless failed to fit the
formula of David Graham Phillips' muckraking *Treason of the
Senate*. His conservatism, like that of his colleague and staunch sup-
porter, Orville Platt of Connecticut, who had no millions and owned
little stock, was ideological, and in the field of finance, narrowly
constructive. By temperament, by experience, and by conviction,
Nelson W. Aldrich was a Hamiltonian.

It was probably inevitable that the distinguished Rhode Islander
should emerge as the leader of Roosevelt's opposition. By 1906 Mark
Hanna was two years in his grave. Spooner and Allison were acting
as Roosevelt's lieutenants on the rate bill largely for reasons of expediency. And Platt, "not as brilliant, but . . . of fine ability, of
entire fearlessness, and of a transparently upright and honorable

nature" in the President's apt description, had died the summer before. Of the genuine conservatives, only Philander C. Knox, who had resigned as Attorney General to become junior senator from Pennsylvania, approached Aldrich in character. And he led no faction.

A number of factors gave added precision to Aldrich's plan to vitiate Roosevelt's railroad program by amendment during the critical months of early 1906. The most fortuitous of these was the Hepburn bill's failure to specify the scope of the review the courts would exercise. Roosevelt believed that the right of limited review of the I.C.C.'s findings was both necessary and proper; and upon being advised that the omission of a definite provision would result in a ruling of unconstitutionality, he had his lieutenants attack the problem when the bill reached the Senate. His object, as Blum writes, was to devise an amendment that would "perpetuate explicitly the ambiguities implicit in the House's version." But in thus tampering with the House bill, Roosevelt opened the door for the Old Guardsmen to cloak their antiregulation, prorailroad arguments in the hallowed language of constitutionalism.

To a few, such as Knox, the constitutional question was substantive. In a memorable speech on March 28 the former Attorney General declared that judicial review was "a right painfully won from tyrannies of the past" and that it "would be as a reproach to those of us who are lawyers . . . should we urge the bill or . . . supinely permit it to become law." But to most conservative Republicans the real issue was how best to circumvent effective regulation of maximum rates. Little or nothing in the backgrounds of Elkins of West Virginia, Penrose of Pennsylvania, Depew of New York, Foraker of Ohio, and numerous other Old Guardsmen suggests that they were remotely animated by concern for the preservation of a great legal tradition.

If the Old Guard's shift of focus from rate-making to judicial review illuminated the art of political sophistry, Aldrich's floor leadership revealed the politics of desperation. Unable to muster a majority for such a broad review clause as would have thwarted the President's purposes, his fertile mind devised still another stratagem. He would turn over floor leadership of the Hepburn bill, then under Dolliver's control, to a Democrat. Not a respectable Democrat with whom the President could cooperate, but a beak-nosed, one-eyed master of personal invective whom Roosevelt had once compared with Robespierre and Marat and had not spoken to for four years—Benjamin R. "Pitchfork Ben" Tillman of South Carolina.

The South Carolina Senator exemplified both the worst and the best in the Southern "popocrat" tradition. A vicious Negro-baiter, an early anti-imperialist, and an inveterate dipper into the federal pork barrel, Tillman was as devoted a servant of his white, back-country constituents' interests as most Northern Republicans were to those of the railroad managers and manufacturers. Like many Southerners of demagogic bent, his compassion was considerable if erratic; had he not been perverted by the curse of Southern history he might have emerged as a respected progressive. "Pitchfork Ben" believed with the President that the real issue was railroad legislation in the public interest, and he proposed to effect it by spelling out the narrowest possible area for judicial review. He even sought to prohibit temporary injunctions, the device by which the railroads could indefinitely delay the I.C.C.'s rulings from going into effect.

Roosevelt was exasperated by the blow the Rhode Island Senator had dealt him. "Aldrich," he fumed privately, had "completely lost both his head and his temper." Indeed, the President feared he might lose everything by identifying himself with the Tillman-La Follette radicals. Not only was it possible that the amendment restraining the use of temporary injunctions would be ruled unconstitutional, there was no assurance that Roosevelt could realign his forces should the alliance with Tillman and La Follette break down. Roosevelt soon decided, however, to take the gamble, and in truth it was not too great. "The more I think over this railroad rate matter and the antics of the men who are, under all kinds of colors, trying to prevent any kind of effective legislation," he wrote to Allison, "the more I think through their own action the so-called 'conservative' or so-called 'railroad senators' have put us in a position where we should not hesitate to try to put a proper bill through in combination with the Democrats." The Republicans, he indignantly complained to another correspondent, "have tried to betray me."

Roosevelt accordingly entered into negotiations with the despised South Carolinian through a mutual friend. The President hoped that they could agree on a bill that would be acceptable to the Spooner-Allison Republicans in the center; but when this failed because Tillman's provisions were too radical for Spooner and Allison, Roosevelt agreed to go all the way with Tillman and La Follette if they could muster a majority. He soon pulled back, however, Tillman failing by two votes to win from the Democratic caucus the support he needed. Both the explicitly narrow review concept and the amendment limiting the use of injunctions consequently collapsed.

The President thereupon returned to his original position—that of an explicit perpetuation, as Blum terms it, of "the ambiguities implicit in the House's version"—and under Allison's persuasive cloakroom leadership the Republican majority then closed ranks behind Roosevelt's program. The Democrats also went along, and on May 18, 1906, with only two states'-rights Democrats from Alabama and one Republican, Foraker of Ohio, voting in the negative, the Hepburn bill passed the Senate. The President had carried his primary objective.

Charges and countercharges inevitably followed: Cries of betrayal from the Tillman-La Follette left; claims of victory by the Aldrich-Knox right. Notwithstanding his failure to form the majority that would have made his amendments possible, Tillman felt that the President had let him down. With injured countenance and ostentatious restraint, "Pitchfork Ben" had arisen from his seat just a few days before the final vote to read an "inside history of recent events" from a carefully prepared manuscript. He "confessed" that he had entered into a "conspiracy" with the President; he charged that the administration had surrendered to Aldrich; and he flatly asserted that Roosevelt had spoken derogatorily of prominent Republicans, namely, Knox, Spooner, and Foraker.

If Tillman's first two charges were routine, the third was sensational. Roosevelt had already strained intraparty harmony to the breaking point; the revelation that he had criticized members of his own party to the leader of the opposition, if proved, could sever the last thin cord. It was with cold discomfort, therefore, that Lodge listened to the colorful South Carolinian's accusations. As soon as Tillman concluded, he rushed to a telephone to read to the President a stenographic report of the South Carolinian's remarks. Lodge returned to the Senate chamber a few minutes later with what the political exigencies demanded—an official denial. Tillman's assertion, said the President in the statement that Lodge read into the record, was "a deliberate and unqualified falsehood."

And so Benjamin R. Tillman of South Carolina was initiated into Roosevelt's "Ananias Club," a society whose rolls were to swell as its director's political career lengthened. It is doubtful that "Pitch-fork Ben's" membership was earned. Roosevelt was never wont to speak with moderation in the heat of controversy. And though the President repeated his denial a few days later in what his daughter Alice dubbed a "posterity letter," he not insignificantly added: "I cannot remember the details of the conversation."

The claims of victory by the Aldrich forces were devoid of foundation. When Roosevelt scuttled the Tillman-La Follette program, he withdrew only to his original position. Blum proves beyond cavil that the bill that finally went through embodied the ambiguous phraseology that Roosevelt had first insisted upon. Thus it was Aldrich, his power compromised by Roosevelt's leadership and Allison's defection to the President's side, who had actually submitted. "[Aldrich] . . . has come nearer being unhorsed and thrown in the ditch in this struggle," Tillman observed, "than ever before since I have been here." Only by climbing on the bandwagon at the end had the haughty Rhode Islander saved his face and a measure of his prestige.

Largely overlooked at the time, moreover, was a clause that put all interstate pipelines under the Commerce Commission's control. On May 4, two weeks before the final vote in the Senate, Roosevelt had sent in a report from the commissioner that described how the Standard Oil Company's possession of a near monopoly of pipelines enhanced its already favored position. He accompanied the report with a forceful special message pointing out that Standard Oil was overcharging New England consumers three to four hundred thousand dollars a year, mainly "by unfair or unlawful methods." Abandoning his opposition to the concept of rate-making, Lodge, who was rarely immune to pressures from his Massachusetts constituents, had framed an amendment that classified all pipelines, including those owned by and designed for the use of a single corporation as in the case of Standard's, as common carriers.

Roosevelt had earned the right to exult and even to exaggerate. The Hepburn bill "contains practically exactly what I have both originally and always since asked for," he later wrote. Senator Tillman knew that it did not contain what the President had "always" requested. But the vituperative South Carolinian also knew what Aldrich tried in the end to ignore: Passage of the Hepburn bill was an extraordinary testament to Roosevelt's generalship. In a speech made after his relations with the President had resumed their customarily low level, the unpredictable Tillman acknowledged that fact. Had it not been "for the work of Theodore Roosevelt, in bringing this matter to the attention of the country," he graciously said, ". . . we would not have had any bill at all," and "whatever success may come from it will be largely due to him." Of course, he added, the idea was proclaimed in three successive Democratic platforms. Other Democrats echoed Tillman's words. "I do not believe a bill of this character would have passed the Senate," Henry M. Teller of Colorado declared, "if the President had not given life to this enterprise." Without Roosevelt, intoned Joseph A. Bailey of Texas, "even this imperfect and insufficient bill could have never become a law."

Roosevelt never had any illusions that the Hepburn Act was perfect. It is probably true that he failed to comprehend certain of its inadequacies, notably its failure to strike at freight differentials. And he undoubtedly overestimated its immediate impact. Even as he had skillfully fought for its broad principles, however, he had frankly regarded it as experimental; always, his plan was to amend it on the basis of practical experience.

To dwell on the Hepburn Act's limitations is to obscure the real measure of the President's achievement. Once again Roosevelt had demonstrated that mastery of the political process that had set off his administration of New York; once again his bold and imaginative leadership had forged the Grand Old Party into an untempered instrument of reform. By feinting and threatening, by advancing and retreating, by inciting the people and cooperating with the opposition, he had wrung from the leaders of his own party legislation that many of them bitterly opposed. He had in addition forged another counterforce to the overweening power of monopoly. To the conservative elements of the nation, government by commission was what would later be called "creeping socialism"; to the extreme left, it was perversion of the socialist dogma. But to disinterested observers it represented a pragmatic and creative response to the need to curb the railroads' antisocial power while yet preserving the economic advantages of large-scale organization. The appraisal of Professor Ripley, who had been disappointed when Roosevelt failed to support amendments he had urged at the time, is still persuasive. The Hepburn Act, wrote Ripley many years later, "was an historic event—the most important, perhaps, in Theodore Roosevelt's public career—and a not insignificant one in our national history."

CHAPTER 15

TRIALS, TRIUMPH, AND TRAGEDY

> But for all that, this contemner of "reforms" made reform respectable in the United States, and this rebuker of "muckrakers" has been the chief agent in making the history of "muckraking" in the United States a national one, conceded to be useful.
>
> —Robert M. La Follette, *Autobiography*

Although the struggle for passage of the Hepburn bill was a striking example of Roosevelt's power to sustain leadership, it illuminated only a few of his many facets and was but one of several events which made 1905 and 1906 the most constructively turbulent years of his presidency. During these first two years of power "in his own right," Roosevelt took America into the world, impressed his image upon a score and more of domestic issues, and engaged in a ceaseless round of controversies. He jousted good-naturedly with Bryan, who accused him of stealing his program. He harpooned the idealistic authors of reformist magazine articles by castigating them as "muck-rakers." And he quarreled publicly with his ambassador to Austria-Hungary, a pleasant gentleman whose career was ruined by the foibles of his ambitious wife. He also made a seriocomic effort to convert the nation to simplified spelling. And he gave his support to public health measures of momentous importance.

Many of the President's controversies hardly merit review though they were sensational enough in their time. His quarrel with Ambassador and Mrs. Bellamy Storer, for example, proves only that Roosevelt was mildly indiscreet in his enthusiasm for the advancement of

Archbishop Ireland to cardinal's rank. As Pringle, after dismissing Storer's charge that Roosevelt had authorized him to inform Pope Pius X of the President's desire for Ireland's promotion, speculates: "It is not difficult to imagine Roosevelt pacing up and down in front of his guests at Oyster Bay and insisting explosively that 'Ireland is just the man for Cardinal . . . the Pope should appoint him . . . I fully sympathize.' "

If the Ireland affair was soon forgotten, the President's vain effort to impose simplified spelling upon an anguished people lives on in the minds of literary purists. Roosevelt took not unnaturally to the recommendations of the Spelling Reform Association, a learned organization headed by his friend, Professor Brander Mathews of Columbia University. And when the Association proposed three hundred changes in spelling in 1906, he directed the Government Printing Office to comply. Although about 90 per cent of the new spellings were already in the standard dictionaries under optional or alternative listings—they mainly embraced such changes as "honour" to "honor," "dropped" to "dropt," "fulfill" to "fulfil"—the ensuing reaction was as heated as the one provoked by another Roosevelt's effort to change the date of Thanksgiving Day some three decades later.

The New York Times weightily observed that all newspapers "will take the kindly view that the President's heterographical freaks are misprints and will correct them into English. . . ." An irate contributor to the Rochester Post-Express charged that the whole scheme is backed "by certain large publishing interests and designed to carry out an immense project for jobbery in reprinting dictionaries and schoolbooks." And Henry Watterson declared in his Louisville Courier-Journal that the President's name should be written "Rucefelt," "the first silabel riming with goose." But the most indignant outcry was raised three thousand miles away. The "President's American," it was freely said on the isle that had spawned the language, is usurping the "King's English."

For six months and more the fateful controversy raged. Presidents Andrew White of Cornell, David Starr Jordan of Stanford, and Nicholas Murray Butler of Columbia aligned themselves with Roosevelt. But his friend Arthur T. Hadley of Yale discreetly refused to comment, while Woodrow Wilson of Princeton expressed open disapproval. The Supreme Court of the United States also issued an opinion. Any citation of a previous decision which invoked the new spelling "was not a literal quotation," the Chief Justice sternly informed the Solicitor General.

Roosevelt knew when a cause was lost. "I could not by fighting have kept the new spelling in," he explained to Mathews after the House angrily directed that all government publications, including those emanating from the executive department, observe the standard practice, "and it was evidently worse than useless to go into an undignified contest when I was beaten." They had made a tactical error. "Do you know that the one word as to which I thought the new spelling was wrong—thru—was more responsible than anything else for our discomfiture?" The President would not, however, concede complete defeat. "In my own correspondence I shall continue using the new spelling," he added. He did.

Meanwhile, more substantial matters were absorbing the President's energy. For a decade and one-half a dedicated group of reformers inspired by the Department of Agriculture's chief chemist, Dr. Harvey Wiley, "a very mountain among men, a lion among fighters," as one admirer described him, had been agitating for a federal law to require the accurate labeling of preserved foods, beverages, and drugs. They had mobilized an articulate opinion in support of their proposals, and they had twice won approval for their bills in the House. They had failed, however, to make headway in the Senate, the Republican spokesmen for the food and drug industries combining with the Southern Democratic proponents of states' rights to keep their bills in committee.

The President's commitment to their cause was belated—a reflection, perhaps, of that accommodation to the conservatives which marked much of his conduct in the election year 1904. Not until the summer of 1905 after talks with his personal physician, Dr. Samuel Lambert, Dr. Wiley, and others, did Roosevelt agree to come out for their proposals; and then he did so with misgivings. As he remarked in November, "it will take more than my recommendation to get the law passed, for I understand that there is some very stubborn opposition." And as he did not say, he was prepared to sacrifice almost everything for passage of his railroad regulation program. Nevertheless, he recommended federal regulation of "interstate commerce in misbranded and adulterated foods, drinks, and drugs" in his annual message on December 5.

Roosevelt's brief recommendation (it was three sentences long) had incited a short, but bitter, fight in the Senate. Refusing to allow a bill sponsored by Weldon Heyburn of Idaho to emerge from committee, Aldrich exposed his acrid anti-intellectualism by sneering openly at the "chemists of the Agricultural Department" and speciously asserting that "the liberty of all the people of the United States" was at stake. Nor was the powerful Rhode Islander's armor pierced when Porter J. McCumber of North Dakota rejoined that the real issue was a man's right to receive what he asks and pays for, "not some poisonous substance in lieu thereof."

For a month and one-half after Aldrich's onslaught the Heyburn bill lay buried in committee. On February 15, 1906, however, Aldrich unexpectedly informed Beveridge that he would permit it to be brought out for consideration, and six days later the measure rolled through the Senate. Four states'-rights Democrats voted against it, and Aldrich, in a not unusual gesture of contempt, abstained. Characteristically, Aldrich offered no explanation for his startling reversal; nor does his adulatory biographer explore his reasoning. The circumstantial evidence, however, is overwhelming. A new wave of public indignation had been set off by Samuel Hopkins Adams's exposures of the patent medicine industry in *Collier's*. The American Medical Association was threatening to take the issue into partisan politics. And Roosevelt himself had entered a personal appeal. In addition, and perhaps as important, Aldrich wanted to clear the decks for the final debate on the railroad bill.

The Pure Food bill might have died in the House. Cannon was indifferent, and Roosevelt was too engrossed in the fight for railroad legislation to give it much attention. But the publication of Upton Sinclair's gruesome indictment of the meat-packing industry, *The Jungle,* in late February dramatically altered the situation. Both the public and Roosevelt were so revolted by Sinclair's findings that the President was almost instantaneously galvanized into action. On March 12 he directed Secretary of Agriculture James "Tama Jim" Wilson to investigate the novelist's charges:

> I wish you would carefully read through this letter yourself [he had enclosed a personal appeal from Sinclair]. . . . The experiences that Moody has had in dealing with these beef trust people convinces me that there is very little that they will stop at. You know the wholesale newspaper bribery which they have undoubtedly indulged in. Now, I do not think that an ordinary in-

vestigation will reach anything. I would like a first-class man to be appointed to meet Sinclair. . . . We cannot afford to have anything perfunctory done in this matter.

Meanwhile, the President engaged in a brisk and revealing exchange with Sinclair, who had written *The Jungle* as a brief for socialism. "I agree with you that energetic, and, as I believe, in the long run radical, action must be taken to do away with the effects of arrogant and selfish greed on the part of the capitalist," Roosevelt wrote the young and sensitive novelist. However, he continued, he deplored the "pathetic belief" of the characters who "preach socialism" in the last chapter of *The Jungle*. There were communities where "self-raising is very hard for the time being," the President added, but "there are many, many men who lack any intelligence or character and who therefore cannot thus raise themselves." He would help those crippled by accident (as the employers' liability bill he was then urging Congress to pass was designed to do), and he would regulate big business; but he was not then ready to go farther. "A quarter of a century's hard work over what I may call politico-sociological problems has made me distrust men of hysterical temperament," he pointedly remarked. Yet, he resolutely concluded, "all this has nothing to do with the fact that the specific evils you point out shall, if their existence be proved, and if I have power, be eradicated."

During the next several weeks the investigation of the meat-packing industry weighed increasingly heavily on the President. He appointed two special investigators of unimpeachable reputation, Commissioner of Labor Charles P. Neill and the veteran social worker, James B. Reynolds, to verify Sinclair's findings. And he took his old friend, Albert J. Beveridge of Indiana, into his confidence. Beveridge was never a member of the Senate's inner circle, his self-assurance, independence, and progressive viewpoint offending the Old Guard. Like Roosevelt, however, he had continued to grow intellectually. He had already voted consistently for railroad regulation, and before the year was out he would become a passionate partisan of the graduated income tax and child labor legislation.

Beveridge had been aware of the nauseous conditions in the stockyards and packing houses for some time, and he had been contemplating legislation even before Sinclair's dramatic indictment captured the national imagination. With the President's hearty assent, but without a promise of active support, he now framed a meat inspection measure which passed the Senate on May 25 as an amendment to the Agricultural Appropriations bill. The House committee on agriculture sat on it, however; and for a while it appeared that the impassioned outpourings of Sinclair, Mark Sullivan, and all the others would come to naught. For in the committee chairman, James W. Wadsworth, a stand-pat, walrus-mustached, gentleman farmer from Geneseo, New York, the packers had a man almost as solicitous of their interests as the paid lobbyists who milled about the corridors of the Capitol.

Meanwhile, the long struggle for the railroad bill described in the preceding chapter had ended. For the first time, accordingly, Roosevelt was free to throw the power of his office behind the pure food and meat inspection legislation; and with customary zest and no little finesse, he did so.

The facts uncovered by Neill and Reynolds are "hideous," the President wrote Wadsworth on May 26. "I was at first so indignant that I resolved to send in the full report to Congress." But after reflection, he continued, he had decided to withhold it if Wadsworth would push through the Beveridge amendment. "I should not make the report public with the idea of damaging the packers," he ominously added. "I should do it only if it were necessary in order to secure the remedy."

In spite of this veiled threat, Wadsworth and the packers' friends in and around Congress were too intent on preventing effective inspection to act rationally. They soon came up with crippling amendments, whereupon Roosevelt sent the House a special message urging passage of the Beveridge amendment. The first part of the Neill-Reynolds report, carefully designated as "preliminary," was appended. Again the inference was clear: The President would publish the full and more damning report should the House fail to swing into line.

As Roosevelt anticipated, the confirmation of the charges made in Sinclair's novel had a devastating impact upon the packing industry's sales, especially in Western Europe. In testimony before the House committee on agriculture a few days later, one packing executive described the decline as "disastrous"; another reported that his company's sales had "been more than cut in two."

Under this pressure, the packers decided to support a federal meat-inspection measure in the hope that it would restore public confidence in their products. Almost overnight many of the same lobbyists who had earlier castigated the Beveridge amendment as "unconstitutional" and "socialistic" reversed themselves. What they and their powerful employers now wanted, and what Wadsworth was prepared to give them, was in Mark Sullivan's words, "an inspection law . . . strong enough to still public clamor, while not so drastic as to inconvenience them too greatly." But what the President wanted, and what he was prepared within limits to fight for, was, in his words, "a thorough and rigid, and not a sham, inspection."

The result was conflict, and in the Roosevelt pattern, compromise. After a bitter exchange of letters in which the President heatedly wrote Wadsworth that his substitute amendment was "very, very bad," and the Congressman replied that Roosevelt was "wrong, 'very, very wrong,'" they reluctantly came together. The President agreed that the government should bear the cost of inspection (Beveridge had wanted the packers to pay the inspectors' salaries, but as Roosevelt, who was looking for minor points of concession anyway, belatedly realized, this would have opened the door to collusion). The President also yielded to the packers' objections to Beveridge's proposal that the date of inspection be stamped on the cans. But Roosevelt won clear-cut victories on two other points. It was agreed that inspectors were to be appointed under the civil service laws and that the government could stop inspections in plants that failed to comply with its recommendations. This meant that the packers would have either to conform or lose the now coveted government stamp of approval.

The President also won a substantive victory on the most important issue of all—court review. Wadsworth had sought to include a clause that would have enabled the packers to evade the law by endless litigation. Roosevelt was outraged by this proposal. "I wish to repeat that if deliberately designed to prevent the remedying of the evils complained of," he testily wrote Wadsworth on June 15, "this is the exact provision which the friends of the packers and the packers themselves would have provided. . . . Why have you not put such a provision in the post-office law as it affects fraud orders; in the law as it affects fraudulent entries of homesteads, and so forth?"

Roosevelt then published his "very, very bad" letter. Wadsworth was crushed, or nearly so. Reluctantly, he submitted to a compromise clause which restricted the packers' right to appeal the inspectors' rulings in the courts. Meanwhile the way was cleared for passage of the original pure food bill. Four months later Wadsworth lost the seat he had held almost continuously since 1881. An embittered and discredited man, he could only growl that the "bloody hero of Kettle Hill" was "unreliable, a faker, and a humbug."

Once again the President basked in the glow of achievement. "The railroad rate bill, meat inspection bill & pure food bill . . . mark a noteworthy advance in the policy of securing Federal supervision and control over corporations," he told Lyman Abbott. "I send you herewith the pen with which I signed the agricultural bill, containing the meat inspection clauses," he wrote Beveridge shortly after the signing ceremony. "You were the man who first called my attention to the abuses in the packing houses. You were the legislator who drafted the bill which in its substance now appears in the amendment to the agricultural bill. . . ."

But to Upton Sinclair, Dr. Wiley, and all the other reformers who had recruited the armies that Roosevelt had so brilliantly maneuvered, the President sent nothing. Nor did he mention them in his *Autobiography*. It was not that Roosevelt was ungenerous; nor, even, that he was contemptuous or wholly impatient of men of theory. Roosevelt himself was the most eminent intellectual to sit in the White House since John Quincy Adams; and his administration reflected it. Never had a President shown such a considered respect for the opinion of experts—of welfare workers and social critics, of natural scientists and experts in general, never had there been such a triumph of applied theory as marked the conservation movement under Theodore Roosevelt.* And never, either, had a President been so acutely sensitive to the compromises forced upon him by political necessity and so rankly partisan in their defense. Incident after incident attests to this.

Roosevelt never publicly acknowledged his debt to Tillman and his Democratic colleagues on the Hepburn bill in spite of the sufferance the coarse South Carolinian and other Democrats had given him. Nor, until late in his second administration, did he begin to have reservations about supporting the Republican Old Guardsmen whose opposition to his own advanced theories had repeatedly compelled their compromise and at times their emasculation. During the congressional elections of 1906 he called in effect for a united Republican

* See Chapter 19.

front; and when Samuel Gompers dared to challenge it with a scorching indictment of "Uncle Joe" Cannon's labor record, he boiled over with resentment. "This administration has had no stouter friend than the Speaker of the House," Roosevelt wrote in apparent sincerity. "I need not say . . . that it is a simple absurdity to portray him as an enemy of labor. . . . He is a patriotic American. He is for every man, rich or poor, capitalist or labor man, so long as he is a decent American; and he is entitled to our support because he is a patriotic man."

Meanwhile, the President continued to give William Jennings Bryan short shrift. The closest Roosevelt ever came to admitting his affinity with the Great Commoner was at a Gridiron Club dinner in January, 1905, when Bryan disarmingly accused the President of abstracting plank after plank from the Democratic platform. Roosevelt had ingenuously confessed the crime. The trouble, he explained with mock regret, was that he had to expropriate the good things in the Democratic platform since Mr. Bryan would never be in a position to make use of them.

As Pringle has cogently written, however, Roosevelt was in the main "curiously intolerant toward the Commoner." Even in late 1905 and early 1906 when Bryan was publicly threatening to read out of the Democratic party those members who opposed the President's effort to regulate railroads, Roosevelt was fulminating against him in private: "He is neither a big nor a strong man . . . he is shallow, but he is kindly and well-meaning, and singularly free from rancor." "Bryan, LaFollette, and others like them, so far as I know, have always refused to attack labor people or to denounce their wrongdoing, no matter how flagrant—for corporations, though their indirect influence may be powerful, have practically no votes, while the labor vote is very strong indeed." "As for Bryan . . . what a shallow demagogue he is. I do not believe he is a bit worse than Thomas Jefferson, and I do not think that if elected President he will be a worse President. The country would survive. . . ."

There was more than partisan Republicanism, more than Roosevelt's concealed discomfort at his own compromises, in those strictures. For even as the President picked up the pieces of the Populist-Democratic platform and began dimly to see that in himself, if not in his party, Hamiltonianism and Jeffersonianism were actually merging, he feared where the advanced reformers might take him. More than ever before he was now the hero of the moderate left; and no more than before did he believe that the critical problems facing the republic could be resolved by supplanting business control of American society with that of the agrarians and labor.

The lust for power and prestige, the self-interest approach to public issues, the potential for political corruption—all these Roosevelt regarded as qualities possessed alike by the right and the left, by the exploiters and the exploited, the favored and the unfavored. They buttressed his fears of unregulated competition; they provoked his consuming aversion to government in the interests of a particular class; and they served inevitably as the intellectual springboard for the great centralizing tendencies of his administrations. They also explain his obsession with personal character, for upon the integrity of the office holder and the disinterested intelligence of the administrator did the success of the classless, centralized state depend. Even Lincoln Steffens, observing in 1904 that Roosevelt "has been sneered at for going about the country preaching . . . good conduct in the individual, simple honesty, courage, and efficiency," was moved to conclude that "the literal adoption of Mr. Roosevelt's reform scheme would result in a revolution, more radical and terrible to existing institutions, from the Congress to the Church, from the bank to the ward organization, than socialism or even anarchy. Why, that would change all of us—not alone our neighbors, not alone the grafters, but you and me."

It was not to be. Indeed, Roosevelt's critics on the right even deny the moral and intellectual base of his mighty thrust toward the national welfare state, arguing as they must that the President's real goal was the personal aggrandizement of power. Contrariwise, his detractors on the left, including the latter-day Steffens, scorn both his rationale and his results. No basic change in the power structure was wrought by Roosevelt's deeds and even less was wrought by his words, they contend to this day. In their analysis, his projection of a classless government was chimerical. And perhaps it was. But the biographical point remains: Roosevelt regarded himself as the steward of all the people's interests—as the active and effective proponent of the regulatory theory of a classless government.

Like the Founding Fathers, Roosevelt believed that man's lust for power had to be contained. But he went far beyond that monumental testament to their conviction—the separation of powers and the creation of an artificial system of checks and balances—in bringing his views to pass. His expansion of the executive branch and his continuing effort to convert the Supreme Court to a public interest philosophy, coupled with his later demand for the recall of judicial decisions on the state level, constituted a direct assault on their creation. And it had to be, given Roosevelt's realization that business domination of the judiciary as well as of the legislature had made separation of powers more theoretical than actual. Yet he remained consistent with the Founding Fathers in one regard: He insisted always that the left be kept in balance. Hence his exaggerated fear of Bryan and La Follette; his refusal until 1912 to align himself with any of the great movements of protest; and his irrepressible habit of striking verbal blows at the left even as he concretely advanced its interests.

Whatever the enduring value of Roosevelt's theory of balance through government regulation, it had practical limitations at the time. For one thing, it presupposed that government control of the corporations would induce more fundamental changes than it actually did. Long after Roosevelt left office big business continued to have a disproportionate voice in Congress, to dominate the regulatory agencies Roosevelt had devised to control it, and to send its political spokesmen to the White House, though never again with quite the same freedom to trample on the public interest as in the pre-Roosevelt era. For another, it profoundly overestimated the power of the left at that point in history. Neither the agrarians nor labor, and certainly not the reformers, were then in a position to assume effective control of American society. Bryan's election in 1896, 1900, or 1908 might have spawned a spate of reform legislation, but it would hardly have fathered the revolution Roosevelt feared. By the President's own analysis, the power of business was inextricably intertwined with the social and political fabric of the nation, and especially of the courts. But Roosevelt, his mind's eye partly on the future and partly on the past (he never fully weaned himself from the conservative historians upon whom he had been nurtured), could not quite see this during the middle years of his presidency. Nor could he realize that the rise of labor, the agrarians, and even the intellectuals to a rough equality with business must perforce be accompanied by excesses and probably by violence, given business' persistent and entrenched opposition to that rise. More than anything else, in fact, his failure to appreciate the inevitability of such convolutions explains his flaming intolerance of the militant left.

Probably no incident of Roosevelt's presidential career more graphically illustrates this intolerance than his blistering attack on the "muck-rakers," leveled first in the semiprivacy of a Gridiron Club dinner in late January, 1906 and repeated publicly in the middle of April. "In *Pilgrim's Progress*," the President exclaimed on the latter occasion, "the Man with the Muck-rake is set forth as the example of him whose vision is fixed on carnal instead of on spiritual things . . . the man who never does anything else, who never thinks or speaks or writes, save of his feats with the muck-rake, speedily becomes, not a help to society, not an incitement to good, but one of the most potent forces for evil."

Roosevelt's indictment had apparently been sparked by the publication in early January of the first article of David Graham Phillips' sensational series, "The Treason of the Senate," in William Randolph Hearst's *Cosmopolitan*. Many of Phillips' insights pierced the veneer of disinterestedness that the most confirmed railroad senators presented to the public. And a hard stratum of truth underlay the great body of his work. But his misstatements of fact, innuendoes, and exaggerations offended many responsible readers, while his character assassinations tended to obscure the fact that a political philosophy, rather than personal corruption, was actually on trial. Roosevelt, who knew "poor old Chauncey Depew," Aldrich, Spooner and the rest for what they really were—unreconstructed Hamiltonians—was understandably exercised.

The President may have feared, moreover, that the coincidence of Phillips' indictment and the administration's renewed attack on the trusts—three major railroads had been indicted in December and suit was filed against the Standard Oil Company in March— would stiffen the Old Guard's resistance to the Hepburn bill, the fight for which was then coming to a climax. There is also a suggestion that the real object of Roosevelt's assault was Hearst himself. Certainly he had long yearned to strike a blow at that demagogic tycoon, whom he mercilessly evaluated in a letter to an English friend a few months later:

> Hearst has edited a large number of the very worst type of sensational, scandal-mongering newspapers . . . being a fearless man, and shrewd and farsighted, Hearst has often been of real use

in attacking abuses which benefited great corporations, and in attacking individuals of great wealth who have done what was wrong. . . . He will never attack any abuse, any wickedness, any corruption, not even if it takes the most horrible form, unless he is satisfied that no votes are to be lost by doing it. He preaches the gospel of envy, hatred and unrest. . . . He cares nothing for the nation, nor for any citizens in it.

Roosevelt seems to have been motivated most, however, by fear that the reform movement was getting out of hand. "The dull, purblind folly of the very rich men; their greed and arrogance, and the way in which they have unduly prospered by the help of the ablest lawyers, and too often through the weakness or short-sightedness of the judges or by their unfortunate possession of meticulous minds"—all this, he worriedly wrote, was exciting the popular mind and sparking an enormous increase in socialistic propaganda. The outpourings of *Cosmopolitan, McClure's,* and *Collier's* contained "a little good, a little truth," but it was mixed in with a "great amount of evil," Roosevelt told Secretary of War William Howard Taft. But to others, and especially to the scholarly journalist, Ray Stannard Baker, whose revelations of railroad malpractices in *McClure's* had done much to marshal public sentiment behind the President's regulatory program, Roosevelt insisted that he was not trying to thwart the advance of the reform movement.

Baker had been shocked and hurt when he learned in the spring of 1906 that Roosevelt had assailed the reform writers before the Gridiron Club in January. "It was difficult for me to understand this attack, considering all that had recently happened, all that the President owed to the investigations and reports of at least some of the magazine writers," he later wrote. Baker had thereupon tried to dissuade Roosevelt from repeating the "muck-rake" speech in April. "Now, the letting in of light and air in the matter of current business conditions, toward which you yourself have contributed more than any other man, and for which your administration will, I sincerely believe, be chiefly remembered," he wrote the President on April 7, "is neither pleasant nor profitable for the rascals upon whom the light is turned." Conceding that some of the exposures had been extreme, Baker asked whether they "have not, as a whole, been honest and useful? and would not a speech, backed by all of your great authority, attacking the magazines, tend to give aid and comfort to these very rascals, besides making it more difficult in the future not only to get the truth told but to have it listened to?"

Seemingly unmoved by Baker's appeal, Roosevelt had promised only that he would try to make clear that he was assailing the extremists. "One reason I want to make that address," he said in reply, "is because people so persistently misunderstand what I said, that I want to have it reported in full."

Actually, Roosevelt's remarks in the public version of the "muckrake" speech in April were carefully qualified. He hailed "as a benefactor" every writer who attacks evil, provided he is honest and refrains from "indiscriminate assault upon character." He warned against misinterpreting his words in one phrase, and predicted in the next that misinterpretation would be their fate. "Some persons are sincerely incapable of understanding that to denounce mud-slinging does not mean the endorsement of whitewashing," he ruefully observed. And he reiterated his respect for forthright and factual exposures of wrongdoing:

> At the risk of repetition let me say again that my plea is, not for the immunity to but for the most unsparing exposure of the politician who betrays his trust, of the big business man who makes or spends his fortune in illegitimate or corrupt ways.

The President's request for a fair hearing was not universally honored. As Baker had predicted, within twenty-four hours the magazine writers were all lumped together by the newspapers—the sensitive, searching ones like Baker himself and Lincoln Steffens, the perfervid emotionalists like Phillips and Thomas Lawson, the author of *Frenzied Finance*. Triumphantly, the conservative press, long starved for utterances by Roosevelt it could endorse without strain, trumpeted the glad tidings across the land. "It was a great day while it lasted, but it came too hot," the New York *Sun* gloated. "Muckrakers worked merrily for a time in their own bright sunshine, and an unthinking populace applauded their performance. Now there are few to do them reverence." The people, the Philadelphia *Press* hopefully said, "are sick of the muck-rake" and "a healthy reaction has begun." But had it?

The President's speech failed to stay the enveloping wave of reformism. Many moderate newspapers, including the *New York*

Times, rallied to the defense of the responsible "muck-rakers," and the term itself became one of approbation rather than derogation. For several years thereafter the muckrakers flourished, maintaining the while that angry excitement which contributed so markedly to Roosevelt's own success as President. When finally they began to take to their deathbed near the end of the Taft administration, it was mainly of old age. Public interest had paled and their writings had ceased to be news. The President's attack in 1906 had done little more than blunt their edge.

Yet many of the muckrakers were embittered even so. "I met the President many times afterward," Baker, who was to become a confidant of Woodrow Wilson, recalled, "and there were numerous exchanges of letters, but while I could wonder at his remarkable versatility of mind, and admire his many robust human qualities, I could never again give him my full confidence, nor follow his leadership." Lincoln Steffens, to whom Roosevelt had given carte blanche to investigate the executive branch of the government just two and one-half weeks before the Gridiron Club speech, professed to be unperturbed. The President, he wrote, "said that he did not mean me."

The indictment of the muckrakers was a minor tragedy. Sensible to the impetus the literature of exposure gave the movement for reform, historians have found it as hard as Baker to understand how Roosevelt could have struck such a devastating blow at the men and women whose writings had so abetted his own program. By uncritically accepting the muckrakers' reminiscences, by fastening on the letter to Taft as a closed statement of Roosevelt's philosophy, and by misconstruing the broad tenor of the speech itself, they have even concluded that the President was at heart a pseudo-progressive. In so doing they have underplayed Roosevelt's plaintive warning against misinterpretation and his explicit exoneration of those "who with stern sobriety and truth assail the many evils of our time." And more important, perhaps, they have discounted or ignored the fact that he concluded the public version of the "muck-rake" address with two proposals hardly calculated to make men of wealth and their spokesmen in the Senate rest easy—federal supervision of *all* corporations engaged in interstate commerce and a progressive inheritance tax on swollen fortunes.

Significantly, those recommendations did not go unheralded by contemporary commentators. Many reformers and moderates who would have (and had) dismissed the inheritance tax proposal disdainfully had it come from Bryan announced their support. The radical Democrats feigned displeasure that "that Republican" in the White House had stolen another plank from the Democratic platform. And numerous conservative newspapers lashed both proposals mercilessly, often in the same editorials that glowingly endorsed Roosevelt's chastisement of the muckrakers. One of the sharpest lashes came from that delight of the political reformers and despair of the economic progressives, the New York *Evening Post:*

> We do not expect any terrible results from the President's happy-go-lucky remark about a subject to which, it is plain, he has given no serious thought. It will be a mortification to his friends, and a real public misfortune, that his mouthing has made Bryan appear a reactionary, Hearst a conservative, and has elevated Debs and Powderly to the level of Presidential statesmanship.

In reality, the President's insight into tax policy was less acute than Bryan's. Except for Roosevelt's firm grasp of the inevitability of centralization in industry and the imperative need to devise effective methods of federal control, his knowledge of economics was rudimentary. He construed the inheritance tax as a moral rather than an economic instrument; and not until later, when he belatedly took up the graduated income tax, was he animated so much by a considered appraisal of revenue needs or a desire to level (though the enactment of his own welfare program would have made the creation of new sources of tax revenue mandatory) as by a moralistic urge to strike at the malefactors of great wealth.

There should be, the President argued in the "muck-rake" speech, a sharp distinction between fortunes "gained as an incident to performing great services to the community . . . and those gained in evil fashion by keeping just within the limits of mere law-honesty." He added that "no amount of charity in spending [ill-won] fortunes in any way compensates for misconduct in making them." He realized, of course, that it was impossible to make the distinction; and because of his reluctance to penalize those whose incomes were by his unspecified criteria earned, he was slow to espouse the income tax. Such was his contempt for the idle rich and their offspring, however, that he came easily to the conclusion that regardless of how huge fortunes were amassed, they should not be passed down in full. "They rarely do good and they often do harm to those who inherit them," he sermonized in his last annual message to Congress. From the attack on the muckrakers on, accordingly, Roosevelt repeatedly urged Congress and nation to adopt a steeply graduated inheritance tax.

CHAPTER 16

THE PEACEMAKER I

> Forty years before Americans were willing to listen . . .
> [Roosevelt] urged active participation in world decisions for
> which he felt we shared responsibility and whose consequences he
> felt we could not escape.
>
> —Howard K. Beale, *Theodore Roosevelt*

Even before the President's domestic program reached its finest flower
in 1906, Roosevelt had sounded the death knell over the old isolationism and won recognition for his country as a world power of the
first magnitude. He had further committed the United States to internationalism of a form. Never thereafter would the American people
live in relative isolation from the affairs of Europe or the Eastern
Hemisphere, though they would often imagine that they were. Never
again would the leaders of the Old World act without regard to
American interests, though they would sometimes tragically miscalcu-
late America's response to their actions.

The Roosevelt who sheathed the sword of ultranationalism to plunge
into the struggle for world peace in 1905 and 1906 was a wiser and
more reflective man than the Roosevelt who had exulted over war in
1898, urged repudiation of a half-century-old treaty with the British
in 1900, and rode roughshod over Latin American sensibilities in
1902. He thought as much as always in terms of power—"I never take
a step in foreign policy unless I am assured that I shall be able eventually to carry out my will by force," he asserted in 1905 and numerous
times before and after. And he continued to press urgently and effectively for military preparedness, especially for the strengthening of

the battle fleet. But he now possessed a clearer perception of the ramifications of power.

No longer did Roosevelt gauge events solely in terms of their impact upon the immediate interests of the United States, as he had frequently done in the past. No longer did he believe that a display of force was invariably more effective than patient negotiation or that America had only to flex its muscles and go it alone. When, just six months before he brought peace to Russia and Japan in 1905, he declared in his inaugural address that America's attitude toward all the nations of the world "must be one of cordial and sincere friendship" and that it must be shown "not only in our words, but in our deeds," he indubitably meant it. And had it not been for the fetters imposed by his own views on colonialism, he might well have fulfilled that high aspiration.

Nowhere were these changes more apparent than in the President's attitude toward the Far East. He still clung to many of the old imperialistic precepts, and he believed to the end that China was fraught with opportunity for American economic penetration. "Before I came to the Pacific Slope I was an expansionist," he exclaimed in San Francisco in May, 1903, "and after having been here I fail to understand how any man . . . can be anything but an expansionist." Thus he continued to give vigorous support to John Hay's "Open Door" and to reflect the ideas of Captain Mahan and, more critically, of Brooks Adams. Yet—and this is the real measure of his intellectual growth—Roosevelt saw the world in more and more complex terms.

"He commenced to realize," writes Beale, "that the struggle for supremacy in Eastern Asia was closely related, sometimes in a complicated and baffling fashion, to a struggle for dominance in Europe, and that both of these component struggles were parts of a world struggle that encompassed much besides either Europe or the Far East. . . . [He] came to comprehend the discouraging but basic fact that, if America was to become a world power among imperial rivals as he wished her to do, she must enter a game in which, through complicated moves and countermoves, each nation was trying to increase its own power but was determined that no other power or group of powers should attain sufficient strength to threaten it and its friends."

One of the portentous results of this maturing process was a *volte-face* toward Russia. Roosevelt had originally been more pleased than displeased by that giant's remorseless advance into Turkestan and the wild reaches of Siberia during the late nineteenth century, viewing the march of the Russian peoples with the fascination that he had written into his own *Winning of the West*. He was keenly aware that the Russians were undemocratic, if not barbaric, and he had vague forebodings that Russia might some day "take possession of Northern China and drill the Northern Chinese to serve as her army." But as late as the eve of his elevation to the presidency he professed to be undisturbed by that latter prospect. "Undoubtedly the future is hers unless she mars it from within," he wrote in July, 1901. "But it is the future and not the present." Meanwhile Russia's advance into China would exert a stabilizing influence on that backward, amorphous, and warlord-ridden nation. Consequently, he concluded, it would actually prove a blessing to "civilization."

Under the heavy responsibility of the presidential office, however, Roosevelt's views began to change. America's dynamic thrust toward world power, the dream of economic penetration of China with the clash of American and Russian aspirations that it portended—these and the growing *rapprochement* with Great Britain shed an ominous new light on the Russian question. Where once Roosevelt had been enamored of the Eurasian giant's latent power and had even speculated that Russia might be "the hope of a world that is growing effete," he now began to ponder the implications of that power. A note of apprehension and distrust of Russian ambitions crept into his correspondence; and when the Russians massacred thousands of Jews at Kishinev in 1903 he was revolted, though he discreetly refused to protest openly. He was further incensed by the tsarist government's failure to withdraw its troops from Manchuria in accordance with an agreement with China of 1902 and by its resultant flaunting of the Open Door. "I wish, in Manchuria, to go the very limit I think our people will stand," he informed Hay in high irritation during the summer of 1903. The Russians have comported themselves with "well-nigh incredible mendacity," the President complained to Albert Shaw about the same time. "I believe in the future of the Slavs if they can only take the right turn," he later confided to Spring-Rice, who had been trying to impress him with the Russian menace for almost a decade. "But I do not believe in the future of any race *while it is under a crushing despotism. . . .*"

Conversely, Roosevelt's once harsh attitude toward Japan softened perceptibly. There was much in the Japanese national character that he had always admired—military competency, industrial efficiency, and sacrificial quality. And though he believed that the Japanese had much to learn from the West, particularly about the treatment of women, he felt that Americans could profit from contact with the Japanese. He was notably impressed by their success in eliminating "the misery" that so cursed America's great cities. But the President was not wont to interject consciously his personal likes and dislikes into his appraisal of the American national interest. Even after he turned against the Tsar's government he continued to feel warm toward the Russian people; and he always did respect Germans heartily, the anti-German tenor of much of his diplomacy notwithstanding.

Roosevelt's growing cordiality toward Japan was animated by several factors. The most critical were the belief that Japan had resigned itself to American possession of Hawaii and the Philippines and the conviction that Japan constituted the natural counterweight to Russia in the Far East. Hence the administration's approval of the Anglo-Japanese Alliance of 1902. Yet the President never dropped his guard completely. "It is always possible that Russia and Japan will agree to make up their differences and assume an attitude of common hostility toward America," he warned his ambassador to Russia in December, 1904. Or, as he had bluntly phrased it to the Japanese ambassador during a luncheon conversation six months before, "Japan might get the 'big head' and enter into a general career of insolence and aggression." But he did not think this was likely as long as the United States treated Japan with respect and recognized its "paramount interest in what surrounds the Yellow Sea."

Convinced that the interests of America and the whole civilized world called for a supreme effort to promote stability in the Far East, the President held himself ready to make the necessary effort. Nor did he feel any compunction about acting on this, his personal estimate of the situation. Indeed, during the summer of 1905, in an action that heavily underlined the irreconcilables faced by numerous architects of twentieth-century foreign policy, he strained the executive authority to its uttermost limit to achieve his object.

Shortly before the President opened the memorable Russo-Japanese peace conference, his special representatives in London and Tokyo, Senator Lodge and Secretary of War Taft, pledged the United States to silent partnership in the Anglo-Japanese Alliance. Of necessity, the commitment was unofficial. Roosevelt would have welcomed a formal treaty with His Majesty's government, for he regarded British and American interests as identical in their larger compass. But he was too able a political leader to cut himself off from the people by proposing such a radical break with tradition. So he settled on the personal arrangements made by Lodge and Taft. They were not binding, except in a gentlemanly sense. Yet their import was clear: On the word of its President and without the knowledge of its people, the United States government had agreed to act in concert with Great Britain and Japan should a Far Eastern crisis develop. As Taft had confidentially explained to Count Taro Katsura, the Japanese Prime Minister, Tokyo could count upon his government "quite as confidently as if the United States were under treaty obligations."

Two decades were to pass before the American people learned of this signal circumvention of the treaty making power. A rumor that the United States had unofficially joined the Anglo-Japanese Alliance was published in Japan a few months after the fact, but it was denied by Washington. Only when the historian Tyler Dennett uncovered the evidence while doing research for his *Roosevelt and the Russo-Japanese War,* published in 1925, was the secret out.

Why the suppression? The startling fact seems to be, as Beale concludes, that Roosevelt simply did not "dare tell" the American people. Whether this restraint was justified depends on the latitude one feels the executive should be granted. There is no question, however, that the President had exceeded the limits of his authority in its narrow construction; that he had comported himself in the grand and sometimes circumspect manner of the strong Presidents from Jefferson through Truman. Nor is there any question that he had acted out of deep-felt concern for his country's well-being, and that he had then acted only after mature reflection and extended consultation with responsible advisers. Confident in the wisdom of his policy, serene in the knowledge that he would within four years return again to the people, he needed no other justification.

The most far-reaching aspect of the Anglo-American-Japanese accord which Roosevelt had thus embraced was the recognition of Japanese suzerainty in Korea—the so-called Taft-Katsura Agreement. Korea had been wrenched from its tie to the Confucian state by China's defeat in the Sino-Japanese War of 1894–95. The triumphant Japanese and the watchfully aggressive Russians had then guaranteed her nominal independence; but the Tsar's government had persistently tightened its hold upon her during the decade that followed. Meanwhile it continued its occupation of Manchuria.

Desperate to resolve what it regarded as the Russian threat, Japan finally offered Russia a free hand in Manchuria in exchange for one in Korea. But the Russians, as Sir Bernard Pares writes, were aiming "at nothing less than establishing a Russian hegemony over Asia . . . including . . . the expulsion of the British from India." Repeatedly the Tsar Nicholas II refused to respond to Japanese entreaties that he evacuate Manchuria or soften his Korean policy. Finally, on February 5, 1904, Tokyo "gave a last and earnest warning," and then withdrew its minister from St. Petersburg. Three days after that, in a maneuver they had used against China in 1894 and would develop to perfection thirty-seven years later, the Japanese launched a surprise attack on the Russian fleet at Chemulpo. They made no formal declaration of this, the start of the Russo-Japanese War.

Spectacularly successful both on land and sea, the Japanese stood as masters of all Korea and part of Manchuria as well by the spring of 1905. They thus made British recognition of their authority in Korea a prime factor in renewal of the Anglo-Japanese Treaty of 1902; and they in effect demanded a similar recognition from the United States.

Roosevelt had followed the course of the war with absorbed interest. He was informed that the Japanese occupation forces were subjecting the Koreans to indignities that made the white imperialism so acidly characterized by "Mr. Dooley" and others seem restrained. And he knew that the Japanese were making a concerted effort to restrict American business activity in Korea. He must also have known, though he could not admit it, that American refusal to recognize Japan's aggrandizement of Korea might have restored the luster to that moral leadership which the subjugation of the Filipino guerillas had so badly tarnished; that it might even have evoked grudging words of praise from his severest domestic critics, the "goo-goos." But he further understood that such action would have spiked his project for a Far Eastern balance of power built on the friendship and mutual recognition of the interests of his own country and Japan. Adapting himself to conditions as he found them, therefore, he warmly agreed with Taft that the United States approved Japan's "suzerainty over" Korea while Tokyo disavowed designs on the Philippines. "Your conversation with Count Katsura absolutely correct in every respect," the President cabled Taft on July 31, 1905. "Wish you would state to Katsura that I confirm every word you have said."

Roosevelt never publicly explained his Korean policy even after he left the presidency; and understandably, given the continued delicacy of Japanese-American relations. Nevertheless, his intimates knew why he had acted as he did. Events had boxed him into a situation analogous to that encountered by Franklin D. Roosevelt at Yalta when the Communists had *de facto* control of Poland. As Elihu Root, irked by charges that his beloved friend had "sold out" the Koreans (young Syngman Rhee was among the most bitter protestants at the time), insisted twenty-five years later, the President had no alternative aside from complete withdrawal. "Many people are still angry because we did not keep Japan from taking Korea," Root reflected. "There was nothing we could do except fight Japan; Congress wouldn't have declared war and the people would have turned out the Congress that had. All we might have done was to make threats which we could not carry out."

By the time the Taft-Katsura memorandum had made formal the Anglo-American-Japanese comity, the President stood on the threshold of his most magnificent, and in a sense most frustrating, diplomatic achievement—mediation of the Russo-Japanese War. The background was long and complex.

Roosevelt had not quite assumed full direction of Far Eastern affairs when the war broke out in February, 1904. His initial reaction followed lines Secretary Hay had earlier laid down. Both Russia and Japan were urged to observe "the neutrality of China," and interested neutral powers were adjured to cooperate to the same end. That, apparently, was all. Afterward the President said in a letter to Spring-Rice that he "notified Germany and France in the most polite and discreet fashion that in the event of a combination against Japan" the United States would "promptly side with Japan and proceed to whatever length was necessary on her behalf." But neither the editors of Roosevelt's *Letters* nor Beale have found evidence that he delivered such a warning. Possibly Roosevelt confused what he actually said with what was in his mind at the time, or with what he later believed he should have said. And possibly neither Ambassador Jusserand nor Speck von Sternburg reported what they may have regarded as informal remarks meant for them rather than their governments.

Meanwhile, the President's enthusiasm for the Nipponese continued to mount. By the technological, militaristic, and administrative criteria that loomed so large in his thinking, they were proving themselves civilized. "What nonsense it is to speak of the Chinese and the Japanese as of the same race," the President said to Hay at one point. "I should hang my head in shame if I were capable of discriminating against a Japanese general or admiral, statesman, philanthropist or artist, because he and I have different shades of skin," he wrote on the eve of the peace conference. The white Russians, not the yellow Japanese, were the inferior people. "They are utterly insincere and treacherous; they have no conception of the truth . . . and no regard for others . . . no knowledge of their own strength and weakness." Was not the Tsar "a preposterous little creature."

Even at the height of his enthusiasm for the Japanese, however, the President thought basically in terms of an American interest related to that of civilization as a whole. To be sure, he sometimes conjectured that it might be best for Russia and Japan to bleed themselves to enfeeblement; and he occasionally contemplated an ultimate war between the United States and Japan. But he never gave serious consideration to either possibility. Maturely and morally, he concluded that the war should be ended rather than prolonged, and that American and world interests would be served thereby. A friendly America would give Japan no provocation for hostile action; and in any event, Russia was more dangerous. "If Russia wins she will organize northern China against us," Roosevelt predicted to Hay when the war was but five months old. "Therefore, on the score of mere national self-interest, we would not be justified in balancing the certainty of immediate damage [from Russia] against the possibility of future damage [from Japan]."

Consequently the President strove to promote a peace that would end the war and yet reflect Japan's military victories. To Chentung Liang-Cheng and Baron Takahira, the cordial Chinese and Japanese ambassadors to Washington, to Count Arturo Cassini, the despised representative of the Tsar, and to those old stand-bys, Speck von Sternburg and Jean Jules Jusserand, Roosevelt repeatedly proposed mediation. But for more than a year he was cast about on the shoals of European rivalries. No nation could afford to antagonize the Russians. France was already allied with them; Germany was striving soulfully to woo them; and Great Britain was in the throes of a fateful

indecision. Nor would the Russians themselves listen to peace proposals. "Cassini throws a pink fit at any reference to peace," Hay
remarked as late as November, 1904.

In these circumstances Roosevelt shrewdly decided that peace
would have to be arranged, if at all, by a seemingly disinterested third
power. And though suggestions were offered that a congress of nations
attempt mediation, he peremptorily dismissed them for fear a congress
would partition China irreparably and destroy America's growing
friendship with Japan in the process. As he explained to Hay, "We
could hardly afford to allow a combination of R. G. & F. to step in
and deprive Japan of the results of this war."

Lacking the financial resources to fight indefinitely, or indeed for
many more months, Japan meanwhile realized the wisdom of negotiating while the fortunes of war were still so munificently with her.
Rumors that she would entertain mediation cropped out in February,
1905, and in March Ambassador Takahira and Baron Kaneko, a
Harvard classmate of Roosevelt's, began secret conferences with the
President. Their government demanded victor's terms, including an
indemnity.

The Tsar, who was an obtuse autocrat at worst and a reckless
gambler at best, was not amenable. He preferred to stake the future
on one more showdown with the Japanese fleet; and this over against
the colossal defeats of his forces, the near bankruptcy of his government, and the massive unrest of his people. The showdown came in
the Battle of the Sea of Japan on May 27 and 28, when, in one of the
most impressive naval victories yet to be won, Admiral Togo practically destroyed Admiral Rozhdestvensky's thirty-two-ship fleet which
had steamed around the world from Europe for the engagement. And
so, wrote Pares, there was fulfilled a fate that had been sure to over-
take it "from the day it set sail on its desperate errand under the
ill-starred flag of the Romanoffs." Three days later the Japanese,
having ascertained that Roosevelt agreed with their principal demands,
asked the President to initiate mediation.

Even imperious Wilhelm II now importuned his stubborn cousin,
"Nicky," to agree to mediation on the grounds that the cessation of
hostilities was the only alternative to revolution. Under this and other
pressure, the Tsar began to weaken, though hardly to break; and there
ensued a difficult preliminary negotiation which has been brilliantly
pieced together by Beale. Through it all Roosevelt showed himself

wisely sensitive to the childlike whims of the Tsar and discreetly firm with the Japanese, who were beginning to stand hard on their new-won dignity. Privately the President raged. "The more I see of the Czar, the Kaiser, and the Mikado the better I am content with democracy, even if we have to include the American newspaper as one of its assets," he complained to Lodge. But in his relations with the principles he acted with "consummate tact."

During the early summer Roosevelt ironed out most of the surface conflict in separate meetings with the delegates: Count Sergei Witte and Baron Roman R. Rosen for the Russians; Ambassador Takahira and Baron Jutaro Komura for the Japanese. Then, on August 5, he surpassed himself with a memorable display of social urbanity and diplomatic finesse aboard the presidential yacht *Mayflower,* anchored in the harbor of Oyster Bay. The occasion was a luncheon for the envoys, and the issue was precedence. Who would be seated to the President's right? Which nation would be toasted first? Who would precede whom into the dining room?

That the fate of tens of thousands of common soldiers and sailors should have depended upon such trivialities (and still often does) is incredible. Witte, who admitted to being "morbidly sensitive" to criticism of his shaken country, was beset by fear that the President, "a typical American, inexperienced in and careless of formalities, would make a mess of the whole business," and that the Japanese might "be given some advantage" over the Russian envoys. "I will not suffer a toast to our Emperor offered after one to the Mikado," he irritably remarked to Baron Rosen on the eve of the conference. Nor were Takahira and Komura, who stood half a foot under Roose-velt and a full foot under the tall and powerful Witte, disposed to waive the proprieties. Their country's resounding defeat of the Rus-sians had symbolized nothing if not the yellow man's rise to equality and more with the white man; and their resultant arrogance had already made its mark on American public opinion.

Roosevelt, however, came up with an ingenious solution. After introducing the Russians to the Japanese when they came aboard the presidential yacht, he engaged in general conversation in French; then, his butchered phrases still pouring out, he simultaneously guided the chief of each delegation across the threshold and into the dining salon, where their plates were filled from a round buffet table. After everyone was served, he exclaimed: "Gentlemen, I propose a toast to which there will be no answer and which I ask you to drink in silence, standing." He then drank "to the welfare and prosperity of the sovereigns and peoples of the two great nations, whose representatives have met one another on this ship." It was, he said, "my most earnest hope and prayer, in the interest . . . of all mankind that a just and lasting peace may speedily be concluded among them."

The President had carried it off. The subsequent conversation was more relaxed even than circumstances warranted, and when Takahira and Rosen later departed, they shook hands warmly. Roosevelt was tremendously relieved; and also pleased with himself. "I looked forward to this affair with a good deal of anxiety," he confided that night to Joseph B. Bishop, who was then secretary of the Isthmian Canal Commission, "knowing that a single slip on my part which could be construed as favoring one set of envoys over the others would be fatal. . . . I think we are off to a good start."

The luncheon on the *Mayflower* was but a prelude to the larger drama that constituted the mediation itself. From any perspective, President Roosevelt had embarked on one of the most perilous courses of his entire career. The stakes were fabulously high. Success promised peace—the end of pointless bloodletting, the extinction of the threat of worldwide conflict. It meant that Roosevelt would be acclaimed by men of good will the world over; that he would be showered with laurels such as no American had ever before received. Failure meant that the war would continue, or, more likely, that the powers of Europe would carve out a peace representative of their own special interests. It also foreshadowed personal humiliation for the President and loss of prestige for his country. Nor was that all. Success in the primary objective—peace—threatened failure in the secondary objective: advancement of the United States' interests. For Japanese-American friendship hung in the balance. What would be the fate of the President's good neighbor policy toward Japan if the terms of the peace he had promoted failed to satisfy the Mikado's government?

It is the measure of Roosevelt's character that knowing all this he still undertook the mission. There are, of course, the stock psychological explanations—his unfailing compulsion to act, his perpetual gravitation toward the center of the stage, his conviction that glory was the supreme end of life. But in all probability, higher motives than those were controlling. Indeed Beale, whose work is marred neither by unreasoned adulation nor by undisciplined prejudice, concludes that the President's purpose was purely and simply to end the carnage and stabilize the balance of power in the Far East. "I thought it my plain duty to make the effort," the President wearily, yet happily, remarked to Bishop the night of the *Mayflower* luncheon. "I should be sorry to see Russia driven completely off the Pacific coast," he had confided to Lodge two months before, ". . . and yet something like this will surely happen if she refused to make peace."

The final terms arranged at Portsmouth were actually more advantageous to Russia than Roosevelt thought necessary. The Tsar had remained adamant, disdaining to the end the Japanese demand for an indemnity; he also opposed transfer of Sakhalin Island to Japan. Fortunately for his obdurate Majesty, Sergei Witte had managed through a combination of good luck and high skill to swing the mercurial American temperament from support of Japan to sympathy for Russia. He had also faithfully reflected his sovereign's obduracy at the council table. The result was prolonged deadlock. Concluding that the negotiations would thus terminate in failure, with all that implied, Roosevelt had made an indirect personal appeal to the Mikado near the end. And well that he had, for the Russian envoys were under orders from the Tsar to "finish the negotiations and come home at once." To Witte's astonishment and Komura's despair, Tokyo had submitted. On August 30 the Japanese agreed to waive the indemnity and accept the southern half of Sakhalin Island, rather than the whole as they had been demanding.

Peace of a sort had finally come to the Far East. As Roosevelt freely acknowledged, France and Germany had contributed to the final achievement; and so had the rugged Russian patriot, Witte, who had earlier been dismissed from the Tsar's service because of his opposition to the aggressive policies which had provoked the war. Nevertheless, it was a uniquely personal triumph for the President, one that earned for him and his government the acclaim of the nations. The Tsar, the Mikado, the Kaiser, the King of England (whose government had been inactive), and hundreds of prominent men the world over effusively poured forth their congratulations. Some were perfunctory; but many were heartfelt.

"This is the happiest news of my life," exclaimed the aging Pope Pius X, who would live just long enough to protest the start of a much greater war. "Thank God for President Roosevelt's courage." "You have probably saved the lives of a quarter of a million men," the American Ambassador to Russia reported. As the editors of the *Literary Digest* concluded, "Whatever the actual influences which induced the Government at Tokyo to accept the terms, the whole world is agreed that President Roosevelt is the man who marshaled them in such a way as to bring about the desired result.

As in all creative acts, however, the cost was high. Even as many Americans basked in their President's glory, even as they conceded that Roosevelt had done for humanity what no one else could have done, they lamented the price of greatness. They spoke critically of "entangling alliances"; they remarked nostalgically of the old isolationism; they read knowingly of the riotous wave of anti-Americanism that rose in Japan in the wake of the settlement. And some, Mark Twain among them, even protested that peace had preserved the tottering regime of the autocratic and irresponsible Nicholas II. Better that the Russians should be liberated from their "age-long chains," said that master satirist of royalty and its works.

And perhaps it would have been better—as it would also have been better if the United States had not become identified with Japan's failure to realize the full fruits of her military victories. More than one historian has added the heavy burden of hindsight to those ponderous judgments. But to what real enlightenment? To accept the premises of those who argue that Roosevelt should have forborne the peacemaker's role that fate had thrust before him is to accept premises which lead logically, albeit extremely, to preventive war. Not yet has moral Western man succumbed to that ultimate degradation of the human spirit. So the wheel perforce turns full circle—back to the night of the luncheon aboard the *Mayflower* and the President's unaffected statement to his friend Bishop that he had felt it "my plain duty to make the effort."

John Hay had not lived to see his country become the focal point of world interest at Portsmouth. Never a robust man, he had been steadily declining since the summer of 1900. Partly out of loyalty to party and friend, largely out of sheer inertia, he had hung on until after the inauguration in March—long enough for the Senate to emasculate a series of arbitration treaties he had laboriously negotiated and then insult him personally by declining to pass a resolution authorizing him to accept the Grand Cross of the Legion of Honor from the French government. Early in the morning of July 1, 1905, two weeks after he had returned to his summer home in New Hampshire following a fruitless trip to Europe in quest of health, he died.

Private secretary to Abraham Lincoln, friend of Roosevelt's revered father, and one of the main architects of that Anglo-American amity to which Roosevelt was now committed, Hay had been for the President a link with the past. "I dearly loved him; there is no one who with any of us can quite fill the place he held," Roosevelt wrote Hay's widow the day of his death. "He was not only my wise and patient advisor in affairs of state; he was the most devoted and . . . charming of friends." The sentiments were genuine, if not inclusive.

The death of the man who had articulated the Open Door policy evoked more than the normal spate of uncritical newspaper appraisals. Hay was given rank with the greatest Secretaries of State; he was credited with achievements that were more Roosevelt's than his and with responsibility for the administration's "signal success." The President was irritated by these lavish encomiums, though he had publicly pronounced Hay's death a "national bereavement." And in letters to Lodge, Taft, Beveridge and others he revealed his pique. But not until the publication in 1909 of three volumes of Hay's letters edited by Henry Adams did he give full vent to his feelings.

Curiously, the burden of Hay's comments was favorable to Roosevelt. "He has plenty of brains, and as you know, a heart of gold," Hay had written in one letter. However, Hay did play down the President's role in the Panama and Alaskan boundary episodes, and otherwise showed less deference presumably, than the President desired. "[Roosevelt] . . . began talking at the oysters, and the *pousse-café* found him still at it," Hay had confided to Adams near the end of Roosevelt's first year in office. "When he was one of us, we could sit on him—but who, except you, can sit on a Kaiser?"

On January 28, 1909, in a nine-page posterity letter to Lodge that was as revealing of its author's values as of its subject's character and achievements, Roosevelt reduced Hay to a stature somewhat below that which many historians would later give him.

I think he was the most delightful man to talk to I ever met, for . . . he continually made out of hand those delightful epigrammatic remarks which we would all like to make, . . . [Roosevelt wrote]. But he was not a great Secretary of State. . . . He had a very ease-loving nature and a moral timidity which made him shrink from all that was rough in life. . . . His close intimacy with Henry James and Henry Adams—charming men, but exceedingly undesirable companions for any man not of strong nature—and the tone of satirical cynicism which they admired . . . marked that phase of his character which so impaired his usefulness as a public man. [Hay] . . . never initiated a policy or was of real assistance in carrying thru a policy; but he sometimes phrased what I desired said in a way that was of real service; and the general respect for him was such that his presence in the Cabinet was a strength to the administration. He was always afraid of Senators and Congressmen who possest any power or robustness. . . .

Roosevelt then came to the core of his grievance: He reproduced documents to prove that he, not Hay, had been principally responsible for settling the Alaskan dispute. He wrote that he himself had done the "vital work" on Panama. He charged that Hay would not act when a crisis had occurred in China. And he claimed that Hay "could not be trusted where England was concerned."

Many of the President's points were well taken; but others, especially on Panama and Alaska, were distorted. There was also an ironic aspect to the complaint that Hay had failed to initiate policy. It was not in Roosevelt's nature to have permitted Hay or anyone else to make the great decisions of state. With less assertiveness than Roosevelt respected, perhaps, Hay had often and sometimes crucially proffered sagacious advice; and the President had on occasion rejected it. Nevertheless, as the burden of Roosevelt's estimate suggests, Hay had been in his own times overrated.

Neither Roosevelt's letter to Lodge nor the remarks in Hay's published letters which provoked it comprise a pleasant chapter. Lincoln, the man both men most admired, could not have written them. But Roosevelt apparently had to. His sense of history and his extraordinary concern for his place in history would not permit him to leave unchallenged statements that he regarded as misleading or derogatory to himself.

If the President's reflections on Hay reveal his own hypersensitivity, his selection of Elihu Root as the new Secretary of State reveals his larger strength. His natural rapport with men of strong character virtually foreordained that he would turn to Root in the urgency of the summer of 1905, though he thought fleetingly of Taft, who had replaced Root as Secretary of War eighteen months before. "I wished

Root . . . partly because I am extremely fond of him and prize his companionship as well as his advice, but primarily because I think that in all the country he is the best man for the position," Roosevelt explained to Beveridge. "He will be a tower of strength to us all," he wrote Lodge. "I not only hope but believe that he will get on well with the Senate, and he will at once take a great burden off my mind in connection with various subjects, such as Santo Domingo and Venezuela."

Root was to meet the President's hopes, though his works as Secretary of State were to be less notable than those of his years in the War Department. Then he had been a host unto himself—efficient, constructive, and within the limits of his cautious outlook, bold. He had contributed substantially to the creation of the American colonial system and he had essayed a noteworthy reorganization of the army. There was a subtle difference, however, in the circumstances of Root's two secretaryships, separated as they were by eighteen months.

Elihu Root had been already in office, already engaged in his constructive labors, when Theodore Roosevelt became President of the United States in September, 1901. And he had continued to be a real power until, with Roosevelt's praises ringing in his ears—"I shall never have, and can never have, a more loyal friend, a more faithful and wiser adviser"—he had resigned on February 1, 1904. But when Root returned to Washington in July, 1905, it was to the service of a man who had been resoundingly endorsed by the American people, was more ebulliently confident than ever, and had for many months been making the broad decisions in foreign policy on his own. The old order had passed; nor could it be re-created.

Yet Root hardly proved subordinate. As Roosevelt later said, "He fought me every inch of the way. And, together, we got somewhere." The President took Root into his confidence on most matters of state, and he fortunately gave him almost free rein in the formulation and carrying out of policy for the Western Hemisphere. Root resolved the nettling Santo Domingo situation by winning Senate approval of a new treaty with the Dominican republic in February, 1907; he promoted cordial relations with Canada; and he emerged as one of the early architects of the modern "Good Neighbor" policy. He was also virtually solely responsible for the administration's Manchurian policy.

CHAPTER 17

THE PEACEMAKER II

"In [Roosevelt's] . . . consciousness of the possibility of world war and of America's involvement in it, and hence of America's concern to help avoid it, he was unusual in an America that was for the most part innocent of the danger of war and certain that a war in Europe or Asia would not concern us if it did come."

—Howard K. Beale, *Theodore Roosevelt*

The muffled outcry of the isolationists over the President's mediation of the Russo-Japanese War became an angry roar when Roosevelt interjected America into a smoldering crisis in French Morocco at virtually the same time. In this action as in the Far Eastern one the President sought to promote peace through an uneasy balance of conflicting interests. And in this crisis as in that one Roosevelt dutifully shouldered responsibilities that a lesser man might have avoided. Once again he emerged as the only statesman possessed of the prestige, power, and presumed disinterest to be acceptable to all concerned. And once again he acted in the realization that fulfillment of his larger objective might compromise the lesser interests of his own country, though he worked adroitly to avoid it.

The issues were not basically different from those which had led to war between Russia and Japan. Nor were the implications less portentous. They involved nothing less than that complex of ententes, alliances, rivalries, and insecurities which was to drag all Europe into war in 1914.

The immediate stake was the Open Door in Morocco. By agreements completed in April, 1904, the British had recognized French control over Morocco in return for French recognition of British preeminence in Egypt. These arrangements offended the Germans, who had come too late on the imperialistic stage to play a role commensurate with their newly consolidated might, and their seething ambitions consequently spilled over. On March 31, 1905, on the urging of his militant Chancellor, Von Bülow, Emperor Wilhelm II disembarked from a German warship off Tangier and delivered, as one historian phrases it, "a defiant, saber-rattling speech" in which he pointedly declared that the Sultan was an independent sovereign in whose domain all foreign powers were entitled to equal rights. The war clouds that had hovered over Europe since the end of the Franco-Prussian War threatened to deluge the continent once more.

Roosevelt was again caught in a dilemma. France's case was so weak, her breach of a trust arranged in 1880 so flagrant, that world opinion might normally have forced her to abandon her Moroccan venture.* But the Moroccan situation could not be isolated from the European power matrix nor, indeed, from Britain's interest in Egypt, where Suez was already regarded as the Empire's life line. To stand against France in Morocco was to oppose Great Britain.

Roosevelt's friendship with the British was emotional in the broad usage of the word; but it was not blindly so, as Hay's sometimes was. The President often railed at the supercilious qualities of eminent and not so eminent Englishmen, and he regarded many British traits as offensively stupid. Like Lodge and numerous other ultranationalists, moreover, he shared feelings of cultural inferiority toward the British —a sure sign of the repressed esteem in which he actually held them. Yet his strident patriotism would not allow of the mother country's supremacy; and even in his historical writings he had only begrudgingly acknowledged the great heritage she had bequeathed her mighty offspring. Nevertheless, by 1905 Roosevelt had become convinced that American and British interests were largely similar; and in the fall of that year the British Ambassador was reporting to Whitehall that although Roosevelt's "prejudices are all the other way," he had at times "seemed really friendly." Two years later when the President received as the new ambassador his old and respected friend, James Bryce, author of *The American Commonwealth,* he cast aside his

---

* Morocco's independence had been affirmed by an international congress at Madrid in 1880.

prepared remarks, so Bryce wrote, "and made a long impromptu speech full of expressions of friendliness to the King and to Great Britain and conveying the earnest desire for best relations and reciprocal understanding between the two countries."

Roosevelt's feelings toward the Germans were at once less critical and more hostile than those toward the British. That genius for order and efficiency he so admired in the Japanese was magnified in the case of the Germans, and many of his own domestic measures bear the mark of the German example. He was also less sensitive than many Americans to the Germans' nationalism, militarism, and compulsive need of self-assertion. Roosevelt could, it is true, laugh surreptitiously at the Kaiser's pompous struttings and imperious boasting; and he was never, as sometimes has been claimed, the subordinate partner in the calculated friendship he and that haughty gentleman long maintained. Still, he did have a kind of admiration for Wilhelm (which he astutely impressed upon German diplomats when it suited his purposes). And he once paid him the American politician's supreme compliment by declaring that he could have carried his ward in a democratic election. Always, however, the President regarded Imperial Germany as a powerful potential rival.

Although Berlin sensed Roosevelt's predisposition toward the British, and in lesser degree the French, it hoped that the American President would serve as Germany's *amicus curiae* in the Moroccan crisis. His cordial relations with the Kaiser and his intimacy with Speck von Sternburg, together with America's devotion to the Open Door in China and absence of ambition in North Africa, suggested that he might. And from early 1905 on the Germans subjected him to unremitting pressure to that end. They pointed out that France and Spain's primacy in Morocco could lead to the exclusion of other commercial nations and that it would enable them to control the passage to the East. They protested that Germany had no ambitions in Morocco beyond maintenance of the Open Door. And they argued that the British would privately welcome action. Would not the United States join Germany in encouraging the Sultan to request an international conference? Would not Roosevelt cooperate by releasing a protest of his own simultaneously with one by Germany?

The President's response to these entreaties was circumspect. He told Speck von Sternburg in early March, 1905, that an active Moroccan policy would only expose him "to the bitterest attacks" in

Congress. And he later advised him that "our interests in Morocco are not sufficiently great to make me feel justified in entangling our Government." Gradually, however, the onward rush of events overtook him. Following his inflammatory speech at Tangier on March 31, the Kaiser became beset by fear that England would support France in a showdown; and through his ambassador, Wilhelm importuned Roosevelt to urge the British against such a fateful course. But the President, who was then on a bear hunt in Colorado, shrewdly refrained. As he explained to Taft, who was handling affairs in Hay's illness, he did not want to make the English "think we are acting as decoy ducks for Germany." He added, however, that he was "sincerely anxious to bring about a better state of feeling between England and Germany," and he suggested that the Secretary of War conduct a cautious inquiry into the British attitude, but only if he found the Ambassador, Sir Mortimer Durand, or the First Secretary "in any rational mood and you think the nice but somewhat fat-witted British intellect will stand it."

During May and early June tension continued to rise, especially after the Sultan issued an invitation for a conference of the powers. The dramatic dismissal on June 6 of Foreign Minister Théophile Delcassé, the resolutely anti-German architect of France's Moroccan policy, reduced it temporarily; but the dismissal served also to embolden the Kaiser. As rumors of an impending showdown spread through the great chancelleries of the Western World, the Imperial government assumed an increasingly belligerent posture. Fearing finally that war might ensue, the French reluctantly began to relax their opposition to an international conference. Roosevelt, who had been keeping an eye on every straw in the wind, thereupon concluded that the time to intervene had come.

The President's friendship with amiable Jean Jules Jusserand, with whom he had often played tennis and scrambled over the boulders of Rock Creek Park, now proved fruitful. Taking the Ambassador into his confidence almost completely, he impressed him with the gravity of the crisis and convinced him of his own disinterested purposes (the President's problem was to avoid creating the impression that he was pro-German). A measure of Roosevelt's success is found in part in the sympathetic report Jusserand later made to this government:

Examining . . . the means by which he might help us in avoiding war, the very idea of which struck him with horror, the President has concluded that the only chance to do what might be useful, would be perhaps to flatter this excessive vanity of William II, to which he attributes, in large measure, the present difficulties.

Roosevelt's intercession, combined with the force of events, had served to swing over the French, at least for the moment. Within a few days, however, a new impasse threatened. France demanded a preliminary understanding before meeting at the council table; Germany insisted that the issues be decided at the formal conference. The fate of the conference, and perhaps of world peace, hung precariously in the balance.

The President reacted with characteristic ingenuity. Using Speck von Sternburg as a sounding board, he played for the Kaiser's ear such a song of praise as was certain to beguile a man of Wilhelm's consummate vanity. He said the Kaiser "stands as the leader among the sovereigns of to-day who have their faces set toward the future." He argued that the French decision to accept a conference was "a genuine triumph for the Emperor's diplomacy." And he suggested that the Emperor's "high and honorable fame might be clouded" should "questions about minor details" produce "the dreadful calamity of war."

Roosevelt's resourcefulness apparently again tipped the scales. Wilhelm agreed to an advance agenda; and he also promised that if there should be differences at the conference he would in every case support whatever decision Roosevelt regarded as "the most fair and the most practical." The President conveyed this promise to the French with the resultant resolution of their doubts.

The President would have preferred to have taken no further part in the proceedings. Congressional opposition to his involvement was strong and vociferous; and in January, 1906, Senator Bacon introduced a resolution designed to remind the President of the Founding Fathers' allegedly isolationist faith. Even Root questioned the wisdom of Roosevelt's participation. But Lodge rose to the President's defense with a high-blown, if somewhat inaccurate, assertion that it was in the American tradition to use "moral influence . . . to prevent war." And when the conference, which opened at Algeciras in southern Spain on January 16, 1906, deadlocked, Roosevelt did not hesitate to accept the challenge.

On February 19, with talk of war once more filling the air, the President offered a four-point compromise program. In consonance with his basic sympathies, as well as his estimate of the total situation, his proposals were more reflective of French than German interests. They provided for the Open Door in principle; but they proposed in effect to turn over control of the Moroccan police to France and Spain. The Kaiser understandably demurred, and it seemed for a while that the conference would now actually fail. On the basis of representations from the Russians, however, Roosevelt decided to make a direct appeal to His Imperial Majesty on March 7. Again playing on Wilhelm's vanity, and also his honor, he quoted Speck von Sternburg's earlier promise that the Emperor would defer to his decision in the event of an insoluble difference between the German government and France. Wilhelm could do little but submit; after failing to convert Roosevelt to a compromise plan of his own, he did so.

The President's imaginative diplomacy had saved the conference, and probably the peace as well. He had strengthened the bonds with his country's natural allies, France and Great Britain, and had managed at least to preserve the bonds with Germany. He had also taken America another long stride into the world. The episode, writes Mowry, "was eloquent testimony to Roosevelt's growing appreciation that the frontiers of twentieth-century American security often lay along the Yangtse and the Rhine, at Algeciras and Rome and Paris, and in a host of other places, some of them unknown or obscure even to members of Congress."

Firm in the conviction that he had acted in the right—that the virtual closing of the Open Door in Morocco was a small price for the maintenance of peace and the support of the British-French entente—Roosevelt was again magnanimous in victory. To Jusserand he wrote that he had been able to give him his confidence only because he knew that "you would treat all that was said and done between us two as a gentleman of the highest honor treats what is said and done in the intimate personal relations of life." And of Speck von Sternburg, whose contribution was perhaps even greater than Jusserand's, he wrote: "Loyal though Speck was to his Government, down in his heart the honest, brave little gentleman did not believe Germany was acting as she should act." But to His Majesty, Wilhelm II, the President was less than candid. In a message that Speck von Sternburg, though presumably not Wilhelm, saw through, he extended his "sincerest felicitations on this epochmaking political success at Algeciras" and asseverated that His Majesty's policy "has been masterly from beginning to end."

As for his own role, the President remained discreetly silent. Only to Ambassador Whitelaw Reid in London, in a long, heavily documented letter which he warned must "be considered as of the most strictly confidential character," did he set forth the record of events. That letter was designed for a posterity which until recently rejected it. Passing over the European sources and dismissing the claims to Reid as a figment of Roosevelt's imagination, American historians have tended to belittle, or at least underestimate, the President's decisive influence in arranging and then saving the Algeciras Conference. Not until 1956, when Beale published his study of Roosevelt after exhaustive research in the sources, including those in Europe, was the President's own account confirmed. He was, Beale concludes, "an amazingly accurate reporter in this instance."

President Roosevelt's mediation of the Russo-Japanese War and his intervention in the Moroccan dispute deservedly earned him the Nobel Peace Prize for 1906. Thereafter his views on domestic issues would continue to develop; his convictions on foreign affairs, however, had by then reached near maturation. This was confirmed by his admonishment of "those who would lightly undergo the chance of war in a spirit of mere frivolity, or of mere truculence," and by his growing concern over the burgeoning costs and frightful implications of the international armaments race. Thus at the same time that Roosevelt worked for the particular peace he made a sincere, though severely limited, effort to secure the general peace through international limitation of naval power and arbitration of minor disputes. In this, however, he failed, European rivalries proving too intense, the United States Senate too chauvinistic, and the President's basic assumptions (they were predicated on continued Anglo-American naval dominance) too transparent.

Roosevelt had first issued a call for an international conference in October, 1904. Because of the Russo-Japanese War, however, he shortly afterward withdrew the call. Then, when the Tsar indicated the next year that he would like to call the conference himself, the President readily deferred. The Tsar's sponsorship would give the United States a freer hand; and it would happily spare Roosevelt, who still scorned the "peace-at-any-price" people on the grounds that they failed to realize that "justice is greater than peace," the odium, as he phrased it, of "posing too much as a professional peacemaker."

During the long interval between the original call and the actual convening of The Second Hague Peace Conference on June 15, 1907, Roosevelt gave considerable thought to the meeting's agenda. He warned that the Conference should not be regarded as a panacea. "Just at present the United States Navy is an infinitely more potent factor for peace than all the peace societies of every kind and sort," he wrote President Eliot of Harvard, whom he viewed as an impractical visionary. "At The Hague I think we can make some real progress, but only on condition of our not trying to go too far." And after he had skirted suggestions for limiting the size and quality of armies, he drew back on the grounds that the world armaments manufacturers' lobby was too powerful and that the Kaiser, especially, would never agree. However, he continued to press for naval limitations and "obligatory arbitration as broad in scope as now appears to be practicable." He further espoused a proposal for exemption of private property from capture in time of war.

The first of these proposals was doomed from the beginning. The Russians wanted to rebuild their fleet, and the Japanese wanted to keep ahead of them and gain on the Americans and British. The Germans aspired to build up to the British. And the Italians were envious of the French. Neither was the prospect of accepting a status quo based on an overwhelming Anglo-American supremacy enticing to any of the other major powers including the British, who equivocated. Hence the death of the President's proposal and the continuance of the fateful armaments race which he correctly surmised would eventuate in a catastrophic war.

Roosevelt's other proposals also died as they were born. He was himself unable to press compulsory arbitration as much as he would have liked because of the attitude of the Senate. As he explained to the British Foreign Secretary, Sir Edward Grey, "it does not represent any real advance for me or anyone else to sign a general arbitration treaty which itself merely expresses a 'pious opinion' that there ought hereafter to be arbitration treaties whenever both parties think they are advisable—and this was precisely the opinion that most even of my own good friends in the Senate took as regards the last batch of arbitration treaties which I sent them." Nevertheless, he added, "I will do my best to get this Government to agree to any feasible scheme which will tend to minimize the chances for war occurring without previous efforts to secure mediation or arbitration."

Whether the President could have persuaded the Senate to accept his view is conjectural. Before he had a chance to act, eight European states led by Germany refused at The Hague to agree to arbitrate legal disputes, to say nothing of those involving national interest. Even the recommendation for exemption of private property from capture in time of war was scuttled; and the Conference adjourned on October 18, 1907, without material accomplishment. As Joseph H. Choate, the American delegate, succinctly put it in one of his reports, "There is very great reluctance on the part of these fighting nations to bind themselves to anything."

The President's cautious internationalism and his mature abhorrence of war continued, of course, to be delimited by his unwavering devotion to the national interest and by his continued contempt for the backward nations. He never agreed to endorse arbitration of disputes involving the national honor or interest. Nor did he ever abandon his belief that it was the duty of the "civilized" nations to discipline the "barbarous" ones. He did, it is true, concede that the problem was relative, that it was difficult to "state exactly which power ceases to be free and civilized and which comes near the line of barbarism or despotism." But in practice he invariably allowed his own conception of the American national interest to rule.

The President's China policy was a case in point. Roosevelt had the intellectual equipment to have evolved a China policy that would have served American interests and kept ill-will at a minimum. He had a keen conception of the Russian menace, an almost prophetic vision of China's future importance, and unparalleled daring and imagination. But because he held firm to his technological criteria of civilization, because he overestimated his country's economic stake in China, and because he insisted on upholding false values of prestige, he failed.

To be sure, Roosevelt inherited his China policy from McKinley and left its conduct largely in Hay's hands until 1904. Yet Hay kept him informed. He agreed in the main with Hay's policies. And he himself made several critical decisions during Hay's tenure. As Beale shows, it was the President who insulted the Chinese by insisting that the mixed foreign court at Shanghai rather than the Chinese government should be authorized to sentence a group of Chinese citizens found guilty of "violent incitements to insurrection" against the Chinese government. It was the President who tried to compel the Chinese to support a nominally American railroad company which had laid but twenty-eight miles of track out of a projected thousand miles in five years of financial chicanery and general mismanagement. (Lodge and Roosevelt agreed that the maintenance of American prestige was at stake.) And it was the President who directed policy throughout the Chinese boycott of American goods in 1905. Of these incidents, the latter was the most significant. The attitudes and actions which provoked it were deeply enmeshed in the American, and indeed the Western, social fabric; and they cut to the core of the imperialistic philosophy, even in its by then softened version.

The precipitating issue was the Chinese Exclusion Treaty of 1883, which came up for renewal in 1904. Roosevelt had long favored the exclusion of Chinese laborers on economic and social grounds. "There is no danger of having too many immigrants of the right kind," he said in his annual message of 1905 and in numerous private letters. Nor, he also wrote, does it make any "difference from what country they come." However, he argued, "we should not admit masses of men whose standards of living and whose personal customs and habits are such that they tend to lower the level of the American wage-worker."

The question was in fact actually more complex than that. Immigration officials and private citizens frequently visited indignities on those Chinese who were admitted, many of them high government officials and distinguished scholars. The United States refused naturalization to *all* Chinese ("Congress has done its work so well that even Confucius could not become an American," Hay remarked to Roosevelt at one point). And West Coast politicians were so intent on playing on the prejudices of their constituents that they demanded unilateral exclusion legislation in the spring of 1904 regardless of the outcome of the then pending treaty negotiations.

Whatever the limitations of the President's own views, they were far in advance of his countrymen's at large. He personally favored admission of qualified Chinese to citizenship. He wanted to extend America's developing cultural hold on China. And he was reluctant to make commercial intercourse with China more difficult than it already was. But in the spring of 1904, fearing more the wrath of the

West Coast voters than the indignation of the impotent Chinese, he sacrificed statesmanship to politics. On April 5 of that election year, he informed his Cabinet that he would approve a separate exclusion bill. Then, in one of the weakest actions of his presidential career, he signed a measure so providing.

Meanwhile, anti-American sentiment in China rose feverishly. It emanated not from the reactionary Boxers, but from the men of China's future—the progressive-minded intellectuals, students, and businessmen who foresaw for China the industrialized development that Roosevelt himself foresaw in his more reflective moments. Led by Sun Yat-Sen among others, these new nationalists resolved to assert China's independence; and they proposed as a first step toward that end the boycotting of American goods in protest against the contemptuous treatment of their countrymen by American immigration officials.

The President's response to the boycott was at once enlightened and authoritarian. He was so angered by the "barbarous methods" which inspired the boycott that he ordered reform even before the textile and other interested American business groups beseeched him to pursue a rational policy in the interest of their commerce with China. "We are a civilized nation," Roosevelt wrote the secretary of the Immigration Bureau on June 12, and "we are trying to teach the Chinese to be civilized. . . . We ought not to treat a Chinese representative in a way which we would not for a moment tolerate if applied by the Chinese to some of our representatives." He then issued an executive order prescribing humane treatment of visiting Chinese by American immigration officials and directing "immediate dismissal" of any official who failed to conform.

Chinese grievances were too long standing and the new nationalists' desire to assert their independence too intense, however, for a change in the form rather than the substance of American policy to divert the Chinese nationalists; on July 20, 1905, the boycott was instituted. It spread rapidly from Shanghai through South China and thence to Hawaii, the Philippines, and the Japanese ports of Nagasaki and Yokahama. It varied widely in effectiveness and was nowhere total; yet it was severe enough to evoke frantic pleas for diplomatic action by the American interests affected. As one consul reported, our businessmen in China have "gone mad" and are acting like "regular wild Indians."

The President's contempt for the "inferior" Chinese now began slowly to surge to the surface. He continued to rail against the obtuseness that had incited the crisis. "I have the right," he testily wrote Senator George C. Perkins of California, "to expect that the Pacific coast representatives will aid me in undoing the injustice in our treaties . . . which has probably been the whole, and certainly the main, cause of the present boycott." But he was unable to hold to that rational viewpoint entirely. To the veteran China hand, William Rockhill, he now laid bare his fatal flaw. The Chinese, wrote Roosevelt, "despise weakness even more than they prize justice, and we must make it evident both that we intend to do what is right and that we do not intend for a moment to suffer what is wrong."

Nevertheless, the President resisted his rising impulse to resort to force until well into November, 1905. Gratified when the Chinese government formally condemned the boycott on August 31, he attempted to marshal public opinion behind a revision of the exclusion laws. The United States had failed to do its "duty toward the people of China," he bluntly told an export-conscious audience in the cotton belt on October 20. At the same time, however, he warned that America must maintain its "rights."

Meanwhile anti-American sentiment in China intensified in spite of the near extinction of the boycott. The President's daughter, Alice, who had accompanied Taft to the Far East, was insulted by the Cantonese and forced to cancel a visit to their city. Riots broke out in several places, including Shanghai, where the Chinese nationalists sought greater jurisdiction over the privileged foreign settlement. And in early December an American admiral who had accidentally shot a Chinese woman was mobbed.

In these circumstances, the President decided to pursue the firmest possible course; on November 15 he ordered the Secretary of the Navy to concentrate "as strong a naval force as possible" off the China coast. Preparations to form an expeditionary force of 15,000 troops followed, and by mid-February the battleship *Oregon* was hovering off Hong Kong and Canton while the gunboat *El Cano* was cruising on the Yangtse River. With the stage thus set, the President submitted a series of humiliating demands to the Imperial government on February 26. Eight days later the Emperor resignedly submitted to this gunboat diplomacy by issuing an Imperial edict condemning expressions of antiforeign sentiment by his subjects.

Roosevelt's threat of force had restored tranquillity, maintained the Open Door, and refurbished the national ego. But it had also embittered China's men of the future. It would be absurd to blame the whole subsequent China tangle on the President's coercive policies; many and graver blunders were to be made in the years to come. It is also difficult to see how Roosevelt could have avoided a firm policy (except for the unnecessary display of force), given the violence of Chinese activity, the frenetic pressures of American businessmen and labor leaders, and the Western milieu of which the United States, however less imperiously, was yet a part. Within this frame of reference, Roosevelt had done almost all that was possible. He had upbraided American officials for their execrable discourtesy; he had urged Congress to modify the exclusion policy (though after he himself had submitted to it); and he had taken the question to the people. How then had he failed?

The President failed, if we may accept Beale's conclusions, in that he, his advisers, and all but a handful of American commentators persisted in regarding China as a colonial with all that the term implied. Ideally, the United States should have courted, rather than condemned, the new nationalists. It should have encouraged, rather than discouraged, Chinese efforts to whittle down the extraterritorial privileges of Occidentals. And as Roosevelt himself wanted to do, it should have opened its doors to cultivated Chinese. But the domestic political maelstrom, coupled with the President's inability to break totally with his imperialistic, might-is-right heritage, prevented it from so doing. Of all the ironies in Theodore Roosevelt's career, none is more revealing than that he should have professed to see the spirit of the American Revolution in the revolt of the Panamanians against Colombia, but refused to see it in the revolt against colonialism of the ancient, the proud, and the civilized Chinese.

The China problem had not yet been resolved when the President became involved in a somewhat similar crisis with Japan. For several years that compound of economic insecurity, racial prejudice and political demagoguery which lay behind the Chinese exclusion law had also been swelling the West Coast's resentment of the Japanese. In 1905 the California legislature openly debated an Oriental exclusion bill before settling on a joint resolution that was almost as offensive as the proposed bill. And in the fall of 1906 the dam finally broke as the San Francisco Board of Education, its resolve weakened by heavy pressure from organized labor, ordered all ninety-three Japanese, Chinese, and Korean students in the public educational system to attend a segregated school.

From across the Pacific there now rolled a great wave of protest which Roosevelt, raging and storming over "the idiots in the California legislature," sought desperately to roll back. "These Pacific Coast people . . . with besotted folly are indifferent to building up the navy while provoking this formidable new power—a power jealous, sensitive and warlike, and which if irritated could at once take both the Philippines and Hawaii from us if she obtained the upper hand on the seas," he protested to Lodge. "Let me repeat that everything in my power will be done," he confidentially wrote Baron Kaneko, who had cabled him from Tokyo. "The action of these people in San Francisco no more represents American sentiment as a whole than the action of the Japanese seal pirates last summer represented Japanese sentiment."

The Californians proved intractable, however, and in his annual message that December the President scorched the San Francisco School Board. He called the Board's action "a wicked absurdity" and "a crime against a friendly nation"; and he threatened to use "all the forces, civil and military" at his command to rectify it. Then, early in the new year, he sent in a special message to Congress which concluded with an expression of hope that the people of San Francisco would resolve the issue "as a matter of comity."

Neither the President's threats nor his pleas moved the emotion-wrought San Franciscans. He decided therefore to intervene directly. Early in February, on his own invitation, he received at the White House an eight-man delegation from the San Francisco School Board. After several conferences (Elihu Root sat always on Roosevelt's left, prepared to interject the light touch or to tap the table when the President became too vehement), the San Franciscans accepted Roosevelt's contention that the segregation order was deleterious to the nation's foreign relations, and a compromise was agreed upon: Aliens of any nationality would be admitted to nonsegregated schools provided they knew English and were in the proper age group; the President would recommend an amendment to the immigration law which would in effect empower him to exclude coolie labor.

The resultant lessening of tension proved temporary. That same month the California Assembly passed a bill limiting ownership of land by Japanese and Chinese, and the next month the California Senate received a bill to exclude Japanese children over ten years of age from the white public schools. In May a mob attacked a Japanese restaurant and bath house in San Francisco, and in June the Board of Police Commissioners refused licenses to six Japanese employment bureaus. Meanwhile, the President and Secretary Root negotiated feverishly with the Japanese government as reports of possible conflict between the United States and Japan filtered in through diplomatic channels. Finally, Roosevelt decided to send Taft to Tokyo to mitigate Japanese resentment.

The amiable Secretary of War reached the Japanese capital in October, 1907, and was at once, so he enthusiastically wrote home, "feted all over the place." Following a round of talks with high Japanese officials he completed arrangements already in the making for the so-called Gentleman's Agreement, under the terms of which both Japan and the United States agreed to limit emigration of their nationals to types acceptable to each other. Practically, this meant that the trickle of coolies into California would almost dry up.

Meanwhile the President had formulated plans for a gesture on the grand scale—the dispatch of the American battle fleet around the world. Roosevelt's reasons for that bold decision included such tactical considerations as giving the fleet practice in coaling at sea and ascertaining the precise time it would take to move it from one ocean to the other. Fundamentally, however, they embodied the desire to stimulate domestic support for his naval construction program and to dramatize to the world, and especially the impressionable Japanese, the magnitude of American naval power.

The President's willingness thus to leave the Philippines and Hawaii unguarded while the fleet was in European waters suggests that he had not taken the war talk of the summer of 1907 seriously. In reality, he had taken it seriously; but he contemplated a future rather than an immediate war, Japanese naval strength being at least a third less than the United States' at that time. He consequently viewed the visit of the fleet to Japan as a deterrent. "My own judgment is that the only thing which will prevent war is the Japanese feeling that we shall not be beaten," he confided to Root in July, 1907.

Nevertheless, precautions were undertaken. Early in July Roosevelt sent Leonard Wood, then in command of the Philippines defenses, coded instructions on the measures to be taken in the event of attack.

And the commander of the Great White Fleet that steamed out of Hampton Roads on December 16, carried firm orders to be prepared for and to resist attack.

No enemy fired a gun except in salute; and on the return of the fleet fourteen months later its main missions had been accomplished or were being accomplished. The Japanese had received the officers and men with a spectacular demonstration of hospitality and blandness, while Congress had been sufficiently moved (with the help of war talk from the President) to have authorized the construction of two additional battleships. There had also been controversy. The chairman of the Senate Naval Affairs Committee was so exacerbated by the President's decision to dispatch the fleet without the formal approval of Congress that he had threatened to refuse funds for its supply—to which the President had responded that enough money was already available to get the fleet to the Pacific, that it would definitely go to the Pacific, and it could then stay in the Pacific. "There was no further difficulty about money," Roosevelt tersely recalled in his *Autobiography*.

The President also declared in his *Autobiography* that the world cruise of the fleet was "the most important service that I rendered to peace." Historians are not so confident. Beale speculates that it served to spur the Japanese naval party and anti-American elements who were even then in conflict with pro-American groups in Japan, while Braisted suggests that "a powerful American fleet defending the Philippines in 1909 was potentially no less threatening to Japan than had seemed Japan's intervention in Hawaii to the United States only twelve years before." It is also likely that that spectacle of American naval might quickened Wilhelm II's already burning resolve to build up the Imperial German Navy.

By the end of Roosevelt's presidency, moreover, the Asiatic balance he had striven so laboriously to create was working against American commercial interests. In silent defiance of the Open Door, Russia and Japan had agreed to divide north China, Mongolia, and Korea between them, and by an exchange of notes between Secretary Root and Baron Takahira on November 30, 1908, the United States had implicitly recognized Japan's economic ascendancy in Manchuria. It is bootless to contend, however, that this posture of affairs was the fault of the administration. Japan was coming of age in any event, and the Root-Takahira Agreement had actually signaled a sort of clearing of the air. The only alternative to Root's measured attempt to persuade Japan to be moderate was war, or a firm threat of war. If the display of force implicit in the fleet's world cruise was a blunder, what would the mustering of sufficient power to disrupt the new Russo-Japanese comity or to drive the Japanese out of Korea and Manchuria have been? To find the wellsprings of Russian and Japanese aggressions in Korea, north China, and Mongolia, the historian must probe far beyond the policies of the Roosevelt administrations. Short of war, the unwisdom of which is clear, or of complete withdrawal from the Far East, the wisdom of which is arguable, Roosevelt had done almost all that could reasonably be demanded. He had also set his country off from all the other powers and atoned partly for his own hardness toward China by accepting the suggestion of a Congregational missionary, Arthur Henderson Smith, that a portion of the Boxer indemnity be used to support Chinese students in American universities.

CHAPTER 18

MORE TROUBLES AND GREATER TRIBULATIONS

> If a man has a very decided character, has a strongly accentuated career, it is normally the case of course that he makes ardent friends and bitter enemies. . . .
> —Theodore Roosevelt to G. O. Trevelyan

The President continued, meanwhile, to be a storm center of controversy on the domestic front. He created it, he fell into it, and he searched it out. When he was not rebuking his once trusted friends, he was taunting his long-sworn enemies. And if he was fleetingly at peace with both, as occasionally he was, it was rarely the peace that passeth understanding. Nor was it possible to predict what the swirling winds that bore his wrath would next envelop. During the same two years the President was making his mark in European affairs, pacifying the Japanese, and flaunting the power of the American navy, he crossed swords with a people whom he had sought sincerely to uplift—the Negroes. He unloosed his fury on a private citizen whose sole offense was an imagination that transcended the observed facts of nature. And he was himself victimized by the financial and industrial barons whose motives he had so long suspected.

The President's clash with the Negroes resulted from an incident at Brownsville, Texas, on August 14, 1906, when a group of Negro soldiers from nearby Fort Brown allegedly killed a white bartender and wounded a policeman in a wild midnight raid on the town. No one of the alleged participants was ever positively identified; nor did any one of them ever admit responsibility. They were never tried before a court of law, military or civil, and to this day their guilt remains unproved. Yet Roosevelt, in a flagrant breach of the Anglo-American code of justice, punished three companies of Negro troops with extraordinary severity. He was substantially influenced to this action by the report of the soldiers' commanding officer, who reluctantly concluded that his troops were blameworthy, and by the findings of two separate investigations, one by a Major August B. Blockson, the other by the Inspector General of the Army.

Major Blockson's report charged that the raid had been "preconcerted" and that many members of the three Negro companies stationed at Fort Brown had entered into a "conspiracy of silence" to protect the men who had actually done the shooting; he recommended that they "be made to suffer with others more guilty." After an intensive effort to break the "conspiracy" failed, possibly because there was none, the President ordered almost the entire complement of the three companies in question "discharged without honor . . . and forever barred from re-enlistment." Of the 160 or more soldiers thus summarily dismissed, several were near retirement and six had won the coveted Medal of Honor in campaigns against the Indians, the Spaniards, or the Filipino insurrectionists.

Although the order was signed on November 5, Roosevelt withheld its release until after the congressional elections of November 6, presumably to mitigate its political impact. So, at least, contended the New York *Herald,* which claimed that a shift in the Negro vote would have reduced the Republican majority in the House of Representatives from 59 to 14, and the Washington *Post,* which pointed out that a switch of one half the Negro votes in Cincinnati could have defeated the President's son-in-law, Representative Nicholas Longworth.

The President's action provoked a country-wide reaction. Many Southern newspapers applauded his course, but the Northern press sharply criticized it and Negro editors and civic leaders vehemently condemned it. The New York *Age* castigated the discharge order as an "outrage upon the rights of citizens who are entitled in civil life to trial by jury and in military life to trial by court-martial." And the pastor of the Abyssinian Baptist Church of New York exclaimed that although Roosevelt was "once enshrined in our love as our Moses," he is now "enshrouded in our scorn as our Judas." Only in Tuskegee,

Alabama, was there silence; and there it was brutally painful. The
President had "blundered," Booker T. Washington, to whom Roosevelt had given advance notice, privately wrote a friend, and ". . . the
enemy will, as usual, try to blame me for all of this. They can talk;
I cannot, without being disloyal to our friend, who [*sic*] I mean to
stand by throughout his administration."

Roosevelt was to ride out the storm, though at no enhancement to
his reputation as a man of justice. For in Joseph B. Foraker, who
unexpectedly emerged as the beleaguered Negro soldiers' *amicus
curiae,* he encountered a bold and resourceful adversary. The veteran
Ohio senator aspired to the presidency in 1908, and as one of his
biographers writes, he needed "an issue which would lend itself to
exploitation before the public at large." Although Foraker believed
at first that the soldiers were guilty as charged, he made an intensive
private investigation during November, 1906, in the hope that he
might turn up something of political advantage; and by early December, when Congress convened, he had convinced himself that the
affair was in truth an "American Dreyfus Case." From then on the
Ohioan carried the torch of justice almost alone. But not until March
2, 1909, two days before Roosevelt left office in triumph and Foraker
left it in disgrace, a victim of the President's wrath and the revelation
of his unseemly relations with the Standard Oil Company, was it
lighted; and then but dimly. On that date Roosevelt signed a compromise measure which authorized the appointment of a high military
court to review the individual cases of all the discharged soldiers.

The two-year controversy between the imperious President and the
audacious Senator was brisk with acrimony. The most regrettable
incident occurred at the Gridiron Club dinner in January, 1907.
Failing for once to accept the newspapermen's barbs in good grace,
Roosevelt delivered a long and humorless defense of his policies and
then virtually flung the gauntlet at Foraker, who sat less than twenty
feet away, his face ashen. With the temerity that had always set him
off from the herd, Foraker retrieved it. For twenty minutes, his words
interrupted only by applause from the tables, he tongue-lashed the
President of the United States, charging finally that Roosevelt's handling of the Brownsville case had been illegal, unconstitutional, and
unjustifiable.

Furious, Roosevelt had sprung to his feet demanding time for a reply. He got it—after the applause for Foraker slowly abated. Through clenched teeth, with squinting eyes and flushing face, the President emphatically denied the Senate's right to interfere and dogmatically asserted that only he had the power to mete out justice to the discharged soldiers. "The only reason I didn't have them hung was because I couldn't find out which ones . . . did the shooting," he emphatically added. Some of them were "bloody butchers." He had thereupon stormed out of the hall, leaving, so Foraker recalled, "no good taste in anybody's mouth and no good feeling in anybody's heart."

Less than twenty-four hours later the President had recovered his balance. "Foraker ought not to have been called upon to speak," he wrote Beveridge, "but, as he was called upon, I do not blame him much for the speech he did make."

The saddest part of the Brownsville affair, sadder even than the President's comportment at the Gridiron Club dinner, was the impression it gave of Roosevelt's attitude toward Negroes. It is conceivable, of course, that the President's indictment would have been less sweeping and his punishment less severe had white troops been involved. Yet his published correspondence fails to suggest it. On the surface, at least, Roosevelt's resort to guilt by association was animated by a conscientious, if misguided, compulsion to maintain military discipline rather than by racial prejudice. A statement he made two days after the discharge order was issued is convincing of his conscious motives:

> When the discipline and honor of the American Army are at stake I shall never under any circumstances consider the political bearing of upholding that discipline. . . . To show you how little the question of color enters into the matter, I need only point out that when a white officer was alleged to be guilty in speaking of the incident of commenting unfavorably on the black troops generally, I directed an immediate investigation into his words and suitable proceedings against him should he prove to have been correctly quoted.

Roosevelt never deviated from that position. To underscore it and to embarrass Foraker politically, he revealed while the conflict was at its peak that he planned to appoint a prominent Negro to a high federal post in Cincinnati (Foraker, who was caught unaware, testily told newspapermen to consult "the third Senator from Ohio—Booker Washington"). The President also tried to redress the balance during these last, troubled years by directing the Army to consider the organization of a Negro battalion of heavy artillery. And in 1908 he threatened the Nashville, Chattanooga & St. Louis Railway Company with legal action unless it provided Negro passengers with facilities. Also, in his annual message of 1906, which came between the issuance of the discharge order and the clash with Foraker at the Gridiron Club, Roosevelt coupled a ringing denunciation of lynching with a rational appeal for improved Negro education:

> It is out of the question for our people as a whole permanently to rise by treading down any of their own number. The free public school, the chance for each boy or girl to get a good elementary education, lies at the foundation of our whole political situation. . . . It is as true for the Negro as for the white man.

The President's effort to redeem his reputation for fair-mindedness met only moderate success. His strictures against lynching failed to mollify the Negro press because he sapped their strength by estimating that one-third of the lynchings in the South were actually incited by rape (he had earlier complained to Owen Wister about Charleston aristocrats who "shriek in public about miscegenation, but . . . leer as they talk to me privately of the colored mistresses and colored children of white men whom they know"). And to the end Brownsville remained an open wound, one that historians would open still wider. There were some, even then, who were able to place the affair in perspective. Among them was Booker T. Washington whose views, admittedly, were influenced by the primacy in Negro circles his friendship with Roosevelt had given him. "The bulk of the Negro people are more and more inclined to reach the decision that even though the President did go against their wishes in dismissing the soldiers at Brownsville," Washington wrote in June, 1908, "he has favored them in nine cases out of ten and the intelligent portion of the race does not believe that it is fair or wise to condemn such good friends as President Roosevelt and Secretary Taft because they might have done what they considered right." The patient educator, whose controversial counsel to fellow Negroes to eschew the professions for the manual arts was already under attack by radicals like William E. B. DuBois (though not by Roosevelt), added that it "is not the part of common sense to cherish ill will against one who has helped us in so many ways as the President has."

Meanwhile Roosevelt was forcing other of his friends to defend his representations against the nature-fakers. Of all the controversies of the presidential years, this was the most needless. No weighty public matter stood in the offing; no election hung in the balance. All that the President could gain was the satisfaction of speaking his mind, and he could gain that only by compromising the dignity of his office.

Like so many of Roosevelt's seemingly impulsive acts, the assault on the nature-fakers had been long in building up. The first round had been fired in the *Atlantic Monthly* some years before by John Burroughs, who flailed the Rev. William J. Long, a pseudo nature writer who attributed human characteristics and other absurdities to wild animals. It is the measure of Roosevelt's devotion to science that in writing Burroughs that he was "delighted" with his forthright exposure of misrepresentation, he also challenged the great naturalist himself. "Don't you think that you perhaps scarcely allow sufficiently for the extraordinary change made in the habits of wild animals by experiences with man?" he wrote. Burroughs had agreed. "I shall never cease to marvel at the variety of your interests and the extent of your knowledge," he replied. "You seem to be able to discipline and correct any one of us in his chosen field. My *Atlantic* paper has some hasty streaks in it."

During the next several years other prominent naturalists also criticized the Long school while Roosevelt, with difficulty, repressed his own rising irritation. Finally, in the spring of 1907, he lost control, giving out an interview under the title "Roosevelt on the Nature Fakirs." "You will be pleased to know," he wrote Burroughs, "that I finally proved unable to contain myself, and . . . sailed into Long and Jack London and one or two others of the more preposterous writers of 'unnatural' history." "I know that as President I ought not to do this," he added, "but I was having an awful time toward the end of the session and I felt I simply had to permit myself some diversion."

The Reverend Long staggered under the presidential censure; but only momentarily. In two forceful public letters he accused Roosevelt of "bad taste and cowardice" and ridiculed the contention that the President was a naturalist. "I find after carefully reading two of his big books," he vitriolically wrote, "that every time Mr. Roosevelt gets near the heart of a wild thing he invariably puts a bullet through it. From his own records I have reckoned a full thousand hearts which he has thus known intimately. In one chapter alone I find that he violently gained knowledge of 11 noble elk hearts in a few days."

Rarely had the President given his hungry critics such an opportunity. Many people felt that Long's false nature writing was less offensive than Roosevelt's wanton killing; and many more concluded that whatever the President's reasons, he had been ungentlemanly and cruel in attacking a private citizen.

Nevertheless, neither Roosevelt nor his friends were willing to drop the matter. On their own initiative the director of the New York Zoological Park, the curator of Mammalogy and Ornithology at the American Museum of Natural History, and a number of other naturalists defended the President in the September, 1906, issue of *Everybody's*. And in the same issue Roosevelt expounded on that commitment to truth that had obviously been his ruling motive:

> We abhor deliberate or reckless untruth in this study of natural history as much as in any other, and therefore we feel that a grave wrong is committed by all who, holding a position that entitles them to respect, yet condone and encourage such untruth.

Resentment against the President's action in the nature-fakers incident was still seething when he became involved in a far more significant imbroglio. This time, however, his role was confidential.

Rumors of an impending break in the stock market had started in December, 1906, when Roosevelt submitted to Congress his most radical annual message so far. An expansion of the constructive parts of his muck-rake speech and of a hard-hitting address he had delivered at Harrisburg, Pennsylvania, during the congressional campaign, it declared that all big business was really engaged in interstate commerce and should consequently be brought under federal control. Specifically, it called for compulsory publicity of corporations' accounts, government inspection of their books, and, as La Follette had argued for the previous spring, physical valuation of railroad properties. It further contended that the "authority" for these measures was inherent in the Constitution. The tough-mindedness which had always distinguished Roosevelt's views on big business from Bryan's pervaded the message. The President dutifully denounced monopoly;

but he proposed no inclusive assault on the trusts. "Our effort should be not so much to prevent consolidation . . . ," he wrote, "but so to supervise and control it as to see that it results in no harm to the people." Only through "such adequate control and regulation . . . as will do away with the evils which give rise to the agitation against them" could government ownership of the railroads be averted. Observing that some people claimed that "such control would do away with the freedom of individual initiative and dwarf individual effort," Roosevelt flatly asserted that "This is not a fact." Indeed, he continued, "the deadening and degrading effect of pure socialism, and especially of its extreme form, communism . . . are in part achieved by the wholly unregulated competition which results in a single individual or corporation rising at the expense of all others."

Whether or not the men of the Street agreed with the Boston *Herald,* which termed the message "a fine example of restrained radicalism and progressive conservatism," the stock market had soon steadied. Nevertheless, rumors persisted that the President would make an unsettling move, perhaps against the great Harriman empire, which was then under investigation by the Interstate Commerce Commission. And when the market suddenly broke sharply on March 14—Harriman's Union Pacific dropped twenty-five points—railroad officials openly cried "persecution." "I would hate to tell you to whom I think you ought to go for an explanation of all this," Harriman bitterly exclaimed to reporters.

The President was now in a quandary. Should he try to stave off panic by directing the Interstate Commerce Commission to let up? (The Fifty-ninth Congress had expired without taking action on the proposals made in his annual message.) Or should he encourage the reform movement on the theory, as expounded in January to the president of the Santa Fe, "that we have got to make up our minds that the railroads must not in the future do things which cannot bear the light?" Apparently, Roosevelt decided to hold to reform but to soften its impact by conciliatory words. On March 15, he directed the Commission to undertake a comprehensive investigation of the railroad industry with particular reference to physical evaluation, legitimacy of stock issues, and vertical and horizontal integration. "I desire from you," he wrote the Commission, "recommendations definite and precise in character to secure a far more thoro-going supervision and control than we now have over the great agencies of interstate transportation." Two and one-half months later, however, with talk of panic still current, he made a psychological concession to business by declaring at Indianapolis that he did not believe the railroads were overcapitalized.

During the summer of 1907 the situation worsened. The President was subjected to heavy pressure from businessmen to let up, especially after Judge Kenesaw Mountain Landis, whom Roosevelt characterized as having "the face of a fanatic—honest, fearless, well-meaning, but tense to a degree that makes me apprehensive," rocked the corporate world by imposing a fine of more than $29 million against the Standard Oil Company for violating the Elkins Act on some fourteen hundred separate counts.

The President refused, however, to give substantial ground. "I have tried my best not to take up any old offenses," he wrote the Boston banker Henry Lee Higginson, on August 12, "but I cannot grant an illegal immunity. If we have to proceed against anyone it is because he has sinned against the light." Eight days later, in an address at Provincetown, Roosevelt dropped a bomb of his own. After charging that "certain malefactors of great wealth" were actually forcing a panic in the hope that it would effect a "reversal" of his regulatory policies "so that they may enjoy unmolested the fruits of their own evil-doing," he strongly urged the criminal prosecution of businessmen law-breakers. Unfortunately, he observed, "the average juryman wishes to see trusts broken up . . . but is very reluctant to find the facts . . . when it comes to sending to jail a reputable member of the business community for doing what the business community has unhappily grown to recognize as well-nigh normal in business."

Nothing untoward followed the President's forceful reaffirmation of his policies, for the financial disturbances were caused by an international overextension of credit rather than by Roosevelt's various pronouncements. Not until the middle of October, when reports of the attempt by a group of swashbuckling banker-speculators to corner the copper market with funds drawn from their own unstable trust companies, as well as the large and sound Knickerbocker Trust Company of New York, were blazoned across the headlines did a major crisis occur. Overnight long lines of frantic depositors formed outside the affected institution's doors, and by the end of the week the runs had forced them all to close. Throughout the nation, but especially in New York, the already overdrawn credit lines became taut. The Westinghouse Company went into receivership; the Stock Exchange in Pittsburgh suspended operations; Western banks demanded more and more money from their New York depositories. And the great Trust Company of America faced imminent collapse.

At this juncture J. Pierpont Morgan brought the force of his commanding abilities to bear. On Wednesday morning, October 23, while Roosevelt was hurriedly returning from a hunt in the Louisiana canebrakes and before Secretary of the Treasury George B. Cortelyou arranged to deposit $25 million of government funds in New York's national banks, Morgan prevented the Trust Company of America from closing by making a heavy deposit of private monies. The next morning some of the government's deposits were added to Morgan's central fund, and these, together with a new pooling of Wall Street's resources, kept both the Trust Company and the Stock Exchange open until the regular closing on Friday.

The President was relieved. On Friday, following consultations with Root and others, he wrote Cortelyou a public letter designed to call attention to the government's role in staying the panic and to help restore general confidence. "I congratulate you upon the admirable way in which you have handled the present crisis," Roosevelt said in part.

> I congratulate also those conservative and substantial businessmen who in this crisis have acted with such wisdom and public spirit. By their action they did invaluable service in checking the panic which, beginning as a matter of speculation, was threatening to destroy the confidence and credit necessary to the conduct of legitimate business.

Within limits, the President was right. Whatever their past errors, the "conservative" bankers of New York had acted wisely and speedily. Indeed, Morgan had been a central bank unto himself. "At a time when the almost universal instinct was to pull one's own chestnuts out of the fire, to escape new commitments, to dodge responsibility," wrote Frederick Lewis Allen, "he risked everything, again and again, on the success of his campaign." He had, in addition, wielded power greater than that of the President of the United States —further testimony to the precarious state of the republic. Roosevelt was destined to go out of office without having substantially modified it.

If the devoutly religious Morgan had greater courage and a higher conception of the commonweal than most of his fellow financiers, he was nonetheless willing to use the situation to his own advantage. The money shortage had carried on into the next week, and by the weekend the prominent brokerage firm of Moore & Schley, which held a great block of the Tennessee Coal and Iron Company's stock, was in danger of failing. Morgan again responded to the challenge.

On Saturday, November 2, an emissary of Moore and Schley suggested to the great financier that his United States Steel Corporation buy out the small, but competing, Tennessee Coal and Iron Company. Its bonds could then be substituted for the Tennessee Company's, saving Moore & Schley and averting a crisis among brokerage firms in general. Morgan pondered over the proposal. He could possibly have bailed out Moore & Schley by other means. Grant B. Schley later admitted to a congressional committee that all the firm really needed was five or six million dollars in "real money," while Judge Elbert H. Gary, the Steel Corporation's president, conceded that a loan would have sufficed. At the time, however, Moore and Schley rejected Morgan's offer of a five-million-dollar loan as insufficient. Spurred by his partner, George W. Perkins, Morgan consequently decided to pursue the merger proposal. He was convinced that the T. C. & I.'s coal and iron deposits alone were worth the price, and after prolonged argument with Henry Clay Frick he prevailed on the Steel Corporation's Finance Committee to buy T. C. & I., at par with United States Steel bonds.

But Judge Gary was at once more cautious and more subtle than the bull-like Morgan; at his insistence the deal was made contingent on President Roosevelt's agreement. Twice before Gary had made arrangements with the President or his representatives—for the Steel Corporation in the fall of 1905 and for the International Harvester Company in the winter of 1907. In each of these "gentlemen's agreements" Gary had agreed to open all the company's books and records to the Bureau of Corporations with the understanding that the resultant information would be used "by the President alone for his guidance in making such suggestions to Congress concerning legislation as might be proper, expedient, and for the actual benefit of the general public." In each case the administration had agreed that the President, rather than the Attorney General, would have the final determination of what matters should be kept confidential. Although neither agreement specified that the corporations would be exempted from prosecution for irregularities, the Morgan-Gary group assumed that Roosevelt would not take such action until after they had been granted time to make their practices conform to the law. The President was too astute to make an explicit promise to that effect. But as his continued failure to institute suit against the companies suggests and his repeated recommendations to Congress for more comprehensive regulatory legislation confirm, Wall Street's assumption that he was more interested in sustained regulation than haphazard dissolution was correct. Indeed, so the historian Robert Wiebe observes, the only broad difference in outlook was that the Wall Street men conceived themselves as equal partners in the business-government relationship (a marked decline, assuredly, from their status as senior partners when Roosevelt succeeded McKinley), and the President regarded them as junior partners.

In these circumstances, Morgan readily agreed that a conference with Roosevelt was desirable, and late that Sunday night Gary and Frick departed for Washington. They met with the President (whom they found at breakfast) and Root early the next morning. Blandly, Gary explained that the United States Steel Corporation had an opportunity to purchase the Tennessee Coal and Iron Company at a "price somewhat in excess of its true value." Should the President approve the purchase before the Stock Exchange opened at ten that morning, he continued, it "would be of great benefit to financial conditions, and would probably save further failure of important business concerns." Gary and Frick had then professed purity of motive. "Judge Gary and Mr. Frick inform me that as a mere business transaction they do not care to purchase the stock," Roosevelt afterward wrote Attorney General Bonaparte for the record. They say, he continued, that "but little benefit will come to the Steel Corporation from the purchase; that they are aware that the purchase will be used as a handle for attack upon them on the ground that they are striving to secure a monopoly of the business and prevent competition. . . . But they feel that it is immensely to their interest, as to the interest of every responsible businessman, to try to prevent a panic and general industrial smashup at this time." "I answered that while of course I could not advise them to take the action proposed, I felt it no public duty of mine to interpose any objection."

The episode haunted Roosevelt thereafter. It was used by the

Democrats without full exposition of the facts as a campaign issue in 1908; it was raised during the investigation of the United States Steel Corporation in 1911 with portentous consequences to the course of American political history; and it was sporadically revived during the rest of Roosevelt's life. Pringle has woven it into a kind of "babe in the woods" account of Roosevelt's relations with "The Wicked Speculators." And some historians regarded it as prima facie evidence of Roosevelt's two-facedness.

Indubitably, Roosevelt had been imposed upon. The United States Steel Corporation's acquisition of the Tennessee Coal and Iron Company strengthened its already favored position within the industry and measurably increased its assets. In spite of the impression conveyed by Gary and Frick, moreover, it remains an open question whether the merger was the only means of saving Moore & Schley. Yet what else could the President have done? He was advised that rejection of the proposal would induce a new panic and possibly a real depression. He was told that time was of the essence and that the decision had to be made before the Stock Exchange opened that morning. And he was assured that Morgan and the others were acting in good conscience. He did, accordingly, what circumstances dictated; he accepted the word of Gary and Frick as that of gentlemen.

The President's tacit consent to the merger should also be viewed in the context of his maturing trust philosophy. As his call for a sweeping regulatory program in December, 1906 suggests, he by then entertained little brief for the Sherman Law except as a political or moral weapon; during the year and one half following the Panic of 1907 he would invoke it only in the most extreme cases. It seems reasonable to contend, therefore, that he was broadly predisposed to approve the merger. And though he hedged in his letter to Bonaparte by emphasizing that the Steel Corporation's holdings would still comprise less than 60 per cent of those of the industry at large, the transaction as he understood it was consistent with his own philosophy on monopoly.

As the long term economic consequences of the merger prove, however, Roosevelt's inability to give a specific definition to the philosophy—to define the indirect no less than the direct limits of tolerance—was critical. The contention that control of less than 60 per cent of the industry failed to constitute a monopoly had a superficial appeal; and in 1920 the Supreme Court itself succumbed to it, refusing to order the Steel Corporation's dissolution after a long and exhausting suit. But the apparent effect of the absorption of Tennessee Coal and Iron by U.S. Steel was the partial subversion of the interests of a section of the nation. Controlled thereafter from Pittsburgh and New York, T. C. & I. was forced to pursue policies consonant with the interests of U.S. Steel rather than the economy of the Southeast. It was subjected to "basing point" prices that by some accounts prevented it from capitalizing fully on its ability to produce more cheaply than the parent corporation's northern subsidiaries; its natural propensity to expand and diversify its production was seriously curbed; and the steel-consuming industries throughout the region it served seemingly grew less rapidly than they would have had T. C. & I. been free to meet their demands.

Probably neither Morgan nor Gary, and surely not Frick, foresaw all this at the time. Whatever their misrepresentations to Roosevelt in the White House Conference, the conspiratorial element is lacking in their talks in New York at the height of the Panic. Nevertheless, the absorption of the southern company gave them and their successors a powerful influence over the fortunes of the Southeast; and in so doing it sharply pointed up the basic weakness in the President's approach to the trust problem.

Otherwise, the Panic of 1907 proved salutary. By dramatizing the inadequacies of the banking and currency system it set the stage for meliorative legislation in 1908 and thoroughgoing reform in 1913 when the Federal Reserve Law was enacted under Woodrow Wilson. After Roosevelt again called for corrective legislation in his annual message of December, 1907, Senator Aldrich introduced a bill authorizing national banks to issue additional notes up to $500 million in times of emergency. The notes were to be based on municipal, state, and railroad bonds, and they were to be taxed in order to expedite their retirement once the money market loosened. This was somewhat less than the President had recommended.

Meanwhile a bill that anticipated the Federal Reserve Act in many essentials was introduced in the House. Politics, insecurity, and a lack of economic imagination combined, however, to force its rejection. Cannon and Aldrich found it too unorthodox. Roosevelt himself considered it inflationary; also "very puzzling." Furthermore, he leaned too heavily on Aldrich. As he facilely wrote in defense of the Rhode Islander's measure a few weeks later:

I would like to see a thoroly good system of banking and currency . . . and yet this is the only measure that has been proposed that we can seriously consider. The trouble is that the minute
I try to get action all the financiers and businessmen differ so that
nobody can advise me, nobody can give me any aid; and only
Senator Aldrich has prepared a bill.

A substitute administration offering, the Vreeland bill, meanwhile
passed the House. As merged with Aldrich's bill and enacted into
law, it modified the former's Eastern bias by broadening the base for
note issues in the South and the West. It still gave heavy advantage
to the East, however, and Southern Democrats and Republican progressives pummelled it unmercifully. Carter Glass of Virginia charged
that the three man committee of bankers empowered to handle the
reserve fund in time of crisis would reflect the interests of the great
financial institutions and could readily strangle small country banks.
He further contended that it "perpetuates and accentuates the rigidity
of a bond-secured currency system," and he finally dismissed it as
"50 per cent House infamy and 50 per cent Senate infamy." John
Sharp Williams of Mississippi claimed that it ought "to be entitled the
'Cannon-Aldrich political emergency bill.'" And La Follette was
equally vitriolic and considerably more voluble.

The criticisms were partisan and overdrawn. The Aldrich-Vreeland
bill was designed as a temporary expedient rather than an inclusive
reform, and its provision for a study commission was of momentous
importance. Nevertheless, many of the opposition's points were well
taken, and the Federal Reserve Act would incorporate them. As
Roosevelt's critics contend, furthermore, his failure to fashion substantial banking and currency reform was one of the signal defeats
of his presidency.

Like Roosevelt's other failures, however, it fades into insignificance
beside his towering contribution to the conservation movement.

CHAPTER 19

FOR THE GENERATIONS
YET UNBORN

> When the historian . . . shall speak of Theodore Roosevelt,
> he is likely to say that he did many notable things, but that his
> greatest work was inspiring and actually beginning a world move-
> ment for staying territorial waste and saving for the human race
> the things on which alone a peaceful, progressive, and happy life
> can be founded.
>
> —Robert M. La Follette, *Autobiography*

Of all Roosevelt's constructive endeavors, the movement for conservation was the most remarkable for sustained intellectual and administrative force. In none other did the President blend the scientific
outlook and his moralistic conception of the public interest quite so
effectively; in only one other, foreign policy, did he submerge partisan
politics nearly so decisively. For more than seven years, often against
the avowed opposition of the most powerful leaders of his own party,
and at the bitter end against the combined opposition of both parties,
he pressed Congress and the states to place the future public interest
above the current private interest. And though he was repeatedly
criticized, rebuffed, and insulted, he refused to be thwarted or even
to compromise significantly.

Roosevelt was always frank to confess that his conservation program was builded upon the labors and visions of scientists who had
given, or were to give, the flower of their lives to its advancement.
"They actually did the job that I and the others talked about," he
pointed out in an address at Harvard two years after he left the White

318

House. "I know what they did because it was something in which I intensely believed, and yet it was something about which I did not have enough practical knowledge to work except through them. . . ." Yet, as virtually everyone who has written about the conservation movement has warmly conceded, the President's was the ultimate responsibility.

Roosevelt would have undoubtedly thrown himself into the movement whatever the circumstances of his presidency. His empiricism, love of nature, obsession with orderly development, and devotion to the public good are all suggestive of that. But he would hardly have promoted it with such extraordinary boldness and imagination had it not been for his inspiring relationship with Gifford Pinchot, Chief Forester of the United States and one of American history's most constructive secondary leaders.

The scion of an old Huguenot family of moderate wealth and high public spirit (the Pinchots in 1900 made the grant that started the Yale Forestry School), Gifford was thirty-six years old when Roosevelt became President. A tall and sinewy figure with piercing eyes, a thin straight nose, and a long sharp chin that a drooping mustache barely softened, he wore an air of compelling urgency. He was constantly converting, or trying to convert, and only his natural graciousness and the high fortune of his friendship with the President early spared him the fate of many another zealot. For more, even, than most men with a mission, Pinchot was fanatically confident of the righteousness of his cause. Upon its altar he would eventually sacrifice his governmental career.

Roosevelt had known Pinchot well enough to sponsor him for membership in the Boone and Crockett Club in the 1890's. But not until Roosevelt became governor of New York did the two men become close. Once, during the winter of 1899, Pinchot stopped in Albany for an overnight visit, arriving, so he later wrote, "just as the Executive Mansion was under ferocious attack from a band of invisible Indians, and the Governor of the Empire State was helping a houseful of children to escape by lowering them out of the second-story window on a rope." After the children had been "saved," the forester had proved his mettle by knocking Roosevelt "off his very solid pins" in a boxing match. He and his host had then discussed forestry.

While one of the nation's most singularly productive friendships was thus being sealed, the conservation cause had been going badly in Washington. By Roosevelt's accession in 1901 more than twenty-six million acres of public lands had been withdrawn from private entry; but the figures were deceptive. Under the prevailing leasing system private exploitation of minerals, timber, and water-power sites went on apace, even in the so-called reserves. Although Cleveland had abruptly halted the leasing process by executive order ten days before his second term expired, McKinley had soon signed a compromise measure which suspended Cleveland's restraining order after nine months had elapsed and thereafter left the reserves open to indiscriminate mining and prospecting. Between 1898 and 1905, when this "vicious piece of legislation," as the Public Land Commission termed it, was repealed, three million acres of government timber land passed permanently into private hands.

President Roosevelt had barely moved into the White House after McKinley's death in September, 1901, before he unloaded his baggage in the conservationists' camp. On Roosevelt's return from his predecessor's funeral, Pinchot and Frederick H. Newell, who may fairly be called the father of the Reclamation Service, spelled out to him the far-reaching forestry and reclamation plans they and their able associates had long hoped to institute. "The new President knew what we were talking about," Pinchot recalled in his autobiography. "We left, two very happy men, authorized to draft for the Message what we thought it ought to say on our twin subjects. It was a Heaven-sent chance."

The message President Roosevelt sent in to the Congress two months later gave forceful expression to Pinchot and Newell's advanced scientific views; and in the manner of all Roosevelt's partly ghost-written statements, to his own as well. "The fundamental idea of forestry is the perpetuation of forests by use," Roosevelt declared as he recommended that the reserves be kept open to "selective cutting." They should also be utilized as natural reservoirs, supplemented where necessary by great storage dams "too vast for private effort" to finance. Nor was this to be accomplished by the states alone. "It is as right for the National Government to make the streams and rivers of the arid region useful by engineering works for water storage," he declared in a passage that foreshadowed his later, more strident centralism, "as to make useful the rivers and harbors of the humid region by engineering works of another kind." Too often, he testily wrote, the states had defaulted on their obligations by allowing streams to pass into private ownership. "Whoever controls a stream practically controls the land it renders productive," he reminded the Congress, and ". . . the doctrine of private ownership of water apart from land cannot prevail without causing enduring wrong." The government's reclamation program should create "the best possible social and industrial conditions" for the people moving into the reclaimed lands; however, he added, it should conform to state laws and should be accomplished "in such manner as will enable the people in the local communities to help themselves."

Roosevelt had then plunged headlong into the seven years struggle to put the proposals of his message into effect. On December 19, 1901, he urged Congress in a special message to create a national forest reserve in the Appalachians. Meanwhile he threw his as yet untested power behind a Democratic-sponsored irrigation and reclamation measure, the Newlands bill, which McKinley had failed to support and which Joseph G. Cannon, then chairman of the Appropriations Committee, was opposing. Cannon's opposition was animated by an unreasoned commitment to economy, by fear that the reclaimed areas would offer competition to Midwestern agriculture, and by that coarse anti-intellectualism which was so much a part of his make-up. As he later snapped in another context, he stood "not one cent for scenery" and he never did have much use for the "college professors, students, wise men and so on through the length and breadth of the country, who investigate. . . ." Nor was "Uncle Joe" moved by a presidential appeal couched both in rational terms and in the pork-barrel language that he understood so well. "I do not believe that I have ever before written to an individual legislator in favor of an individual bill," Roosevelt wrote the Ohioan, "but I break through my rule to ask you as earnestly as I can not to oppose the Irrigation measure. Believe me this is something of which I have made a careful study, and great and real though my deference is for your knowledge of legislation, and for your attitude in stopping expense, I yet feel from my acquaintance with the far West that it would be a genuine and rankling injustice for the Republican party to kill this measure. I believe in it with all my heart from every standpoint."

I am just about to sign the River and Harbor bill. . . . Now this is a measure for the material benefit of your State and mine and of the other states with harbors and navigable rivers. Surely it is but simple justice for us to give to the arid regions a measure of relief, the financial burden of which will be but trifling, while the benefit to the country involved is far greater than under the River and Harbor bill. I cannot too strongly express my feeling upon this matter.

Cannon refused to clarify his position, and the Newlands bill rolled through the House without his support, and on June 17, 1902, Roosevelt enthusiastically signed it into law. The first important enactment of his presidency, it authorized the creation of a reclamation service, assigned revenues from land sales to the construction of reservoirs and irrigation works by the federal government, and established a broadly creative, if heavily subsidized, policy toward the arid lands. By its authority, thirty irrigation projects embracing three million acres, including the Roosevelt Dam in Arizona, were in progress or already completed when Roosevelt left office in March, 1909.

During the remainder of his first term Roosevelt continued to see much of Pinchot, a charter member of his "Tennis Cabinet." And at the forester's suggestion he shortly set aside the Dismal River and Niobrara Forest Reserves for a controlled experiment in tree planting in Nebraska where an earlier and more limited experiment had shown that marketable trees could grow on sand hills regarded as worthless. This second experiment proved similarly successful, serving, in Pinchot's words, as the forerunner of the "great Shelter Belt Plan begun under President Franklin D. Roosevelt, and so brilliantly suggested and successfully directed by Raphael Zon."

Not until after he was elected in his own right, however, did Roosevelt's flaming conviction really scorch the anti-conservationists. Reinforced by his popular mandate and by the Public Land Commission's (appointed in 1903) considered recommendations for orderly development, the President now launched a full-scale program to stay the exploitative processes of a century and a quarter and to impress upon the nation an intelligent awareness of nature's beauteous bounty and munificent industrial potential. From the winter of 1905 on, indeed, scarcely a detail eluded Roosevelt's creative attention as he vigorously promoted the cause of conservation through regulated use in his public speeches, messages to Congress, and executive actions. The consequence was such an enlightenment as the nation had not theretofore seen and would not again witness until Franklin Roosevelt, himself nurtured on Theodore's conservationist principles, came to power.

The first harvest was reaped on February 1, 1905, when Roosevelt signed a measure transferring the Forest Reserves from the jurisdiction of the inefficient Land Office in the Department of the Interior to the Bureau of Forestry, renamed the Forest Service, in the Department of Agriculture. The measure also conferred upon Pinchot that tremendous grant of power which was to make him the Galahad of the conservationists and the bête noire of their opponents. Two months after its enactment, the Forest Service was authorized for the first time to make arrests for the violation of its regulations.

The forestry movement was now coming of age. The most powerful interests in the West, including the National Wholesale Lumber Dealers' Association, had finally concluded that the selective cutting and other techniques urged upon them by the evangelical Pinchot and his dedicated colleagues were feasible. It was no accident that the transfer bill was passed just after they expressed their approval of its intent at the meetings of the American Forest Congress early in January, 1905; nor that Roosevelt had waited until after the election of 1904 to push it.

The Forest Service became even more independent of Congress than anticipated in ensuing months. By a little-noticed clause soon given an inclusive interpretation by the Attorney General, William H. Moody, the Agriculture Appropriations Act of 1905 authorized the Service to use the revenues from the sale of the lands or products of the reserves for administration of existing reserves and the creation of new ones. The result was a small revolution. "While we could still say nothing but 'Please' to private forest owners," Pinchot recalled, "on the national Forest Reserves we could say, and we did say, 'Do this,' and 'Don't do that.' We had the power, as we had the duty, to protect the Reserves for the use of the people, and that meant stepping on the toes of the biggest interests in the West. From that time on it was fight, fight, fight."

Under Roosevelt's driving leadership the Forest Lieu Act of 1897 was repealed. This measure, writes Roy Robbins, was believed by many Westerners to have "done more to aid the speculators and corporations than to aid the actual settler." Hard on its demise came an administration order establishing a leasing system for use of the grass lands within the forest reserves. Under and in violation of prevailing regulations, pastures had been ruthlessly overgrazed, government lands had been fenced in by private operators, cattlemen had fought bloody battles against sheepmen, and both had made life miserable for the homesteaders who were regarded as a menace by the large grazing interests. A first, and partial, step toward remedying these conditions, the new order was buttressed by Roosevelt's resolve to enforce the laws against fencing. "I cannot consent to a clause continuing for a year, or for any length of time, the present illegal fencing," he explained to Senator Francis E. Warren of Wyoming, whose solicitude for the sheep industry would later earn him the sobriquet, "the greatest shepherd since Abraham." The President continued:

> The opposition we have . . . now comes primarily from the big men who graze wandering flocks of sheep, and who do not promote the real settlement of the country. These are the men whose interests are diametrically hostile to those of the homemakers, who wish to eat out and destroy the country where he desires permanently to live, and who, when they have thus ruined the land of the homesteader and small stockman, move elsewhere to repeat the process of devastation.

Actually, as Samuel P. Hays' penetrating study of the conservation movement makes clear, Roosevelt's understanding of the problem was deeper than his strictures against illegal fencing implied. He knew that many homesteaders and small cattlemen had also resorted to illegal fencing, if only in self-defense. He shared the cattlemen's animus toward the sheepmen. And he realized that the Public Land Commission's investigation had indicated that the fenced-in lands were generally less overgrazed than the open range. As he conceded in a special message the next year, fencing the public domain "would be thoroughly desirable if it were legal."

The President was also aware that the 160-acre limitation in the existing homestead legislation was grossly inadequate for the semiarid country. He persistently labored to correct this, and shortly before he left office Congress raised the allotment to 320 acres. As Roosevelt contended, however, the only rational solution was a system basing the allotment on the particular needs of the area. Otherwise, he observed as early as December, 1905, "needless suffering and failure on the part of a very considerable proportion of the bona-fide settlers who give faith to the implied assurance of the government that such an area is sufficient" would probably result. In later years students of the Western land problem would confirm his judgment.

Meanwhile the President focused his sights on the fast-growing electric power industry. For some years, writes Pinchot, utility companies had been securing the best water-power sites "through every workable use or misuse of the public-land laws and the laws relating to navigable rivers. . . . The Government's problem, as we saw it, was to ensure the fullest possible development of water power and its sale to the consumer at the cheapest possible price. That meant the prevention of monopoly where we could, and effective regulation of it where we couldn't." To these ends Roosevelt had vetoed a bill on March 3, 1903, that would have turned Muscle Shoals, which later became the heart of the TVA, over to piecemeal private development. And in June, 1905, Pinchot was given the authority to issue permits for the use of water-power sites.

From 1906 on, when a number of sites were leased to the Edison Electrical Company of California, a policy of controlled, fifty-year leases obtained. To assure orderly development, Pinchot withdrew 2,565 sites from entry during the next two years, often on the pretext that he planned to establish ranger stations on them. In these actions, as in most others, he leaned heavily on the President's broad shoulders. "Without T.R.'s support," he wrote forty years later, "all reasonable regulation of the development of water power on the National Forests would have broken down."

Thus Roosevelt, after first approving a number of loosely framed special acts for private contraction, several times vetoed bills which failed to conform to the administration's regulatory program; and on January 15, 1909, in one of the most memorable of such actions, he sweepingly rebuked both Congress and the puissant electric power lobby. "I esteem it my duty," he said in rejecting a measure that would have authorized the construction of an unleased and unregulated dam in Missouri, "to use every endeavor to prevent this growing monopoly, the most threatening which has ever appeared, from being fastened upon the people of the Nation." This bill "does not contain the conditions essential to protect the public interest."

Shortly after Roosevelt and Pinchot began to apply the principle that "the public rights come first and private interest second" to the electric power industry, the President imposed it upon the mining industry. Under the prevailing agricultural land laws, valuable coal lands had long been passing into private hands at prices wholly disproportionate to their true value. Now, by direction of the President on June 29, 1906, the process was finally slowed. During the next two years more than fifty million acres believed to contain coal and other minerals were temporarily withdrawn from public entry in order that they might be classified, and before Roosevelt left office eighteen million additional acres were withdrawn in Alaska. To be sure, the President's frequent requests that Congress establish a royalty fee system under government price and transportation controls fell on deaf ears. But as Hays concludes, the Geological Survey at least "valued the coal lands according to the quality of the deposits and their accessibility, and established prices which would aid development, while preventing speculation."

By 1907 Congress, the timber, grazing, and mining interests of the West, countless other interests, and the overwhelming majority of conservatives in the East were surfeited with Theodore Roosevelt. From 1907 on the President faced a manifestly hostile Congress, one that was to resist him on almost all major issues and actually repudiate him on some. Had Roosevelt been a less resourceful man, he might consequently have served out his final years of the presidency in fretful impotence. But because he held it the executive's duty to lead, and because he accepted the stewardship theory without reservation, he managed to maintain the authority of his office. By his discriminating use of the veto power he held the main line against his opponents' embittered assaults; and by continuing that audacious use of the executive power that had characterized his tenure from the strike against the Northern Securities Company in 1902 on, he even advanced in some areas. His conservation program reached full maturity, in fact, at the very time it fell under the sharpest attack.

The first of the succession of showdowns between President and Congress came during the short session of 1907. Senatorial resentment of Roosevelt and Pinchot's policies toward the forest reserves had seemingly increased in direct proportion to their effectiveness; and when the Agricultural Appropriations bill was sent in from the House, Senator C. W. Fulton, an Oregon Republican who bowed not to "Uncle Joe" Cannon in the vigor of his anti-intellectualism, castigated the Chief Forester and his colleagues as impractical "dreamers and theorists" ensconced within "marble halls" and opposed a provision to increase Pinchot's salary.

Less than a month later Fulton proposed to amend the Agricultural Appropriations bill with a clause specifying that no forest
reserve should thereafter be created within the states of Oregon,
Washington, Idaho, Montana, Colorado, or Wyoming (extremist
Westerners actually wanted the reserves returned to the states, under
whose benign authority private interests had already ravaged great
blocks of land). The anti-Roosevelt feeling in the Senate was so concerted that Fulton's amendment was adopted without a roll-call vote,
and shortly before the session ended the amended Agricultural Appropriations bill reached the President's desk. Fulton and his friends
waited, serene in the belief that Roosevelt would sign it, since the
Department of Agriculture and all its subordinate agencies, including
the forest reserves, depended on its authorization for funds during
the coming fiscal year. They were completely unprepared for the explosion that followed.

Responding instinctively to what he and Roosevelt conceived as a
sullen threat to the American future, Gifford Pinchot formulated an
ingenious counterattack: He would have the President proclaim National Forests in all suitable remaining public lands during the ten
days Roosevelt had to sign or reject the bill. "We knew precisely
what we wanted," Pinchot recalled. "Our field force had already
gathered practically all the facts. Speedily it supplied the rest. Our
office force worked straight through, some of them for thirty-six and
even forty-eight hours on end, to finish the job." As the proclamations were completed, Pinchot took them to the White House for
Roosevelt's signature. They were then sent to the State Department
for safekeeping until, all told, twenty-one new forest reserves, embracing sixteen million acres in the six states affected by Fulton's amendment, were provided for. They were formally proclaimed on March 2
just before the President signed the Agricultural Appropriations bill
into law.

Six years later Roosevelt wrote with transparent glee of how "the
friends of the special interests in the Senate" had been outwitted. "The
opponents of the forest service turned handsprings in their wrath, and
dire were their threats against the Executive; but the threats could not
be carried out, and were really only a tribute to the efficiency of our
action." As a memorandum he dictated at the time reveals, however,
he was genuinely concerned lest historians interpret his action as
arbitrary. "If I did not act . . . and if Congress differs from me in

this position," he wrote, "it will have full opportunity in the future
to take such position as it may desire. . . ."

Failure on my part to sign these proclamations would mean that
immense tracts of valuable timber would fall into the hands of the
lumber syndicates . . . for our entire purpose in this forest reserve
policy is to keep the land for the benefit of the actual settler and
home-maker, to further his interests in every way, and, while using
the natural resources of the country for the benefit of the present
generation, also to use them in such manner as to keep them un-
impaired for the benefit of the children now growing up to inherit
the land. This is the final and exclusive object not merely of our
forest policy but of our whole public land policy.

The President's "midnight" proclamations rang down the curtain
for many Westerners. Forgotten in the bitterness of the hour were
the ties of affection that had once made them regard the young
reformer-ranchman as their own; that had moved them to pour out
of the mountains and off the great plains to serve under his command
in 1898; that had turned "Boss" Platt's cynical maneuvering into an
uncontrollable stampede at the Republican Convention of 1900. Not
only to the lumber syndicates, the mining corporations, and the great
sheep and cattle barons, but to many of the "plain people" Roosevelt
professed so to love, the President by 1907 was a deadly enemy of
their region. The spurious charge that the governor of Washington
now leveled against Pinchot—he "has done more to retard the growth
and development of the Northwest than any other man"—could only
have had Roosevelt as its real object. Within a month of the proclamations a call (proposed several months before by the governor of
Colorado at the instigation of the sheepmen and farmers rather than
the lumber interests) had gone out all over the West for a great
protest convention to meet in Denver on June 19.

Not all the opposition to the Roosevelt-Pinchot policies was un-
founded; nor did it all emanate from the servants of "special privilege"
as the President and his devoted forester friend too sweepingly implied. The problems were so diverse and the interests involved so
irreconcilable that there remain to this day areas of unresolved conflict. The complaint of the states that the national reserves reduced
their tax base is reasonable, if not in the broad view consequential.
Understandable also are the protests of all those operators, small even
more than large, who by habit or custom had come to regard the

nation's resources as theirs to exploit. Man once unfettered does not gracefully submit to bureaucracy, no matter how great its flexibility or laudable its social and scientific purposes. The leasing fees, the proscriptions of illegal fencing, the prohibition of excessive grazing—these and numerous other regulations were anathema to free-wheeling Westerners on the make.

Furthermore, all Westerners did not regard the administration's forest policies as a boon to the small entrepreneur. Again and again there arose in the mountain states the complaint that the great lumber companies benefited unfairly from the creation of reserves because they had already engrossed the lands that gave ingress. Besides, the selective-cutting techniques prescribed by the Forest Service were easier for the large interests to finance. The gigantic Weyerhaeuser Timber Company could act in accordance with the principles of a long-term investment, but few small companies or independent operators had the financial resources to take the long view. Inevitably, they resented having it imposed upon them.

Roosevelt's reaction to these complaints was ambivalent at best and disingenuous at worst. He continued in his public pronouncements to emphasize the antimonopolistic tenor of his policies; and with some justification, for a million and one-half acres were opened to settlement by small farmers under his administration while his water-power program was clearly designed to bring natural monopolies under public control. At the same time, however, he privately complained that the "people refuse to face squarely the proposition that much of these lands ought to be leased and fenced as pastures, and that they cannot possibly be taken up with profit as small homesteads." But the point is hardly worth laboring. The President's commitment to scientific forestry was so total, his insight into the advantages of corporate organization in a technological age so deep, that the knowledge that the big companies were profiting and growing could not have altered his course. Regulation was to him the only socially desirable solution.

There were also other complaints against the administration. The grazing interests vehemently protested that much grassland was locked up in the forest reserves, as in truth it temporarily was. On the eve of the militant protest convention in Denver the Forest Service released thousands of acres of such land—a well-timed maneuver, admittedly, but also part of an already considered policy. Beyond or beneath these arguable complaints was the West's vexation at Roosevelt's good-government philosophy, or at least its practical application.

Starting in 1903 the administration had relentlessly proceeded against a great host of land swindlers including every member but one of Oregon's all-Republican congressional delegation. Their indictment and subsequent prosecution had won plaudits for Roosevelt throughout most of the country. But in the Northwest they had evoked an enthusiasm similar to that displayed by the Tammany Democrats when Police Commissioner Roosevelt had tried to clean their Augean stables in the mid-1890's. "Even men who were in no way implicated . . . felt a sympathy for the ones who were caught," writes an historian of the movement, "for unquestionably such frauds had been too common . . . to be viewed seriously." One high government official whom Roosevelt had dismissed, though not prosecuted, was elected to represent an Oregon district in Congress within six months of his forced retirement; and Senator Fulton never did forgive Roosevelt for the blow he had dealt his colleagues.

There was also the paradox inherent in Pinchot's personnel policies. For years the old Forestry Division had been plagued by an inferior staff, especially in the field, where ward politicians, ex-bartenders, and other misfits had comprised an embarrassing large part of the ranger force. Westerners on the spot had understandably chafed at being policed by such a motley crowd; and at Pinchot's instance Roosevelt had placed foresters under the civil service laws in December, 1904. So salutary did that reform prove that by 1908 a New York consulting firm compared the administration of the Forest Service "most favorably" with private industry and reported that its investigators had "rarely, if ever, met a body of men where the average of intelligence was so high or the loyalty to the organization and to the work so great."

From Cannon on down, however, the professional politicians resented the resultant loss of patronage. More ironical still, Westerners who had earlier protested the low quality of the Forestry Division fulminated in later years against the high quality of the reconstituted Forest Service. No longer could they evade regulations on the excuse that the men who devised and enforced them were appallingly incompetent. Like the meat packers, the railroad officials, and many other businessmen who had felt Roosevelt's controlling hand, their philosophy was thus proved under fire to encompass little more than their own self-interest.

Meanwhile the President's appreciation of nature was carrying him into less utilitarian channels. For all his zest for hunting, Roosevelt possessed both the naturalist's compulsion to conserve and the democrat's desire to share. Now, as he fought Congress for a rational policy toward both the conservation and maximization through controlled use of the nation's natural resources, he also skirmished for the preservation of its magnificent natural monuments—for Niagara Falls and Arizona's Grand Canyon, for Oregon's Crater Lake and New Mexico's Petrified Forest, for the undulating Blue Ridge Mountains and dozens upon dozens of others. In his private letters, his speeches, and even in his messages to Congress he expressed his heartfelt conviction that nature's wonders were the American people's own rightful heritage. "I cannot too often repeat that the essential feature in the present management of the Yellowstone Park, as in all similar places, is its essential democracy," he said on April 24, 1903, as he laid the cornerstone of the gateway to that spectacular park. It is, he elaborated, "the preservation of the scenery, of the forests, of the wilderness life and the wilderness game for the people as a whole, instead of leaving the enjoyment thereof to be confined to the very rich who can control private reserves."

And so there were created during Roosevelt's two administrations five National Parks—Crater Lake in Oregon, Platt National Park in Oklahoma, Wind Cave in South Dakota, Sully Hill in North Dakota, and Mesa Verde in Colorado. These doubled the number established by all his predecessors. There was passed under Roosevelt's spur the National Monuments Act of June, 1906, by authority of which he eventually proclaimed sixteen National Monuments, including Wyoming's Devil Tower, California's Muir Woods, and Washington's Mount Olympus. There were established by executive orders issued between March 14, 1903, when Roosevelt first realized he had the power, and March 4, 1909, when he turned over the power, fifty-one wildlife refuges ("Is there any law that will prevent me from declaring Pelican Island a Federal Bird Reservation?" he had asked. Informed that there was none, he had replied: "Very well, then I so declare it"). And there was launched from the base built by William T. Hornaday, George Bird Grinnell, Frank M. Chapman, the National Audubon Society, and others a nature-appreciation movement that offers one of the few remaining hopes that the march of the billboards, the gas stations, and the bulldozers may somehow be stayed and that such commercial barbarisms as Wisconsin's Dells may yet be redeemed.

As the time for Roosevelt to yield his stewardship drew near, he came increasingly to realize that the future of the conservation movement lay preeminently with the states. They must be persuaded to abandon their particularism in order that regional, multipurpose river developments might be undertaken; they must be imbued with a sense of responsibility that the despoliation of their own public lands might be halted. To these ends Roosevelt appointed a path finding body, the Inland Waterways Commission, on March 14, 1907. Six months later he announced that he would call a conference of governors to meet in Washington that winter. The long-range effect of both these actions was momentous.

The President's decision to create the Inland Waterways Commission was sparked by W J McGee of the Bureau of Soils, though commercial groups in the Mississippi Valley had been urging action for some time. At issue was the need of a comprehensive plan for the improvement and control of the nation's rivers. Roosevelt had long realized this, and his letter to the chairman of the Commission spelled out the charge:

> Works designed to control our waterways have . . . been undertaken for a single purpose, such as the improvement of navigation, development of power, the irrigation of arid lands, the protection of lowlands from floods, or to supply water for domestic and manufacturing purposes. While the rights of the people to these and similar uses of water must be respected, the time has come for merging local projects and uses of the inland waters in a comprehensive plan designed for the benefit of the whole country.

Within the year the Inland Waterways Commission confirmed and amplified the President's original charge in a report that reflected the creative imagination of McGee and the engineering brilliance of Marshall O. Leighton, Chief Hydrographer of the Geological Survey. Presumably because he feared that Congress might miss the point, Roosevelt appended to it a sharp blast of his own against the electric power industry. "Among these monopolies . . . ," he wrote, "there is no other which threatens, or has ever threatened, such intolerable interference with the daily life of the people as the consolidation of companies controlling water power."

. . . I call your special attention to the attempt of the power corporations, through bills introduced at the present session, to escape from the possibility of Government regulation in the interests of the people. These bills are intended to enable the corporations to take possession in perpetuity of national forest lands for the purposes of their business, where and as they please, wholly without compensation to the public.

Neither the report of the Inland Waterways Commission nor the angry assertions of the President turned Congress from its pork-barreling, philosophically conservative ways. Resentful of Roosevelt's hold on the popular mind, contemptuous of his concern for social planning, and solicitous as always of the varied special interests, the Republican majority yearned openly for the day when its leader would no longer lead—when it would have again a President in the mold of McKinley. Sullenly, it sat on its hands. It got off them only to prohibit the President from appointing new commissions without congressional assent following Roosevelt's return to the subject in his message of December 8, 1908. The historic handling of the inland waterways has been "short-sighted, vacillating, and futile," the President charged in that last annual message. The army engineers responsible for the program (the Chief of the Corps was actually on record as stating that flood control, hydroelectric power, and irrigation should be subordinate to navigation) were "unsuited by their training and traditions to take the broad view" and they had failed above all "to grasp the great underlying fact that every stream is a unit from its source to its mouth, and that all its uses are interdependent." Congress should provide funds, the President fruitlessly concluded, "to frame and supervise the execution of a comprehensive plan."

It was those last two principles—"that every stream is a unit from its source to its mouth, and that all its uses are interdependent"—which later comprised the springboard for the TVA, that monument to George W. Norris's persistence and the New Deal's acceptance of its legacy from the Square Deal.

Had Theodore Roosevelt's service to conservation ended with the proclamation of the sixteen million acres of Forest Reserves in 1907, or with his vigorous exposition of the findings of the Inland Waterways Commission, his administrations would still have been distinguished beyond those of all of his predecessors. But it did not. The

Governors' Conference of 1908 added one more star to his already glittering constellation.

On the morning of May 13, 1908, President Roosevelt, attired in the formal clothes he deemed appropriate to the occasion, mounted a temporary podium in the East Room of the White House. For fifty minutes in the modulated, cultured tones that were as characteristic of his speech as the shrill falsetto ascribed to him by caricaturists, he spoke—to the members of his Cabinet; to the Associate Justices and the Chief Justice of the Supreme Court of the United States; to the governors of thirty-eight states and territories, many of whom spared no love for either him or conservation; to that loyal leader of the opposition, William Jennings Bryan, who would make his third and last bid for the presidency that autumn; to Andrew Carnegie, dedicated for some years past to peace, philanthropy, and public welfare; to John Mitchell, still the dignified idol of the United Mine Workers; to James J. Hill, the most enlightened of the great railroad magnates; and to a host of scientists, publicists, and representatives of the nation's learned societies. Grover Cleveland would also have been present had he not then been in his final illness.

The President's address was a testament of faith and a statement of hope. He started by declaring that conservation was "the chief material question that confronts us, second only—and second always—to the great fundamental question of morality." He emphasized the urgent need for a "coherent plan" of development. He reaffirmed that his object was not to lock up natural resources, but to use them in a way that would increase their yield for the next generation. "No wise use of a farm exhausts its fertility," he observed. "So with the forests." He showered encomiums upon Gifford Pinchot, "to whom we owe so much of the progress we have already made." And he concluded with a moralistic assertion that the rights of the public were paramount to those of private individuals:

> In the past we have admitted the right of the individual to injure the future of the Republic for his own present profit. The time has come for a change. As a people we have the right and the duty, second to none other but the right and duty of obeying the moral law, of requiring and doing justice, to protect ourselves and our children against the wasteful development of our natural resources, whether that waste is caused by the actual destruction of such resources or by making them impossible of development hereafter.

Probably no event of Roosevelt's turbulent career evoked a more spontaneous and universally favorable reaction that the three-day conference he had then opened. Throughout the nation his address was acclaimed as one of his greatest public utterances, perhaps the greatest. Even the New York *Evening Post* grudgingly wrote that "this is distinctly a case where Mr. Roosevelt's love of the spectacular and skill in advertising have proved of public advantage." The New York *Sun,* noted the editors of the *Literary Digest,* "is the only paper we yet have seen which holds absolutely aloof from the enthusiasm of the occasion."

The monumental significance of the Governors' Conference can only be suggested. Not all the governors were sympathetic to the Roosevelt-Pinchot program; and before the sessions closed several of the Westerners militantly defended states' rights, that "darling of the great special interests" as Pinchot caustically termed them. Thus Governor Gooding of Idaho demanded that the National Forests be transferred to the states and Governor Norris of Montana castigated the grazing fee as a "levying of tribute." Yet even they gave their names to the notable Declaration of the Governors, a landmark in the history of the conservation movement and the changing conception of federal-state relationships. That document declared:

We agree that the sources of national wealth exist for the benefit of the People, and that monopoly thereof should not be tolerated.

We declare the conviction that in the use of the natural resources our independent States are interdependent and bound together by ties of mutual benefits, responsibilities, and duties.

We agree that further action is advisable to ascertain the present condition of our natural resources and to promote the conservation of the same; and to that end we recommend the appointment by each State of a Commission on the Conservation of Natural Resources, to co-operate with each other and with any similar commission of the Federal Government.

Roosevelt proved quick to take a first stride toward activating the declaration's recommendations. On June 8, 1908, he appointed the Federal Commission on the Conservation of Natural Resources under the chairmanship of the indefatigable Pinchot. Organized into four divisions—water, forest, land, and mineral resources—the Commission was charged by Roosevelt to cooperate heartily with the states in the interests of "the permanent welfare of the people" and to submit a preliminary report by January, 1909. The end product, writes Robbins, was a three-volume report that comprises "the most exhaustive inventory of our natural resources that has ever been made." Its value to scholars, government officials, and all those civic-minded citizens who have since concerned themselves with the conservation movement has been inestimable.

Most of the state executives kept the faith of their declaration during the first great outburst of enthusiasm that followed the conference. Within a year or so of the final session forty-one state conservation commissions had been formed; and until their recommendations began actually to be applied, everyone, or almost everyone, was avowedly for conservation. Only "when it began to interfere with the profits of powerful men and great special interests," complained Pinchot with some exaggeration and considerable truth, did the honeymoon come to an end.

Yet that is less than the whole. If, a half century later, many state governments stand paralyzed before the special interests that Roosevelt fought; if, thirty years after Roosevelt's death, private power companies continue to build dams without regard for the multipurposes he urged; if, only rarely, a governor emerges with the courage and vision to rise above the short-sighted economy that Roosevelt deplored; if, all this in our times is true, it is also true that the very substantial achievements of the past fifty years reflect the animating spirit of Theodore Roosevelt and that those of the next half century will doubtless continue to reflect it.

There was much difference of opinion about President Roosevelt the politician. Dr. Charles Van Hise, pioneer conservationist, noted geologist, and president of the University of Wisconsin from 1903 to 1918, wrote two years after Roosevelt left the presidency:

> He has been severely criticized by many, warmly commended by others, but his aggressive action for the conservation of our resources has been commended by all parties alike . . . what he did to forward this movement and to bring it into the foreground of the consciousness of the people will place him not only as one of the greatest statesmen of this nation but one of the greatest statesmen of any nation of any time.

CHAPTER 20

TOWARD THE WELFARE STATE

> There has been a curious revival of the doctrine of State rights . . . by the people who know that the States cannot with justice to both sides practically control the corporation and who therefore advocate such control because they do not venture to express their real wish, which is that there shall be no control at all. . . .
>
> —Theodore Roosevelt in a speech at Harvard, 1907

Although the President's inadvertent submission to Wall Street during the Panic of 1907 and its aftermath had thrown him back into the arms of the congressional conservatives, his sustained struggle for conservation suggests that the *rapprochement* was not of the spirit. True, Roosevelt maintained the working alliance with the Old Guard on some issues until near the end, though it daily grew more precarious. And in the manner of his entire career, he continued to compromise, holding out for some measures, sacrificing others, and accepting the form in lieu of the substance on still others.

The President wanted, for example, to reorganize the administration of the Navy as the Army had earlier been reorganized by Elihu Root. But he wanted even more to build up the battle fleet and establish a naval base at Pearl Harbor. Both programs were opposed by powerful members of his own party. Rather than risk total defeat, accordingly, he concentrated his energies on the latter. The result was that Congress in 1908 gave him two battleships (after he had manufactured a war scare with Japan) and the Pearl Harbor Base while the reorganization problem was left to his successors.

A letter Roosevelt wrote to Cannon while the question hung in the balance is revealing of the President's continued mastery of the political process: "If you knew the stormy time I have been having on your behalf with all kinds of people in connection with the tariff commission, I think you would look favorably on this Pearl Harbor request."

Again, Roosevelt would have been gratified had Congress enacted a national child labor law. But on that, as on many other measures, he was thwarted by his party's massive conservatism. So powerful was the manufacturers' hold upon the Republican leadership that no executive pressure, no marshaling of sociological data, no high-minded appeals from disinterested reformers could have broken it. The President had little alternative, therefore, but to dismiss as impractical the impassioned pleas of Beveridge, who had taken the child labor movement to his heart, and to support instead a bill sponsored by Lodge which applied only to the District of Columbia, an area where child labor was virtually nonexistent. The President rationalized this near-mockery of justice by contending that it would serve to warn the states that they must either pass similar legislation or be subjected to a federal law in the future.

To dwell on Roosevelt's forced compromises with the Sixtieth Congress is to obscure the larger significance of his final years as President. The fact is that on front after front he was moving far out in advance of his party—moving so far and so rapidly that by 1908, a year before Herbert Croly published his *The Promise of American Life,* Roosevelt had skirted all, and occupied most, of the ground he was to deploy his armies over in 1912. Nor is it surprising that the President's ideas continued to develop during these last, frantic years. For if the challenges were not more imposing than they had been at the beginning, they were more sharply delineated; and in great measure because of Roosevelt's own actions and speeches. It was partly the momentum of his own earlier attacks on special privilege that now impelled Roosevelt to set forth piecemeal the positivist-regulationist program that the theoretician Croly would later formalize and expand.

The essence of this program was a broad extension of federal authority by executive action and by act of Congress. And one of the most widely accepted interpretations of it, as I have mentioned before, is that it represented a signal reflection of Roosevelt's lust for personal power. Only a man who believed in power could have countenanced such a concentration of authority as Roosevelt repeatedly urged; only a man unafraid of power could have unloosed the broadsides that Roosevelt again and again rained upon the states'-righters. So the analysis runs.

There is, to repeat, a measure of truth in those assertions. The reader familiar with Blum's perceptive writings on Roosevelt must be impressed by the influence abstract and concrete concerts of power exerted upon the President's policies. Nor can he disregard Blum's suggestion that Roosevelt resented being inhibited by the law; that he, especially, "may have benefited from the limits on Presidential power which men who understood the problem in 1787 created." The Brownsville affair and numerous other incidents attest weightily to that. So does one of Roosevelt's candid revelations. "I don't think that any harm comes from the concentration of power in one man's hands," he wrote as his tenure neared its end, "provided the holder does not keep it for more than a certain, definite time, and then returns to the people from whom he sprang."

Nevertheless, an even larger truth emerges: A great exertion of federal authority was the only feasible means of meeting the challenge of the times. That challenge was dramatized by the overweening arrogance of the Morgans, the Harrimans, the meat packers, and their like. But its primal force was the impersonal corporate power of the burgeoning industrial age and that shattering revolution in communications which made California closer to New York in Roosevelt's day than Virginia had been to Georgia when the Constitution was framed. To ignore this, to attribute the growth of centralized power under Roosevelt to his apparent compulsion for power, is to do enormous violence to history and to the President himself. For if Roosevelt's glands decreed that he must forever act, his high sense of justice and his empirical approach to problems determined the direction of his acts.

Theodore Roosevelt had never been alone in urging the positivist-regulationist state upon a reluctant Congress. By comparison to the negative-minded Cleveland and the judicial-minded Parker he may have been a Caesar. But by comparison to the affirmative-minded Bryan he was a comrade in arms. For all that mental fuzziness which prevented him from seeing the problem in detail, the Great Commoner also understood that the upheavals wrought by the machine civilization made national action mandatory; and on numerous particular issues he heartily cheered Roosevelt on. And so, even, with William Howard Taft. Notwithstanding that conservative gentleman's distaste for personal power, the rise of the regulationist state was to continue throughout the four years of his presidency.

Curiously, the high-minded and rational motivation of Roosevelt's conservation policies has rarely been challenged, even by the President's most psychoanalytically oriented critics, though they embodied the broadest of all his extensions of federal authority. It is perhaps fruitful, therefore, to re-examine his evolving corporation and labor policies, and especially his attitude toward the judiciary.

The President's move against the Northern Securities Company in 1902 had been followed by a spate of antitrust proceedings—forty-three all told. The burden of these had been instituted hard on the election of 1904 and they had served in part to justify Roosevelt's faith in himself, to prove that he was a free moral agent in spite of the hostage the corporation's tremendous contributions to his campaign had purportedly represented. They had failed, however, to resolve the trust problem. Antisocial practices continued in the face of the dissolution orders, and the vast majority of corporations were in no wise affected anyway.

The President was accordingly beset by misgivings even as he encouraged a succession of attorney generals to prosecute the most flagrant violators of the antitrust laws. At the risk of repetition, it should be remarked again that the constructive in him had always rebelled against the muckraking mentality's total indictment of big business. Roosevelt rarely, if ever, attacked from a purely anticorporation bias. To assert the supremacy of the federal government; to court (unconsciously perhaps) the favor of the "plain people"; to suppress the most flagrant cases of "wrongdoing"; or to strike down the most patent monopolies—these, and the need to force Congress to support his program, as with the Hepburn bill, were seemingly his motives. But now, slowly yet ineluctably, that regulationist philosophy which had all along dominated his policy toward the railroads came in his mind to reign over most other areas as well. Without abandoning trust-busting completely, for he continued to believe that some trusts warranted dissolution, Roosevelt gave regulation greater and greater emphasis.

By March, 1907, seven months before he tacitly agreed to the

merger of the United States Steel Corporation and the Tennessee Coal
and Iron Company, the President was writing the Interstate Commerce
Commission that he did "not believe in the sweeping and indiscriminate prohibition of all combination which has been so marked
and as I think so mischievous a feature of our anti-trust legislation."
Could not the Commission explore further the possibility of authorizing combinations by consent?" he inquired. And in December of
that year he realistically asserted that "This is an age of combinations." Then, with greater emphasis than ever before, he urged Congress in December, 1907, to get behind a bold and comprehensive
regulatory program, one that would place all interstate business under
federal supervision. "This is not advocating centralization," he declared stridently. "It is merely looking facts in the face and realizing
that centralization in business has already come and cannot be avoided
or undone, and that the public at large can only protect itself from
certain evil effects of this business centralization by providing better
methods for the exercise of control. . . ."

The pure-food law was opposed so violently that its passage was
delayed for a decade; yet it has worked unmixed and immediate
good. The meat-inspection law was even more violently assailed;
and the same men who now denounce the attitude of the National
Government in seeking to oversee and control the workings of
interstate common carriers and business concerns, then asserted
that we were "discrediting and ruining a great American industry."

The President's assertions drew strong support from a small coterie
of sophisticated Wall Street men, among them George W. Perkins,
who was already moving along the road that would carry him to
Armageddon with Roosevelt in 1912. That very winter, in fact, the
House of Morgan supported proposals that would have regularized
the procedures embodied in the earlier "gentlemen's agreements" with
Judge Gary by authorizing the Bureau of Corporations to pass on
business projects in advance. By then, however, the great majority
of corporate leaders outside the Morgan-Gary-Perkins axis were so
exercised by Roosevelt's penetrating criticisms of businessmen and by
his increasing receptivity to labor's demands that they were blinded
to their own interests. Nor did small business take kindly to measures
that would have accelerated the inevitable rise of giant corporations
by sanctioning "reasonable" restraints on trade. The result was that
neither the regular session of the Sixtieth Congress nor the short

session a year later gave serious consideration to the proposals. The trouble, the President wrote Henry Lee Higginson in exasperation, was that the corporations preferred that the existing laws be "administered crookedly" rather than be revised in their own and the public interest. "Of course," he added, "as far as I am concerned such expectation is in vain."

The President's charge may have been oversimplified; but it was hardly impetuous and certainly not ill-considered. As his reflections at the time of Holmes' appointment to the Supreme Court suggest, he had long seen the partial truth in Brooks Adams's contention that the law is "the expression of the will of the strongest for the time being" and that as wealth increases "the representatives of the monied class acquire that absolute power once wielded by the Roman proconsul, and now exercised by the modern magistrate." He recoiled, however, from Adams' pessimistic conclusion that a legal system serving poor and rich alike was impossible of realization and probably of conception. Excepting his personal transgressions, which were more largely those of the man of action than of theory, the whole tenor of Roosevelt's approach to the law was one of reconstruction. His goal was a legal system that knew neither class nor favor; he had sought often in the past, and he would seek more often in the future, to attain it.

For years Roosevelt had been angered by the moral anomaly of imposing heavy prison terms on petty criminals while allowing businessmen to violate the statutes (criminal as well as civil) with relative impunity. He had been uncertain, however, as to a course of action. He believed that since the antitrust laws had so long lain dormant it would be unfair to prosecute for offenses which the government had condoned, in effect, by default. And he had consequenty overlooked many businessmen's earlier transgressions. But now, as he stepped his campaign to bring corporations under the law, he concluded that the dictates of justice required that businessmen who flaunted the law be treated with neither more nor less consideration than other criminals. So he repeated in that December message the strictures against juries which fail "to jail a member of the business community" that he had uttered at Provincetown the previous summer. "The two great evils in the execution of our criminal laws today are sentimentality and technicality," he informed the Congress. Both should be remedied; the former by "the gradual growth of a sound public opinion," the latter by strengthening and more clearly defining the law.

Nor did the President then cover his guns. On January 31, 1908, over the protests of his lieutenants, he fired at Congress one of the most bitter and radical special messages on record. Reiterating his standing, if still general, demand for a constructive revision of the Sherman Antitrust Law, Roosevelt charged that "the representatives of predatory wealth—of the wealth accumulated on a giant scale by all forms of iniquity, ranging from the oppression of wage workers to unfair and unwholesome methods of crushing out competition, and to defrauding the public by stock jobbing and the manipulation of securities," were thwarting his program. He excoriated those "apologists of successful dishonesty" who declaim against all measures to strike down corruption "on the grounds that any such effort will 'unsettle business.' " He called again for stringent regulation of securities, adding that there "is no moral difference between gambling at cards . . . and gambling in the stock market" (a sentiment that he often expressed privately as well). He upbraided "decent citizens" for permitting "those rich men whose lives are evil and corrupt" to control the nation's destiny. And he generalized disdainfully about that great body of editors, lawyers, and politicians "purchased" by the corporations as "but puppets who move as the strings are pulled."

The President then vented his towering rage on the judiciary. There has been, he caustically declared, a growing tendency for judges to "abuse" the injunction process in labor cases. The injunction was a necessary device for the prevention of violence and should under no circumstances be eliminated. Nevertheless, he continued, steps should be taken to remedy the "grave and occasionally irreparable wrong" sometimes inflicted upon those enjoined. It was a travesty on justice for the law to acknowledge labor's right to engage in peaceable, organized action on the one hand and for the courts, "under the guise of protecting property rights," to override that right on the other hand.

The blazing indictment continued. The "high office of judge" should be regarded with the "utmost respect," as should those "brave and upright men" who in the main comprised the judiciary, the President wrote. However, he added, the judge who "truckles to the mob" and "shrinks from sternly repressing violence and disorder," or who makes the wage worker bitter "by misuse of the process of injunction or by his attitude toward all measures for the betterment of the conditions of labor," or by failing "to stop the abuses of the criminal rich," could not expect to escape public censure. And this, he concluded, "is but right, for except in extreme cases this is the only way he can be reached at all."

Not in all Roosevelt's seven and one-half years in office was there an emotional outburst comparable to the one that followed that message. In Congress, where the Bryan wing of the Democracy punctuated its reading with round after round of spontaneous applause, the great body of Republicans sat glumly, applauding perfunctorily, and then but infrequently. On the outside, conservative Easterners like Nicholas Murray Butler lost all sense of proportion and the *New York Times* actually wrote editorially that the President's "delusions of persecution . . . would ordinarily be commended to the attention of a psychiatrist."

Across the nation, however, the reaction was favorable. The agents of special privilege who wore the Republican label in Congress had never been broadly representative of the "plain people" who comprised the bulk of the Grand Old Party's membership. And independent Republican editorial voices by the dozens joined their Democratic counterparts in hailing the message of January 31 "as a classic," as one of "the really memorable state papers in the history of the nation," and as "a clarion call to duty." And once again that faithful tribune of the people, William Jennings Bryan, rose to his great rival's support. Roosevelt's message, exclaimed Bryan, was a "brave" and timely "call to arms"; he urged his fellow Democrats "to accept promptly the issues that have been presented by the President."

Fundamentally, the memorable message of January 31 was what the President claimed it was—an exhortation to "national honesty in business and politics." As such it was in the pattern cut out more than a quarter of a century before when he had so courageously defied his party leaders by moving the investigation of Judge Westbrook. There was, however, one significant difference. The Roosevelt of 1882 had seen only the superficial manifestations of corruption; the Roosevelt of 1908 knew something of their root causes. This was exemplified by his sweeping arraignment of both the puppets and the men who actually pulled the strings; by his charge that the courts were partial to the corporations; and by his asseveration that the judiciary's overwhelming commitment to the status quo was perverting justice and thwarting organized labor. As Roosevelt had explained to Justice William R. Day a few weeks before, unless the spirit behind the decisions that had recently overruled New York's bakery and tenement laws was changed, "we should not only have a revolution, but it would be absolutely necessary to have a revolution, because the condition of the worker would become intolerable." What he wanted "from some of you judges, whom I respect more than I do any other public men," the President had added, is "some satisfactory scheme, which would permit of the necessary protest against the few unrighteous, and the less few unwise decisions, without impairment of that respect for the law which must go hand in hand with respect for the courts. . . ." The failure to get that "scheme" would be responsible for Roosevelt's espousal of the recall of judicial decisions in 1912.

Meanwhile the President continued his efforts to meliorate the lot of the working man and woman. He still refused to accept the principle of the closed shop while his fear of labor violence and dislike for "professional labor agitators" remained as great as ever. Less than two months before the message of January 31, in fact, he had ordered federal troops into Nevada to suppress reported violence during a strike in the mine fields. When it became evident, however, that there was little violence and that the pro-corporation governor of the state had designed to use the troops to break the mine workers' union, Roosevelt had peremptorily withdrawn them.

Roosevelt did not even then subscribe to the near total environmentalism that comprises the warp and the woof of so much of twentieth-century liberalism. To the end he believed in the individual's free moral capacity, in his ability to control and rise above his environment. And he was unfailingly disdainful of theoretical socialism. To Lincoln Steffens, whose increasingly critical attacks on Roosevelt reflected his own growing commitment to socialism, the President wrote in June, 1908 that "under government ownership corruption can flourish just as rankly as under private ownership." Privilege must be eliminated; but privilege was not all. "I know from actual experience—from experience of the most intimate kind in the little village of Oyster Bay and out in the West at Medora, where there was not a special privilege of any kind in either place—that what is needed is the *fundamental fight for morality*." Yet, as he wrote another friend, the tenets of many people who call themselves socialists "are not only worthy of respect but represent real advances." Among such "advances," presumably, were major features of Roosevelt's own conservation program.

Even as Roosevelt clung to the vestiges of the "survival of the fittest" theory, even as he continued to believe that much of man's weakness and evil was inherent, he drastically modified his application of those concepts. By 1908 he perceived more clearly than ever before that the environment was of tremendous, if not quite overpowering influence, especially on the weak and the straitened. So in the newer mode of Reform Darwinism and the older tradition of *noblesse oblige* and human compassion, he strove to mitigate the conditions of labor through government action. Warmly and persistently he supported proposals for the eight-hour day and for workmen's compensation measures. "I spoke of the hard case of P. B. Banton, who was crippled for life while doing his duty on the Panama Canal and is now helpless with a wife and three children," he wrote a congressman in February, 1908. "Will it not be possible to have a general bill passed to remedy the injustice . . . ? No more righteous act could be passed by Congress." Or, as he wrote in his message of January 31:

> The special pleaders for business dishonesty, in denouncing the present Administration for enforcing the law against the huge and corrupt corporations which have defied the law, also denounce it for endeavoring to secure sadly needed labor legislation, such as a far-reaching law making employers liable for injuries to their employees. . . . It is hypocritical baseness to speak of a girl who works in a factory where the dangerous machinery is unprotected as having the "right" freely to contract to expose herself to dangers to life and limb. She has no alternative but to suffer want or else to expose herself to such dangers . . . it is a moral wrong that the whole burden of the risk necessarily incidental to the business should be placed with crushing weight upon her weak shoulders. . . . This is what opponents of a just employers' liability law advocate. . . .

Even more significant than Roosevelt's widening acceptance of the deterministic postulates of Reform Darwinism was his strengthening conviction of the need for big unionism He continued to condone the closed shop, but he came more and more to believe that big unionism was as necessary as big business was inevitable; and within the limits imposed by his ultimate faith in individualism, he warmly encouraged the labor movement. The principle of unionism was "beneficial," he repeatedly asserted; it was the "abuses" of power that must be guarded against.

The first President to keep an open door to union officials, Roosevelt conferred many times with Gompers, Mitchell, and other labor leaders during his seven and one-half years in office. And though he never again played such a dramatic role as he had in the Anthracite Strike of 1902, he continued to the end to make a modest contribution to labor's uplifting. For example, in the winter of 1908 when several railroads contemplated wage reductions in order to redeem losses caused by the administration's regulatory program—or so the Louisville and Nashville angrily charged—Roosevelt ordered the Interstate Commerce Commission to investigate. "These reductions in wages may be warranted, or they may not," the President wrote. But in any event, the Commission should be prepared to mediate. It finally did so, arranging a settlement that held the line on wages and creating in the process a precedent for the handling of future controversies in the railroad industry.

Had Roosevelt had his way, the principle of government mediation would have been made broadly inclusive. In his annual message of 1906 and again in that of 1907 he had urged "compulsory investigation of such industrial controversies as are of sufficient magnitude and of sufficient concern to the people of the country as a whole"— clear evidence that in the President's mind labor had come of age. When his attitude is contrasted to that of the National Manufacturers Association, which was then girding its loins for an anti-unionism campaign that persists to this day ("better to fight than be assassinated in the interests of a coalition of politics and labor," the Association's journal warned in May, 1908), the magnitude of Roosevelt's progressivism stands in perspective.

Although organized labor was gratified by the advances in the President's thought, it still refused to take him to its bosom. Roosevelt's deep distrust of union officials as a class remained ill-concealed. And his reluctance to place labor violence in its social context continued. Roosevelt might have agreed with that part of the publisher E. W. Scripps's defense of the bomb-setting McNamara brothers which read: "We, the employers . . . have the jobs to give or withhold; the capital to spend, or not spend, for production, for wages, for ourselves; we have the press to state our case and suppress theirs;

we have the Bar and the Bench, the legislature, the governor, the police and the militia." But he could only have spewed epithets over Scripps's conclusion that "violence and mob force" were labor's sole weapons and that "Workingmen should have the same belligerent rights in labor controversies that nations have in warfare."

A much more direct cause of labor's disenchantment with the President was his failure to force the G.O.P. to write his advanced recommendations into law. As Samuel Gompers, whose own career was the epitome of moderation and gradualism, later charged, Roosevelt "desired to maintain party leadership and that led to compromise with the reactionaries in the Republican party."

There was large truth in that analysis; and the President's devious handling of the injunction issue in the 1908 campaign would underscore it. Nevertheless, Gompers' evaluation begs the central political question of Roosevelt's presidency. Could Roosevelt have broken with the Old Guard and yet fulfilled so many other of his foreign and domestic objectives?

CHAPTER 21

THE CAMPAIGN OF 1908

> I believe in a strong executive; I believe in power; but I
> believe that responsibility should go with power and that it is
> not well that the strong executive should be a perpetual executive.
> —Theodore Roosevelt

The sands were running out, and with them the President's waning
influence over Congress and party. Within five months of the
memorable special message of January 31 Roosevelt's successor would
be nominated, and within ten months he would be elected. For the
four months following Roosevelt would be in name what he already
was in fact—a "lame duck" President. Then, on March 4, 1909, just
a year after the meeting of the governors at the White House, the
middle-aged man who had committed himself to the "governing class"
as a youth would return to the people, though not really to become
one of them.

A difficult matter for normal men, the loss of power was an ex-
cruciating prospect for this man of such extraordinary drive and
talent—one which all his surging emotions rebelled against; one
which his character alone supported, and then only after a supreme
and sustained exertion of strength. Rarely has history witnessed a
more painfully high-minded action than Roosevelt's voluntary re-
linquishment of a power that he had proudly proclaimed was greater
than that of any crowned head in all of Europe. And rarely has
history seen a great man come nearer to true nobility than Theodore
Roosevelt did when he resolutely refused over a period of many

349

months to submit to the enormous pressures that he violate his election-eve promise of 1904 and accept another term.

It was to his fellow historian, Sir George Otto Trevelyan, that the President wrote most revealingly of his abnegation. "It is a very unhealthy thing that any man should be considered necessary to the people as a whole, save in the way of meeting some given crisis," he wrote. "I regard the memories of Washington and Lincoln as priceless heritages for our people, just because they are the memories of strong men, of men who cannot be accused of weakness or timidity . . . who, nevertheless, led careers marked by disinterestedness just as much as by strength. . . ."

> Now, my ambition is that, in however small a way, the work I do shall be along the Washington and Lincoln lines. . . . I may be mistaken, but it is my belief that the bulk of my countrymen, the men whom Abraham Lincoln called "the plain people"—the farmers, mechanics, small tradesmen, hard-working professional people—feel that I am in a peculiar sense their President, that I represent the democracy in somewhat the fashion that Lincoln did, that is, not in any demagogic way but with the sincere effort to stand for a government by the people and for the people. Now the chief service I can render these plain people who believe in me is, not to destroy their ideal of me.

Continuing, Roosevelt related an incident that had greatly moved him. "A few months ago three old back-country farmers turned up in Washington and after a while managed to get in to see me," he said. "They were rugged old fellows, as hairy as Boers and a good deal of the Boer type. They hadn't a black coat among them, and two of them wore no cravats; that is they just had on their working clothes, but all cleaned and brushed. When they finally got to see me they explained that they hadn't anything whatever to ask, but that they believed in me, believed that I stood for what they regarded as the American ideal, and as one rugged old fellow put it, 'We want to shake that honest hand.' "

If Roosevelt's decision to step down was an act of high statesmanship, the manner and choice of his successor was something less. It was marked by poor judgment, was influenced by extraneous considerations of personality, and was accomplished in typical power-political fashion.

The President's real preference for the succession was Elihu Root.

Down through the tumultuous years of the second administration that ablest of Roosevelt's intimates had continued to give the President constructive counsel as well as to explain him to his own Wall Street friends. To the end, however, Root had remained a skeptic. And though he often endorsed Roosevelt's advanced recommendations, including that for an inheritance tax, he was largely unmoved by the humanism that had already pushed Beveridge and would soon drive George W. Perkins in new directions. Never did Root urge Roosevelt on; never did he display that passion for social and economic justice that made the Square Deal an end in itself. After he lost close contact with Roosevelt and entered the United States Senate in 1909, moreover, he lost even the veneer of his ideological sophistication. As his most recent biographer, Richard W. Leopold, concludes, from then until his retirement in 1915, Root was "astonished, puzzled, irritated and eventually overborne" by the progressive ferment that challenged the values of his early manhood.

That Roosevelt could have believed Root capable of carrying on the Square Deal is a measure of the Secretary of State's forceful personality as well as of Roosevelt's credulity. It is also a measure of the President's deep concern with foreign policy, for in that area Root was above all others qualified. Roosevelt was so favorably disposed toward Root, in fact, that he once called him "without question the greatest living statesman" and purportedly remarked that "I would walk on my hands and knees from the White House to the Capitol to see Root made President." But he was shrewd enough to realize that Root's corporate background and conservative associations made him politically unpalatable, and he wisely refrained from making him his heir apparent. "What the people do not understand of . . . [Root]," he ruefully concluded, "is that if he were President they would be his clients."

The best qualified man all around was probably Charles Evans Hughes of New York. A stern, unbending Baptist, Hughes's heavy beard and pale blue eyes masked a will of steel. He had been catapulted to prominence in 1905 on the force of his brilliant special investigation of the corrupt and mismanaged life insurance industry in the Empire State. Backed handsomely by the Roosevelt administration the next year, he had narrowly defeated William Randolph Hearst in a gubernatorial contest that Roosevelt had exuberantly pronounced "a victory for civilization." As governor, Hughes had fused the old

political reformism with the new economic progressivism much in
the manner of Roosevelt himself, and he became in consequence the
presidential choice of many progressive Westerners as well as of
Eastern reformers of the *Evening Post* variety. Unfortunately, however, Hughes's most striking personal characteristic—his fierce independence—proved his Achilles heel.

In the spring of 1907 after Roosevelt removed a minor federa
officeholder in Rochester who was opposed to both Hughes and
himself, the Governor had righteously announced that he had been
neither consulted nor informed. This studied rebuff to the President
had then been blown up into a major declaration of independence by
a feature writer for the *Evening Post,* and Hughes was thus forced
into the camp of the enemy—not of the left or the right, but of the
impracticable, Roosevelt-baiting "goo-goos." The President never
forgot the incident. Hughes is "a thoroly selfish and cold-blooded
creature," he warned Taft more than a year later. "I strove to help
him and he started the entire mugwump press cackling with glee about
the way in which he had repudiated my help and did not care for it,
and relied purely upon the people." The affair had sealed Hughes's
fate, if it had not already been sealed by Roosevelt's affection for
William Howard Taft.

The selection of this distinguished and eminently likable public
servant was not as incongruous as events later suggested. By performance and apparent conviction, Taft was sympathetic to Roosevelt's program. As he wrote with some irritation in 1907, "Mr. Roosevelt's views were mine long before I knew Mr. Roosevelt at all." From
the President's strictures against the abuse of injunctions through his
espousal of the inheritance tax, Taft had conscientiously, if reservedly,
supported him. And he had been on the tariff issue more forthright
than Roosevelt himself. Furthermore, he had proved in the Philippines that he could be moved by enlightened compassion. And if he
believed with the President and others of the inner circle that reform
was necessary to preserve the capitalistic structure, he also believed
with Roosevelt, though not with all the others, that some reforms
were ends in themselves.

Behind Taft's affable countenance, walrus mustache, and three
hundred and more pounds of undulating flesh, however, was a man
of marked limitations. They were not great; and they would not have
disqualified Taft from the presidency in normal times. But the times

were not normal. By the sheer force of his political genius, Roosevelt
had made his party moderately responsive to the challenges that
everywhere confronted it. But not even he had radically changed the
Grand Old Party's basic character. The election of a La Follette, the
conversion of a Beveridge, the surging progressivism of the rank and
file—notwithstanding all that, the party's congressional leadership and
corporate supporters remained militantly conservative and in many
cases reactionary. Never during the Progressive Era, not even at the
height of insurgency in 1910, would more than a quarter of the Republican delegation in either the Senate or the House raise the progressive battle flag. Taft lacked the wherewithal to bear it for the other
three-fourths.

Taft was neither bold nor dynamic; nor in the political sense resourceful. He was extraordinarily lazy, and he was given to petulance
rather than, like Roosevelt, to wrath. His mental processes were painfully conventional, and he displayed little of Roosevelt's synthesizing
intelligence and even less of his urge to create. For all his humanism
and unexpected moral courage, he was then and would always be
thereafter a conservative in all his instincts. No more than Elihu
Root, and others of legalistic frame of mind, could he approve all of
Roosevelt's tactics, even though he thought he believed in his objectives. Had the battle been won, Taft might have been competent to
hold the line. The point is debatable, perhaps. But the lines were
actually advancing and the intermediate objectives changing. The
President's great battle order of January 31, which Taft had professed
to approve, had called for an offensive that Roosevelt himself would
have been hard pressed to push to victory. Was Taft, whose experience had been that of a loyal lieutenant and a top-drawer liaison
officer, the man for the command?

Taft's ambitious wife and his father-like half-brother were confident
that he was; but only because they were enamored of the presidency
itself. They seemed not to understand, or at least to accept, the
formidable obstacles that would confront any Republican successor
to Theodore Roosevelt. Indeed Mrs. Taft, the real instrument of her
husband's tragedy in that she placed her own desire to be First Lady
above his more reasonable aspiration to a post on the Supreme Court,
seems to have been impervious to the tidal wave of reformism that
was then engulfing the country. Recoiling from the President's special
message of January 31, she advised her husband as early as Feb-

ruary, 1908, not to "make any more speeches on the Roosevelt policies."

But there was another Taft who was sure that William Howard was not the man for the command. "Roosevelt is a good fighter and enjoys it, but the malice of politics would make you miserable," Taft's aged mother warned her son shortly before she died. "They do not want you as their leader, but cannot find anyone more available." Nor was Roosevelt absolutely certain. A letter he sent Taft during the heat of the campaign in 1908 is implicitly revealing of his doubts: Be sure to let the people realize "that for all your gentleness and kindliness and generous good nature, there never existed a man who was a better fighter when the need arose," he wishfully advised his beloved friend.

By then Roosevelt had long since made his decision. As early as 1905, in fact, he had decided that the Secretary of War was his most likely successor, and thereafter he had given him every encouragement short of absolute commitment. True, he had appeared to waver in early 1906 when he again offered Taft a seat on the High Bench. There was a compelling need for distinguished men to sit on "the greatest court in Christendom" and pass judgment on the questions "which seem likely vitally and fundamentally to affect the social, industrial and political structure of our commonwealth," Roosevelt had then written. However, he had also explained, he thought that Taft really wanted to become a member of the Court. "What you say in your letter and what your dear wife says [Mrs. Taft had impressed her views on the President in an urgent, half-hour interview arranged at her instigation] alter the case."

Following that fateful exchange, the President's resolve to make Taft his successor deepened, though he did not act decisively until March, 1907. During the interim the generous-minded Secretary of War several times told Root, his wife, and the President himself that Roosevelt should run again. Although Roosevelt gave that suggestion short shrift, he did write William Allen White, who was cool to Taft, that he was "not going to take a hand in his nomination for it is none of my business." Then, in October, 1906, he strained his relations with the aggressive Mrs. Taft, if not with her husband, by warning that if Hughes's popularity continued to soar and Taft remained aloof he might have to back the New Yorker. In March, 1907, however, before Roosevelt's vendetta with Hughes completely soured him, the President virtually made the final commitment by directing that "a peculiar regard" for Taft's "judgment" be shown in all executive appointments in Ohio.

The pre-convention campaign that the President now waged for his "beloved Will" was as ruthless, and probably more so, than the one he had fought against Mark Hanna for his own nomination in 1904. And the justification was less, for Hughes was closer to Roosevelt ideologically than Hanna had been. Once again the President played the patronage game to the hilt; and once again he artfully denied that he had. "I appointed no man *for the purpose* of creating Taft sentiment; but . . . I have appointed men in *recognition* of the Taft sentiment already in existence." But Roosevelt needed even more than that to win, or so he thought. Late in January, in one of those brilliant political maneuvers so characteristic of himself and that later Roosevelt, he stole Hughes's audience in the Governor's very hour of self-revelation.

In spite of Hughes's public indifference and the President's preference for Taft, the movement for Hughes's nomination had continued to burgeon during all of 1907. The Governor was repeatedly urged to declare his intentions, and he finally agreed to state his views on national issues in a widely advertised address to the Republican Club of New York on January 31, 1908. It was expected that the Governor's statement of faith (it turned out to be friendly to Roosevelt and his policies) would be spread broadside over the front pages of the newspapers the morning following. The headlines on February 1, however, heralded a startlingly different event: "Roosevelt's onslaught . . ."; "Big Men Roasted . . ."; "Message Dazes"; "Hottest Message Ever Sent to Congress. . . ."

On the afternoon of January 31, too late for publication in the evening papers, the President had released that most challenging of all his messages to Congress. "If Hughes is going to play the game," he blandly remarked to reporters, "he must learn the tricks."

And so—Roosevelt the king-maker. Years before, in his biography of Benton, he had bitterly criticized Andrew Jackson for acting similarly. But the point merits no belaboring. The selection of Taft, even more than some of the President's other aberrations, was the price the nation paid for Roosevelt's inherent strength and manifest distinction. Furthermore, as Mowry remarks, Roosevelt's popularity was so great that he had either to choose and support a successor or submit to his own renomination.

Mrs. Taft's gnawing suspicions to the contrary, the President's support of her husband was so effective that Taft's nomination was a foregone conclusion months before the Republican Convention opened at Chicago on June 19. Only a stampede for the President could have altered the outcome; and, as Pringle writes, the convention consequently proved a study in irony—"Roosevelt the politician used machine methods to crush Roosevelt the popular hero."

Determined to prevent his own nomination, Roosevelt had commissioned Lodge to stave off any movement for his selection. It was a tough assignment. "If you think it was pleasant to be the one to close the door & do what we both thought right you are in error," Lodge later wrote his friend. "The hardest thing I ever had to do in public life was to use all the great tho' temporary powers of my place at Chicago to shut you out of the White House & put some one else (much as I love & admire that some one else) in."

But Lodge had succeeded admirably—succeeded in the face of a record forty-nine-minute demonstration for Roosevelt that had interrupted his keynote address just before the end. "The President . . . retires by his own determination," this devoted friend who more than any one else except, perhaps, Edith Roosevelt, appreciated the nobility of Roosevelt's self-abnegation, had exclaimed to the delegates after order was restored. "His refusal of renomination . . . is final and irrevocable. Any man who attempts to use his name as a candidate for the presidency impugns both his sincerity and his good faith. . . . That man is no friend to Theodore Roosevelt."

Throughout the campaign that summer and fall the President directed a steady stream of thinly veiled instructions at the uncomfortable Taft, who had won the nomination on the first ballot. Many were exhortatory—"Hit them hard, old man!" he wrote at one point—and many more were shrewdly practical. Roosevelt warned Taft not to affront Speaker Cannon, no matter how insufferable that aging tyrant's support. He suggested that Taft curtail his golf playing, or at least refuse to be photographed "in costume" (he had always been careful about his own tennis, he pointedly explained). And he warned the Secretary of War not to appear on the same platform with the loathsome Foraker, whose unsavory relationship with the Standard Oil Company had recently been aired by Hearst. Roosevelt further urged Taft to be cautious in his recommendations for tariff revision (Taft had embarrassed the President and party by forth-rightly coming out for downward tariff revision in 1906).

It was hard, even so, for the warrior-politician to avoid the smoke of battle. Mastering his swelling frustration, he held to an early decision to make no speeches. He also tried conscientiously to prevent his own booming personality from overpowering Taft's. "I think that the number of times my name is used should be cut down," he wrote the nominee after reading the draft of his formal message of accept-ance. "You are now the leader, and there must be nothing that looks like self-depreciation or undue subordination of yourself." But in the end, Roosevelt reached the front through a series of public letters; and in so doing he again scarred his reputation.

There was much in the Democratic platform of 1908 and Bryan's exegesis of it that warranted attack from Roosevelt's point of view. This was particularly true of the foreign policy planks. Not only did they display little understanding of the realities of world power, they threatened a disruption of Roosevelt's delicately negotiated master-piece, the "Gentlemen's Agreement" with Japan. As the President caustically observed to Taft, the Democrats "desire to insult Japan by excluding all Japanese immigration, and at the same time recom-mend cutting down the navy so it could only be used for coast defense." In addition, the Democratic platform called for an im-mediate declaration in favor of Philippine independence, a proposal Roosevelt regarded as fatefully premature.

The Democratic planks on domestic matters were not above criticism either. The President regarded the statements on the trusts, which promised a limitation on the size of corporations rather than regulation of their activities, as impractical. He had no sympathy for the Democrats' promise of over-all reductions in the tariff, preferring instead his own party's ephemeral promise of a controlled revision that would retain the protectionist principle. And he took specious exception to the Democrats' proposal for a federally guaranteed bank deposit scheme which presaged the Federal Deposit Insurance Cor-poration of the New Deal. Professing to approve it in principle, he urged Taft to attack it on the grounds that the banking structure must be radically changed before it could be implemented. But it was the injunction issue that inspired Roosevelt to show his political colors and suffer his heaviest wound.

True to the faith of his message of January 31, and four previous recommendations to Congress, the President had sent Lodge to the Republican Convention at Chicago under firm instructions to frame an injunction plank with teeth in it. But the Massachusetts Senator had failed, partly because he was unsympathetic, and largely because of the National Association of Manufacturers' decisive authority in Republican councils. The plank, as rewritten by the Association's president, James W. Van Cleave, Aldrich, and other conservative Republican leaders, pledged the party to "uphold at all times the authority and integrity of the courts. . . ." Nor did it propose to limit the use of injunctions. That plank "will legalize what we have been trying to abolish," Samuel Gompers had cried out in anguish at the time. Bitterly, he had then charged that labor had been "thrown down, repudiated and relegated to the discard by the Republican party." The Democrats, meanwhile, had proved as superficially responsive to labor's demands as the Republicans had been substantively responsive to industry's. At Gompers's urging, their convention at St. Louis adopted a sweeping plank that could readily be interpreted as outlawing the use of the injunction in labor disputes.

Roosevelt had seized upon the Democratic plank as extreme, and he was partly honest in so doing. Nothing he ever said or wrote suggests that he favored the outright abolition of injunctions. Always his brief was against their "abuse" by procorporation or antilabor judges. In a characteristically partisan and self-deluding twist, however, he now contended that the Republican plank was truly "moderate" and that the G.O.P. had steered a middle course between the demands of labor and the manufacturers.

The issue had simmered through the summer of 1908. It flamed up on October 13 when the press across the land carried an open letter from Gompers in which he repeated the charge that the Republicans had sold out labor and boldly urged workingmen to vote for Bryan. Roosevelt was furious. A week and a half later he released a long and indignant letter to Senator Philander Knox in which he challenged Bryan, who had been silent on the injunction issue, to indicate whether he agreed with Gompers's broad construction of the Democratic plank. He also criticized Gompers for charging in words that were actually less vehement than his own that the judiciary was subservient to corporate power. And he particularly excoriated Gompers's support of legislation that would have attacked the secondary boycott.

"No court could possibly exercise any more brutal, unfeeling, or despotic power than Mr. Gompers claims for himself and his followers in this legislation," he said. Roosevelt failed, however, to reply effectively to the basic political challenge—to wit, the Republican party was so submissive to the National Association of Manufacturers that not even the President of the United States had been able to have his reasonable views on the injunction problem written into the party's platform. For that letter, for past compromises, and for future blasts, tens of thousands of working men would in 1912 rally behind Eugene V. Debs or Woodrow Wilson.

Meanwhile Gompers had replied in kind. "The mere fact that Mr. Roosevelt denounces a proposition as wicked does not so constitute it," he said in a second public letter. He noted that Roosevelt himself had called the reversal of the $29 million fine Judge Landis had imposed on the Standard Oil Company "a gross miscarriage of justice." He quoted the President's statement of January 31 that "It is futile to concede . . . the right and the necessity of organized effort on the part of wage earners and yet by injunctive process to forbid peaceable action to accomplish the lawful objects for which they are organized. . . ." He twitted Roosevelt for permitting "Genial Uncle Joe" Cannon and other Old Guardsmen to "slap" him in the face by nominating the archconservative James "Sunny Jim" Sherman for Vice-President. And he charged that Roosevelt, after failing to get the Republican platform committee to accept his own liberal platform, "not only swallows the whole pot pourri, but . . . directly and indirectly attack[s] me in the fight which my fellow workers and I are making in defense of equality before the law of the men of labor with all other citizens. . . ." He added an ironic footnote. In January, 1908, Roosevelt himself had called Gompers's attention to a chapter in George A. Alger's *Moral Overstrain* that sharply criticized the courts for guaranteeing the workingman "an academic and theoretic liberty which he does not want" and "denying him industrial rights to which he thinks he is ethically entitled." Then, four days before the memorable Special Message of January 31, Roosevelt had written Gompers that he would "be amused to know" that he had sent copies of Alger's book to the antilabor Supreme Court Justices Day and McKenna.

The injunction controversy was unpleasant, but it had been waged openly both by Roosevelt and by Taft. There was, in fact, a refreshing quality in Taft's frank defense of his issuance of injunction orders while a Federal judge in Cincinnati almost a decade before. But there was another issue in the campaign of 1908 on which a frank defense seemed politically inexpedient—religion. A Unitarian of considered conviction, William Howard Taft did not believe in the divinity of Jesus Christ. He stood in distinguished company—with Benjamin Franklin, Thomas Jefferson, John Adams, and John Quincy Adams probably; with Abraham Lincoln and Theodore Roosevelt possibly; and with numbers of other eminent Americans whose services to their country had been not less noteworthy for their failure to conform to the reigning theology. But Taft in 1908 was running against William Jennings Bryan. The consequence was a painful experience for Taft and a frustrating one for Roosevelt.

All during the summer of 1908 the President fumed privately at the undercover campaign. Bryan was playing "strong in Chautauqua circles and elsewhere for the church vote," he irritably wrote Taft. Meanwhile others raised the issue—"the bigoted, narrow-minded, honest, evangelical . . . Methodists, Lutherans, Baptists, and some Presbyterians," as Roosevelt, who received hundreds of letters protesting Taft's unbelief, referred to them. "Think of the United States with a *President* who does not believe that Jesus Christ was the Son of God," wrote the editor of one religious journal, "but looks upon our immaculate Savior as a common bastard and low, cunning impostor!" From Chautauqua came the report that the Methodist ministers attending an Epworth League Convention had "gone wild" for Bryan. "They assert that no good Methodist can vote for a man who openly declares he does not believe in the divinity of Christ," the secretary of the Assembly said. On the other hand, the *Literary Digest* reported that the majority of religious publications viewed Taft's religion with equanimity, while at least one Catholic paper argued that the issue was irrelevant since the "dominant Protestantism of the day is unconfest [*sic*] Unitarianism."

To compound Taft's troubles, many Protestants also argued that the Republican candidate had been pro-Catholic in his conduct of affairs in the Philippines. The charge was patently unfair. Although the Vatican had driven a hard bargain when it finally consented to sell the friars' lands, militant Catholics had bitterly disapproved the secular emphasis of the public school system established on the Islands during Taft's commissionership.

Confused, surprised, and hurt, Taft proposed to issue a public statement. But under advice from Root and Roosevelt, he decided against it. Meanwhile, the President kept silent with difficulty. He continued to inveigh against bigotry in his private letters, alluding repeatedly to Lincoln's unorthodox religious beliefs. And he once attended Unitarian services with Taft in the hope, as he phrased it, "that it would attract the attention of sincere but rather ignorant Protestants who support me." But in deference to Taft's interests he waited until the campaign was over before speaking out. Then, in a letter that reflected that Jeffersonian strain which was often submerged but never drowned, he poured forth his convictions in a public letter to a correspondent from Ohio: "You ask that Mr. Taft shall 'let the world know what his religious belief is.'"

This is purely his own private concern; it is a matter between him and his Maker, a matter for his own conscience; and to require it to be made public under penalty of political discrimination is to negative the first principle of our Government, which guarantees complete religious liberty, and the right to each man to act in religious affairs as his own conscience dictates. . . .

Discrimination against the holder of one faith means retaliatory discrimination against men of other faiths. The inevitable result of entering upon such a practice would be an abandonment of our real freedom of conscience and a reversion to the dreadful conditions of religious dissension which in so many lands have proved fatal to true liberty, to true religion, and to all advance in civilization.

Except for his seething resentment over the intrusion of the religious issue, the President was jubilant in Taft's hour of victory. "We have them beaten to a frazzle," he had exclaimed again and again the night of the election as the returns were brought into him at Sagamore Hill. And on November 10 he wrote the President-elect a warm, congratulatory letter declaring that with the possible exception of Hughes, Taft was the only man who could have been elected. "You have won a great personal victory as well as a great victory for the party," he said, "and all those who love you, who admire and believe in you and are proud of your great and fine qualities, must feel a thrill of exaltation over the way in which the American people have shown their insight into character, their adherence to high principle."

Roosevelt was partially right. It was "a great personal victory"; but as much for himself as for Taft—the President-elect's margin was only half of Roosevelt's record plurality in 1904. Taft had, however, run far ahead of his party. Four states—Ohio, Indiana, Minnesota, and North Dakota—elected Democratic governors while returning majorities for Taft. And in New York, where Hughes was re-elected, Taft ran considerably ahead of the Governor and the ticket as a whole. Nor was the Republican majority in the congressional elections especially large, a number of reactionaries having failed to be returned. The import was clear: Neither Roosevelt nor Taft had succeeded in convincing the country that the Grand Old Party had a monopoly on reform and progress.

The President-elect's reaction to his triumph was not less ominous. He was not jubilant. At three o'clock the morning after the election Taft wearily told a crowd outside his half-brother's house in Cincinnati that he hoped his administration would prove "a worthy successor of that of Theodore Roosevelt." He then went to bed.

A few weeks later he confided his sense of inadequacy to a friend. "If I were now presiding in the Supreme Court of the United States as chief justice, I should feel entirely at home," wrote the man whose mother had warned him he was not qualified for the presidency, "but with the troubles of selecting a Cabinet, and the difficulties in respect to the revision of the tariff, I feel just a bit like a fish out of water." He concluded by saying that "my wife is the politician and she will be able to meet all these issues." It was not to be.

CHAPTER 22

THE CHANGING OF THE GUARD

> I have had the best time of any man of my age in all the world. . . . I have enjoyed myself in the White House more than I have ever known any other President to enjoy himself, and . . . I am going to enjoy myself thoroly when I leave the White House.
>
> —Theodore Roosevelt

The most striking aspect of the postelection interim was that attention continued to center on Roosevelt. Between the election in November and the inauguration in March there was no abatement of the controversy that had enveloped him from 1902 on; nor was there any relaxation of the President's determination to spread on the record his blueprint for a future America. Until the end of the regime Roosevelt was a raging lion—spurred by prods at his rear, wounded by attacks on his flanks, angered by barriers at his front—but roaring all the while.

The roar was as lordly as it was angry. The hunting in other seasons had been good; and the Congress that convened in December, 1908, to bid all speed to this powerful personality who had revitalized the powers of this office and made it responsive as never before to the needs of the industrial age, knew it. The legislative and administrative achievements of the past seven years—the Hepburn Act, the Pure Food and Drug Act, the Meat Inspection Amendment, the Employer's Liability Act, the antitrust measures, the conservation program, the work on the Panama Canal, the expansion of the fleet, the Roosevelt Corollary to the Monroe Doctrine, and the intervention in European and Far Eastern affairs—could not be written off. The pressures that Roosevelt had generated for even greater reforms could not be dismissed.

The President's final annual message on December 8 proved to be more a call to action than a valediction. Roosevelt, the Washington *Post* observed, "looks forward and not back." There were, assuredly, the prideful cadences of most of the other messages. And there were few new ideas. The recommendations for judicial reform, labor legislation, conservation, and naval expansion had all been made before, though not always as specifically. Nevertheless, that message was a compelling statement of the President's still advancing progressivism, one that boldly laid down proposals of action on every important issue then current except the tariff, and one that categorically declared that the workingman should be guaranteed "a larger share of the wealth" he produced. It provoked the New York *Commercial and Financial Chronicle* to complain that if a fraction of Roosevelt's recommendations could be put into statute "they would commit the country to a course of new experiments and make over the face of social creation." And it inspired in the New York *Sun* a ray of hope— hope that within a few weeks "the seven-year flood of words" would at last dry up!

But the most suggestive comments on the President's urgent call for social and economic justice through centralization were made by independent Democratic newspapers. Roosevelt had asserted that the telegraph and telephone companies should be placed under the jurisdiction of the Interstate Commerce Commission. And he had again charged that corporate wealth was using the "appeal to the old doctrine of States' rights" as a "cover" in its fight against "adequate control and supervision. . . ." The charge was neither new nor inaccurate. Roosevelt had leveled it many times before, often, as in the case of the meat packers, with fateful precision. But the significant point, as the *Literary Digest* reported, was that "a number of Southern and other Democratic papers are willing to give it a tolerant, and even a sympathetic hearing, while some of the most strenuous protests come from Republican sources."

That historic reversal in philosophy which has been the signal feature of twentieth-century party politics was thus in the process of delineation. Repulsed by Roosevelt's neo-Jeffersonian ends, the Republicans were openly abandoning their commitment to Hamiltonian means in order to thwart the fulfillment of those ends; attracted by those same ends, the Democrats were abandoning their belief in Jeffersonian means that they might be realized. The trend was by no means universal. The Republicans would waver until 1912, and on some issues, long after; and the Democrats would not even be certain where they stood under Woodrow Wilson. By the middle of the century, however, the reversal would be relatively complete: The overwhelming majority of Democrats in Congress, except for the Southern states'-rightists, would be wedded to the centralized welfare state; the great majority of Republicans would be in varying degrees opposed or unsympathetic to it. Theodore Roosevelt, grown increasingly sensitive of, and frustrated by, the tenets of his own party during his last two years in office, served mightily to hasten this momentous development. Indeed, his messages, speeches, and public letters had established him as a kind of advance agent for reform. The Detroit *News* said that "Measured by his own standard, his work will be seen to be one of awakening rather than accomplishment." The New York *Tribune* said the great service of his administration "has been in calling public attention to social problems and bringing them into politics."

There was truth in those appraisals. The history of twentieth-century reform that fails to account Roosevelt's moral and political influence upon his own times and, through then young men like Franklin Delano Roosevelt, Harold Ickes, Felix Frankfurter, Henry L. Stimson, Learned Hand, and countless others upon later times, falls woefully short. But the argument is not all inclusive. For if Roosevelt failed either to convert his party to his own regulatory philosophy or to effect such an orthodox reform as revision of the tariff, his legislative and administrative accomplishments had been nonetheless concrete.

Unfortunately, the President had distorted the larger sense of his last annual message by an acrimonious attack upon Congress itself. During the previous session an amendment had been adopted limiting the activities of the Secret Service to the protection of the President and the investigation of counterfeiting. In part because he felt the Secret Service was needed to combat anarchists, and mainly because he wanted it to investigate corporation executives who had violated the law, Roosevelt had vehemently opposed the amendment. The House, however, had insisted on passing it. Some members of that body were still riled over the President's earlier prosecutions of congressmen for postal, land, and timber frauds. Others were presumably reluctant to expedite the indictment of businessmen whose interests they had so long served. And still others opposed the expansion of the Secret Service on high civil libertarian grounds.

Unable longer to hold back what he believed was the truth, the President had baldly charged in his annual message of December, 1908, that the chief argument for the amendment had been "that the congressmen did not themselves wish to be investigated." Congress was outraged. Never during Roosevelt's seven and more years in office did his relations with the legislature sink to a lower level than they did under the weight of that accusation. Unanimously, an outraged House approved the formation of a committee to investigate. Angrily, Senator Aldrich drafted a resolution of inquiry that even Cabot Lodge supported.

In the White House, meanwhile, the President fumed. On January 4 he replied to the House with a special message that modified his charge against Congress, but repeated the assertion that weakening the Secret Service was a boon to "the criminal class." The members of the House were not edified; in an action that goes back to Jackson for a precedent, they voted by a majority of 211 to 36 to lay on the table that portion of the annual message which referred to the Secret Service and the whole of the special message of January 4. They further resolved that the message be viewed as an invasion of the privileges of the House. Not even that ponderous rebuke chastened the President, however, and for weeks, so Ambassador Bryce reported to Whitehall, people hardly ventured to mention Roosevelt's name at many dinner tables.

To make matters worse, the President was by then embarked upon a course more misguided even than his conduct in the Brownsville affair. Infuriated by charges in the Indianapolis *News* and the New York *World* that the $40 million paid the New Panama Canal Company had gone to interested American businessmen, including his brother-in-law, Douglas Robinson, Roosevelt decided to have the government institute libel proceedings. His decision was made after consultation with high government attorneys, and his provocation was understandable, the *World* having finally charged him with deliberate misstatement of fact. Grand juries in Indianapolis and New York actually returned indictments against the publishers of both newspapers, while Bryce wrote Sir Edward Grey that "The moral effect of convictions in cases of this kind would be excellent." In the end, however, federal district judges dismissed the cases. And well, probably, that they did. For as the editors of Roosevelt's *Letters* suggest, a government victory "would . . . in the opinion of many men at the time and since, have placed the freedom of the press in jeopardy."

Until the end of the reign the charges and countercharges continued. Repeatedly, Roosevelt lost his powers of discretion; but only rarely his sense of humor. "Taft told me with a chuckle," he wrote his son Kermit the second week in January, ". . . that one of his friends in New York has said to him that he supposed that between the election and his inauguration there would be a period of stagnation in Washington. I have felt like wiring him," he continued, "that the period of stagnation continues to rage with uninterrupted violence." Congress, however, lost both its discretion and its humor. Critical of the man, resentful of his conception of his office, and largely unsympathetic to his broad social purposes, it struck wildly, even irresponsibly at the President.

In early January Congress approved the bill authorizing a private power project in Missouri under conditions that mocked Roosevelt's plan for a carefully controlled development of such sites. The result was the irate veto message discussed in Chapter 19. On January 12 the Senate agreed to a resolution directing the Secretary of the Treasury to give a comprehensive report of all disbursements under the President's emergency fund. (No irregularities were found.) Shortly later a bill designed to create 4,000 positions in the Census Bureau, all without competitive examination, was passed. Refusing to submit, Roosevelt sent in another angry veto message. Then, when the President transmitted to Congress on February 8 the Report of the Country Life Commission, a document of surpassing excellence which reflected Roosevelt's concern for the conservation of human no less than of natural resources, the House refused to appropriate funds to publish it.

Those were not the only examples of Congress' consuming desire to insult, to defy, and to expose the President in those last turbulent months. The supreme act of spite was the passing of the amendment to the Sundry Appropriation Bill discussed in Chapter 19, which forbade the President's appointing commissions of inquiry without specific authority from Congress. If evidence is lacking that Congress understood the great accretion of power and expansion of executive authority which had occurred during the Roosevelt years, that action should fill the void. Yet even it failed to beard the mighty lion. "I replied to Congress," Roosevelt wrote in his *Autobiography,* "that if I did not believe the Amendment to be unconstitutional, I would veto the Sundry Civil Bill which contained it, and that if I remained in office I would refuse to obey it."

Even in the midst of the raging storm there were moments of triumph and actions of real consequence. The most memorable came on February 22, 1909, when the Great White Fleet steamed into Hampton Roads, its voyage around the world completed. From the deck of the presidential yacht *Mayflower* Roosevelt reviewed it, serene in the knowledge that Congress had again appropriated funds for two new battleships, and probably mistakenly confident that the fleet's grand tour had exerted a profoundly salutary impact upon world politics. "Not until some American fleet returns victorious from a great sea battle will there be another such homecoming, and such a sight," the President proudly exclaimed.

On October 27, 1908, Theodore Roosevelt had turned fifty years of age. He was unsettled about his future plans; but he was nonetheless sure that he should do something useful "to help onward certain movements for the betterment of the people." As he wrote Ted, who had gratified him by entering business in Hartford after graduation from Harvard "instead of leading a perfectly silly and vacuous life around the clubs or in sporting fields," he was also determined to enjoy himself. "Every now and then solemn jacks come to me to tell me that our country must face the problem of 'what it will do with its ex-Presidents,' " he confided to his oldest son.

> I always answer them that there will be one ex-President about whom they need not give themselves the slightest concern, for he will do for himself without any outside assistance; and I add that they need waste no sympathy on me—that I have had the best time of any man of my age in all the world, that I have enjoyed myself in the White House more than I have ever known any other President to enjoy himself, and that I am going to enjoy myself thoroly when I leave the White House, and what is more, continue just as long as I possibly can to do some kind of work that will count.

Nor did he fail in those goals during the decade of life that remained.

Actually, Roosevelt had already laid his immediate plans. He would first go into the dark depths of Africa, there to hunt big game and collect data and specimens for the Smithsonian Museum ("I feel that this is my last chance for something in the nature of a 'great adventure,'" he explained to St. Loe Strachey). He would then go to Oxford on the invitation of its chancellor to deliver the Romanes Lectures (these, he wrote Lodge with mixed pride and awe, had been given by Gladstone, Huxley, Morley, and Bryce among others). The engagement would also give substantial purpose to his European visit, for he said, he was anxious to avoid a "kind of mock triumphal procession." Upon his return to the United States in the late spring of 1910, he would become a contributing editor to Lyman Abbott's *Outlook* at a salary of $12,000 per year (he had rejected vastly more remunerative offers on the grounds that the *Outlook* connection was the more appropriate for a former President).

Roosevelt's decision to become a popular editorial writer was not ideal. But he had too much contempt for the money-making process, too much suspicion of businessmen and their values, to have accepted a position in industry. There was, moreover, that irresistible compulsion to express himself, to continue to influence the flow of events. "I feel that I can still for some years command a certain amount of attention from the American public," he explained, "and . . . I want to use it so far as possible to help onward certain movements for the betterment of our people." Short of a return to politics there was only one other possibility—a college presidency. There had been speculation in 1906 that Roosevelt would succeed Charles Eliot at Harvard. But the offer was never made. Henry Lee Higginson probably expressed the common doubt when he questioned whether Roosevelt would be happy in such a cloistered atmosphere. He also wondered if the necessary "judgment is to be found coupled with such enormous energy?" A greater man than Higginson, however, thought that it might be. Roosevelt, said the philosopher William James, was qualified in many ways.

While the President was formulating his plans and his enemies were figuratively wishing luck to the lions ("Only Four Weeks More of Roosevelt," an editorial in the *Sun* proclaimed on February 4), a quieter and largely unspoken drama was playing out at 1600 Pennsylvania Avenue. It revealed Roosevelt's personality in yet another dimension.

It will be recalled that the President had been unable to refrain from counseling Taft during the campaign of 1908, or, in the end, from openly participating himself. Taft had welcomed, or at least accepted graciously, his benefactor's activities; and during the campaign he had made little effort to disengage himself from the Roosevelt record or from the President's personal influence. Indeed, he had broadly endorsed the Roosevelt policies. After the election, Roosevelt had continued his role as chief of staff for a week or two, long enough to advise the President-elect against a move to prevent Cannon's re-election as Speaker on the grounds that the effort would probably prove abortive. And even if it should prove successful, he had added, "I do not believe it would be well to have him in the position of the sullen and hostile floor leader bound to bring your administration to grief." This was sound advice; but it was also frighteningly ominous advice. Sooner even than Roosevelt feared, Taft would be caught in a web from which there would be no escape. He would be forced to take open sides with either the insurgent or Old Guard wings of his party.

The decision to accept Cannon having been made, Roosevelt had rather abruptly abandoned the role of adviser. His wisdom and sense of propriety told him that Taft must be his own master; and with an exertion of self-discipline that was the more remarkable for his earlier dominance over his easygoing friend, Roosevelt gave the President-elect his rein. Difficult moments followed, especially when it became apparent that Taft was unsympathetic to the Roosevelt-Pinchot conservation policies and that he planned to drop several members of the Cabinet (he had never really promised to keep them on, though at one point he had implied that he would). But as Henry Pringle, who sometimes captures Roosevelt in fuller perspective in his sober life of Taft than in his lively biography of Roosevelt, concludes, the President "loyally suppressed, save on one or two occasions, any temptation to give expression to the first seeds of doubt regarding the man he had pushed into glory." Roosevelt told Archie Butt, his military aide, that "Taft is going about this thing just as I would do, and while I retained McKinley's Cabinet the conditions were quite different. I cannot find any fault in Taft's attitude to me."

Indeed the President did not request his successor to appoint his friends to office outside the Cabinet except in a very few cases. He arranged indirectly for his private secretary, William Loeb, to become

Collector of the Port of New York. And on December 10 he sent Taft a memorandum listing the names of eleven men and a woman who, he wrote, had "been staunch adherents of Mr. Taft under stress of adverse assault in positions not of the first rank." He asked for nothing; but the implication was clear. Taft caught it. He eventually took care of most of the people on the list, which included a few former Rough Riders, though he dropped Deputy Commissioner of Immigration Joe Murray, who had given Roosevelt his start in politics in 1881, and one other. Only for his old hunting guide and companion, Bill Sewall, did Roosevelt make a direct plea; and on December 18 he was able to write "Friend William" that Taft had agreed to keep him on as Collector of Customs for the Eastern District of Maine. After thanking Sewall and his wife for their gift of a pair of heavy woolen socks, he warned Sewall to show his letter of recommendation to no one except Taft. Otherwise, he explained, "I should be deluged with requests for letters."

There were additional touches of loyalty, affection, and appreciation as the time for the changing of the guard drew near. To Gifford Pinchot, Roosevelt implied that he was distressed that Taft was not reappointing the able and progressive James Garfield Secretary of the Interior. "There had been a peculiar intimacy between you and Jim and me, because all three of us have worked for the same causes, have dreamed the same dreams, have felt a substantial identity of purpose," the President wrote. "Jim has made a sacrifice in entering public life that you and I have not made. . . . I think that he has been the best Secretary we have ever had in the Interior Department." Now, Roosevelt concluded, Garfield's "law practise has gone to the winds."

But it was on his relations with Pinchot himself, in a letter that cast a long shadow over the future, that the retiring President poured out his heart. "As long as I live I shall feel for you a mixture of respect and admiration and of affectionate regard," he wrote the eminent forester two days before he left office. "I am a better man for having known you . . . *and I cannot think of a man in the country whose loss would be a more real misfortune to the Nation than yours would be.* For seven and a half years," he continued, "we have worked together, and now and then played together—and have been altogether better able to work because we have played; and I owe to you a peculiar debt of obligation for a very large part of the achievement of this administration."

The President wrote one other important letter in those final days. Conscious, perhaps, of the partial failure of his Far Eastern policy, fearful with reason of Germany's growing lust for naval power, and faithful as always to the views of Mahan, he addressed himself to the President-elect the day before the inauguration. "Dear Will," he said, "one closing legacy. Under no circumstances divide the battle fleet."

There remained only the personal farewells and the inaugural ceremony itself. On March 1 the President gave a dinner to his "Tennis Cabinet" and out-of-town associates. He seated Ambassador Jean Jules Jusserand on his right, Captain Seth Bullock, United States Marshal of Oklahoma at his left, and twenty-nine other guests, including Bill Sewall, a professional wolf hunter named Jack Abernathy, and Elihu Root at the rest of the table ("there will never be such a smashing precedence again as to rank," wrote Archie Butt).

At the end of the luncheon the guests gave the President a bronze cougar by Proctor, Henry L. Stimson making the presentation when Seth Bullock choked with emotion. Later that afternoon the President went to the home of the Garfields, where eleven more or less regular members of the "Tennis Cabinet" presented him with a silver bowl as Jusserand, who was to have presided, broke down. The next afternoon at a reception for the diplomatic corps in the East Room of the White House many in the line, including the Japanese Ambassador's wife, Baroness Takahara, wept openly. Meanwhile, the President himself lost his composure when he found his wife and their daughter Ethel crying over a diamond necklace that a group of Washington society women had presented the First Lady. "He has the humour to carry these little scenes off well," Butt wrote, "and says he feels heartily ashamed of such apparent weakness." However, Butt reflected, "the love which does manifest itself on all sides, coming just now after the bitter attacks from the political world, has gone to their hearts."

There was one final civility. With characteristic generosity, Roosevelt had invited the Tafts to spend the night of March 3 at the White House. In a letter signed "With love and affection, my dear Theodore," Taft accepted with warm protestations of their continuing friendship. Their ladies also tried to be friendly; but Mrs. Taft lacked the grace. Even before she moved into the White House she had made arrangements for many of the Roosevelts' favorite servants to be replaced the instant the change in mistresses became official. Both the President and his wife were hurt, but they did not show it. Taft later described the dinner that night as a "funeral"; and the Tafts did not invite the Wilsons in 1913 though Taft made several other generous gestures to his successor. Archie Butt reported that the dinner went better than expected, however, the President "talking as naturally and entertainingly as he does usually at his luncheons" and the salad course being reached before it was realized. When it was time to retire, Mrs. Roosevelt gently took Mrs. Taft's hand and expressed the hope that her sleep would be sweet. "Thoughtful and gentle to the last," wrote Butt, ". . . she has stood, the embodiment of womanly dignity and social culture, before the entire nation, never unbending in the matter of official etiquette, yet always the gentle, high-bred hostess; smiling often at what went on about her, yet never critical of the ignorant and tolerant always of the little insincerities of political life."

The inaugural ceremony the next day was ruled by the pomp and circumstance of tradition though it was held indoors because of a blustery storm that Cabot Lodge, with more prescience than he knew, pronounced a "calamity." Solemnly President Taft promised in his undistinguished inaugural address to maintain and enforce his predecessor's reforms; and enthusiastically former President Roosevelt rushed forward to congratulate him. "God bless you, old man," he exclaimed. "It is a great state document." Then, by an arrangement suggested by Roosevelt and warmly endorsed by Mrs. Taft, the parties divided. Instead of riding down Pennsylvania Avenue with the new President, Roosevelt was escorted by the New York delegation to the railroad station where he and his wife were given a rousing sendoff. Meanwhile Mrs. Taft took the former President's place at her husband's side to the disgust of the members of the Congressional committee. The seven and one-half years of Theodore Roosevelt's presidency thus ended; the era of Theodore Roosevelt was yet to reach a climax.

THE HIGH TIDE OF PROGRESSIVISM

CHAPTER 23

THE NEW NATIONALISM

The whole tendency of [Roosevelt's] programme is to give a democratic meaning and purpose to the Hamiltonian tradition and method. He proposes to use the power and resources of the Federal government for the purpose of making his country-men a more complete democracy in organization and practise. . . .
—Herbert Croly, *The Promise of American Life*

Within three weeks of Taft's inauguration Theodore Roosevelt, his twenty-year-old son Kermit, and a party of professional naturalists had embarked for Africa from the grimy port city of Hoboken, New Jersey. The new President had not seen the former President off. But he had sent gifts—a gold ruler and an autographed photograph of himself—and a pathetically revealing letter. "When I am addressed as 'Mr. President,' " Taft wrote, "I turn to see whether you are not at my elbow." He predicted that Roosevelt would find him under suspicion by their Western friends when he returned. He guilelessly remarked that Cannon and Aldrich had promised to stand by the platform and follow his lead, and he confessed that he lacked Roosevelt's facility for educating the public and arousing popular support. "I can never forget that the power that I now exercise was a voluntary transfer from you to me," he concluded, "and that I am under obligation to you to see that your judgment . . . shall be vindicated. . . ."

Edith Roosevelt had also remained at home. She had not wanted Theodore to go; but as in 1898 she had known that he must. His mother "was perfectly calm and self-possessed," Kermit confided to Archie Butt aboard ship that morning; however, he added, "her heart was almost broken."

Others had also been moved. "In all the striking incidents of your career," wrote Cabot Lodge the following week, "I never saw one which impressed me more. It was not merely the crowd but the feeling which was manifested which was so striking. I can see you now, as the ship moved slowly down the river, waving your hand to us from the bridge, . . . The newspapers have been filled daily with minute accounts of your progress. . . . The American people . . . follow it all with the absorbed interest of a boy who reads 'Robinson Crusoe' for the first time."

The field part of the expedition proved a spectacular success. "Bwana Makuba" (Great Master), as the Africans called the Colonel, took seriously the Smithsonian Institution's sponsorship—repeatedly he had protested that he was "going primarily as a naturalist"—and he was able to ship to the National Museum a collection of flora, fauna, and mammals that raised that institution's East African collection to among the world's greatest. He impressed his companions with the breadth of his knowledge. "[Roosevelt] . . . had at his command the entire published literature concerning the game mammals and birds of the world, a feat of memory that few naturalists possess," Edmund Heller, with whom he later collaborated on a two-volume scientific work, reported. "I constantly felt while with him that I was in the presence of the foremost field naturalist of our time, as indeed I was. . . ." During the long nights in camp, the Colonel wrote the Lodges, he even came into his "inheritance in Shakespeare" whose works were among the sixty classics in the "pigskin library" he carried with him. Roosevelt's mood was poetically re-created in the foreword to his *African Game Trails*:

> "I speak of Africa and golden joys"; the joy of wandering through lonely lands; the joy of hunting the mighty and terrible lords of the wilderness, the cunning, the wary, and the grim. . . .
> But there are no words that can tell the hidden spirit of the wilderness, that can reveal its mystery, its melancholy, and its charm . . . the strong attraction of the silent places, of the large tropic moons, and the splendor of the new stars; where the wanderer sees the awful glory of sunrise and sunset in the wide waste spaces of the earth, unworn of man, and changed only by the slow change of the ages through time everlasting.

The ten-months' adventure had been free of conflict except for Roosevelt's bouts with the wild beasts of the jungle. Almost the instant the Colonel emerged at Khartoum in mid-March, however, the old order returned. In speeches that he himself reported "caused an outburst of anger and criticism among the Egyptian Nationalists, the anti-English and fanatically Moslem party," he applauded British rule in the Sudan as "really the rule of civilization" and declared that it was "incumbent on every decent citizen of the Sudan to uphold the present order of things."

Two weeks after those impolitic remarks, the Colonel, Mrs. Roosevelt and Ethel, who had met him at Khartoum, were received by the King and Queen of Italy. He found them, as he was to find most of the other royalty he met during the next two months, "delightful people" of ordinary endowment. And so, perhaps, he might also have found the Pope, Pius X. But when the Papal Secretary, Merry del Val, informed him that as the condition of an audience with His Holiness, the ex-President must agree not to see a group of offensive American Methodist Missionaries in Rome (one of the Methodists had referred to Pius X as "the whore of Babylon"), the former President refused. The Pope, he said, was a "worthy, narrowly limited parish priest; completely under the control of . . . Merry del Val." Roosevelt then refused to see the Methodists who issued what he termed a "scurrilous" address of exultation when it was learned that he had rebuffed the Pope. "The only satisfaction I had out of the affair," the Colonel wrote Lodge, ". . . was that on the one hand I administered a needed lesson to the Vatican, and on the other hand I made it understood that I feared the most powerful Protestant Church just as little as I feared the Roman Catholics." He added that it was a good thing he had no further interest in public office, for the incident would have compromised his usefulness as a candidate.

The grand tour continued. In Paris Roosevelt captivated the French with a homely exhortation at the Sorbonne on the "Duties of Citizenship." Even he was surprised by the favorable reception it evoked. In Holland he was enchanted by Haarlem's tulip show. And in Christiania, where he accepted the Nobel Peace Prize at Andrew Carnegie's instance, he sparked the simmering peace movement by calling for the limitation of naval armaments, expansion of the work of The Hague Tribunal, and the formation of a League of Peace backed by force if necessary. He did not, however, spell out the details.

After a brief visit in Stockholm, the Colonel and his party went to Germany where he and Wilhelm II held their much remarked review of army maneuvers. Afterward the Kaiser sent Roosevelt two photographs of them watching the troops. On one, in the Imperial hand, was the inscription: "When we shake hands we shake the world." The German Foreign Office urgently requested Roosevelt to return the photographs even before he left Berlin, but the Colonel refused. "His Majesty, the Kaiser, gave the photographs to me," he said, "and I propose to keep them." On the other hand, Roosevelt apparently made no effort to impress Wilhelm with his disapproval of his naval expansion program, perhaps because he was swept up by His Majesty's enthusiasm, more probably, as Elting Morison suggests, because he believed the cause was hopeless. He had, moreover, thrown down the gauntlet at Christiania. "The ruler or statesman," Roosevelt exclaimed after coming out for a League of Peace, "who should bring about such a combination would have earned his place in history for all time and his title to the gratitude of mankind."

In London a week later Roosevelt served as the American representative at the funeral of Edward VII. The formal dinner given by King George V the night before, he later told Taft, was the most "hilarious banquet" he ever attended. Eight visiting monarchs were there, and "Everyone went to the table with his face wreathed and distorted into grief." But even before the first course was over, he continued, "we had all forgotten the real cause of our presence in London." In the line of procession the next day, the former President of the United States rode with the French Minister of Foreign Affairs and a Persian Prince in the eighth carriage.

A week and a half after Edward's funeral Roosevelt shook the British by lecturing them on their administration of Egypt. "Now, either you have the right to be in Egypt or you have not," he declared at the Guildhall in London on May 31; "either it is or it is not your duty to establish and to keep order." He then advised them to get out if they were not prepared to rise to their responsibilities. He expressed the earnest hope, however, that in the interest of civilization and "fealty to your own great traditions," they would decide to rise to them.

Seven days later Roosevelt delivered the Romanes lecture, "Biological Analogies in History," that had figured so prominently in his original decision to visit Great Britain and Europe. It was not an intellectual success. "In the way of grading which we have at Oxford," the Archbishop of York later said, "we agreed to mark the lecture

'Beta Minus,' but the lecturer 'Alpha Plus.' While we felt that the lecture was not a very great contribution to science, we were sure that the lecturer was a very great man."

On June 18, 1910, the "very great man" disembarked at New York. During the fourteen months he had been conquering the jungle, slighting the Pope, enlightening the British, and sounding the hopeful moral note at Christiania, his chosen successor had been proving a political failure. And even as the Colonel waved, grinned, thumped, and expostulated amidst the most tumultuous of receptions, troubles were closing in on him. For by the summer of 1910 the shifting coalitions which Roosevelt had so skillfully maneuvered during his presidency had crystallized into uncompromising conservative and progressive factions; and in the face of his promises to continue the Roosevelt policies, Taft had aligned himself with the former.

The new President's misfortunes were only partly of his own making. Almost any man would have suffered by comparison to Roosevelt, one of the three or four greatest natural leaders of all American history. Nor could Taft be blamed for the temper of the times or the character of his party. At the very moment the national progressive movement was building up to its first roaring climax, the long-champing Republican majority in Congress was angrily re-affirming that marriage to the lords of the market place that Roosevelt had fought so hard to sunder. Only Roosevelt himself could have saved the situation; and not even he could have saved it without taking sides.

Human frailty and differences also figured importantly in the party's polarization. As Taft's mother had feared, William Howard's lack of zest for conflict proved a heavy burden. He tended to submit rather than fight; or, because of his laziness, to follow the course of least resistance. He delegated too much authority; and for want of information or willingness to explore a problem, he sometimes made offhand or impulsive decisions. He had a poor sense of timing. And he lacked the ability to inspire. Nor did he read so voluminously or productively as Roosevelt, nor welcome to the White House such a churning stream of people with ideas (if Taft ever had an intellectual exchange with an Upton Sinclair or his like, it is not a matter of record).

Taft's decision to surround himself with legalists also hurt, for his Cabinet supplemented rather than complemented his own viewpoints.

His later lament that "Roosevelt has no one to advise him of the conservative type, like Root or Moody or Knox or myself, as he did when in office," is as revealing of Taft as of TR; and it gives point to the classic remark dropped by Senator Jonathan Dolliver, the Iowa insurgent, who observed that the President was a "ponderous and amiable man completely surrounded by men who know exactly what they want." Taft's brother Henry, his half-brother Charles and the President's wife, who was ill throughout most of his term, added to his difficulties. They wielded a heavy and conservative influence, wrongly advising him as to the temper of the country and fanning the flames of his growing suspicions of the absent Roosevelt.

Ironically, however, it was Taft's stubborn courage which first disrupted the party. True at first to his personal ideals and campaign promises, Taft had called a special session to revise the tariff shortly after his inauguration. The House had responded in reasonably good faith by approving substantial reductions on iron and steel goods and writing in an inheritance tax provision. When the House bill reached the Senate, however, Aldrich and his friends blandly amended it 847 times, mostly upward. They also eliminated the inheritance tax clause, though they reluctantly replaced it with a modest tax on corporations. The President was irritated; but after he secured some modifications he lost the will to fight or even to veto the measure. Then, in a move that adds point to Mowry's observation that Taft suffered himself through life to be "often persuaded to act against his own basic instincts," he rationalized his acquiescence by asserting that the bill represented "a sincere effort on the part of the Republican party to make a downward revision." Nor was that all. That autumn Taft went into the Middle West where the Payne-Aldrich tariff was regarded as a bare-faced perversion of the spirit of the Republican platform of 1908, one whose rates served Eastern interests and compromised those of the West, and exclaimed in Winona, Minnesota, that "I think the Payne bill is the best bill that the Republican party ever passed."

Roosevelt was already on safari in Africa when the controversy reached its peak. Such comment as he did make was hardly to his credit. From the Juja Farm on May 15, 1909, he wrote Lodge, who had smugly informed him that the Senate would virtually maintain the old schedules, that there was no real issue:

. . . what we have to meet is not an actual need, but a mental condition among our people, who believe there ought to be a change; and I also agree with you that the inevitable disappointment and irritation will die down after a few months provided, as of course will be the case, that the Bill is fundamentally sound, and provided also, as you say, that there comes a return of prosperity when once the tariffs are out of the way.

Triumphantly, Lodge had shown TR's letter to Aldrich. "He put the whole situation in those few lines," the Rhode Islander wrote with enthusiasm. "He is the greatest politician we have had. We are dealing with a mental condition and that is the exact trouble with the situation." Thus was the irony compounded. It was Roosevelt who emerged as the beneficiary of the ensuing reaction against Taft.

If the Colonel's views were clouded on this first of the two issues that set his successor on the road to political disaster, they were clear and consistent on the second—conservation. Taft apparently came into the presidency with no conscious intention of undoing Roosevelt's great work, although, as Hays aptly suggests, he certainly intended to modify it. From the beginning Gifford Pinchot (whom he regarded as "a good deal of a radical and a good deal of a crank") was suspicious, and with cause. "There is one difficulty about the conservation of natural resources," President-elect Taft had declared to the second Joint Conservation Conference of Governors on December 8, 1908. "It is that the imagination of those who are pressing it may outrun the practical facts." It was Taft's failure to make a fighting speech on that occasion, Pinchot later claimed, coupled with numerous other straws in the wind, including the dropping of Garfield, that sparked the Roosevelt administration's last-minute withdrawals of potential water-power sites on the theory "that the incoming Executive would have to act affirmatively to give them away."

To make matters worse, Taft had selected a dubious conservationist, Richard Achilles Ballinger, to replace Garfield, the dedicated Secretary of the Interior. Ballinger was a strict constructionist; or, in Pinchot's somewhat overdrawn characterization, a friend of the special interests. While Commissioner of the Land Office under Roosevelt in 1907 he had opposed the President's mineral-lease program, preferring outright sale to rental. And on that and other accounts he had resigned his position after exactly a year in office. Returning under Taft to the government service in a higher position than Pinchot held, it was probably inevitable that he should clash with the zealous Chief Forester.

Taft's legalism further complicated matters. Whatever the President's views on conservation, he had no stomach for the Roosevelt-Garfield-Pinchot methods. "After T.R. came Taft," Pinchot was later to write in high irritation. "It was as though a sharp sword had been succeeded by a roll of paper, legal size." Neither did Taft approve of the Hamilton-Marshall conception of implied powers—a doctrine Roosevelt would have had to invent had it not already been in the public realm—or of Roosevelt and Pinchot's reliance on scientific, as opposed to congressional, advice. As he admonished the California conservationist, William Kent, three months after his inauguration, "We have a government of limited power under the Constitution, and we have got to work out our problems on the basis of law."

> Now, if that is reactionary, then I am a reactionary. . . . Pinchot
> is not a lawyer and I am afraid he is quite willing to camp outside
> the law to accomplish his beneficent purposes. I have told him so
> to his face. . . . I do not undervalue the great benefit that he has
> worked out, but I do find it necessary to look into the legality of
> his plans.

The first clash between Pinchot and the new administration had come over the water-power sites. "I do not hesitate to say," Taft wrote Kent late in the spring of 1909, that the presidential power to withdraw public lands "was exercised far beyond legal limitation under Secretary Garfield—and, more than that, unnecessarily so." Resolutely, Taft authorized Secretary Ballinger to restore them to public entry pending a report by the Geological Survey. So the die was cast early. For in rejecting the view that the spirit of the law and the public interest could best be served by temporary withdrawals while the time-consuming permanent surveys essential to controlled development were completed, Taft had repudiated one of Roosevelt's basic policies.

With clocklike regularity clashes between Pinchot and Ballinger had followed. Ballinger so harassed the Reclamation Service that a group of its engineers contemplated resigning in a body. He made establishment of legitimate ranger stations difficult. He played into the hands of the corrupt "Indian Ring" by canceling an arrangement whereby the Forest Service had efficiently managed the forests in the

Indian Reservations to the Indians' advantage. And he allowed the administration's prime dispenser of the patronage, Postmaster General Hitchcock, to have an outsized hand in appointments.

Ballinger justified his actions on strict constructionist grounds. Perhaps he did act in good faith. But if so, his tendency toward loose construction when private interests were at stake has never been adequately explained. The most generous interpretation is that he mirrored the Western milieu out of which he came: He was intelligent enough to approve conservation in principle, and less broadly in practice. But when the issue was drawn his commitment almost invariably proved to be to the private entrepreneur; and hence, in the Roosevelt-Garfield-Pinchot view, to the ruthless exploitation or inefficient development of the nation's natural resources. Both before Ballinger entered and after he left the government service, moreover, he recommended that the public domain be opened to all comers, and at least twice during his tenure as Secretary of the Interior, Taft himself requested that he cease associating with the known opponents of conservation.

The most famous example of Ballinger's tergiversation was his attitude toward the Morgan-Guggenheim Syndicate's acquisition of the Cunningham coal lands claims in Alaska. The details of this *cause célèbre* of the Taft administration need not concern us here. But it should be observed that the case dramatically demonstrated that more than legalism, or even states' rights, differentiated Ballinger's policies from Garfield's. When, in the spring of 1910, the evidence was finally in, Ballinger was revealed to have played fast and loose with the law in a way that made Pinchot and Garfield's elastic interpretations seem rigid by comparison; and he had done so in the private, though assuredly not in his personal, interest, rather than the public interest. Worse still, President Taft was revealed to have compromised his integrity by signing a spuriously dated document designed to bolster the administration's case against Pinchot's charges that Ballinger was promoting a "give-away" of the disputed Cunningham claims. And most portentously of all, Pinchot had been forced to resign.

By every criterion except that of the public interest, the fault was the Chief Forester's. With characteristic single-mindedness, he had decided within six months of Taft's inauguration to force the larger issue into the open. During the summer and autumn of 1909 he had delivered one conservationist speech after another as the newspapers buzzed with rumors of his differences with Ballinger. And in late September, after it became clear that Taft intended to support Ballinger's handling of the Cunningham claims (Ballinger refused to recognize their flagrantly fraudulent character), Pinchot told Taft he would stick to his guns even if the President had to fire him. Three months later, in defiance of a presidential order, Pinchot sent Senator Dolliver a letter defending two of his own subordinates who had released information about Ballinger and the Cunningham claims to the press. By prearrangement, the Iowan read it on the floor of the Senate chamber. "It is clear not only that they acted from a high and unselfish sense of public duty," Pinchot's defense of his subordinates ran, "but that they deliberately chose to risk their official positions rather than permit what they believed to be the wrongful loss of public property."

By his own admission, Pinchot had been insubordinate. "There is only one thing for you to do now," Elihu Root told the President as the issue was joined; and on January 7 the President called for the Chief Forester's resignation. "I would not have removed Pinchot if I could have helped it," he plaintively observed three days later. Taft replaced Pinchot with an outstanding conservationist, but he kept Ballinger on, and by doing so fatally stamped his administration as anticonservationist and indirectly as anti-Roosevelt. The Congressional insurgents thus had their second major grievance against the President.

With thirty newspaper editors over the country calling for Pinchot's nomination for President in 1912 and the periodical press, which was already enraged by the President's call for an increase in the postal rates for magazines, rising almost as one in criticism of Taft, the pressure was now on the administration and the Old Guardsmen in Congress. On June 25, in compliance with an earlier request from Taft, Congress restored the President's authority to withdraw public lands temporarily from entry—the same power it had so angrily wrested from Roosevelt three years before. And from then on Taft moved so relentlessly that by the end of his term of office his record of withdrawals compared most favorably with Roosevelt's. Whether this represented the fulfillment of his original intent or reflected his political desperation, as Pinchot asserted and Roosevelt implied, is impossible to say. What is certain, however, is that he failed even then to grasp Roosevelt's conception of controlled development.

Indeed, Taft actually reversed TR's policies by signing a number of bills authorizing perpetual and unlimited franchises for the construction of dams, among them one for the James River in Missouri, the project that Roosevelt had so angrily vetoed two months before he left office.

Unquestionably, the removal of Pinchot was the major catalyst in Roosevelt's estrangement from Taft. The Colonel tried to be fair; and he even sought to withhold judgment until his return to the United States. The burden was unbearable. On each side there were ties of loyalty and affection. But on Pinchot's side there was also a great cause—one of the greatest of Roosevelt's presidency. It was inconceivable that Taft should have dealt it such a blow. "We have just heard by special runner that you have been removed," TR wrote Pinchot from the Lado Enclave in Africa on January 17, 1910. "I cannot believe it. I do not know any man in public life who has rendered quite the service you have rendered. . . . Do write. . . ."

Pinchot had already written. On December 31, 1909, a week before he was forced out, he sent the Colonel a sixteen-point bill of particulars against Taft, the gist of which was that "the tendency of the Administration thus far, taken as a whole, has been directly away from the Roosevelt policies." Then on April 11, to the regret of Lodge, who advised TR not to see him, Pinchot met his former chief at Porto Maurizio in Italy.

There is no record of what Roosevelt and Pinchot said at that momentous meeting. "One of the best and most satisfactory talks with T.R. I ever had," was Pinchot's terse comment in his diary. "Lasted all day, and till about 10:30 at night." But Pinchot had already said enough in his letter of December 31 to make his position clear. And if he had not, he bore letters from Beveridge, Jonathan Dolliver, and William Allen White charging that the Payne-Aldrich Tariff was "just plain dishonest" and that Taft had taken "the certificate of character which Mr. Roosevelt had given him and turned it over to the Senator [Aldrich] from Rhode Island."

Roosevelt never felt the same toward Taft after that. On the day he saw Pinchot he wrote Lodge that Taft had virtually failed. "The qualities shown by a thoroughly able and trustworthy lieutenant are totally different, or at least may be totally different, from those needed by the leader, the commander," he remarked. Admitting that "a man with strong convictions is always apt to feel overintensely the difference between himself and others with slighter convictions," he had then renounced ambitions of his own:

> I have played my part, and I have the very strongest objection to having to play any further part; I very earnestly hope that Taft will retrieve himself yet, and if, from whatever causes, the present condition of the party is hopeless, I most emphatically desire that I shall not be put in the position of having to run for the Presidency, staggering under a load which I cannot carry, and which has been put on my shoulders through no fault of my own.

Nor was Roosevelt then disposed to help the Republican regulars. The Colonel had had almost a year to reflect on the character of his party and his presidency. And in a passage that the Democrats would have given their party treasury to have made public, he testily rejected Lodge's suggestion that he campaign for the G.O.P. in 1910. "Twice I have asked the American people to elect a Republican Congress," he reminded his friend, "in one case in spite of an indifferent record [1906], and in the other in spite of a poor record [1908]. . . . In each case the leaders of Congress have promptly gone back on their promises and have put me in the position of having promised what there was no intention of performing. I don't see how I can put myself in such a position again."

Three weeks later the former President passed another revealing judgment: "Our own party leaders did not realize that I was able to hold the Republican party in power only because I insisted on a steady advance, and dragged them along with me. Now the advance has been stopped. . . ."

Meanwhile Roosevelt's wife reported that people were urging her to keep her husband out of the country for a year and a half longer ("Why not for life?" said Henry Adams). Finally, on May 30, Elihu Root met TR at the Dorchester House in London. Root defended Taft for an hour, after which, so he later contended, the Colonel promised to stay out of politics for sixty days following his return home.

In Washington at about the same time, the troubled President, whom Adams described as "feebly wabbling all over the place, and tumbling about the curbs," penned a long, poignant letter to his predecessor. Taft remarked on the heavy burden of Mrs. Taft's illness. She "is not an easy patient and an attempt to control her only increased the nervous strain." He dismissed the criticisms of the Payne-Aldrich Tariff measure, terming it "a good bill and a real downward revision." And he pointed with understandable pride to the constructive measures already enacted or about to be enacted—railroad legislation, a postal savings bank system, statehood for New Mexico and Arizona, protection for railroad employees, and restoration of the President's authority to withdraw land from the public domain. He concluded by incorrectly implying that the insurgents, rather than the Old Guard, had failed to abide by the party platform:

> The fight for a year to move on and comply with our party promises has been a hard one. LaFollette, Cummins, Dolliver, Bristow, Clapp and Beveridge, and I must add Borah, have done all in their power to defeat us. They have probably furnished ammunition enough to the press and the public to make a Democratic House. . . .

Roosevelt dictated a generous but pointed reply to Taft's letter, which he had received just before sailing. We are, he wrote, aware that the "sickness of the one whom you love most has added immeasurably to your burden . . . and feel very genuine pleasure at learning how much better she is." He also told Taft of his talk with Root, adding significantly that he did not know the situation at home. "I am, of course, much concerned about some of the things I see and am told." "I have felt it best to do . . . absolutely nothing—and indeed to keep my mind as open as I kept my mouth shut!"

The mind was willing, but the heart and the flesh were weak. For a few weeks after his return home a fortnight later the Colonel managed to avoid public affront to Taft, though he rejected the President's invitation to visit him in Washington. And in spite of the importunities of the insurgents—Pinchot, Garfield, Beveridge, La Follette and almost every one else of consequence—who made the hegira to Sagamore Hill that summer, he refused to identify himself openly with the opposition. In fact, he worked conscientiously to promote party unity of a sort. Yet TR proved incapable of repressing his feelings completely. Before the summer was out he had so thoroughly reaffirmed the advanced progressivism of the last two years of his presidency (and, at Pinchot and Herbert Croly's urging, a little more besides) that he and the President had lost all rapport.

The first break occurred in August when Roosevelt challenged the reactionary Barnes machine for the temporary chairmanship of the New York State Republican Convention. If Taft had been capable of reading the signs, he would have seen that the Colonel's action was providential. A firm and open declaration of support for Roosevelt would have placed TR under personal obligation and would have narrowed their ideological gulf, since Barnes was an incorrigible conservative. But with characteristic maladroitness Taft made it appear that he favored the Barnes forces; nor did he suppress his perverse satisfaction when news that the New York County organization had refused to endorse Roosevelt reached him in Washington. The Colonel's opinion of his successor's ineptitude was thus confirmed. "Taft is utterly helpless as a leader," he confided to Ted soon afterward.

> I fear that he has just enough strength to keep with him the people of natural inertia, the good conservative unimaginative people who never do appreciate the need of going forward, and who fail to realize that unless there is some progressive leadership, the great mass of the progressives for lack of this legitimate leadership will follow every variety of demagogue and wild-eyed visionary.

Less than two weeks later TR was campaigning in support of his own progressive policies, and, so he professed to believe, of Taft and party unity. On August 23, in a special railroad car provided by the *Outlook,* he set out on a three weeks' speaking tour of the West that carried him into sixteen states and saw him deliver at Osawatomie, Kansas, perhaps the most radical speech of his career. More, even, than on his previous forays into the West, he was wildly, almost ecstatically acclaimed by plainly dressed crowds that stood long hours in the baking prairie sun awaiting his whistle-stop appearances; and more, perhaps, than ever before they saw in Roosevelt the Moses who would lead them to the promised land.

The Colonel scaled the status quo's outer defenses at Denver on August 29 when he attacked the Supreme Court for its decisions in the *Knight* case of 1895 and the *Lochner* case of 1905. Both cases, he said, were against national rights and against states' rights. But in reality, he asserted, they were "against popular rights, against the Democratic principle of government by the people, under the forms of law." The result was the creation of a "neutral ground . . . which can serve as a place of refuge for the lawless man, and especially for the lawless man of great wealth, who can hire the best legal talent to advise him how to keep his abiding place equally distant from the uncertain frontiers of both state and national power."

Two days later, on the grounds at Osawatomie where John Brown's centennial was being celebrated, TR stormed conservatism's inner bastion. "The essence of any struggle for liberty has always been, and must always be to take from some one man or class of men the right to enjoy power, or wealth, or position, or immunity, which has not been earned by service to his or their fellows," he declared in a passage that was as close to a Marxist interpretation of history as he ever got.

Anticipating the furore those words would incite, Roosevelt had preceded them with a quotation:

Labor is prior to, and independent of, capital. Capital is only the fruit of labor, and could never have existed if labor had not first existed. Labor is the superior of capital, and deserves much the higher consideration.

With characteristic directness, he had then rammed the point home. "If that remark was original with me, I should be even more strongly denounced as a Communist agitator than I shall be anyhow. It is Lincoln's. I am only quoting it. . . ."

Roosevelt's dream was actually the ancient one of equality of opportunity within a propertied framework. In the tradition of the Jacksonians far more than of Lincoln, he sought to purge business of its corrosive influence upon men, morals, and politics; but not to destroy it. Even at Osawatomie Roosevelt preached no proletarian uprising nor envisioned no broad destruction of private property. Nor, significantly, did he call for the upbuilding of labor as a countervailing force. The "essence of the struggle is to destroy privilege, and give to the life and citizenship of every individual the highest possible value both to himself and to the commonwealth." Only then could America's mighty creative forces fulfill their unparalleled potential, he exclaimed in a passage that marked the full flowering of his views and gave title to his speech and the progressive movement's philosophy, the "New Nationalism puts the national need before sectional or personal advantage."

It is impatient of the utter confusion that results from local legislatures attempting to treat national issues as local issues. It is still more impatient of the impotence which springs from over division of governmental powers, the impotence which makes it possible for local selfishness or for legal cunning, hired by wealthy special interests, to bring national activities to a deadlock. This New Nationalism regards the executive power as the steward of the public welfare. It demands of the judiciary that it shall be interested primarily in human welfare rather than in property, just as it demands that the representative body shall represent all the people rather than any one class or section of the people.

TR had then called the list of reforms without which equality of opportunity would remain the haphazard process the industrial revolution had made of it. The elimination of corporate expenditures for political purposes; physical valuation of railroad properties; regulation (though not even by inference, the breaking up) of industrial combinations; establishment of an expert tariff commission (to function within the protectionist framework); a graduated income tax and, especially, a graduated inheritance tax; reorganization of the nation's financial system; conservation of natural resources and stringent regulation of their exploitation; comprehensive workmen's compensation laws; state and national legislation to regulate the labor of women and children; and complete publicity of campaign expenditures.

Much of the West applauded what it heard at Denver and Osawatomie. "The West loves and understands Roosevelt," the Denver *Republican* observed. This region "takes it for granted that Theodore Roosevelt will be the next Republican candidate for President," the correspondent of the New York *World* wired from Cheyenne, "so what is the use of getting excited about it." The New York *Tribune* urbanely agreed. Criticisms of Colonel Roosevelt "afford great comfort to a select class of persons," it remarked, "for not to approve, or to give only a qualified approval to, the Colonel is a mark of distinction. It sets you apart from the common herd, with its love of moral platitudes and its incapacity for distinguishing between them and deep and original thought."

Other Eastern criticisms were not so light-hearted. Elihu Root continued to be patronizing of his turbulent friend, aptly remarking that "the only real objection" was that Roosevelt had called the New Nationalism "new!" But he was nonetheless disturbed. "I shall be curious to know whether he really meant" that he would deprive the courts of their power to pass on constitutional questions, he wrote

Taft. Cabot Lodge also managed a degree of equanimity by claiming that Western papers had quoted Roosevelt out of context. But he too was worried; and he so informed the Colonel. Meanwhile the New York *Commercial,* in a fair sample of the unsophisticated Eastern reaction, called Roosevelt a "peripatetic revolutionist" and his tour "a firebrand's triumphal march."

It was President Taft, however, who was hurt and angered the most. He complained that Roosevelt had gone far beyond the advocations of his White House days (which was not substantially true). He commented on Roosevelt's "ego," "swelled-headedness," and "wild ideas." And he argued that the Colonel's proposals were "impracticable" since they could be brought about only through "revolution or revision of the Constitution." But above all he was enraged that the Colonel had aligned himself with the enemy. "In most of his speeches he has utterly ignored me," he lamented to his brother Horace. "His attitude toward me is one that I find difficult to understand and explain. . . ." "He is at the head of the insurgents, and for the time being the insurgents are at the top of the way. They have carried Wisconsin and Kansas and California and Iowa, and they may carry Washington. . . ."

Subsequent events wrought little change in the general situation. In spite of his fear that the G.O.P. was foredoomed to defeat in 1910 and 1912, Roosevelt seems to have been congenitally unable to stay out of the congressional campaign. His own ambitions were as yet unformed—he may have been thinking vaguely of 1916—but he still believed that only the Republicans were capable of governing. He foresaw with fateful accuracy, furthermore, that complete division foreboded long-term disaster. He accordingly decided to veer back toward the middle and even to endorse the Payne-Aldrich tariff; but to little constructive result, so turbulent was the backlash of Osawatomie and his entente cordiale with the insurgents.

In New York the Old Guardsmen simply would not forgive the Colonel—either for the "crime" at Osawatomie or for "sins" committed as far back as his governorship. Worse still, Roosevelt's reluctant decision to resume relations of a sort with Taft backfired. The President and the former President had met once since Roosevelt's return from Africa—at Taft's summer residence in Beverly, Massachusetts, on June 30. Taft had made a heartfelt effort to break through the formal veneer. "See here now," he exclaimed to the Colonel,

394 POWER AND RESPONSIBILITY

"drop the 'Mr. President.' " But for all his effervescent good will, his "bullies" and exclamations of "de-e-light," TR had refused to resume the old relationship. They had parted as far apart as they had been before they saw each other.

They met again on September 19 at New Haven, where Taft was attending a meeting of the Yale Corporation. This time their conference set off a small bomb. TR stole the early headlines by streaking out from Oyster Bay in a motorboat, putting in at Stamford because of rough weather, and proceeding on to New Haven by motor. He and the President had conferred alone for an hour, then departed for the station in an automobile. The Colonel "told stories and the President wreathed his face with a purely physical smile and laughed aloud," Archie Butt reported, "but it was all strained."

Up to that point, the meeting had been fruitful, for Taft had agreed to support Roosevelt in his bid for the temporary chairmanship of the New York State Convention. Unfortunately, however, a member of Taft's entourage told newspapermen on the President's train that the conference had been arranged at Roosevelt's request and that he had asked the President to help him out of his difficulties in New York. That did it as far as TR was concerned.

Roosevelt issued a denial the next day and then poured out his feelings to Lodge. He had agreed to meet Taft on the representations of a third party, he said. "I did not ask Taft's aid or support in any shape or way, and it would never have entered my head to do so; although of his own accord he volunteered the statement that Barnes and Company were crooks, and that he hoped we would beat them." For his part, Taft wrote his wife that "It was perfectly characteristic that after having sought the interview, as . . . [Roosevelt] undoubtedly did, . . . [he] should at once advertise that it was not at his instance. . . ." He added that Roosevelt had asked for his support. To Butt, however, Taft explained that he had offered his support unsolicited, and that he had done so because he knew that the Colonel intended to ask for it.

Taft's later support of Roosevelt at the New York State Convention failed to mend the breach, partly because Roosevelt prevented that body from endorsing the President for re-election. And when Root in "a jollying letter" written at Taft's request asked TR to speak for the President in Ohio, he categorically refused. "As for what you say about the President having helped here in New York," he replied,

"I can only say that I went into the fight at all simply at the earnest request of the Taft men." The Colonel added that he had "been cordially helping the election of a Republican Congress, having split definitely with the Insurgents, including good Gifford Pinchot, on this point."

I have never had a more unpleasant summer. The sordid baseness of most of the so-called Regulars, who now regard themselves as especially the Taft men, and the wild irresponsible folly of the ultra-Insurgents, make a situation which is very unpleasant. . . . I do not see how I could as a decent citizen have avoided taking the stand I have taken this year, and striving to reunite the party and to help the Republicans retain control of Congress and of the State of New York, while at the same time endeavoring to see that this control within the party was in the hands of sensible and honorable men who were progressives and not of a bourbon reactionary type.

CHAPTER 24

THE TRAVAILS OF INDECISION

> Even so clear-headed a man as Root thinks that Theodore has not the Presidency in his mind, but that he aims at a leadership far in the future, as a sort of Moses and Messiah for a vast progressive tide of a rising humanity.
>
> —Henry Adams

Had Theodore Roosevelt been not quite so ambitious, or even a shade less self-righteous, the history of twentieth-century American politics must surely have been different. The Taft forces had been humiliatingly defeated in the congressional elections of 1910, first by the insurgents in the Republican primaries and then by the Democrats in the regular contests. For the first time since Grover Cleveland the Democrats had won control of the House, and for the first time in the Roosevelt era the American people had broadly affirmed their progressivism by electing a string of progressive governors, most of them Democrats. They had also returned almost all the incumbent progressive Republican senators and had added three new ones to their ranks. The import was clear: Taft and the Old Guard were headed for defeat in 1912 and Theodore Roosevelt was destined to have his party's nomination thrust upon him four years after that.

Assuming that the Colonel's thoughts were on 1916, and he was too young and dynamic for them not to have been, his tactics and strategy were sharply limned. He must avoid giving mortal affront to the Old Guard, which was bowed but far from crushed, and he must continue to cultivate relations with the party's growing band of progressives. Following Taft's defeat in 1912 he would resume leadership of the party. Resignedly, the Old Guard would accept him in the realization that he was the party's strongest candidate; enthusiastically, the progressives would embrace him in the belief that he reflected their views.

This course, if it was in fact a course, was not without obstacles. On the one side stood the Roosevelt-haters. Conservatives by and large, they also included politicians of no apparent ideology—men to whom politics was purely a play for power, men who might even support another progressive, so eager were they to have done with TR's disruptive force. Could the Colonel compromise with such types indefinitely? He had done so for seven and one-half years as President, and with generally constructive results. Without office, however, he would have nothing constructive to show; nothing but party regularity and intellectual inconsistency.

On the other side stood the militant progressives—the men and women of creative vision and evangelical good will whose doctrinaire politics Roosevelt had so often deplored and whose fertile ideas he had so regularly expounded. Could the Colonel indefinitely please these—the Jane Addamses, the Gifford Pinchots and all those other idealists whose lives and heritage have so enriched the Republic—and yet maintain his precarious political relationship with the conservatives, including his beloved friends Root and Lodge? Already, by 1910, this was a meaningful question. For the reform sentiment that Roosevelt had so spectacularly affirmed at Osawatomie would have to be consolidated on more than party regularity and nurtured on more than intellectual equivocation. Should TR pull his punches too much, should he imply by his relations with the conservatives that he had not really meant what he had said, then, surely, the reformers would gravitate to the relentlessly uncompromising La Follette, as many were already doing or threatening to do. Probably Roosevelt could have won them back; it was not the Colonel's nature, however, to view his political future with optimism.

In the center stood Roosevelt himself—Roosevelt the progressive conservative and Roosevelt the conservative progressive; Roosevelt, the man of surprising subtlety and predictable bluntness; Roosevelt, the ruthless politician and the idealistic preacher; Roosevelt, the contemner of reformers and the purveyor of reforms; Roosevelt, the most consummate man of action the American public has ever known. Could he avoid stumbling over himself? Could he for five years do and say the contradictory things necessary to the preservation of his hold on both the right and the left? Could he accept the inevitable even after he had convinced himself that Taft's nomination in 1912 was in fact inevitable?

For well on to a year the Colonel pursued this, the course of political wisdom and expediency, if not of valor. The Colonel resumed friendly relations with Taft even as he was cultivating them with La Follette. He was less than consistent on some issues and he reversed himself ignobly on at least one, tariff reciprocity. He both defended and criticized Taft in private, and he did the same with La Follette, Pinchot, and other militant progressives. And he even backslid a bit from Osawatomie. In the end, however, he proved emotionally incapable of walking the tightrope that both he and circumstances had strung.

The *rapprochement* with Taft proved short-lived; nor did it ever quite recapture the easy informality of earlier years. Roosevelt could rekindle the flames of friendship as readily as he could stamp them out, but he could not re-create the old respect for Taft's competency. Never, not even with his beloved brother Elliott, who had died of alcoholism eighteen years before, was Theodore Roosevelt tolerant of weakness. And never, almost certainly, was he tolerant of ineptitude in men of public responsibility. For all those flashes of courage that made his downfall a minor tragedy, Taft had proved both weak and inept. "I do not believe he has been a bad President, and I am sure he has been a thoroughly well-meaning and upright President," TR wrote Arthur Lee in September, 1910, as his relations with Taft started to become more cordial. "I think he is a better President than McKinley and probably than Harrison, but the times are totally different, and he has not the qualities that are needed at the moment." After Taft's continuing political obtuseness and Roosevelt's bustling vanity had brought about a situation beyond repair, the Colonel would alter even that measured judgment of his chosen successor.

Meanwhile, however, TR wrote Taft that he was "a trump" to invite him again to the White House. He commended him in December, 1910, after reading the proof of his annual message (though most of that message was intransigently conservative, portions of it were eminently progressive). And he rendered friendly advice on foreign policy. Taft responded in kind, for he was even more desirous of harmony than Roosevelt. Reporting to the Colonel on the progress of the Panama Canal in late November, he observed that it would be completed around July, 1913, "a date at which both you and I will be private citizens and . . . can then visit the canal together." And in March, 1911, when Roosevelt requested permission to raise and command a cavalry division in the event the festering Mexican situation exploded into a major war, the President cordially acquiesced.

Three months later the President and the former President met in Baltimore at a celebration honoring Cardinal Gibbons, where as Mowry writes, they "shook hands heartily, whispered together, and at times broke into unrestrained laughter." A few days later Roosevelt sent the Tafts a silver wedding anniversary gift. Taft's thank-you note, dated June 18, 1911, was the last personal communication exchanged by the two men in years. By the third week in August Roosevelt was writing that the President "is a flubdub with a streak of the second-rate and the common in him, and he has not the slightest idea of what is necessary if this country is to make social and industrial progress." Taft's real trouble, he explained to Hiram Johnson in October, 1911, lay in his values. Like those of McKinley, Hanna, and most of America's business leaders, they were essentially materialistic.

What caused this final estrangement? Certainly Roosevelt's personality was a major factor. TR's whole career was marred by a seemingly congenital inability to view his competitors with normal dispassion, and Mowry's speculation that he "could not have thoroughly approved of the leadership of any successor, much less that of a personal friend," is powerfully compelling. It is not unlikely, in fact, that from that one great flaw of character flowed much of the rest—the intolerance, the hypercriticism, the indignation at the reversal of "my policies." Even at their unalloyed worst, however, personality considerations were only partially determinative. They fixed the direction of Roosevelt's broad bias, and they governed the magnitude of the final eruption; but they would have been historically inconsequential had they not been compounded by ideological issues in which TR had long been involved. During the eight or ten months of his *rapprochement* with Taft, for example, the Colonel proved quite capable of checking his more egregious compulsions. It is reasonable to assume that he might have continued to hold them in bounds had there not unfolded in the spring and fall of 1911 a new series of disruptive issues. One of the most important of these was foreign policy.

In the face of Roosevelt's labors in the vineyard of peace, he had never lost that contempt for weakness which had marred his conduct of diplomacy with the less advanced nations. He never regarded U.S. vital interests as justiciable, in spite of his own efforts in behalf of the Second Hague Peace Conference and the endorsement he had given limited arbitration treaties while President, to say nothing of his Nobel Prize speech in the spring of 1910. To the end of his life the Colonel remained a *Realpolitiker,* his moral principles partly suppressed by his own strident nationalism or merged in that *Zeitgeist* which identified America's national interests with the ultimate welfare of humanity. When, therefore, Taft backed a series of comprehensive arbitration treaties in the spring of 1911, Roosevelt was hard pressed to maintain the façade of approval that circumstances demanded. Indeed, he soon commenced to destroy it brick by brick.

Privately, the Colonel warned Lodge, who needed no urging, against sanctioning such "maudlin folly" as the negotiation of "honor and independence." He also said much the same publicly, first in a signed article in the March issue of the *Outlook,* later in a seven-page letter published in the *New York Times.* Hurt and embittered, Taft refused to reply in kind though he privately attributed Roosevelt's opposition to his primitive drives and personal animosity toward himself. "The truth is he believes in war and wishes to be a Napoleon and to die on the battlefield," he wrote of his predecessor. "I shall continue . . . to discuss the treaties, and shall not notice the personal turn of his remarks. . . . It is curious how unfitted he is for courteous debate. I don't wonder he prefers the battle-ax." Roosevelt's private opinion of Taft was hardly more complimentary.

Actually, the controversy transcended both personalities and politics. The two men's raging disrespect for each other doubtless contributed subconsciously to the fanning of the flames; but neither it nor Roosevelt's as yet unformed ambition for 1912 was causal. Above all else, above conservation even, this was an ideological conflict.

Like Bryan, Carnegie, and eventually Woodrow Wilson, William Howard Taft envisioned the ultimate substitution of international law for sheer force. He devoutly believed that all disputes were justiciable, including those involving the national honor and interest. And in a series of extraordinarily frank and sensitive speeches in defense of the arbitration treaties before the Senate in 1911, he persuasively expounded his internationalist views. "We had the war of 1812, in which our neighbor, England, asserted rights that she would not now think of pressing," Taft said at Marquette on September 11. "I think that war might have been settled without a fight and ought to have been. So with the Mexican War. So, I think, with the Spanish war." The climax came at the University of Idaho on October 7, when Taft directly foreshadowed Woodrow Wilson's "too proud to fight" assertion of four years later. "I don't think," the President exclaimed to the students and faculty, "that it indicates that a man lacks personal courage if he does not want to fight, but prefers to submit questions of national honor to a board of arbitration."

To a Theodore Roosevelt, a Cabot Lodge, an Admiral Mahan, and even an Oliver Wendell Holmes, Taft's subordination of the national ego was the rankest heresy. How could patriotism be fostered? How could the manly virtues, without which the nation would follow the course of Rome and all the other past civilizations grown flaccid from effeteness and ultramaterialism, be maintained if national wrong were admitted and the will to assert renounced?

That was not the whole of Roosevelt's brief against Taft's arbitration treaties. If the Colonel bore the national honor as a truculent youngster carried a chip on the tip of his shoulder, his understanding of power politics as it was then played was as deep as that of the most cynical of his European contemporaries. He entertained no objection per se to a treaty with England, for he now believed America and Britain's larger national interests were either identical or complementary. But he objected strenuously to Taft's plan to consummate similar treaties with all the other powers. As he wrote Lodge late in the spring of 1911:

> Of course as regards England . . . there is not any question that we could not arbitrate. . . . But with either Germany or Japan it is perfectly conceivable that questions might arise which could not submit to arbitration. If either one of them asked us to arbitrate the question of fortifying the Isthmus; or asked us to arbitrate the Monroe Doctrine, or the fortification or retention of Hawaii; or Germany's right to purchase the Danish islands in the West Indies; or Japan's right to insist upon unlimited Japanese immigration—why! we would not and could not arbitrate.

There was and is no easy answer. In the tradition of the great idealists, Taft was pushing hard on the only course that offers ultimate hope for the preservation of world civilization. In the tradition of the great realists, Roosevelt was arguing that national survival was

paramount to commitment to a world order. Actually, neither statesman was quite as extreme as his words of the moment suggested. The
President, for example, was wholeheartedly committed to the fortification of the Panama Canal and the defense of the Monroe Doctrine.
The Colonel, as his acceptance of Root's treaties and his Nobel Prize
speech suggest, was willing to push for arbitration as an eventual
goal. Like Root and the many other responsible senators who helped
emasculate the treaties at issue, however, he felt that Taft was moving
too rapidly and, hence, irresponsibly.

Other issues continued to widen the ideological gulf between the
two antagonists throughout 1911. One was conservation; another,
Roosevelt's continuing criticism of the courts. As Taft's administration progressed he had become increasingly responsive to the needs
of the conservation movement. In June, 1910, at the President's request, Congress restored to his office the power to withdraw public
lands from entry (it forbade the creation of or addition to forest reserves in Oregon, Washington, Idaho, Montana, Colorado, or Wyoming, however, except by act of Congress), and during the remainder
of his administration Taft actually exercised the power of withdrawal
more liberally than Roosevelt had done.

Notwithstanding this salutary effort, however, Taft failed to give
the conservation movement the moral support that had made it a
crusade under Roosevelt and Pinchot. Had he spoken for conservation
with the same zeal he defended the Payne-Aldrich Tariff or the
arbitration treaties, he might have spared himself a heavy burden of
pain. Nevertheless, by late April, 1911, after he finally accepted
Secretary of the Interior Ballinger's resignation "with great reluctance," and appointed an able and dedicated conservationist in his
place, Roosevelt was writing that if only "Poor Taft" had done some
of the things he was now doing two years earlier, his lot might have
been substantially different. But even this faint glimmer of approval
was soon obscured by the black cloud that fell over Taft's Alaskan
policy.

Distressed by Taft's appointment of "a thoroughly untrustworthy
man" as governor of Alaska in 1909, and disgusted by the subsequent
revelations of Ballinger's handling of the Guggenheim claims, Roosevelt needed but the slightest breeze to fan the white coals of his conservationist zeal. It came in the spring of 1911 when the Taft administration restored to public sale forest lands on Controller Bay

that his own administration had withdrawn from public entry. The Colonel interpreted this as playing into the hands of the Guggenheim monopolists, and on July 22, a little more than a month after he and Taft had conversed so amiably at the Gibbons reception in Baltimore, he published in the *Outlook* a severe attack on Taft's conservation policies in general and his Alaskan policy in particular. The President, he wrote, had created conditions which would make it possible for the Guggenheim interests to acquire control of the only remaining outlet to the Bering coal fields. Four days later Taft responded to this indictment with a special message to Congress sharply defending his own course and criticizing by implication the Roosevelt administration's action. "I fear," the President confided to poor Archie Butt, who was still striving manfully to be loyal to Taft without being disloyal to Roosevelt, that the Colonel "will regard this portion of my message as a direct slap at himself and will answer it as such."

The President's fears were justified. Encouraged by the single minded Pinchot, who would no longer even concede that Taft was "upright," Roosevelt struck back on August 5 and again on August 12 through editorials in the *Outlook*. One was signed, the other unsigned, and neither spared the nettled President's feelings. Even as the controversy thus degenerated, however, it was punctuated by new advances in Roosevelt's thought. Eschewing a simple recommendation for lease, as opposed to sale, of the Alaskan coal lands, he came out for government construction and operation of the port facilities and the railroad line into the coal fields. This, he emphatically believed and openly declared, was the only alternative to private monopoly.

If Taft's foreign and conservation policies were central to Roosevelt's ideological estrangement from the President, the Colonel's attitude toward the law continued to be the most critical factor in Taft's divorcement from Roosevelt. A few months were yet to pass before TR would carry his slashing criticisms of the judiciary to their logical conclusion—the substitution of the people's will for the courts' judgment under limited conditions. But as conservatives long feared, Roosevelt was advancing rapidly along that fateful path in the spring of 1911; and Taft realized it.

Curiously, the legal issue was confounded by the trust question. In spite of his protestations in 1908 that his policies were the same as Roosevelt's, Secretary of War Taft had always entertained reservations about the wisdom, and in some cases the legality, of many of

Roosevelt's policies. He had, it is true, demurred only mildly, and he had even acquiesced in the President's handling of the Brownsville affair. He had also submitted to Roosevelt's views on the trusts, which he seems not to have grasped fully. "What we believe in, if I understand it," he wrote TR shortly after his own nomination, "is the regulation of the business of the trusts as distinguished from its destruction." Once Taft had assumed Roosevelt's sceptre, however, his compulsion to uphold the letter of the law—a compulsion that at times caused him to pursue policies more redolent of form than of substance —became again his *leitmotif*. The result was the most unrelenting destruction of the trusts to that time and the most shattering of blows to the relations between the President and the former President.

The signs were already posted when, in ordering the dissolution of the Standard Oil and American Tobacco companies in the spring of 1911, the Supreme Court laid down the so-called "rule of reason" doctrine. In so far as that doctrine read flexibility into the interpretation of the Sherman Antitrust law, it confirmed Roosevelt's long-held view; he can perhaps be forgiven the smugness that crept into his comments. "I think it is a good thing to have had those two decisions . . . ," he wrote a friend, "but they do not reach the root of the matter." What was needed, he wrote in the *Outlook* on June 3, was an independent commission with powers similar to those of the Interstate Commerce Commission. Regulation of corporations could then be "accomplished by continuous administrative action, and not by necessarily intermittent lawsuits." Furthermore, he added, the commission should be empowered to fix prices indirectly.

If President Taft was impressed by Roosevelt's article in the *Outlook,* there is no record of it. Conscious that he was enforcing the Sherman Law as it had not been enforced, even by Roosevelt himself, he gave his energetic Attorney General, George W. Wickersham, his rein. The consequence was that while Standard Oil and American Tobacco Company executives were privately snickering at the government (the orders seemed not to affect their company's real power positions within the steel and tobacco industries; and, as Pringle writes, who among them "was indicted, fined or punished?"), the administration was taking its most fateful step of all. In the full flower of that stubborn innocence that was both his charm and his political undoing, Taft allowed a special assistant to the Attorney General to file suit against the United States Steel Corporation on October 26, 1911. He did not even read the government's bill of particulars. There followed the most disastrous explosion in the Republican party's history.

The government's petition of October 26 made the startling inference that President Roosevelt had been hoodwinked by Messrs. Frick and Gary when they assured him in October, 1907 that the purchase of the Tennessee Coal and Iron Company by the United States Steel Corporation was essential to stoppage of the panic of that year and that no advantage would accrue to U.S. Steel from the merger. In spite of the hard truth of this inference, the Colonel was too vain, or to put it more charitably, too human, to do other than deny it. He did so at once—vitriolically in his private letters and vehemently in an *Outlook* article of November 18. He complained to friends that Taft had been "enthusiastic" and "emphatic in his commendation of the merger" when Secretary of War. "It ill becomes him either by himself or through another afterwards to act as he is now acting," he contended. And he charged in the article in the *Outlook* that Taft's insistence on meeting the trust problem "by a succession of lawsuits . . ." was about as practical as "a return to the flintlocks of Washington's Continentals."

The wheel had finally turned full circle. Roosevelt now appeared at one with Justice Holmes who had raised similar objections to the dissolution of the Northern Securities Company in 1904. Yet the wheel had also moved forward; and in so doing it had left the great jurist, who held no brief for regulation either, to muse alone over the raw Social Darwinian theories of Herbert Spencer and William Graham Summer. "I don't disguise my belief," Holmes had written his friend Pollock just the year before, "that the Sherman Act is a humbug based on economic ignorance and incompetence, and my disbelief that the Interstate Commerce Commission is a fit body to be entrusted with rate-making. . . ."

The Colonel's solution was the one that he had been pointing toward as early as 1902 when "Mr. Dooley" had chided him for his apparent ambivalence toward the trusts, for his then fuzzy categorization of "good" and "bad" industrial combinations. TR called not only for continuous and comprehensive government regulation as he had done so often during the last years of his presidency and again at Osawatomie, for the first time in a public statement he faced the ultimate question—government control of wages, hours and prices. After defending his own comportment in the Steel case (he implied that the Steel Corporation was a "good" trust) and criticizing the Taft administration's failure to dissolve the "bad" Tobacco Trust in fact no less than in theory, he concluded that in extreme cases the government should be empowered to exercise "control over monopoly prices, as rates on railways are now controlled. . . ."

Impressed by the paeans of praise for TR that immediately rose out of the man-made canyons on lower Manhattan, historians have widely interpreted the *Outlook* article as a direct bid for Wall Street's support. And so it was, in timing at least. Wiebe's studies show that the Morgan-Gary-Perkins forces were already disaffected by the Taft administration's relentless enforcement of the Sherman Law and that they had earlier sought to avoid suit by reviving the "gentlemen's agreements" of the Roosevelt years and offering to correct in advance such practices as the Department of Justice found offensive. But Wickersham, whose devotion to the letter of the law was as sustained as Taft's, had flatly refused. Furthermore, they had already proved themselves sympathetic to Roosevelt's broad regulatory proposals, including government price-fixing. As Judge Gary told the congressional committee that investigated the Steel Corporation that June, price-fixing would diminish cut-throat competition; and as he did not tell the committee, it would also have assured tremendous profits for his organization since the prices would have to be set high enough to cover the costs of the small, and less efficient, companies. Gary also argued that it was "a great mistake to suppose that we can dominate the market price, a great mistake." Under cross-examination, however, he conceded that the Steel Corporation's vertical organization, coupled with the benefits derived from comparative bookkeeping in its numerous plants, did give it a considerable advantage.

As I suggested in the treatment of the U.S. Steel-T. C. & I. merger in Chapter 18, Roosevelt seems never to have shown any real insight into the purely economic effects of the subordination of the interests of a subsidiary company to those of a parent company. He was concerned with the more obvious abuses of power—railroad rebates, for example—rather than with the subtle and intangible, yet surely substantive, economic consequences of monopoly or oligopoly. Believing that the manufacturing industries were impelled by the same natural forces as the utilities to become monopolistic or oligopolistic, he came readily to the conclusion that what was right for one was right for the other; that the Steel Corporation should be regulated in the manner of the railroads rather than dissolved.

There were refinements and exceptions of course; also inconsistencies. As a moralist, TR was concerned preeminently with processes. Since the Standard Oil and American Tobacco trusts, unlike the Steel Corporation, had been created by willfully dishonest, anti-social means, they were "bad" trusts and deserved to be atomized. This was right; this was retributive justice, so essential in his value system to the good and ordered society. Yet—and here was the inconsistency—he did not believe their effective dissolution was possible even though he had made the original decision to prosecute them as President. Hence his assertion that the Tobacco Trust had been dissolved in theory but not in fact.

The Colonel was not alone in this view. Many informed observers believed at the time and for long thereafter that the decrees against the Standard Oil and American Tobacco companies failed to alter their real power positions within their industries. Most economic historians now hold, however, that the disruption of the oil and tobacco trusts had a constructive impact on the industries concerned. They further contend that both the application and the threatened application of the Sherman and Clayton acts by the Roosevelt, Taft, and Wilson administrations reduced the incidence of business malpractices and retarded the growth of monopoly. As Eugene V. Rostow puts it, "The example of these basic decisions served as a powerful negative factor in business affairs. Certain lines of development were denied to ambitious men."

In these circumstances, TR's distinction between "good" and "bad" trusts belongs more to the limbo of morals than economics. Conversely, Taft's wholesale prosecution of the trusts gives his administration a luster often denied it. (It is no accident that his majority opinion in the *Addyston Pipe & Steel Co.* case, rendered when he was a Federal judge in 1898, is one of the classic statements of antitrust literature.) Nevertheless, there is widespread agreement that more than mere trust-busting was needed; that an incorporation statute such as Roosevelt had proposed and Taft had failed to push, or an agency like the Federal Trade Commission, which TR had also envisioned and

Wilson later created, was also necessary. This being so, it is fair to conclude that Roosevelt's perception of the complexity of aspects of the trust problem and his sustained call for the rule of reason were as economically hard-headed as his belief that the Steel Corporation was a "good" trust was economically naïve.

Roosevelt had anticipated that his article would provoke charges of collusion between himself and Wall Street, and he had acted to dispel them with a statement at once forthright and disingenuous:

> Sincere zealots who believed that all combinations could be destroyed and the old-time conditions of unregulated competition restored, insincere politicians who knew better but made believe that they thought whatever their constituents wished them to think, crafty reactionaries who wished to see on the statute-books laws which they believed unenforceable, and the almost solid "Wall Street crowd" or representatives of "big business" who at that time opposed with equal violence both wise and necessary and unwise and improper regulation of business—all fought against the adoption of a sane, effective, and far-reaching policy.

The Colonel's main point was relevant. The business community and its representatives in Congress had in fact prevented the enactment of his regulatory program in 1908. What TR failed to observe, however, was that the Morgan-Gary-Perkins part of the "Wall Street crowd" he had so sweepingly arraigned had actually cooperated in the preparation of much of that program and had then supported it.

On the other hand, only a few big businessmen were willing to accept in good faith Roosevelt's most crucial hypothesis—big business should be subordinate to, rather than a partner of, the government. Among them were men of high civic purpose and personal disinterest, like the canny, freethinking Scot, Andrew Carnegie; also some younger men like the sophisticated, yet increasingly humanistic, George Perkins. Competition, exclaimed Perkins in the spring of 1911 in a speech that blended Gary's concern for business stability with Roosevelt's desire for social justice, had largely induced "the past horrors of the factory system"—low wages, restricted production, child labor, and "inadequate care for the safety of life and limb." Within a month of TR's outburst Carnegie was to write Perkins, who forwarded his letter to Taft, that Roosevelt's proposal for government price-fixing was the only effective solution to the trust problem. And by the end of the year Perkins would place at the Colonel's disposal his own bulging pocketbook, the product of that service to the Morgan and other interests that he was then abandoning.

However all that may be, it is apparent that the steel suit and Roosevelt's resultant enunciation of a trust program so advanced that it remains unrealized to this day catapulted him into that presidential arena which he had been theretofore only skirting. As the Charleston *Post* correctly surmised, ". . . 'Theodore' and 'Will' have parted political company sharply at last, and . . . there is going to be a struggle between them as representing conflicting schools of thought within the Republican party."

The Colonel himself was at once amused, pleased, and confused. He was amused that there should be so much interest in what he contended "was really merely a repetition of what I had been saying for nine years at least." He was pleased that it "seemed to be the one really practical platform put forth by any leader, the one platform that represented sincerity of belief as to the need of reform and practical good sense in advocating what could be really achieved." And he was confused, or so he protested, by the demands that he issue a categorical declaration of his intentions. "Most men seem to live in a space of two dimensions; and so they wish either for me to declare myself a candidate, or to declare that I will not accept the nomination under any circumstances," he wrote on December 11, 1911. "I cannot, as a matter of duty, take either position. I am not a candidate, I shall not become one, I do not think it will be necessary to accept the nomination; but if the matter of my candidacy should appear in the guise of a public duty, then however I might feel about it personally, I would not feel that I ought to shirk it. But I see no signs of it so appearing."

Indubitably, TR was honest, even to himself. Whatever his subconscious desires, his rational self opposed a bid for the nomination. His place in history was already high and secure, and he quite agreed with Nick Longworth and other conservative intimates that it would be "a veritable calamity" to run again. He would even have moments of regret after the die had been cast. "I've got no glory to get out of being President again," he told Felix Frankfurter that winter. "I have no particular religious beliefs" and no sense of assurance that there is a hereafter. "The one thing I want to leave my children," accordingly, ". . . is an honorable name. They have that now."

Also, the Colonel's near superhuman energy was beginning to flag. This was not perceptible to the public. At fifty-three TR's stamina was still incredible. The arduous speaking tour in the spring of 1911; the scramble walks, long hikes, rowing trips, and hunts; the whirling talks with visitors at Sagamore or in the *Outlook* office on Fourth Avenue; the voluminous outpouring of articles—all are suggestive of that. Roosevelt would not measurably weaken until after he had been stricken with malarial fever during his exploration of the River of Doubt in South America in 1914. And even in the five years of life that followed that setback the fighting instinct which compelled him again and again to rise to the challenge would drive him to remarkable feats of energy. Nevertheless, Roosevelt in 1911 was admitting to himself and close friends that he felt tired.

Finally, the political realities had not changed significantly. The Taft forces firmly controlled the party machinery, and only a minor revolution could unseat them. Such an upheaval would not be easy to accomplish, given La Follette's growing resolve to strike boldly on his own. The Wisconsin Senator's personal following was large, though not large enough to gain him the nomination, as Roosevelt coldly surmised. And much of it, including Roosevelt partisans like Gifford Pinchot, who had announced for La Follette only after concluding that TR would not run, would move unhesitatingly into the Roosevelt camp should the Colonel give the sign. But not all of it would. Inevitably, there would be resentment and recriminations among La Follette's hard-core supporters. Nor could La Follette himself be expected to submit gracefully. In vanity, in creative drive, in moral fervor, and in lust for power—in virtually everything but personal charm and that breadth of view which was TR's greatest distinction, the Midwestern regionalist was Roosevelt's peer. And in uncompromising quality—or stubbornness—he was his superior. Should TR decide to fight Taft for the presidential prize, he must first give battle to the rock-hewn senator from Wisconsin.

There were even more compelling reasons, on the other hand, why Roosevelt's resolve to remain aloof weakened during the long summer and fall of 1911. Of these, the most powerful was the mounting evidence that he, and he alone, was the popular choice. TR still thrived on personal popularity. He loved to be engulfed by surging crowds, to preach to great assemblages, to bask in their roaring shouts of approval and demonstrations of faith. And when, therefore, the cry for his nomination went up all over the country following his statements on the trusts, it was practically foreordained that he should reconsider his position.

Nor could the prospect of another term have been as unappealing in late 1911 as it had been in 1908. Notwithstanding the great popular favor under which Roosevelt had left the presidency, there had been that rankling undercurrent of resentment by Congress which had so comprised the dignity and effectiveness of his last year in office. Had he been re-elected in 1908 it would hardly have abated substantially. But by 1911 the old order had markedly changed. The archconservative Aldrich had retired. Allison was dead. Foraker had been forced out. And Joe Cannon's power had finally been circumscribed by a coalition of Democrats and insurgent Republicans led by an emerging progressive star, George W. Norris of Nebraska.

More important still, the progressive movement was surging forward. In spite of Roosevelt's belief in 1908 that the country was surfeited with reform, or at least with him, notwithstanding Taft's post-election contentions that he had been elected to consolidate rather than to advance, the demand almost everywhere was for more, not less, reform. This was exemplified by the early reaction against Taft's conservation policies, by the signal defeat of the conservative Republicans in the 1910 congressional elections, and by the meteorlike rise of La Follette; it was further attested by the emergence of men like Woodrow Wilson in the ranks of the Democrats and by the increasing strength of the progressive Republicans in and out of Congress; and it was confirmed by the popular approval accorded Roosevelt's views on the relations of capital and labor and kindred problems.

There was, it is true, no assurance that the conservative Republicans in Congress would go along with Roosevelt much more than they had before should he again become President. Yet TR would undoubtedly carry many progressive Republicans into office with him. And he could in addition count on considerable support from the Democrats, who, in combination with the small group of progressive Republicans, had been responsible for enacting most of Taft's reforms possible. Here it was—power, prestige, and a political matrix that promised greater opportunity for the fulfillment of Roosevelt's ideas than ever before. The times, as TR acutely sensed, were crying for action. Could he turn his back on them? Could he again contain, as he had so nobly done in 1908, that vaulting personal ambition which had been the springboard for so many long plunges in the past? Could he live indefinitely at Sagamore surrounded by the mementos of a past glory?—a glory which however great, was less than that which now beckoned.

CHAPTER 25

THE PEOPLE SHALL RULE

> The life of the law has not been logic; it has been experience.
> The felt necessities of the time, the prevalent moral and political
> theories, intuitions of public policy, avowed or unconscious, even
> the prejudices which judges share with their fellow-men, have
> had a good deal more to do than the syllogism in determining
> the rules by which men should be governed.
> —Oliver Wendell Holmes, *The Common Law*

Seven months were still to pass before Colonel Roosevelt would stand
at Armageddon. But by December, 1911, the forces that would drive
him there were proving hard to contain. From all sides and from all
sections of the country letters imploring TR to run were pouring in.
They came from Republican regulars who coldly calculated that
Roosevelt's was the bandwagon to ride. They came from nationalists
who viewed La Follette as a regionalist, and from moderates who regarded him as an extremist. They came from radical Westerners who
concluded that only the Colonel could win. They came from men with
little or no place in politics—from TR's favored "plain people"; from
friends of long and abiding affection; from personal supporters of no
acquaintance whatsoever. And they came from social reformers like
Colorado's great children's judge, Ben Lindsey. Inevitably, under
this heartening demonstration of confidence, the Colonel began to
weaken.

By the middle of December Roosevelt was casting an appraising
eye at the trial balloons his friends had sent up. And by the end of
the month he was clearly implying that he would accept the nomina-

tion if it came as the result of "an overwhelming public sentiment." But even then he would not admit that he earnestly wanted it. "I should regard it as utterly unfortunate"; it "would be a veritable calamity";—such was his constant refrain. Besides, he might lose. "If I were nominated, very possibly I should be beaten," he confided to the president of the University of California; "and if I were elected, such impossibilities would be expected of me that I do not see how I could avoid causing bitter disappointment to sincere and good people."

TR had lost little of those fears which lingered always near the surface and sometimes surged above it. Nor was this fiercest campaigner of the era yet prepared to command a lost cause; to lead his still inadequate armies against all those hoary bastions of privilege and complacency he had so often verbally harassed. Until July, 1912, Colonel Theodore Roosevelt led no Pickett's charges and ordered no Rapido crossings. Only when he became convinced that victory was possible, if not absolutely certain; only when he convinced himself that he had heard the clarion call of duty, then, and then only, did he unfurl his battle flag and plunge his sword. In December, 1911, the chances of success were still slight, the call of duty still muted, though they were daily growing greater and louder.

Yet Roosevelt had already made a major, preparatory step. His moving renunciation of 1904, he now said, applied only to three consecutive terms. The real danger "would come from a man who had been in office eight years and may be thought to have solidified his power by patronage, contracts and the like, using that power to perpetuate himself," he explained to a friend, Herbert Parsons. "Oh! good Herbert," he added parenthetically, "I cannot help grinning as I dictate these words at your solemnity over the possible danger to free institutions from the Contributing Editor of The Outlook who has just come to Town hanging onto a strap in a crowded car."

TR's confessions that he felt tired and old had also abated. He never conceded the point, but the pleasures of Sagamore and the stimulations of his editorial work were not enough. As Frankfurter, who understood his drives better than most, remarked after their meeting that winter, "when a fellow was gifted like TR was gifted for public life, he had to do that, just as Gutzon [Borglum] had to sculpt, work with his hands. You could see that [after the Colonel had exclaimed, 'Oh, if only Taft knew the joys of leadership!'] he just sort of jumped out and was going to lead the armies for regeneration. All this about, 'We stand at Armageddon,' wasn't just flapdoodle. That's the way he felt."

Moreover, the prestige and power Roosevelt was then savoring would wane after November, 1912. The steady stream of visitors, the tidal wave of mail, the headlines that heralded his every word—all this, TR well knew, stemmed from the muddled situation created by the hapless man in the White House. Had Taft's administration been popular and his control of the party commanding, then, surely, the politicians and the idealists, the disaffected and the men of good hope, would not have made the hegira to Sagamore Hill.

The future also looked less promising than it had a year earlier. La Follette's bid for the nomination was earnest and powerful, if not powerful enough. Should the Colonel decline the authority that was being urged upon him, the moral and political leadership of the party's progressive hosts would repose in the Wisconsin Senator following Taft's defeat in the national campaign. Could TR wrest it back between 1912 and 1916? Probably he could have; yet the question remains.

If all the above is speculative, Roosevelt's conscious conclusion that it was his plain duty to run is not. Again and again it was impressed upon him that only he could hold the Republican party together. He was told that Taft's defeat for re-election would split the G.O.P. beyond repair; that La Follette's drive for the nomination was destined to end in bitter frustration. He was told that only he could advance the progressive principles he had so persuasively expressed at Osawatomie; that he, not La Follette, represented a progressivism that was both sane and constructive. And most important of all, probably, for his thirst for power was never quenched, it was borne upon him that he had a chance to win.

All through December and on into January, however, Roosevelt continued to hold back. He repeatedly protested privately that he was not a candidate and that he emphatically did not want to run; and he pointedly refused to give overt encouragement to his friends. Yet he refrained from closing the door with a Sherman-like declaration. And under a rapidly rising volume of appeals to declare himself, the emphasis of his replies perceptibly changed; no longer did he interlard with reservations his statements that he "might conceivably" accept the nomination. By early January he obviously wanted to run —but only on his own terms.

The crux of the Colonel's terms was that the people should demand his nomination. "My usefulness . . . would depend not merely upon the people wishing me to be President, but upon their having good reason to believe that I was President because of their wishes, because of their desire that I should do a given job, which they felt I could do better than anyone else, and not because of any personal ambition on my part." Therefore, he wrote the publisher Frank Munsey on January 16, "I must not put myself in a position which would look as if I were seeking the office."

From then on events moved swiftly to their fateful climax. Two days later, in response to a plea from Michigan's Governor Chase Osborn, TR virtually threw his hat into the ring. "I am inclined to come to the conclusion that it is impossible for me much longer to remain silent," he wrote. "In this morning's mail came two letters from Governor Glasscock of West Virginia and Governor Hadley of Missouri, written to the same general effect as yours." He would, he continued, agree to reply openly to a joint letter signed by these and other governors stating that the people of their states "desire to have me run for the Presidency, and [want] to know whether in such a case I would refuse the nomination."

> I want to make it very clear that I am honestly desirous of considering the matter solely from the standpoint of the public interest, and not in the least from my own standpoint; that I am not seeking and shall not seek the nomination, but that of course if it is the sincere judgment of men having the right to know and express the wishes of the plain people that the people as a whole desire me, not for my sake, but for their sake, to undertake the job, I would feel in honor bound to do so.

This "spontaneous appeal" of the governors was a disingenuous device. Yet it was neither dishonest nor really deceptive, for the demand was already there. Roosevelt had merely manufactured a political vehicle for its expression.

There was now no holding the Colonel back. The cat jumped out of the bag early in February when a copy of TR's letter to Munsey was published. The next week the governors' prearranged request that TR "soon declare whether, if the nomination for the Presidency

come to you unsolicited and unsought, you will accept it" was released. Then, as the Colonel arrived in Columbus on February 21 to
deliver an address at the Ohio Constitutional Convention, he casually
remarked to a reporter that "My hat is in the ring." Three days later
he replied formally to the petition from the governors. "I will accept
the nomination for President if it is tendered to me," he wrote, "and
I will adhere to this decision until the convention has expressed its
preference." The die was thus cast.

The Colonel was in Boston for a meeting of the Harvard Board of
Overseers on the day his response to the governors' appeal was released. A month later his host, Robert Grant, graphically reported
his impressions to James Ford Rhodes. "Before I give you in detail
his reasons and comments," Grant wrote, "let me say that I never
saw him in better physical shape."

He is fairly stout, but his color is good, and he appeared vigorous.
I saw no signs of unusual excitement. He halts in his sentences occasionally; but from a layman's point of view there was nothing to
suggest mental impairment, unless the combination of egotism, faith
in his own doctrines, fondness for power and present hostility to
Taft . . . can be termed symptomatic . . . I have never spent a
more absorbing twenty-four hours. He was a most delightful guest.
He had his usual laugh at the people who said he drank,—and this
story has been revived with the new one that he is crazy. He drank
nothing but the wines we had at dinner and he took tea in the afternoon. As you well know, his habits are simply normal. . . .

"But you will agree that Taft has made a good President this
last year?" He acquiesced without enthusiasm. . . . That if he
were to wait for four years the Republican party would be in a
hopelessly moribund condition and that this was the crucial moment to do it. . . . He protested that he owed nothing to Mr. Taft,
but that the President owed everything to him; that Mr. Taft had
in all States immediately after becoming President affiliated himself
with the factions hostile to his (Roosevelt's) friends. . . . Indeed,
he asserted that he was interested in carrying out his ideas, and that
the plea of disloyalty did not weigh with him. . . .

"But will any of the party leaders support you?" I inquired.

"No," he said. "None of them; not even Lodge, I think. I don't
see how he can." . . . "I like power; but I care nothing to be
President as President. I am interested in these ideas of mine and
I want to carry them through." He said that he believed the most
important questions today were the humanitarian and economic

problems, and intimated that the will of the people had been thwarted in these ways, especially by the courts on constitutional grounds, and that reforms were urgent. . . .

That Theodore is in earnest and sincere, there is no room for doubt in my mind. People who hate him,—and their number is legion in our walk of life—credit him neither with sincerity nor honesty. . . . At the same time it is to be remembered that he has the reputation of being the most farsighted politician in the Country, and he unquestionably believes that we are on the eve of an economic revolution, and that it is better for the Country that the Republican party should point the way rather than the Socialists should control the situation and leadership. . . .

. . . I am so in sympathy with his desire to right humanitarian wrongs, and such a true admirer of his . . . though I disapprove of what he has done, and feel a little as if a baby had been left on my doorsteps. . . . On the other hand, I was on very pleasant terms with Mr. Taft, who I hear on the best authority is *much* wounded and very sad over Theodore's defection. . . .

Roosevelt's declaration was indeed a heavy blow to the distraught man in the White House, though it was expected. "I told you so four years ago and you would not believe me," Mrs. Taft is said to have exclaimed upon hearing the news. "I know you did, my dear, and I think you are perfectly happy now," the President replied. "You would have preferred the Colonel to come out against me than to have been wrong yourself." In point of fact, the waters ran deeper.

No less than Theodore Roosevelt, William Howard Taft believed that his cause was righteous and high; and he at once announced his resolve to keep the campaign for the nomination on the highest possible plane. "I believe the arguments pro and con will force themselves upon the electorate without the use of denunciation and personal attack," he warned his supporters even before TR made his formal announcement. And unlike Roosevelt, in whom the vein of sentiment had hardened into ice, the President still brooded over the destruction of their friendship. He hoped, so a mutual friend reported to TR after visiting Taft, that "when all this turmoil of politics has passed, you and he would get together again and be as of old."

With La Follette, however, it was different. No memories of happier years, no gratitude for past favors or respect for peerless abilities bound the iron-willed Senator to the dynamic ex-President. They had sometimes waged common cause in the past, it is true; and they seemed during 1911 to be doing it again. But the alliance had been cautious and always informal. Roosevelt's belief that statesmanship was the art of the possible and La Follette's conviction that it was the leadership of a crusade come victory or defeat made mutual trust impossible. Thus the Colonel had commended the National Progressive Republican League, formed in January, 1911, to advance progressive principles and to promote La Follette's candidacy; but he had refused to join it. And though he had been friendly to the Wisconsin Senator's candidacy, he had always backed off from a categorical commitment. For his part, La Follette never considered anyone except himself an acceptable candidate in 1912.

So swollen was La Follette's ego, in fact, that he seems to have believed that the Colonel had actually pledged himself to his candidacy. When, therefore, the enthusiasm of many of his own supporters had begun to wane in late November while that for Roosevelt commenced to rise, he had feared conspiracy. And when it became apparent early in the near year that Gifford Pinchot, Frank Munsey, and Medill McCormick, publisher of the Chicago *Tribune,* would scuttle La Follette's already battered ship on a signal from the former President, his fears were confirmed. The showdown came not at the memorable Periodical Publishers' dinner in Philadelphia on February 2, where the overworked and harassed Senator virtually broke down, but on January 29 in La Follette's Washington headquarters.

The outlook had been so bleak from November on that in the second week of December La Follette had actually contemplated withdrawing in favor of Roosevelt. On December 11 he had authorized the California conservationist, William Kent, and the two Pinchot brothers, Gifford and Amos, to draw up a letter to that effect; but he had changed his mind the next morning. Thereafter, as the Roosevelt boom became steadily more powerful, La Follette became correspondingly less tractable. He agreed to have lunch with Roosevelt at Amos Pinchot's apartment in New York on December 17, then backed down. The Colonel, who kept the engagement, proved still noncommittal about his own plans, declaring only that Taft should be beaten but that he doubted that he could be. Meanwhile, the evidence that La Follette had no following of consequence in the East continued to mount.

Finally, without consulting the Senator, La Follette's lieutenants called the meeting of January 29 in Washington. There now began, wrote Amos Pinchot in his *History of the Progressive Party,* "another painful and long drawn out series of conferences with La Follette. . . . Most of his supporters were by this time convinced that his strength, always confined to the rural districts of the West and Middle West, had sunk to a point where it was to La Follette's own interest to get out of the campaign as quickly as possible. . . ." But the Senator could not, or would not agree, so intense was his hatred of Roosevelt and so confirmed his commitment to his own cause. Indignantly, he rejected the suggestion that he withdraw. "I told them," he wrote in a 1913 edition of his autobiography, "that I had never played that kind of politics and never would; that I did not recognize Roosevelt as standing for Progressive principles; that I had resisted from the time of its proposal every effort on the part of Pinchot and others to make me serve as a stalking horse for Roosevelt's candidacy. . . ."

And so another chapter of the tumultuous progressive movement was written. In truth, La Follette had been used as a stalking horse, but by Roosevelt's supporters rather than by the Colonel himself. And though many of them had actually preferred La Follette, for they believed his progressivism more confirmed than Roosevelt's, they had known all along what the Wisconsin leader's unconquerable spirit would not openly admit: He had never had a chance. The sensational publicity given La Follette's temporary breakdown at the publishers' dinner four days later was but the *coup de grâce.*

Meanwhile, Roosevelt was assuming the roles of strategist, politician, and ideologist—or, as he would have preferred it, practical idealist. They proved not always complementary; and within the month his commitment to progressive principles had carried him into a situation from which his consummate political skill never succeeded in extricating him.

The occasion was Roosevelt's speech in Columbus, Ohio, on February 21, where, in a militant address that bore the mark of Croly and the Pinchots' advanced progressivism, TR severed the faint reed of hope that G.O.P.'s conservatives might support him out of fear that Taft could not be re-elected.

The Colonel started by evoking the heritage of Lincoln and repeating phrases become familiar, if not respectable, with the passing of time: "We Progressives believe that . . . human rights are supreme . . . that wealth should be the servant, not the master, of the people.

. . ." As Lincoln said, this nation "belongs to the people." "So do the natural resources which make it rich." Our charge is to "stop the waste of human life in industry and prevent the waste of human welfare which flows from the unfair use of concentrated power and wealth in the hands of men whose eagerness for profit blinds them to the cost of what they do." "The only prosperity worth having is that which affects the mass of the people. We are bound to strive for the fair distribution of prosperity." But this can be accomplished only by encouraging legitimate business enterprise. We must "exercise over big business a control and supervision" based on the realization that bigness is not necessarily bad. Nor should we shrink "from bringing governmental regulation to the point of control of monopoly prices if it should ever become necessary to do so." Unquestionably, "our fundamental purpose must be to secure genuine equality of opportunity."

More followed in similar vein. Then, about one-third of the way through, Roosevelt plunged into the political question of the era— popular representation. "I believe in . . . direct preferential primaries." "I believe in the initiative and the referendum, which should be used not to destroy representative government, but to correct it whenever it becomes misrepresentative." "I do not believe that there is any great necessity for [the recall] as regards short-term elective officers. . . . I believe it should be generally provided, but with . . . restrictions."

All that was uncomfortable, if not quite fatal. Most conservatives, including Cabot Lodge, recoiled from one or all of those proposals; but they regarded them as only mildly revolutionary. Had the Colonel stopped there, the situation might yet have been salvaged. But instead, he deliberately crashed headlong into conservatism's strongest and most hallowed bastion—the judiciary. In phrases that even Pringle calls "fine and courageous," he boldly came out for the recall of judicial decisions involving constitutional interpretation on the state level. "In New York, in Illinois, in Connecticut, lamentable injustice had been perpetuated . . . ," Roosevelt asserted. There have been "foolish and iniquitous decisions" and they "have almost always been rendered at the expense of the weak," of the "wage-workers," of the men who "toil on the farm and on the railway, or in the factory." The judges who wrought these injustices were "well-meaning men," but their "prime concern was with the empty ceremonial of perfunctory legalism, and not with the living spirit of justice." He would not vote for the recall of judges themselves, TR added, even "for as flagrant a decision" as that which declared unconstitutional New York State's Workmen's Compensation law. "But most emphatically I do wish that the people should have the right to recall the decision itself." The prevailing system was nothing if not "a monstrous perversion of the Constitution into an instrument for the perpetuation of social and industrial wrong and for the oppression of the weak and helpless."

Roosevelt realized that his proposals pitted the rule of men against that of law; or, as he regarded it, the rule of the majority of men against the law as construed by a minority of men. He knew, too, that the latter position had powerful advocates, many of them his own friends—men who "believe, and sometimes assert, that the American people are not fitted for popular government, and that it is necessary to keep the judiciary 'independent of the majority of all the people.' " But he cared not.

> I take absolute issue with all those who hold such a position. I regard it as a complete negation of our whole system of government; and if it became the dominant position in this country, it would mean the absolute upsetting of both the rights and the rule of the people.
>
> If the American people are not fit for popular government, and if they should of right be the servants and not the masters of the men whom they themselves put in office, then Lincoln's work was wasted and the whole system of government upon which this great democratic Republic rests is a failure.

Whatever the merit of these proposals, TR's purity of purpose is beyond cavil. The Roosevelt who spoke at Columbus on February 21, 1912, was not the politician who supported Blaine in 1884. Nor was he the master statesman who had so deftly guided the Hepburn bill to passage, constructively cooperated with Cannon, Aldrich, and other Old Guardsmen, and made his party moderately responsive to reform. He was, rather, the compulsive idealist: the kinetic leader whose career, for all its temporizing and equivocating, for all its bold pronouncements and weak follow-throughs, was studded with more acts of courage, with more audacious maneuvers, and with more frontal assaults on the sanctuaries of privilege than any of his major contemporaries except La Follette or Bryan.

Politically, there had been no need for Roosevelt to say the things he said at Columbus. Except for the most intransigent supporters of La Follette—and their numbers were never great—the Colonel held the insurgent West in the palm of his hand. All that he had to do was reaffirm the progressive faith, for it was the East, not the West, that had to be won; and Roosevelt knew it.

The Colonel was also well aware that his espousal of the recall of judicial decisions would stir up a whirlwind in moderate circles all over the country. Henry L. Stimson, tough-minded Learned Hand, and other men of similar quality had all warned him against his earlier flirtations with the recall; and so had numbers of lesser men. But to little result. TR's passion for moral justice was so intense, his conviction that the courts had become the servants of privilege so acute, that he had to act. In the failure of his long campaign to convert the judiciary from a static to an organic conception of the law, he had fastened upon the recall of judicial decisions as a last resort.

The reaction against the "Charter of Democracy" address at Columbus proved more severe than any Roosevelt had theretofore provoked. The New York *World* suggested that it might better have been called "the charter of demagogy." The New York *Times* observed that it would be "alarming" and "appalling," a threat "to our institutions" were it not certain that Roosevelt "had gone far beyond" public opinion. And the New York *Sun* labeled it "the craziest proposal that ever emanated from himself or from any other statesman." But the Colonel must have expected as much.

Nor could TR have been surprised with Cabot Lodge's heartfelt lament. "I have had my share of mishaps in politics but I never thought that any situation could arise which would have made me so miserably unhappy as I have been during the past week," the Senator wrote the Colonel on February 28. "I knew of course that you and I differed on some of these points but I had not realized that the difference was so wide." To this and Lodge's assertion that he would remain silent rather than openly oppose Roosevelt in convention, TR had generously replied:

> My dear fellow, you could not do anything that would make me lose my warm personal affection for you. For a couple of years I have felt that you and I were heading opposite ways as regards internal politics. I shan't try to justify my viewpoint because it would seem as if I were attacking yours.

But TR could hardly have anticipated the wave of disapproval that swept through the progressive ranks. From Washington came the report that "even the more radical of the Progressives in Congress acknowledge that the Colonel's utterances are distasteful to the lawyers among the Republican insurgents," while Roosevelt's own files reveal that many, many others were deeply disturbed. As that quondam progressive and sometime lion, Senator William E. Borah of Idaho, snorted, the recall of judicial decisions was "bosh."

Wounded and hurting though he was, the Colonel remained on the firing line. On the urging of Learned Hand and other realistic progressives, he expended much breath and even more stationery explaining exactly what he had and had not recommended. He emphasized that he did not favor the recall of judges in all states; that his proposals had absolutely no relation to "ordinary suits, civil or criminal, as between individuals"; and that they did not apply to the Supreme Court (though his disgust with that body had loomed large in his thinking). But he held to his conviction that the door to social and economic reform hinged on political reform; and in speech after speech he drove deeper and deeper this wedge that was breaking the Grand Old Party asunder.

"I have scant patience with this talk of the tyranny of the majority," TR heatedly exclaimed to a roaring audience at Carnegie Hall on March 20. "The only tyrannies from which men, women, and children are suffering in real life are the tyrannies of minorities." He named them—the coal trust, the water-power trust, the meat-packing trust. "I am not thinking of . . . bribery and crime," he added. "I am thinking as much of their respectable allies and figureheads, who have ruled and legislated and decided as if in some way the vested rights of privilege had a first mortgage on the whole United States, while the rights of all the people were merely an unsecured debt." Either they would be stripped of their overweening hold on the body politic or the Republic would fail. "I stand on the Columbus speech."

If on this new continent we merely build another country of great but unjustly divided material prosperity, we shall have done nothing; and we shall do as little if we merely set the greed of envy against the greed of arrogance, and thereby destroy the material well-being of all of us. . . . We stand against all tyranny, by the few or by the many. We not merely admit, but insist, that there must be self-control on the part of the people . . . but we also insist that the people can do nothing unless they not merely have, but exercise to the full, their own rights.

Eight days later TR was in St. Louis pleading the cause "of the crippled brakeman on a railroad, of the overworked girl in a factory, of the stunted child toiling at inhuman labor, of all who work excessively or in unhealthy surroundings, of the family dwelling in the squalor of a noisome tenement, of the worn-out farmer in regions where the farms are worn out also. . . ."

Less than a fortnight later Roosevelt appeared in Philadelphia, where he had bludgeoned the defenders of the status quo more than once in the past. Now, in a bold and forthright address entitled "The Recall of Judicial Decisions," he did so again. Remarking that a group of eminent New York lawyers, headed by Joseph Choate, had formed an association to combat the referendum and the recall of judicial decisions, TR charged that their real purpose was "to uphold privilege and sustain the special interests against the cause of justice and against the interest of the people as a whole." In similar manner, he added, a group of distinguished New Yorkers had defended the Dred Scott decision sixty-five years before.

"This is a strong statement," Roosevelt conceded, "and I would not make it of ordinary men who are misled by reading those New York papers owned or controlled by Wall Street." But Choate and his associates were not ordinary men. "These men are not to be excused on the plea of ignorance." As Choate knows, the proposal "is precisely and exactly in line with Lincoln's attitude toward the Supreme Court in the Dred Scott case, and with the doctrines he laid down for the rule of the people in his first inaugural as President." Its purpose was not to make the legislature supreme, Roosevelt contended, but to "make legislature and court alike responsible to the sober and deliberate judgment of the people, who are masters of both legislature and courts."

> In the long run this country will not be a good place for any of us to live in unless it is a reasonably good place for all of us to live in; and it will neither become nor remain a good place for all of us to live in if we permit our government to be turned aside from its original purpose and to become a government . . . by corporation attorneys on the bench . . . serving the cause of special privilege and not the cause of the people.

Such, then, were the intellectual highlights of Theodore Roosevelt's preconvention campaign for the Republican presidential nomination in 1912. Men will always differ about their merits. Roosevelt had no more faced the long-range question of the tyranny of the majority and the probable corrosion of the law than his opponents had come to grips with the immediate question of the tyranny of the minority. ("An ignorant judge may be informed, a corrupt judge may be detected and exposed, but a judge cowed into impotence or tempted to excess by dependence upon the constant favor of the appointing power or the continued smile of public approval is of all men most pitiable and most dangerous," warned Congressman John W. Davis of West Virginia a few months later.) But that Roosevelt had pointed up the then current perversions of the law, that he had offered a concrete, if ill-considered, plan for their resolution, and that he had kept his own and the progressive faith while comporting himself with high and resolute courage, no man can deny.

TR's strictures did not lack constructive result. Nicholas Longworth and the bulk of conservative Republicans in Congress remained supinely inactive. But that very spring John W. Davis framed, and a majority of Democrats and a few handfuls of progressive Republicans supported, a bill, subsequently incorporated in the Clayton Antitrust Act, to eliminate that abuse of the labor injunction against which Roosevelt had so long inveighed. In spite of the American Bar Association's condemnation of the recall of judicial decisions in a resolution passed a few months later, moreover, many thoughtful lawyers were moved to reflect on the problems the former President had raised.

"I was one of those who favored the resolution . . . ," Felix Frankfurter wrote the next winter. "But as I left the meeting, I had a conviction that the . . . American Bar Association fell short of its responsibility in not going beyond negative criticism and inquiring into the cause of the ferment. . . . The fallacy of a specific remedy may be crushingly exposed," Holmes's eminent disciple continued, "but we cannot whistle down the wind of a widespread, insistent, and ill-vouched feeling of dissatisfaction." When the conditions of life are changing, Frankfurter added in a comment that marked the coincidence of his own, Holmes's and Roosevelt's perception, the law cannot remain static.

Eleven years later when La Follette revived the issue in his presidential campaign against Coolidge and Davis, Frankfurter pronounced the historical verdict on the impact of TR's campaign against judicial excesses in 1912. "No student of American constitutional law can have the slightest doubt that Mr. Roosevelt's vigorous challenge of judicial abuses was mainly responsible for a temporary period of liberalism which followed in the interpretation of the due process clause," he wrote, "however abhorrent the remedy of judicial recall appeared to both bar and bench."

The public opinion which the Progressive campaign aroused subtly penetrated the judicial atmosphere. In cases involving social-industrial issues, public opinion, if adequately informed and sufficiently sustained, seeps into Supreme Court decisions. Roosevelt shrewdly observed: "I may not know much about law, but I do know one can put the fear of God into judges." The "fear of God" was needed to make itself felt on the bench in 1912.

CHAPTER 26

THOU SHALT NOT STEAL

> The cause of our opponents has now become naked—the
> cause of the political bosses and the special privilege in the
> business world.
>
> —Theodore Roosevelt

The Colonel had been too long in the jungle to permit the enemy to
do the stalking. Even as he had commandeered the high ground with
his principled public addresses, his scouts were scouring the under-
brush for the convention delegates that alone would sustain his cause.
And when in the process they uncovered the main quarry—the President of the United States—TR rushed pell mell from the heights to
engage in that hand-to-hand combat which was not in his blood to
resist. What might have been a reasoned debate between high-minded
public servants of divergent outlook degenerated into a ferocious personal brawl.

Ironically, it was the judicial-minded Taft who made the first lunge.
On Lincoln's birthday, 1912, less than two weeks before Roosevelt
formally threw his hat into the ring, the President had also invoked
the heritage of the Great Emancipator. He contended, however, that
Lincoln was a constitutional reformer, one who would have dismissed
those "political emotionalists or neurotics" who would "reconstruct
our whole society on some new principle, not definitely formulated,
and with no intelligent or intelligible forecast of the exact constitutional or statutory results to be attained." No one who heard Taft
could have misinterpreted the implication.

Meanwhile Taft gave his managers free rein to corral convention

427

delegates; and in a manner reminiscent of TR's tactics against Mark Hanna, they soon forced almost the whole great conglomeration of Southern officeholders into line. He also allowed Congressional Republicans to revive the old charge, never really proved or disproved, that TR had compromised with E. H. Harriman in 1904. And then, after Lodge's son-in-law, Rep. Augustus P. Gardner of Massachusetts, charged in late April that Roosevelt had personally interceded to prevent the International Harvester Company from being prosecuted under the Sherman Law in 1907, the President engaged in an acrimonious exchange with his once beloved friend.

It is doubtful, however, that any one or all such incidents sparked the flow of venom that soon issued from Roosevelt. Elihu Root, whose flashes of insight into TR's personality are illuminating in spite of the limitations that prevented him from understanding his friend's philosophic base, had known it would come. "I have an immense admiration for him," he wrote in March.

> I think that, rightly directed, his tremendous personality would be a great national asset. All these things combined fill me with regret over what he is now doing. He is essentially a fighter and when he gets into a fight he is completely dominated by the desire to destroy his adversary. He instinctively lays hold of every weapon which can be used for that end. Accordingly he is saying a lot of things and taking a lot of positions which are inspired by the desire to win. I have no doubt he thinks he believes what he says, but he doesn't. He has merely picked up certain popular ideas which were at hand as one might pick up a poker or chair with which to strike.

Taft had yet to feel the full force of Roosevelt's attack when those lines were written on March 9. But the first blows were already raining. TR's strategy was to wage primary battles in those states which had primaries and to try to institute primaries in states that did not. Failing in the latter, he would appeal directly for the support of the convention delegates. His tactics were less clear, though a pattern emerged after he began his campaign. He identified himself with progressivism, and in a side-swipe at La Follette, contended that he was the only progressive who had a chance to win the nomination and carry the election. He labeled Taft a conservative, and as the campaign became more intense, a reactionary. And he further identified the President with the political bosses and finally with corruption at the polls.

Nevertheless the Colonel's campaign went badly through March and on into April. The Wisconsin delegation was La Follette's to the man. North Dakota went almost two to one for the insurgent Senator (blandly, TR instructed his campaign manager to declare that the North Dakota delegation would support him after "a complimentary vote for La Follette"). New York, Indiana, Michigan, and Kentucky selected Taft delegations. And the South made ready to affirm its loyalty to the organization.

Under the impact of these defeats Roosevelt became increasingly bitter. He vehemently charged the Taft people with "bare-faced fraud"—in New York and in a host of other states. He denounced as "deliberate faking" rumors that he would bolt the Grand Old Party if Taft were nominated. He shamelessly linked Taft with the notorious Senator Lorimer of Illinois, though the President had earlier explained to TR his own desire to have the Senate unseat him. And throughout the West he unabashedly denounced Taft's Canadian Reciprocity tariff agreement—a measure adverse to midwestern agricultural interests.

But not until the tide suddenly changed and Roosevelt began to roll off primary victories in late April did Taft again claw back. En route to Boston on April 25, the President pathetically told the milling crowds at the whistle stops that he had come "to reply to an old and true friend of mine, Theodore Roosevelt, who has made many charges against me. I deny those charges. I deny all of them. I do not want to fight Theodore Roosevelt, but sometimes a man in a corner fights. I am going to fight." And fight he did, giving a reasoned, if not conclusive, rebuttal to many of the Colonel's charges in two surprisingly effective speeches in Boston. He asserted that during the course of "his long and useful and honorable life," Roosevelt had not learned "to be a good loser." He ridiculed the Colonel's trust policy. He indirectly aligned himself with the conservatives by claiming that Roosevelt's nomination would cause a depression. And he expressed grave fear that the third term tradition should be broken:

> One who so lightly regards constitutional principles, and especially the independence of the judiciary, one who is so naturally impatient of legal restraints, and of due legal procedure, and who has so misunderstood what liberty regulated by law is, could not safely be intrusted with successive presidential terms.

The strain proved unbearable. That night Taft returned to his train weary, depressed, and shaken. The thick flesh on his unlined face sagged almost lifelessly and his step, usually light and graceful, was heavy, even ponderous. He sat down alone on one of the lounges. There, writes Pringle, Siebold of the *World* found him "slumped over, with his head between his hands." The President looked up as the newspaperman entered. "Roosevelt was my closest friend," he blurted out. He then broke down and wept.

Still, Taft kept going. He argued that his administration had put through a great body of progressive measures, many of which Roosevelt himself had tried, but failed to get through Congress. He did not, of course, admit that they were a tiny creek compared to the surging waters of progressivism's mighty mainstream—a mainstream whose channels Roosevelt had done so much to carve. Nor did he point out that most of them had been pushed through by a majority of Democrats and only a minority of Republicans, mostly progressives; or that dynamic executive leadership could have produced more comprehensive legislation. On the other hand the President could not regard himself as other than he was—a man of pacific temperament constrained to fight desperately for the semblance of self-respect.

"Condemn me if you will," Taft exclaimed at Lowell, Massachusetts, on April 30, "but condemn me by other witnesses than Theodore Roosevelt. I was a man of straw, but I have been a man of straw long enough. Every man who has blood in his body, and who has been misrepresented as I have been is forced to fight." A week later from Hyattsville, Maryland, newspapers reported a yet more humiliating remark. "I am a man of peace, and I don't want to fight. But when I do fight I want to hit hard. Even a rat in a corner will fight." The President reached his nadir a few days after that. As Roosevelt had done under much less extenuating circumstances eight years before, he prepared to sign a pension bill which he thoroughly disapproved. A veto "would certainly lose the soldier vote in Ohio and elsewhere," he pointed out to Horace Taft. "I feel seriously that I represent the people's cause, that I represent the cause of constitutional government, that I represent the cause of liberty regulated by law." ". . . under these conditions, and facing as I do a crisis with Mr. Roosevelt," he explained in a deleted passage of the draft of a letter to Charles Francis Adams, ". . . the question is whether I ought not to yield and sign the bill." He finally did so.

On the other extreme, where the indomitable La Follette was waging a futile battle against fate, there was no sorrow, no yielding, no heart-rending appeal. The political tenor of "Fighting Bob's" campaign was captured in a statement sent out by his Nebraska campaign manager: "I WANT THE NAMES OF ALL WHO ARE READY TO FIGHT FOR LA FOLLETTE TO THE END"; and its ideological tone was embodied in the Senator's repeated reaffirmations of his progressive faith and his charges that Roosevelt was a trimmer. To the end he remained an heroically stubborn figure, a "unique" politician, as one newspaperman termed him.

> Supposedly coming from a sickbed, . . . [he] looks anything but a sick man. He is tense, vigorous and full of fighting ire. Picture this "little giant" with the bushy head of hair, tramping up and down the platform, face, hands and figure in nervous action as he drives home his points. Picture him leading carefully up to his arraignment of the popular idol of the day [Roosevelt] and as one prominent North Dakotan described it, "getting away with it," and you have "Bob" La Follette on the stump.

Meanwhile the gargantuan struggle between Roosevelt and Taft raged thunderously to its tumultuous conclusion. Early in April the Colonel captured most of the Pennsylvania delegation from the President, who had the support of the corrupt Penrose machine (TR was backed by the less notorious, but hardly less corrupt, Flinn machine). And from then until early June victory followed victory. California, Minnesota, Nebraska, Maryland, and South Dakota all went into Roosevelt's column. The Colonel swept New Jersey. And in Taft's own state, Ohio, he carried thirty-seven out of forty-eight delegates.

TR's resounding triumph in the President's home grounds was the most exhilarating and portentous of all his victories. The campaign itself had been degrading. Exhausted and frayed by thousands of miles of travel and scores of speeches, both men had lowered the bars more than ever before. The beleaguered President had called Roosevelt a "dangerous egotist," a "demagogue," and a "flatterer of the people"; the high-riding Colonel had labeled Taft a "puzzlewit," a "fathead," and worse. Yet they had also spoken on the philosophical questions that separated them and their respective wings of the party. As the independent Philadelphia *Public Ledger* observed editorially:

Ohio was not excited by a coal strike, as was Pennsylvania; nor was it aroused over the Lorimer case, as was Illinois; nor were there complications of a primary ballot, as in Maryland; nor was there the new element of woman-suffrage, as in California. The issue was fairly drawn; the voters had every opportunity to be fully informed in a campaign of unexampled activity, . . .

The outcome in Ohio had raised the lid, and the smashing triumph in New Jersey had blown it sky high. Roosevelt could now claim that he had won enough delegates to be nominated. "The result in Ohio has settled the contest," he exclaimed to newspapermen. "I will have a great deal to say, and I won't stand it for a moment" if "the discredited bosses and politicians . . . decide against me."

Actually, the Colonel was about seventy delegates short of the majority needed for nomination. So boldly had his managers pressed his case, however, that 254 seats were open to contest. About one hundred of these were legitimate challenges. The remainder were manufactured—the product of TR and his followers' frenetic charges of fraud. But that Roosevelt could win even the legitimate challenges was doubtful, for all seats at issue were to be reviewed by the Taft-controlled Credentials Committee, a body selected in 1908 when TR was using the power of his office to compel the nomination of Taft. Final decision rested with the Convention itself. More ironically, still, many of the delegates against whom Roosevelt had no real case were from the South. Just four years before TR had opposed a movement to reduce that privileged domain's yield; now its lush harvest was Taft's to reap.

By the time the Credentials Committee began hearings on June 7, eleven days before the Convention convened, TR was caught ineluctably in his own momentum. He had either to carry the Convention with him or crash through and out on his own. There was no honorable alternative. That he knew this is uncertain; nor is it of any moment given the powerful compulsions and the mighty external forces that were propelling him onward.

Of the compulsions, that for victory was the most gripping. TR's mental state was such that he must take over the active leadership of the Republican majority or bequeath it his ghost. Compromise, the great constructive tactic of the past, was out, for to swing the nomination to a moderate progressive like Charles Evans Hughes or Governor Herbert S. Hadley of Missouri would be to relegate himself to political oblivion. "I'll name the compromise candidate," Roosevelt had expostulated just after his triumph in Ohio. "He'll be me. I'll name the compromise platform. It will be our platform."

Not even this consuming need to fulfill himself completely explains TR's absolute determination to fight to a finish, however; nor does his searing desire to destroy Taft. The fact is that Roosevelt and many of his friends were sincerely convinced that he was being robbed; that the National Committee, which found in favor of Taft with callous regularity from June 7 on, was positively dishonest. "Under the direction, and with the encouragement, of Mr. Taft," declared a statement the Colonel released on June 22, "the majority of the National Committee, by the so-called 'steamroller' methods, and with scandalous disregard of every principle of elementary honesty and decency stole eighty or ninety delegates. . . ."

In the face of those partial truths, the parallel between Taft's comportment in 1912 and Roosevelt's in 1904 loses some of its exactness. In both cases TR's engine was fired by the coals of public opinion; Hanna's in 1904 and Taft's in 1912 were sparked by the Republican machine and little else. Indeed, it was this vast preponderance of support from the man in the street—Roosevelt had polled 1,157,397 votes in the primaries to Taft's 761,716—that makes TR's cause at least as righteous as it was self-righteous. It was inconceivable that the Colonel, riding such a tidal wave of popular support, should have failed to invoke prematurely the forms of democracy which the wave bore along on its churning crest. "I have felt that we are fighting for a very high ideal," he wrote privately three days before the National Committee commenced its hearings. "The cause of our opponents has now become naked—the cause of the political bosses and of special privilege in the business world. It is the cause of corruption and of bad government. . . ."; or, as he phrased it in his statement of June 22, his opponents placed "on the temporary roll call a sufficient number of fraudulent delegates to defeat the legally expressed will of the people, and to substitute a dishonest for an honest majority."

The story of the Convention itself bears little retelling. There was the Colonel, his countenance wrought with indignation and determination, arriving in Chicago three days before the formal opening on the urgent entreaties of his angry, explosive lieutenants. "The issue is both simpler and larger than that involved in the personality of any man," he exclaimed to an overflow crowd of screaming supporters in the Chicago Auditorium the night before the Convention opened. "Tonight we come together to protest against a crime which strikes straight at the heart of every principle of political decency and honesty, a crime which represents treason to the people, and the usurpation of the sovereignty of the people by irresponsible political bosses, inspired by the sinister influences of moneyed privilege." "We fight in honest fashion for the good of mankind; . . . we stand at Armageddon, and we battle for the Lord."

There was the felt presence of Robert Marion La Follette, more dogmatic and neither less self-righteous nor egocentric than Theodore Roosevelt, spouting orders into the long-distance telephone at Washington. The Wisconsin progressive was willing to let Taft and the Old Guard win rather than throw his support to TR, so consuming was his hatred of his progressive adversary, and in a decision that probably cost Roosevelt the nomination, he refused to combine forces in support of a temporary chairman. Then, when some of his subordinates defied his wishes, he forthwith repudiated them. "This nomination is not with Senator La Follette's consent," a lieutenant dutifully announced. "We make no deals with Roosevelt. We make no trades with Taft." And thus, La Follette's biographers conclude, the Roosevelt forces were "robbed . . . of the psychological band-wagon advantage they had hoped to gain by uniting. . . . The convention knew that delegates instructed for La Follette would not go to Roosevelt on the ballot for President."

There was Elihu Root in morning coat and gray striped trousers, wielding the chairman's gavel and vainly calling for order following the defeat of TR's candidate for temporary chairman by 558 to 502 votes. As he had once served Roosevelt and the nation, and before and between them the great corporations, this eminent lawyer, whose principles were at once so high and so narrow, was now serving Taft and the Old Guard; or, so the Colonel phrased it, "the representatives of reaction." With heavy heart, for he had accepted the chairmanship only as "a difficult and embarrassing duty," Root fatefully ruled that delegates whose seats were in contest would be allowed to vote on all cases except their own. The ruling was consonant with traditional procedure.

There was the spectacle on and around the convention floor: the fist fights and near fist fights; the vitriolic cries of "liar," "swindler," "robber," and "thief"; the chants of "We Want Teddy" that swept

down from the galleries and set off a roaring forty-five-minute demonstration in the aisles; the imitation steamroller toots and whistles that
rent the air whenever the Taft forces offered a motion. There were
the flowery words and empty sentences of that pathetic pleaser of
crowds, Warren Gamaliel Harding of Ohio, whom Taft had selected
to place his name in nomination; and there was, finally, the grim
determination of the 344 Roosevelt delegates who refrained from voting on the Colonel's order and then marched out of the hall as it was
announced that the President had been renominated on the first ballot
with 561 votes.

There were also the scenes in the Colonel's suite in the Congress
Hotel, where TR and his advisers were gathered in council of war.
"We are frittering away our time," Hiram Johnson of California,
whose state had returned a 77,000 majority for Roosevelt only to
have Root rule in favor of the Taft slate, grimly asserted. "We are
frittering away our opportunity. And, what is worse, we are frittering
away Theodore Roosevelt." There was the Colonel himself silently
walking up and down the floor. Could he bolt from the party he had
led as President for seven and one-half years; could he form a new party
without financial support except from the grass roots? Of a sudden,
the decision was made for him. The millionaires Frank Munsey and
George Perkins, who had been bent over in earnest conversation in a
corner of the room, straightened up. "And with a decisive gesture
from Munsey, who seemed the more agitated of the two," wrote Amos
Pinchot, "both men . . . moved over to Roosevelt, meeting him in
the middle of the room. Each placed a hand on one of his shoulders
and one, or both of them, said, 'Colonel, we will see you through.'
At that precise moment the Progressive Party was born. . . ."

Finally, there was the climactic scene in Orchestra Hall on Saturday
night, June 22, where a near hysterical throng of Roosevelt men—the
344 delegates who had strode out of the convention, the scores upon
scores of delegates who had been refused their seats, and thousands
of alternates and spectators—met in rump convention. Shouting,
stamping, and singing, they interrupted the Colonel again and again
as he started the most historic of all his speeches by hissing "Thou
Shalt Not Steal" and ended it by declaring that he would make the
third-party fight "even if only one State should support me."

What is the historical verdict? Historians generally agree that
Roosevelt had been "robbed"; not of the seventy to a hundred dele-

gates he loosely claimed, but of about twenty-five. These would have been enough to control the convention and at least have created a deadlock. Probably the nomination would then have gone to Roosevelt. As Mowry points out, the Taft commitment of many delegates reflected the blandishments of their local machines rather than devotion to the President. Swept up by the moral fervor of the Roosevelt movement at Chicago, many had begun to weaken. Each day of the convention one or more went over to the Colonel; and had the voting gone beyond one ballot, many others must surely have done the same. Nor could Taft have held indefinitely his sixty Negro delegates. The product of the most insidious politics—they had actually sold out the interests of their own people—they were being subjected to heavy pressure by sophisticated Chicago Negro leaders to abandon the President who had largely reversed Roosevelt's moderately uplifting policies toward members of their race. And they were also, apparently, being offered cash bribes by the Roosevelt forces. It is doubtful that La Follette's forty-one delegates would have suffered the fetters he imposed upon them until the end of the convention had there been a deadlock. Devoted to La Follette though they were, they were not all as uncompromising and vindictive as their extraordinary leader.

If the approximately twenty-five "stolen" delegates would thus have enabled TR to win the convention, he could also have won it for a progressive other than himself or La Follette without them. In fact, some of the Taft leaders did offer to support Governor Hadley of Missouri as a compromise candidate. But Roosevelt angrily rejected their proposal. Had the Colonel remained at Oyster Bay he might have consented, though it is unlikely that his vanity would really have allowed it. On the scene at Chicago, in any event, he was caught up in the swirling adulation of his outraged followers and was blinded by the wrathful fervor of his own burning indignation. To have divested authority over this holy cause in a more ordinary man, to have compromised with the satanic forces who had defied the Eighth Commandment, would in TR's emotion ridden state have been to make hollow mockery of the tragic drama that was unfolding before his eyes. He was right when he ringingly affirmed before the rump convention on Saturday night that the cause was far nobler than any one man; and he was probably also right when he implied that he alone could lead it.

CHAPTER 27

ARMAGEDDON

> He had the hold of the hero. By his words and deeds he gave
> a defining and supporting frame for the aspirations of those
> insufficiently clear or strong to support their aspirations by their
> own endeavor. Men, in the hope of finding their better selves,
> attached themselves to him.
> —Elting E. Morison, *Turmoil and Tradition*

As Roosevelt knew it must, the Progressive party convention that met
seven weeks later in the same auditorium where the Republican steamroller had flattened the Eighth Commandment, was destined to prove
a failure of politics and a triumph of ideals. The practical politicians
upon whom success depended were notable for their absence. A few
came, including Flinn of Pennsylvania and Walter Brown of Ohio,
neither of whom had any other place to go. A handful of insurgent
Republicans led by Beveridge of Indiana, handsome, well groomed,
and confident as always of his intellectual prowess, also came. For
Beveridge, as for many of the others, the interim between the two
conventions had been a time of painful indecision. He had opposed
the formation of the new party and had refused to participate in the
rump convention in June for reasons of expediency. But now, out of
devotion to principle, not a small measure of vanity, and fealty to the
Colonel and their mutual friend Perkins, he prepared to deliver the
keynote address and serve as the temporary and permanent chairman.

Otherwise the signs were ominous. Of the seven governors who had
signed the round-robin call for TR to wage war against Taft seven
months before, only two were courageous or foolish enough to join

the Progressive party: Chase Osborn of Michigan and high-strung Hiram Johnson of California, who militantly agreed to become Roosevelt's running mate. Hadley of Missouri refused to come over, arguing that progressive control of his state could be achieved only through the Republican party; and so with most of the other governors. William E. Borah, took the same position; and the majority of progressive Republican senators and representatives in Congress did likewise though some, like Nebraska's Norris, escaped the decision by winning the endorsement of both the Republican and Progressive parties.

Roosevelt was understandably bitter. "What a miserable showing some of the so-called Progressive leaders have made," he grumbled. "They represent nothing but sound and fury . . . they have not the heart for a fight, and the minute they were up against deeds instead of words, they quit forthwith."

Yet the Colonel also had moments of understanding for some. "Nothing has touched me more than the willingness of men in whom I earnestly believe to leave their official positions and come out in this fight," he wrote a Department of Justice agent who offered to support him a few weeks before the convention convened. "But . . . I feel that the sacrifice ought not to be made unless the good that will be done outweighs the damage. . . . I do not feel that our cause is sufficiently bright to warrant me to have men like you and those . . . named [among them, Felix Frankfurter] come out for me. . . . Events shaped themselves so that I had no alternative except to lead, but I am under no illusion about it. It is a forlorn hope." Nevertheless, he was determined to sustain it. ". . . do not let it get beyond the men I have mentioned," he warned, "for even in a forlorn hope it does not do to let your soldiers think that their commander won't lead them to victory—although there are occasions when it is his highest duty to fight no matter how great the risk of defeat."

If the Colonel's army lacked regulars, it suffered nothing for volunteers. Rarely, and perhaps never, has a modern political convention contained such a concentration of substantial and dedicated citizens, of men and women so fervently devoted to cause and leader alike, as now closed ranks at Chicago. "Here were the successful middle-class country-town citizens," wrote William Allen White, "the farmer whose barn was painted, the well-paid railroad engineer, and the country editor."

It was a well dressed crowd. We were, of course, for woman suffrage, and we invited women delegates and had plenty of them. They were our own kind, too—women doctors, women lawyers, women teachers, college professors, middle-aged leaders of civic movements, or rich young girls who had gone in for settlement work. Looking over the crowd, judging the delegates by their clothes, I figured that there was not a man or woman on the floor who was making less than two thousand a year, and not one, on the other hand, who was topping ten thousand. Proletarian and plutocrat were absent—except George Perkins. . . .

. . . On the speaker's stand, we had notables from all over the land: college presidents, heads of scientific foundations. Our prize exhibit was Jane Addams. . . . When she came down the aisle back of the speaker's stand where the other notables wearing Bull Moose badges were arrayed in proud and serried ranks, the delegates and the scattered spectators in the galleries rose and cheered. Not even the Colonel got much more rousing cheers than Jane Addams, when she rose to second his nomination.

Why had they come? Some, obviously, to tie their kites to Roosevelt: the cynical, flint-faced underlings of Flinn and his like; men of vast materialistic design and little if any moral purpose. Their numbers were not great, but they were large enough to be embarrassing. The true fanatics were also there, come to this convention as to the great protest assemblages of the past to indulge in an orgy of political emotionalism. Later Roosevelt would ungraciously designate them "the lunatic fringe."

But what of the convention's real leaders, the middle-class respectables White so graphically describes? One of the most provocative analyses, that of Richard Hofstadter, is that they were animated by personal resentment over their loss of general status to the new elite—the coarse, crude, compassionless men of business and finance who surged to the top on the mighty convulsions of the industrial revolution; the crass materialists whom Roosevelt and the Adams brothers so feared and deplored; the vulgar new leaders whose ostentatious mansions had become the focal points of the new high society in the great urban centers and summer resorts of the nation; the amoral men of power whose puissant wealth, so Roosevelt had charged, had bought off the editors, the lawyers, and the college professors; the *nouveaux riches* whose bulldozing tactics were reducing to an ant heap the once mountainous influence of the people of long-established, but by the new standards, relatively modest means.

What was more natural than that the younger members of these submerged genteel families should emerge as the secondary leaders of the Progressive movement? They had the time, the money, and the political habit in a local, dilettantish way. Their grandfathers and their fathers had been abolitionists, mugwumps, and civil service reformers. They themselves were active in civic affairs, their declining power notwithstanding. Moreover, they now realized, if only because of the widespread rise of prices which was attributed to the trusts, that they themselves stood in the lengthening shadow of the concentration of power and wealth in the hands of the new barbarians.

Unquestionably, as Hofstadter emphasizes, resentment born of their declining status contributed to their reform impulses. Undeniably, vanity, ambition, and other worldly considerations figured large in their acceptance of Roosevelt's commissions. Cut off from service in the Democratic party by the rise of the recent immigrants under the rampant big-city bosses, frustrated by the spokesmen of the men of new wealth in their desire to exert influence within Republican councils, they inevitably gravitated to Roosevelt. With him they could bask in the prominence and assert the authority they deemed their rightful inheritance; with him they could curb the plutocrats' power and recapture in part their own lost status.

Yet, as other studies and much internal evidence indicate, they could also strive for fulfillment of the rational ideas and humanitarian ideals to which as working intellectuals or men of reflective leisure they had long been attached.

Assuredly, the striking aspect of the program the Progressives met at Chicago to adopt was its high intellectual and broad humanitarian tone. Their platform contained a full measure of angry indictments, sweeping generalizations, and partisan distortions. But it also embodied a constructive distillation of the current social wisdom—a wisdom that derived from the decade and more of analysis of American society by the muckrakers, by economists and historians, by the new psychologists and sociologists, and by all those investigatory commissions that Roosevelt as President had appointed. For all that platform's naïvetés, including the colossal one of the recall of judicial decisions, it comprised a blueprint for a more humane, enlightened, and constructive America. It is hardly an accident that virtually all of its planks have since been written into law.

Nor is it less remarkable that the Progressive party should have attracted the type of people it did, given man's capacity for compassion, his compulsion for order, and his urge both to conserve and create. Roosevelt expected to receive, and he did broadly receive, the support of college professors and presidents the nation over (it was, happily, an era when intellectual attainment was a requisite for the latter position) because his program offered them an opportunity to implement theories that their minds had long nurtured and cultivated. And so with Pinchot's scientific management conservationists, those scientists and gentlemen who had been at once a cause and an effect of the Progressive movement. It would have been remarkable had they not followed their unfailing patron into a party which offered them complete freedom to write its conservation plank. Nor was it much different with Jane Addams and all those other well-born women social workers who had become reformers out of resentment against man's inhumanity to man. Aggrieved though they were by the Colonel's militant preparedness views, they saw in the planks calling for minimum wages for women and the national abolition of child labor the fruition of much of their life's labors. The same may be said for the clergy who joined the crusade in liberal numbers in spite of Woodrow Wilson's powerful pull. Theodore Roosevelt, the greatest preacher and the most strident moralist of them all, was offering nothing less than an opportunity to write the preachments of the Social Gospel movement into the political law.

Nevertheless, there were profound differences in viewpoint, especially toward the trusts. As Alfred D. Chandler, Jr. has shown in an investigation that probes beneath William Allen White's graphic generalizations, the vast majority of Progressive party leaders were upper-class Protestants of urban background, and a substantial portion of them were moderate-to-big businessmen. This was notably true of the Easterners. They followed Roosevelt because they believed his regulatory program offered a means of curbing the corporations' abuses while yet preserving the economic beneficences of the corporate structure; they opposed La Follette because he and his agrarian-minded followers, the bulk of whom nevertheless swung in behind Roosevelt, continued to adhere to the atomistic philosophy of the Sherman Law.

If great numbers of Progressive leaders were thus men of creative moral vision and social respectability, they were nonetheless emotional for it. At Chicago, where TR arrived the night before the convention opened on August 5 exuberantly exclaiming that he felt "as strong as a bull moose," their impassioned outcries soared to the rafters and thence across the land. At the slightest provocation, and sometimes with no provocation at all, ten thousand and more voices poured out the soul-stirring cadences of those great martial hymns, "Onward Christian Soldiers" and "The Battle Hymn of the Republic." Again and again thousands of delegates, alternates, and alternates' alternates who had come at their own expense cheered, waved, and stamped as a succession of speakers affirmed the exaltation of their cause.

"We stand for a nobler America," thundered the emotion-wrought Beveridge (listening to Beveridge rehearse the keynote address in his room the night before, George Perkins is said to have broken into a sob and left the room with tears coursing down his cheeks). We know "the price we must pay, the sacrifice we must make, the burdens we must carry . . . yet we enlist and we enlist for the war. For we know the justice of our cause, and we know, too, its certain triumph."

The climax came on the afternoon of the second day when Roosevelt himself appeared before the convention. He had come, he afterward wrote, to say the things that were "deepest" in his heart, and he had entitled his address his "Confession of Faith." Mowry describes the scene.

> As he stood on the platform in the old familiar attitude, his body swaying with delight, his left hand in his pocket and his right vigorously waving a reply, fifteen thousand people roared their welcome. For fifty-two minutes, wildly waving red bandannas, they cheered him as they had never cheered anyone else. Here were no claques, no artificial demonstration sustained by artificial devices. . . . Men and women simply stood on their feet for an hour to welcome a man because they liked him and believed in him. When Roosevelt himself finally sought to stop the demonstration, the crowd once more broke into song:
>
> Thou wilt not cower in the dust,
> Roosevelt, O Roosevelt!
> Thy gleaming sword shall never rust,
> Roosevelt, O Roosevelt.

At long last the singing stopped and Roosevelt prepared to speak. A newspaperman observed that he seemed bewildered, unable to understand the temper of his audience. "They were crusaders; he was not," the reporter wrote. Yet Roosevelt the politician knew what the amateurs who filled the Coliseum did not know or could not admit if they did know—the failure of progressive Republican politicians to join the Progressive party on the state level had foredoomed him and the party to disaster even before the convention had begun. And because of that knowledge, Roosevelt at that moment and for the three months that followed was more truly a crusader than he had ever before been. "Now, friends," he exclaimed at the end of a speech that the Wilson scholar, Arthur S. Link, terms a classic synthesis of the most advanced progressive thought of the times, "this is my confession of faith." ". . . I hope we shall win. . . . But win, or lose, we shall not falter. . . . Our cause is based on the eternal principle of righteousness; and even though we who now lead may for the time fail, in the end the cause itself shall triumph. . . . We stand at Armageddon, and we battle for the Lord."

Yet the ways of the Lord are sometimes mysterious. Even before this most religious-like convention in American political history was ended, Roosevelt's handling of the trust question had sown seeds of doubt in the minds of a great body of the faithful.

Reflecting their agrarian frame of reference, the radical, or as Mowry designates them, reactionary, Midwestern Progressives and a sprinkling of Easterners insisted that the party platform call for a strengthening of the Sherman Law. The day after Roosevelt's address the Committee on Resolutions framed a plank to that effect. The platform was then sent up to Roosevelt's rooms where George Perkins, who served as TR's chief aide throughout the convention and campaign, persuaded the Colonel to delete it.

The next day Perkins sat confidently in the Coliseum as Dean William Draper Lewis of the University of Pennsylvania Law School read the platform to the convention. Suddenly Perkins started. Lewis was apparently reading the antitrust plank as originally approved by the Committee on Resolutions. "That does not belong in the platform," Perkins shouted to Amos Pinchot, according to one account. "We cut it out last night." Thereupon he rushed out of the auditorium.

Perkins later prevailed on Roosevelt to direct the party's secretary to delete the plank; and as printed and distributed the Progressive party platform neither endorsed nor called for the strengthening of the Sherman Antitrust Act. The radicals' distrust of Perkins, whom they believed only to be protecting his vast holdings in the United States Steel Corporation and the International Harvester Company, was thus confirmed. "Perkins . . . smiling and simpering in triumph like a sinister specter—in his gray alpaca suit to match the slightly sprinkled gray of his brown hair and gray mustache, and . . . steel-gray heart . . . was not one of us," William Allen White wrote. He "misunderstood" Roosevelt. White's characterization, accepted by virtually all the Midwestern Progressive leaders and written thence into the history books, is a palpable injustice to Perkins as Garraty's recent biography proves. It is also a misreading of Roosevelt himself, one that blithely ignores the long evolution of TR's views on the trusts as well as the categorical denunciation of the Sherman Act philosophy in his address accepting the Bull Moose charge.

"Half of . . . [the Progressives] are really representative of a kind of rural toryism, which wishes to attempt the impossible task of returning to the economic conditions that obtained sixty years ago," Roosevelt had angrily written of the Sherman Act proponents just the summer before. "The other half wishes to go forward along the proper lines, that is, to recognize the inevitableness and the necessity of combinations in business, and meet it by a corresponding increase in governmental power over big business; but at the same time these real progressives are hampered by being obliged continually to pay lip loyalty to their colleagues, who, at bottom, are not progressive at all, but retrogressive."

Many Progressives were also pained by Roosevelt's handling of the party's relations with Southern Negroes. Partly to win the Northern Negro vote, and partly because of their militantly humanitarian sentiments, Progressive leaders had encouraged Northern Negroes to come into the Progressive fold; and when the convention convened at Chicago the delegates' ranks were studded with Negroes—mute testimony to their faith in Roosevelt, Brownsville notwithstanding. Large numbers of Negroes had also sought to join the party in the South, where they were not welcomed. The result was that three Southern states sent contesting delegations, mixed and all white, to Chicago. Their leaders appealed to Roosevelt in advance, and on August 1 he announced his decision in a moving letter to Julian L. Harris, son of the author of *Uncle Remus*.

Observing that the Republican party in the South "exists only to serve the purposes of a small group of politicians, for the most part white, but including some colored men, who have not the slightest interest in elections," Roosevelt contended that a similar fate would befall the Progressive party should it appeal "to the Negroes or to the men who in the past have derived their sole standing from leading and manipulating the Negroes."

I earnestly believe that by appealing to the best white men in the South, the men of justice and of vision as well as of strength and of leadership, and by frankly putting the movement in their hands from the outset we shall create a situation by which the colored men of the South will ultimately get justice as it is not possible for them to get justice if we are to continue and perpetuate the present conditions.

That decision plagued TR for the duration of the campaign. The majority of Northern Negro delegates swallowed hard and stayed on; but a small number angrily walked out of the party—a few into the arms of Woodrow Wilson, who was to treat them worse, and most into those of Taft, who already had done so. The Colonel was hurt, especially when Booker T. Washington came out for Taft; nevertheless, he resolutely adhered to the policy.

Meanwhile, TR girded himself for battle with his principal adversary—Governor Woodrow Wilson of New Jersey. Roosevelt and his followers had hoped that the bibulous Champ Clark of Missouri would be the Democratic nominee; and their depression ran deep when Wilson won a grueling contest on the forty-sixth ballot at Baltimore the week after they had stormed hopefully out of the Republican convention in Chicago.

Wilson and Roosevelt had once been cordial, if not intimate, friends, "Woodrow Wilson is a perfect trump," TR had written in 1902 when Wilson was named president of Princeton University; and Wilson had reciprocated. Gradually, however, their friendship weakened, for Wilson strongly disapproved Roosevelt's strident nationalism. He also became disenchanted with TR's personality, and in November, 1907, gave out an interview, which he afterward partially disavowed:

I have not seen much of Mr. Roosevelt since he became President, but I am told that he no sooner thinks than he talks, which is a miracle not wholly in accord with the educational theory of forming an opinion.

As Governor of New Jersey in 1911, however, Wilson had won national recognition by his masterful imposition of a formidable body of progressive legislation upon a divided legislature; and that accomplishment, together with his conservative mien and commanding eloquence, made him the strongest nominee the Democrats could have named. The day after he was nominated, Governor Osborn, one of the two of the original seven governors who finally voted for TR, had spread consternation through the Colonel's ranks by publicly declaring that there was now "no necessity for a new party" and urging Roosevelt not to run. Praising Wilson as "a christian, [*sic*] a scholar and a fearless citizen," the Michigan Governor added that Wilson was "not owned by anybody" and would "lead the people against the financial overlords in orderly but earnest fashion."

In spite of TR's realization that he could not win and that the party he was founding could not survive—"I would have had a sporting chance if the Democrats had put up a reactionary candidate," he lamented to Sir Horace Plunkett on the eve of the Bull Moose convention—the Colonel remained adamant. His prejudices against the Democrats were too deep, his desire to destroy Taft too consuming, his conviction too compelling, and his urge for leadership too irresistible. He replied to Osborn, who had meanwhile written that "Woodrow Wilson represents . . . what you represent," that Wilson's election would result in a resurgence of the Democratic bosses and that two-thirds of his own supporters would go to Taft if he withdrew. And though he admitted to Plunkett that Wilson "is an able man . . . and would not show Taft's muddle-headed inability to understand," he deplored the fact that he was not "a Nationalist." Indeed, Roosevelt continued with considerable accuracy, until Wilson was fifty years old "he advocated with skill, intelligence and good breeding the outworn doctrines which are responsible for four-fifths of the political troubles of the United States." Then, as governor, he "turned an absolute somersault so far as at least half of these doctrines was concerned."

Perhaps the most significant feature of the campaign that ensued that summer and fall was the modification Roosevelt induced in the "other half" of Wilson's doctrines—and also the partial retreat the New Jersey Governor, who was counseled by that great people's attorney, Louis D. Brandeis, forced the Colonel to make. Writing off Taft as undeserving of serious debate, TR charged Wilson with "rural toryism"; he argued that his proposal to resolve the trust problem by breaking up the giant corporations was anachronistic; and he exaggeratedly contended that Wilson's low-tariff views, which he interpreted as embracing free trade, would destroy the American workingman. But he hammered most forcefully at Wilson's reluctance to countenance big government. "Mr. Wilson is fond of asserting his platonic devotion to the purposes of the Progressive party," TR declared at San Francisco on September 14. But, he continued, Wilson also holds that " 'The history of liberty is a history of the limitation of governmental power, not the increase of it.' " He then asked how his opponent could square that view with the Progressive proposals for workmen's compensation, the limitation of the hours of labor, regulation of work conditions in factories, control of railroads and the trusts, and all the rest. "We propose to use the whole power of the government to protect all those who, under Mr. Wilson's laissez-faire system, are trodden down in the ferocious, scrambling rush of an unregulated and purely individualistic industrialism," Roosevelt concluded.

Actually, as John Wells Davidson's work on Wilson shows, TR had inadvertently quoted Wilson out of context. The "history of liberty" remark, made in New York on September 16, had been preceded by a qualifying paragraph which the newspapers had failed to reproduce. Nevertheless, Wilson and Roosevelt were still separated by a tremendous gulf. Wilson sought to bridge it, for he was wounded by Roosevelt's hammering. The first break came in a speech at Scranton in early October, "I realize that while we are followers of Jefferson," Wilson asserted, "there is one principle of Jefferson's which no longer can obtain in the practical politics of America."

> You know that it was Jefferson who said that the best government is that which does as little governing as possible. . . . That was said in a day when the opportunities of America were so obvious . . . that all that was necessary was that the government should withhold its hand and see to it that every man got an opportunity to act if he would. But that time is past. America is not now, and cannot in the future be, a place for unrestricted individual enterprise.

Wilson also focused increasingly on social justice as the campaign progressed. He refused to endorse the Progressives' demand for a minimum wage law for women, arguing that it would drive the general wage level down to the minimum. Nor did he come out for a national child labor law as Roosevelt and his party advocated. By the end of the campaign, however, he had several times endorsed the Progressive party's broad social objectives. "I want to say here, as I have said on so many other occasions," the Democratic candidate declared in Minneapolis, "that there is a great deal in the program of the new third party which attracts all public-spirited and hopeful men, that there is a great program of human uplift included in the platform of that party."

Meanwhile Wilson maintained a relentless fire on Roosevelt's proposal to place trust regulation under a commission of experts without specifying in law the abuses to be regulated. Under Wilson's harassment and the concurrent complaints of the radical Progressives, the Colonel finally submitted. In mid-October he issued a statement that virtually reaffirmed the antitrust plank Perkins had struck out of the platform in the backstage episode at Chicago.

> If, for instance, a corporation should be found crushing out competition by refusing to sell when the patron bought off competitors, or by underselling in districts, or in the dozen of other ways that Congress should learn were being practised and should say were illegal, I would have the statute say point blank, with no loophole for escape, that the corporation was guilty.

Roosevelt's statement had been issued from a hospital bed in Chicago where, surrounded by his wife and younger children, he lay recuperating from a bullet wound. On October 14, in Milwaukee, as he stepped into his car, he had been shot by a fanatic. The bullet went through the former President's overcoat, spectacles case, and folded manuscript, fracturing his fourth rib and lodging a little short of his right lung. Stunned, TR had fallen backward momentarily, coughed, and then stood up again. "Stand back. Don't hurt the man," he shouted at the crowd. Then, over the protests of attending physicians, he had insisted that he be driven to the auditorium, where he was scheduled to deliver an address.

"Friends," he exclaimed to the crowd that sat rigid before him five minutes later, "I shall ask you to be as quiet as possible. I don't know whether you fully understand that I have just been shot; but it takes more than that to kill a Bull Moose. . . . I had my manuscript—and there is a bullet—there is where the bullet went through . . . and it probably saved me from it going into my heart. The bullet is in me now. . . . And now, friends . . . I want you to understand that I am ahead of the game, anyway. No man has had a happier life than I have led. . . . I cannot understand a man fit to be a colonel who can pay any heed to his personal safety. . . . Friends, I am thinking of the movement. . . . He shot to kill. He shot—the shot, the bullet went in here—I will show you. . . . Now, friends, I am not speaking for myself at all. I give you my word, I do not care a rap about being shot; not a rap. . . . Now, friends—[speaking to someone on the stage], I am not sick at all. I am all right. . . . Now friends, what we Progressives are trying to do is to enroll rich or poor . . . to stand together for the most elementary rights of good citizenship. . . . My friends are a little more nervous than I am. Don't you waste any sympathy on me. I have had an A-1 time in life and I am having it now. . . ."

Of a sudden TR seemed to forget all about his wound. "At one time I promoted five men for gallantry . . . two of them were Protestants, two Catholics, and one a Jew. . . . If all five of them had been Jews I would have promoted them. . . ." He continued, moving now into the theme of his prepared address. "I make the same appeal in our citizenship." ". . . It is essential that there should be organizations of labor. This is an era of organization. Capital organizes and therefore labor must organize." Roosevelt then called for capital to treat labor fairly and for labor to repudiate crime and violence. Finally, he struck at his principal opponent. "I know these doctors, when they get hold of me, will never let me go back, and there are just a few things more that I want to say to you," TR declared. "Mr. Wilson has distinctly committed . . . [himself] to the old flintlock, muzzle-loaded doctrine of States' rights. . . . We are for the people's rights. If they can be obtained best through the National Government, then we are for national rights." ". . . Mr. Wilson has distinctly declared that you shall not have a national law to prohibit the labor of children. . . . I ask you to look at our declaration and hear and read our platform about social and industrial justice and then, friends, vote for the Progressive ticket without regard to me. . . ."

The Colonel had spoken for almost an hour. Yet, as Pringle writes, "Men did not judge . . . [his performance] histrionic or childish." Such was Theodore Roosevelt's uniqueness.

The election returns a few weeks later confirmed Roosevelt's fears.

Wilson won in a landslide with 435 electoral votes. He failed, however, to win a popular majority, receiving 6,286,124 votes to Roosevelt's 4,126,020 and Taft's 3,483,922. And although one embittered Socialist pointed out that "the new party, which goes boldly forth to its first campaign with the inscription on its banners, 'Thou Shalt Not Steal!' begins its career with the brazen theft of half the working program of the Socialist party," Eugene V. Debs polled close to a million votes. It was a remarkable demonstration of the left wing's distrust of the three major candidates, their parties, and their programs. On the other hand, the Democrats captured both houses of Congress and numerous governorships while the Progressives won but a scattering of congressional seats and elected only one governor.

Roosevelt ran best in the urban areas—he swept Pennsylvania, Michigan, California, and three smaller states—and he fared poorer than expected in the West. His ringing defenses of his conservation policies antagonized anticonservationist Westerners, and great numbers of them reportedly voted Democratic in order to spite him. More significant still, he failed to win over the Democratic and independent progressives; party loyalty, Wilson's eloquence, and the lingering belief that the Colonel was a trimmer all worked against him. As the reformer Anna Howard Shaw wrote Jane Addams shortly after the Progressive convention, "I wish I could believe . . . [TR] intended to do a single honest thing, or that he would carry out a single plank in the platform if he were elected . . . I cannot." That statement mirrored the views of thousands of nonpolitical reformers who never understood the constructive compromises of Roosevelt's presidency.

The crusade, nevertheless, had not been in vain. Roosevelt's vigorous and explicit statement of the case for social justice had sharpened the mounting offensive against privilege and exploitation. And just as importantly, it had forced Wilson and many of the leaders of his party to face the paradox inherent in their commitment to both national reform and the philosophy of states' rights.

Theodore Roosevelt's personal services to the great movement that was the signal feature of the era that bears his name virtually ended with the Bull Moose campaign. Within the following four years the Democratic party under Woodrow Wilson would write the burden of the Bull Moose party's planks into law, and Roosevelt himself would go into temporary eclipse. He would come out of it near the end of Wilson's first administration to perform one last memorable service and some disservice to the country he loved.

PART VI

ONE LAST GREAT CAUSE

CHAPTER 28

THE VARIETY OF HIM—

> . . . the vitality of him, the charm, the humor, the intellectual
> avidity, the love of people, the flaming devotion to his country.
>
> —Hermann Hagedorn

Although its leader would return at the head of another great command, the Progressive party itself was doomed to die. Its fate had been sealed in the summer of its birth by the failure of Republican office-holders to support it; and with all his personal magnetism, Theodore Roosevelt had not the power to sustain it indefinitely. The real questions were how long the death rattle would last, and whether the Great Bull Moose would make a final ferocious lunge before it rolled over and died. The answers lay in Roosevelt's personality, the metamorphosis of Woodrow Wilson and the Democratic party, and in the coming of World War I.

The Colonel's first inclination was to drift with the tide of events. He considered himself finished as a politician and early in 1913 he plunged into the writing of his autobiography. Yet he was under heavy obligations to those more than four million Americans who had affirmed their faith at the polls, and especially to those thousands of nonprofessionals who had cut loose from the Grand Old Party to serve under his banner. Great hosts of these still believed that the party could eventually supplant the G.O.P.; a sizable number were determined to see that it did. Their leader felt duty bound to go along with them, at least until the Congressional elections of 1914 clearly exposed the party's fatal weakness.

The first order of business was to suppress a movement by Gifford

Pinchot and the Western radicals to deprive George Perkins of his influence in party councils. Ascribing the movement to "baseless prejudice," Roosevelt emphatically refused to "throw to the wolves one of the staunchest allies and supporters we have had. . . ." The radicals thereupon submitted, although they won from both Roosevelt and Perkins the right to include a plank favoring the strengthening of the Sherman Antitrust Act in the platform they adopted at their Chicago meeting a month following the election. The Colonel himself attended the Chicago meeting, and on December 10 reaffirmed the Progressive creed in a typically fervent speech before fifteen hundred delegates. From then until the 1914 congressional elections, moreover, he repeatedly declared that the party was permanent. "We believe that there are literally millions of progressives now associated with the Democratic and Republican parties who agree with our principles," he wrote a group of leading Minnesota Progressives in January, 1913. "There shall be no retreat from the position we have taken. High of heart and strong of hand, we front the future; and the future is surely ours."

Yet Roosevelt scarcely believed his own words as he uttered them. "I regret to add that I agree with your forecast," he replied to a pessimistic letter from Hiram Johnson in January, 1913. "Our chance depends upon there being a break in the Democratic party . . . [Wilson] showed his adroitness during the campaign, and he may well be able to show similar adroitness during the next four years in the Presidency, and with the same result."

> Well, my dear Governor, if these views are correct, the chances of immediate victory or at least of victory obtained under my leadership, are not great. . . . In any event I do believe that great good has come from the fight we have made, and that the principles for which we stand have made and will make real progress.

But it was not in the Colonel's nature to withdraw permanently from the surging stream of events. When the lower Mississippi Valley was again inundated by flood waters in the winter of 1913, he reiterated his demand for multipurpose development of the entire watershed. It was "criminally wasteful" for the "richest nation on earth" to "hesitate or haggle" over adoption of such a program, he angrily wrote John M. Parker, the Progressive leader of Louisiana. There must be a "national effort to turn floods into power, arid regions into gardens, and marshes into farms" through a single enabling act of Congress, "establishing a policy and providing continuing funds, exactly as was done in the case of the Panama Canal."

Meanwhile TR commented on the issues of the day through the columns of the *Outlook*. He contributed to the settlement in the workers' interest of a major garment strike in New York. And in line with his belief that the traditional method of revising the tariff was outmoded, he encouraged the little band of Progressives in Congress to foster a tariff commission, which proposal Wilson finally accepted in 1916. Conversely Roosevelt failed to acknowledge the magnitude of the President's achievement in forcing through Congress the first significant downward revision of the tariff since before the Civil War. And though TR came out for repeal of the exemption of Panama Canal tolls granted American coastwise shipping in violation of the treaty of 1900 with Great Britain, he said nothing after Wilson took up the matter.

But in the main, TR devoted himself to the pleasures of life at Sagamore—to walks with his wife, to whom he was even closer in his middle age than he had been in his youth; to letters to Quentin and Archie at Groton and Harvard, to Kermit in Brazil, where he was employed as an engineer; and to Ted, a successful businessman in California and father of the Colonel's first grandchild ("the very dearest baby you ever saw," said TR); to luncheons with that great host of politicians, scientists, and men of letters who poured ceaselessly into Oyster Bay or the *Outlook* offices; and to the preparation of speeches, articles, and books.

On December 27, 1912, seven weeks after the Bull Moose Campaign became history, Roosevelt appeared in Boston to deliver the presidential address to the American Historical Association. "I am to deliver a beastly lecture—'History as Literature'—" he confided to Lodge. He added that none of the Association's members "believe that history is literature" but that he had spent "much care" on the address even so. He did not spare the disbelievers, whom he had long ago characterized to Trevelyan as the "small men who do most of the teaching," when he confronted them.

Roosevelt's own poetic strain was too strong and his potential as a stylist too powerful for him to have approved the dryness of much of the new historical writing—itself a reflection, ironically, of that scientific spirit with which he was otherwise so imbued. Inevitably, he overstated the case for literary excellence, though with such lyric force as almost to win it. He understood, assuredly, the importance of the monograph, if not of economic analysis. And he paid formal deference at the outset of his address to the men who wrote them. "I pay high honor to the patient and truthful investigator," he said. "He does an indispensable work." But he wanted more, far more than most men could give. What was needed was "the great master who can use the materials gathered, who has the gift of vision, the quality of the seer, the power himself to see what has happened and to make what he has seen clear to the vision of others." His protest, Roosevelt explained, was against those "who believe that the extension of the activities of the most competent mason and most energetic contractor will supply the lack of great architects." The distinguished historian of the future must have vision and imagination, the power to grasp the essentials and reject the nonessentials, the "power to embody ghosts, to put flesh and blood on dry bones, to make dead men living before our eyes." He must, the author of *The Winning of the West* declaimed, "have the power to take the science of history and turn it into literature."

Then, in passages as revealing of his ultimate affirmation of human kind as any he ever wrote, he called both for deeper understanding and firmer moral judgment. "Side by side with the need for the perfection of the individual in the technic of his special calling," Roosevelt said, "goes the need of broad human sympathy, and the need of lofty and generous emotion in the individual." The great historian must perforce be a great moralist. "It is no proof of impartiality to treat wickedness and goodness as on the same level." Agreed, there were dangers. It was wrong, for example, to allow abstract principles to intrude upon facts as Carlyle had done in his *Frederick the Great*. Nevertheless, Roosevelt warned, when great events lack a great historian the poet will fix them in the minds of men. Shakespeare had so fixed the character of Richard III; and it is the lines of Keats, who had even forgotten Balboa's correct name, "which leap to our minds when we think of the 'wild surmise' felt by the indomitable explorer-conqueror from Spain when the vast new sea burst on his vision."

Warning his fellow historians that the revolt against the spectacular and the exceptional, against war, oratory, and politics, had gone too far, Roosevelt declared that "there are hours so fraught with weighty achievement, with triumph or defeat, with joy or sorrow, that each such hour may determine all . . . that are to come thereafter." Then, in a Churchillian peroration that rings down through the years, he challenged his listeners to re-create the truly epochal movements of the past. "Some day," he concluded, "the historians . . . will portray the conquest of the continent. . . . They will show how the land which the pioneers won slowly and with incredible hardship was filled in two generations by the overflow from the countries of western and central Europe. The portentous growth of the cities will be shown, and the change from a nation of farmers to a nation of business men and artisans. . . . The formation of a new ethnic type in this melting-pot of nations will be told. The hard materialism of our age will appear, and also the strange capacity for lofty idealism which must be reckoned with by all who would understand the American character. . . ."

In February, 1913, Roosevelt's autobiography began to appear in the *Outlook* in serial form. Like all autobiographies it justified its subject's career, and like most autobiographies it was marked by grievous omissions. Its literary quality was uneven, though some sections were superbly written, and its point of view was that of the Progressive rather than the Republican Roosevelt. But for all of that, it was and is the most illuminating autobiography ever written by a former President and probably by any major American political leader.

At odd hours into the late spring of 1913 TR also wrote his part of *Life Histories of African Game Animals,* a two-volume work done in collaboration with the naturalist Edmund Heller. Published in 1914 under Roosevelt and Heller's name (TR had offered to list the naturalist's name first), it was commended by the *Bulletin of the American Geographic Society* as "a very valuable contribution both to geography and zoology," and by C. Hart Merriam as "far and away the best book ever written on the big-game animals of any part of the world."

Meanwhile Ethel was married to Richard Derby in the little Episcopal church in Oyster Bay where the family worshiped. The guest list reflected the shattering political upheaval of the previous year; also Roosevelt's conviction that he had been cheated out of the Republican nomination. Cabot Lodge was invited, but he lacked congenial company. "We did not send invitations to Root or Taft or Nicholas Murray Butler . . ." TR explained to Winthrop Chanler, "because they would have been just as unwelcome guests as Barnes or Penrose or Guggenheim." "Root took part in as downright a bit of theft and swindling as ever was perpetrated by any Tammany ballot box stuffer, and I shall never forgive the men who were the leaders in that swindling."

In late May the Colonel pressed a libel suit against an obscure Michigan editor who had written during the campaign of 1912 that "Roosevelt lies and curses in a most disgusting way; he gets drunk too, and that not infrequently, and all of his intimates know about it." Determined, as he phrased it, "to expose the infamy of these slanders," the Colonel easily won the suit. The editor failed to produce a single witness to confirm his assertions, though in actual fact TR was given to mild profanity when excited, and Roosevelt produced a host of depositions to disprove them. At TR's request, damages were set at six cents.

It was in the spring of 1913, also, that Roosevelt made a memorable sally into art criticism. He had never been as sensitive to the fine arts as to literature and history. Yet his curiosity was so avid and his belief in the ennobling force of aesthetics so firm that he was unfailingly responsive. He considered the Gothic cathedrals of Western Europe "the most magnificent architecture that our race has ever been able to produce," though he also liked the Greek temples, and he admired Raphael, Michelangelo, and Rembrandt among the painters. His favorite contemporary sculptor was Saint-Gaudens. As President, in fact, Roosevelt had directed the United States Mint to employ Saint-Gaudens to design coins. Then, when the sculptor decided for artistic reasons to omit the phrase "In God We Trust" from the new coins, Roosevelt had supported him in the face of a popular outcry. Roosevelt had also appointed a Fine Arts Council of distinguished architects, painters, and sculptors to advise the government on the design and placement of public buildings. ("I am going to do what these men want, Gifford; it is a move for civilization; it is the right thing to do," he said to Pinchot at the time. "It is a great deal better than appointing third-class postmasters.") Before the council was disbanded under Taft at the behest of pork-barrel congressmen and commercial interests, an enlightened plan for the preservation and development of the Mall was adopted. The result, a former member of the Council wrote in the *American Architect* the year after TR's death, was "an epoch" in our history. Theodore Roosevelt's administrations marked the first real case "of Executive appreciation of the Fine Arts" since John Quincy Adams.

On March 27, 1913, after viewing the historic international exhibition of modern art at the Sixty-ninth Regiment Armory, Roosevelt described his impressions for the *Outlook* under the title, "A Layman's View of an Art Exhibition." Unabashedly, the former President compared the Cubists and the Futurists or Near-Impressionists to the "lunatic fringe" of the progressive movement in one passage and to the "later work of the paleolithic artists of the French and Spanish caves" in the next. And he took particular exception to a Duchamp which "for some reason is called 'A Naked Man Going Down Stairs,'" [*sic*] but could just as fittingly have been called "'A Well-Dressed Man Going Up a Ladder.'" Yet he perceived, even as he failed wholly to understand; his appreciation of the exhibition's raging creativity was far in advance of some of the best professional opinion of the times. "It is vitally necessary to move forward and to shake off the dead hand, often the fossilized dead hand, of the reactionaries," Roosevelt wrote. The necessary penalty of creativity "is a liability to extravagance."

There was one note entirely absent . . . and that was the note of the commonplace. There was not a touch of simpering, self-satisfied conventionality anywhere in the exhibition. Any sculptor or painter who had in him something to express and the power of expressing it found the field open to him. . . . There was no stunting or dwarfing, no requirement that a man whose gift lay in new directions should measure up or down to stereotyped and fossilized standards.

And so with TR's understanding of literature. It is true that he allowed the moral and political conventions of the times to delimit his appreciation—that he failed in part to come into rapport with the naturalistic novelists whose rise roughly paralleled his own because they described the "unspeakable" or because he found their deterministic philosophy indigestible. As he explained to the minor novelists Owen Wister and Winston Churchill, Mrs. Roosevelt could evaluate literary works purely on their aesthetic quality, but he could not. "I am old-fashioned, or sentimental, or something, about books!" he admitted. "Whenever I read one I want, in the first place, to enjoy myself, and, in the next place, to feel that I am a little better and not a little worse for having read it." TR believed with Bernard

Shaw that comedy is more realistic than tragedy, and he more than once advised Wister, perhaps with deleterious effect, and other of his novelist friends to "Let in some sunlight, somehow . . . life, after all, does—go—on."

The result was a string of social, moral, and political pronouncements that have sadly compromised Roosevelt's reputation in academic circles. Henry James was "a miserable little snob" for abandoning his native land and writing of the drawing room. The characters of Zola were "hideous human swine." To find the merits of Rabelais and Boccaccio was to examine "a gold chain encrusted in the filth of a pigpen." Kipling's *Stalky & Co.* was unhealthy, "for there is hardly a single form of meanness which it does not extol. . . ." Even *Peck's Bad Boy* was unfortunate. "I want every boy to be manly and able to fight for his own rights and those of his country," TR wrote a youngster who expressed fondness for the book, "but I want him to be gentle and upright also."

It was Roosevelt's attitude toward Tolstoy, however, which has exposed him to the severest criticism. TR conceded that the Russian giant was "a great writer, a great novelist," and that "even as a professional moralist and philosophical adviser of mankind in religious matters he has some excellent theories and on some points develops a noble and elevating teaching. . . ." But he feared that if Tolstoy's preachments were broadly diffused among the people they "would have an influence for bad." Hence his disapprobation. There was in the *Kreutzer Sonata,* the Colonel wrote in the *Outlook* in 1909, a "moral perversion" that must inevitably have come "from a man who, however high he may stand in certain respects, has in him certain dreadful qualities of the moral pervert." Significantly, however, when the former President lectured the militaristic Germans in Berlin in 1910, he chose to say of the pacifistic Russian novelist that "it would also be a bad thing not to have Tolstoy, not to profit by the lofty side of his teachings."

The criticism of Roosevelt's views on literature may be overdrawn. Indeed, there is an ironically perverse quality in the harsh judgments academicians have rendered against this most widely read and most book-loving President. TR was invariably interested, and for all his moralizing and banality, for all his forced optimism, his letters and essays are studded with perceptions that transcend the conventions that controlled his conclusions. And if it is true, as many reflective men have said, that insights rather than generalizations or systematic expositions survive, Roosevelt's literary criticisms cannot be totally dismissed.

Certainly the mere fact of TR's love of reading is important. Here was a statesman whose interests were more catholic than all but a handful of his country's men of letters and probably most of its college professors. He may have lacked, and by his own disarming confession he did, the critical capacity (more likely the introspective turn of mind) to assess *Hamlet* and *Macbeth* in depth. But as Wagenknecht, one of the few scholars to cut through the clichés that are the life-blood of judgments on TR, convincingly shows, Roosevelt's breadth was incredible. He knew, often in the original, Villon, Ronsard, Mistral, Körner, Topelius, Goethe, Dante, Dumas, and hundreds of others. He was versed in the minor Scandinavian sagas, the Arabian tales, the core of Rumanian literature. And he even earned his honorary presidency of the Gaelic Literature Association by anticipating the revival of interest in Celtic literature.

Here also was a statesman who had read the bulk of his own country's literature and knew personally perhaps a majority of the nation's best writers. A rare quality in any man of action, this was a unique quality in a President. There had been Presidents before who were intellectuals—most notably Jefferson and the Adamses; and there was one after him—Woodrow Wilson. There were a few others who were receptive to intellectuals. But there was no modern President save TR who had such deep bonds with and unaffected interest in the nation's writers. Just as Roosevelt's attacks on the courts worked a subtle change on the judicial mind, just as his responsiveness to social and natural scientists quickened the acceptance of their ideas, so did his patronage of writers (and also of sculptors and architects) influence the national mood. One has only to contrast the cultural vacuum that the apotheosis of the businessman by some Presidents made of the White House to the virile intellectualism that filled its corridors and flowed out onto its lawns under Roosevelt to appreciate this.

Admittedly, TR's boyish exuberance in all things made him a somewhat deserving foil for aesthetes like brooding, cynical Henry Adams. Roosevelt, wrote Adams in one of those searing aphorisms that live more for the prejudices they confirm than the truths they reveal, was "pure act." And there was hardly a first-rate literary mind

in the country that was not contemptuous of TR's heavy-handed imposition of social conventions upon aesthetic standards. Yet the
central fact remains: Roosevelt stimulated, and even inspired, dozens
of young authors over the years. If he did not discover, he nevertheless
exposed to the public eye the genius of Edwin Arlington Robinson,
whom he appointed to a minor government post with the admonition
"to think poetry first and Treasury second."

Indeed, it was Roosevelt's patronage of his friend Robinson,
Robert Frost recalled, that was the first thing he himself remembered
about TR. "As I think of him," Frost said, "I remember him as the
only President I ever met, as the only President who ever took that
much interest in a poet . . . [TR] was our kind. He quoted poetry
to me. He knew poetry. Poetry was in his mind; that means a great
deal to me."

Stephen Vincent Benét felt much as Frost did. "I do not mean to
say in the least that his [TR's] judgment of books was infallible—no
man's is. . . ." Benét wrote. But, he added, Roosevelt had "a love
for the thing itself." The testimony is endless. Hamlin Garland recalled the Colonel exclaiming excitedly at lunch one day during
World War I: " 'Do you know that the rhythms of archaic French are
much finer and manlier than the rhythms of modern French?'
Whereupon, he quoted with immense gusto and dramatic force a
page or two from the Song of Roland and followed it up by the
quotation of a poem from a modern French writer." Van Wyck
Brooks remembered a similar performance—"the most remarkable
exhibition of presence of mind and phenomenal memory I had ever
heard of," he wrote. "If ever there was obviously a man of genius,"
said Brooks in a judgment that TR himself never accepted, "it was
Theodore Roosevelt."

The interim between the Bull Moose campaign and the outbreak
of World War I was marked by the most harrowing physical experience of Roosevelt's life. Early in the summer of 1913 he decided to
combine a lecture trip to South America with an ascent of the
Paraguay River. "It won't be anything like the African trip," TR
wrote Kermit, who postponed his marriage in order to join his father.
"There will be no hunting and no adventure."

When the Colonel reached Rio de Janeiro on October 21, however, he heard of an unmapped river, the River of Doubt, which

flowed north toward the Amazon from the Brazilian plateau. "We will go down that unknown river!" he excitedly exclaimed; and the Brazilian government thereupon agreed to organize a major expedition, "the Expedicão Scientifica Roosevelt-Rondon."

On February 27, 1914, after an uneventful trip into the interior, the Colonel, Kermit, and twenty others began the hazardous exploration of the River of Doubt. They were soon beset with troubles. The insects proved almost unbearable, eating through their clothes and biting painfully into their flesh. Two boats were lost when the river rose unexpectedly one night. Hostile Indians killed one of their dogs. Kermit's boat was capsized and one of the boatmen was lost—"In these Rapids died Simplicio," read the inscription they placed on a marker. Kermit himself escaped death after being swept over a falls only by grasping an overhanging limb. Food ran dangerously low. Another boat was lost. Equipment was discarded. One of the men went insane, killed a member of the party, and fled into the wilderness. Finally, the Colonel, who had been weakened by intermittent attacks of fever, slipped and gashed his weak leg (broken while riding years before) in an heroic effort to prevent two capsized boats from being ground against the rocks.

The Colonel's wound became infected; he was striken with malaria and dysentery and his temperature rose to 105 degrees. The naturalist George K. Cherrie expected to find him dead each morning, and once Roosevelt reportedly told Kermit and Cherrie to go on without him. "I feel I am only a burden to the party." TR also contemplated suicide, but decided against it for fear that Kermit would insist on bringing his body out. "The fever was high and father was out of his head," Kermit later wrote.

The scene is vivid before me. Father first began with poetry; over and over again he repeated, "In Xanadu did Kubla Khan a stately pleasure dome decree," then he started talking at random, but gradually he centered down to the question of supplies, which was, of course, occupying everyone's mind. Part of the time he knew that I was there, and he would then ask me if I thought Cherrie had had enough to eat to keep going. Then he would forget my presence, and keep saying to himself: "I can't work now, so I don't need much food, but he and Cherrie have worked all day with the canoes, they must have part of mine." Then he would again realize my presence and question me as to just how much Cherrie had had.

On April 30, two months after they had started the descent, the Colonel and his party ended their journey at Manaos. They had completed a major exploration, made significant collections for the American Museum of Natural History, and traveled 1,500 miles. TR had lost fifty-seven pounds, satisfied his last great urge for non-military adventure, and suffered the illnesses that would be responsible for his gradual physical disintegration. He had also written the major portion of a minor adventure classic, *Through the Brazilian Wilderness,* and had had his name formally given by the Brazilian government to the River of Doubt. "My dear Sir," the fever-wracked former President of the United States telegraphed the Brazilian Minister of Foreign Affairs on reaching Manaos, "I thank you from my heart for the chance to take part in this great work of exploration."

Even while Roosevelt had been fighting for his life in the jungle, his name had been embroiled in controversy at home. On April 6, 1914, the new Secretary of State, William Jennings Bryan, guilelessly signed a treaty with Colombia which virtually admitted that the United States had dealt that nation less than substantial justice in acquiring the Panama Canal Zone. The treaty, as approved by President Wilson, expressed "sincere regret that anything" should have marred relations between the two nations and agreed to pay Colombia a $25 million indemnity.

The Colonel first learned of the treaty with Colombia after his descent of the River of Doubt, and from that moment until his death he suffered paroxysms of rage at its mention. "I regard the proposed Treaty as a crime against the United States, an attack upon the honor of the United States, . . . and a serious menace to the future well-being of our people," he wrote the Democratic leader, Senator William J. Stone, in July, 1914. "Either there is warrant for paying this enormous sum and for making the apology, or there is not." And he believed emphatically that there was not. "Every action we took was in accordance with the highest principles of public and private morality," the Colonel concluded in a statement that both the facts and his own earlier assertions belied.

The United States Senate eventually rejected the Colombian treaty. But in 1921, after Roosevelt's death, the Harding administration re-negotiated it in order to win oil concessions for American corporations. Although the apology was then omitted, the $25 million settlement which TR had called "blackmail" was still included. But in one of the most casuistic speeches in his long career Cabot Lodge argued in the Senate that his deceased friend would have approved.

The treaty with Colombia was not the only brief Roosevelt held against Wilson and Bryan. The Colonel had early and inconsistently taken issue with Wilson's handling of a resurgence of anti-Japanese sentiment in California. And in September, 1913, he had projected, but failed to deliver, a blistering attack on the President's messianic Mexican policy. Nor was he any more sympathetic with Wilson and Bryan's faith in arbitration than he had been with Taft's.

On August 1, 1914, four days after Austria-Hungary declared war on Serbia, he unburdened himself on that and other counts to Arthur Lee. "As I am writing, the whole question of peace and war trembles in the balance; and at the very moment . . . our own special prize idiot, Mr. Bryan, and his ridiculous and insincere chief, Mr. Wilson, are prattling pleasantly about the steps they are taking to procure universal peace by little arbitration treaties which promise impossibilities, and which would not be worth the paper on which they are written in any serious crisis," the Colonel wrote. "It is not a good thing for a country to have a professional yodeler, a human trombone like Mr. Bryan as Secretary of State, nor a college president with an astute and shifty mind, a hypocritical ability to deceive plain people, unscrupulousness in handling machine leaders, and no real knowledge or wisdom concerning internal and international affairs as head of the nation."

Three days later Kaiser Wilhelm's superbly conditioned armies goose-stepped across the Belgian border.

CHAPTER 29

THE BUGLE THAT WOKE AMERICA

There were some of them did shake at what was told,
And they shook best who knew that he was right.
— Edwin Arlington Robinson

Within three months of the Imperial German Government's invasion of Belgium Theodore Roosevelt had thrown himself into the mightiest struggle of his career—the campaign to persuade the American people to enter World War I and to prosecute it with vigor after they had entered it. In the four and one-half years of life that remained, Roosevelt was to deal his great adversary, Woodrow Wilson, even heavier blows than he had earlier dealt Taft. He was to suppress his progressivism for the first two of those years, and he was then to liquidate the Bull Moose party in one of the angriest major conventions in American history. He was to see his influence sink to its lowest point since 1900, and he was to see it resurge and soar to new heights in a remarkable testament to his powers of leadership. And he was to set for his countrymen an unparalleled example of intolerance and hatred, of duty and devotion, and of high and resolute courage.

Roosevelt's early reactions to the coming of the war to Europe elude facile generalization, partly because he said one thing in private and, out of a commendable sense of propriety, another thing in public; also, he seems to have reversed himself on some issues as the significance of the war gradually emerged in sharper relief. Nevertheless, his views on two or three of the principal issues are clear. He sympathized wholeheartedly with Belgium. He believed emphatically

466

that England had to go in to prevent Germany from stamping its iron heel on all Europe. And he also feared the long-term implications of German defeat.

Felix Frankfurter, who with Herbert Croly, one or two other young Americans, and Charles Booth, the English reformer and shipping executive, was visiting the Colonel on August 4, the day England entered the war, long afterward recalled Roosevelt's reaction. "You've got to go in! You've got to go in!" TR passionately exclaimed to Booth in the library at Sagamore Hill. "I say all this," he continued, "though probably in a few years Germany will be an ally of ours in our fight against Japan." A letter Roosevelt wrote Hugo Münsterberg, the Harvard psychologist and German sympathizer, three months after the event, confirms and supplements Justice Frankfurter's account. "At the outset of the war," TR said, "I happened to have visiting me a half a dozen of our young men. . . . We all of us sympathized with Belgium, and therefore with England and France . . . , but I was interested to find that we all of us felt that the smashing of Germany would be a world calamity, and would result in the entire Western world being speedily forced into a contest with Russia."

Even more revealing of the emotional depths of Roosevelt's feeling toward Germany is an incident that occurred two or three days after the invasion of Belgium. An emissary bearing a letter from the German Embassy sought out Roosevelt at Progressive party headquarters in New York. After bowing formally, the German said that his Imperial Majesty wished him to know that he had always remembered the great pleasure it gave him to receive and entertain the Colonel at the palace in Potsdam. He added that the Emperor felt assured that he could count on Roosevelt's sympathetic understanding of Germany's position. TR had then bowed, looked the emissary straight in the eye, and icily replied: "Pray thank his Imperial Majesty for me for his very courteous message and assure him that I am deeply conscious of the honor done me in Germany and that I shall never forget the way in which His Majesty the Emperor received me in Berlin, *nor the way in which His Majesty King Albert of Belgium received me in Brussels.*"

Regrettably, however, Roosevelt soon put himself on the record in a manner he later rued. On August 22, 1914, he wrote in the *Outlook* that he would not then pass judgment on the violation of the

treaties guaranteeing Belgium's integrity. "When giants are engaged
in a death wrestle, as they reel to and fro they are certain to trample
on whoever gets in the way of either of the huge straining com-
batants." He amplified his views the next month in a curiously contradictory article. "We can maintain our neutrality only by refusal to
do anything to aid unoffending weak powers which are dragged into
the gulf of bloodshed and misery through no fault of their own."

> Of course it would be folly to jump into the gulf ourselves to no
> good purpose; and very probably nothing that we could have done
> would have helped Belgium. We have not the slightest responsibility
> for what has befallen her, and I am sure the sympathy of this coun-
> try for . . . Belgium is very real. Nevertheless, this sympathy is
> compatible with full knowledge of the unwisdom of uttering a single
> word of official protest unless we are prepared to make that protest
> effective; and only the clearest and most urgent National duty would
> ever justify us in deviating from our rule of neutrality and non-
> interference.

Three weeks later Roosevelt repeated himself in the first of nine
prolix articles hastily written for the *New York Times;* and not until
November 8 did he openly castigate President Wilson's failure to
protest the invasion of Belgium. Thereafter, however, his criticism
of the President on that count was unbounded.

Early in 1915 TR published these essays under the title *America
and the World War*. A call to action rather than a historical document, that work saw the equivocal passage in the *Outlook* essay of
August 22 replaced with a sweeping indictment of Wilson's call for
"a neutrality so strict as to forbid our even whispering a protest against
wrong-doing, lest such whispers might cause disturbance to our ease
and well-being."

> We pay the penalty of this action—or, rather, supine inaction—
> on behalf of peace for ourselves, by forfeiting our right to do any-
> thing on behalf of peace for the Belgians in the present. . . . It is a
> grim comment on the professional pacifist theories as hitherto de-
> veloped that, according to their view, our duty to preserve peace
> for ourselves necessarily means the abandonment of all effective
> effort to secure peace for other unoffending nations which through
> no fault of their own are trampled down by war.

The Colonel's critics were quick to pounce upon him for his apparent change of front. "I was pretty lonely, and almost everybody

attacked me for not 'standing by the President,' " he later mused. "For the first sixty days, I . . . supported President Wilson . . . on the assumption that he was speaking the truth, had examined the facts, and was correct in his statement that we had no responsibility for what had been done in Belgium." Then, he continued, "I went over the Hague Conventions myself" and found that "they did demand action on our part." Indeed, he concluded, "if I made any error whatever, it was standing by . . . [Wilson] just sixty days too long. I have never committed the error since. . . ."

TR's explanation of his dramatic reversal is both enlightening and confusing. It ignores that fatalistic acceptance of brute power implicit in his assertion that "giants . . . engaged in a death wrestle . . . are certain to trample on whoever gets in the way." It curiously fails to mention his own qualifications—qualifications that prove he was far from pro-German. We should make no official protest, Roosevelt had written in the original version, "unless we are prepared to make that protest effective." And it even omits reference to the sympathy for Belgium implicit in the statement that only by refusing "to do anything to aid unoffending weak powers which are dragged into the gulf of bloodshed and misery through no fault of their own" can the United States maintain its neutrality.

The Colonel's explanation further ignores the fact that even as he was publishing his ambivalent defenses of Wilson's neutrality program in the summer of 1914, he was privately concluding that the President should have protested the invasion of Belgium. As he wrote Arthur Lee on August 22, the day his controversial *Outlook* article appeared, "I do not know whether I would be acting right if I were President or not, but it seems to me that if I were President I should register a very emphatic protest, a protest that would mean something, against the levy of the huge war contributions on Belgium. . . . The Germans, to suit their own purposes, trampled on their solemn obligations to Belgium and on Belgium's rights . . . any power which now or hereafter may be put at the mercy of Germany will suffer in similar shape." Roosevelt then cautiously prophesied German defeat, adding that he saw "no reason for believing that Russia is more advanced than Germany as regards international ethics." He also suggested that Germany might have to be supported later as a bulwark against Russia. There is "little chance of hostility between us and Russia," he added, but "there is always the chance of hostility between us and Japan."

The Colonel appended to that letter a postscript which suggests that he was holding in his real views because of a high-minded desire to avoid compromising President Wilson's conduct of diplomacy. "Of course this letter is only for you and Ruth," he wrote. "I am an ex-President; and my public attitude must be one of entire impartiality—and above all no verbal or paper 'on to Berlin' business." Meanwhile, he informed a newspaperman who attempted to draw him out that "what we have to do is not to put obstacles in the way of the Administration."

Roosevelt's indignation at Belgium's fate and Wilson's refusal to protest it had continued to increase as the summer waned. On September 5, the publisher E. A. Van Valkenberg and Dean Lewis met the Colonel on a train bound for New Orleans, where he was to deliver a Labor Day speech for the Progressive congressional candidates. "Germany is absolutely wrong," TR expostulated as the two Progressive leaders entered his compartment. "Her own White Book places her squarely in the wrong . . . [nothing] she can possibly do in the future will extricate her."

About two weeks later Roosevelt's newspaperman friend, O. K. Davis, pointedly asked him what he would have done had he been President at the outbreak of war. The Colonel replied that Sir Edward Grey had needed only a few more days to force a conference on Germany. "We certainly could have supplied those few days, if Washington had cared to do so, or had known how . . . I should have felt myself a criminal, if I had been President, and had not done so." Furthermore, the United States could have demanded a conference as one of the signatories to the Hague Convention. Or perhaps it could have suggested that it was prepared to act to fulfill its obligations. "The necessary result was bound to be the few days of delay Grey so desperately needed," TR added. "The Kaiser's haste in declaring war shows that he recognized the fact that, if he did not begin hostilities at once, he would be prevented from doing so."

Still, the Colonel had doubts. "Of course," he reflected, "it might not have prevented it permanently, for the Kaiser and Germany were bent on attacking France, and possibly England also. . . . If Germany—that is, the Kaiser and von Moltke and the army war-lords—

really believe that they can dominate the whole world, then nothing would permanently keep them from making the effort."

Two weeks later the Colonel repeated similar sentiments to Spring-Rice. "I would not have made such a statement," he added, "unless I was willing to back it up. I believe that . . . the American people would have followed me. But whether I am mistaken or not as regards this, I am certain that the majority are now following Wilson. Only a limited number of people could or ought to be expected to make up their minds for themselves in a crisis like this; and they tend, and ought to tend, to support the President." Adding that it would be "mere clamor and nothing else" for him to talk about "what ought to be done or ought to have been done," TR warned that his views should be kept confidential. This was, he remarked, the freest expression of opinion he had yet allowed himself. Then, almost as an afterthought, he sapped the strength of his contention that Wilson could have delayed the outbreak of war:

> Of course, I only acted in the Japanese-Russian affair when I had received explicit assurances, verbally from the Russians and in writing from the Japanese, that my action would be welcome; and three or four months of talk and negotiation had preceded this action on my part.

The Colonel might have openly attacked Wilson's policies long before November, for he was daily growing more resentful of the President's unrealistic adjuration to be neutral in thought as well as in deed, had it not been for his obligations to his Progressive supporters. In spite of his own pessimism, his lieutenants insisted that he again lead an advance—Beveridge, Bainbridge Colby, Garfield, Johnson, Gifford Pinchot, and Victor Murdock were all running on state tickets. And so TR had dutifully and wearily undertaken the assignment.

On the stump that fall, TR, "always cheerful in public, always with his head high, and with his old appearance of confidence and unshaken determination," said most of the same old things in the same old manner. But they lacked the same old meaning. Wilson and the Democratic party were outflanking Roosevelt and the Bull Moose legions; and even if the Colonel had not been consumed with revulsion for the President's diplomacy, even if he had not believed the Progressive party's internal weaknesses assured its extinction, he had sooner or later to face that fact.

The first fruits of Roosevelt's ideological victory over Wilson in 1912 had come on September 26, 1914 with the enactment of the Federal Trade Commission Law. Envisaging, in the words of Arthur S. Link, "such a positive regulation of business as Roosevelt had advocated and Wilson had condemned," that measure outlawed unfair business practices in a sweeping general statement that delegated the responsibility for interpretation to the members of the Commission. Three weeks later Wilson, who was actually less sympathetic to unions than Roosevelt, signed the Clayton Antitrust Bill into law. Under that measure's famous labor section, which Samuel Gompers enthusiastically and prematurely labeled "labor's Magna Carta," use of the injunction against labor unions was theoretically modified. This was ironical indeed, for it was broadly what Roosevelt had called for in the great messages of his last two years in office, what he had tried unsuccessfully to write into the Republican platform of 1908, and what he had campaigned so eloquently for in 1912.

However grimly satisfying the Colonel's vindication by Wilson and the Democrats, it made the campaign of 1914 more difficult. To complicate matters further—and probably to explain the disparity between his private and public statements from September on—Roosevelt was also constrained to soften his projected attack on Wilson's foreign policies. As Midwestern Progressive leaders sharply warned him early in the fall, many voters felt that the United States would be at war with Mexico and involved in Europe were he President. The result was the most fruitless canvass Roosevelt had undertaken since 1884.

Tired and disheartened, TR sat talking with O. K. Davis on a train going from Philadelphia to New York near the end. The Colonel remarked on the futility of it all, on the crowds' enthusiasm for himself and their lack of interest in the Progressive candidates he urged them to support. After a while, however, his mood changed dramatically. "Well, O.K.," he exclaimed, leaning over and whacking the newspaperman on the knee in a gesture of triumphant liberation, "I've got only a few hours more of this campaign, and then I shall be through. . . . Hereafter no man can claim anything from me in politics. Not a single obligation is left. I have done everything, this fall, that everybody has wanted. This election makes me an absolutely free man. Thereafter I am going to say and do just what I damned please."

The wraps were now off. Five days after the elections the Colonel for the first time publicly criticized Wilson's failure to protest Germany's invasion of Belgium. Early in December he arraigned the President for tolerating violence in Mexico. And from then until the night before his death four years later he maintained an unremitting fire on Wilson's policies. Roosevelt's strictures were unvaryingly colored by partisanship. But they were almost unfailingly constructive and they were never remotely obstructionist. TR's consuming purpose was the advancement of his country's interests as he conceived them, and neither his volcanic hatred of Wilson nor his emerging ambition to return to the White House more than fanned flames that were already raging. It was no different with Cabot Lodge, with whom TR again became bound in common object. For all his contempt of Woodrow Wilson and disdain for the President's party, that cold Brahmin only incidentally allowed his personal feelings to influence his actions on the great questions of foreign policy during the neutrality years. Not until the epochal struggle over the League of Nations would Lodge emerge as a bitter-end obstructionist.

The controversy over Belgium was a skirmish as compared to the battle that soon raged over preparedness policy. The lines were first drawn early in the fall of 1914. In spite of the soft-pedaling of his views on Belgium and Mexico, TR had come out forthrightly for defense increases during the congressional campaign. His statements had evoked little support and no small measure of derision; and though they had probably sparked a handful of like-minded men to speak out, notably Lodge's son-in-law, A. P. Gardner, they had particularly incited the President's ire. "We shall not alter our attitude . . . because some amongst us are nervous or excited," Wilson coldly remarked in his annual message on December 8, 1914. A change of policy "would mean merely that we had lost our self-possession, that we had been thrown off our balance by a war with which we had nothing to do, whose causes cannot touch us, whose very existence affords us opportunities of friendship and disinterested service which should make us ashamed of any thought of hostility or fearful preparation for trouble."

This meant that the President had chosen to stake everything on the hope that the United States could end the war by mediation. It was a noble dream, one that Roosevelt had pursued at Portsmouth and was even then criticizing Wilson for not having tried at the outbreak of hostilities. Men must always honor the President for it. Yet mediation and preparedness were not mutually exclusive. As Roosevelt had consistently and realistically held, strength could portend greater force for peace than weakness in the world as it then was.

"Upon my word," TR lamented to Lodge when Wilson first ridiculed the preparedness agitation in October, "Wilson and Bryan are the very worst men we have ever had in their positions." "If Germany smashes England I should regard it as certain that this country either had to fight or to admit that it was an occidental China," he confided to another friend. "In any event I feel that an alliance between Germany and Japan, from which we would suffer, is entirely a possibility, if Germany comes out even a little ahead in the present war."

The Colonel's growing concern over the implications of an Allied defeat was widely shared. If the submarine controversy had not interjected a major diversionary element into the neutrality question in the spring of 1915, the preparedness crusade might well have been fought out on that broader issue. As it was, Roosevelt and Lodge missed no opportunity to advance the Allies' cause. They supported the President's refusal to institute an embargo on munitions on the grounds that it would hurt Britain and France. They opposed Wilson's plan to purchase foreign-owned ships confined to American ports for fear it would lead to conflict with the British. And they even attacked Wilson's measured protest against Great Britain's unnecessarily inclusive contraband policy. The President "has remained silent in regard to the violation of Belgium's neutrality by Germany," Lodge complained to TR in January, 1915, ". . . and then he suddenly finds his voice in a protest to England, one of the Allies, about interference with our trade."

As it became apparent that winter that the war might develop into one of attrition, Roosevelt advised the British to reconsider their contraband policy. To both Spring-Rice and Edward Grey in January, 1915, he pointed out that His Majesty's government had been inexpedient and lacking in foresight. "Our trade . . . is of vastly more service to you and France than to Germany," he wrote Grey. Should German submarines "now begin to destroy ships carrying foodstuffs to Great Britain," he continued, "the effect might be not merely serious but appalling."

Under such conditions, it would be of the utmost consequence to England to have accepted the most extreme view the United States could advance as to her right to ship cargoes unmolested . . . the trade in contraband is overwhelmingly to the advantage of England, France and Russia, because of your command of the seas. You assume that this command gives you the right to make the advantage still more overwhelming.

TR added with some truth and more exaggeration that the majority of administration leaders "see that political advantage will unquestionably lie with those who try to placate the German-American vote and the professional pacificist vote."

The German-Americans wish to put a stop to all exportation of contraband because such action would result to the benefit of Germany. The pacificists are inclined to fall in with the suggestion, because they feebly believe it would be in the interest of 'Peace'—just as they are inclined heartily to favor any peace proposal, even though it should leave Belgium in Germany's hands and pave the way for certain renewal of the war.

At the same time the Colonel suggested to Spring-Rice that the British and French governments capitalize upon reports of German war atrocities and objectives by publishing official versions of such stories. He warned, however, that he "should most heartily reprobate putting out any fact which was not absolutely established." With the passing of time and the deepening of his emotional involvement, he was to disregard that warning.

By 1915, in fact, the Colonel was practically convinced that the United States should enter the war. Early in the year J. Medill Patterson, the publisher of the Chicago *Tribune,* raised the question. "You even seem to want to get us into war on the Allied side," Patterson remarked. "Is it just Belgium, or do you feel that America itself is menaced?" TR replied that although Germany would probably not attack the United States at once, she would soon challenge American interests in the Caribbean. "In this way," he continued, "we would be thrown into hostilities with Germany sooner or later and with far less chance of success *than if we joined with the powers which are now fighting her.*"

TR was too astute to destroy his effectiveness by openly calling for war at a moment when Congress was willingly acquiescing in the

President's rejection of preparedness. So he continued to focus on preparedness, the embargo, and Mexico.

He chafed under his self-imposed fetters; and he almost broke out from them when the American tanker *Gulflight* was torpedoed on May 1 with the loss of three American lives. The attack was "an act of piracy, pure and simple," he declared in a ringing public statement. But on the whole he disclosed his real feelings only to his friends.

"Lord, how I would like to be President in view of . . . the huge German-Irish element and the possible sinking of the *Lusitania,*" the Colonel wrote the famed reporter Cal O'Laughlin on May 6, 1915. Less than twenty-four hours later the giant, unarmed British liner was torpedoed without warning off the coast of Ireland with a loss of more than eleven hundred men, women, and children, one hundred and twenty-eight of them American citizens.

The first report of the *Lusitania* tragedy came to Roosevelt in a crowded courtroom at Syracuse where he was standing trial for libel against the notorious New York Republican boss, William Barnes, Jr. He made no comment. That night, however, he was called from his bed by a telephone call from an editor in New York City. "That's murder!" the Colonel exclaimed as the immensity of the disaster was borne upon him. "Will I make a statement? Yes, yes, I'll make it now. Just take this":

> This represents not merely piracy, but piracy on a vaster scale of murder than old-time pirates ever practiced. . . . It is warfare against innocent men, women, and children, traveling on the ocean, and our own fellow countrymen and countrywomen, who are among the sufferers. It seems inconceivable that we can refrain from taking action in this matter, for we owe it not only to humanity but to our own national self-respect.

The next morning TR advised his lawyers that his statement had probably alienated the two German-Americans on the jury. "I cannot help it," he added. "There is a principle at stake here which is more vital to the American people than my personal welfare is to me." His fears, of course, were groundless; the jury returned a verdict in his favor.

Meanwhile the President embarked upon that policy of note-writing which was to eventuate in Bryan's resignation and Germany's partial submission to the American position. Like Roosevelt, Wilson was outraged by Germany's inhumanity; but unlike the Colonel, he believed the general solution was a negotiated peace. The President had no intention of asking Congress for a war resolution, and he was in fact warned by powerful Democratic leaders in Congress that the people would not support a war over the *Lusitania* incident. The great majority of newspapers throughout the country also counseled moderation. Even Cabot Lodge confined his public remarks to a general affirmation of the right of American citizens to travel on the ships of belligerent nations, though he privately argued that the President should sever relations with Germany and seize German ships in American ports unless the Imperial government apologized and agreed to pay reparations. As the Kansas Progressive leader, Victor Murdock, reported to Roosevelt, the Middle West's sense of outrage "died down as suddenly as it had risen."

TR's later contention that Wilson could readily have taken the nation into war at the time is thus inconclusive. Indeed, when the President made his memorable declaration at the height of the crisis that "There is such a thing as a man being too proud to fight," Roosevelt was virtually alone in denouncing him publicly. America could not act on the President's theory, he indignantly declared, "if it desires to retain or regain the position won for it by the men who fought under Washington and by the men who, in the days of Lincoln, wore the blue under Grant and the gray under Lee."

Roosevelt's personal letters were even more direct. "There is a chance of our going to war; but I don't think it is very much of a chance," he wrote his son Archie on May 19. "Wilson and Bryan . . . are both of them abject creatures and they won't go to war unless they are kicked into it. . . ." Had he been President, TR wrote his English friend, Arthur Lee, "I would . . . have taken a stand which would have made the Germans either absolutely alter all their conduct or else put them into war with us." "If the United States had taken this stand," he significantly added, "in my judgment we would now have been fighting beside you."

The sinking of the *Lusitania* obscured the real issue—war in the broad national interest. From that fateful day on, TR concentrated almost solely on the neutral rights issue. And though he never lost his conviction that the national interest demanded American entry into the war on the Allies' side, the preservation of American rights against

Germany now became an end in itself. On that issue Roosevelt based his renewed demands for preparedness; and upon it he eventually based his call for war. He sensed, at times, that he sounded extreme; that, as he phrased it to Arthur Lee, he was "making people think that I am a truculent and bloodthirsty person, endeavoring futilely to thwart able, dignified, humane Mr. Wilson in his noble plan to bring peace everywhere by excellently written letters. . . ." But he believed himself morally obligated to give the country the leadership that he felt the President was failing to offer. "I put the case as strongly as I can," he explained. "I speak as often as I think will do good."

During the next twenty-one months Roosevelt did more than any other citizen, not excepting the President of the United States, to condition the American people to the coming of war. He became the avowed enemy of the rabid German-Americans and the Irish-Americans, of the agrarian isolationists and the urban pacifists, and of those men and women of good hope led by Hamilton Holt and William Howard Taft who anticipated Woodrow Wilson's great vision of an international order by forming the League to Enforce Peace. He emerged, conversely, as the leader and spokesman of many of those same Republican conservatives who had rejected him in 1912. Even before the *Lusitania* crisis broke, TR was writing that he might find it necessary to vote for Elihu Root over Wilson and Bryan. And by February, 1915, his relations with Lodge so improved that the Senator spent a weekend at Sagamore Hill for the first time in four years.

The Colonel found boundless opportunities to fire verbal blasts at the despised professor in the White House during these twenty-one months. He tried to be fair. When Bryan resigned as Secretary of State in protest against the second *Lusitania* note, he issued a statement pledging his "heartiest support" to Wilson in any steps he might take "to uphold the honor and the interests of this great Republic, which are bound up with the maintenance of democratic liberty and of a wise spirit of humanity among all the nations of mankind." But he was so completely out of sympathy that he could not realize that the President's note-writing was more complicated than it appeared. Nor would Roosevelt concede the political obstacles under which Wilson labored. For all TR's charges of cowardice and lack of leadership, Wilson courageously pursued policies that powerful congressional blocs representing the Democratic and Republican agrarians, the urban Irish-Americans, and the Middle Western German-Americans bitterly opposed. His suppression of the Gore-McLemore resolutions of March, 1916, which comprised a full-scale rebellion against his insistence on maintaining the very rights TR was castigating him for not upholding, is but the most dramatic evidence of that.

In these circumstances, the unrelieved stream of expletives that continued to pour forth from Roosevelt's lips is understandable only in the context of his larger aim—war in the national interest, and, as the generation that has witnessed Hitler's ultimate defilement of Bismarck's creation of "blood and iron" is now coming to believe, in the interest of the civilized world. Certainly TR, who had feared the rise of German naval power as early as 1908, so regarded the issue.

Unhappily, however, the Colonel seems also to have been animated by that rampant nationalism and inflated conception of the national honor which forever prevented him from scaling the spiritual heights. Thus the ugly suspicion persists that he would have been just as extreme had the issue been merely the upholding of American rights in Mexico, where the impoverished masses were then in rebellion against their aristocratic, clerical, and foreign overlords. Even as TR referred to the President as that "infernal skunk in the White House" and irritably dismissed one of his protests to Germany as "No. 11,765, series B," he excoriated the "feebleness, timidity, and vacillation" of the President's relations with the Mexican revolutionists.

If the reasonableness of the Colonel's scorn for the President's diplomacy is an open question, his broadsides against Wilson's preparedness policy were justifiable, given the President's own assumptions. Wilson's decision to hold Germany to "strict accountability" destroyed the premises on which his original opposition to preparedness rested, i.e., the United States was not in danger of becoming involved in the war. From that moment on Wilson was obligated to prepare for the war that must inevitably come if Germany refused to back down. But in the face of all the warnings raised by Roosevelt and the other advocates of preparedness, the President moved with the speed of a glacier. The *Lusitania* was five months in the depths of the Atlantic before he made his first public call for defense increases, and his "strict accountability" policy was twelve months old before he took the issue forcefully to the people. And then it was largely to restate propositions that Roosevelt had been arguing for the seventeen preceding months.

Ironically, when the President finally acted on Roosevelt's logic, TR and Lodge convinced themselves that he was inspired by purely political considerations. "Wilson evidently has come to the conclusion that there is a rising popular feeling for preparedness and, seeing votes in it, is prepared to take it up," Lodge wrote TR in the summer of 1915 when the President made his first tentative overtures toward preparedness. "Last winter he did everything he could to stop any improvement in the Army and Navy, sneered at Gardner and held him up as merely trying to make political capital because he was urging them, as he is now, the necessity of doing something."

There was probably more "political capital" in playing preparedness down than up, so intense was the antiwar sentiment throughout the country. But whatever the President's motives, it is clear that his dramatic *volte-face*, which occurred in the fall of 1915, confirmed Roosevelt's judgment on the preparedness issue. From the fall of 1915 on, as Bryan lamented to his friends, Wilson spoke partially in Rooseveltian terms. The President failed, however, to act with Rooseveltian dispatch, or to propose an army program commensurate with Roosevelt's conception of the nation's needs.

The Colonel quickly seized upon the opportunity afforded by Wilson's belated espousal of preparedness to press a proposal that he had never deemed possible of enactment in the past—universal military service. As the preparedness debate came to a head in the winter of 1915–1916, he made a herculean effort to persuade the public and the administration to support it. "I would have the son of the multimillionaire and the son of the immigrant who came in steerage, sleep under the same dog-tent and eat the same grub," TR exclaimed in October, 1915. "It would help mightily to a mutual comprehension of life." In the end, however, the fight for universal service failed for lack of support from the "plain people" in the West and the South and from organized labor throughout the country. Nor could Wilson, who was having to coerce and cajole Congress into passing a modest army program, have got it through.

Meanwhile, the administration's program was taking shape. Instead of calling a special session of Congress in the summer or fall of 1915 when he first convinced himself of the need for a preparedness program, the President had waited for the regular session to convene in December. Then, on the urging of Secretary of War Lindley M. Garrison, he had come out for the creation of a volunteer force of 400,000 semireservists—the so-called Continental Army. Roosevelt, whose relationship to Wilson was not unlike that of La Follette's to himself during the fight for the Hepburn Act ten years before, at once charged that the proposal was inadequate; and when Lodge, the National Security League, and a number of prominent Republicans endorsed it in the realization that they could not expect more, given the anti-preparedness sentiment of Congress, the Colonel was furious. "I am so out of sympathy with what seems to be the prevailing currents of American opinion that I keep my judgment suspended . . . ," he wrote Lodge.

Apparently the Republicans are expecting to beat Wilson by keeping as neutral as he is as regards international duty, by supporting him in his sham-preparedness program and letting him pose before the country as the author of that program and as the champion of preparedness, and by then trusting that on the tariff and by some more or less secret understanding with the German vote they may be able to replace him by some one to whom the Germans won't object. . . .

But Lodge's sensitivity to the strength of the agrarian-progressive opponents of preparedness was keener than Roosevelt's. Rather than hold out for the impossible, he decided over TR's protests to compromise. "I have repeatedly said that this Administration has wasted one year in providing for the defense of the country and I want to prevent them if I can from wholly wasting another year," he explained to TR. "We may not be able to get much but every little counts."

Meanwhile, Southern agrarians under the firm leadership of Claude Kitchin of North Carolina bore out Lodge's reasoning by resolutely refusing to approve the Continental Army scheme. Claiming that it was militaristic and unnecessary, they insisted instead on expanding the inefficient National Guard. In this they were supported by the majority of Republicans in the House, many of whom succumbed to the blandishments of the powerful National Guard lobby. The President was thus forced to compromise or suffer the complete defeat of his army program, and when he did so the inflexible Secretary of War resigned in disgust. Garrison became in consequence a minor martyr to many preparedness advocates, but not to TR.

Legislation to increase the Army's strength from a little over 100,000 officers and men to about 220,000 was finally enacted, but only after a protracted battle which saw Wilson bring all the great force of his personality and the power of his office to bear on the resentful agrarian-progressives in the House. Provision was also made to place the National Guard under federal supervision and to increase substantially its strength.

Understandably, Roosevelt was too exacerbated by the unconscionable delay—the National Defense Act of 1916 followed the outbreak of war by two years and the enunciation of the "strict accountability" policy by eighteen months—to appreciate the leadership the President had at long last exerted. He did not regard the measure as a victory for his own point of view. It was, he said, "as foolish and unpatriotic a bit of flintlock legislation as was ever put on the statute book. It is folly, and worse than folly, to pretend that the National Guard is an efficient second line of defense." Roosevelt realized, moreover, that Congress' failure to provide for a capable reserve force implicitly repudiated the thesis that the United States should prepare for participation in the war then raging.

The naval bill was another matter. Wilson's request in December, 1915, for a vast construction program incited only moderate opposition; and after he gave a spectacular series of addresses in the Middle West, climaxed in St. Louis, where German-American resentment of British naval power was strong, by an oratorical call for "incomparably the greatest navy in the world," the majority of Democrats and Republicans in Congress swung behind his recommendations. The result was the largest and most comprehensive naval program to that time, a program based on two propositions Roosevelt had been arguing since the start of the war: the United States should be prepared to negotiate from strength, and it should be capable of defending its far-flung strategic interests upon the end of hostilities in Europe.

Only on one important issue had TR failed the preparedness crusade. From the start of the demands for increases in military strength the agrarian-progressives and their allies in labor and reform circles had contended that the movement was inspired by big business in general and the munitions makers in particular. After Wilson's belated conversion to preparedness in 1915, they had laid plans to impose the cost of the program upon those groups. Republicans "will vote for the biggest preparedness appropriation and then fight all methods to finance it . . . ," Kitchin resentfully wrote Bryan. "I am persuaded to think that when the income tax will have to pay for the increase in the army and navy, they will not be one-half so frightened over the future invasion by Germany."

Kitchin's analysis was partially overdrawn. Nevertheless, when he pushed a revenue bill late in the summer of 1916 that drastically raised the income tax in the upper brackets, instituted a steeply graduated inheritance tax, and assessed the profits of munitions makers as well, the overwhelming majority of Republicans in both houses of Congress, including Roosevelt's son-in-law, Nicholas Longworth, bitterly fought it. Though TR himself had long advocated the income and inheritance taxes, he failed to call on them to support it.

That Lodge and other like-minded conservatives should have opposed a more equitable tax structure was to be expected. But that Roosevelt, in whom the Progressive leadership was vested until July, 1916, should have failed to sound a clarion call for a great democratization of effort (as he was to do after the United States entered the war) is one of the minor tragedies of his career. A generation was to pass before the naïve belief that the munitions makers and the House of Morgan had inspired the preparedness movement and American entry into the war would begin to down. TR could have at least struck it a blow at its birth.

How much the preparedness program of 1916 owed to Roosevelt's driving leadership can only be conjectured. His bitter strictures against Wilson, the pacifists, and the so-called hyphenated Americans undoubtedly provoked an adverse reaction among many moderates. His extremism also alienated many who agreed with his position. Yet, he just as certainly roused the fears and inspired the courage of many, many others. There was not a preparedness society in the country that did not look to TR for leadership, scarcely a major newspaper that was not moved to discuss editorially the issues he had raised; nor, probably, was there a politician in Washington who was not influenced one way or the other by his searing pronouncements. By 1916 "preparedness" and "Roosevelt" were virtually synonymous; and if the Colonel was not literally "The Bugle That Woke America," he was surely the leader of the corps that did.

CHAPTER 30

THE CAMPAIGN FOR AMERICAN RIGHTS

> The delegates [Progressives] who go to Chicago will have it in their power to determine the character of the administration which is to do or leave undone the mighty tasks of the next four years.
>
> —Theodore Roosevelt

While the preparedness program was coming to a head in the spring of 1916, Roosevelt was girding for yet another battle—one that would concentrate all his surging idealism and flaming patriotism, all his political artistry and personal venom, into a mighty drive to supplant Wilson with a President whose devotion to preparedness and American rights matched his own.

With each twist and turn in President Wilson's diplomacy during 1915 and early 1916 Roosevelt's urge to remove him from power had become more compelling. Months before the election of 1916 the Colonel had fastened upon a strategy that made suppression of his progressivism mandatory and led logically to his ultimate insult to the crusaders of 1912—the proposal that they give Henry Cabot Lodge the Bull Moose presidential nomination. It was to win the Republican nomination for himself, and, failing in that, to force the Republicans to select a candidate who was "right" on the great issues of the times. He would use the Progressive party's potential strength at the polls as the bludgeon wherewith to achieve one or the other of these ends, and would then take the party triumphantly back into the organization that had given it birth. The broad outlines of this strategy were disclosed as early as January, 1916, when TR compelled the Progressive National Committee to issue a statement calling on its members to return to the Republican fold in a supreme effort to turn out the Democrats.

If the Colonel was thus willing to draw the veil on the progressive movement in the vain hope that he could compel the Republican party to rise to responsibilities that the Democrats had eschewed, he was nonetheless determined that his own nomination, if it came, would come in full recognition of his views on preparedness and Americanism. He fervently wanted the nomination. "Don't imagine that I wouldn't like to be at the White House this minute," he exploded to a friend that winter. "This was my year—1916 was my high twelve," he resignedly confided to another intimate after Wilson had been re-elected. "In four years I will be out of it. . . . I did not want to run in 1912. Circumstances compelled me to run then. This year it was different."

But except for that deference to the Old Guard's economic prejudices implicit in his failure to endorse the agrarian-progressives' tax program, Roosevelt cast politics to the winds in the spring of 1916. From Trinidad, where he and Mrs. Roosevelt took a brief vacation in March, he, in effect, invited the American people to elect him President and then go to war. "I . . . say that it would be a mistake to nominate me unless the country has in its mood something of the heroic—unless it feels not only devotion to ideals but the purpose measurably to realize those ideals in action," he declared in a public statement. And in May he took his militant message to the Middle West, the seedbed of the nation's three great isolationist strains—ruralism, pacifism, and German-Americanism.

In Detroit, where Henry Ford's pacifist views had received a long, full hearing, TR gave a rousing speech for universal military service highlighted by a personal exchange with a slender woman, who arose in the balcony, American flag in hand, and cried out: "I have two sons. I offer them." Gravely, the Colonel replied after a wave of thunderous applause died down, "Madam, if every mother in the country would make the same offer, there would be no need for any mother to send her sons to war."

Later that month Roosevelt went to Kansas City, where he was engulfed by a roaring crowd of fifty thousand, and then to St. Louis, where he lashed the German-Americans with incredible fury. "It is our purpose this fall," he declared in that German-American center on the Mississippi, "to elect an American president and not a viceroy of the German emperor." One week later the Republican convention, its ranks heavily laden with German-Americans, and its managers prepared to defer to German-American sensibilities at any cost, convened at Chicago.

The Colonel's performance had destroyed his last slim hope of winning the presidential prize, and he knew that it had. "If there had been a chance of winning the Republicans' support," he remarked after his return to Oyster Bay, "I killed it by my tour of the West."

In reality, there had been little chance. A small group of Easterners were willing to let bygones be bygones. And a great host of the G.O.P. rank and file wanted the Colonel. Just two spontaneous outbursts would punctuate the Republican convention the following week, one when a speaker inadvertently mentioned Roosevelt's name, the other when it was placed in nomination. But the Midwestern professionals had no intention of letting Roosevelt capture the heights. Long before TR dropped his hat on the edge of the ring, they had decided to nominate a man tinged with enough progressivism to be acceptable to the Bull Moosers, orthodox enough on the tariff to keep contributions from manufacturers rolling in, and mild enough on the war to appease the German-Americans. They went to the Supreme Court of the United States to find him.

"I wish I knew something about [Charles Evans] Hughes," Representative Gardner had written his daughter in January, 1916, as the movement for the jurist's nomination had first begun to gather momentum. "All I know is that he wears a beard and stopped horseracing in New York. . . . The machine is getting ready to nominate . . . [him]." Roosevelt added in May that the movement for Hughes "is primarily a politicians' movement made for the very reason that no one knows where he stands, and therefore represents the ideal, dear to the soul of the politician, of the candidate against whom no one can say anything." Gardner and Roosevelt were not far wrong. The Republican party would have to wait until it met in convention on June 7 to find out what its leading candidate stood for, and even then it would not quite be certain. Nor would it know much more after he had campaigned for four months.

Meanwhile, some Republican leaders sought to pave the way for Roosevelt's endorsement of the Republican candidate by framing a platform consonant with the Colonel's views. In Washington, before they entrained for Chicago, Lodge and Borah drew up an aggressive document which they submitted for approval to George Perkins, who served as TR's liaison man. When they reached Chicago, however, they found the majority too intent on appeasing the German-Americans and rural isolationists to accept their draft. Resignedly, they rewrote it.

The first plank to go was a call for universal military service. "They all admitted, readily enough, that we must come to universal military training, but they did not think the people were ripe for it, and were afraid to risk it," Lodge afterward explained to TR. "I did what I could with the aid of Jimmy Wadsworth." Calls for an army of 250,000 and a navy second to none were also deleted. As finally adopted, the planks on foreign policy paid lip-service to the Colonel's philosophy; but they ignored most of his charges against Wilson's diplomacy. They also called for "a straight and honest neutrality between the belligerents," the antithesis of what Roosevelt, Lodge, and the Eastern interventionists desired. Not without perception did a Progressive national committeeman later write TR that the Republican platform measured "up to your demands to about the same degree the Kaiser's answers did to Wilson's notes."

While the Republicans were meeting in the Coliseum, the Bull Moosers were staging a remarkable demonstration of fealty to TR in the Chicago Auditorium. A great body of Progressives—probably the overwhelming majority of the convention—was opposed to war, whether against Germany or Mexico. But their affection for the Colonel was so great and their realization that they could not survive without him so acute, that they unhesitatingly prepared to swallow the bitter with the sweet. Protesting only in undertones, they endorsed a platform that evaded the critical taxation issue, that only perfunctorily endorsed the memorable reform planks of 1912, and that called for universal military service, a regular army of 250,000, and the second largest navy in the world (TR continued to believe that Great Britain should have the largest). Angrily, the *New Republic* summed it up:

> The platform of an ostensibly progressive party fails to utter one single conviction which need cause any uneasiness to the established order. It does not tamper with the foundations of political and eco-

nomic power. . . . Militant progressivism is converted into a nebulous nationalism which can be made to mean all things to all men.

The blackest hour was yet to come. The Republican professionals in the Coliseum could neither forget 1912 nor ignore the seething hatred the German-Americans now felt for the Colonel. In the face of a minor boom for Roosevelt on the lower echelons, they resolutely held to their plan to nominate Hughes, who remained substantially uncommitted on the great questions of the times. TR was outraged when apprised by telephone. "I guess there is no need to tell you," he said to Medill McCormick over a private line connecting Sagamore Hill with George Perkins' rooms in the Blackstone Hotel, "that I think Hughes a good deal of a skunk in the attitude he has taken." He would "breathe a sigh of relief" if he were not nominated himself, he added when Lodge came on the wire, ". . . but in international matters and in the present situation I know I am worth two of Hughes."

The Colonel's contempt for Hughes proved less than consuming. To be sure, he vehemently reiterated his opposition to the jurist in telephone conversations with Perkins and other Progressive and Republican leaders. And he even offered the notorious Boise Penrose, who was "right" on preparedness and Americanism if little else, the majority leadership of the Senate in return for his support in the Republican convention. He refused, however, to force the G.O.P.'s hand by letting it out that he would again run on the Progressive ticket should Hughes receive the Republican nomination. Gifford Pinchot implored him to do so. "We have been playing poker with them," he heatedly asserted, ". . . without chips in that direction." But Roosevelt brusquely dismissed the proposal. "I wish to say this," he said to his forester friend when he again raised the issue, ". . . there is a very wide difference between making a young Colonel and a retired Major General lead a forlorn hope." He added later that he would refuse to support Hughes until "he repudiated the German-American alliance," but that he was "not going to dictate to that Convention as if I were a Tammany Chieftain."

In point of fact, the Colonel was already dictating to the Progressive convention. The Bull Moosers wanted Roosevelt and no one else, and they were straining powerfully to nominate him and have done with it. But against the urgent entreaties of Pinchot, William

Allen White, and others, TR insisted that Perkins prevent the Progressives from balloting until after the Republicans had made their nomination. Dutifully, Perkins, who was later to be charged by the western radicals with destroying the Progressive party, followed his leader's instructions. By Friday night, June 9, however, it was apparent that Perkins could not indefinitely hold back the flood. The Bull Moosers were going to nominate Roosevelt the next morning regardless of his or Perkins' protests; and the Republicans were just as surely going to bestow their accolade on Hughes.

In desperation Perkins put Nicholas Murray Butler on the phone with the Colonel at three A.M. Saturday to discuss alternative candidates. "How do you do, President of Columbia College," TR remarked when the pompous Butler came on the wire. He then dismissed Butler's three suggestions—Elihu Root, Philander C. Knox, and former Vice President Charles W. Fairbanks—and countered with Leonard Wood. "Of course he would understand very speedily that the tariff and such matters were entirely outside his realm and would get on the Army and Navy question and Americanism at once," Roosevelt added. "He wouldn't have to do as Brother Hughes will have to do—improvise." Although W. A. White had said earlier that Wood's selection would "suit me beautifully," Perkins blanched at the prospect. ". . . I think it was a very grave mistake to suggest Wood," he admonished the Colonel a little later. "He is not acceptable to anybody. He is a military man. It puts you in a bad light." Roosevelt saw Perkins' point. "It has been rejected and I will not follow it up at all," he replied.

Meanwhile, Roosevelt suggested Cabot Lodge as his alternative candidate. Perkins again demurred, proposing instead that the Progressive convention adopt a resolution of opposition to Hughes and then nominate Roosevelt as Pinchot and White had earlier urged. Vehemently, the Colonel rejected the idea. "That is one of the most extraordinary things I have ever heard," he exclaimed. "I want to say right here, although you may not agree with me, that I am sure I was right in speaking of Wood and Lodge."

Perkins thereupon backed down, conceding that Lodge was "the only man familiar with the international situation" who might be acceptable to both conventions. "I know Lodge's record like a book," TR replied. "There has never been anything against it at any time, except, of course, George, that he does not have as advanced views as you and I."

Nevertheless, Perkins remained unenthusiastic, and early that morning he and other Progressive leaders made a last effort to dissuade TR from submitting Lodge's name to the Progressive convention. Roosevelt proved implacable. "I do not ask our people to accept one of the burglars," he testily remarked to former Governor Robert Bass of New Hampshire. "I do not ask them to accept any man who isn't of the highest character and who does not stand absolutely square on the issues of the day." That ended it.

Late that morning the faithful Perkins went resignedly before the Bull Moose convention and read a statement from Roosevelt that warmly commended Lodge as one of the "staunchest fighters for different measures of economic reform in the direction of justice." As he finished, a great gasp of incredulity went up from the floor. The delegates felt that Roosevelt "had done something not merely fantastic but grossly insulting," Amos Pinchot recalled. "They had been kept in the dark, treated like children—pawns in a game into the nature of which they had had no inkling. I saw men and women sitting as if stunned, like unjustly punished children, with tears streaming down their cheeks." With catcalls and boos filling the air, they shouted down a new appeal from Perkins that they nominate Hughes. They were done with dealings, or so they thought. Deliberately, and with a touch of irony in his voice, Bainbridge Colby thereupon placed Roosevelt's name in nomination. Hiram Johnson seconded it with a speech calling on TR to rise to his responsibilities. And then, three minutes after the Hughes movement reached floodtide in the Republican convention, the Progressives angrily and overwhelmingly gave their unqualified nomination to Theodore Roosevelt. Roosevelt's response came by telegraph that afternoon, Saturday, June 10.

"I cannot accept it at this time," the message read. "I do not know the attitude of the candidate of the Republican party toward the vital questions of the day. Therefore, if you desire an immediate decision, I must decline the nomination." Roosevelt suggested, however, that his conditional refusal to run be submitted to the national committee. "If Mr. Hughes's statements, when he makes them, shall satisfy the committee . . . they can . . . treat my refusal as definitely accepted."

The Colonel had partially carried his objective; but at the cost of wounds that would never heal. His artfulness had been bared as rarely before. And his commendation of Lodge as "one of the staunchest fighters . . . for economic reform . . ." lives on as the hollow mockery of a once glorious crusade. Cabot Lodge was no black reactionary, nor even an unyielding defender of the status quo. But if his heart ever throbbed with the passion for social justice and economic reform that inspired the Bull Moose legions and their leader, its beat has never been recorded. That very summer, in fact, he would fail to support the child labor bill that Wilson would drive through Congress.

Yet, as the radical pacifist, Amos Pinchot, whom TR was soon to consign to the Progressive party's "lunatic fringe," would later concede, the circumstances were extenuating. No man can gainsay that in Roosevelt's mind the cause that now enveloped him was not noble; that preparedness for war did not transcend all other issues. The Colonel may have suppressed his progressivism more than was necessary; and he undoubtedly allowed his contempt for Wilson to becloud his judgment of the President. But he was absolutely faithful to his own conception of the main issues. And more than any other major political figure of the era, Henry Cabot Lodge stood as one with him in support of those issues. That Roosevelt should have turned to Lodge in the hour of crisis is as understandable from his point of view as it was unforgivable from that of the Progressives. As Amos Pinchot wrote in the reflective mood of a later year, "There are generally extenuating circumstances for every political act in which the element of betrayal seems present." The Colonel's treatment of the Bull Moosers "was bad; at the time . . . unforgivable."

And yet, in the light cast on these events by Roosevelt's own peculiar philosophy, there was a certain justification. . . . He believed that the most important thing in the world was for America to enter the war on the side of the Allies. Comparatively speaking, domestic issues did not exist for him. He was wrapped up in the war. . . . In 1916 Wilson was a pacifist.

. . . Roosevelt felt—and how much his personal animosity toward Wilson warped his judgment cannot be told—that the essential thing was to get rid of Wilson. For him to run as a Progressive would have meant to re-elect Wilson. . . .

Actually there was a degree of logic in TR's eventual acceptance of Hughes, whom he had earlier passed off as "another Wilson with whiskers." The Colonel was bitter that Hughes had been nominated without showing his colors. "A more sordid set of creatures than the

Republicans who nominated Hughes could not be imagined," he angrily wrote. "They are a trifle better than the corrupt and lunatic wild asses of the desert who seem most influential in democratic councils, under the lead of that astute, unprincipled and physically cowardly demagogue Wilson; but they are a sorry lot." As always, however, Roosevelt looked to the future. He took hope in reports that Hughes would appoint Elihu Root Secretary of State. He held that Hughes's understanding of the progressive philosophy, though deficient, was at least "far ahead of all the other leading Republicans." And he persuaded himself that Hughes was "an able, upright man" capable of learning with "comparative quickness" and possessed of the temperament to "rise to a very big height" in time of crisis.

The Colonel had also had a gratifying luncheon conversation with Hughes on June 28, two days after the Progressive National Committee reluctantly submitted to TR's judgment and agreed to support the Republican nominee. "I believe as you do that he will make a straight-out fight for preparedness and national defense," he confided to Lodge soon afterward. "He told me he personally believed in universal service, but was doubtful as to the expediency of coming out for it at this time." Furthermore, Roosevelt was outraged by the Democrats' comportment at St. Louis, where ex-Governor Martin Glynn of New York had electrified the convention and given the party its campaign theme with a rolling reiteration of the thesis that "We didn't go to war" every time an American right had been violated in the past, that he had no real choice.

TR's hard-forced enthusiasm for the Republican candidate was destined to be short-lived, for the unwritten terms of Hughes's candidacy made a forthright campaign politically impossible. "To satisfy Mr. Roosevelt, Hughes must quarrel with the Old Guard," Joseph Pulitzer's St. Louis *Post Dispatch* said editorially during the later stages of the campaign.

> To satisfy the pro-Germans he must quarrel with the pro-British, who demand war with Germany. To satisfy Wall Street, he must quarrel with the Western radicals. To satisfy the jingoes and the Munitions Trust, he must quarrel with most of the country. To satisfy privilege and plutocracy, he must quarrel with the people. Even as a candidate Mr. Hughes dare not have a policy, because to have a policy is to antagonize one element or another of his followers.

Although he had a recurring throat condition that made speech painful, Roosevelt meanwhile agreed to campaign for Hughes. Even as he decided to take the Republican case to the people, G.O.P. leaders cringed at the offense he would give Hughes's German-American supporters. As TR was to confess midway through the campaign, "it has been no light task for me in my speeches to avoid seeming to clash with Hughes and, at the same time, not to go back on any of the things for which I stand." On the whole, however, the Colonel gave full and free expression to his views on the hyphenates, universal military training, and European and Mexican policy. Requested to confine his remarks to the tariff at one point, he exploded: "I did not come here to talk tariff, the crowd did not come here to hear me talk tariff, and I'll be hanged if I do talk tariff. I'll talk what is in me."

The one question on which Roosevelt was inconsistent was intervention. Sometimes he argued that a firm policy would have prevented the *Lusitania's* destruction. More often, however, he implied that the United States should have gone to war when the British liner was torpedoed. In Battle Creek, Michigan, he charged that "men who now with timid hearts and quavering voices praise Mr. Wilson for having kept us out of war are the spiritual heirs of the Tories of 1776, and the Copperheads of 1864." And in Denver he declared that he would have gone to war in a minute had he been President when the *Lusitania* was torpedoed. Elsewhere TR asserted that when he was President other nations knew he was not "too proud to fight." He also attacked the professional hyphenated Americans over the protests of harried Republican managers, and he raised the question of whether Wilson would not fight for the babies murdered on the *Lusitania.*

The climax came on November 3 when Roosevelt, by then utterly consumed with revulsion by Wilson's failure to make a sweeping repudiation of the "He kept us out of war" theme, spoke at Cooper Union in New York. Unable to contain himself, he cast aside his manuscript near the end of his speech and remarked in a voice vibrant with emotion that the President was then residing at Shadow Lawn, a summer home in New Jersey.

There should be shadows now at Shadow Lawn; the shadows of the men, women and children who have risen from the ooze of the ocean bottom and from graves in foreign lands; the shadows of the helpless whom Mr. Wilson did not dare protect lest he might have to face danger; the shadows of babies gasping pitifully as they sank under the waves; the shadows of women outraged and slain by bandits. . . . Those are the shadows proper for Shadow Lawn; the shadows of deeds that were never done; the shadows of lofty words that were followed by no action; the shadows of the tortured dead.

There was neither cant nor hypocrisy, and certainly not conscious partisanship, in those harsh words. In the mind of Theodore Roosevelt, and in the minds of thousands of responsible citizens the country over, Woodrow Wilson had failed to uphold the national honor as it was then construed.

The Colonel had given more of himself in the campaign than he had planned. Yet he had not given quite enough. Unlike Wilson, who understandably believed that he had kept the country out of war, or Hughes, who mistakenly believed that a firmer policy would continue to prevent war, Roosevelt stood for war. The war that he was asking for, however, was more largely for the maintenance of American rights rather than the preservation of the Anglo-Franco-American balance of power or even of international law. Not once during the campaign did TR state his rational conviction: The United States should have been fighting on the Allies' side regardless of the submarine issue.

It is easy now to say that Roosevelt and his friends should have stated their objectives fully. And it is probably true that their failure to treat the war in a larger context than American rights contributed to the disillusionment of the postwar generation. But that only underscores the realities of 1916. The American people were wracked with dissension over the submarine issue; and Roosevelt, almost alone, had spoken frankly to that question. Had it not been for his scorching strictures, the nation might never have been roused to a war pitch. He had led the country just as far as it was willing to be led, or dragged. He could not have done more and maintained a position of leadership. Nor did he believe that he was otherwise obligated. As he exclaimed in effect again and again, "A nation is not wholly admirable unless in time of stress it will go to war for a great ideal wholly unconnected with its immediate national interest."

The Colonel's postmortem comments on the campaign are revealing of the fervor of the convictions that had inspired him. "I was grimly accepting, at great personal cost, a man whose election would have been hailed as a great personal triumph over me by the stand-patters," he wrote William Allen White, "because I felt that Wilson's reelection would be a damage to the moral fibre of the American people." Roosevelt agreed with White that Hughes's failure to talk progressivism had cost him the election; that the West "fixed its eyes on Hughes' pussy-footing and lack of vision, and on the machine and reactionary support of him." And he heartily approved the postelection movement to "progressivize" the Republican party launched by White, Gifford Pinchot, James Garfield, Harold Ickes and other Progressive leaders. But he was distraught over the nation's failure to respond to the American rights issue and by the character of the Democrats' campaign. "Hiram Johnson wrote me that in California one large factor in the vote for Wilson was the 'he kept us out of war cry,' especially affecting the women," TR explained to White. "This is yellow, my friend! plain yellow!"

During the interim between the election and Woodrow Wilson's classic call for war on April 2, 1917, TR's impatience with the President's failure to read a great moral issue in the Allied cause daily grew greater. When accounts of the deportation of tens of thousands of Belgian workers to Germany were published in the United States in late December, Roosevelt joined Root, Bacon, Stimson and others in urging Wilson to act. And when the President presciently warned the world on January 22 that there must be "a peace without victory"; that a victor's peace would rest "only as upon quicksand," he stormed furiously. "Any peace, which does not mean victory over those responsible for these outrages, will set back the march of civilization," he wrote.

> Any announcement by the United States, that Belgium and Germany are fighting for the same thing, is a falsehood, and by inference an approval of wickedness. Any announcement that the United States desires peace to come without a victory which will restore Belgium to her people, puts the United States in an attitude of aiding and abetting international immorality, and ranks this people against the cause of international righteousness.

Wilson's indecisiveness after the severance of relations with Germany on February 4 further infuriated the Colonel. "I don't think he is capable of understanding the emotion of patriotism, or the emotion of real pride in one's country," he wrote Hiram Johnson on February

17. "Whether we will really go to war or not, Heaven only knows, and certainly Mr. Wilson doesn't."

The Zimmerman Note was the final blow. Informed by newspapermen at Oyster Bay of Germany's startling proposal that Mexico recapture its "lost territory in New Mexico, Texas, and Arizona" in return for an alliance if the United States entered the war, TR unloosed a stream of expletives at the President. "Boys," he said, after recovering himself and flashing his famous grin, "I'm sorry, but you have now heard some of the more or less—mostly less—justly famed Roosevelt profanity. . . . I don't apologize for it—this man is enough to make the saints and the angels, yes, and the apostles, swear, and I would not blame them. My God, why doesn't he do something? It's beyond me."

Roosevelt refrained from attacking the President publicly for a few weeks more because, as he explained to Lodge on February 28, "I have applied for leave to raise a division, [and] I doubt the propriety of doing so." He added that he wished "Root would speak up unequivocally, as he thinks." "I am as yet holding in," he wrote Lodge two weeks later, "but if he does not go to war with Germany I shall skin him alive." Fearful that the President would hold indefinitely to a policy of armed neutrality or resort to limited naval warfare, Roosevelt finally decided to speak out. "I shall write a brief and courteous, but unequivocal statement of our present condition in the face of Germany," he confided to the Massachusetts Senator on March 18. "I have kept silent for seven weeks. Whatever the effect on myself, I think that the situation now calls for some statement by me."

Two days later TR went to the Union League Club to make his statement. Here he had been flailed as a revolutionist in the turbulent days of what by then seemed another era. He failed to refer directly to the President or to the events of the preceding two and one-half years. But he argued persuasively and eloquently that the United States was hiding behind Great Britain's shield. "Let us dare to look the truth in the face," he declared. "Let us dare to use our own strength in our own defense and strike hard for our national interest and honor. There is no question about 'going to war.' Germany is already at war with us. The only question for us to decide is whether we shall make war nobly or ignobly."

Meanwhile the tragedy was playing out at 1600 Pennsylvania Avenue. On March 20, the day that Roosevelt issued his war call before the Union League Club, President Wilson listened to his Cabinet argue that war existed in fact and advise him to call Congress into session on April 2 to declare it. Wilson was hesitant. "Every reform we have won will be lost if we go into this war," predicted the man whose administration had implemented so much of Roosevelt's platform of 1912. "War means autocracy. The people we have unhorsed will inevitably come into the control of the country for we shall be dependent upon the steel, oil, and financial magnates. They will run the nation."

The harried President continued to search his soul through the last days of March. Finally, after reluctantly concluding that "the right is more precious than peace," he wrote his war message and sent for Frank Cobb of the New York *World*. Cobb reached the White House in the early hours of the morning of April 2. And there, in a scene that will live forever in the minds of sensitive men, Wilson confided his feelings to the New York editor:

" 'Once lead this people into war,' the President said, 'and they'll forget there was ever such a thing as tolerance. To fight you must be brutal and ruthless, and the spirit of ruthless brutality will enter into the very fibre of our national life, infecting Congress, the courts, the policeman on the beat, the man in the street.' Conformity would be the only virtue, said the President, and every man who refused to conform would have to pay the penalty.

"He thought the Constitution would not survive it; that free speech and the right of assembly would go. He said a nation couldn't put its strength into war and keep its head level; it had never been done.

" 'If there is any alternative, for God's sake, let's take it,' he exclaimed."

That night, April 2, 1917, the President asked a joint session of Congress to declare a war "for democracy, for the right of those who submit to have a voice in their own Governments, for the rights and liberties of small nations, for a universal dominion of right by such a concert of free peoples as shall bring peace and safety to all nations and make the world itself at last free."

Four days later the United States entered the war upon the outcome of which, Theodore Roosevelt also believed and had longer, if more narrowly, maintained, the ultimate survival of freedom depended.

CHAPTER 31

THE LAST BATTLE

> I have no message for France; I have already given her the best I had.
>
> —Theodore Roosevelt

Woodrow Wilson's anguished decision to take the American people into war was Theodore Roosevelt's ultimate vindication. During the next eighteen months as his countrymen waged war on the Imperial German Government and its allies the Colonel gave heroically of his time, his energy, and his health in support of their efforts. He emerged as the acknowledged leader of the administration's constructive and, until the coming of peace, loyal opposition. And for one fleeting moment at the start he even stood as one with the Democratic President.

"The President's great message of April 2 was literally unanswerable," the Colonel wrote in the *Metropolitan.* "All good Americans will back . . . [him] with single-minded loyalty in every movement he makes to uphold American honor, defend American rights, and strike hard and effectively in return for the brutal wrong-doings of the German Government."

But the wounds had cut too deep for the unity long to endure. Wilson's message was "a terrible indictment of everything he has done and said, and everything he has left undone and unsaid, during the past two years and eight months," Roosevelt meanwhile confided to James Bryce. "I will forgive him everything if he will see that America fights not only with swords but with hatchets also."

If Roosevelt demanded total submission before he would forgive,

Woodrow Wilson demanded that and more. The President was neither so cold and arrogant nor so inflexible and domineering as his critics have often portrayed him. The British Foreign Secretary, Arthur Balfour, found him "firm, modest, restrained, eloquent, well-informed, and convincing." And others found him similarly appealing. It is even said that his sense of his own dignity was less than TR's. Wilson "did not seem to value it, while Roosevelt sometimes overvalued his," wrote one who knew them both. Yet the failings that mark those who value ideas above men were surely there. The passing of a generation and the waging of a Second World War were to see the triumphant resurgence of the President's noble ideals, but they would not see the vindication of his remorseless Calvinism. The long chain of broken friendships that he left behind—the awe, loyalty, and even reverence frequently lived on—contrasts starkly with the web of affection that even the "lying thieves" of 1912 spun over the grave of the Colonel. Roosevelt never suffered from Wilson's inability to thrive on the give and take of strong men; nor was TR, for all his ruthlessness in the heat of conflict, unable to forgive and forget once the lines had shifted.

The first clash between Roosevelt and Wilson after the nation's entrance into the war was personal, though it had powerful public overtones. For more than a year TR had been drawing up plans for organizing a volunteer division. It was to be officered on the higher levels by regulars and on the lower echelons by business and professional men ("The broncho-buster type will be very much lacking," the Colonel pointedly asserted). After six weeks training in the United States it was to be transported to France for combat training in order, TR explained, "that it could be sent to the front in the shortest possible time."

As war impended in the winter of 1917, Roosevelt had bombarded Secretary of War Newton D. Baker with letters and telegrams requesting authorization to act. He offered to finance the division privately until Congress took action. And he urgently called Baker's attention to his record in the Spanish-American War—"I served in the first fight as commander first of the right wing and then of the left wing of the regiment; in the next, the big fight, as Colonel of the Regiment; and I ended the campaign in command of the brigade." "I wish respectfully to point out that I am a retired Commander in Chief of the United States Army, and eligible to any position of command over American troops to which I may be appointed." But to little avail.

"This is one of the most extraordinary documents I have ever read!" Wilson commented to Baker after examining one of TR's communications. "Thank you for letting me undergo the discipline of temper involved in reading it in silence!"

Finally, on April 10, Wilson granted the former President an interview. Both men exuded cordiality, the President's secretary, Joseph P. Tumulty, later reported. They exchanged anecdotes and "seemed to enjoy what the Colonel was accustomed to call a 'bully' time." They also sparred. TR told Wilson his war message would rank "with the great state papers of Washington and Lincoln" *if he made it good.* The President explained that his desk was piled high with applications from assorted Indian fighters, Texas Rangers, and Southern "colonels" though none, of course, of Roosevelt's eminence. He outlined his plans for a selective service law (which TR agreed to support and did support). And he remarked that the war in France was no "Charge of the Light Brigade."

After an hour the Colonel left in high spirits, thumping Tumulty on the back and promising him a place in the division (but not, he later explained to a confidant, near headquarters where Tumulty could report his observations to the White House). "I had a plain talk with the President, and if it were anyone but Mr. Wilson, I'd say that it is all fixed up," TR exclaimed to newspapermen upon his return to Sagamore Hill. "Yes," the President remarked after Roosevelt breezed out of his office, "he is a great big boy. I was . . . charmed by his personality. There is a sweetness about him that is very compelling. You can't resist the man."

Roosevelt had also talked with the Secretary of War while in Washington. At the instance of Franklin D. Roosevelt, whose preparedness views had been closer to TR's than to Wilson's, Baker had called on the Colonel at his daughter's home shortly after TR saw the President. He found him surrounded by senators and friends discussing plans to have the selective service bill provide for volunteer divisions. "[TR] came out when I arrived and greeted me cordially, put his hand through my arm and took me upstairs to one of the bedrooms," Baker, who inadvertently addressed him once as "My dear Mr. President," recalled. Roosevelt then repeated the reasons for granting his request. The Secretary made no promises although Roosevelt, doubtless mistakenly, felt that he "could twist him about my finger could I have him about for a while." The trouble with Baker, TR subsequently wrote, is that he has a blind faith in the General Staff and graduates of the Military Academy. "He does not realize that a muttonhead, after an education at West Point—or Harvard—is a muttonhead still. . . . The Secretary has changed his position so rapidly he reminds me of the flywheel of an engine. But," he added of the courageous ex-reform mayor of Cleveland, "the dear little fellow isn't to blame."

Inevitably, the "Roosevelt Division" became a *cause célèbre.* Applications for service poured in by the tens of thousands and a rising tide of public opinion called on Wilson to give the old warrior his rein. "The appearance of an ex-President of the United States leading American soldiers to the battle front," wrote "Marse" Henry Watterson in his Louisville *Courier-Journal,* would "electrify the world." The battered hero of the Marne, Marshal Joffre, who headed a French mission to the United States early that spring, emphatically agreed that it would; and when he said as much at a formal dinner in his honor, the State Department reportedly censored newspaper accounts of his remarks. Meanwhile passage of the selective service bill was delayed for two weeks while Lodge and other Roosevelt men in the Senate amended it to authorize volunteer divisions of troops above and below the draft ages. "It is a pity," General Pershing wrote privately at the time, "that . . . [Roosevelt] has not been able to take a broader view . . . but I presume a man's ambition eventually will warp his view of things."

The amended selective service measure became law on May 18, 1917, and TR at once telegraphed the President for authority "to raise two divisions for immediate service at the front." Wilson replied, as Hagedorn remarks, in words chosen "to reduce the patriot to the romantic adventurer." The President said that though he would like to pay Roosevelt the compliment, "this is not the time for compliment or for any action not calculated to contribute to the immediate success of the war." He added that the "business now in hand is undramatic, practical, and of scientific definiteness and precision." And so in a sense it was.

Yet, as the man soon to emerge as the "Tiger of France" understood all too well, "scientific definiteness and precision" were no substitute for courage, inspiration, and hope. In a graphic open letter to Wilson published in his Paris newspaper *L'Homme Enchaîné,* Georges Clemenceau summed up the case for TR:

. . . in all candor, that at the present moment there is in France one name which sums up the beauty of American intervention. It is the name of Roosevelt, your predecessor, even your rival but with whom there can now be no other rivalry than heartening success . . . [Roosevelt] is an idealist, imbued with simple vital idealism. Hence his influence on the crowd, his prestige, to use the right expression. . . . The cause of humanity, which is also your cause, will owe to . . . [the soldiers of France] something approaching a miracle. Since it is in your power to give them before the supreme decision the promise of reward, believe me—send them Roosevelt.

Most of the announced reasons for refusing Roosevelt's request appear untenable today. The selective service principle was a sober and sensible manifestation of democratic doctrine, but its effectiveness hardly hinged on the rejection of all volunteer forces. The only other living ex-President of the United States, William Howard Taft, was prepared to serve in a nonmilitary capacity (and also to wish Theodore "no worse luck than to be sick in bed while Woodrow runs his war"). Neither was TR so inflexible that he would not have agreed to staff his divisions with other than the regular officers he had chosen—the finest in the army. Even the argument that Roosevelt lacked military experience breaks down before the facts, which TR heatedly urged upon Baker, that the regulars would have to undergo almost as much training in the new warfare as the draftees and that he was prepared to accept a subordinate command. On the evidence then available, many a general officer was tragically less qualified for command than Roosevelt, the most brilliant administrator ever to occupy the White House and the most inspiring leader ever to quicken the nation's courage. There was plausibility, moreover, in a painful confession TR made Ambassador Jusserand shortly before the issue was settled. "I am too old. . . . I should crack. But," Roosevelt continued,

I could arouse the belief that America was coming. I could show the Allies what was on the way and then, if I did crack, the President could use me to come back and rouse more enthusiasm here and take some more men over. That is what I am good for now, and what difference would it make if I cracked or not?

One factor was not irrelevant—the Colonel's irrepressibility. The President touched it the day he rejected Roosevelt's final appeal when he remarked to a guest at lunch that "it would be dangerous to send over someone likely to try to show Europe how it should manage its

affairs." And TR himself adverted to it indirectly by assuring Jusserand that "The President need not fear me politically." But could the
Colonel have kept that faith? Would he have accepted Wilson's decision not to drive on to Berlin in November, 1918, as Pershing and
Foch wanted to do? Could he have been silent or discreet about a
dozen other political-military matters? Could he have comported himself as an Eisenhower rather than as a MacArthur? General Hugh L.
Scott, then Chief of Staff, thought not. "Consider what a ridiculous
figure you would cut," he warned Secretary Baker, "attempting to
punish Mr. Roosevelt by court-martial!"

   The episode was as unfortunate as it was inevitable. It exposed the
President's cold self-possession. (". . . I really think the best way to
treat Mr. Roosevelt is to take no notice of him," he told Tumulty at
one point. "That breaks his heart and is the best punishment that can
be administered.") It fanned the flames of TR's already raging hatred
of Wilson. And it sharpened the impression that the Colonel was in
fact a military adventurer.

   The impression was not inaccurate. The romance and glory of the
battlefield still burned bright in TR, and even before the United States
entered the war he had written William Allen White that "I think
I could do this country most good by dying in a reasonably honorable
fashion, at the head of my division in the European War." Now, in
the bitterness and frustration of Wilson's denial of his heart's desire,
he projected himself into the military careers of his four sons: "I am
immensely delighted, . . . for I had no idea that you could make a
regular regiment in a line position," he wrote Ted, who had been
given command of the 1st battalion of the 26th regiment of the First
Division. "I think it was most wise of . . . [Kermit] to get transferred
to the armored car service," he told his second son's wife. "Kermit
is a natural officer of the fighting line." "One of your Generals gave
. . . [Archie] the Croix de Guerre," he wrote Clemenceau in March,
1918, "and I am prouder of his having received it than of my having
been President."

   Just as the warrior sent forth his sons to battle to prove their
courage and share with him the greatest satisfaction he ever knew,
so did the statesman send them forth to perform their national duty.
"We must dare to be great; and we must realize that greatness is the
fruit of toil and sacrifice and high courage," wrote the man whose
career had come as close, probably, as any political leader's could to

exemplifying those values. The ultimate measure of national character, he wrote in typically romanticist-realist vein, was war: "No
qualities called out by a purely peaceful life stand on a level with
those stern and virile virtues which move the men of stout heart and
strong hand who uphold the honor of their flag in battle." What
anguish would have been his had he not had four sons to give when
the offer of his own life was declined!

Meanwhile, the Colonel threw himself into the battle of the home
front with a zeal unsurpassed in all his career. He briefly considered
offering his services to Wilson in any capacity. But partly because he
feared "the President would treat me as an importunate and self-
seeking beggar," he decided against it. He also abandoned thoughts of
asking General Pershing for command of a brigade of regulars.
". . . I am not certain that to give it to me would mean a service to
any one except myself," he explained to A. P. Gardner, who was
soon to die on active duty, "whereas if allowed to raise four divisions
of volunteers I would be doing a service of prime importance both to
this country and to the Allies." Instead, he cast himself in the roles
of preacher-at-large to the American people and critic-in-general of
the Wilson administration.

Roosevelt characteristically chose the Kansas City *Star,* which
served the heartland of the still powerful isolationist sentiment, as his
main outlet. Between September, 1917, and January, 1919, he wrote
more than one hundred syndicated articles for its pages. He also made
repeated appearances on the public platform, often while wracked
with pain from the malignant malarial fever he had suffered in Brazil
and from recurring abscesses of his thigh and ear. In the fall of 1917
and again the spring and fall of 1918 he made major tours of the
Middle West, and on each trip close observers perceived that his iron
determination, and little more, was holding him together. Indeed,
TR himself thought the end had come in February, 1918, when a
friend found him lying in agony on a bed in the Hotel Langdon in
New York. "I don't mind having to die," he slowly remarked as he
roused himself. "I've had my good time . . . and I don't mind having
to pay for it. But," he concluded with a sudden display of fire, "to
think that those swine will say that I'm out of the game."

Throughout the war the Colonel's unvarying theme was Americanism, a "one hundred per cent, undivided loyalty" that tolerated neither
dissent from nor obstruction of the war effort. He expounded it with

incredible vigor and awesome virulence, and he scored his record in so doing (as Wilson also did his) with scars so ugly that the passing of forty years has failed to erase them.

Roosevelt could neither sympathize with the antiwar attitudes nor comprehend the moral courage of the conscientious objectors, whom he regarded as "slackers, pure and simple." He flailed them unmercifully and he relegated them finally to the camp of the enemy. He endorsed loyalty oaths for teachers and urged the dismissal of those who refused to take them. He advocated the abolition of the teaching of German in the public schools. He suggested that German-language newspapers be compelled gradually to publish in English on the theory that "moral treason in English is at least open, whereas in a foreign language it is hidden." He approved the prosecution of two Columbia University students who had advised their fellow students not to register for the draft; and he similarly endorsed the indictment of the Milwaukee Socialist and pro-German, Victor Berger. He regretted that the German apologists George S. Viereck and Bernard Herman Ridder were not given the same treatment. Yet—and the point is not irrelevant in view of the informed speculation that he would face the electorate as the Republican presidential candidate in 1920—he was unfailingly forthright. Repeatedly his bitterest excoriations of German-American "disloyalty" were made in the German-American centers of the Middle West.

Even as TR fanned the already raging flames, moreover, he strove to keep the fire within bounds. In the summer of 1917 he denounced the series of race riots that swept eastward from East St. Louis. In the spring of 1918 he condemned the lynching of a German alien in Collinsville, Illinois. And from the beginning to the end of the war he warned against blanket indictments of the hyphenates. "It is," he asserted again and again, "an outrage to discriminate against a good American in civil life because he is of German blood." But his words fell as water on burning kerosene; the conflagration he himself had set off evaporated them.

TR was also quick to read "Bolshevist" and "German Socialist" into labor strife. And at the end of the war he was preaching that campaign of intolerance which catapulted Attorney General A. Mitchell Palmer to passing fame and enduring notoriety in 1919. "Any foreign-born man who parades with or backs up a red flag or black flag organization ought to be instantly deported to the country from which he came," Roosevelt wrote in the *Star* on November 14, 1918. "Appropriate punishment should be devised for the even more guilty native-born."

Again and again during the war the Colonel spoke out for a press free to print the truth; but it was a truth that collated only with his own one hundred per cent Americanism. He approved the administrations' suppression of the famed Socialist periodical *Masses;* he excoriated it for its failure to take the same action against the powerful Hearst papers for their incitement of "the hatred of our people against allies who are faithfully fighting beside us." He also castigated the administration (and he properly placed the responsibility on the President rather than on Postmaster General Albert B. Burleson) for censoring publications for partisan political purposes. But on the main line—the right to impose cloture on those who opposed the war effort —he held firm. Thus his celebrated attack on the Sedition Bill of 1918, an attack that ironically won him the plaudits of the *Nation,* was directed at a clause that proposed to prohibit "contemptuous or slurring language about the President," not at its strictures against disloyalty. "If it is passed," TR wrote in the *Star,* "I shall certainly give the Government the opportunity to test its constitutionality."

The Colonel's concern for the right to criticize was real and personal. By the late autumn of 1917 he had emerged as Wilson's most powerful and effective critic—so embarrassingly effective that it was rumored that Burleson planned to impose the iron glove of censorship on the *Metropolitan* and Kansas City *Star*. And by the end of hostilities Roosevelt's scathing pen had exposed all of the administration's major failings (and attributed to it a number of others that were not its fault). He seems only to have feared that the President would silence him by appointing him to official position. As he remarked to a friend who observed him hurrying through a mass of proof, "It's a collection of my war articles and speeches. I'm afraid Wilson is going to appoint me to something, and I want to get the book out before he shuts me up."

Roosevelt had inaugurated his editorial series for the *Star* with a powerful blast at America's failure to have "a single man on the fighting line" after eight months of war. He followed it with an indignant protest against the War Department's failure to equip the draftees with rifles—"Broomstick Preparedness," he called it. Thereafter he hammered furiously at the administration's indecisiveness and lack of a sense of urgency—its failure to decide quickly on a specific rifle for infantrymen; its seeming indifference to the task of transporting a great army to France; its leisurely approach to the shipping crisis; and its failure to produce aircraft and artillery. The titles of TR's editorials reveal his bent: "Broomstick Apologists," "A Square Deal for the Training Camps," "Fighting Work for the Man of Fighting Age," "Mobilize Our Manpower," "Tell the Truth and Speed up the War," "The Cost of Unpreparedness," "Let George Speed up the War," "Gird Up Our Loins."

Again, it is impossible to measure Roosevelt's influence accurately. Indubitably, it was heavy. Senator George E. Chamberlain, one of the Democrats' few earnest preparedness leaders, would probably have demanded an investigation of the mobilization effort in December, 1917, regardless of TR's strictures. ("The Military Establishment of America has fallen down," Chamberlain exclaimed to members of the National Security League in January. ". . . It has almost stopped functioning.") But his charges could not have received such widespread and nonpartisan endorsement as they did were it not for the seeds that the Colonel had sown. Indeed, when TR went to Washington the third week in January to rally congressional support of Chamberlain's bill to create a nonpartisan war cabinet, the fruits of his labor were clear to see. Angrily, the President deflected this frontal assault on his war leadership by responding with a bold and constructive proposal—the Overman bill—which vested vast power over production in himself. He also reorganized the War Industries Board and appointed Bernard M. Baruch its chairman—with such salutary results that within a few months criticism lost much of its substance.

It was hardly in TR to speak well of Wilson; and though he sometimes did so, most notably when the President also called for complete victory in his annual message to Congress in December, 1917, such occasions were far from frequent. Yet, Roosevelt's partisanship should not be overexaggerated. It prevented him from appreciating the President's many estimable qualities, and it infused his otherwise constructive criticisms with personal venom and rancor. But it bears repeating that the record of Roosevelt's wartime activities fails utterly to suggest that he was even remotely obstructive.

That record fails to reveal TR as the reactionary that his harsh injunctions against the pacifist-progressives and his renewed communion with the Republican Old Guard imply. He privately classified

La Follette and other antiwar progressives with "that unhung traitor, Hearst." Thus he first recommended that La Follette be expelled from the Senate, then settled on a recommendation for censure as the more expedient course (he feared La Follette would be martyrized and re-elected). And he still refused to recognize, much less endorse, the memorable progressive enactments of Wilson's first administration. Yet, the embers of his own progressivism continued to smolder, and in 1918 again to flame. At war's end it was Woodrow Wilson, pre-occupied with the great questions of the peace as Theodore Roosevelt had been preoccupied with those of preparedness from 1914 to 1917, whose progressivism had burned down. The Colonel's attitude toward tax policy and kindred questions are revealing of this.

TR's understanding of finance was still hazy ("I have not made any speech *only* on the Liberty Loan, because while I may not share any other quality with Abraham Lincoln, I do share his lack of intimate acquaintance with finance," he wrote Herbert Hoover in the fall of 1917). However, he remained actively interested in the social and moral aspects of such problems. He regarded the administration's bill for a 60 per cent ceiling on excess profits taxes as inadequate. And against the counsel of Lodge, he backed Hiram Johnson and, in-directly, Norris, La Follette, and Borah, in their demand for an even higher tax. With the blessing of George Perkins, he stated on the platform and in his published writings that it would be "mischievous not to put a stop to the making of unearned and improper fortunes out of the war," and that America must have "a heavily—a very heavily—graduated tax on the excess profits . . . a tax as heavy as Great Britain has now imposed."

The Colonel was similarly concerned with the inequities, actual and proposed, in the draft system. He chided the Y.M.C.A. for including men of military age on its staff. "It is an ignoble thing for an able-bodied man to be in . . . a position of bodily safety." He excoriated President Wilson for allegedly holding up Edsel Ford's induction into service until he could be legally deferred. "These other young Ameri-cans face death and endure unspeakable hardships and misery and fatigue . . . and have surrendered all hope of money-getting, of comfort and of safety," he indignantly wrote. "But young Mr. Ford, in ease and safety, is in the employ of his wealthy father." And he bitterly attacked the program, devised late in the war, to send new draftees to college preparatory to commissioning them without service in the ranks on the grounds that it was unfair to those already serving overseas and essentially undemocratic.

The average working-man or small farmer has not had money enough to educate his son so that the boy can now enter college without further training. Yet that boy may have in him the qualities of leadership which especially fit him for command. Such a working-man or farmer ought to wish, and does wish, that his son be tested on his merits by actual service in the ranks, alongside of all other boys, no favors being shown either him or them. . . . [There should be no] privilege given to money. . . .

By 1918 Roosevelt's booming exhortations had made him the loyal opposition's uncrowned leader and the Republican party's foremost candidate for the presidency in 1920. "I suspect," Raymond Robbins remarked in July to William Barnes, the Old Guardsman who had sued Roosevelt for libel three years before, "we are going to nominate TR in 1920 by acclamation."

"Acclamation, hell!" Barnes reportedly replied. "We're going to nominate him by assault."

The Colonel was pleased, even sanguine, until personal tragedy finally dulled his edge. "Yes, I will run," he reportedly said, "if the people want me, but only if they really want me. I will not lift a finger for the nomination." He had, he continued, discussed the matter with a number of Republican senators and representatives who "appeared to be sincerely desirous of accepting the fact that we were about to face a changed world and that mere negation and obstruction and attempts to revive the dead past spelled ruin." And he had told them that "I am not in the least concerned with *your* supporting *me* either now or at any future time; all I am concerned with is that you should so act that *I* can support *you*."

Roosevelt meant what he had always meant: the Republican party should become "the Party of sane, constructive radicalism, just as it was under Lincoln." Otherwise, he firmly added, "I have no place in it."

It was an idle dream. Had TR been elected President in 1920 the shape of events would surely have been different. But could they have been much different than in the last years of his presidency? Roosevelt's party had shown its colors during his own turbulent administration and under Taft's as well. It had shown them in its opposition to the progressive legislation of the first Wilson administration; and it would show them again in the administrations of Harding, Coolidge, and Hoover and thence through the long, bitter years of obstruction to the New and Fair Deals. It is hard to believe that Roosevelt, for all the excellence of the administration he would have given the nation, could have done in the 1920's what he had failed so dramatically to do from 1901 to 1912—change the Republican party's social and economic bias. A handful of Republicans—La Follette, Johnson, Norris, and their like—would burn the progressive candle down through the twenties; but they were the very senators whom TR most despised because of their opposition to the war. Nevertheless, the Colonel, satisfied finally that the preparedness fight was won and the Bull Moose party buried, could not but dream of a progressive Republican future.

On March 28, 1918, at Portland, Maine, in his last creative address on domestic affairs, Roosevelt urgently warned party and nation that they must tread the moderate progressive path during the postwar years. He reaffirmed his belief in a tightly and federally regulated capitalism. He called for the encouragement of private enterprise, but not at the expense of labor's "full right to cooperate and combine and full right to collective bargaining and collective action." And he again adumbrated the New Deal by advocating aid to farmers, multipurpose river valley developments, public housing projects, reductions in the hours of labor, and sundry social security measures including old age, sickness, and unemployment insurance.

The Portland address was Theodore Roosevelt's progressive legacy. Though they would soon repudiate it, it was grist for the Old Guard's propaganda mill in the spring of 1918; and the more so because it also featured a broadside attack on the Democrats' conduct of the war. The Republican National Committee had TR's Portland address printed and distributed by the tens of thousands during the congressional campaign that summer and fall.

The Colonel was delighted with the fire he had lit. "I think I do not overstate the matter, he enthusiastically wrote William Allen White, "when I say that the Maine Progressives felt that my speech and its reception amounted to the acceptance, by the Republicans of Maine, of the Progressive platform of 1912 developed and brought up to date." He did not, however, really deceive himself. Even as he railed against the Bolsheviks to the end of his life, he continued to have forebodings that the Grand Old Party would reject his counsel and allow "the Romanovs of our social and industrial world" to return to power.

Meanwhile the pall of death enveloped Sagamore Hill. The old warrior never expected all of his sons to return and he and Mrs. Roosevelt, he later said, were "quite prepared that none of them should come back." Had he not been so captivated by children throughout his life, one might read into the affection he now lavished on his grandsons and daughters an urgency born of the war. "I came back here Monday evening," he wrote Ted's wife who was with the Y.M.C.A. in France, in October, 1917, "and day before yesterday your three darling children arrived."

> I can't say how I have enjoyed them. Gracie is the most winning little thing I have ever known. . . . The first evening I read her Peter Rabbit and Benjamin Bunny, while Mother as an interlude read her Little Black Mingo—Gracie felt that to have us read alternately prevented monotony. Ted's memory was much clearer about the pigs than about me; he greeted me affably, but then inquired of a delighted bystander . . . "What is that man's name?" . . . This afternoon I took the three down to that haven of delight, the pig pen; . . . Little Edie by the way is sometimes laid on the sofa in my room for me to take care of while I am dressing.

But it was on twenty-year-old Quentin, the most promising of his own boys, that the Colonel's thoughts fastened in the summer of 1918. TR had earlier sought unsuccessfully to have suspended the "idiotic ruling" that prevented Quentin's fiancée, Flora Payne Whitney, from going to France to marry him. For, he explained to Ted, "It is well to have had happiness, to have achieved the great ends of life, when one must walk boldly and warily close to death." It was not to be.

The second week in July, just as TR was preparing to serve as a pallbearer for former Mayor John Purroy Mitchel who had been killed in a training accident in Louisiana, he was told that Quentin had destroyed a German plane in combat near Château-Thierry. "Whatever now befalls Quentin," the Colonel wrote Ethel a few days later, "he has now had his crowded hour, and his day of honor and triumph. Mitchell [sic] had neither; he died before he was able to get to the front and to render service and to feel the thrill generous souls *ought* to feel when they have won the honorable renown of doing their duty with exceptional courage and efficiency."

Five days later a newspaperman informed Roosevelt at Sagamore Hill that Quentin had gone down behind the German lines. The father received the news in silence, striding up and down the veranda. Finally, after wondering aloud how he would break the news to Mrs. Roosevelt, he summoned his courage and entered the house. A half hour later he reappeared with a written statement for the press: "Quentin's mother and I are glad that he got to the front and had a chance to render some service to his country, and show the stuff that was in him before his fate befell him." The date was July 17, 1918.

Three suspenseful days followed. On July 18 Roosevelt kept an engagement to deliver the keynote address to the Republican State Convention at Saratoga Springs, resolutely asserting that "It is more than ever my duty to be there." He received at Saratoga the most heartfelt personal ovation of his career; and also a flicker of hope. A cablegram from Ted's wife reported that Quentin's death was "absolutely unconfirmed." The Colonel returned to Sagamore Hill the next day to find similar reports from his son-in-law, Richard Derby, and from General Pershing. But on the afternoon of July 20, just twenty minutes *before* TR received and addressed a delegation from the Japanese Red Cross, a warm and sympathetic telegram from President Wilson confirmed the original report. Quentin was dead! He had been buried, the Germans reported, "with military honors by German airmen at Cambrai at the spot where he fell."

It was then, wrote the Colonel's young friend, Hermann Hagedorn, that the boy in TR died.

For five and a half more months the man in TR lived on. Never was the mature Roosevelt's conception of duty and honor put to a harder test. For a while Quentin's last letters continued to arrive; and once Ethel's young son Richard, Quentin's favorite nephew, heard an airplane overhead and exclaimed to the Colonel, "perhaps that's Uncle Quentin." Finally, in late July, the Roosevelts fled their beloved Sagamore for the first time since their marriage to spend two weeks in Dark Harbor, Maine, with Ethel and Quentin's bereaved fiancée. "It is no use pretending that Quentin's death is not very terrible," TR wrote Kermit's wife. ". . . There is nothing to comfort Flora at the moment; but she is young; I most earnestly hope that time will be very merciful to her, and that in a few years she will keep Quentin only as a loving memory of her golden youth, as the lover of her golden dawn, and that she will find happiness with another good and fine man. But of course it would be all wrong for me to tell her this *now*. As for Mother, her heart will ache for Quentin until she dies."

And so it was also with the father. The public never heard him express his grief. But his valet observed him sitting on a chair, an open book before him, gazing out at the horizon, murmuring, "Poor Quinikins!" There were also fleeting moments of doubt. "To feel that one has inspired a boy to conduct that has resulted in his death, has a pretty serious side for a father," TR wrote to a stranger. However, he added, "I would not have cared for my boys and they would not have cared for me if our relations had not been just along that line." To the novelist Edith Wharton he remarked that there was no use in his writing about Quentin, for "I should break down if I tried." And to General Pershing, whose wife and three daughters had perished in a fire three years before, he wrote that "I should be ashamed of myself if I did not try in a lesser way to emulate . . . [your] courage." But it was to Arthur Lee that he expressed his philosophy most cogently: "It is very dreadful that [Quentin] should have been killed; it would have been worse if he had not gone."

The father's informal memorial, an editorial in the Kansas City *Star* entitled "The Great Adventure," fittingly made no mention of his son's name.

Only those are fit to live who do not fear to die; and none are fit to die who have shrunk from the joy of life and the duty of life. Both life and death are parts of the same Great Adventure. Never yet was worthy adventure worthily carried through by the man who put his personal safety first. Never yet was a country worth living in unless its sons and daughters were of that stern stuff which bade them die for it at need; and never yet was a country worth dying for unless its sons and daughters thought of life not as something concerned only with the selfish evanescence of the individual, but as a link in the great chain of creation and causation. . . .

But honor, highest honor, to those who fearlessly face death for a good cause; no life is so honorable or so fruitful as such a death. Unless men are willing to fight and die for great ideals, including love of country, ideals will vanish, and the world will become one huge sty of materialism. And unless the women of ideals bring forth the men who are ready thus to live and die, the world of the future will be filled by the spawn of the unfit. . . .

For Roosevelt there now remained one last struggle—the winning of the peace. He did not survive to its end; and the tactics he would have pursued can only be conjectured. But he said and wrote enough during its early stages to make his ultimate objective clear. He stood for a peace that would redress Belgium for the wounds she had suffered, reduce Germany to military impotence, and perpetuate the grand alliance that had won the war.

Roosevelt had never forgiven Woodrow Wilson for his call for a "peace without victory" in January, 1917, for his assertion that all the belligerents were fighting for the same general ends. Upon America's entrance into the war TR's conviction that the vital interests of the United States and the Allies were virtually identical had gained wide acceptance; and what he had so often said privately during the long ordeal of neutrality he thereafter said publicly and emphatically. He upbraided the President for insisting that the United States was an associate, rather than a partner, of the Allies. He vehemently and repeatedly demanded that America declare war on Turkey and Bulgaria. And he briefly advocated that American combat troops be placed under British and French command to expedite the prosecution of the war.

Nor did TR delude himself that the United States alone was winning or had won the war. Five weeks after Quentin was shot from the skies, he reminded the American people of their debt to Great Britain. "If she had not controlled the seas," he wrote in the Kansas City *Star*, on August 18, "not an American battalion could have been sent to the aid of France as she struggled to save the soul of the world, and no help could have been given gallant Italy or any others of these Allied nations to whose stern fighting efficiency we owe it that this earth is still a place on which free men can live."

Several weeks after the armistice Roosevelt publicly evaluated the factors responsible for victory: (1) the French army; (2) the British navy; (3) the British army; (4) the Italian army. "Our own gallant army and navy did exceedingly well," he added, "but came in so late that the part they played, taking the four and a half years as a whole, does not entitle them to rank with the instrumentalities given above."

It was this appreciation of the decisive role of Allied power, coupled with his fear that Germany would come back with a vengeance, that underlay TR's call for the unconditional surrender of Germany. He was, no doubt, influenced by a thirst for revenge. And surely his passion was heightened by his contempt for Wilson. "Let us," he had pointedly exclaimed, "dictate peace by the hammering guns and not chat about peace to the accompaniment of the clicking of typewriters." Yet at root he was rational, however unwise. "A premature and inconclusive peace now," he wrote in May, 1918, "would spell ruin for the world, just as in 1864 a premature and inconclusive peace would have spelled ruin to the United States. . . . Twenty years hence by mere mass and growth Germany would dominate the Western European powers." "Germany must accept whatever terms the United States and its allies think necessary in order to right the dreadful wrongs that have been committed and to safeguard the world for at least a generation to come from another attempt by Germany to secure world dominion," he declared on the eve of the armistice. "The surest way to secure a peace as lasting as that which followed the downfall of Napoleon is to overthrow the Prussianized Germany of the Hohenzollerns as Napoleon was overthrown."

More, even, than Roosevelt's anger at Wilson's call for a Democratic Congress in 1918, those views governed Roosevelt's attitude toward the President's peace program. Arguing that Wilson's Fourteen Points portended "not the unconditional surrender of Germany but the conditional surrender of the United States," he openly ridiculed them as "Fourteen Scraps of Paper." He was particularly incensed by the proposals for freedom of the seas and general disarmament. Freedom of the seas "would have meant Germany's victory and the subjugation of not only Germany's foes, but of all neutrals like ourselves," he realistically contended. He was so exacerbated by Wilson's failure to appreciate the importance of British naval power to America's well-being, in fact, that he now left the ranks of the loyal opposition. The Republican party, he wrote Sir Arthur Balfour, Lloyd George, and Clemenceau, does "not believe in what we understand to be Mr. Wilson's interpretation of 'the Freedom of the Seas.' " He declared that "in any free country, except the United States," the Democratic defeat in the Congressional elections on November 5 "would have meant Mr. Wilson's retirement from office and return to private life." And he unashamedly informed them that his party did not support the President's startling proposal to force Britain's hand by threatening a naval race. (Of all men in the United States, Roosevelt, the onetime master diplomatist, should have allowed Wilson to bluff.) "We feel that the British Navy . . . should be the most powerful in the world, and we have no intention of rivaling it, any more than we have any intention of rivaling the French military preparedness, because we recognize that France must prepare her army in a way not necessary for the United States," he told the British and French leaders. He added in the *Star* that the "worse thing we could do would be to build a spite navy, a navy built not to meet our own needs, but to spite some one else."

Elements of realism, as well as a fateful shortsightedness, marked Roosevelt's attitude toward the League of Nations. Here too, he was surely influenced by his hatred of Wilson. But to imply that his spleen was controlling is to defile one of the purest and noblest, if also egocentric, patriots the nation has yet produced. It is also to ignore the consistency of the Colonel's career.

It will be recalled that Roosevelt had never totally dismissed the ancient dream of a parliament of the nations. Even in his Nobel Peace Prize address at Christiana in 1910, however, his commitment had been cautious and measured. He did not believe that the nations of the world were yet ready to subordinate their national drives to the collective will; nor, in his own country's case, did he think that it was desirable to do so. He was too nationalistic—perhaps realistic—to scuttle the Monroe Doctrine. "All the coasts and islands which in any way approach the Panama Canal must be dealt with by this Nation, and by this Nation alone," he wrote as the League issue was coming to a head. And notwithstanding the great blow he himself had rendered the old isolationism, the fateful limitations of his nationalism prevented him from perceiving that America's future frontiers lay beyond the Rhine. "If the League of Nations means that we will have to go to war every time a Jugoslav wishes to slap a Czecho-slav in the face," he said to his personal physician, "then I won't follow them." He added that "we don't want any more scraps of paper." He also wrote in the *Star* that "the affairs of hither Asia, the Balkan Peninsula, and of North Africa are of prime concern to the powers of Europe, and the United States should be under no covenant to go to war about matters in which its people have no concern and probably no intelligent interest."

Even so, the Colonel's attitude toward the League was cautiously affirmative. Partly because Taft and Root, with both of whom he had resumed cordial relations, favored the League, and partly perhaps, because of his own commitment to the ideal in 1910, he prepared in the summer of 1918 to support it with reservations. "I think I have found a *modus vivendi!*" he wrote Taft on August 15. "I will back it as an *addition to,* but not as a *substitute for,* our preparing our own strength in our own defense."

From then until his death Roosevelt gave a carefully measured endorsement to the plan for a league, arguing always that it should be built around the concert of powers that had won the war. He publicly recommended that the United States and Great Britain sign a *universal* arbitration treaty, though not, he hastened to advise Kipling privately, "on the hands-across-the-sea or Anglo-Saxon brotherhood theory." As a matter of fact, he added, "I doubt if there is such a thing as an Anglo-Saxon, but at any rate I am not one. . . . I am just plain straight American."

Otherwise, TR disapproved of President Wilson's decision to go to Paris, approved the appointment of Henry White, whom he referred to as an independent, to the peace commission, and supported a proposed congressional resolution to separate the peace treaty from the League of Nations Covenant. He repeatedly demanded that the Covenant recognize the Monroe Doctrine and that its members be authorized to regulate their own internal affairs, including tariff and immigration policy. And in his last public statement, an editorial dictated three days before his death, he endorsed Taft's proposed reservations, which were substantially the ones he had been advocating himself.

Whether, as Henry Pringle flatly asserts, the Colonel "would have joined the battalion of death that killed the League of Nations" had he lived, is impossible to say. Shortly before Christmas, 1918, Lodge spent two mornings at TR's hospital bedside in New York reportedly formulating the general reservations upon which he later stood. The report is probably correct; Lodge's major reservations, as distinct from his minor ones, were not really different from those Taft and Roosevelt had already advocated. But that TR would have indulged his friend in all his obstructionist maneuvering, and especially in his pandering to the Irish-Americans, is conjectural. TR was probably too deeply committed to Anglo-Franco-American comity, to the moderate reservations of William Howard Taft, and perhaps to his own words over the years for that. Still, he would surely have opposed the treaty as Wilson brought it home. And it remains an open question whether as President in 1921 he would have compelled the Republican party to abide by the campaign promises of a great phalanx of its leaders and have taken the United States into a modified League of Nations. His commitments, and especially Britain's willingness to accept America's nationalistic reservations, suggest that he would have; his belief that an alliance with Great Britain would prove more substantive than membership in any peace organization, coupled with his loathing of all that Woodrow Wilson represented, suggests that he would not have.

On October 27, 1918, Roosevelt observed his sixtieth birthday. "I am glad to be sixty," he wrote Kermit, "for it somehow gives me the right to be titularly as old as I feel. I only hope that when you are sixty you'll have as much happiness to look back upon as I have had," and he added, "be as proud of your sons and daughters as I am of mine; and somehow I believe you'll then still be as much in love with Belle as I am with your Mother, and will feel that you owe her as much as I owe your Mother."

The next day, in the last major address of his thirty-six-year political career, the Colonel answered Wilson's appeal for a Democratic Congress before a full house in Carnegie Hall. For two tense hours, his jaw thrust forward, his teeth clicking, and his manuscript waving as of old, he blasted the President's record, motives, and proposals. He seemingly forgot that just twenty years before, a Republican President had requested that there be no "divided councils" as the nation prepared to make peace, and that the then Republican candidate for governor of New York had appealed for a Republican Congress on the grounds that the world would interpret a Republican defeat "as a refusal to sustain the efforts of our peace commission to secure the fruit of war." Still the circumstances were not quite identical. For if Woodrow Wilson's appeal was justified, as in a sense it was, Theodore Roosevelt's thunderous attack on that appeal was at least understandable in terms of his party's war record. ". . . [The President] asks for the defeat of pro-war Republicans," the Colonel expostulated in Carnegie Hall. "He does not ask for the defeat of anti-war Democrats. On the contrary, he supports such men if, although anti-war, they are pro-Administration."

TR had returned to Sagamore Hill after his Carnegie Hall appearance to take to his bed with lumbago. Six days after the Republicans swept the Congressional elections, on the day the armistice was signed, he was admitted to the Roosevelt Hospital, where his illness was diagnosed as inflammatory rheumatism. He was advised that he might be confined to a wheel chair for the rest of his life, upon which he mused a moment, then replied: "All right! I can work that way, too." Old friends dropped in to see him, among them William Howard Taft. The novelist Hamlin Garland came with a proposal that a garden be planted around Quentin's grave, but Mrs. Roosevelt vetoed it. Someone else talked of the reports, which many political observers by then regarded as a foregone conclusion, that TR would be nominated by the Republicans in 1920. To these the Colonel professed indifference. "Since Quentin's death the world seems to have shut down on me," he said. "But if I do consent," he added with a flash of the old fire, "it will be because as President I could accomplish some things that I should like to see accomplished before I die." Then, probably recalling the G.O.P.'s long hostility toward so much of what he represented, TR raised himself up in bed and asserted: "And, by George, if they take me, they'll take me without a single modification of the things I have always stood for!"

Uncured and still wracked with pain, Roosevelt returned to Sagamore Hill on Christmas Day. There, chatting with neighbors and family, browsing among his books, and surrounded by the trophies and mementos of his tumultuous career, he lived on for almost two weeks. He wrote the editorial endorsing Taft's reservations to the League which appeared in the *Star* after his death, and he composed a scorching and intolerant message on Americanism that was read to a meeting of the American Defense Society in the Hippodrome in New York the night before he died. He also dictated a final memorandum that suggests that he was prepared again to hold his party together, his militant progressive declarations notwithstanding: "Hays —see him; he must go to Washington for 10 days; see Senate & House; prevent split on domestic policies."

On the eleventh day, Sunday, January 5, the Colonel remained in his bedroom overlooking Long Island Sound. He read aloud with his wife, dictated a letter to Kermit, and worked over the proof of an article for the *Metropolitan*. Late in the afternoon as Mrs. Roosevelt, who had been playing solitaire, rose to leave, the Colonel looked up from his book and said, "I wonder if you will ever know how I love Sagamore Hill."

A little earlier than usual that night, the Colonel asked his Negro valet if he thought "I might go to bed now." The valet, James Amos, almost lifted him into bed, then Mrs. Roosevelt came in and kissed him good night as she had done to Quentin the night he slept at

Sagamore Hill for the last time. Between eleven and twelve o'clock the Colonel said, "James, please put out the light." He never spoke again. Sometime after four the next morning, January 6, 1919, Theodore Roosevelt died in his sleep.

He was buried without eulogy, music, or military honors in a plain oak casket on a hillside plot near Sagamore Hill that he and Mrs. Roosevelt had earlier selected. About four hundred personal friends, fifty children from the public school in Oyster Bay where he had sometimes played Santa Claus, and one hundred dignitaries attended the simple ceremony. Among them was the man he had hurt the worst and who had loved him the most—William Howard Taft. Some time after the assemblage had dispersed, Taft was seen standing alone meditating over the grave.

For weeks the tributes poured forth. "ONE WORD is repeated a thousand times. . . ," the *Literary Digest* reported. "It is the simple but eloquent word 'American.' " America's contribution to the Great War, said the Philadelphia *North American* in a statement echoed throughout the nation, was "the product of the will, the passionate conviction, and the devoted services of Theodore Roosevelt, private citizen, more than any other force." In England Rudyard Kipling wrote a memorial, "Great-heart." And in the chamber of the Senate a grief-stricken Cabot Lodge closed his eloquent eulogy with the quotation: "So Valiant-for-Truth passed over and all the trumpets sounded for him on the other side." Even the man who had served as the buffer between the Colonel and President Wilson was affected. "You will, no doubt, be greatly distressed at the news," gentlemanly Newton D. Baker wrote General Pershing the morning Roosevelt died. "About many things my disagreements with him were fundamental, but like all Americans I had a sympathy for his irresistible energy and courage. . . . In practically every field of human endeavor he has made his mark. . . ."

As Irvin S. Cobb put it, "You had to hate the Colonel a whole lot to keep from loving him."

Like most men of heroic proportions, Theodore Roosevelt had made major blunders and miscalculations. He had suffered an acute and far-ranging vision to be blurred by a too sweeping commitment to force or the threat of force. He had blinded himself, except in the memorable year of his Bull Moose heresy, to the moral limitations imposed on his party by its hostage to the men and values of the market place. He had repelled men who should have taken him seriously by his boyish enthusiasms and matchless lust for life. And he had often conveyed the impression of opportunism by the ease with which he had shifted causes and allegiances in the harsh conviction that politics is the art of the possible.

Yet, as in all generalizations about this extraordinary man, the need to qualify and elaborate remains. If Roosevelt the conservative retained to the end a Burkean fear of revolution, Roosevelt the progressive had proclaimed from the beginning a democratic functionalism that was grounded in almost fuller faith in man—in his free moral capacity, his educability, and his power to act finally with disinterest —than Jefferson's. No great American statesman has ever been more committed to an open society based on talent; no American President has ever flirted more seriously with majority rule. Nor, paradoxically, has any major American political leader ever reposed greater confidence in government by experts; nor, still more paradoxically, expounded so emphatically a philosophy of moral absolutes.

If, in the summing up, Roosevelt indulged too indiscriminately in platitudes, as surely he did, and if he extolled character at the sacrifice of depth and breadth of mind, as conservatives have immemorially done, his preachments are nonetheless viable. It is true that they rested on nothing more substantial than his own intuition and intelligence— as he once exclaimed when asked how he knew that justice had been done, "Because I did it." And it is also true that although this was well enough for him, the intuition being deep and the intelligence penetrating, it was not enough for all the men who subsequently held the office he had himself so distinguished. Men of estimable character with one exception and men of narrow intellectual horizons with some exceptions, only a few of them understood, as the mature Roosevelt finally did, that a moralism unsupported by social and economic reality is the most meaningless of platitudes.

For all of that, for all, even, of the relativism of the modern mind, the feeling persists that men of character, if blessed also with depth and breadth of view, will always come to a working concensus as to the nature of justice in a given situation. And if such is in truth the case, the ideal of the morally responsible and duty-conscious citizen that Roosevelt so imbued in the minds of his own generation must live on in those that follow.

Whatever the Colonel's ultimate place in the hearts of his countrymen—and it yearly grows larger and warmer—there is no discounting those incisive perceptions and momentous actions that made him such a dynamic historical force from his civil service years to the day of his death. In an age when the excesses of the profit system were undermining the moral foundations of American society, when one great body of reformers was invoking the antiquated ways of the agrarian order and another was uncritically accepting a mechanistic interpretation of man himself, when two of the nation's most ripened historical minds, Brooks and Henry Adams, were evolving theories that closed the ring on all hope, Roosevelt the practical idealist was molding the new determinism and the old individualism into the only synthesis compatible with the American political temperament; the only program that offers hope that industrialism will ultimately serve American society for good rather than ill. Eschewing laissez-faire capitalism no less than doctrinaire socialism, he saw with the pragmatist's genius that "Ruin faces us if we . . . permit ourselves to be misled by any empirical or academic consideration into refusing to exert the common power of the community where only collective action can do what individualism has left undone, or can remedy the wrongs done by an unrestricted and ill-regulated individualism." More, perhaps, than anything else, it was the coincidence of that insight and Roosevelt's disposition to act that explains his dramatic and exhilarating impact on his times.

Long after the rationalizations, the compromises, the infights, the intolerance and all the rest have been forgotten, Theodore Roosevelt will be remembered as the first great President-reformer of the modern industrial era—the first to concern himself with the judiciary's massive property bias, with the maldistribution of wealth, and with the subversion of the democratic process by businessmen and their spokesmen in Congress, the pulpits and the editorial offices; the first to comprehend the conservation problem in its multiple facets, the first to evolve a broad regulatory program for capital, and the first to encourage, however cautiously, the growth of countervailing labor unions; the first President, in fine, to understand and react constructively to the challenge to existing institutions raised by the technological revolution. And if, for the affront his militarism and chauvinism gave the human spirit, he will never be truly revered as is Lincoln, he will yet for his unique personal qualities and remarkably constructive achievements, among them the realistic pursuit of peace in a world that he understood better than most, be greatly loved and profoundly respected.

NOTES

GENERAL

As my references within the text indicate, I have written this book mainly from published works. There are, of course, significant exceptions. I have done supplementary research in the Roosevelt Papers at the Library of Congress, in Roosevelt's several diaries at the Library of Congress and the Houghton Library of Harvard University, and the voluminous scrapbooks kept by Roosevelt's family and friends and now on deposit in the Widener Library at Harvard. I have also used many of the relevant public documents—legislative journals, Civil Service Commission and Police Commission reports, *Congressional Record,* and Roosevelt's published messages as governor and President. In connection with another work, moreover, I have done systematic, basic research for most of Part VI—the World War years. But in general I have relied on two invaluable sets of Roosevelt's writings: Elting E. Morison and John M. Blum (eds.), *The Letters of Theodore Roosevelt* (8 vols., Cambridge, 1951–54); and Hermann Hagedorn (ed.), *The Works of Theodore Roosevelt* (20 vols., National Edition, New York, 1926). I doubt that I could have written this biography without either of them. They will be cited hereafter as *The Letters* and *The Works* respectively. Albert Bushnell Hart and Herbert Ronald Ferleger (eds.), *Theodore Roosevelt Cyclopedia* (New York, 1941) has been useful as a reference guide.

Since the following chapter notes include only the works I have actually used, as distinct from the hundreds and perhaps thousand or more books I have consulted over the years, the serious student's attention is directed to a number of bibliographies. The most exhaustive such work on Roosevelt himself, one that merits separate publication, is in Edward Wagenknecht, *The Seven Worlds of Theodore Roosevelt* (New York, 1958). The best general bibliography for the presidential and immediate post-presidential years is in George E. Mowry, *The Era of Theodore Roosevelt* (The New American Nation Series, New York, 1958); the best for the years 1912–1916 in Arthur S. Link, *Woodrow Wilson and the Progressive Era* (The New American Nation Series, New York, 1954). Oscar Handlin, *et al.* (eds.) *Harvard Guide to American History* (Cambridge, 1954) is indispensable for the whole of Roosevelt's life and times.

PART I: **THE MAKING OF A MAN**

Chapter 1. THE FIRST BATTLE

Although I disagree strongly with many of his inferences and conclusions, Henry F. Pringle's scintillating *Theodore Roosevelt: A Biography* (New York, 1931) has contributed immeasurably to the conception of this chapter and indeed to many that follow. In revision I have profited from Carleton Putnam, *Theodore Roosevelt: The Formative Years* (New York, 1958), the superb first volume of a projected multi-volume biography. Besides *The Letters* and *The Scrapbooks*, I have drawn liberally on TR's unpublished diaries (the diaries covering the legislative period have been published in part as Appendix I, *The Letters*, Vol. II. Other primary sources include Theodore Roosevelt, *An Autobiography*, first published in 1913 and later reissued as Volume XX of *The Works; Proceedings of the Theodore Roosevelt Memorial Meeting of the State Charities Aid Association* (privately printed, New York, 1878); and New York State Assembly, *Journal of the Assembly, 1882* (6 vols. Albany, 1882–1884). The recollections of Isaac Hunt and others, quoted herein, are in the "Harvard Club Transcripts," a transcript of the proceedings at a Harvard Club dinner in New York in 1920, at the Theodore Roosevelt Memorial Association Library in the Roosevelt House, New York; also the recollections of Joe Murray as told to Hermann Hagedorn. Roosevelt's *The Naval War of 1912* is in Volume VI of *The Works.*

Of the secondary materials, Howard Lawrence Hurwitz, *Theodore Roosevelt and Labor in New York State, 1880–1900* (New York, 1943) has proved informative and suggestive. It is, I think, unnecessarily harsh, and it should be read against the broader and more understanding treatment in Putnam's *The Formative Years*. In addition, I have drawn on or quoted from the following works: Howard K. Beale, "TR's Ancestry, A Study in Heredity," *New York Genealogical and Biographical Record,* LXXXV (1954); Hermann Hagedorn, *The Boy's Life of Theodore Roosevelt* (New York, 1918); Corrine Roosevelt Robinson, *My Brother, Theodore Roosevelt* (New York, 1923); Paul Russell Cutright, *Theodore Roosevelt the Naturalist* (New York, 1956), a good appreciation by a professional zoologist; Frances Theodora Parsons, *Perchance Some Day* (privately printed, New York, New York, 1951), cited by Putnam; William Roscoe Thayer, *Theodore Roosevelt, an Intimate Biography* (New York, 1919); Charles G. Washburn, *Theodore Roosevelt, the Logic of His Career* (New York, 1916); Owen Wister, *Roosevelt: The Story of a Friendship* (New York, 1930); William Wingate Sewall, *Bill Sewall's Story of T.R.* (New York, 1919); Donald Wilhelm, *Theodore Roosevelt as an Undergraduate* (Boston, 1910); Curtis Guild, Jr., "TR at Harvard," *Harvard Graduate Magazine*, X (1938); and J. Laurence Laughlin, "Roosevelt at Harvard," *Review of Reviews*, LXX (1924). Also, Poultney Bigelow, *Seventy Summers*, (2 vols., New York, 1925).

Chapter 2. A LEADER EMERGES

Besides the obvious sources—*The Letters, Autobiography, Journal of the Assembly* for the relevant years, and *Scrapbooks*—I have again used Pringle, *Theodore Roosevelt* and Hurwitz, *Theodore Roosevelt and Labor* extensively. Again, too, I have made several revisions on the basis of Putnam's *The Formative Years*. My characterization of Cleveland reflects Allan Nevins' excellent and highly moralistic *Grover Cleveland: A Study in Courage* (New York, 1932). Among the many other works used are: Samuel Gompers, *Seventy Years of Life and Labor* (2 vols., New York, 1925); Jacob Riis, *Theodore Roosevelt the Citizen* (New York, 1904); Chauncey Depew, *My Memories of Eighty Years* (New York, 1922); Henry Cabot Lodge (ed.), *Selections from the Correspondence of Theodore Roosevelt and Henry Cabot Lodge, 1884–1918* (2 vols., New York, 1925); and the *Proceedings of the Eighth Republican Convention* (Chicago, 1884). I have evolved my account of the Republican Convention of 1884 from the varying interpretations given in Pringle's and Putnam's biographies; in John A. Garraty, *Henry Cabot Lodge* (New York, 1953); James C. Malin, "Roosevelt and the Elections of 1884 and 1888," *Mississippi Valley Historical Review*, XIV (1927); DeAlva Stanwood Alexander, *A Political History of the State of New York* (4 vols., New York, 1906–1923), and by the same author, *Four Famous New Yorkers* (New York, 1923); contemporary newspaper accounts as found in the *Scrapbooks;* and numerous general works. A few of Roosevelt's campaign speeches are in *Campaigns and Controversies*, Vol. XIV, *The Works;* excerpts from others may be found in the *Scrapbooks*. John Blum's essay, "Theodore Roosevelt: Years of Decision," published as Appendix IV, *The Letters*, Vol. II, has been a continuing source of stimulation. For reasons implicit in my treatment throughout, however, I incline to be more tolerant of the "eclectic intellectual home," so incisively described therein, that Roosevelt created to accommodate the divergent pulls of pure theory and pure politics.

Chapter 3. THE WESTERNER: RANCHER, HUNTER, HISTORIAN

The best account of the death and funeral of Roosevelt's wife and mother is in Putnam, *The Formative Years*. Pringle's treatment is also moving. I have supplemented their accounts with clippings from the *Scrapbooks,* excerpts from *The Letters,* and quotations from Theodore Roosevelt, *In Memory of My Darling Wife* (privately printed), and Arthur H. Cutler's typewritten statement as cited by Putnam. Hermann Hagedorn's pioneering narrative, *Roosevelt in the Bad Lands* (Boston, 1921), forms the base for my brief treatment of TR's western experience. In revision I drew on the seemingly definitive story in Putnam, *The Formative Years.* Otherwise I used *The Letters; Scrapbooks;* Lincoln Lang, *Ranching with Roosevelt* (Philadelphia, 1926); Cutright, *Theodore Roosevelt the Naturalist;* and Ray H. Mattison, "Roosevelt and the Stockmen's Association," *North Dakota History,* XVII (1950). I have also read Roosevelt's three books, *Hunting Trips of a Ranchman, Ranch Life and the Hunting Trail,* and *The Wilderness Hunter.* They comprise Volume I and part of Volume II of *The Works.*

The expositions of Roosevelt's *Thomas Hart Benton* and *Gouverneur Morris,* published as Volume VII of *The Works,* are my own. Briefer analyses may be found in the biographies by Putnam and Pringle. I have chosen to quote liberally from Frederick Jackson Turner's review of the fourth volume of Roosevelt's *The Winning of the West,* which appeared in *The American Historical Review,* II (1896), in order to emphasize how seriously professional historians regarded the work at the time. I do not agree with all of Turner's judgments. Further evidence of Roosevelt's high repute among contemporary professional historians may be found in the analysis of the reviews of Volumes I and II offered by George B. Utley, "Theodore Roosevelt's *The Winning of the West:* Some Unpublished Letters," *The Mississippi Valley Historical Review,* XXX (1944). A brief, favorable assessment may also be found in Wagenknecht's uniquely interesting *The Seven Worlds.* Two severely critical appraisals of TR as an historian are the essays by H. J. Thornton and Raymond C. Miller published respectively in William T. Hutchison (ed.), *The Marcus W. Jernegan Essays* in *American Historiography* (Chicago, 1937); and James Lea Cate and Eugene N. Anderson (eds.), *Medieval and Historiographical Essays in Honor of James Westfall Thompson* (Chicago, 1938). Harvey Wish, *The American Historian* (New York, 1960), also gives a brief evaluation.

PART II: **THE ROAD TO THE WHITE HOUSE**

Chapter 4. For the Good of the Nation

The classic account of the Haymarket tragedy is Henry David, *The History of the Haymarket Affair* (New York, 1936). I have used it along with *The Letters* and Ray Ginger, *Altgeld's America* (New York, 1958). Putnam's treatment of TR's attitude is more sympathetic than mine. The account of the mayoralty campaign of 1886 is drawn from *The Letters; Scrapbooks;* Hurwitz, *Theodore Roosevelt and Labor;* Allan Nevins, *Abram S. Hewitt, With Some Account of Peter Cooper* (New York, 1935); Louis F. Post and Fred C. Leubuscher, *An Account of the George-Hewitt Campaign in the New York Municipal Election of 1886* (New York, 1886); Albert Jay Nock, *Henry George* (New York, 1939); and Jacob Riis, *Theodore Roosevelt.* I have found the chapter on George in Daniel Aaron, *Men of Good Hope* (New York, 1951) especially illuminating. The estimate of Edith Carow Roosevelt is based on two confidential sources; on Hermann Hagedorn, *The Roosevelt Family of Sagamore Hill* (New York, 1954); and on scattered references in *The Letters* and in memoirs too numerous too cite. Putnam is partial to TR's first wife. My evaluation of Lodge, in so far as it is moderate, reflects Garraty's multi-dimensional study, *Henry Cabot Lodge.* Roosevelt's relations with Lodge may also be traced in Lodge (ed.) *Selections.* Because of the unspecified changes made by Lodge in the original letters, they should be used with caution.

For the description of TR's activities as Civil Service Commissioner, I have relied heavily on *The Letters* and *Scrapbooks* and particularly on the *Annual Reports* for the relevant years. I have also quoted from the *Letters of Theodore Roosevelt: Civil Service Commissioner, 1889–1895,* a pamphlet issued in 1958 under the direction of then Commissioner Harrison Ellsworth. It contains several theretofore unpublished letters. In addition, I have drawn on Theodore Roosevelt, "Six Years of Civil Service Reform," *Scribner's Magazine,* XVIII (1895); Eric F. Goldman, *Charles J. Bonaparte, Patrician Reformer* (Baltimore, 1943); Dorothy Canfield Fowler, *The Cabinet Politician: The Postmasters General, 1829–1909* (New York, 1943); Carl Schurz, *Speeches, Correspondence and Political Papers* (Frederic Bancroft, ed., 6 vols., New York, 1913); Herbert A. Gibbons, *John Wanamaker* (2 vols., New York, 1926); and William Dudley Foulke, *Roosevelt and the Spoilsmen* (New York, 1925). In revision I have modified my treatment slightly on the basis of Leonard D. White, with the assistance of Jean Schneider, *The Republican Era, 1869–1901* (New York, 1958). White is more sympathetic to (and probably more understanding of) the problems faced by Wanamaker and others who crossed TR than I am. He is especially appreciative of Wanamaker's organizational and executive ability.

Chapter 5. THE FIGHT FOR THE RIGHT

There is no adequate secondary account of Roosevelt's tenure as Police Commissioner although the late Howard K. Beale's unpublished first volume of TR's life is said to contain an exhaustive treatment. The chapter in Pringle, *Theodore Roosevelt,* is palpably unfair; that in Lincoln

Steffens, *The Autobiography of Lincoln Steffens* (2 vols., New York, 1931), perceptive but cynical and not wholly reliable. Riis, *Theodore Roosevelt*, is informative, but uncritical. My reconstruction of the commissionership is based mainly on *The Letters, Scrapbooks, Reports* of the New York City Police Department, and especially on the scrapbooks kept by TR's fellow commissioner, Avery D. Andrews. These are now in the collection at Harvard. I also found Andrews's unpublished manuscript, "Theodore Roosevelt as Police Commissioner," of considerable value. A copy is in the Theodore Roosevelt Memorial Association Library. In addition, I have consulted and occasionally quoted from Roosevelt's *An Autobiography;* Gustavus Myers, *The History of Tammany Hall* (New York, 1901); Joseph Bucklin Bishop, *Theodore Roosevelt and His Time* (2 vols., New York, 1920); Wister, *Roosevelt;* Lodge (ed.), *Selections;* and Charles F. Parkhurst, *My Forty Years in New York* (New York, 1923). I have further used *Campaigns and Controversies*, Vol. XIV, *The Works.*

Chapter 6. THE GREAT ADVENTURE

Besides such standard sources as *The Letters, Scrapbooks*, and *An Autobiography*, I have relied on Bishop's and Pringle's biographies of TR and Garraty's of Lodge. I have also quoted from William Allen White, *Masks in a Pageant* (New York, 1930), William L. Langer, *The Diplomacy of Imperialism, 1890–1902* (2 vols., New York, 1935), Hermann Hagedorn, *Leonard Wood: A Biography* (2 vols., New York, 1931), Philip C. Jessup, *Elihu Root* (2 vols., New York, 1938), and Catherine Drinker Bowen, *Yankee from Olympus: Justice Holmes and the Supreme Court* (Boston, 1944). The excerpts from Long's diary are taken from Stefan Lorant, *The Life and Times of Theodore Roosevelt* (New York, 1959); the statement by Will James from the excellent chapter, "Racism and Imperialism," in Richard Hofstadter, *Social Darwinism in American Thought*, rev. ed. (Boston, 1955). Among the numerous other works I have used are James Ford Rhodes, *The McKinley and Roosevelt Administrations* (New York, 1922), Julius W. Pratt, *Expansionists of 1898* (Baltimore, 1936), Samuel Flagg Bemis, *A Diplomatic History of the United States* (rev. ed., New York, 1950) Richard Hofstadter, *The American Political Tradition and the Men Who Made It* (New York, 1948), and Matthew Josephson, *The Politicos,* (New York, 1938), and *The President Makers* (New York, 1940).

I have found the analysis of Roosevelt's views on Darwinism and imperialism in Blum's essay, "Theodore Roosevelt: The Years of Decision," especially discerning. Margaret Leech, *In The Days of McKinley* (New York, 1959) supercedes George S. Olcott, *The Life of William McKinley* (Boston, 1916). I used it in revision. Although I continue to believe that McKinley could have and should have averted war, *In The Days of McKinley* offers the best account yet published of the enormous pressures to which he was subjected. A fine brief history of the war is Frank Freidel, *The Splendid Little War* (Boston, 1958). Roosevelt's own view is given in Theodore Roosevelt, *The Rough Riders*, Vol. XI, *The Works*. The interested student might also consult his reviews of Alfred T. Mahan's *The Influence of Sea Power Upon History* and of Brooks Adams' *The Law of Civilization and Decay*, reprinted in Volumes XII and XIII of *The Works*. Charles A. Beard's appreciative comments on TR's review of Adams's work are in his introduction to the Vintage Edition of Brooks Adams, *The Law of Civilization and Decay* (New York, 1955). Also see Albert K. Weinberg, *Manifest Destiny: A Study of Nationalist Expansionism in American History* (Baltimore, 1935); Richard Hofstadter, "Manifest Destiny and the Philippines," in *America in Crisis*, Daniel Aaron, ed. (New York, 1952); and John P. Mallan, "The Warrior Critique of a Business Civilization," *American Quarterly*, VIII (1956). I have also quoted from William Reynolds Braisted, *The United States Navy in the Pacific, 1897–1909* (Austin, Texas, 1958).

Chapter 7. THE FINAL PREPARATION

TR's governorship has been covered exhaustively in a doctoral dissertation, regrettably unpublished, G. Wallace Chessman, "Theodore Roosevelt, Governor," (Harvard University, 1950). I have used it in revision. There is no published work of consequence. Pringle's chapter is superficial. Alexander's *A Political History* is limited. Hurwitz *Theodore Roosevelt and Labor* is informative, but unappreciative of the multiple demands made on TR. It is nonetheless useful. A number of other works have also contributed to various phases of my treatment. They include: Harold F. Gosnell, *Boss Platt and His New York Machine* (Chicago, 1924); Thomas Collier Platt, *The Autobiography of Thomas Collier Platt*, edited by Louis J. Long (New York, 1910); Roosevelt, *An Autobiography;* Richard Hovey, *John Jay Chapman, an American Mind* (New York, 1959); Henry Herman Kohlsaat, *From McKinley to Harding* (New York, 1923); Jessup, *Root;* Chauncey M. Depew, *My Memories of Eighty Years* (New York, 1922); and Joseph I. C. Clarke, *My Life and Memories* (New York, 1925).

The substance of my exposition is drawn from *The Letters*, Vol. II, and a number of illuminating notes therein, including O'Neil's report to Van Duzer; the *Scrapbooks; Public Papers of Theodore Roosevelt, Governor* (2 vols., Albany, 1899–1900); *Journal of the Assembly of the State of New York* (7 vols., Albany, 1899–1900); and the *Journal of the Senate of the State of New York* (4 vols., Albany, 1899–1900). My characterization of Root, originally quite harsh, now reflects in part the brief estimate in Elting E. Morison, *Turmoil and Tradition: A Study of the Life and Times of Henry L. Stimson* (Boston, 1960). The "Note on Roosevelt's Nomination for the Governorship" (no author named), in Appendix II, *The Letters*, Vol. II, offers the most plausible explanation I have read of the controversy between TR, Chapman, *et al* over the issue of a separate, Independent ticket nomination.

Chapter 8. THE PEOPLE'S CHOICE

The most inclusive account of the events leading to TR's nomination is G. Wallace Chessman, "Theodore Roosevelt's Campaign Against the Vice Presidency," *The Historian*, XIV (1952). Margaret Leech, *In The Days of McKinley* offers new insights into McKinley's attitude toward TR. I have been unable to weave them into my copy, however. Basically, I have depended on Chessman's article and *The Letters, Scrapbooks,* and numerous memoirs, including Nicholas Murray Butler, *Across the Busy Years: Recollections and Reflections* (2 vols., New York, 1939, 1940); Kohlsaat, *From McKinley to Harding;* Herbert Croly, *Marcus Alonzo Hanna, His Life and Works* (New York, 1912); Platt's *Autobiography;* and White's *Autobiography.*

The story of the campaign has been reconstructed in part from most of the above mentioned works and largely from newspaper clippings in *The Scrapbooks.* My appraisal of Altgeld reflects two constructive appraisals, Harry Barnard, *Eagle Forgotten: The Life of John Peter Altgeld* (Indianapolis, 1938), and Ginger, *Altgeld's America.* My understanding of the populist movement derives from John D. Hicks, *The Populist Revolt* (New York, 1931); from chapters in C. Vann Woodward, *Origins of the New South* (Baton Rouge, La., 1951); Francis B. Simkins, *Pitchfork Ben Tillman, South Carolinian* (Baton Rouge, La., 1944); Theodore Saloutos and John D. Hicks, *Agricultural Discontent in the Middle West* (Madison, Wisc., 1951); and articles, monographs, and doctoral dissertations too numerous to cite here. I agree with the assertion in Samuel P. Hays, *The Response to Industrialism: 1885–1914* (Chicago, 1957), that the economic analysis in works such as Carl C. Taylor, *The Farmer's Movement, 1620–1920* (New York, 1953) and Allan G. Bogue, *Money at Interest: The Farm Mortgage in the Middle Border* (Ithaca, 1955) proves that the farmers' suffering was caused less by money lenders, whether Eastern or Southern and Western, and tariff-protected industrialists than by marketing problems that we have yet to resolve. I also find the exposition of the racist and other egregious impulses of the Populists and their agrarian successors set forth in Richard Hofstadter, *The Age of Reform; From Bryan to F.D.R.* (New York, 1955) suggestive, if hardly inclusive. But I see little in these newer works that refutes the validity of the Populist-Bryan program (as distinct from its analysis of the reasons for the farmers' plight) in so far as it embraced lower tariffs, government-supported regional credit devices, graduated income tax, and a general expansion of the money supply. I find, accordingly, that the older works continue to be illuminating.

Bryan awaits a good biography. Richard Hofstadter, *The American Political Tradition* (New York, 1948) presents a devastating portrait. The picture in Eric Goldman's graphic *Rendezvous with Destiny* (New York, 1952) is similarly penetrating and not more flattering. I lean toward the affirmative assessment in Henry S. Commager, *The American Mind* (New Haven, 1952). Bryan's major speeches for the two campaigns are in William Jennings Bryan, *The First Battle* (Chicago, 1896) and *The Second Battle* (Chicago, 1900). Since the above was written, an extended essay, Paul W. Glad, *The Trumpet Soundeth: William Jennings Bryan and His Democracy, 1896–1912* (University of Nebraska Press, 1960), has been published. Glad makes Bryan intelligible to the urban mind and broadly succeeds, I think, in giving him his due. Conversely, Leech, *In the Days of McKinley,* seems to me to give McKinley far more than his due. Yet it has many excellences. It contributes particularly to an understanding of the decision to take the Philippines. But also see the relevant chapters in Bemis, *A Diplomatic History* and Thomas A. Bailey, *A Diplomatic History of the American People* (New York, 3rd ed., 1946).

It occurs to me as this goes to press that the reader may infer from my treatment of the campaign of 1900 that the election actually turned on the imperialism issue. Historians familiar with Thomas A. Bailey, "Was the Presidential Election of 1900 a Mandate on Imperialism?" *Mississippi Valley Historical Review,* XXIV (1937) and the numerous works that touch on the question know that the available evidence indicates that it did not. They are similarly aware, as most of the standard diplomatic histories point out, that Bryan's response to the charge that other powers would take the Philippines should the United States move out was a nebulous proposal for a protectorate.

A General Note on the Presidential Years

George E. Mowry, *The Era of Theodore Roosevelt: 1900–1912* (New York, 1958) is the best work on the presidential years. It supercedes the chapters in Pringle, *Theodore Roosevelt* and in Rhodes, *The McKinley and Roosevelt Administrations.* Mowry's book appeared too late to influence my conception. I have, however, made some revisions and included some new materials on the basis of it. Mowry takes Roosevelt seriously, as Pringle and most of the historians who draw on him did not always do; he succeeds admirably in relating him to his times. In lighter vein, there is much colorful material on the Roosevelt years in Volumes II and III of Mark Sullivan, *Our Times* (New York, 1927, 1930).

For general background I have consulted, but not used, a number of political-intellectual histories, the most important of which are: Henry Steele Commager, *The American Mind;* Goldman, *Rendezvous With Destiny;* Arthur Ekirch, Jr., *The Decline of American Liberalism* (New York, 1956); and Richard Hofstadter's *Age of Reform.*

I have also found Harold U. Faulkner's *The Quest for Social Justice: 1898–1914* (New York, 1931), and the same author's *The Decline of Laissez-Faire: 1897–1914* (New York, 1951) informative. Hays, *The Response to Industrialism* revises many of the older judgments found in Faulkner and others.

It is needless to add that I have based much of the following chapters on *The Letters,* Vols. III–VI, and on the Homeward Bound Edition of Roosevelt's *Presidential Addresses* (8 vols., Review of Reviews Co., 1910). *The Works,* Vol. XV, contains a comparatively small number of TR's messages to Congress. I have continued to use the *Scrapbooks* and have supplemented them with *The Literary Digest* for the years under review. I have also used the *Congressional Record* liberally, though not systematically, a detailed and exhaustive study of the legislative process being beyond the scope of this volume.

PART III: THE SQUARE DEAL BEGINS

Chapter 9. THE FIRST FELL BLOWS

The broad outlines of the sparkling account of TR's first blows against the trusts given in Pringle, *Theodore Roosevelt,* have not changed. Mark Sullivan, *Our Times: America Finding Herself* (Vol. II of *Our Times*) is also rich in human interest. I have extracted the Pulitzer correspondence from it. I have also used Talthasar Meyer, *A History of the Northern Securities Case* (University of Wisconsin Bulletin, No. 142, Madison, 1906); the court record, *Northern Securities Co., et al. v. United States,* 193 U.S. 360, 1904; and several treatises on the trust problem. Of the latter, Hans B. Thorelli, *Federal Anti-Trust Policy: Organization of an American Tradition* (Baltimore, 1955) offers a thorough, up-to-date, and generally favorable appraisal of TR's early antitrust program. A keen insight into the business mind is found in Edward C. Kirkland, *Dream and Thought in the Business Community, 1860–1900* (Ithaca, N.Y., 1956).

Biographies of the central figures include Frederick Lewis Allen, *The Great Pierpont Morgan* (New York, 1949); James G. Pyle, *The Life of James J. Hill* (New York, 1917); and George Kennan, *E. H. Harriman*

(2 vols., Boston, 1922). All should be used with caution. In addition, see Elmer Ellis, *Mr. Dooley's America: A Life of Finley Peter Dunne* (New York, 1941).

The background of Roosevelt's decision to appoint Holmes is given in John Garraty, "Holmes' Appointment to the Supreme Court," *The New England Quarterly*, XXII (1949). Garraty's treatment is fuller than mine and properly emphasizes TR's interest in Holmes's attitude toward the Insular Cases. Also see Mark A. DeWolfe Howe, *The Correspondence of Mr. Justice Holmes and Sir Frederick Pollock* (2 vols., Cambridge, 1941); Felix Frankfurter, *Mr. Justice Holmes and the Supreme Court* (Cambridge, 1938); and Worthington C. Ford (ed.), *The Letters of Henry Adams: 1892–1918* (2 vols., Boston, 1932).

An informative note on Littlefield's activities is in *The Letters*, Vol. III. Arthur M. Johnson, "Theodore Roosevelt and the Bureau of Corporations," *Mississippi Valley Historical Review*, XLV (1959), is illuminating.

Chapter 10. AN HISTORIC DEPARTURE

The dramatic account in Sullivan, *American Finding Herself*, has not been altered substantially by recent scholarship. I have supplemented it from my usual primary sources, *The Letters, Scrapbooks, The Literary Digest*, and in this case the *Report* of the Anthracite Coal Commission, U.S. Department of Labor Bulletin No. 46 (Washington, 1903). I have also used Marguerite Green, *The National Civic Federation and the American Labor Movement, 1900–1925* (Washington, 1956); a number of standard labor histories, including Foster Rhea Dulles, *Labor in America: A History* (New York, 1949); and especially Robert J. Cornell, *The Anthracite Coal Strike of 1902* (Washington, 1957). Eliot Jones, *The Anthracite Coal Combination in the United States* (Cambridge, 1914) has been useful, and so has Edward Berman, *Labor Disputes and the President of the United States* (New York, 1924).

Among the other works I have drawn upon or quoted from are: Lodge (ed.), *Selections;* Jessup, *Root;* Elsie Gluck, *John Mitchell, Miner* (New York, 1929); Irving Stone, *Clarence Darrow for the Defense* (New York, 1941); Mother [M. H.] Jones, *Autobiography*, M. F. Parton (ed.), (Chicago, 1925); Gompers, *Life and Labor;* Mowry, *The Era of Theodore Roosevelt;* and Roosevelt, *An Autobiography*. Judge Pine's statement is in the *New York Times*, April 30, 1952.

Chapter 11. AFFAIRS OF STATE

The secondary literature on foreign affairs during Roosevelt's presidency is enormous. No effort will be made to survey it. As I hope my text makes clear, however, I have been strongly influenced by Howard

K. Beale, *Theodore Roosevelt and the Rise of America to World Power* (Baltimore, 1956). Except for a set of neo-isolationist conclusions that seem curiously distended from the body of the work, Beale's book is the most exhaustive and balanced treatment extant of selected phases of Roosevelt's conduct of diplomacy. I have, of course, profited from many other works also. Of these, special mention should be made of Julius W. Pratt, *America's Colonial Experiment* (New York, 1950); Dexter Perkins, *The United States and the Caribbean* (Cambridge, 1947); the same author's classic *The Monroe Doctrine, 1867–1907* (Baltimore, 1937); Samuel F. Bemis, *The Latin American Policy of the United States* (New York, 1943); Garel A. Grunder, *The Philippines and the United States* (Norman, Okla., 1951); M. M. Knight, *The Americans in Santo Domingo* (New York, 1928); Russell H. Fitzgibbon, *Cuba and the United States, 1900–1935* (Menasha, Wis., 1935); and many other specialized studies.

I have also used S. W. Livermore, "Theodore Roosevelt, The American Navy and the Venezuelan Crisis," *American Historical Review,* LI (1946); Thomas A. Bailey, "Theodore Roosevelt and the Alaskan Boundary Settlement," *Canadian Historical Review,* XVIII (1937); H. C. Hill, *Roosevelt and the Caribbean* (Chicago, 1927); and Charles C. Tansill, *Canadian-American Relations, 1875–1911* (New Haven, 1943). Of the biographies, Henry F. Pringle, *The Life and Times of William Howard Taft* (2 vols., New York, 1939); Garraty, *Henry Cabot Lodge;* Jessup, *Root;* and Tyler Dennett, *John Hay, From Poetry to Politics* (New York, 1933) have been most helpful.

Additional sources include: Nelson Manfred Blake, "Ambassadors at the Court of Theodore Roosevelt," *Mississippi Valley Historical Review,* XLII (1955); *The Literary Digest* for the relevant years; *Special Report of William H. Taft on the Philippines,* Sixtieth Congress, First Session, Sen. Doc., VII, No. 200; Frederick James Zwierlein, *Theodore Roosevelt and Catholics* (St. Louis, 1956); and a microfilm reel of reports to Whitehall by British ambassadors, now in the library of the Theodore Roosevelt Memorial Association at the Theodore Roosevelt House. I have also used Roosevelt's *An Autobiography* and *The Letters,* vols. III and IV.

Chapter 12. NOBLE ENDS AND LESS NOBLE MEANS

To most of the works cited for the previous chapter should be added the fine study by Dwight C. Miner, *The Fight for the Panama Route* (New York, 1940). I have followed it closely. Also see Philippe Bunau-Varilla, *Panama; the Creation, Destruction and Resurrection* (London, 1913), the note in Vol. III of *The Letters,* and Gerstle Mack, *The Land Divided* (New York, 1944), a superb book. I have found the version in Chapter 26 of Julius W. Pratt's *A History of United States Foreign Policy* (New York, 1955) the best of the brief accounts. Pratt is understanding of the force of the engineering opinion in favor of Panama, critical of TR's refusal to try further negotiations with Colombia. Pringle's treatment is overdrawn and suffers from his failure to consider the impact on TR of the engineering aspects of the situation. Nevertheless, his insight into certain of Roosevelt's drives cannot be dismissed. Arthur H. Dean, *William Nelson Cromwell* (New York, 1957) views Cromwell's comportment as exemplary, or as he puts it, "unselfish and patriotic."

Chapter 13. IN HIS OWN RIGHT

The account of the inaugural is reconstructed from contemporary newspaper reports in the *Scrapbooks* and *The Literary Digest*. For the Hanna incident and TR's manipulation of the patronage in general see Croly, *Hanna;* Thomas Beer, *Hanna* (New York, 1929); A. Bower Sageser, *The First Two Decades of the Pendleton Act* (Lincoln, Nebraska, 1935); *The Letters* and relevant notes; Mowry, *The Era of Theodore Roosevelt;* and, in particular, Blum, *Republican Roosevelt*. For the appointment of Straus, also see Oscar S. Straus, *Under Four Administrations: From Cleveland to Taft* (Boston, 1922). Straus quotes TR in January, 1906, when he first asked him to enter the Cabinet: "There is still a further reason: I want to show Russia and some other countries what we think of the Jews in this country."

Alfred D. Chandler Jr.'s essay, "Theodore Roosevelt and the Panama Canal: A Study in Administration," is in *The Letters*, Vol. VI, Appendix 1. An analysis of the report of the Immigration Commission is in Oscar Handlin, *Race and Nationality in American Life* (Boston, 1957). John Higham, *Strangers in the Land* (New Brunswick, N.J., 1955) has also contributed to my understanding of the immigration problem. Roosevelt's religion is discussed in Hermann Hagedorn, "The Unknown Theodore Roosevelt," an unpublished essay, in Christian F. Reisner, *Roosevelt's Religion* (New York, 1922), a compilation of conventional observations by contemporaries; and in Gamaliel Bradford, *The Quick and the Dead* (Boston, 1931). I have also used TR's diaries. The best biographies of Booker T. Washington are Basil Mathews, *Booker T. Washington, Educator and Interracial Interpreter* (Cambridge, 1948); and Samuel R. Spencer Jr., *Booker T. Washington and the Negro's Place in American Life* (Boston, 1955). I have also found the relevant chapters in John Hope Franklin, *From Slavery to Freedom* (New York, 1947) stimulating. Professor Franklin is more critical of TR and Booker T. Washington than my conviction that economic uplift was precedent to civil rights at that time permits me to be. Pringle, Mowry, and Blum all write perceptively of the campaign of 1904 as does Josephson in his *The President Makers*.

I have filled out their various accounts with stories from contemporary newspapers and material from Jessup's biography of Root. I have also quoted from Ford (ed.), *The Letters of Henry Adams*. Parker has no biographer. The reader still rankled by TR's opportunism in the Clarkson appointment might take succor in his statesmanship and sure purpose as appraised by William Seal Carpenter, *The Unfinished Business of Civil Service Reform* (Princeton, 1952), to wit, "Before he left the presidency, Theodore Roosevelt had brought many thousands of positions within the classified service until 63.9 per cent of the whole executive civil service was included."

PART IV: **THE SQUARE DEAL MATURES**

Chapter 14. ANOTHER MEASURED ADVANCE

This chapter is largely based on two brilliant essays by John Blum, "Theodore Roosevelt and the Legislative Process; Tariff Revision and Railroad Regulation, 1904–1906," and "Theodore Roosevelt and the Hepburn Act: Toward an Orderly System of Control," published as appendices I and II of *The Letters*, vols. IV and VI. I have added to them and revised somewhat with materials from the *Scrapbooks* and the *Congressional Record*. I have also drawn from the following biographies or memoirs: Nathaniel Stephenson, *Nelson W. Aldrich* (New York, 1930); Simkins, *Pitchfork Ben Tillman;* S. H. Acheson, *Joe Bailey: The Last Democrat* (1932); Blair Bolles, *Tyrant from Illinois: Uncle Joe Cannon's Experiment with Personal Power* (New York, 1951); Robert M. La Follette, *Autobiography* (Madison, 1913); Belle Case La Follette and Fola La Follette, *Robert M. La Follette* (2 vols., New York, 1953); Leland L. Sage, *William Boyd Allison: A Study in Practical Politics* (Iowa City, 1956); Ray Stannard Baker, *An American Chronicle* (New York, 1945); and Garraty, *Lodge*.

I have quoted at length from William Z. Ripley, *Railroads: Rates and Regulation* (New York, 1912), and have also used Russel B. Nye, *Midwestern Progressive Politics* (East Lansing, Mich., 1951). The best account of the pipeline amendment controversy is in Arthur Menzies Johnson, *The Development of American Petroleum Pipelines: A Study in Private Enterprise and Public Policy, 1862–1906* (Ithaca, N.Y., 1956), although my account is based on the *Congressional Record*. Johnson points out that the amendment had little economic impact on the oil industry, but that it was nonetheless a landmark in the expansion of federal regulatory power. An illuminating note on the grievances of Nebraskans against the railroads is Richard Lowitt, "George W. Norris, James J. Hill, and the Railroad Rate Bill," *Nebraska History*, XL (1959).

Chapter 15. TRIALS, TRIUMPHS, AND TRAGEDY

I have added little to Pringle's sprightly account of the controversy over simplified spelling—a few contemporary editorial comments, but no more. My description of the fight for the Pure Food Act and the Meat Inspection Amendment to the Agricultural bill comes partly from *The Letters, The Literary Digest,* and the *Scrapbooks,* partly from the exciting story in Mark Sullivan, *Our Times,* vol. II, and partly from the following memoirs, biographies, and monographs: Dr. Harvey Wiley, *An Autobiography* (Indianapolis, 1930); Oscar E. Anderson, Jr., *The Health of A Nation: Harvey W. Wiley and the Fight for Pure Food* (Chicago, 1958), an able study that describes TR's subsequent falling out with Wiley; Louis Filler's thoughtful and interesting *Crusaders for Liberalism* (Yellow Springs, Ohio, 1950); and Claude G. Bowers's full dress *Beveridge and the Progressive Era* (New York, 1932). I have also used Faulkner, *The Quest for Social Justice.*

The quotation by Steffens is from his introduction to his *The Shame of the Cities* (New York, 1904). The muck-raking incident is drawn from Filler, *Crusaders for Liberalism;* C. C. Regier, *The Era of the Muckrakers* (Chapel Hill, N.C., 1932); Baker, *American Chronicle;* Steffens, *Autobiography;* and Arthur Wallace Dunn, *Gridiron Nights* (New York, 1915) and the usual contemporary sources. My appraisal has also been influenced by the reflective comments of Walter Lippmann, "The Themes of Muckraking," in his *Drift and Mastery* (New York, 1914), and by the evaluation in Hofstadter, *The Age of Reform.* TR's speech is in *The Works,* Vol. XVI. The suggestion that the "muck-rake" speech may have been animated by TR's desire to soften the Senate in preparation for the fight over the Hepburn bill is Richard Lowitt's.

Chapter 16. THE PEACEMAKER I

This chapter closely follows Beale, *Theodore Roosevelt and the Rise of America to World Power.* I have supplemented his work with excerpts from *The Letters, Scrapbooks,* and *The Literary Digest.* I have also taken advantage of such standard works as Alfred W. Griswold, *The Far Eastern Policy of the United States* (New York, 1938); Tyler Dennett, *Roosevelt and the Russo-Japanese War* (New York, 1925); Thomas A. Bailey, *Theodore Roosevelt and the Japanese-American Crises* (Stanford, 1934); and a number of scholarly articles.

I have further used John Hay, *Letters and Extracts from the Diary,* edited by Henry Adams (3 vols., Washington, D.C., 1908). Jessup's *Root* contains much good material on Root's tenure as Secretary of State, while Richard W. Leopold, *Elihu Root and the Conservative Tradition* (Boston, 1954) offers a thoughtful evaluation. William Appleman Williams, *The Tragedy of American Diplomacy* (Cleveland, 1959), and George F.

Kennan, *American Diplomacy, 1900–1950* (Chicago, 1951) have proved
stimulating in different ways; so, too, Williams's *American-Russian Relations, 1781–1947* (New York, 1952), though I disagree with many of his
underlying assumptions.

Chapter 17. THE PEACEMAKER II

Besides the works of Beale and the other authors cited under the
preceding heading, I have drawn on: E. C. Sandmeyer, *The Anti-Chinese
Movement in California* (Urbana, Ill., 1939); Eleanor Tupper and George
E. McReynolds, *Japan in American Public Opinion* (New York, 1937);
Pringle, *Taft;* Thomas A. Bailey, "The Root-Takahira Agreement of
1908," *Pacific Historical Review,* IX (1940); Eugene N. Anderson, *The
First Moroccan Crisis, 1904–1906* (Chicago, 1930); Outten J. Clinard,
Japan's Influence on American Naval Power, 1897–1917 (Berkeley, Cal.,
1947), Braisted, *The United States Navy in the Pacific, 1897–1909;*
Gordon Carpenter O'Gara, *Theodore Roosevelt and the Rise of the
Modern Navy* (Princeton, 1943); William Clinton Olson, "Theodore
Roosevelt's Conception of an International League," *World Affairs
Quarterly,* XXIX (1959); and Raymond A. Esthus, "The Changing Concept of the Open Door, 1899–1910," *The Mississippi Valley Historical
Review,* XLVI (1959), an important essay. Also three other important
works: Fred H. Harrington, *God, Mammon, and the Japanese* (Madison,
Wis., 1944) Charles Vevier, *The United States and China, 1906–1913*
(New Brunswick, N.J., 1955); and Robert E. Osgood, *Ideals and Self-Interest in America's Foreign Relations* (Chicago, 1953), which covers
these and all the other chapters on foreign policy. The citations of the
reports of the British ambassadors are taken from the microfilm reel of
same in the Roosevelt Memorial Association Library.

Chapter 18. MORE TROUBLES AND GREATER TRIBULATIONS

Pringle's treatment of the Brownsville episode has not been surpassed. I have filled it out and modified it slightly on the basis of my
reading of *The Letters.* I have further drawn from Emma Lou Thornbrough, "The Brownsville Episode and the Negro Vote," *The Mississippi
Valley Historical Review,* XLIV (1957); James A. Tinsley, "Roosevelt,
Foraker, and the Brownsville Affair," *Journal of Negro History,* XLI
(1956); and Everett Walters, *Joseph Benson Foraker: An Uncompromising Republican* (Columbus, Ohio, 1948). Morison, *Turmoil and Tradition*
describes Stimson's support of Roosevelt. It is less critical of TR than my
account and those cited above. It is significant, I think, that Roosevelt
did not mention the episode in his *An Autobiography.*

Cutright's exposition in depth of the nature-fakers affair in his
Theodore Roosevelt The Naturalist supercedes the account in Pringle,
Theodore Roosevelt. I have drawn on his sources. My treatment of the

Panic of 1907 was originally based on the conventional sources, notably, Pringle, *Theodore Roosevelt;* Allen, *Pierpont Morgan;* William C. Schluter, *The Pre-War Business Cycle, 1907–1914* (New York, 1923); Alfred D. Noyes, *Forty Years of American Finance, 1865–1907* (New York, 1909); and several extended notes in *The Letters,* Vol. V. I have tempered my evaluation of Morgan, however, on the basis of the account set forth in John A. Garraty, *Right-Hand Man: The Life of George W. Perkins* (New York, 1960). As the text indicates, I have also drawn on two important essays by Robert H. Wiebe, "Business Disunity and the Progressive Movement, 1901–1914," *Mississippi Valley Historical Review,* XLIV (1958), and "House of Morgan and the Executive, 1905–1913," *American Historical Review,* LXV (1959). Wiebe's statement that "a respectable number of country bankers . . . applauded" the Aldrich-Vreeland Act modifies the assertions by Glass, Williams, and La Follette which I have taken from the *Congressional Record,* Sixtieth Congress, First Session. For the trust problem I have used Henry R. Seager and Charles A. Gulick Jr., *Trust and Corporation Problems* (New York, 1929), and with particular profit, George W. Stocking, *Basing Point Pricing and Regional Development: A Case Study of the Iron and Steel Industry* (Chapel Hill, N.C., 1954). On the other hand, Ward S. Bowman, Jr. argues in a review article in *The University of Chicago Law Review,* XXII (1954) that Stocking's evidence fails to support the thesis that relative retardation in the South was caused by acquisition or basing point prices. He does not, however, disagree with the proposition that the merging of U.S. Steel and T. C. & I. or the use of a basing point system had no anti-competitive effects on production in the South as elsewhere. Rather, Bowman's point is that the relative retardation of the South is not established by Stocking's analysis. He holds, as do many other economists, that the South's plight was attributable to numerous other factors.

Chapter 19. FOR GENERATIONS YET UNBORN

In addition to *The Letters* and their several informative notes, I have relied heavily on Gifford Pinchot, *Breaking New Ground* (New York, 1947). Pinchot's book is partisan and fails to do justice to some of the pro-conservation men with whom he disagreed. Nevertheless, for its anecdotes, for its insights into the best sides of Roosevelt's character, and for its revelation of Pinchot's missionary zeal, without which in my view the conservation movement might never have matured, it is a work of surpassing importance. I have, of course, modified its conclusions in the light of such standard works as E. Louise Peffer, *The Closing of the Public Domain: Disposal and Reservation, 1900–1950* (Stanford, 1951); Roy M. Robbins, *Our Landed Heritage: The Public Domain, 1776–1936* (Princeton, 1942); John Ise, *The United States Forest Policy* (New

Haven, 1920); Jerome Kerwin, *Federal Water-Power Legislation* (New York, 1926); Benjamin Horace Hibbard, *A History of the Public Land Policies* (New York, 1939); Samuel Trask Dana, *Forest and Range Policy: Its Development in the United States* (New York, 1956); and Peggy Heim, "Financing the Federal Reclamation Program, 1902 to 1919: The Development of Repayment Policy" (unpublished Ph.D. dissertation, Columbia University, 1953). I have also drawn on William T. Hornaday, *Thirty Years War for Wildlife* (New York, 1931), and Arthur B. Darling (ed.), *The Public Papers of Francis G. Newlands* (2 vols., New York, 1932), and J. A. O'Callaghan, "Senator Mitchell and the Oregon Land Frauds, 1905," *Pacific Historical Review,* XXI (1952). Pringle, *Theodore Roosevelt,* reviews TR's conservation record (favorably) in two paragraphs. Roosevelt, *An Autobiography,* has a good chapter, perhaps the best in the book. Arthur De Witt Frank, *The Development of the Federal Program of Flood Control on the Mississippi River* (New York, 1930), confirms, in so far as it expresses any judgments, the validity of Roosevelt's and Pinchot's strictures against the Army engineers. Erich W. Zimmermann, *Conservation in the Production of Petroleum* (New Haven, 1957), is an informed and scholarly study. I think, however, that Zimmerman reads too much of the preservationist, as distinguished from conservationist, into Roosevelt and Pinchot. Cutright, *Theodore Roosevelt, The Naturalist,* has much fascinating and relevant material. Whitney R. Cross, "Ideas in Politics: The Conservation Policies of the Two Roosevelt's," *Journal of the History of Ideas,* XIV (1953) is suggestive and I think meritorious. Indubitably, the ideals and example of TR influenced FDR. The statement by Dr. Van Hise is from his *The Conservation of Natural Resources in the United States* (New York, 1911).

As my text suggests, I have also revised a number of judgments on the basis of Samuel P. Hays, *Conservation and the Gospel of Efficiency: The Progressive Conservation Movement, 1890–1920* (Cambridge, 1959), the most exhaustive and in many respects, penetrating, study of the movement yet published. Hays plays down too much the anti-monopolistic tenor of the Roosevelt-Pinchot waterpower policies, but he puts their forest and range policies in sharp perspective. He is especially informative in his analysis of the roles of McGee and Leighton, in his appreciation of the movement's scientific base, and in his analysis of the differences between the conservationists and preservationists (a subject I have been forced to ignore for reasons of space). On the other hand, I find little in Hays or anything else I have read to negate the contention in J. Leonard Bates, "Fulfilling American Democracy: The Conservation Movement, 1907 to 1921," *Mississippi Valley Historical Review,* XLIV (June, 1957), that "The organized conservationists were concerned more with economic justice and democracy in the handling of resources than with mere prevention of waste."

Chapter 20. TOWARD THE WELFARE STATE

This chapter has been written mainly from *The Letters, The Works, Scrapbooks,* and *The Literary Digest.* I have not treated Herbert Croly at length, either here or in later chapters, mainly because I am convinced that Roosevelt's actions and speeches had as much impact on Croly, probably, as Croly's writings had on Roosevelt. I am also of the opinion that Roosevelt would have taken almost the same positions he did had Croly never lived. On the other hand, Croly undeniably had a sharp impact on the intellectuals of his times and thus on the climate of opinion in which TR functioned. See, for example, Goldman's *Rendezvous With Destiny.* David W. Noble, *The Paradox of Progressive Thought* (Minneapolis, 1958) ably dissects Croly's ideas. The statements attributed to Scripps are taken from Stone, *Clarence Darrow;* that by Gompers from his *Autobiography.* I have also quoted from Brooks Adams, *The Law of Civilization and Decay* (Vintage Edition, New York, 1955). Berman, *Labor Disputes and the President* offers a measured evaluation of TR's decision to send troops into Nevada. Berman concludes: "The incident again shows the necessity for investigation by some impartial agent before the President orders troops sent to the scene of a strike. The alarming tone of Governor Sparks' first telegram to the President probably caused the latter to fear the evil consequences of delay, but, as he himself said to the officer in charge of troops . . . 'Better twenty-four hours of riot, damage, and disorder than illegal use of troops.' Though his action in sending soldiers so hastily is deserving of criticism, his insistence that they be strictly impartial and his pressure on the Governor to have the legislature convened and to make provision for doing its own policing, when he realized that he had been placed in a false position, are worthy of praise."

Chapter 21. THE CAMPAIGN OF 1908

Besides the obvious sources—*The Letters, Scrapbooks, The Literary Digest,* and *The Works*—I have drawn on Leopold, *Root;* Lodge (ed.), *Selections;* and numerous other secondary works. Pringle's fine biography of Taft, earlier cited, has been especially useful. Merlo J. Pusey's *Charles Evans Hughes* (2 vols., New York, 1951), unfailingly informative, though not always critically so, has also been helpful. The comments by Archie Butt in this and the following chapter are taken from Lawrence F. Abbott (ed.), *The Letters of Archie Butt* (New York, 1924). The correspondence on the Roosevelt-Gompers controversy is in *Injunc-*

tions: Hearings before the Committee on the Judiciary, House of Representatives. Sixty-Second Congress, Second Session (Washington, D.C., 1912). Yet another irony in the Roosevelt-Gompers relationship is that by 1908 Roosevelt perceived the greater equity in workmen's compensation, as distinguished from employer's liability, laws. He persuasively argued for same in his message of January 31 and in a second special message two months later. Congress responded by establishing a limited compensation system for government employees. Gompers, however, failed to support the President. Not until after Roosevelt left the presidency did the A.F. of L. leader finally comprehend the superiority of the compensation principle.

Chapter 22. THE CHANGING OF THE GUARD

I have supplemented *The Letters, The Works, Scrapbooks,* and *The Literary Digest* with liberal extractions from Pringle's two biographies, *Theodore Roosevelt* and *William Howard Taft;* also from Butt, *Intimate Letters.* The italics in Roosevelt's farewell letter to Pinchot are mine. The quote from Lord Bryce is taken from the microfilm reel previously cited. Morison, *Turmoil and Tradition* offers a more charitable interpretation than I of Roosevelt's decision to press the libel suits. But see the note in *The Letters,* Vol. VI. Hays, *Conservation and the Gospel of Efficiency* confirms Roosevelt's and Pinchot's realization before the inauguration that Taft was unfriendly toward their conservation policies. The best analysis of the report of the Country Life Commission, which Congress refused to publish, is Clayton S. Ellsworth, "Theodore Roosevelt's Country Life Commission," *Agricultural History,* XXXIV (1960). Ellsworth reveals Taft's indifference to the Commission's recommendations. He also shows that the Wilson administration put many of the Commission's recommendations, some indirect and others direct, into law. Farm organizations were exempted from the Clayton Anti-Trust Act; extension education was provided by the Smith-Lever Act of 1914; vocational education was promoted by the Smith-Hughes Act; federal aid to roads was given by an act of 1916; more adequate credit facilities were established through the Federal Reserve Act of 1913, the Federal Warehouse Act of 1916, and the Federal Land Bank Act of the same year; also, the Underwood-Simmons Tariff of 1914 reduced the rates on industrial products purchased by farmers.

PART V: **THE HIGH TIDE OF PROGRESSIVISM**

GENERAL

The ground here has been clearly staked out by George E. Mowry, *Theodore Roosevelt and the Progressive Movement* (Madison, 1946). I have followed his guide lines, though wandering here and there and modifying certain of his conclusions. I have also benefited enormously from Pringle's *Taft*, and from Arthur S. Link's *Wilson: The Road to the White House* (Princeton, 1947), and Link's *Woodrow Wilson and the Progressive Era: 1910–1917* (New York, 1954). My greatest debt continues to be to the editors of *The Letters*, Vol. VII of which covers the period under review. I have also, of course, drawn liberally on Roosevelt's *The Works*.

Chapter 23. THE NEW NATIONALISM

This chapter is based on the works mentioned above, on press commentaries in *The Literary Digest*, and on numerous books cited earlier. The most valuable of the latter include, Goldman, *Rendezvous;* Cutright, *Theodore Roosevelt the Naturalist;* Lodge (ed.), *Selections;* Butt, *Intimate Letters;* Pinchot, *Breaking New Ground;* Jessup, *Root;* White, *Autobiography;* and Roosevelt's *The Works.* I have also used Kenneth W. Hechler, *Insurgency: Personalities and Politics of the Taft Era* (New York, 1940); Ford (ed.), *The Letters of Henry Adams;* and F. W. Taussig, *The Tariff History of the United States* (New York, 1914). Conflicting interpretations of the Ballinger-Pinchot affair are Pringle, *Taft,* and Mowry, *Progressive Movement;* also, Alpheus T. Mason, *Bureaucracy Convicts Itself: The Ballinger-Pinchot Controversy of 1910* (New York, 1941). Hays, *Conservation and the Gospel of Efficiency* also treats it. Archibald W. Butt, *Taft and Roosevelt: the Intimate Letters of Archie Butt* (2 vols., Garden City, N.Y., 1930) is the source of the remarks by Archie Butt in this and the three following chapters.

Chapter 24. THE TRAVAILS OF INDECISION

The Letters, The Works, Scrapbooks, The Literary Digest, and *The Outlook* together with Pringle's *Taft* and Mowry's *Progressive Movement* are the main sources for this chapter. I have also drawn from Mowry's *Theodore Roosevelt and the Progressive Era,* wherein he is much more sympathetic to and understanding of Roosevelt's approach to the trust problem than in the earlier *Progressive Movement.* Wiebe's articles have again proved enlightening, while Garraty's *Right-Hand Man* has confirmed my own conclusion that Perkins was sincere and conscientious. I have further drawn on Amos R. E. Pinchot, *History of the Progressive Party, 1912–1916,* edited by Helene Maxwell Hooker (New York, 1958), and Felix Frankfurter, *Felix Frankfurter Reminisces: Recorded in Talks with Dr. Harlan B. Phillips* (New York, 1960). Among the numerous other works I have used are Pinchot, *Breaking New Ground;* Hechler, *Insurgency;* Hays, *Conservation and the Gospel of Efficiency;* and L. E. Ellis, *Reciprocity, 1911* (New Haven, 1939). Of further interest is the statement by John J. Leary, Jr., that TR told him in 1916 that Taft's failure to reappoint the Country Life Commission was "the last straw." It is in

Talks with T.R. From the Diaries of John J. Leary Jr. (Boston, 1930). Judge Gary's statements are extracted from *Special Committee on Investigation of the U.S. Steel Corporation. Hearings.* House of Representatives (Washington, 1911).

For a favorable and reflective appraisal of Chief Justice White's "rule of reason" doctrine, see Eugene V. Rostow, *Planning for Freedom, The Public Law of American Capitalism* (New Haven, 1959). The most exhaustive and judicious synthesis of antitrust policy I have read is Simon N. Whitney, *Antitrust Policies, American Experience in Twenty Industries* (2 vols., New York, 1958). Whitney concludes, as does Rostow, that the broad deterrent effect of the antitrust laws has been greater than the visible effects of special prosecutions would suggest. I am particularly impressed by Whitney's implicit confirmation of the broad outlines of Roosevelt's attitude toward big business. His closing statements read in part: "Few if any responsible writers would push such a program [for pure competition] to the extreme, lest the benefits of large-scale operation and the profit motive be lost. . . ." "The pure competition of small firms . . . would not be dynamic or progressive." "Not competition alone, but the combined force supplied by competition and by ambitions of a noncompetitive nature, will make a progressive economy."

Chapter 25. THE PEOPLE SHALL RULE

I have here drawn on almost all the works cited under the three previous headings. Of the new materials, Robert Grant's letter to James Ford Rhodes is in *The Letters,* Vol. VIII, Appendix II; Felix Frankfurter's retrospective comments on the recall of judicial decisions in Archibald MacLeish and E. F. Prichard, Jr., Eds., *Law and Politics: Occasional Papers of Felix Frankfurter, 1913–1918* (New York, 1939). The quotation by John W. Davis is from one of his speeches in 1912 in support of his bill to eradicate the abuse of the injunctive power. My general statements on Davis are based on an examination of his papers which are temporarily in my possession.

The reader dissatisfied with my analysis of Roosevelt's motivation in seeking again the presidency might profitably consult Morison's *Turmoil and Tradition.* Morison puts the case for TR's personal ambition more compellingly and more succinctly than any historian I have read. An interview with Judge Learned Hand on January 25, 1958, is the basis for my statement that he advised TR not to come out for the recall of judicial decisions and to clarify his position after he had come out for them.

Chapter 26. THOU SHALT NOT STEAL

Here again the sources are essentially the same as those listed under *General,* Chapter XXIII, and Chapter XXIV. I should say, however, that in addition to *The Letters* and *The Literary Digest*, I have drawn particularly heavily on Pringle's *Taft*. Belle Case La Follette and Fola La Follette, *Robert M. La Follette* has also contributed new material; and so, also, Jessup's *Root*. My account of the convention is reconstructed partly from contemporary newspaper accounts, partly from memoirs and autobiographies earlier cited, and largely from Mowry's *Progressive Movement*.

Chapter 27. ARMAGEDDON

To all my standard sources should be added Hofstadter's *Age of Reform;* George E. Mowry, *The California Progressives* (Berkeley, 1951); Bowers, *Beveridge;* and Link, *Woodrow Wilson and the Progressive Era*. Also, Woodrow Wilson, *A Crossroads of Freedom*, edited by John Wells Davidson (New Haven, 1956); Ira Kipnis, *The American Socialist Movement: 1897–1912* (New York, 1920); David Shannon, *The Socialist Party of America* (New York, 1955); Ray Ginger, *The Bending Cross: A Biography of Eugene Victor Debs* (New Brunswick, N.J., 1949); and Nye, *Midwestern Progressivism*. Additional sources include Henry May, *Protestant Churches and Industrial America* (New York, 1949); White, *Autobiography;* Robert M. Warner, "Chase S. Osburn and the Presidential Campaign of 1912," *Mississippi Valley Historical Review*, XLVI (1959); and Alfred D. Chandler, Jr., "The Origins of Progressive Leadership," *The Letters*, Vol. VIII, Appendix III. The most recent and most inclusive treatment of the controversy over the anti-trust plank is in Garraty, *Right-Hand Man*. Garraty points out that the records have been lost and that, in any event, the changes were matters of detail rather than of principle. He confirms, however, that regardless of the wording of the platform, the real issue was trust-busting *versus* government regulation. Roosevelt's speech at Milwaukee is in *The Works*, Vol. XVII. Also see Robert Donovan, *The Assassins* (New York, 1955). For insight into why one group of conservationists—the pure nature lovers or preservationists —who were at odds with Pinchot because of his insistence that the forests be opened to controlled commercial use, supported Taft rather than TR, see Linnie Marsh Wolfe, *Son of the Wilderness: The Life of John Muir* (New York, 1945).

PART VI: **ONE LAST GREAT CAUSE**

Chapter 28. THE VARIETY OF HIM

See Garraty, *Right-Hand Man* for evidence that Perkins was far more dedicated to preserving the Progressive Party than Harold Ickes, W. A. White, and other Westerners believed. The most discerning short treatment of Wilson's domestic program is in Link, *Woodrow Wilson and the Progressive Era*. A vastly more detailed account of the first phase is in the same author's *Wilson: The New Freedom* (Princeton, 1956). TR's address to the American Historical Association is in *The Works*, Vol. XII. His disparaging remarks to Trevelyan about history professors should be weighed, perhaps, against his several deferential letters to Frederick Jackson Turner printed in *The Letters*, Vol. I. I have drawn on the brief and interesting account of TR's South American expedition in Cutright, *Theodore Roosevelt the Naturalist*. The record of the libel suit is in *Roosevelt* vs. *Newett: A Transcript of the Testimony Taken at Depositions Read at Marquette, Michigan* (Privately printed, 1914). TR's review of the Armory Show is in *The Works*, Vol. XII. Sam Hunter, *Modern American Painting and Sculpture* (New York, 1959) gives a good account of the Armory Show's critical reception. He recognizes the force of TR's affirmation, but emphasizes more his negative views.

As I said in the text, Wagenknecht, *The Seven Worlds* offers the most inclusive appreciation of TR's feeling for the arts I have read. Wagenknecht is not as penetrating as many of Roosevelt's negative critics, but TR himself never professed to be a critic. If Roosevelt's sophistication was less than that of the critics and academicians, it was greater, certainly, than that of the average college graduate and incomparably superior to that of most politicians. At the risk of being didactic I repeat the judgments implied in my text: It is a good thing to have a President or former President interested in the arts; TR did more to advance them than any President between Jefferson and Franklin Roosevelt, whose great service was performed through the WPA.

I have also used Homer Saint-Gaudens, "Roosevelt and Our Coin Designs," *Century*, XCIV (1920); Glenn Brown, "Roosevelt and the Fine Arts," *American Architect*, CXVI (1919); and Carl J. Weber, "Poet and President," *New England Quarterly*, XVI (1943). I have also drawn on Owen Wister, *Story of a Friendship;* Henry Adams, *The Education of Henry Adams* (Boston, 1918); and Hermann Hagedorn and Sidney Wallach, *A Theodore Roosevelt Round-Up* (New York, 1958), wherein are printed the statements by Robert Frost, *et al.* These have the ring of the memorium—they were written after TR's death—but they are surely of value. Hamlin Garland's affection for and appreciation of TR is also brought out in Jean Holloway, *Hamlin Garland, A Biography* (Austin, Texas, 1960). The most recent criticism of TR's literary values is Don D. Walker, "Wister, Roosevelt and James: A Note on the Western," *American Quarterly*, XII (1960). Walker describes how TR prevailed on Wister to eliminate the gory details from an episode in *The Virginian* and suggests that TR may have been responsible for Wister's subsequent failure to realize his potential. In the same article, however, Walker quotes W. D. Howells, the then dean of realism, as advising Wister that he not show his first novel to a publisher because "it was certain to shock the public gravely" and because "a whole fig tree would not cover the Widow Taylor." Many of TR's letters to Wister and numerous other writers are in the eight volumes of *The Letters*. I have formed my conclusions on the whole body of them.

Chapter 29. THE BUGLE THAT WOKE AMERICA

The title for this chapter is taken from Hermann Hagedorn, *The Bugle That Woke America: The Saga of Theodore Roosevelt's Last Battle for His Country* (New York, 1940). The chapter as a whole is a condensation of part of my doctoral dissertation, "Wilson, Roosevelt, and Interventionism, 1914–1917" (Northwestern University, 1954). Readers interested in published works covering the same period might consult Link, *Woodrow Wilson and the Progressive Era*, or William E. Leuchtenberg, *The Perils of Prosperity* (Chicago, 1958); also most of the works cited in the notes for Chapter 31. For a revealing insight into Roosevelt's matured views on the need to extend popular control of the government, his continued contempt for legalism, his belief "that strong labor unions are indispensable to progress," and his reaffirmation of Charles Van Hise's theories on the regulation of trusts—all of which positions, as I have tried to show, he had come to during the last years of his presidency—see his *Outlook* review (November 18, 1914) of Herbert Croly's *Progressive Democracy* and Walter Lippmann's *Drift and Mastery*. It is republished in *The Works*, Vol. XII under the title "Progressive Democracy." The letter by TR describing his meeting with the German emissary is in Mrs. Theodore Roosevelt, Jr., *Day Before Yesterday* (Garden City, 1958).

Chapter 30. THE CAMPAIGN FOR AMERICAN RIGHTS

This chapter is also a condensation of a part of my dissertation as cited under the preceding heading. The report of the telephone conversations at the convention was originally taken from John A. Garraty (ed.), "TR on the Telephone," *American Heritage*, IX (1957). I have since used the original. It is in the Perkins Papers in the Special Collections Room of the Butler Library at Columbia University. I am impressed by the evidences of TR's hope, expressed over the phone to Lodge and others, that a militant nominating speech by Senator Albert Fall on the Mexican situation might swing the Republican convention behind him. It tends to confirm, regrettably, my speculation that TR would have been as ready to go to war against Mexico as against Germany had there been no conflagration in Europe. The report of President Wilson's conversation with Cobb is taken from John L. Heaton, *Cobb of "The World"* (New York, 1924).

Chapter 31. THE LAST BATTLE

I have based this chapter partly on the collections of the Papers of Theodore Roosevelt, Woodrow Wilson, Newton D. Baker, John J. Pershing, and Hugh S. Scott, all on deposit in the Manuscripts Division of the Library of Congress. I have also drawn liberally from TR's wartime writings as published in Ralph Stout (ed.) *Roosevelt in the Kansas City Star* (Boston, 1921). My views on the excesses of the war years have been formed, if they needed to be formed, by such works as H. C. Peterson and G. C. Fite, *Opponents of War, 1917–1918* (Madison, Wis., 1957); Carl Wittke, *The German-Language Press in America* (Lexington, 1957); Zachariah Chafee, *Free Speech in the United States* (Cambridge, 1941); J. Weinstein, "Anti-War Sentiment and the Socialist Party, 1917–1918," *Political Science Quarterly*, LXXIV (1959); Robert K. Murray, *Red Scare: A Study in National Hysteria, 1919–1920* (Minneapolis, 1955); John Blum, "Nativism, Anti-Radicalism, and the Foreign Scare, 1917–1920," *Midwest Journal*, III (1950–51), and Arthur Ekirch, *Civilian and the Military* (New York, 1956). I have also read with interest, but not used, Harry N. Scheiber, *The Wilson Administration and Civil Liberties, 1917–1921* (Ithaca, N.Y., 1960). Scheiber places a heavy burden of blame on President Wilson.

I have drawn most of my personal anecdotes from Hagedorn, *The Bugle That Woke America;* Oscar K. Davis, *Released for Publication* (New York, 1925); Frederick S. Wood (ed.), *Roosevelt As We Knew Him* (Philadelphia, 1927); Charles Willis Thompson, *Presidents I Have Known* (Indianapolis, 1929); Leary, *Talks With T.R.;* Bishop, *Life and Times;* James Amos, *Theodore Roosevelt* (New York, 1927). The description of Taft at the grave is from a letter by Kent B. Stiles to Hermann Hagedorn, December 24, 1955. Mr. Stiles, who was in 1919 a reporter for the Associated Press, writes that the "scene was too sacred" for him to report at the time.

I am aware, of course, that the reports of TR's various sayings as recorded in the above cited memoirs and reproduced in my text may not be literally accurate in all cases. Yet every one of them seems to be in character with TR's personality and the historical situation. Most of them were recorded, moreover, by trained newspapermen accustomed to taking down verbatim accounts of conversations. On the theory that the historian's charge to recreate the past is more nearly, if still imperfectly, achieved by using such materials with discrimination rather than by dismissing them in the interest of what may become a sterile literalism, I have chosen to include them.

Scholarly support for the speculations that TR would have been the leading contender for the Republican nomination in 1920 may be found in Howard Scott Greenlee, "The Republican Party in Division and Re-union, 1913–1920," (Doctoral dissertation, University of Chicago, 1950). My generalizations about the nature of the Republican party in the post-war era are substantiated by the facts, if not always the interpretations, set forth in almost any textbook on the period. Also see Arthur S. Link, "What Happened to the Progressive Movement in the 1920's?" *American Historical Review*, LXIV (1959). Link recounts the persistence of pro-gressivism in Congress, but also speculates that neither Wilson nor Roose-velt could have formed a viable progressive government. The most dis-passionate account I have read of the wellsprings of Lodge's opposition to Wilson's conception of the League of Nations is in Garraty's *Henry Cabot Lodge*. Although Garraty does not discount the personal equation, he succeeds in showing that Lodge's position was consistent with the one he (and Roosevelt) had always taken on national sovereignty. Thus he writes of the Lodge reservations: "Though some of them were unneces-sary and others plainly motivated by political considerations, the chief purpose of most of them was to define the obligations of the United States more specifically and to make clear the right of Congress to control American performance of these duties."

Elting E. Morison and John M. Blum (eds.), *The Letters of Theodore Roosevelt*, from Vol. VIII of which is taken Clemenceau's editorial, have been to the end of inestimable value.

INDEX